MILLER'S LAW
OF FREIGHT LOSS AND
DAMAGE CLAIMS

MILLER'S LAW OF FREIGHT LOSS AND DAMAGE CLAIMS

Fourth Edition

Richard R. Sigmon, LL.M.

wcb

WM. C. BROWN COMPANY PUBLISHERS
Dubuque, Iowa

Library of Congress Catalog Card Number: 73-84327

ISBN 0—697—08511—2

Fourth Printing, 1979

Printed in the United States of America

Contents

To my wife,
Maha

Preface

As John Miller pointed out in the preface to the first edition, there is no essential difference in the adjustment of claims filed with rail and motor carriers and freight forwarders. The liability of all three modes for loss and damage on interstate shipments is governed by section 20(11) of the Interstate Commerce Act. John designed this work as a handbook to assist in the voluntary adjustment of claims for loss and damage. This latest revision brings the material up-to-date, but adheres to the purpose of the first edition.

I want to acknowledge the innumerable contributions of my wife, Maha, and the great help of Mrs. Lori Piatkowski who typed the manuscript, checked references, and generally assisted in bringing this edition to press.

Richard R. Sigmon

1

Source of Carrier Liability for Loss and Damage

The law governing the common carrier's liability for loss and damage of property delivered to it for transportation is an outgrowth of the law of bailments. There are numerous definitions of a bailment, varying according to the point of emphasis of the writer and, to some extent, according to the time of writing. Many of the early writers defined a bailment in terms of a contract, an approach which is criticized because it fails to cover certain situations which have always been treated as bailments; for example, the gratuitous bailment or the finding of lost property.

A good definition of a bailment is that given by Dobie in his handbook.

> A bailment is the relation created through the transfer of the possession of goods or chattels, by a person called the bailor to a person called the bailee, without a transfer of ownership, for the accomplishment of a certain purpose, whereupon the goods or chattels are to be dealt with according to the instructions of the bailor. (*Bailments and Carriers* [St. Paul: West Publishing Co., 1914], p. 1)

The shipper-carrier relation is created through the delivery of possession of the freight by the shipper (bailor) to the carrier (bailee), while the shipper-bailor retains ownership of the freight, for the purpose of securing transportation of the freight, whereupon the freight is delivered according to the instructions of the shipper-bailor.

There are two general types of bailments, namely, the *ordinary bailment* and the *extraordinary bailment*. Ordinary bailments include three classes: (1) those which are for the sole benefit of the bailor or some other person than the bailee; (2) those which are for the sole benefit of the bailee; and (3) those which are for the benefit of both parties. Extraordinary bailments may be classified as (1) those which are quasi-public in their nature, as in the case of innkeepers and common carriers; and (2) those which are public in nature, as in the case of postmasters and similar government agencies.

All but the most primitive societies must face problems involving bailments since, whenever a person has possession of goods belonging to someone else, questions must arise concerning their rights and duties toward each other. Much of the modern law of bailments has its origins in the early Roman law, yet the question of the bailee's liability, as best as can be determined from the historical material available to us, was subject to no clear rules until the eighteenth century. In the famous 1703 case of *Coggs* v. *Bernard,* 2 Ld. Raym. 909, Lord Holt took the opportunity to consider the whole question of the bailee's liability.

Carriers' Liability at Common Law

Just a century before the decision in *Coggs* v. *Bernard,* it was held, in *Southcote* v. *Bennet,* 4 Coke 83b, Cro. Eliz. 815 (1601), that a bailee was liable for loss of goods even though his defense was that they had been stolen from him without his fault. The rule of absolute liability of the bailee was thus recognized in clear terms and, with a minor exception, was the rule made applicable to all bailments. As a result of this rule, bailees began making express stipulations limiting their liability. This, in turn, qualified and narrowed the rule of Southcote's case and led to classifications of bailees according to the liability they assumed.

The only point in issue in *Coggs* v. *Bernard* was the liability of a gratuitous bailee for damage to goods while he was moving them. The defendant, without reward, had undertaken to move a cask of brandy from one cellar to another. The cask was damaged during the move and the plaintiff sued for damages. All three of the judges agreed that the rule of absolute liability against a gratuitous bailee announced in Southcote's case was wrong and was no longer the law. Lord Holt went further and reviewed the whole field of bailment and laid down a number of rules which established varying standards of care applicable to the different types of bailments. These reflected a scale of degrees of care due, ranging from the bailee who receives goods to keep for the use of the bailor, to whom he is liable only for gross neglect; to the common carrier for hire, who is chargeable with the highest degree of care. The carrier, said Lord Holt, "is bound to answer for the goods at all events," and went on to explain:

> The law charges this person thus entrusted to carry goods, against all events, but acts of God, and of the enemies of the King. For though the force be ever so great, as if an irresistible multitude of people should rob him, nevertheless he is chargeable. And this is a politic establishment, contrived by the policy of the law, for the safety of all persons, the necessity of whose affairs oblige them to trust these sorts of persons, that they may be safe in their ways of dealing; for else these carriers might have an opportunity of undoing all persons that had any dealings with them, by combining with thieves, etc., and yet doing it in such clandestine manner as would not be possible to be discovered. And this is the reason the law is founded upon in that point.

As Lord Holt's decision shows, our medieval law imposed special, strict liability upon certain classes of people who, by reason of their employment, are assigned a special status. The legal justification for this rule of strict liability applicable to those who practiced *common callings* has been the subject of much learned discussion and some acrimonious dispute in legal texts and journals. Lord Holt's statement that it results from a policy of the law does not explain the reason for the policy. On the other hand, his explanation that the greater possibility for undetectable misappropriation requires the special liability of the carrier does not explain why the same degree of responsibility is not assigned to carriers who are not common carriers. As to the liability of the bailee-carrier who does not exercise a public employment or calling, Lord Holt said:

> The second sort are bailees, factors and such like. And though a bailee is to have a reward for his management, yet he is only to do the best he can. And if he is robbed, etc., it is a good account. . . . But the true reason of the case is, it would be unreasonable to charge him with a trust, farther that the nature of the thing puts it in his power to perform it. But it is allowed in the other cases, by reason of the necessity of the thing. . . .

In the Middle Ages there were numerous employments classed as common callings: common carriers, common innkeepers, common merchants, common bakers, common schoolmasters, common surgeons, and many others. Today the only examples which remain are the common carrier and, to some extent, the common innkeeper. Yet there is little, if any, logical explanation why the common carrier and the common innkeeper are today still labelled as such and still retain special duties to the public, while the many other public employments have lost both the name and the special status. A baker or a storekeeper is no less a common trader than is a carrier or an innkeeper, yet he is not charged with the special duties assigned to the latter.

On the other hand, conditions surrounding transportation have greatly changed in the more than 250 years since Lord Holt laid down the rule of strict liability for common carriers. There is little comparison between the carriage of goods by pack horse and wagon over the primitive trails and through the bandit-infested forests of Lord Holt's time and the transportation by modern carriers in our relatively peaceful, well-policed society. But, at least in this country (although not in England, the source of the principle), strict liability has continued to be the basic law with respect to common carriers. The only significant changes have been the additions to the exceptions stated by Lord Holt (act of God and act of the public enemy), those of the act or default of the shipper, the act of the public authority, and the results of the inherent nature or vice of the goods.

If today the special duties and the strict liability assigned to common carriers are to be regarded as unique to the employment involved, it must be borne in mind that they do not result from the common carrier's being singled out for these special responsibilities, but rather that the numerous other public callings were gradually, over the years, removed from the class subjected to this special status. Probably the reason that the obligations of the common calling have been dropped from many occupations which formerly were subjected to them is that a choice, conscious or not, has been made of different means of achieving the ends of public policy; it is not the result of any differences in the ends sought.

Unfortunately, there is a strong tendency to retain legal rules long after the reasons for the rules have disappeared. Justice Oliver Wendell Holmes described this tendency in his treatise, *The Common Law*:

> A very common phenomenon, and one very familiar to the student of history, is this. The customs, beliefs, or needs of a primitive time establish a rule or a formula. In the course of centuries the custom, belief, or necessity disappears, but the rule remains. The reason which gave rise to the rule has been forgotten, and ingenious minds set themselves to inquire how it is to be accounted for. Some ground of policy is thought of, which seems to explain it and to reconcile it with the present state of things; and then the rule adapts itself to the new reasons which have been found for it, and enters on a new career. The old form receives a new content, and in time even the form modifies itself to fit the meaning which it has received. ([Boston: Little, Brown and Co., 1881], p. 5)

This tendency to continue to adhere to rules long after the reasons for the rules have disappeared results in a rigidity in the law, a rigidity which is little in keeping with the dynamic and developing nature of our society and our economy. It would be far better to keep our law governing the relations between people more flexible in order to better meet the needs of contemporary society. Mere antiquity does not make a law sound. In addition, unless the basis for a law is meaningful to man in terms of his own social situation, wholehearted support of the law is not freely given.

In their monograph, *The Obligation to Carry* ([London: The Institute of Transport, 1956], pp. 12-13), Milne and Laing contend that the special regulation attached to the common callings resulted not so much from the fact that they were common as from the fact that they were monopolistic. They further suggest that as the various other common callings became less monopolistic, the need for regulation tended to disappear. It is not within the scope of the present volume to test this thesis or, assuming it sound, to determine whether the forces of competition are sufficiently at work in the field of transportation to justify a major change in the law of carrier liability. But it is important to recognize that the special obligations and liabilities of common carriers are not inherent in common carriage so that we can never consider change in the law to meet changed circumstances. Transportation is a dynamic industry and the regulation of transportation cannot be frozen into a rigid mold.

Despite the contention of some of the judiciary in recent years, the common law is *not* a sharply defined, easily ascertainable, accessible, and comprehensible code. In fact, in some fields, there is excellent reason to believe that more time is devoted in this country to a hit-or-miss effort to determine the ancient common-law rulings than is devoted by those in the country in which it developed. This is especially true in the field of commercial transactions which today admittedly are little comparable with the ancient circumstances which gave rise to the common law decisions of that age. Basically, the common law is a mass of principles determined from innumerable judicial decisions, learned treatises, and even from common usage of peoples in daily life, tempered by common sense and interpreted in light of judicial concepts of fairness and public policy. In this country, the common law has varied from state to state, varied likewise in the various branches of federal jurisdiction, and admittedly has been revised from time to time to conform to new conditions.

Under the common law, the liability of common carriers was so rigid that they were often regarded as *insurers* of the goods entrusted to them and it was only natural and to be expected that with the passage of time the carriers would seek ways to lessen their burdens. Under the common law, a common carrier was free to contract against liability for loss or damage due to causes other than his own negligence. Initially, the common carriers sought to escape their extraordinary liability by publication of notices to the effect that their liability would be limited to indicated amounts unless the shipper elected to pay a higher rate which would impose upon the carrier the assumption of greater liability. By the posting of these notices, the common carriers hoped the courts would consider that knowledge of the conditions under which the goods would be carried and would be brought home to the owner and by custom become a part of the transportation contract. Even though this was a loose arrangement with the result that a shipper might ship his goods without actual knowledge of such notice, the courts recognized early that it was sufficient to limit the carrier's liability when there was reason to believe that the notice had been brought to the attention of the shipper or reasonably should have been known to him.

As a result of controversy over whether the shipper was actually informed or reasonably should have been, Parliament in 1854 enacted the Railway and Canal Traffic Act which provided that carriers could limit their common-law liability only by written contract with the shipper. In this country, from early times, courts have required that any restriction of liability must be agreed to by the shipper who once having accepted the terms was bound by them; and assent was considered sufficient when the shipper accepted a receipt or bill of lading containing the terms and conditions under which the goods would move, which extended a valuable consideration in the form of reduced charges for the agreement to accept reduced liability.

Because the common law is our heritage, there is a tendency to assume a uniformity and finality comparable to that of a legal code. Particularly in the area of carrier liability, there is a tendency in many of the court decisions to assume a conclusiveness which is belied by the numerous writers who have questioned the basic premises of that liability. It is unfortunate that some of the early writers used the term *insurer* in describing the carrier's liability since the term implies a form of liability, indeed a relationship, which does not belong to the carrier. Partly because of this vague understanding of liability of the common carrier and partly, the writer fears, because of a tendency to charge the loss to the common carrier who is assumed to be in the best position to absorb the loss or pass it on, some courts tend to give only lip service to the common carrier's common-law liability and to statutes intended to give carriers limited additional protection, such as the statutes relating to time limits for filing claims.

On the other hand, there is a surprising reluctance on the part of common carriers to insist that claimants make even a prima facie case of carrier liability before paying claims. Shippers, no doubt at least partly because of past experience, tend to expect claims to be paid almost on demand and without question. Today there is probably no greater loophole for discrimination, rebates, etc., than in the matter of claims against carriers for loss and damage to freight.

The strict common-law rule of carrier liability had its foundation in a public policy which has been variously imputed to the absolute possession and control of the carrier during transit, to the survival of a rule once applied to all bailees, and to the consequences of the rigid forms of pleading at common law. Whatever its true origin, the strict liability of the common carrier survives as an anachronism today.

Carriers' Liability Under Federal Legislation

The early decisions concerning the liability of common carriers arose from transportation by stagecoaches, carts, and wagons. With the advent of the railroad and its virtual monopoly of the transportation field in the latter half of the last century, there were few decisions in connection with carrier liability which did not involve rail carriers. The development of motor transportation, however, in recent years brought many phases of the law of carrier liability back to highway transportation where it had originated.

When rail transportation commenced, carrier liability under the common law founded on transportation by highway was applied to this mode of conveyance. Similarly, when the motor transportation industry entered the field, the law of carrier liability developed in connection with rail transportation was applied to motor carriers. In determining the liability of a common carrier under the common law, it makes no difference whether the transportation agency is a horse, truck, or train. If it is a common carrier for hire, then it is subject to common-law liability.

Even today many motor carriers are reluctant to cite cases involving rail carriers in connection with their liability to their customers. It should be remembered, however, that while much of present day law in connection with loss and damage claims is based on litigation involving rail transportation, nevertheless, this law is equally applicable to motor transportation. In any event, these decisions were written by the courts, not the carriers.

The severity of liability imposed upon carriers by the common law, arising from the carriers' position to violate the trust reposed in them, led to resistance on the part of the carriers to the application of the old common law. According to Kent (*Commentaries on American Law*, vol.

1, Lecture 21), the common law "includes those principles, usages, and rules of actions applicable to the government and security of person and property; which do not rest by their authority upon any express and positive declaration of the will of the legislature." Blackstone (*Commentaries on the Laws of England,* Intro. § *III*) defines common law in this manner:

> Whence it is that in our law the goodness of a custom depends upon its having been used time out of mind; or, in that solemnity of our legal phrase, time whereof the memory of man runneth not to the contrary. This is that (which) gives its weight and authority. . . .

After the War of Independence, it was generally the intent of the original colonies to embrace as fully as possible the basic common law of the mother country. Even today the decisions of the courts of Great Britain before such independence and even afterwards are frequently cited as authority in this nation, although seldom is reference made to development of the statutory law found necessary because of the inadequacy or other failing of that ancient common law. The reluctance of this country to evaluate the common law in the light of present day necessities, and particularly in the light of its development in the nation of its origin, has resulted today in a roadblock to our own progress. Especially is it true as a result of the limited sources of authority to determine the old common law with preciseness and with knowledge of those exceptions "which make the rule."

Following our own independence, the various state legislatures passed laws with respect to common carriers, some of which were more advantageous to them than the common law used by the federal courts. These laws and the state courts' interpretation of the common law were in many instances applied to interstate shipments; but in those instances where appeal to the federal courts was made, any ruling contrary to the federal courts' interpretation was quickly overruled. The federal courts from the beginning assumed authority over disputes regarding shipments in interstate commerce on the basis that such authority was given by Section 2, Art. 3, of the Constitution, which declared that:

> The judicial power shall extend to all cases in law and equity, arising under this constitution, the laws of the United States, and treaties made or which shall be made, under their authority; to all cases of admiralty and maritime jurisdiction. . . .

As a result of the chaos brought about through the railroad monopoly of transportation, Congress enacted the Interstate Commerce Act in 1887.

The Act applied to common carriers "engaged in the transportation of persons or property wholly by rail or partly by rail and water when both are used under a common control, management, or arrangement for continuous carriage or shipment." (54 Stat. 899) Section 20 of the Act as originally enacted, while important in that it delegated to the federal courts adjudication of all disputes on matters pertaining to interstate commerce, was far from satisfactory in disposing of the questions relating to liability of interstate common carriers. For almost twenty years after the enactment of this legislation, rail carriers continued to issue bills of lading containing clauses intended to relieve them from some of their common-law liability, not only as insurers but also for negligence. Particular concern was caused by the carrier's liability for any loss or damage occuring beyond its own line. For this lack and others, the original Interstate Commerce Act was supplemented and strengthened by the Hepburn Act, passed in 1906, and the Clayton Act, passed in 1914.

The Hepburn Act of 1906 contained what is commonly designated as the Carmack Amendment. The purpose of this amendment was to provide a more uniform standard of liability for rail and water carriers. It required carriers to issue a bill of lading or receipt for property received for transportation and imposed liability on the initial carrier for all injuries to a shipment not only while in its own possession, but even when in the possession of a connecting line. Prior to the enactment of this legislation, authorities were in conflict as to the liability of the initial carrier for injury to the goods while in the possession of a connecting carrier. One school of thought followed what is called *the English rule,* which holds that a common carrier receiving goods consigned to a point beyond its line is liable for loss or injury occurring while the goods are in possession of the connection unless the carrier specifically contracted to limit its liability to its own line. Most federal and state decisions, however, at that time held that in the absence of any contract, usage or statute to the contrary, the liability of the initial carrier was limited to its own line. It is interesting to note that prior to federal regulation of motor carriers, one federal court held that since these decisions limiting liability of the initial carrier were the outgrowth of railroad transportation, they should not be applied to carriers by motor truck, on the grounds of public policy and in view of the different conditions under which they operate. (*Tubize Chattilon Corporation* v. *White Transp. Co.,* 6 F. Supp. 15)

The Carmack Amendment did not sufficiently cover all the controversies arising in connection with carrier liability. The law with respect to released valuation in bills of lading was the source of many disputes and as a result additional federal legislation was enacted. In 1915 Congress enacted the First Cummins Amendment, which imposed liability on the carrier for the full loss, damage, or injury caused by it or any connecting carrier regardless of any agreement for limitation of liability or value. In 1916 Congress passed the Second Cummins Amendment to provide that carriers might lawfully limit their liability by released rates which had been specifically authorized by the Interstate Commerce Commission. Congress subsequently further amended this section of the Interstate Commerce Act (Sec. 20, Par. 11) to make the delivering as well as the initial carrier liable to the holder of the receipt or bill of lading and to specify the time limits for filing claims and suits.

Through the Motor Carrier Act of 1935, Congress provided federal regulation of interstate highway transportation. This legislation is now part II of the Interstate Commerce Act. Congress did not write a new section in this law to provide for carrier liability, but Section 219 (49 U.S.C. §319) provided as follows:

> SEC. 219. The provisions of section 20(11) of part I shall apply with like force and effect to receipts or bills of lading of common carrier by motor vehicles.

This section was later amended to make Section 20(12) of part I also applicable to motor common carriers. These provisions have no application with relation to contracts, obligations, and liabilities of carriers with regard to shipments which are exclusively intrastate. Rail and motor carrier liability with respect to intrastate transportation is founded on the laws of the various states. As a practical matter, the state laws and court decisions thereunder are substantially the same as those relating to interstate shipments.

Statutory Provisions of the Interstate Commerce Act

Section 219 of part II of the Interstate Commerce Act, 49 U.S.C. §319:

> SEC. 219. The provisions of section 20(11) and (12) of part I of this Act, together with such other provisions of such part (including penalties) as may be necessary for the enforcement of such provisions, shall apply with respect to common carriers by motor vehicle with like force and effect as in the case of those persons to which such provisions are specifically applicable.

Section 20(11) of part I of the Interstate Commerce Act, 49 U.S.C. §20(11):

SEC. 20(11). That any common carrier, railroad, or transportation company subject to the provisions of this Act receiving property for transportation from a point in one State or Territory or the District of Columbia to a point in another State, Territory, District of Columbia, or from any point in the United States to a point in an adjacent foreign country shall issue a receipt or bill of lading therefor, and shall be liable to the lawful holder thereof for any loss, damage, or injury to such property caused by it or by any common carrier, railroad or transportation company to which such property may be delivered or over whose line or lines such property may pass within the United States or within an adjacent foreign country when transported on a through bill of lading, and no contract, receipt, rule, regulation, or other limitation of any character whatsoever, shall exempt such common carrier, railroad, or transportation company from the liability hereby imposed; and any such common carrier, railroad, or transportation company so receiving property for transportation from a point in one State, Territory, or the District of Columbia to a point in another State or Territory, or from a point in a State or Territory to a point in the District of Columbia, or from any point in the United States to a point in an adjacent foreign country, or for transportation wholly within a Territory, or any common carrier, railroad, or transportation company delivering said property so received and transported shall be liable to the lawful holder of said receipt or bill of lading or to any party entitled to recover thereon, whether such receipt or bill of lading has been issued or not, for the full actual loss, damage, or injury to such property caused by it or by any common carrier, railroad, or transportation company to which such property may be delivered or over whose line or lines such property may pass within the United States or within an adjacent foreign country when transported on a through bill of lading, notwithstanding any limitation of liability or limitation of the amount of recovery or representation or agreement as to value in any such receipt or bill of lading, or in any contract, rule, regulation, or in any tariff filed with the Interstate Commerce Commission; and any such limitation, without respect to the manner or form in which it is sought to be made is hereby declared to be unlawful and void. . . .

This section contains a number of qualifying provisos, the first two of which relate the liability of water carriers and to liability for passengers' baggage. The second proviso also sets out the conditions under which a carrier may limit its liability:

Provided, That if the loss, damage, or injury occurs while the property is in the custody of a carrier by water the liability of such carrier shall be determined by the bill of lading of the carrier by water and by and under the laws and regulations applicable to transportation by water, and the liability of the initial or delivering carrier shall be the same as that of such carrier by water: *Provided, however,* That the provisions hereof respecting liability for full actual loss, damage, or injury, notwithstanding any limitation of liability or recovery or representation or agreement or release as to value, and declaring any such limitation to be unlawful and void, shall not apply, first, to baggage carried on passenger trains or boats, or trains or boats carrying passengers; second, to property, except ordinary livestock, received for transportation concerning which the carrier shall have been or shall hereafter be expressly authorized or required by order of the Interstate Commerce Commission to establish and maintain rates dependent upon the value declared in writing by the shipper or agreed upon in writing as the release value of the property, in which case such declaration or agreement shall have no other effect than to limit liability and recovery to an amount not exceeding the value so declared or released, and shall not, so far as related to values, be held to be a violation of Section 10 of this part to regulate commerce, as amended; and any tariff schedule which may be filed with the Commission pursuant to such order shall contain specific reference thereto and may establish rates varying with the value so declared and agreed upon; and the Commission is hereby empowered to make such order in cases where rates dependent upon and varying with declared or agreed values would, in its opinion, be just and reasonable under the circumstances and conditions surrounding the transportation. The term "ordinary livestock" shall include all cattle, swine, sheep, goats, horses, and mules, except such as are chiefly valuable for breeding, racing, show purposes, or other special uses. . . .

The other provisos to this section are primarily jurisdictional:

Provided further, That nothing in this section shall deprive any holder of such receipt or bill of lading of any remedy or right of action which he has under the existing law: *Provided further,* That all actions brought under and by virtue of this paragraph against the delivering carrier shall be brought, and may be maintained, if in a district court of the United States, only in a district, and if in a State court, only in a State through or into which the defendant carrier operates a line of railroad: *Provided further,* That it shall be unlawful for any such receiving or delivering common carrier to provide by rule, contract, regulation, or otherwise a shorter period for the filing of claims than nine months, and for the institution of suits than two years, such period for institution of suits to be computed from the day when notice in writing is given by the carrier to the claimant that the carrier has disallowed the claim or any part or parts thereof specified in the notice: *And provided further,* That for the purpose of this paragraph and of paragraph (12) the delivering carrier shall be construed to be the carrier performing the line-haul service nearest to the point of destination and not a carrier performing merely a switching service at the point of destination: *And provided further,* That the liability imposed by this paragraph shall also apply in the case of property reconsigned or diverted in accordance with the applicable tariffs filed as in this part provided.

Section 20(12) of part I of the Interstate Commerce Act, 49 U.S.C. §20(12):

SEC. 20(12). The common carrier, railroad, or transportation company issuing such receipt or bill of lading, or delivering such property so received and transported, shall be entitled to recover from the common carrier, railroad, or transportation company on whose line the loss, damage, or injury shall have been sustained, the amount of such loss, damage, or injury as it may be required to pay to the owners of such property, as may be evidenced by any receipt, judgment, or transcript thereof, and the amount of any expense reasonably incurred by it in defending any action at law brought by the owners of such property.

2

The Transportation Contract

The liability of interstate carriers for loss, damage, or delay to freight while in their possession is based on (A) the common law, (B) statutory law, (C) lawful conditions of the contract of shipment (bill of lading), and (D) pertinent provisions of applicable tariffs legally on file with the Interstate Commerce Commission as to interstate transportation.

A common carrier generally cannot, under the common law, exempt itself from the consequences of its own negligence or willful act in the handling of goods. Therefore even when injury is the result of one of the common-law excepted perils, the carrier will nevertheless be liable for any failure to use the degree of care that would have prevented or mitigated the injury resulting from the excepted cause.

The law is now well settled that a carrier may, unless forbidden by statute, limit or restrict or even extend and enlarge, its common-law liability. Such contracts which limit or enlarge the carrier's common-law liability must, however, meet with all the requirements applicable to other forms of contracts. The enlargement or limitation of liability must be supported by mutual assent and valuable consideration. In view of statutory provisions today, however, this right is practically meaningless.

The Bill of Lading

The efforts of carriers to limit their common-law liability by contract led to many different provisions in bill of lading forms; and prior to the Carmack Amendment, these varying terms were subject to construction by state courts and the application of varying policies by state legislatures and state courts. This lack of uniformity was the source of confusion and controversy resulting in the enactment of the Carmack Amendment in 1906 which, among other things, required common carriers receiving property for transportation in interstate commerce to issue a receipt or bill of lading therefor and imposed liability on the carrier to the lawful holder thereof for any loss, damage, or injury to such property caused by it (the carrier).

Prior to the adoption of the Carmack Amendment the liability of common carriers was determined by the common law or the statutes of the different states. A usual provision incorporated in bills of lading then in use provided that no carrier should be liable for any loss or damage occurring while the goods were not in its possession. Under this limitation the initial carrier was not liable for loss or damage through the fault of the connecting lines to which it had safely delivered the goods for further transportation. These connecting lines were considered the agent of the shipper for the continuance of the transportation. The claimant, in an action for recovery on account of injury to the goods, was therefore subjected to the inconvenience of ascertaining upon which line in the through route the injury occurred. This difficulty imposed a serious hardship upon the claimant in the prosecution of his suit.

The Carmack Amendment took away from the initial carrier its former right to make a contract limiting its liability to injury to the goods occurring while in its possession and made the connecting lines the agents of the initial carrier. Claimants were thereby relieved of the burden of proving the particular carrier upon whose line the injury occurred. The Carmack Amendment also withdrew from the states all regulatory authority and jurisdiction over questions of loss, damage, or injury to property shipped in interstate commerce and brought such matters under the uniform operation and regulation of federal law.

It should be noted that under the Carmack Amendment a carrier may not escape liability if it fails to issue a bill of lading. The statutory liability attaches to the contracts of shipment regardless of whether or not a bill of lading is actually issued.

Immediately following the enactment of the Carmack Amendment, opinion as to its effect on the liability of interstate carriers differed greatly. Subsequent litigation had the result of clearly defining the exact meaning of this legislation. Simply stated, the amendment provided that the applicable and valid terms of the bill of lading issued by the initial carrier governed the adjustment of claims for loss, damage, and delay to that shipment, regardless of where it occurred, and afforded the claimant a convenient means of collecting its claim by freeing it of the burden of determining which carrier was responsible.

The Carmack Amendment did not increase the extent of the carrier's liability as imposed by common law. The amendment did not prohibit carriers from limiting the amount recoverable by a claimant in case of loss or damage to an agreed value made for the purpose of obtaining the lower of two or more rates or charges proportioned to the amount of the risk.

The enactment of the First Cummins Amendment in 1915 further modified the common-law liability of carriers. The practical effect of this legislation was to abolish in interstate commerce the whole system of released rates based on agreed valuation as distinguished from actual value. This amendment made a common carrier liable for the full actual loss, damage, or injury caused by it unless, when the shipment was made, the goods were hidden from view and the carrier not informed as to their character, in which event the carrier could require the shipper to state in writing the value of the goods and could limit its liability to the amount so stated. The amendment also provided certain periods of limitation for giving notice of claims, for filing claims, and instituting suits.

The Second Cummins Amendment was enacted in 1916 and the provisions relating to goods hidden from view were eliminated. By this amendment, carriers were authorized to limit their liability and the amount of recovery with respect to all property except "ordinary livestock." The amendment further prescribed the specific conditions under which carriers could limit their liability in the transportation of property other than "ordinary livestock." These conditions are the establishment and maintenance of rates (1) dependent upon value declared in writing by the shipper, or (2) agreed upon in writing as the released value of the property under the express authorization or requirement of the Interstate Commerce Commission. Since Section 10 of the Interstate Commerce Act makes it unlawful for a shipper to misrepresent in any way the nature or value of property shipped for the purpose of securing lower rates, the amendment provides that such declarations or agreements shall have no other effect than to limit liability and recovery to an amount not exceeding the value stated and shall not be deemed in violation of Section 10. Thus the Second Cummins Amendment restored, in a restricted manner, the system of released rates which had been abolished by the First Cummins Amendment.

The Newton Amendment enacted in 1927 and legislation enacted in 1930 had the effect of extending liability to the delivering carrier as well as the initial carrier, and specifically providing the time limits for filing claims and bringing suits which are in effect at the present time.

Initially there was some doubt as to the power of the Interstate Commerce Commission to prescribe the form and contents of bills of lading to be used by railroad carriers operating under its jurisdiction. The Commission had, however, as early as 1904, instituted an investigation, Docket No. 787, which resulted in two reports, 13 I. C. C. 550 and 14 I. C. C. 348. A formal investigation was later instituted, Docket No. 4844, *In the Matter of Bills of Lading,* and many hearings have been conducted and many orders issued in connection with this proceeding which is still upon the Commission's docket.

In its first report in Docket No. 4844, decided 14 April 1919, 52 I. C. C. 671, the Commission held that it had authority under the law to require carriers subject to its jurisdiction to comply with the provisions of the law respecting issuance of bills of lading; to file with it the rules and regulations which they write into their bills of ladng; to require that uniform rules and regulations be adopted by them; and to determine what are reasonable and nondiscriminatory rules and regulations. In this report, the Commission prescribed for the use of carriers subject to its jurisdiction a bill of lading with contractual provisions which it found just and reasonable. These provisions were modified in the Commission's subsequent report, 64 I. C. C. 357, decided 21 October 1921, to conform with the requirements of the Interstate Commerce Act as amended on 28 February 1920.

The Commission, in reviewing the background leading to its decision to prescribe the form and content of the rail bill of lading, made the following observations, 52 I. C. C. 681:

An important function of the bill of lading is to give formal expression to the stipulations and conditions under which the carrier seeks to obtain a modification or limitation of the liability that otherwise would be imposed upon it under the common law. While the limitations of the carrier's liability must be agreed to by the shipper and the agreement be invested with the sanctity of a valid contract, neither by common law nor by federal statute in the country is any particular form of contract or solemnity of execution required. Contracts between shipper and carrier, however, are almost invariably evidenced by the more or less formal bill of lading, written or printed, which serves three distinct functions: First, a receipt for the goods; second, a contract for their carriage; and, third, documentary evidence of title to the goods. As a receipt for the goods, it recites the place and date of shipment; decribes the goods, their quality, weight, dimensions, identification marks, condition, etc., and sometimes their quality and value. As a contract, the bill names the contracting parties, specifies the rate or charge for transportation, and sets forth the agreement and stipulations with respect to the limitations of the carrier's common-law liability in the case of loss or injury to the goods and other obligations assumed by the parties or to matters agreed upon between them. That part of the bill which constitutes a receipt may be treated as distinct from the part incorporating the contractual terms. *Porter, Law of Bills of Lading,* 14, citing *Myer* v. *Peck,* 1 *Tiffany* (28 N.Y.), 590, *Higgins* v. *U.S.M.S.S. Co.,* 3 *Blatchf.* (U.S.S.C.), 282. Ordinarily parol evidence will not be admitted to vary the terms or legal effect of a bill of lading, considered as a contract between the parties to it, although, it seems, that as a receipt for the goods it may be contradicted by oral testimony. *The Delaware,* 14 *Wall.,* 579. It is sufficient if the shipper accepts the carrier's bill of lading without himself signing it. It becomes binding upon him by his acceptance, he being presumed to know and accept the conditions of the written bill of lading. The bill of lading is regarded as representative of the goods while they are in the carrier's possession. It is not a negotiable instrument in the common acceptance of the term, but it may be, and frequently is, made negotiable in form and thus becomes invested with peculiar attributes of great practical importance commercially.

With respect to interstate motor common carriers, the Interstate Commerce Commission has never undertaken in a formal proceeding to prescribe the form and contents of their bills of lading and undoubtedly this has resulted solely from the fact that there has never seemed to be any necessity for doing so. After the Commission was given jurisdiction over interstate motor carriers the following notice dated March 25, 1936, was issued by the Commission.

Receipts and Bills of Lading

Section 219 of the Motor Carrier Act, 1935, effective April 1, 1936, requires common carriers of property by motor vehicle to issue a receipt or bill of lading for any property received for transportation by them in interstate or foreign commerce. The Commission is in receipt of numerous inquiries regarding the proper form and contents of receipts and bills of lading to be issued by common carriers of property in compliance with this requirement of the law.

Such carriers, in order to comply with the above requirements must provide and have ready for use on and after April 1, 1936, appropriate forms of receipts or bills of lading, the contents and provisions of which must be just and reasonable. The responsibility for including any unlawful conditions or provisions in receipts or bills of lading rests with the carriers. If experience proves that it is necessary for the Commission to take action in this matter, conferences and formal hearings may be held at which interested parties will have an opportunity to present their views.

A bill of lading may not contain any condition or provision which purports to limit the liability of a common carrier of property by motor vehicle for any loss, damage, or injury to the property transported, unless such carrier has been previously authorized by the Commission, after application, to establish and maintain rates dependent upon the value declared or agreed upon in writing as the released value of the property.

On 25 November 1946, the Commission issued the following order to motor common carriers concerning the issuance of receipts and bills of lading:

It is ordered, That every common carrier by motor vehicle subject to the jurisdiction of this Commission shall, on and after the first day of January, 1937, cause to be shown on the face of each and every receipt or bill of lading issued for the transportation of property by such carrier in interstate or foreign commerce, information which shall include the names of the consignor and consignee; the points of origin and destination; the number of packages, description of the articles, and weight, volume or measurement (if the lawfully applicable rates or charges are published to apply per unit of weight, volume or measurement) of the property received; and that a record of this information be kept by the carrier by the preservation of a copy of such receipt or bill of lading.

The adoption of the Motor Carrier Act, 1935, was followed by considerable confusion in getting the implementing regulations under way, and it would have been impossible to hold formal hearings with thousands of carriers and shippers participating therein to determine in minute detail the terms and conditions with respect to the basic document to every shipment made, the bill of lading. As one authority has stated:

For years and at great length the Commission had already heard everybody as to all phases of the subject as it related to common carriers by railroad, and had made formal findings as to the just and reasonable conditions, substance, and form of the bill of lading, which had stood up against court attack. The motor carriers and their shippers were under strong moral duty to be practical and put in operation the general findings of the Commission so as to apply to motors, as well as to the types of competing carriers which had been heard formally. This is exactly what was done; and the informal nature of the proceeding emphasized the duty of any aggrieved person, carrier, or shipper, to proceed formally if he had reason to question the action of the Commission. No such action has ever been taken.

Generally, the bill of lading adopted by motor common carriers followed closely the bill of lading prescribed by the Commission for rail carriers. The form generally in use by the motor carriers is that published in the National Motor Freight Classification. No provision of the bill has been attacked or subjected to court review because of any claim of variance with the common, statutory, or general jurisprudence.

The Pomerene Bills of Lading Act (41 U. S. C. 81 *et seq.*), approved in 1916, applies to *all* common carriers. This important legislation has been described as a "codification of our Federal law covering the issuance, negotiation, accomplishment, and cancellation of bills of lading." To a large extent, this legislation, discussed in detail herein (see p. 49), is concerned primarily with the "title to the goods" aspect of the bill of lading and the rights and liabilities relating thereto.

As a practical matter, many shippers purchase their own bills of lading forms, fill them in, and tender them for signature at the time the carrier accepts the shipment. It is the carrier's duty, however, to issue the bill of lading as stated in Section 20(11) of the Interstate Commerce Act. Due to this practice of shippers, considerable confusion at one time existed because a shipper would often tender a motor carrier a shipment on a bill of lading which upon minute examination would be found to be that of rail carriers and vice versa. Actually, the terms and conditions of the two bills differ only slightly but, technically, the shipment should have been accepted only on the bill of lading prescribed in the tariff of the carrier accepting the shipment. The shipper, however, quite often did not feel that he should be required to go to the trouble of securing more than one bill of lading form and be placed to the additional trouble of determining which one to use. In 1949 both motor and rail carriers prescribed in their respective classifications what is designated as a "short form" bill of lading and which omits the printing of the contract terms and conditions which appear in very small type on the reverse side of the standard bill. The "short form" incorporates the applicable bill of lading terms and conditions by reference by the following words:

> . . . every service to be performed hereunder shall be subject to all the terms and conditions of the Uniform Domestic Straight Bill of Lading set forth (1) in Official, Southern, Western and Illinois Freight Classifications in effect on the date hereof, if this is a rail or a rail-water shipment, or (2) in the applicable motor carrier classification or tariff if this is a motor carrier shipment.

The quoted provision appears in the receipt portion of the bill and precedes the following paragraph which is printed in bold face type:

> Shipper hereby certifies that he is familiar with all the terms and conditions of the said bill of lading, including those on the back thereof, set forth in the classification or tariff which governs the transportation of this shipment, and the said terms and conditions are hereby agreed to by the shipper and accepted by himself and his assigns.

The bill of lading as a commercial document serves three distinct purposes in connection with the carriage of goods: (1) it is a receipt for the goods; (2) it represents the contract of carriage; and (3) it serves as a document of title.

The Bill of Lading as a Receipt

The relation of shipper and common carrier commences with the delivery of goods by the shipper to the carrier with shipping directions, and ordinarily a receipt is not essential to complete delivery to the carrier for transportation. A carrier cannot escape liability because of its failure to issue a receipt or bill of lading.

The portion of the commonly used rail and motor carrier bill of lading which constitutes a receipt is that portion on the face of the bill reading as follows:

Received, subject to the classifications and tariffs in effect on the date of the issue of this bill of lading.

From ....Date .... 19 ......

At .... Street .... City .... County ....

State .... the property described below in apparent good order, except as noted (contents and conditions of contents of packages unknown) marked, consigned, and destined as shown below. . . .

As a receipt for property the bill of lading provides that the property described is received (1) subject to the classifications and tariffs in effect on the date the bill of lading is issued, (2) in apparent good order, except as noted, the contents and conditions of contents of packages being unknown, and (3) marked, consigned, and destined as shown in the space provided for that purpose.

Since the date of the bill of lading determines the classification and tariffs applicable to the shipment, it is important that the date shown be the exact date on which the shipment is received. To knowingly insert a false date on the bill for the purpose of securing a lower rate is unlawful.

As a receipt the bill of lading is not conclusive as to the amount of goods receipted for, it being competent to show as between the parties that a different quantity was actually delivered. A receipt showing delivery of the property to the carrier and reciting that they were received in apparent good order is not conclusive of the question but only prima facie evidence that the goods were in apparent good order. Receipts, as such, are subject to explanation as between the parties.

In the law of evidence there exists a rule commonly known as the *Parol Evidence Rule*. Briefly, this rule provides that the terms of a written integrated document, contractual in nature, cannot be varied by parol (oral) evidence as between the parties making the agreement. The theory of this rule is in the substantive law of contracts which conclusively presumes that the negotiations of the parties are merged in the writing and that this was intended by them as the final and authoritative statement of their agreement. This rule, however, in its application does not prevent third persons from attacking the written instrument by parol testimony of prior or contemporaneous matters; nor does the rule prohibit the parties themselves from showing that there was fraud, mistake, or duress which would invalidate the written contract. The Parol Evidence Rule is applicable only to written instruments which are contractual in nature. As has been explained, the bill of lading is both a contract and a receipt. Accordingly, that portion of the bill which is contractual in nature cannot be varied by oral testimony as between the parties to its execution. On the other hand, that portion of the bill of lading which constitutes the receipt can be varied or explained by the parties as this part of the bill is noncontractual.

The receipt is said to be prima facie evidence of the facts herein recited. Prima facie evidence is rebuttable. In other words, a receipt creates a rebuttable presumption that the facts stated therein are true and shifts the burden of proving otherwise to the party contesting its accuracy. It therefore follows that insofar as the bill of lading constitutes a receipt for the goods, the recitals with respect to condition, quantity, and quality of goods are not conclusive and it is always permissible to show the true facts.

The rule of law that a receipt for the goods is explainable holds good only as between the parties thereto, namely, the consignor and the carrier. A different rule applies where a third party acquires rights under the bill of lading, as is explained hereafter.

The Bill of Lading as the Contract of Carriage

The bill of lading, as a contract, specifies the contracting parties and sets forth the terms and conditions of their agreement. It contains the stipulations with respect to the limitations of the carrier's common law liability and other obligations which the carrier assumes. It describes the property which the carrier agrees to transport and may name the rates to be applied and the charges to be collected, which must be the lawfully published rates and charges.

The contractual nature of the bill of lading most commonly used by carriers is set forth in the following provision on its face:

> It is mutually agreed, as to each carrier of all or any of said property over all or any portion of said route to destination, and as to each party at any time interested in all or any of said property, that every service to be performed hereunder shall be subject to all the conditions not prohibited by law, whether printed or written, herein contained, including the conditions on back hereof, which are hereby agreed to by the shipper and accepted for himself and his assigns.

As mentioned earlier, the so-called short form combination rail-motor bill of lading does not set forth contract terms and conditions of the bill on its reverse side as does the standard bill, but incorporates such terms and conditions by reference. Even on the so-called long form the terms and conditions are printed in exceedingly small type and are quite often illegible and, for that matter, seldom read, understood, or analyzed by the shipper or carrier. Nevertheless the provisions of this contract of transportation are of tremendous importance to all transportation users and carriers. The more important of these provisions, from a claim standpoint, are the following:

1. The carrier shall be liable as at common law, except as otherwise provided in the bill of lading.
2. The carrier shall not be liable for loss, damage, or delay due to acts of God, the public enemy, the authority of law, the acts of defaults of the shipper or owner, or for natural shrinkage.
3. Except in case of negligence of the carrier (and the burden of proving freedom from negligence shall be on the carrier), the carrier shall not be liable for loss, damage or delay occurring while the property is stopped in transit upon the request of the shipper or owner, or resulting from a defect or vice in the property, or for country damage to cotton, or from riots or strikes, or for delay due to faulty or impassable highways or lack of capacity of any highway, bridge or ferry.
4. Except in case of negligence, the carrier shall not be liable for anything required to be done by quarantine regulation.
5. No carrier is bound to transport property by any particular vehicle, or in accordance with any particular schedule, or otherwise than with reasonable dispatch.
6. Claims must be filed within nine months, and the carrier may not waive this requirement. Suits must be instituted within two years and one day from the date carrier declines the claim or a portion thereof in writing.
7. Refused or unclaimed property may be sold by the carrier at public auction in the manner provided.
8. The carrier's liability shall be that of a warehouseman only for loss, damage, or delay occurring after the expiration of free time.

While the foregoing eight provisions reflect the most important provisions of the bill of lading from the standpoint of claims, each provision of the bill of lading should be carefully studied and analyzed to fully understand the contractual liability of the carrier. Each section of the usual rail and motor bill of lading is reproduced in the following analysis together with a brief summary of its meaning. The few differences between the motor and rail bill of lading are indicated and explained.

Analysis of Terms and Conditions of Bill of Lading

Analysis of Section 1(a) of Bill of Lading Terms

SEC. 1(a). The carrier or party in possession of any of the property herein described shall be liable as at common law for any loss thereof or damage thereto, except as hereinafter provided.

This paragraph provides that carrier is liable as at common law for any loss or damage, except as otherwise provided. By this provision, the carrier insures against everything not specifically exempted in the bill of lading.

Analysis of Section 1(b) of Bill of Lading Terms

SEC. 1(b). No carrier or party in possession of all or any of the property herein described shall be liable for any loss thereof or damage thereto or delay caused by the act of God, the public enemy, the authority of law, or the act or default of the shipper or owner, or for natural shrinkage. The carrier's liability shall be that of warehouseman, only, for loss, damage, or delay caused by fire occurring after the expiration of the free time (if any) allowed by tariffs lawfully on file (such free time to be computed as therein provided) after notice of the arrival of the property at destination or at the port of export (if intended for export) has been duly sent or given, and after placement of the property for delivery at destination, or tender of delivery of the property to the party entitled to receive it, has been made. Except in case of negligence of the carrier or party in possession (and the burden to prove freedom from such negligence shall be on the carrier or party in possession), the carrier or party in possession shall not be liable for loss, damage, or delay occurring while the property is stopped and held in transit upon the request of shipper, owner, or party entitled to make such request, or resulting from a defect or vice in the property, or for country damage to cotton, or from riots or strikes. *Except in case of carrier's negligence, no carrier or party in possession of all or any of the property herein described shall be liable for delay caused by highway obstruction, faulty or impassable highway, or lack of capacity of any highway, bridge or ferry, and the burden to prove freedom from such negligence shall be on the carrier or party in possession.*

The words shown in italics appear only in the motor carrier bill of lading. This paragraph sets forth four major provisions relative to the carrier's liability as a common carrier. Provision is made:

1. That the carrier shall not be liable for any loss, damage, or delay caused by
   A. The act of God
   B. The public enemy

C. The authority of law
D. Act or default of owner or shipper
E. Natural shrinkage

2. That the carrier shall be liable as a warehouseman only, for loss, damage or delay caused by fire occurring after the expiration of free time (if any) allowed by lawfully published and filed tariffs after
   A. Notice of the arrival of the property at destination has been duly sent or given, *or*
   B. Notice of the arrival of the property at port of export (when for export) has been duly sent or given, *and*
   C. After placement of the property for delivery at destination has been made, *or*
   D. After tender of delivery of the property to the party entitled to receive it has been made.
3. That except in case of negligence the carrier shall not be liable for loss, damage or delay
   A. Occurring while the property is stopped and held in transit upon the request of the shipper, owner, or party entitled to make such request.
   B. Resulting from a defect or vice in the property.
   C. Caused by country damage to cotton.
   D. Resulting from riots or strikes.
4. That carrier shall not be liable except in case of negligence for delay, caused by
   A. Highway obstructions.
   B. Faulty or impassable highways.
   C. Lack of capacity of any highway, bridge, or ferry.

Under Section 1(b), the duty of proving freedom from negligence is placed upon the carrier. In other words, the negligence of the carrier is presumed and the carrier must prove itself free from negligence in cases of loss, damage, or delay occurring under the specific exemptions.

Analysis of Section 1(c) of Bill of Lading Terms

SEC. 1(c). In case of quarantine the property may be discharged at the risk and expense of owners into quarantine depot or elsewhere, as required by quarantine regulations or authorities, or for the carrier's dispatch at nearest available point in carrier's judgment, and in any such case carrier's responsibility shall cease when property is so discharged, or property may be returned by carrier at owner's expense to shipping point, earning freight both ways. Quarantine expenses of whatever nature or kind upon or in respect to property shall be borne by the owners of the property or be a lien thereon. The carrier shall not be liable for loss or damage occasioned by fumigation or disinfection or other acts required or done by quarantine regulations or authorities even though the same may have been done by carrier's officers, agents, or employees, nor for detention, loss, or damage of any kind occasioned by quarantine or the enforcement thereof. No carrier shall be liable, except in case of negligence, for any mistake or inaccuracy in any information furnished by the carrier, its agents, or officers, as to quarantine laws or regulations. The shipper shall hold the carriers harmless from any expense they may incur, or damages they may be required to pay, by reason of the introduction of the property covered by this contract into any place against the quarantine laws or regulations in effect at such place.

This paragraph provides in substance that except in case of negligence, the carrier shall not be liable for any loss, damage, delay or expense which may occur as a result of quarantine laws or regulations.

Analysis of Section 2(a) of Bill of Lading Terms

SEC. 2(a). No carrier is bound to transport said property by any particular *schedule,* train, *vehicle* or vessel, or in time for any particular market or otherwise than with reasonable dispatch. Every carrier shall have the right in case of physical necessity to forward said property by any carrier or route between the point of shipment and the point of destination. In all cases not prohibited by law, where a lower value than actual value has been represented in writing by the shipper or has been agreed upon in writing as the released value of the property as determined by the classification or tariffs upon which the rate is based, such lower value plus freight charges if paid shall be the maximum amount to be recovered, whether or not such loss or damage occurs from negligence.

The two italicized words *schedule* and *vehicle* appear only in the motor carrier bill of lading. This paragraph has three separate provisions to the effect that

1. Carriers are under no legal obligation to transport property by any particular schedule, train, or vessel or in time for any particular market or otherwise than with reasonable dispatch. Reasonable dispatch cannot be defined by any definite rule. Some of the factors which must be considered in determining reasonable dispatch are
   A. Distance traveled.
   B. Mode of conveyance.
   C. Character of the weather.
   D. Season of the year.
   E. Available facilities for transportation.
   F. Any unusual traffic conditions.
2. The carrier shall have the right, in case of physical necessity, to forward property by any carrier or route between the points of shipment and destination. This provision is undoubtedly valid since it is based upon physical necessity.

3. In all cases not prohibited by law, where a lower value than the actual value has been represented in writing by the shipper as the released value of the property as determined by the classifications or tariffs upon which the rate is based, such lower value plus freight charges, if paid, shall be the maximum amount to be recovered. This applies even though such loss or damage occurs from negligence.

Analysis of Section 2(b) of Bill of Lading Terms

SEC. 2(b). As a condition precedent to recovery, claims must be filed in writing with the receiving or delivering carrier, or carrier issuing this bill of lading, or carrier on whose line the loss, damage, injury or delay occurred, or *carrier in possession of the property when the loss, damage, injury or delay occurred,* within nine months after delivery of the property (or, in the case of export traffic, within nine months after delivery at port of export) or, in case of failure to make delivery, then within nine months after a reasonable time for delivery has elapsed; and suits shall be instituted against any carrier only within two years and one day from the day when notice in writing is given by the carrier to the claimant that the carrier has disallowed the claim or any part or parts thereof specified in the notice. Where claims are not filed or suits are not instituted thereon in accordance with the foregoing provisions, no carrier hereunder shall be liable, and such claims will not be paid.

The words in italics in this section appear only in the motor carrier bill of lading. To secure payment of claims for loss, damage, injury, or delay, observance of the provisions of paragraph 2(b) is absolutely required. To secure payment, claims must be made

1. In writing to
   A. The originating carrier, *or*
   B. The delivering carrier, *or*
   C. The carrier issuing the bill of lading, *or*
   D. The carrier on whose line the loss, damage, or injury occurred.
2. Within nine months
   A. After delivery in case of domestic traffic.
   B. After delivery at port of export, in case of export traffic.
   C. After, in the case of failure to make delivery, a reasonable time for delivery has elapsed.

It is also provided that suits shall be instituted only within two years and one day from the time claimant is notified in writing that the carrier has disallowed the claim or any part thereof. It is not optional with the carrier to adhere to or disregard the time limitations set forth. To adhere to them in one instance and disregard them in another would be a violation of the provisions forbidding unjust discrimination and undue preference.

Analysis of Section 2(c) of Bill of Lading Terms

SEC. 2(c). Any carrier or party liable on account of loss of or damage to any of said property shall have the full benefit of any insurance that may have been effected upon or on account of said property, so far as this shall not avoid the policies or contracts of insurance: PROVIDED, That the Carrier reimburse the claimant for the premium paid thereon.

Under Section 2(c), the carrier is given the benefit of any insurance which has been taken out on the shipment. This provision applies only so far as it does not annul the policies or contracts of insurance and the carrier must pay to the claimant any amount which he has paid as a premium on the insurance. Validity of this provision has been upheld in *Y. & M. V. R. R. Co.* v. *Blum*, 86 So. Rep. 805, and *Luckenbach* v. *McCahon Sugar Ref. Co.*, 248 U.S. 139.

Analysis of Section 3 of Bill of Lading Terms

SEC. 3. Except where such service is required as the result of carrier's negligence, all property shall be subject to necessary cooperage and baling at owner's cost. Each carrier over whose route cotton or cotton linters is to be transported hereunder shall have the privilege, at its own cost and risk, of compressing the same for greater convenience in handling or forwarding, and shall not be held responsible for deviation or unavoidable delays in procuring such compression. Grain in bulk consigned to a point where there is a railroad, public or licensed elevator, may (unless otherwise expressly noted herein, and then if it is not promptly unloaded) be there delivered and placed with other grain of the same kind and grade without respect to ownership (and prompt notice thereof shall be given to the consignor), and if so delivered shall be subject to a lien for elevator charges in addition to all other charges hereunder.

Under Section 3, provision is made that

1. The owner is required to pay the cost of any cooperage or baling of property found necessary. This does not apply when it is necessitated by the negligence of the carrier, as when rough handling is the cause.
2. The carrier has the privilege of compressing cotton or cotton linters, in transit, at its own risk and cost, in order to facilitate handling or forwarding. Carrier cannot be held responsible for any unavoidable delays or deviation in procuring such compression. Compressing is entirely optional with the carrier.
3. If bulk grain is not unloaded, or unless other instructions have been given in the bill of lading, carrier is entitled to place grain in elevator with other grain of same kind and grade, regardless of ownership, and give prompt notice to the consignor. Such grain is then subject to elevator charges, in addition to carrier's charges.

Analysis of Section 4(a) of Bill of Lading Terms

SEC. 4(a). Property not removed by the party entitled to receive it within the free time (*if any*) allowed by tariffs, lawfully on file (such free time to be computed as therein provided), after notice of the arrival of the property at destination or at the port of export (if intended for export) has been duly sent or given, and after placement of the property for delivery at destination has been made, *or property not received, at time tender of delivery of the property to the party entitled to receive it has been made,* may be kept in vessel, *vehicle,* car, depot, warehouse or place of *business* [delivery] of the carrier, subject to the tariff charge for storage and to carrier's responsibility as warehouseman, only, or at the option of the carrier, may be removed to and stored in a public or licensed warehouse at *point* [place] of delivery or other available *point* [place], *or if no such warehouse is available at point of delivery or other available point, then in other available storage facility,* at the cost of the owner and there held without liability on the part of the carrier, and subject to a lien for all freight and other lawful charges, including a reasonable charge for storage. *In the event consignee cannot be found at address given for delivery, then in that event, notice of the placing of such goods in warehouse shall be mailed to the address given for delivery and mailed to any other address given on the bill of lading for notification, showing the warehouse in which such property has been placed, subject to the provisions of this paragraph.*

The words shown in italics in this section appear only in the motor carrier bill of lading while those shown within brackets appear only in the rail bill of lading. Section 4(a) provides that after notice of the arrival of the property has been sent or given and placement of the property for delivery has been made of property not received when delivery attempted, if not removed within free time (if any) it may be kept in vessel, vehicle, care, depot, warehouse or place of business of the carriers subject to storage charges provided by tariff and liability limited to that of warehouseman only. Carrier has option of removing the property to a licensed or public warehouse and storing it at owner's expense and without further liability on part of carrier. Property is then subject to lien for all freight and reasonable storage charges. It is provided that if consignee cannot be found at the address given in the bill of lading for delivery, notice of placing goods in warehouse shall be mailed to address given for delivery and to any other address given on the bill of lading for notification.

Analysis of Section 4(b) of Bill of Lading Terms

SEC. 4(b). Where nonperishable property which has been transported to destination hereunder is refused by consignee or the party entitled to receive it *upon tender of deliver,* or said consignee or party entitled to receive it fails to receive *or claim it* with 15 days after notice of arrival shall have been duly sent or given, the carrier may sell the same at public auction to the highest bidder, at such place as may be designated by the carrier: PROVIDED, That the carrier shall have first mailed, sent, or given to the consignor notice that the property has been refused or remains unclaimed, as the case may be, and that it will be subject to sale under the terms of the bill of lading if disposition be not arranged for, and shall have published notice containing a description of the property, the name of the party to whom consigned, or, if shipped order notify, the name of the party to be notified, and the time and place of sale, once a week for two successive weeks, in a newspaper of general circulation at the place of sale or nearest place where such newspaper is published: PROVIDED, That 30 days shall have elapsed before publication of notice of sale after said notice that the property was refused or remains unclaimed was mailed, sent or given.

The words shown in italics in this section appear only in the motor carrier bill of lading. Section 4(b) provides for disposition of nonperishable property which is refused or unclaimed at destination. The carrier may sell the property to the highest bidder, at public auction, at a place selected by the carrier where it has been refused by consignee or the party entitled to receive it upon tender of delivery and where either one fails to receive it within 15 days after notice of arrival has been sent or given. This sale, however, cannot take place until the carrier has first mailed, sent, or given to the *consignor* a notice that

1. The property has been refused or remains unclaimed, as the case may be.
2. That the property will be subject to sale under the terms of the bill of sale or nearest place where such newspaper is published, notice containing.

Further, before sale the carrier is required to publish, once a week for two successive weeks, in a newspaper of general circulation at the place of sale or nearest place where such newspaper is published, notice containing

1. Description of the property.
2. Name of party to whom consigned, or if order notify, name of party to be notified.
3. The time and place of sale.

Thirty days must elapse after notice given to the consignor that property was refused or remains unclaimed before the notice of sale is published.

Analysis of Section 4(c) of Bill of Lading Terms

SEC. 4(c). Where perishable property which has been transported hereunder to destination is refused by consignee or party entitled to receive it, or said consignee or party entitled to receive it shall fail to receive it promptly, the carrier may, in its discretion, to prevent deterioration or further deterioration, sell the same to the best advantage at private or public sale: PROVIDED, That if time serves for notification to the consignor or owner of the refusal of the property or the failure to receive it and request for disposition of the property, such notification shall be given, in such manner as the exercise of due diligence requires, before the property is sold.

Section 4(c) provides for disposition of perishable property which is refused or remains unclaimed at destination. Where perishable property is refused or unclaimed at destination, or not received promptly, carrier may, in its discretion, to prevent deterioration or further deterioration, sell the property at private or public sale to the best advantage. If sufficient time is available, carrier shall notify the consignor or owner of the refusal or failure to receive and request disposition before property is sold.

Analysis of Section 4(d) of Bill of Lading Terms

SEC. 4(d). Where the procedure provided for in the two paragraphs last preceding is not possible, it is agreed that nothing contained in said paragraphs shall be construed to abridge the right of the carrier at its option to sell the property under such circumstances and in such manner as may be authorized by law.

Where it is not possible to follow the provisions of Section 4(b) and (c), the carrier has the right, at its option, to sell the property under such circumstances and in such manner as may be authorized by law.

Analysis of Section 4(e) of Bill of Lading Terms

SEC. 4(e). The proceeds of any sale made under this section shall be applied by the carrier to the payment of freight, demurrage, storage, and any other lawful charges and the expense of notice, advertisement, sale, and other necessary expense and of caring for and maintaining the property, if proper care of the same requires special expense, and should there be a balance it shall be paid to the owner of the property sold hereunder.

Since the carrier has a lien on the property for its charges, proceeds of the sale shall be applied by the carrier to the payment of its freight, demurrage, storage, and any other lawful charge, and the expense of notice, advertisement, sale, and other items, and for caring for and maintaining the property, if necessary. If there is any balance, carrier must pay it to the owner.

Analysis of Section 4(f) of Bill of Lading Terms

SEC. 4(f). Property destined to or taken from a station, wharf, [or] landing *or other place* at which there is no regularly appointed freight agent shall be entirely at risk of owner after unloaded from cars, *vehicles* or vessels or until loaded into cars, *vehicles* or vessels, and, except in case of carrier's negligence, when received from or delivered to such stations, wharfs, [or] landings, *or other places,* shall be at owner's risk until the cars are attached to and after they are detached from locomotive or train or until loaded into and after unloaded from vessels, *or if property is transported in motor vehicle trailers or semi-trailers, until such trailers or semi-trailers are attached to and after they are detached from power units. Where a carrier is directed to unload or deliver property transported by motor vehicle at a particular location where consignee or consignee's agent is not regularly located, the risk after unloading, or delivery, shall be that of the owner.*

The words shown in italics in this section appear only in the motor carrier bill of lading while those shown in brackets appear only in the rail bill of lading. This section provides that where property is destined to, or shipped from (1) a station, (2) a wharf, or (3) a landing, at which there is no regularly appointed freight agent, it shall be entirely at the owner's risk. Where carrier is directed to unload or deliver property at a particular location where consignee or consignee's agent is not located, it is done at the owner's risk.

Analysis of Section 5 of Bill of Lading Terms

SEC. 5. No carrier hereunder will carry or be liable in any way for any documents, specie, or for any articles of extraordinary value not specifically rated in the published classification or tariffs unless a special agreement to do so and a stipulated value of the articles are endorsed hereon.

Section 5 provides that the carrier declines to carry or be liable for transportation of any documents, specie, or for any articles of extraordinary value which are not specifically rated in the published classifications or tariffs. However, special agreement can be made that the stipulated value of the articles is to be endorsed on the bill of lading.

Analysis of Section 6 of Bill of Lading Terms

SEC. 6. Every party, whether principal or agent, shipping explosives or dangerous goods, without previous full written disclosure to the carrier of their nature, shall be liable for and indemnify the carrier against all loss or damage caused by such goods, and such goods may be warehoused at owner's risk and expense or destroyed without compensation.

Section 6 protects the carrier in the event explosives or dangerous articles are shipped without full written disclosure of their nature. Every party shipping such merchandise without full disclosure is required to indemnify the carrier against all damage and the carrier has authority to warehouse the goods at owner's expense or destroy them without compensation.

Analysis of Section 7 of Bill of Lading Terms

SEC. 7. The owner or consignee shall pay the freight and average, if any, and all other lawful charges accruing on said property, but, except in those instances where it may lawfully be authorized to do so, no carrier shall deliver or relinquish possession at destination of the property covered by this bill of lading until all tariff rates and charges thereon have been paid. The consignor shall be liable for the freight and all other lawful charges, except that if the consignor stipulates, by signature, in the space provided for that purpose on the face of this bill of lading that the carrier shall not make delivery without requiring payment of such charges and the carrier, contrary to such stipulation shall make delivery without requiring such payment, the consignor (except as hereinafter provided) shall not be liable for such charges. PROVIDED, That, where the carrier has been instructed by the shipper or consignor to deliver said property to a consignee other than the shipper or consignor, such consignee shall not be legally liable for transportation charges in respect of the transportation of said property (beyond those billed against him at the time of delivery for which he is otherwise liable) which may be found to be due after the property has been delivered to him, if the consignee (a) is an agent only and has no beneficial title in said property, and (b) prior to delivery of said property has notified the delivering carrier in writing of the fact of such agency and absence of beneficial title, and, in the case of a shipment reconsigned or diverted to a point other than that specified in the original bill of lading, has also notified the delivering carrier in writing of the name and address of the beneficial owner of said property; and, in such cases the shipper or consignor, or, in the case of a shipment so reconsigned or diverted, the beneficial owner shall be liable for such additional charges. If the consignee has given to the carrier erroneous information as to who the beneficial owner is, such consignee shall himself be liable for such additional charges. [On shipments reconsigned or diverted by an agent who has furnished the carrier in the reconsignment or diversion order with a notice of agency and the proper name and address of the beneficial owner, and where such shipments are refused or abandoned at ultimate destination, the said beneficial owner shall be liable for all legally applicable charges in connection therewith. If the reconsignor or diverter has given to the carrier erroneous information as to who the beneficial owner is, such reconsignor or diverter shall himself be liable for all such charges.]

[If a shipper or consignor of a shipment of property (other than a prepaid shipment) is also the consignee named in the bill of lading and, prior to the time of delivery, notifies, in writing, a delivering carrier by railroad (a) to deliver such property at destination to another party, (b) that such party is the beneficial owner of such property, and (c) that delivery is to be made to such party only upon payment of all transportation charges in respect of the transportation of such property, and delivery is made by the carrier to such party without such payment, such shipper or consignor shall not be liable (as shipper, consignor, consignee, or otherwise) for such transportation charges but the party to whom delivery is so made shall in any event be liable for transportation charges billed against the property at the time of such delivery, and also for any additional charges which may be found to be due after delivery of the property, except that if such party prior to such delivery has notified in writing the delivering carrier that he is not the beneficial owner of the property, and has given in writing to such delivering carrier the name and address of such beneficial owner, such party shall not be liable for any additional charges which may be found to be due after delivery of the property; but if the party to whom delivery is made has given to the carrier erroneous information as to the beneficial owner, such party shall nevertheless be liable for such additional charges. If the shipper or consignor has given to the delivering carrier erroneous information as to who the beneficial owner is, such shipper or consignor shall himself be liable for such transportation charges, notwithstanding the foregoing provisions of this paragraph and irrespective of any provisions to the contrary in the bill of lading or in the contract of transportation under which the shipment was made. The term "delivering carrier" means the line-haul carrier making ultimate delivery.]

Nothing herein shall limit the right of the carrier to require at time of shipment the prepayment of guarantee of the charges. If upon inspection it is ascertained that the articles shipped are not those described in this bill of lading, the freight charges must be paid upon the articles actually shipped. [Where delivery is made by a common carrier by water the foregoing provisions of this section shall apply, except as may be inconsistent with Part III of the Interstate Commerce Act.]

The portion of Section 7 shown within brackets appear only in the rail bill of lading. Section 7 deals with the payment of freight charges. It provides

1. That the owner of the goods or the consignee must pay the freight charges and average, if any, and in addition all other charges accruing on the property.
2. Except where carrier is lawfully authorized to do so, it must not deliver nor relinquish possession at destination of the property until all tariff rates and charges on it have been paid.
3. The consignor shall be liable for the freight and all other lawful charges unless space provided for stipulating otherwise on face of bill has been signed.
4. Carrier has right to require prepayment or guarantee of the charges at time of shipment.
5. If inspection reveals that the articles shipped are not correctly described in the bill of lading, the freight charges on goods actually shipped must be paid.

Analysis of Section 8 of Bill of Lading Terms

Sec. 8. If this bill of lading is issued on the order of the shipper, or his agent, in exchange or in substitution for another bill of lading, the shipper's signature to the prior bill of lading as to the statement of value or otherwise, or election of common law or bill of lading liability, in or in connection with such prior bill of lading, shall be considered a part of this bill of lading as fully as if the same were written or made in or in connection with this bill of lading.

Section 8 provides for the liability of a shipper in connection with the issuance of an exchange or substituted bill. Under this provision, the shipper's signature on prior bill as to statement of value or otherwise, or election of common law liability, is incorporated and considered a part of the new bill the same as if written therein.

Analysis of Section 9(a)-9(f) of Bill of Lading Terms

SEC. 9(a). If all or any part of said property is carried by water over any part of said route, [and loss, damage or injury to said property occurs while the same is in the custody of a carrier by water the liability of such carrier shall be determined by the bill of lading of the carrier by water (this bill of lading being such bill of lading if the property is transported by such water carrier thereunder) and by and under the laws and regulations applicable to transportation by water. Such] *such* water carriage shall be performed subject to all the terms and provisions of, and all the exemptions from liability contained in the Act of the Congress of the United States, approved on Februray 13, 1893, and entitled "An act relating to the navigation of vessels, etc.," and of other statutes of the United States according carriers by water the protection of limited liability, [as well as the following subdivision of this section;] and to the conditions contained in this bill of lading not inconsistent with this section, [when the bill of lading becomes the bill of lading of the carrier by water].

(b) No such carrier by water shall be liable for any loss or damage resulting from any fire happening to or on board the vessel, or from explosion, bursting of boilers or breakage of shafts, unless caused by the design or neglect of such carrier.

(c) If the owner shall have exercised due diligence in making the vessel in all respects seaworthy and properly manned, equipped and supplied, no such carrier shall be liable for any loss or damage resulting from the perils of the lakes, seas, or other waters, or from latent defects in hull, machinery, or appurtenances whether existing prior to, at the time of, or after sailing, or from collision, stranding, or other accidents of navigation, or from prolongation of the voyage. And, when for any reason it is necessary, any vessel carrying any or all of the property herein described shall be at liberty to call at any port or ports, in or out of the customary route, to tow and be towed, to transfer, trans-ship, or lighter, to load and discharge goods at any time, to assist vessels in distress, to deviate for the purpose of saving life or property, and for docking and repairs. Except in case of negligence such carrier shall not be responsible for any loss or damage to property if it be necessary or is usual to carry the same upon deck.

(d) General Average shall be payable according to the York-Antwerp Rules of 1924, Sections 1 to 15, inclusive, and Sections 17 to 22, inclusive, and as to matters not covered thereby according to the laws and usages of the Port of New York. If the owners shall have exercised due diligence to make the vessel in all respects seaworthy and properly manned, equipped and supplied, it is hereby agreed that in case of danger, damage or disaster resulting from faults or errors in navigation, or in the management of the vessel, or from any latent or other defects in the vessel, her machinery or appurtenances, or unseaworthiness, whether existing at the time of shipment or at the beginning of the voyage (provided the latent or other defects or the unseaworthiness was not discoverable by the exercise of due diligence), the shippers, consignees and/or owners of the cargo shall nevertheless pay salvage and any special charges incurred in respect of the cargo, and shall contribute with the shipowner in general average to the payment of any sacrifices, losses or expenses of a general average nature that may be made or incured for the common benefit or to relieve the adventure from any common peril.

(e) If the property is being carried under a tariff which provides that any carrier or carriers party thereto shall be liable for loss from perils of the sea, then as to such carrier or carriers the provisions of this section shall be modified in accordance with the tariff provisions, which shall be regarded as incorporated into the conditions of this bill of lading.

(f) The term "water carriage" in this section shall not be construed as including lighterage in or across rivers, harbors, or lakes, when performed by or on behalf of [rail] carriers *other than water.*

The words shown in italics appear only in the motor carrier bill while those within brackets appear only in the rail carrier bill of lading. Section 9 consists of six paragraphs relating to transportation by water. Provisions of paragraph (a) provide that transportation by water is subject to liability set forth by the Harter Act which makes water carriers liable for loss or damage occasioned by

1. Negligence, fault, or failure in proper loading, stowage, custody, care or delivery.
2. Failure to exercise due diligence properly to equip, man, provision, and outfit its vessels.
3. Failure to exercise reasonable care in making a vessel seaworthy and capable of performing her intended voyage.

The object of paragraph (b) is to relieve carrier by water from liability for loss or damage resulting from any fire happening to, or on board, the vessel, or from explosion, bursting of boilers, or breakage of shafts. These exemptions, however, do not apply where occasioned by the design or negligence of the carrier.

Paragraph (c) provides that if the owner has exercised due diligence in making the vessel seaworthy in all respects and in having it properly manned, equipped and supplied, the carrier shall not be liable for loss or damage from

1. The perils of the lakes, seas, or other waters.
2. Latent defects in hull, machinery, or appurtenances, whether existing prior to, at time of, or after sailing.

3. Collision, stranding, or other accidents of navigation.
4. Prolongation of the voyage.

When for any reason it is necessary, the vessel is at liberty to

1. Call at any port or ports in or out of the customary route.
2. Tow and be towed.
3. Transfer.
4. Trans-ship.
5. Lighter.
6. Load and discharge goods at any time.
7. Assist vessels in distress.
8. Deviate for the purpose of saving life or property.
9. Deviate for docking and repairs.

In the absence of negligence, the carrier shall not be liable for loss or damage to property where it is necessary, or where it is customary, to carry such property on its decks.

Paragraph (d) provides that General Average shall be paid according to York-Antwerp rules of 1924 and, as to any matters not covered, according to law and usage of the Port of New York. If the owners have exercised due diligence to make the vessel seaworthy and properly manned, equipped, and supplied, in case of danger, damage, or disaster resulting from certain named causes, the shippers, consignee, and owners of the cargo shall pay salvage and any special charges incurred in connection with the cargo. They shall also contribute with the shipowner in general average to payment incurred for the common benefit or to relieve the adventure from any common peril. Paragraph (f) is self-explanatory.

Analysis of Section 10 of Bill of Lading Terms

SEC. 10. Any alteration, addition, or erasure in this bill of lading which shall be made without the special notation hereon of the agent of the carrier issuing this bill of lading, shall be without effect, and this bill of lading shall be enforceable according to its original tenor.

This section prohibits alteration of the bill of lading without the knowledge or consent of the carrier. In the event such alteration is made, the bill shall be enforceable according to its original tenor.

The Bill of Lading as Evidence of Title

The Pomerene Bills of Lading Act, effective 1 January 1917, governs bills of lading issued by any common carrier for the transportation of goods in interstate commerce insofar as property rights are concerned. The passage of this act was necessitated by the wrongful negotiation of bills of lading, the perpetrators of which were escaping punishment due to the inadequacy of the law.

Prior to the passage of the Bills of Lading Act it was established that a bill of lading served as documentary evidence of title; as by mercantile law and usage, the bill stands as the substitute and symbolic representative of the goods described in the bill and carries the legal title to the shipment so that a transfer of bill is a transfer of the goods evidenced by it. Possession symbolized by a bill of lading is the same as actual possession.

Unlike some state bill of lading enactments, the federal law has never specified the terms and conditions of the bill of lading as it is concerned primarily with the rights of the parties relating to ownership. The primary purpose of the act is to enlarge and enhance the negotiability of *order* bills of lading by definitely prescribing the law with respect to negotiability and imposing on carriers greater responsibility in that connection to afford protection to those who, in the course of commercial transactions, handle and deal in such bills.

In each bill of lading a person must be named as *consignee* to whom the goods are to be delivered. A consignee is that person to whom a carrier may lawfully deliver the shipment in accordance with the terms of the contract of carriage. The goods must be delivered to the designated consignee, and to him only, where there is nothing to indicate that he is not entitled to receive them. It is the carrier's absolute duty to deliver freight to the proper person entitled to receive it.

From the earliest times shippers have enjoyed the choice of naming a consignee to whom the goods were to be delivered or shipping the goods to the shipper's order, in which case something more remained to be performed to justify delivery by the carrier. These two methods originally were accomplished by the use of one standard form, but the Interstate Commerce Commission in the *Bill of Lading Case* decided in 1914, approved the plan of using different forms distinguished by color, and designated separately as *straight bill of lading* and as *shipper's order bill of lading*. These designations were adopted into the provisions of the Bills of Lading Act, which prescribes the following forms of bills of lading.

1. Straight bill — ". . . a bill in which it is stated that the goods are consigned or destined to a specified person. . . ."
2. Order bill — ". . . a bill in which it is stated that the goods are consigned or destined to the order of any person named in such bill. . . ."

The provisions of the Bill of Lading Act fall within three groups.

1. Those relating to straight bills of lading.
2. Those relating to order bills of lading.
3. Those applicable to both straight and order bills.

By far the greater number of shipments move under the straight bill of lading and ownership disputes are seldom encountered. The following sections of the Bills of Lading Act contain provisions to straight bills of lading.

SEC. 6. *Straight Bills Not Negotiable.* This section requires that a straight bill of lading shall have plainly placed upon its face the words *nonnegotiable* or *not negotiable.* This provision does not apply with respect to memoranda or acknowledgements of an informal character. It will be noted in this connection that the rail and motor straight bills of lading contain the following words in their headings: *Original—Not Negotiable—Domestic.*

SEC. 29. *Equities Pass to Transferee.* This section provides that a straight bill cannot be negotiated free from existing equities, and the endorsement of such a bill gives the transferee no additional rights. The holder of the bill can transfer it by delivery, accompanied by an expressed or implied agreement, to transfer the title to the bill or the goods covered by it.

SEC. 32. *Transferee's Title and Duties.* Under this section, it is provided that a transferee of a straight bill (as provided in Section 29) has the duty of notifying the carrier of the transfer of the bill of lading to him. The carrier then owes the transferee the same duties as previously owed to the transferor. Prior to such notification, the title of the transferee may be defeated if the carrier has been served with garnishment or attachment or execution upon the goods by a creditor of the transferor, or if the carrier has been notified by the transferor or a subsequent purchaser from the transferor of a subsequent sale of the goods by the transferor. The notification to the carrier by the transferee of his rights must be made to an officer or agent of the carrier, the actual or apparent scope of whose duties includes action upon such notification; no notification shall be effective until the officer or agent notified has had time, with the exercise of reasonable diligence, to communicate with the agent or agents having actual possession or control of the goods.

Under the federal Bills of Lading Act, straight bills of lading are deemed nonnegotiable, even though endorsed, and the transferee can take no better title than the transferor had. This is more or less academic, as endorsement or attempted endorsement of a straight bill of lading seldom occurs. Practically all shipments moving under a straight bill of lading are intended to be delivered and in fact are usually delivered to the consignee named in the bill. In many instances, the named consignee will not even have possession of the original straight bill of lading issued by the carrier to the shipper at the time the shipment was accepted. While some shippers do promptly forward the original or memo copy of the straight bill of lading after it is signed by carrier to the named consignee (usually attached to invoice), this practice is by no means universal. However, it is highly recommended as it does serve to notify the consignee of date shipment was made and the identity of the originating carrier so that tracing of the shipment in the event of delay is facilitated. The originating carrier accepting the shipment and issuing the straight bill of lading as a matter of routine retains the shipping order copy of the bill and except in highly unusual circumstances is always justified in making delivery to the consignee named therein.

A bill of lading in which it is stated that the goods are consigned or destined to the order of a person is an order bill. The Bills of Lading Act provides that a person to whom an order bill has been duly negotiated acquires thereby, in addition to title to the goods shipped, the direct obligation of the carrier to hold possession of the goods for him according to the terms of the bill as fully as if the carrier had contracted directly with him.

Both the rail and motor carrier classifications contain rules which provide that the name of anly one shipper, one consignee, and one destination shall appear on a bill of lading and that bill of lading consigned *To Order* will not be issued unless the name of the person, firm or corportation to whose order the shipment is consigned is plainly shown after the words *To Order Of.* The order bills of lading of both rail and motor carriers contain lines in the heading for indication of the name and address of the party to be notified. Carrier rules further require that the original bill of lading properly endorsed be surrendered to the carrier before delivery of the property, but that if the original bill has been lost or delayed the property may be delivered in advance upon receipt of a certified check, or cash, in an amount equal to 125 percent of the invoice or value of the property or, at the carrier's option, upon the receipt of a bond acceptable to the carrier, in an amount equal to twice the amount of the invoice or value of the property, or a blanket bond may be accepted when satisfactory to the carrier as to surety, amount, and form. These provisions will assist in securing a better understanding of the provisions of the Bills of Lading Act summarized below.

SEC. 4. *Issuance in Parts Forbidden.* This section prohibits the issuance of order bills in parts or sets when the transportation covered is to any place in the United States on the continent of North America, except Alaska and Panama. If so issued, the carrier issuing them shall be liable for failure to deliver the goods described therein to anyone who purchases a part for value in good faith, even though the purchase be after the delivery of the goods by the carrier to holder of one of the other parts. This section specifically exempt order bills of lading covering shipments to Alaska, Panama, Puerto Rico, the Philippines, Hawaii, or foreign countries, from its provisions.

Sec. 5. *Duplicates to be Marked.* Under this section when more than one order bill is issued, all except the original must be plainly marked *duplicate* or otherwise to indicate that the document is not an original bill. Failure to indicate copies as being such subjects the carrier to liability for damages caused to anyone who has purchased the copy for value in good faith as an original, even though the purchase be made after delivery of the goods by the carrier to the holder of the original bill. This section likewise is not applicable to shipments to Alaska, Panama, Puerto Rico, the Philippines, Hawaii or foreign countries.

Sec. 7. *Negotiability.* This section provides that the insertion in an order bill of the name of a person to be notified of the arrival of the goods shall not limit the negotiability of the bill or constitute notice to a purchaser thereof of any rights or equities of such person in the goods. In *Kemper Mill & Elevator Co.* v. *Hines,* 239 S.W. 803, this section was held to apply only to contests with a purchaser of the bill, and not to contests between the carrier and the shipper, while the latter was still the holder and possessor of the bill. In *Temple* v. *Southern R. Co.,* 129 S. E. 815, it was held that an order bill is negotiable by endorsement under Section 3 (49 U. S. C. 83) and its negotiability is not affected by provision therein that a person other than consignee is to be notified of the arrival of the goods at destination, in view of this section. See also *Slutzkin* v. *Gerhard,* 191 N. Y. S. 104, 199 App. Div. 5.

Sec. 11. *Failure to Deliver Goods.* This section provides that where delivery of the goods is made by the carrier without taking up and canceling the order bill of lading covering the shipment, the carrier becomes liable to anyone who for value and in good faith purchases the bill, regardless of whether such purchase of the bill is made before or after delivery of the goods by the carrier. This provision does not apply if the carrier has lost possession of the goods in any of the following ways

1. By delivery compelled by legal process.
2. By selling the goods to satisfy its lien for freight and other charges.
3. By selling the goods because unclaimed.
4. By selling the goods because they are perishable or hazardous.

Under this section, a carrier making delivery of the goods without taking up and canceling the order bill of lading is liable to purchaser of the bill of lading in good faith. However, in *Pere Marquette Ry. C.* v. *J. F. French & Co.,* 254 U.S. 538, it was held that where a bank holding a draft to which the original order bill was attached delivered the bill without collecting the amount of the draft and the buyers obtained delivery without surrender of the bill and subsequently rejected the goods and returned the bill of lading, the shipper who took back the draft and the bill from the bank with knowledge of the circumstances was not a bona fide purchaser of the bill and had no right against the carrier.

SEC. 12. *Partial Delivery.* This section is similar to Section 11 and applies to delivery of a portion of the goods for which the order bill has been issued and the carrier has either failed to take up and cancel the bill or to place plainly upon it a statement that a portion of the goods has been delivered with a description which may be in general terms either of the goods or packages that have been so delivered or which remain in the carrier's possession. The same exceptions as specified in Section 11 apply, and the carrier is made liable to a bona fide purchaser for value who is damaged because of the carrier's failure.

SEC. 14. *Lost, Stolen, or Destroyed Bill.* This section provides that where an order bill has been lost, stolen, or destroyed, a court of competent jurisdiction may order the delivery of the goods upon satisfactory proof of such loss, theft, or destruction and upon the giving of a bond, with sufficient surety, to be approved by the court, to protect the carrier or any person injured by such delivery from any liability or loss incurred by reason of the original bill remaining outstanding. The court is authorized in its discretion to order the payment of the carrier's reasonable cost and counsel fees. The carrier may accept a voluntary indemnifying bond, given without order of the court and, under such circumstances, the parties thereto are bound. Delivery under court order will not relieve the carrier from liability to a purchaser of the original bill for value without notice of the proceedings or of the delivery of the goods.

SEC. 23. *Garnishment.* This section provides that the carrier shall not in any case be compelled to deliver the actual possession of the goods until the original bill is surrendered to it or impounded by the court. Goods which are delivered to a carrier by their owner or his authorized representative and on which an order bill has been issued cannot be attached by garnishment or otherwise. Neither can an execution be levied upon them unless the original bill is first surrended or its negotiation enjoined.

SEC. 24. *Injunction.* This section provides that a creditor whose debtor is the owner of an order bill shall be entitled to such aid from courts of proper jurisdiction by injunction and otherwise in attaching such bill or securing such equitable relief as is provided in those cases where property cannot be readily attached or levied upon by ordinary legal process.

SEC. 25. *Carrier's Lien.* This section provides that the carrier shall have a lien on the goods covered by an order bill for the following.

1. Freight.
2. Storage.
3. Demurrage.
4. Terminal charges.
5. Necessary expense for preservation of the goods.
6. Expenses incident to their transportation subsequent to the date of the bill.
7. All other charges incurred in transportation and delivery.
8. All charges enumerated in the bill so far as they are allowed by law and the contract between consignor and carrier.

SEC. 27. *Negotiation by Delivery.* This section provides that an order bill may be negotiated by delivery where, by the terms of the bill, the carrier undertakes to deliver the goods to the order of a specified person, and such person or a subsequent endorsee of the bill has endorsed it in blank.

SEC. 28. *Negotiation by Endorsement.* Under this section, an order bill is made fully negotiable by endorsement of the person to whose order the goods are deliverable and such endorsement may be in blank or to a specified person. In the event of a special endorsement, the specified person may negotiate it either by special or blank endorsement and subsequent negotiations may be made in like manner.

SEC. 30. *Bill Negotiable by Possessor.* Under this section, an order bill may be negotiated by any person in possession of it irrespective of how such possession may have been acquired, if by the terms of the bill the carrier undertakes to deliver the goods to the order of such person, or if at the time of negotiation the bill is in such form that it may be negotiated by delivery.

SEC. 31. *Title to Goods.* This section provides that a person to whom an order bill has been duly negotiated acquires thereby:

1. Such title to the goods as the person negotiating the bill to him had or had ability to convey to a bona fide purchaser for value, and also such title to the goods as the consignee and consignor had.
2. The direct obligation of the carrier to hold possession of the goods for him according to the terms of the bills as fully as if the carrier had contracted directly with him.

SEC. 32. *Transferee's Title.* This section provides that a person to whom a bill has been transferred, but not negotiated, acquires thereby as against the transferor the title to the goods, subject to the terms of any agreement with the transferor. Other provisions of this section relating to straight bills of lading have been discussed in the foregoing.

SEC. 33. *Compelling Endorsement.* Where an order bill is transferred for value by delivery, and the endorsement of the transferor is essential for negotiation, this section provides that the transferee acquires the right to compel transferor to endorse the bill, unless a contrary intention appears, and the negotiation shall take effect as of the time when the endorsement is actually made. This obligation may be specifically enforced. Such compulsion is usually afforded in courts of equity or courts with jurisdiction of matters involving equitable relief.

SEC. 38. Where a person has sold, mortgaged, or pledged an order bill or goods which are in carrier's possession and for which an order bill has been issued, and such person continues in possession of the bill, under this section the subsequent negotiation of the order bill by that person to any person receiving it in good faith for value and without notice of the previous sale is as valid as if authorized by the first person to whom the bill or goods covered were sold, mortgaged or pledged. This section makes it incumbent on the purchaser, mortgagee, or pledgee to secure possession of the order bill as security when entering into such transactions.

SEC. 39. *Seller's Lien and Stoppage in Transitu.* This section provides that where an order bill has been issued, no seller's lien or right of stoppage *in transitu* shall operate to defeat the rights of a bona fide purchaser for value to whom such bill has been negotiated. Further, the carrier shall not be obliged to deliver or justified in delivering the goods to an unpaid seller unless the order bill is first surrendered for cancellation.

Of equal importance (if not greater from the viewpoint of loss and damage claims) are those provisions of the Bills of Lading Act relating to both straight and order bills of lading.

SEC. 8. *Carrier's Duty to Deliver Goods on Demand.* Unless the carrier has a lawful excuse, it must deliver goods upon the demand of the consignee named in straight bill of lading, or of the holder of an order bill of lading, providing such demand is accompanied by the following:

1. An offer in good faith to pay the carrier's lawful lien on the goods.
2. Possession of the bill and an offer in good faith to surrender it, properly endorsed, if the bill is an order bill of lading.
3. A readiness and willingness to sign an acknowledgment that the goods have been delivered, if such receipt is requested by the carrier.

If the carrier refuses or fails to deliver the goods in compliance with the foregoing provisions, then the burden is upon the carrier to establish the existence of a lawful excuse for such failure or refusal.

Notwithstanding that this section has no provisions concerning consignee's duty to accept delivery, the duty of the carrier to deliver and the consignee to accept are reciprocal. (*Crinella* v. *Northwestern Pac. R. Co.*, 259 P. 774) In *Patterson* v. *American Ry. Express Co.*, 123 S. E.

844, it was held that the demand of the shipper for a diversion of the shipment was a *lawful excuse* for carrier's failure to deliver to the original consignee named in the straight bill where the shipper had retained title to the goods. In *Pere Marquette R. Co.* v. *J. F. French & Co.*, 254 U.S. 538, it was held that where sellers of potatoes attached the original order bill to a draft and the bank delivered the original bill without payment of the draft, and carrier delivered the goods without securing surrender of the bill and the potatoes were later rejected, the seller could not hold the carrier liable for conversion where it accepted the return of the bill and draft. In this case, the Court said:

> There is nothing in the act which imposes upon the carrier a specific duty to the shipper to take up the bill of lading. Under 8 (49 U.S.C. 88) the carrier is not obliged to make delivery except upon production and surrender of the bill of lading; but it is not prohibited from doing so. If, instead of insisting upon the production and surrender of the bill, it chooses to deliver in reliance upon the assurance that the deliveree has it, so far as the duty to the shipper is concerned, the only risk that it runs is that the person who says that he has the bill may not have it. If such proves to be the case, the carrier is liable for conversion, and must, of course, indemnify the shipper for any loss which results. Such liability arises not from the statute, but from the obligation which the carrier assumes under the bill of lading.

In *Winget* v. *Grand Trunk Western R. Co.*, 177 N.W. 273, *cert. den.* 254 U.S. 629, it was held that a carrier's liability for delivery without requiring surrender of the bill of lading is measured by the value of the goods and not by the amount of the drafts attached under the bill of lading.

SEC. 9. *To Whom Carrier Shall Deliver the Goods.* This section provides that a carrier is justified in delivering the shipment to:

1. A person lawfully entitled to their possession.
2. The consignee named in a straight bill.
3. A person in possession of an order bill for the goods, by the terms of which the goods are deliverable to his order, or which has been endorsed to him, or endorsed in blank by the consignee or an endorsee holding under the consignee.

Where a consignor ships under a straight bill of lading, the goods remain subject to his control and he generally has the right to stop them in transit, and the consignee likewise has the right to stop or divert the goods during transportation unless the carrier has been notified by the consignor that the consignee does not have these rights. (*Southern Pac. Co.* v. *Agencia Joffroy, S. A.,* 174 P. 2d 278) In *Tennessee Egg Co.* v. *Monroe*, 268 S.W. 372, *cert den.* 269 U.S. 580, the Court said:

The owner can choose which form of bill he will ship under. If an "order bill," and he negotiates same, his control over the goods is gone, and the person acquiring the bill obtains good title as against the owner, his vendee, or his creditors. If he ships under a "straight bill" the goods are still under his control, and he can reclaim them, convey them to a third party, or stop them in transitu.

In *Carter* v. *St. Louis-San Francisco Ry. Co.*, 18 S.W. 2d 376, it was held at a carrier delivering shipment to another at direction of the consignee named on straight bill of lading cannot be held liable to owner giving such directions even though they were not in writing. In *Erskine William Lumber Co., Inc.* v. *John I. Hay & Co., Inc.*, 160 So. 650, 1935, where lumber was consigned by consignor to itself in care of third party whose name appeared on bill of lading under words, "Mail or street address of the consignee—for purpose of notification only," and carrier delivered lumber to such party, it was held that the position of third party's name on the bill did not give carrier sufficient notice that delivery was to be made to consignee only and carrier was freed from liability for delivery to the third party. An order bill must be properly indorsed in order that physical possession thereof may justify carrier in making delivery. (*Davis* v. *Fruita Mercantile Co.*, 220 P. 983) Delivery of freight consigned under an order bill is prima facie wrongful unless original order bill properly indorsed is first surrendered to delivering carrier. (*Norfolk & Western Ry. Co.* v. *Aylor*, 150 S. E. 252, cert. den. 282 U.S. 847)

SEC. 10. *Carrier Liability for Unlawful Delivery.* Under this section where a carrier delivers goods to one who is not lawfully entitled to them, it is liable to anyone having right of property or possession in the goods if delivered otherwise than as authorized under the second and third conditions outlined in the preceding section. Even when delivered as authorized under these two provisions, the carrier shall be liable if before delivery:

1. It has been requested, by or on behalf of a person having a right of property or possession in the goods, not to make such delivery.
2. It has information at the time of delivery that it was to a person not lawfully entitled to possession.

This request or information, to be effective, must be given to an officer or agent of the carrier whose actual or apparent duties include action upon such request or information, and must be given in time to enable the one to whom it is given, with the exercise of reasonable diligence, to stop delivery of the goods.

This section does not relieve the shipper or holder of the bill of lading from compliance with the time limit for filing claim as specified in the bill of lading contract. (*Norfolk & Western R. Co.* v. *Cosmopolitan Bank & Trust Co.*, 174 N.E. 801; *Davis* v. *John L. Roper Lumber Co.* 269 U.S. 158)

SEC. 13. *Alteration of a Bill.* Provision is made under this section that any alteration, addition, or erasure in a bill after its issue without authority from the carrier issuing it in writing or noted on the bill shall be void, regardless of the nature and the purpose of the change, and the bill shall be enforceable according to its original tenor. (See Section 10 of Terms and Conditions of Bill of Lading.)

SEC. 15. *Liability for Duplicates.* Under this section, carrier's liability for a bill, upon the face of which the word *duplicate* or some other designation appears indicating that the document is not an original bill, is the liability of one who represents and warrants that such document is an accurate copy of an original bill properly issued, but no other liability.

SEC. 16. *Carrier's Title to the Goods.* This provision specifies that no title to the goods or the right to their possession asserted by the carrier in its own interests shall excuse it from liability for refusing to deliver according to the terms of a bill issued for them, unless such title or right is derived from a transfer made by the consignor or consignee after the shipment, or from the carrier's lien.

SEC. 17; SEC. 18. *Carrier's Rights Where Ownership in Dispute.* Under these sections, where the ownership is in dispute, carrier may require all claimants to interplead either as defense to action for nondelivery or as an original suit. If the carrier has notice of adverse claimants, it is excused from liability for refusing to delivery until it has reasonable time to ascertain the validity of the claims or to bring legal proceedings to compel all claimants to interplead.

SEC. 19. *Defenses Against Holders of Bills.* The carrier cannot set up the right or title of a third person as a defense to an action brought by the consignee of a straight bill or by holder of an order bill for failure to deliver on demand unless:

1. The right or title of the third person is enforced by legal process.
2. Carrier interpleads all the claimants.
3. Carrier has made delivery to a person lawfully entitled to possession as covered by Section 9.

SEC. 20; SEC. 21. *Shipper's Weight, Load, and Count.* The provisions of these two sections are discussed in Chapter 4, p. 99

SEC. 22. *Liability for Issuance of Bill When All or Part of Goods Not Received.* By express provision in this section, the issuing of a bill of lading by an agent acting within the scope of his actual or apparent authority renders the carrier liable to the owner of goods covered by a straight bill or to the holder in good faith for value of an order bill for damages caused by the nonreceipt by the carrier of all or part of the goods, or their failure to correspond to the description in the bill, at time of issue.

SEC. 26. *Bill for Goods Sold under Carrier's Lien.* This section relieves the carrier from liability for failure to deliver to either holder of straight or order bill where it has sold the goods to satisfy a carrier's lien, or because unclaimed, perishable, or hazardous.

SEC. 29. *Transfer of Bill by Delivery.* This section authorizes transfer of title to a bill by delivery, accompanied by an agreement express or implied to transfer ownership.

SEC. 32. *Transferee's Title.* Subject to the terms of any agreement with the transferor, under this section the transferee of a nonnegotiated bill acquires the transferor's title to the goods.

SEC. 34. *Warranties of Endorser or Transferor.* Unless a contrary intention appears the transferor by endorsement or delivery makes the following warranties.

1. That the bill is genuine.
2. That he has a legal right to transfer it.
3. That he possesses no knowledge of any fact which would impair the validity or worth of the bill.
4. That he has the right to transfer title to the goods, and that the goods are merchantable or fit for a particular purpose whenever such warranties would have been implied if the contract of the parties had been to transfer the actual goods.

SEC. 35. *Endorser's Liabilities.* This section provides that the endorser of a bill is not liable for failure of the carrier, or previous endorsers, to fulfill their respective obligation. The endorser does make the warranties set forth in previous section, however.

SEC. 36. *Pledgee's Warranty.* A holder of a bill for security such as a mortgagee or pledgee who in good faith demands or receives payment of the debt for which the bill is security, under this section does not warrant the genuineness of such bill or the quantity or quality of the goods described. Thus a bank receiving drafts with bill of lading attached for collection does not warrant the genuineness of the bill nor the quantity or quality of the goods described therein.

SEC. 37. *Validity of Negotiation.* The validity of the negotiation of a bill is not impaired by:

1. Breach of duty on part of person making the negotiation.
2. Owner losing possession of the bill by fraud, accident, mistake, duress, loss, theft, or conversion.

However, this section applies only to persons to whom the bill was negotiated, or subsequently negotiated, who gave value therefor in good faith, without notice of the breach of duty, fraud, accident, mistake, duress, loss, theft, or conversion.

SEC. 40. *Lien Holder's Rights.* This section provides that the rights and remedies of a mortgagee or lien holder are not limited against one who purchased the goods which are subject to the mortgage or lien for value in good faith from the owner immediately prior to delivery and secured possession of them.

SEC. 41. *Forging or Counterfeiting Bills.* Under this section any person who, knowingly or with intent to defraud, falsely makes, alters, forges, counterfeits, prints or photographs any bill of lading purporting to represent goods received for interstate or foreign shipment, or aids or issues such bill, shall be punished by imprisonment not exceeding five years or by fine not exceeding five thousand dollars or both.

The fraudulent issuance of a bill of lading by an agent or employee acting within the scope of his actual or apparent authority makes the carrier liable to anyone who purchases the bill in good faith for value.

The Federal (Pomerene) Bills of Lading Act, as Amended [Title 49, U.S. Code] [Effective January 1, 1917]

SEC. 1. (U.S. Code, title 49, sec. 81.) That bills of lading issued by any common carrier for transportation of goods in any Territory of the United States, or the District of Columbia, or from a place in a State to a place in a foreign country, or from a place in one State to a place in another State, or from a place in one State to a place in the same State through another State or foreign country, shall be governed by this Act.

SEC. 2. (U.S. Code, title 49, sec. 82.) That a bill in which it is stated that the goods are consigned or destined to a specified person is a straight bill.

SEC. 3. (U.S. Code, title 49, sec. 83.) That a bill in which it is stated that the goods are consigned or destined to the order of any person named in such bill is an order bill. Any provision in such a bill or in any notice, contract, rule, regulation, or tariff that it is nonnegotiable shall be null and void and shall not affect its negotiability within the meaning of this Act unless upon its face and in writing agreed to by the shipper.

SEC. 4. (U.S. Code, title 49, sec. 84.) That order bills issued in a State for the transportation of goods to any place in the United States on the Continent of North America, except Alaska and Panama, shall not be issued in parts or sets. If so issued, the carrier issuing them shall be liable for failure to deliver the goods described therein to anyone who purchases a part for value in good faith, even though the purchase be after the delivery of the goods by the carrier to a holder of one of the other parts: *Provided, however,* That nothing contained in this section shall be interpreted or construed to forbid the issuing of order bills in parts or sets for such transportation of goods to Alaska, Panama, Puerto Rico, the Philippines, Hawaii, or foreign countries, or to impose the liabilities set forth in this section for so doing.

SEC. 5. (U.S. Code, title 49, sec. 85.) That when more than one order bill is issued in a State for the same goods to be transported to any place in the United States on the Continent of North America, except Alaska and Panama, the word "duplicate," or some other word or words indicating that the document is not an original bill, shall be placed plainly upon the face of every such bill except the one first issued. A carrier shall be liable for the damage caused by his failure so to do to anyone who has purchased the bill for value in good faith as an original, even though the purchase be after the delivery of the goods by the carrier to the holder of the original bill: *Provided, however,* That nothing contained in this section shall in such case for such transportation of goods to Alaska, Panama, Puerto Rico, the Philippines, Hawaii, or foreign countries be interpreted or construced so a to require the placing of the word "duplicate" thereon, or to impose the liabilities set forth in this section for failure so to do.

SEC. 6. (U.S. Code, title 49, sec. 86.) That a straight bill shall have placed plainly upon its face by the carrier issuing it "nonnegotiable" or "not negotiable."

This section shall not apply, however, to memoranda or acknowledgements of an informal character.

SEC. 7. (U.S. Code, title 49, sec. 87.) That the insertion in an order bill of the name of a person to be notified of the arrival of the goods shall not limit the negotiability of the bill or constitute notice to a purchaser thereof of any rights or equities of such person in the goods.

SEC. 8. (U.S. Code, title 49, sec. 88.) That a carrier, in the absence of some lawful excuse, is bound to deliver goods upon a demand made either by the consignee named in the bill for the goods, or, if the bill is an order bill, by the holder thereof, if such a demand is accompanied by

(a) An offer in good faith to satisfy the carrier's lawful lien upon the goods;
(b) Possession of the bill of lading and an offer in good faith to surrender, properly indorsed, the bill which was issued for the goods, if the bill is an order bill; and
(c) A readiness and willingness to sign, when the goods are delivered, an acknowledgement that they have been delivered, if such signature is requested by the carrier.

In case the carrier refuses or fails to deliver the goods in compliance with a demand by the consignee or holder so accompanied, the burden shall be upon the carrier to establish the existence of a lawful excuse for such refusal or failure.

SEC. 9 (U.S. Code, title 49, sec. 89.) That a carrier is justified, subject to the provisions of the three following sections, in delivering goods to one who is—

(a) A person lawfully entitled to the possession of the goods, or
(b) The consignee named in a straight bill for goods, or
(c) A person in possession of an order bill for the goods, by the terms of which the goods are deliverable to his order; or which has been indorsed to him, or in blank by the consignee, or by the mediate or immediate indorsee of the consignee.

SEC. 10. (U.S. Code, title 49, sec. 90.) That where a carrier delivers goods to one who is not lawfully entitled to the possession of them, the carrier shall be liable to anyone having a right of property or possession in the goods if he delivered the goods otherwise than as authorized by subdivisions (b) and (c) of the preceding section; and, though he delivered the goods as authorized by either of said subdivisions, he shall be so liable if prior to such delivery he—

(a) Had been requested, by or on behalf of a person having a right of property or possession in the goods, not to make such delivery, or
(b) Had information at the time of the delivery that it was to a person not lawfully entitled to the possession of the goods.

Such request or information, to be effective within the meaning of this section, must be given to an officer or agent of the carrier, the actual or apparent scope of whose duties includes action upon such a request or information, and must be given in time to enable the officer or agent to whom it is given, acting with reasonable diligence, to stop delivery of the goods.

SEC. 11. (U.S. Code, title 49, sec. 91.) That except as provided in Section 26, and except when compelled by legal process, if a carrier delivers goods for which an order bill has been issued, the negotiation of which would transfer the right to the possession of the goods, and fails to take up and cancel the bill, such carrier shall be liable for failure to deliver the goods to anyone who for value and in good faith purchases such bill, whether such purchaser acquired title to the bill before or after the delivery of the goods by the carrier and notwithstanding delivery was made to the person entitled thereto.

SEC. 12. (U.S. Code, title 49, sec. 92.) That except as provided in Section 26, and except when compelled by legal process, if a carrier delivers part of the goods for which an order bill had been issued and fails either –

(a) To take up and cancel the bill, or
(b) To place plainly upon it a statement that a portion of the goods has been delivered with a description which may be in general terms either of the goods or packages that have been so delivered or of the goods or packages which still remain in the carriers possession, he shall be liable for failure to deliver all the goods specified in the bill to anyone who for value and in good faith purchases it, whether such purchaser acquired title to it before or after delivery of any portion of the goods by the carrier, and notwithstanding such delivery was made to the person entitled thereto.

SEC. 13. (U.S. Code, title 49, sec. 93.) That any alteration, addition, or erasure in a bill after its issue without authority from the carrier issuing the same, either in writing or noted on the bill, shall be void, whatever be the nature and purpose of the change, and the bill shall be enforceable according to its original tenor.

Sec. 14. (U.S. Code, title 49, sec. 94.) That where an order bill has been lost, stolen, or destroyed a court of competent jurisdiction may order the delivery of the goods upon satisfactory proof of such loss, theft, or destruction and upon the giving of a bond, with sufficient surety, to be approved by the court, to protect the carrier or any person injured by such delivery from any liability or loss incurred by reason of the original bill remaining outstanding. The court may also in its discretion order the payment of the carrier's reasonable cost and counsel fees; *Provided*, a voluntary indemnifying bond without order of court shall be binding on the parties thereto.

The delivery of the goods under an order of the court, as provided in this section, shall not relieve the carrier from liability to a person to whom the order bill has been or shall be negotiated for value without notice of the proceedings or of the delivery of the goods.

Sec. 15. (U.S. Code, title 49, sec. 95.) That a bill, upon the face of which the word "duplicate" or some other word or words indicating that the document is not an original bill is placed, plainly shall impose upon the carrier issuing the same liability of one who represents and warrants that such a bill is an accurate copy of an original bill properly issued, but no other liability.

Sec. 16. (U.S. Code, title 49, sec. 96.) That no title to goods or right to their possession asserted by a carrier for his own benefit shall excuse him from liability for refusing to deliver the goods according to the terms of a bill issued for them, unless such title or right is derived directly or indirectly from a transfer made by the consignor or consignee after the shipment, or from the carrier's lien.

Sec. 17. (U.S. Code, title 49, sec. 97.) That if more than one person claims the title or possession of goods, the carrier may require all known claimants to interplead, either as a defense to an action brought against him for non-delivery of the goods or as an original suit, whichever is appropriate.

Sec. 18. (U.S. Code, title 49, sec. 98.) That if someone other than the consignee or the person in possession of the bill has a claim to the title or possession of the goods, and the carrier has information of such claim, the carrier shall be excused from liability for refusing to deliver the goods, either to the consignee or person in possession of the bill or to the adverse claimant, until the carrier has had a reasonable time to ascertain the validity of the adverse claim or to bring legal proceedings to compel all claimants to interplead.

Sec. 19. (U.S. Code, title 49, sec. 99.) That except as provided in the two preceeding sections and in section 9, no right or title of a third person, unless enforced by legal process, shall be a defense to an action brought by the consignee of a straight bill or by the holder of an order bill against the carrier for failure to deliver the goods on demand.

SEC. 20. (U.S. Code, title 49, sec. 100.) That when goods are loaded by a carrier such carrier shall count the packages of goods, if package freight, and ascertain the kind and quantity if bulk freight, and such carrier shall not, in such cases, insert in the bill of lading or in any notice, receipt, contract, rule, regulation, or tariff, "Shipper's weight, load, and count," or other words of like purport, indicating that the goods were loaded by the shipper and the description of them made by him or in case of bulk freight and freight not concealed by packages the description made by him. If so inserted, contrary to the provisions of this section, said words shall be treated as null and void and as if not inserted therein.

SEC. 21. (U.S. Code, title 49, sec. 101.) That when package freight or bulk freight is loaded by a shipper and the goods are described in a bill of lading merely by a statement of marks or labels upon them or upon packages containing them, or by a statement that the goods are said to be goods of a certain kind or quantity, or in a certain condition, or it is stated in the bill of lading that packages are said to contain goods of a certain kind or quantity or in a certain condition, or that the contents or condition of the contents of packages are unknown, or words of like purport are contained in the bill of lading, such statements, if true, shall not make liable the carrier issuing the bill of lading, although the goods are not of the kind or quantity or in that condition which the marks or labels upon them indicate, or of the kind or quantity or in the condition they were said to be by the consignor. The carrier may also by inserting in the bill of lading the words "Shipper's weight, load, and count," or other words of like purport, indicate that the goods were loaded by the shipper and the description of them made by him; and if such statement be true, the carrier shall not be liable for damages caused by the improper loading or by the nonreceipt or by the misdescription of the goods described in the bill of lading: *Provided, however,* Where the shipper of bulk freight installs and maintains adequate facilities for weighing such freight, and the same are available to the carrier, then the carrier, upon written request of such shipper and when given a reasonable opportunity so to do, shall ascertain the kind and quantity of bulk freight within a reaonable time after such written request, and the carriers shall not in such cases insert in the bill of lading the words "shipper's weight," or other words of like purport, and if so inserted contrary to the provisions of this section, said words shall be treated as null and void and as if not inserted therein.

SEC. 22. (as amended March 4, 1927) (U.S. Code, title 49, sec. 102.) That if if a bill of lading has been issued by a carrier or on his behalf by an agent or employee the scope of whose actual or apparent authority includes the receiving of goods and issuing bills of lading therefor for transportation in commerce among the several states and with foreign nations, the carrier shall be liable to (a) the owner of goods covered by a straight bill subject to existing right of stoppage in transitu or (b) the holder of an order bill, who has given value in good faith, relying upon the description therein of the goods or upon the shipment being made upon the date therein shown, for damages caused by the nonreceipt by the carrier of all or part of the goods upon or prior to the date therein shown, or their failure to correspond with the description thereof in the bill at the time of its issue.

SEC. 23. (U.S. Code, title 49, sec. 103.) That if goods are delivered to a carrier by the owner or by a person whose act in conveying the title to them to a purchaser for value in good faith would bind the owner, and an order bill is issued for them, they cannot thereafter, while in the possession of the carrier, be attached by garnishment or otherwise or be levied upon under an execution unless the bill be first surrendered to the carrier or its negotiation enjoined. The carrier shall in no such case be compelled to deliver the actual possession of the goods until the bill is surrendered to him or impounded by the court.

SEC. 24. (U.S. Code, title 49, sec. 104.) That a creditor whose debtor is the owner of an order bill hall be entitled to such aid from courts of appropriate jurisdiction by injunction and otherwise in attaching such bill or in satisfying the claim by means thereof as is allowed at law or in equity in regard to property which cannot readily be attached or levied upon by ordinary legal process.

SEC. 25. (U.S. Code, title 49, sec. 105.) That if an order bill is issued the carrier shall have a lien on the goods therein mentioned for all charges on those goods for freight, demurrage and terminal charges, and expenses necessary for the preservation of the goods or incident to their transportation subsequent to the date of the bill and all other charges incurred in transportation and delivery, unless the bill expressly enumerates other charges for which a lien is claimed. In such case there shall also be a lien for the charges enumerated so far as they are allowed by law and the contract between the consignor and the carrier.

SEC. 26. (U.S. Code, title 49, sec. 106.) That after goods have been lawfully sold to satisfy a carrier's lien, or because they have not been claimed, or because they are perishable or hazardous, the carrier shall not hereafter be liable for failure to deliver the goods themselves to the consignee or owner of the goods, or to a holder of the bill given for the goods when they were shipped, even if such bill be an order bill.

SEC. 27. (U.S. Code, title 49, sec. 107.) That an order bill may be negotiated by delivery where, by the terms of the bill, the carrier undertakes to deliver the goods to the order of a specified person, and such person or a subsequent indorsee of the bill has indorsed it in blank.

SEC. 28. (U.S. Code, title 49, sec. 108.) That an order bill may be negotiated by the indorsement of the person to whose order the goods are deliverable by the tenor of the bill. Such indorsement may be in blank or to a specified person. If indorsed to specified person, it may be negotiated again by the indorsement of such person in blank or to another specified person. Subsequent negotiation may be made in like manner.

SEC. 29. (U.S. Code ,title 49, sec. 109.) That a bill may be transferred by the holder by delivery, accompanied with an agreement, express or implied, to transfer the title of the bill or to the goods represented thereby. A straight bill cannot be neogtiated free from existing equities, and the indorsement of such a bill gives the transferee no additional right.

SEC. 30. (U.S. Code, title 49, sec. 110.) That an order bill may be negotiated by any person in possession of the same, however such possession may have been acquired, if by the terms of the bill the carrier undertakes to deliver the goods to the order of such person, or if at the time of negotiation the bill is in such form that it may be negotiated by delivery.

SEC. 31. (U.S. Code, title 49, sec. 111.) That a person to whom an order bill has been duly negotiated acquires thereby –

(a) Such title to the goods as the person negotiating the bill to him had or had ability to convey to a purchaser in good faith for value, and also such title to the goods as the consignee and consignor had or had power to convey to a purchaser in good faith for value; and

(b) The direct obligation of the carrier to hold possession of the goods for him according to the terms of the bill as fully as if the carrier had contracted directly with him.

SEC. 32. (U.S. Code, title 49, sec. 112.) That a person to whom a bill has been transferred, but not negotiated, acquires thereby as against the transferor the title to the goods, subject to the terms of any agreement with the transferor. If the bill is a straight bill such person also acquires the right to notify the carrier of the transfer to him of such bill and thereby to become the direct obligee of whatever obligations the carrier owed to the transferor of the bill immediately before the notification.

Prior to the notification of the carrier by the transferor or transferee of a straight bill the title of the transferee to the goods and the right to acquire the obligation of the carrier may be defeated by garnishment or by attachment or execution upon the goods by a creditor of the transferor, or by a notification to the carrier by the transferor or a subsequent purchaser from the transferor of a subsequent sale of the goods by the transferor.

A carrier has not received notification within the meaning of this section unless an officer or agent of the carrier, the actual or apparent scope of whose duties includes action upon such a notification, has been notified; and no notification shall be effective until the officer or agent to whom it is given has had time, with the exercise of reasonable diligence, to communicate with the agent or agents having actual possession or control of the goods.

SEC. 33. (U.S. Code, title 49, sec. 113.) That where an order bill is transferred for value by delivery, and the indorsement of the transferor is essential for negotiation, the transferee acquires a right against the transferor to compel him to indorse the bill, unless a contrary intention appears. The negotiation shall take effect as of the time when the indorsement is actually made. This obligation may be specifically enforced.

SEC. 34. (U.S. Code, title 49, sec. 114.) That a person who negotiates or transfers for value a bill by indorsement or delivery, unless a contrary intention appears, warrants —

(a) That the bill is genuine;
(b) That he has a legal right to transfer it;
(c) That he has knowledge of no fact which would impair the validity or worth of the bill.
(d) That he has a right to transfer the title to the goods, and that the goods are merchantable or fit for a particular purpose whenever such warranties would have been implied if the contracts of the parties had been to transfer without a bill the goods represented thereby.

SEC. 35. (U.S. Code, title 49, sec. 115.) That the indorsement of a bill shall not make the indorser liable for any failure on the part of the carrier or previous indorsers of the bill to fulfill their respective obligations.

SEC. 36. (U.S. Code, title 49, sec. 116.) That a mortgagee or pledgee or other holder of a bill for security who in good faith demands or receives payment of the debt for which such bill is security, whether from a party to a draft drawn for such debt or from any other person, shall not be deemed by so doing to represent or warrant the genuineness of such bill or the quantity or quality of the goods therein described.

SEC. 37. (U.S. Code, title 49, sec. 117.) That the validity of the negotiation of a bill is not impaired by the fact that such negotiation was a breach of duty on the part of the person making the negotiation, or by the fact that the owner of the bill was deprived of the possession of the same by fraud, accident, mistake, duress, loss, theft, or conversion, if the person to whom the bill was negotiated, or a person to whom the bill was subsequently negotiated, gave value therefor in good faith, without notice of the breach of duty, or fraud, accident, mistake, duress, loss, theft, or conversion.

SEC. 38. (U.S. Code, title 49, sec. 118.) That where a person, having sold, mortgaged, or pledged goods which are in a carrier's possession and for which an order bill has been issued, or having sold, mortgaged, or pledged the order bill representing such goods, continues in possession of the order bill, the subsequent negotiation thereof by that person under any sale, pledge, or other disposition thereof to any person receiving the same in good faith, for value and without notice of the previous sale, shall have the same effect as if the purchaser of the goods or bill had expressly authorized the subsequent negotiation.

SEC. 39. (U.S. Code, title 49, sec. 119.) That where an order bill has been issued for goods no seller's lien or right of stoppage in transitu shall defeat the rights of any purchaser for value in good faith to whom such bill has been negotiated, whether such negotiation be prior or subsequent to the notification to the carrier who issued such bill of the seller's claim to a lien or right of stoppage in transitu. Nor shall the carrier be obliged to deliver or justified in delivering the goods to an unpaid seller unless such bill be first surrendered for cancellation.

Sec. 40. (U.S. Code, title 49, sec. 120.) That, except as provided in Section 39, nothing in this Act shall limit the rights and remedies of a mortgagee or lien holder whose mortgage or lien on goods would be valid, apart from this Act, as against one who for value and in good faith purchased from the owner, immediately prior to the time of their delivery to the carrier, the goods which are subject to the mortgage or lien and obtained possession of them.

Sec. 41. (U.S. Code, title 49, sec. 121) That any person who, knowingly or with intent to defraud, falsely makes, alters, forges, counterfeits, prints or photographs any bill of lading purporting to represent goods received for shipment among the several States or with foreign nations, or with like intent utters or publishes as true and genuine any such falsely altered, forged, counterfeited, falsely printed or photographed bill of lading, knowing it to be falsely altered, forged, counterfeited, falsely printed or photographed, or aids in making, altering, forging, counterfeiting, printing, or photographing, or uttering or publishing the same, or issues or aids in issuing or procuring the issue of, or negotiates or transfers for value a bill which contains a false statement as to the receipt of the goods, or as to any other matter, or who, with intent to defraud, violates, or fails to comply with, or aids in any violation of, or failure to comply with any provision of this Act shall be guilty of a misdemeanor, and, upon conviction, shall be punished for each offense by imprisonment not exceeding five years, or by a fine not exceeding $5,000, or both.

Sec. 42 (U.S. Code, title 49, sec. 122.) First. That in this act, unless the context of subject matter otherwise requires —

"Action" includes counterclaim, set-off, and suit in equity.

"Bill" means bill of lading governed by this Act.

"Consignee" means the person named in the bill as the person to whom delivery of the goods is to be made.

"Consignor" means the person named in the bill as the person from whom the goods have been received for shipment.

"Goods" means merchandise or chattels in course of transportation or which have been or are about to be transported.

"Holder" of a bill means a person who has both actual possession of such bill and a right of property therein.

"Order" means an order by indorsement on the bill.

"Person" includes a corporation or partnership, or two or more persons having a joint or common interest.

To "purchase" includes to take as mortgagee and to take as pledgee.

"State" includes any Territory, District, insular possession, or isthmian possession.

Sec. 43. (U.S. Code, title 49, sec. 123.) That the provisions of this Act do not apply to bills made and delivered prior to the taking effect thereof.

Sec. 44. (U.S. Code, title 49, sec. 124.) That the provisions of this Act are independent and severable, and the declaring of any provisions or part thereof, or provisions or part thereof, or section or part thereof, or sections or part thereof, unconstitutional shall not impair or render unconstitutional any other provision or part thereof or section or part thereof.

Sec. 45. That this Act shall take effect and be in force on and after the first day of January next after its passage.

3

Common Carrier's Liability Generally

One of the briefest statements of the common carrier's liability is that of Justice Oliver Wendell Holmes in *The Common Law* ([Boston: Little, Brown and Co., 1881], p. 180): "A common carrier is liable for goods which are stolen from him, or otherwise lost from his charge except by the act of God or the public enemy." This statement is close to that given by Lord Holt in *Coggs* v. *Bernard,* 2 Ld. Raym. 909, in 1703: "The law charges this person thus entrusted to carry goods, against all events, but acts of God, and of the enemies of the King." Neither of these statements include the three further exceptions from the common carrier's liability, which were noted in Hutchinson's *Law of Carriers* ([Chicago: Callaghan and Co., 2d ed., 1891], pp. 198-99):

> The liability of the common carrier by law is, as has been seen, an unusual and extraordinary one, based upon considerations of public policy which have survived the wonderful change in the circumstances under which they first arose. By that law the common carrier is regarded as a practical insurer of the goods against all losses of whatever kind with the exception of (1) those arising from what is known as an act of God, and (2) those caused by the public enemy; to which in modern times have been added (3) those arising from the act of the public authority, (4) those arising from the act of the shipper, and (5) those arising from the inherent nature of the goods.

In *Beard* v. *Railway Co.,* 44 N.W. 803, the Court spelled out the obligations of the common carrier of freight. His duty is not limited merely to transportation, but "he must exercise such diligence as is required by law to protect the goods from destruction and injury resulting from conditions which, in the exercise of due care, may be averted or counteracted." Further, said the Court, he must guard the goods from destruction or injury by the elements, from the effects of delay, and "from every source of injury which he may avert, and which, in the exercise of care and ordinary intelligence, may be known or anticipated."

The Interstate Commerce Act continues the common-law principles of common carrier liability for loss or damage to freight and, indeed, in one respect it extends that liability by requiring common carriers to accept liability for loss or injury occurring beyond their own lines. Section 20(11) of the Act (made applicable to motor carriers and freight forwarders by incorporation) makes the originating and delivering carrier on a movement under a through bill of lading liable for "any loss, damage, or injury to such property caused by it or by any common carrier" party to the through movement. The same section restricts the common carrier's ability to limit its liability for loss or damage to freight (other than baggage carried on passenger vehicles). Such limitation of liability is prohibited except as to property concerning which the carrier has been expressly authorized or required by the Interstate Commerce Commission to establish and maintain rates dependent upon the value declared by the shipper in writing, or agreed upon in writing as the released value of the property.

The phrase *caused by it* not only relieves a common carrier from liability for loss or damage due to the five excepted causes listed in the foregoing but also makes it possible for a carrier to contract against liability for loss or damage due to other causes except the carrier's own negligence. An example of this is the provision in many bills of lading stating that except in the case of negligence the carrier shall not be liable for loss, damage, or delay from riots or strikes. A carrier cannot exempt itself from liability for its own negligence although, in the case of authorized released rates, it may limit the *amount* of its liability. A common carrier cannot avoid its obligations as a common carrier by entering into an agreement with the shipper providing for its transportation to be as a private carrier or a contact carrier. Even in the case of such specialized transportation as the movement of circus trains, if the railroad holds itself out to transport any circus train, it is a common carrier and its liability, notwithstanding any agreement, is that of a common carrier. (*Chicago & N.W. R. Co.* v. *Davenport,* 295 F. 2d 589) On the other hand, a contract carrier can agree to assume the obligation toward a shipment normally assumed by a common carrier. The contract carrier's use of a uniform straight bill of lading, however, is not conclusive proof of such intent. (*Aetna Insurance Co.* v. *Cooper Wells & Co.,* 234 F. 2d 342)

As a general dule, a common carrier must accept for transportation any property tendered to it, provided the property is such as it holds itself out as willing to carry. This duty is not absolute, but is subject to reasonable qualifications. Whenever necessary to the proper conduct of its business, a common carrier may embargo certain traffic ordinarily accepted. An embargo is defined as "a notice issued by a common carrier refusing to receive or carry certain kinds of freight on its line, or between certain points." (*Chesapeake, etc., R. Co.* v. *O'Gara,* 139 S. W. 803)

Generally the Carmack Amendment and the liability it imposes upon common carriers has no application to foreign shipments; that is, shipments originating at or destined to points outside the United States. (*Missouri Pacific R. Co.* v. *Porter,* 273 US 341; *Atlantic C. L. R. Co.* v. *Pioneer Products, Inc.,* 265 F. 2d 431; *Harry Becker & Co.* v. *Wabash R. Co.,* 55 N. W. 2d 776) This is subject to a certain amount of qualification, however. In *Reider* v. *Thompson,* 339 U.S. 113, the Supreme Court had for its consideration the problem as to whether Section 20 (11) of the Interstate Commerce Act was applicable to a shipment in Argentina, transported by steamship to New Orleans, and reshipped from that point to Boston. The ocean bill of lading indicated the port of shipment as Buenos Aires and the port of discharge as New Orleans and the consignee: "Shipper to the order of: The First National Bank of Boston. Notice of Arrival should be addressed to (if consigned to Shipper's Order) Rudolph Reider, 39 South Street, Boston, Mass., U.S.A." Upon arrival at New Orleans, the shipment was unloaded and shipped by Missouri Pacific Railroad Company which issued its domestic bill of lading indicating that the goods were received from H. P. Lambert Co. and consigned to the H. P. Lambert Co. at Boston. The Court of Appeals for the 5th Circuit, 176 F. 2d 13, applied the tests laid down in *United States* v. *Erie R. Co.,* 280 U.S. 98, and *Texas & New Orleans R. Co.* v. *Sabine Tram Co.,* 227 U.S. 111, and held that the domestic rail bill of lading was a "supplemental bill of lading" issued by the domestic carrier to cover its portion of the transportation and delivery of a "through foreign shipment" and that the Carmack Amendment did not apply as it covered only domestic shipments and shipments originating in the United States destined to an adjacent foreign country, citing *Missouri Pacific R. Co.* v. *Porter,* 273 U.S. 341. In reversing the Court of Appeals and holding the Carmack Amendment applicable, the Supreme Court said:

> Reliance on the cited cases is misplaced. The issue in the *Porter* case, *supra,* was totally different from the question here. And whether the commerce is properly characterized as foreign or domestic is, in our view of the case, not material.
>
> The issue is whether this transaction is within the Carmack Amendment. But basically, the problem here is one of liability. The contract giving rise to liabili-

ty—the bill of lading—is our primary aid in solving that problem. So we turn to the contract to ascertain whether it evidences a transaction within the Carmack Amendment.

Does the fact that the shipment in this case originated in a foreign country take it without the Carmack Amendment? We think not. There was no through bill of lading from Buenos Aires to Boston. The record does not show the slightest privity between respondent (railroad) and the ocean carrier. The contract for ocean transportation terminated at New Orleans. Having terminated, nothing of it remained for the new, separate, and distinct domestic contract of carriage to "supplement." Even the parties to the ocean bill of lading and the domestic bill of lading were different. If the various parties dealing with this shipment separated the carriage into distinct portions by their contracts, it is not for courts judicially to meld the portions into something they are not. The test is not where the shipment originated but where the obligation of the carrier as receiving carrier originated. *Rice* v. *Oregon Short Line R. Co.*, 33 Idaho 565, 198 P. 191; *Barrett* v. *Northern Pacific R. Co.*, 29 Idaho 139, 157 P. 1016; *Baltimore & Ohio R. Co.* v. *Montgomery & Co.*, 19 Ga. App. 29, 90 S. E. 730. Thus it is not significant that the shipment in this case originated in a foreign country, since the foreign portion of the journey terminated at the border of the United States. The obligation as receiving carrier originated when respondent issued its original through bill of lading at New Orleans. That contract of carrier was squarely within the provisions of the statute

The case of *Alwine* v. *Pennsylvania R. Co.*, 141 Pa. Super. 558, 15 A. 2d 507, much relied upon by respondent and the Court of Appeals, is not in point. We need not now determine whether that case was correctly decided. For purposes of this case it is sufficient to note that there the Pennsylvania court emphasized that the shipment came into this country on a *through* bill of lading from Canada. The contract of carriage did not terminate at the border, as in the instant case. Nor does *Mexican Light & Power Co.* v. *Texas Mexican R. Co.*, 331 U.S. 731, 67 S. Ct. 1440, 91 L. Ed. 1779, aid respondent. There an export shipment on a through bill of lading from Pennsylvania to the international boundry, destined for a point in Mexico, was damaged in Mexico. The Texas Mexican Co., the last in a series of carriers handling the shipment in this country, issued a second bill of lading at Laredo, Texas, for the carriage on into Mexico. Recovery was sought against the Texas Mexican Co. as initial carrier under the Carmack Amendment. This Court held that it was not a receiving carrier because its duties were controlled by the first bill, and the second bill was without consideration and void. As the dissenting judge below said: "That case rules nothing as to a reverse shipment. . . ." And it could hardly be contended that respondent's domestic bill of lading here was void. As a matter of fact, the shipment in this case could not have moved an inch beyond New Orleans under the ocean bill; and the Carmack Amendment required respondent to issue a through bill of lading for the carriage from New Orleans to Boston.

We disavow, as did both the concurring judge and the dissenting judge below, any intimation that our holding might impose liability on a domestic carrier for damage attributable to an ocean carrier. The complaint in this case alleges that the shipment was received by respondent in good order and condition and was damaged when delivered. Unless petitioner can prove the case stated by his complaint, respondent is not liable.

The purpose of the Carmack Amendment was to relieve shippers of the burden of searching out a particular negligent carrier from among the often numerous carriers handling an interstate shipment of goods. To hold otherwise than we do would immunize from the beneficial provisions of the amendment all shipments originating in a foreign country when reshipped via the very transportation chain with which the Amendment was most concerned. Respondent was the receiving carrier squarely within the wording and meaning of the Carmack Amendment. The judgment of the Court of Appeals is *Reversed.*

In the foregoing proceeding Justice Frankfurter dissented on the ground that he felt that the Court of Appeals' decision was supported by the *Porter* case, *supra.* He remarked that ". . . the answer to our problem is not to be had by taking the words of the Carmack Amendment out of the illuminating context of the regulatory scheme of which they are a part. A legal faggot ought not to be broken into verbal sticks."

Duty to Provide Facilities

The first obligation of a common carrier which holds itself out to the public as ready to engage in the transportation business is to provide itself with reasonable facilities and appliances for the transportation of such goods as fall within the scope of its holding out to the general public. The carrier must put itself in a situation to be at least able to transport an amount of the freight which it proposes to carry equal to that which may be normally expected to be offered to it for transportation upon its route; for, while the law will sometimes excuse a carrier's delay in the transportation and even the refusal to accept goods which may be offered for transportation, when an unprecedented and unexpected press of business occurs, the law will not do so when the carrier's failure or refusal results from failure to provide itself with sufficient equipment and facilities to handle the regular and expected normal business. Section 216(b) of part II of the Interstate Commerce Act provides, in part, that:

> It shall be the duty of every common carrier of property by motor vehicle to provide safe and adequate service, equipment and facilities for the transportation of property in interstate and foreign commerce. . . .

A similar provision applicable to rail carriers appears in Section 1 (4) of part I of the Act.

Motor carriers are not required to maintain an unlimited supply of equipment, nor are they required to provide special equipment such as refrigerated or heated trucks. Shipment may be declined if the carrier does not have suitable equipment available. However, if a shipment is accepted, the carrier then becomes responsible for its prompt transportation and affording such protection as is provided for in its tariffs. Even if the tariff does not hold out that protective services will be provided, the carrier may be held liable for loss or damage to perishable cargo, the carrier obviously being negligent in accepting such shipment if he had no refrigerated equipment. In *Johnson Motor Transport* v. *United States,* 149 F. Supp. 175, the court said that as the carrier's tariffs did not provide or offer to protect shipments from heat or cold, it is clear that when consignments of meat were tendered to the carrier for transportation under bills of lading requiring the meat be transported in refrigerated trucks, the carrier could have refused the shipments. However, having accepted the shipments, the carrier cannot rely on its commitment being beyond the scope of its tariffs. Apart from the scope of the contractual obligation assumed by an interstate common carrier for the protection of cargo under the provisions of the pertinent bill of lading, the common law imposes upon the carrier a duty in relation to the protection of the cargo against loss or damage, and the carrier is liable in tort for a breach of that duty.

In *New England Express Co.* v. *Maine Central Railroad,* 57 Me. 188, discussing the duty of the carrier to serve all alike, the court said:

> Common carriers are bound to carry indifferently, within the usual range of their business for a reasonable consideration, all freight offered and all passengers who apply. For similar equal services, they are entitled to the same compensation. All applying have an equal right to be transported, or to have their freight transported, in the order of their application. They cannot legally give undue and unjust preference, nor make unequal and extravagant charges. Having the means of transportation, they are liable to an action if they refuse to carry freight or passengers without just ground for such refusal. The very definition of a common carrier excludes the right to grant monopolies or to give special or unequal preferences. It implies indifference as to whom they may serve, and an equal readiness to serve all who may apply, and in the order of their application.

In *Great Western Railroad* v. *Burns,* 60 Ill. 284, it was held that a common carrier could not, under any circumstances, delay the transportation of goods which had already been delivered to it and was awaiting shipment, in order to receive and forward other goods. From these and other authorities, it seems clear that a common carrier must serve all alike in the order the shipments are offered.

Motor common carriers operating in interstate commerce under certificates issued by the Interstate Commerce Commission are restricted to the transportation of the commodities specified in their certificates. Obviously there is no duty on an interstate motor common carrier to accept for transportation commodities which are outside the scope of its certificate. Such transportation would be unlawful and both the shipper and carrier would be subject to prosecution. Likewise, carriers are under no duty to accept for transportation shipments for which rates are not provided in tariffs lawfully filed with the Commission. Further, motor carriers cannot by special contract agree to transport a particular shipment by a particular vehicle or on a particular day when such service is not provided for in its tariff. (*Wilson & Co., Inc.* v. *Werner Transp. Co.* 69 N. E. 2d 713)

As to the common carrier's obligation to conform its tariff holding out to the operating authority, in Ex Parte Docket No. MC-77, *Restrictions on Service by Motor Common Carriers,* 111 M.C.C. 151, on 18 February 1970, the Commission promulgated the following regulation:

> Tariffs must contain only rates, charges, and related provisions that cover services in strict conformity with each carrier's operating authortiy. No provision may be published in tariffs, supplements, or revised pages which results in restricting service to less than the carrier's full operating authority or which exceed such authority. Tariff publications containing such provisions are subject to rejection or suspension for investigation.

A common carrier is under no compulsion to transport property of extraordinary character but if rates are provided for such property then there is a holding out to transport it, and the carrier is under obligation to accept it for transportation. A carrier may refuse to receive and transport property injurious to the public health, peace or morals. (*Coweta County* v. *Central of Georgia R. Co.,* 60 S. E. 1018)

There is no obligation on a common carrier to receive and transport property not prepared for shipment in the manner ordinarily required by it. (*Wiggins Ferry Co.* v. *St. Louis Union R. Co.,* 107 Ill. 450; *Thomas & Houston Elec. Co.* v. *Simon,* 25 Pac. 147) Property which has been packed or loaded in such manner, or which is in such condition, that its transportation would entail extra care and risk can also be refused. (*Louisiana & N. R. Co.* v. *Hendricks,* 171 So. 273; *Calif. Powder Works* v. *Atlantic R. Co.,* 45 Pac. 691)

Beginning of Liability

The liability of a common carrier begins on the delivery of the goods to it for transportation, that is, as soon as the delivery is complete and the possession of the goods has been transferred from the shipper to the carrier. To constitute an actual delivery, there must be an acceptance by the carrier as well as transfer of the physical possession and control of the goods. No formal acceptance is necessary and the fact that a bill of lading has not been issued does not indicate that that carrier has not accepted the goods.

Delivery cannot be complete if anything remains to be done by the shipper before the goods can be forwarded. Yet, if the thing remaining to be done is something which it is the duty of the carrier to do, without further act on the part of the shipper, then the liability of the carrier has begun. In *W. F. Bogart & Co.* v. *Wade*, 200 S. W. 148, the Court set forth the rule for determining whether the carrier's liability had commenced as:

> Had the control and possession . . . been completely surrendered by the shipper to the railroad company? Whenever the control and possession of goods passes to the carrier and nothing remains to be done by the shipper, then it can be said with certainty that the relation of shipper and carrier has been established.

In *Louisiana & N. R. Co.* v. *Edward's Adm'x,* 209 S. W. 519, it was held that where the carrier is directed by the shipper to do that which is incompatible with its common law duty as carrier, as, for example, not to forward the goods until further orders, there is no such delivery and acceptance as will render the carrier liable as such. Until such instructions are given the carrier's liability is that of an ordinary bailee. Under these circumstances, it is clear that delivery to the carrier is not complete to the extent necessary in order to impose full common-law liability until shipping instructions are actually given to the carrier.

The liability of the carrier does not begin with the giving of shipping instructions and signing of the bill of lading if the shipper has failed to make a complete delivery of the goods to the carrier for transportation. The issuance of a bill of lading, however, is prima facie evidence of an acceptance of the goods by the carrier.

A delivery of goods for shipment to an agent of the carrier, who is duly authorized to receive them or clothed with apparent authority to do so, and who has been accustomed to receiving goods tendered for carriage, constitutes sufficient delivery to bind the carrier. In shipper's action against motor carrier for loss of goods, where shipper proved that truck with carrier's identifying mark received delivery of the goods, the shipper was held entitled to rely on presumption that the ordinary course of business had been followed and that that carrier would not allow one of its trucks to answer call of shipper without a duly authorized driver.

(*Brown-Forman Distillers Corp.* v. *Walkup Drayage & Whse. Co.*, 163 Pac. 2nd 878)

Ordinarily, delivery to a motor carrier can be made to one of two places. Usually the delivery is made to the carrier's pick-up driver. In other instances, the shipper delivers the goods to the carrier at its terminal. In either of these cases, it is easy to determine when the carrier's liability attaches. The situation is more difficult, however, where the carrier spots a vehicle at the shipper's platform for loading and accepts the shipper's load and count. The weight of authority holds that when the shipment has been placed for transportation in the usual and customary manner, the carrier's liability begins after a reasonable time for it to take the shipment has ended. This problem presents a question of fact which, in the event of litigation, would be within the province of a jury to determine. In making such determination, the usual and customary arrangements between the parties would be entitled to consideration. It would seem that once the vehicle was loaded and the carrier notified, liability would commence within a reasonable time thereafter and any delay in moving the vehicle would be for the carrier's own convenience.

Liability of Initial Line

Under the English law, it has long been settled that a carrier accepting goods for transportation to a destination not on its own route nevertheless was liable to the owner for any damage regardless of the fact that it may have occurred while the goods were in the possession of a connecting carrier. In the development of transportation law in this country prior to federal regulations, some courts followed the English rule. The majority of state courts held that in the absence of any other contract than such as is generally to be implied from the acceptance of the goods, the obligation of the carrier accepting the shipment extended only to the end of its route and a delivery there to the next succeeding carrier to further or complete the transportation. Today, however, insofar as interstate shipments are concerned, the initial carrier is liable to the claimant for loss or damage by a connecting carrier regardless of "clear delivery" to a connecting carrier. This liability is specifically provided for in Section 20(11) of the Interstate Commerce Act.

The object of legislation making the initial carrier liable for any loss, damage, or injury to property transported is to enable one contracting with a common carrier for the carriage of goods to a point in a distant state to recover damages for injury thereto directly from the carrier to which the goods were delivered and by which the bill of lading was issued without being compelled to investigate to determine the identity of the carrier responsible for the damage. The effect of Section 20(11) is to impose upon the carrier the legal liability to perform and complete by delivery at destination every contract of interstate carriage into which it may enter. The carrier cannot escape from this liability either by rules or regulations of its own or by the contract or consent of the shipper.

Recently there has been some question as to the duty of the initial carrier to accept a shipment when the connecting line is being struck or boycotted. At the very minimum, indicated the court in *Southern Pacific Co.* v. *M. Rothstein & Sons,* 304 S. W. 2d 383, it is the duty of the carrier accepting a shipment to inform the shipper of any cause, such as a strike on the connecting lines on the route ordinarily followed, likely to delay the transportation, which is within the carrier's knowledge or within its fair and reasonable means of knowledge; the carrier is liable for the decline in market value resulting from the delay in the transportation of the shipment. Where the carrier's employees balk at handling goods destined for a particular connecting line, the carrier must do everything within its power to render service in accordance with its holding out and is relieved of its obligation to serve the public only upon a clear showing that it was prevented from so doing by circumstances clearly beyond its control. (*Galveston Truck Line Corp.* v. *Ada Motor Lines, Inc.,* 73 M. C. C. 617) Secondary boycotts were outlawed by labor relations legislation enacted in 1959.

An originating carrier paying a claim to a shipper for injury for which it was not responsible may, under the provision of Section 20(12), secure reimbursement from the carrier at fault. Carriers should, however, pay the claim directly to claimant immediately upon determining carrier liability and not delay settlement of the claim pending payment from the carrier at fault. Necessarily carriers must investigate all claims carefully before payment. Frequently the originating carrier may not be in possession of the documents necessary to determine whether a claim is valid. This is true particularly when the claim is for an alleged shortage, as it is necessary not only to determine from the delivering carrier if there was in fact a shortage at time of delivery, but also to ascertain from consignee if the shortage has been subsequently received from any other source. An investigation of this nature takes time, and frequently settlement of a claim may be expedited by filing it with the delivering carrier, who is usually in a better situation to investigate it.

Where a bill of lading was issued at Sharon, Pennsylvania, and specified Laredo, Texas, as destination with notation that machinery was "for export to El Oro," the initial carrier was held not liable for damage which occurred during movement from Laredo to El Oro, Mexico, notwithstanding that the shipment was transported from Sharon on an export rate since, ordinarily a bill of lading is a "through bill of lading" only from point of origin to the destination named. (*Mexican Light & Power Co.,* v. *Pa. R. Co.,* 33 F. Supp. 483)

Liability of Delivering Carrier

Not only is the originating carrier liable for any loss, damage, or injury to shipments received by it for transportation; but, under the provisions of Section 20(11), the delivering carrier is also made liable. The statute provides that claims may be filed with either the originating or delivering carrier and the carrier with whom claim is filed is made liable to the claimant for the full actual loss, damage, or injury irrespective of whether or not the shipment was injured while in its possession. Section 20(12) gives the carrier paying a claim for which another is responsible the right to secure recovery from the responsible carrier.

When a claim is filed with a delivering carrier, the carrier should investigate the claim and, if it is established that the shipment was injured while in its possession or the possession of some other carrier party to the through movement, then the delivering carrier should pay the claim and, if not responsible itself for the injury, proceed to secure reimbursement from the carrier at fault.

When the interstate transportation has come to an end, even though the shipment remains in the carrier's possession, its liability as a common carrier under Section 20(11) of the Interstate Commerce Act ceases. (*General American Transportation Corp.* v. *Indiana Harbor Belt R. Co.,* 191 F. 2d 865, cert. den., 343 U.S. 905; *Miller* v. *Greyvan Lines, Inc.,* 130 N. Y. S. 2d 378)

Liability of Intermediate Carriers

Claimant has always had the right to hold the carrier which actually caused the injury liable, and that right still exists. But if the intermediate carrier did not cause the loss, damage, or injury it cannot be held liable and claims should not be filed with it. If the injury is what is known as concealed loss or damage, there may well be an arrangement among the carriers for a proration of the claim amount. However, such an arrangement affords the claimant no rights against the intermediate carrier since it pertains only to the division of the settlement, which by law is the responsibility of the originating or delivering carrier among the carriers party to the through movement.

While Section 20(11) of the Interstate Commerce Act provides in part that ". . . nothing in this section shall deprive any holder of such receipt or bill of lading of any remedy or right of action which he has under existing law . . . ," and might be construed as authorizing a right against the intermediate carrier, the Supreme Court of the United States, in *Adams Express Co.* v. *Croninger,* 226 U.S. 491, held that this proviso only preserved to such holder "any right or remedy which he may have had under existing Federal law at the time of his action." In other words, this proviso, according to the highest United States court, is a "grandfather clause" to protect those having rights under existing law at the time Section 20(11) was enacted from losing any rights by the new legislation. The claimant's right to look to the intermediate carriers must be found in the existing common law or statute law outside the Interstate Commerce Act since Section 20(11) only provides for liability in the originating and delivering carrier. No case has been found clearly defining the effect of Section 20 (11) on the preexisting law or carrier liability. In the matter of the carrier's duty to serve, the 9th Circuit Court of Appeals in *Pensick & Gordon, Inc.* v. *California Motor Express,* 323 F. 2d 769, cert. den., 375 U.S. 984, indicated that the extent to which common law rights have been affected or qualified or supplemented by the Interstate Commerce Act is yet to be determined.

Of growing importance in the next few years will be the question of the liability of railroads performing Plan I trailer-on-flat-car (TOFC) or piggyback service jointly with motor common carriers. Under this form of TOFC service, the motor carrier's trailers are transported over rail lines in a substituted rail-for-motor service. Although the Interstate Commerce Commission has long held that Plan I TOFC service is a valid through-route, joint-rate arrangement, the question of its legality has been raised and is now pending in a federal district court. At least one federal court, the United States District Court for the Northern District of Illinois, has held that the railroad performing TOFC service under a motor carrier's substituted freight service directory is liable to the motor carrier under Section 20(12) of the Interstate Commerce Act only as a connecting carrier and hence is liable only to the extent that its actual negligence was the proximate cause of the loss or damage for which the motor carrier has honored a claim and therefore seeks reimbursement from the railroad. (*Briggs Transfer Co.* v. *Chicago Great Western Ry. Co.,* 11 Fed. Carr. Cas. 81,071)

Liability of Local Cartage Operator

As a common carrier, a local cartage operator is responsible for the goods tendered to him for transportation even though such service is performed by the local operator as a pickup and delivery agent of the line-haul carrier. In *Olive Kent Park, Inc.,* v. *Moshassuck Transportation Co.,* 71 N. Y. S. 2d 15, the New York Supreme Court found that Moshassuck Transportation Company, an over-the-road carrier operating between the New York City area and New England, had an agreement with Conboy Trucking Corp., a local truckman, to perform a portion of its pickup and delivery work. On 13 August 1946, Moshassuck turned over to Conboy, for delivery, 195 pieces of textiles, valued in excess of $35,000. The goods were not delivered to the consignee because on the date mentioned Conboy's truck was hijacked and the goods stolen. There was no negligence on Conboy's part. The owner of the goods called on Moshassuck to make good the loss and Moshassuck, in turn called on Conboy. The evidence indicated that Conboy did not, at least in its dealings with Moshassuck, issue its own bills of lading but used the forms of Moshassuck. The issue in this case was whether Conboy was operating as a common carrier, or, as contended, a contract or private carrier. In ruling Conboy to be a common carrier and responsible for the damage, the court commented:

> Does the manner in which the Conboy Corporation operates its transportation business constitute it a common carrier?
>
> The Public Service Law of this state, in article 1, section 2, subdivision 2, subdivision 30-b, provides: "The term common carrier by motor vehicle means any person who or which undertakes, whether directly or by lease or any other arrangement, to transport property, or any class or classes of property, for the general public by motor vehicle for compensation, whether over regular or irregular routes, or within a defined terrritory, including such motor vehicle operations, of carriers by railroad or water, and of express or forwarding companies to the extent they are not otherwise included within the provisions of Parts 1 and 2 of the Interstate Commerce Act of the United States and the laws of this state."
>
> The cases contain many definitions of a common carrier, but while their phraseology differs their substance does not. In the case of *Jackson A. Iron Works* v. *Hurlbut* (158 N.Y. 34), a common carrier is defined as follows (at p. 38): "A common carrier is one who, by virtue of his calling, undertakes for compensation to transport personal property from one place to another for all such as may choose to employ him, and everyone who undertakes to carry for compensation the goods of all persons indifferently is, as to liability, to be deemed a common carrier." At page 37 the court further said: "Truckmen, wagoners, cartment and porters who undertake to carry goods for hire as a

common employment in the city, or from one town to another, are common carriers."

In the case of *Heuman* v. *The Power Company* (175 App. Div. 628, First Department) the court said: "The defendant is a general truckman, transporting goods for hire under special contracts. He was therefore a common carrier."

An interesting case is *Stevenson Company* v. *Hartman* (231 N.Y. 378). There the defendant conducted a trucking business for the delivery of packages of merchandise in the Borough of Manhattan. He maintained a stand at Fifteenth Street and Sixth Avenue. His customers were located in that vicinity, and were engaged in various kinds of business activities. The defendant there asserted that he delivered goods only within a circumscribed area in the city, that he followed no special routes, and transported all the goods which his facilities enabled him to carry. He further claimed that he made his own choice of customers, and that his transportation charges were arrived at as a result of individual bargaining with customers. He was nevertheless held as a common carrier. In its opinion the court said (at page 381): "It seems to us perfectly clear that the position thus described was that of a common carrier of goods. Defendant was either a private carrier, carrying occasionally for some particular person under some particular arrangement, or he was a common carrier engaged in the general business of carrying goods generally for those who desired his services. It seems plain that his case is not fitted by the former description, but that he comes within the latter definition."

The characteristics of a common carrier, gathered from the decisions in many jurisdictions are well summarized in section 3 of Carriers, subdivision (b), in 13th *Corpus Juris Secundum,* in the following words: "The test by which it is determined whether a party is a common carrier of goods is: (1) He must be engaged in the business of carrying goods for others as a public employment, and must hold himself out as ready to engage in the transportation of goods for persons generally, as a business and not as a casual occupation. (2) He must undertake to carry goods of the kind to which his business is confined. (3) He must undertake to carry by the methods by which his business is conducted and over his established routes. (4) The transportation must be for hire. The distinctive characteristics of a common carrier are those stated in the first text set out above, namely, that he holds himself out as ready to engage in the transportation of goods for hire as a public employment and not as a casual occupation, and that he undertakes to carry for all persons indifferently within the limits of his capacity and the sphere of the business required of him."

It has been held that a transporter may confine its business to a special type or class of merchandise and still be a common carrier. A case in point is *United States* v. *Carolina Freight Carriers Corporation* (315 U.S. 475), where the court said at page 483: "It is plain that a carrier's holding out and actual performance may be limited to a few articles only. That is to say, he may be a common carrier only of a restricted number of commodities."

It has also been held that the absence of regular schedules of operation or of definite terminals does not necessarily take a carrier out of the classification of a common carrier. (*Anderson* v. *Fidelity & Casualty Co.,* 228 N.Y. 475) In

Jackson A. Iron Works v. *Hurlbut* (supra) that court said (at page 37): "The circumstance that the defendants had no regular tariff of charges for their work but that a special price was fixed by agreement, does not change the relation. The necessity for a different charge in each case arises, of course, out of the difference in labor in handling the articles of great bulk. The charge in each case may be proportioned to the risk assumed, and commensurate with the carrier's responsibility as such."

Nor is it necessary for a carrier to serve all of the public in order to warrant its classification as a common carrier. This was made clear in the often-quoted case of *Terminal Cab Company* v. *Kutz* (241 U.S. 252), where the court said: "No carrier serves all the public. His customers are limited by place, requirements, ability to pay and other facts. The public does not mean everybody all the time."

In the very recent case of *Surface Transportation Corp.* v. *Reservoir Bus Lines, Inc.* (271 App. Div. 556, First Department), the defendant carried passengers consisting only of the tenants of certain landlords with whom it had contracted for such service. The learned court, however, held that the defendant was a common carrier.

The Conboy Corporation, in support of its contention that it is a private or contract carrier instead of a common carrier, relies most strongly upon the case of *Matter of Motor Haulage Co.* v. *Maltbie* (293 N.Y. 338). In that case the petitioner, Motor Haulage Company, had been classified by the Public Service Commission as a common carrier. Upon a review, that determination was upheld by the Appellate Division (226 App. Div. 1040). Upon appeal to the Court of Appeals, however, that learned court, by a division of four to three, reversed the Appellate Division, and held that the petitioner was not a common carrier. A careful study of that case shows that the holding arrived at by a bare majority of the court was based upon certain peculiar facts which are elaborately set forth in the majority opinion, relating to the manner and method of the conduct of the petitioner's business. The distinguishing features of that carrier's activities which influenced the court's decision are not evidenced in the manner in which the Conboy Corporation operated its business.

The evidence before me satisfies me that the Conboy Trucking Corporation, viewed in the light of the authorities is a common carrier. This conclusion constrains me to grant the motion of the Moshassuck Transportation Company for judgment against the Conboy Trucking Corporation for the sum of $34,346.43, with interest and costs. At the conclusion of the trial the court granted the motion of the plaintiffs for judgment against the Moshassuck Transportation Company for the sum of $19,658.02. The difference between that amount and $34,346.43, as already noted, represents the value of goods belonging to persons other than the plaintiffs which had been turned over on August 13, 1946, by the Moshassuck Transportation Company to the Conboy Corporation for delivery and which were included in the goods that were lost as a result of the hijacking already referred to.

The liability of a local motor carrier rendering pickup and delivery service for an air carrier was discussed by the Court of Appeals for the

9th Circuit in *Twentieth Century Delivery Service, Inc.*, v. *St. Paul Fire and Marine Ins. Co.*, 242 F. 2d 292, wherein the court said:

It seems to us that it would be absurd to assume that the elaborate provisions made by Congress for regulation of such shipments could be permitted to result in the shipper having a new contract with new terms and varying degrees of liability each time his property was passed to a connecting carrier or delivered to a delivery service company such as the appellant. Analogous situations have arisen in respect to carriers other than air carriers, and it has been held, without exception, that provisions contained or incorporarted by reference in the bill of lading issued by the initial carrier and limiting the amount of liability for loss, extend to and operate for the benefit not only of connecting carriers, but of other persons, not carriers, performing unloading or other accessorial services connected with the shipment. In such cases it is deemed to be a circumstance wholly unimportant that the persons doing the accessorial services did not sign or execute the bill of lading, or are not named parties thereto. . . .

The Civil Aeronautics Act and its provision authorizing regulation of air carriers . . . demonstrates a similar purpose on the part of Congress that the conditions and limitations applicable to carriage by air, should likewise apply, without variation to any shipment from beginning to end, and in this case, from the consignor's door to the consignee's street address. To accomplish this, the provision of Rules Tariff 1-A that the liability should not exceed the value on which the rate is based, shall inure to the benefit of any person performing pickup or delivery service in connection therewith must be given effect.

Duty of Carriers to Interchange

Common carriers are required to accept shipments within the scope of their holding out, whether such shipments are tendered by ordinary shippers or by other carriers. In other words, the duty to render service includes the handling of interchanged freight. (*Nebraska Short Lines Carriers, Inc. Common Carrier Application,* 79 M. C. C. 599, rev'd on other grounds, 371 U.S. 156) Where two or more carriers hold themselves out jointly to render a through transportation service from a point on the line of one of them to a point on the line of the other, they normally publish joint rates. Publication of joint rates and through routes constitutes a definite holding out to the public, on the part of each carrier participating therein, to perform transportation service within the scope of such applicable tariff provisions. In the performance of such joint service connecting carriers, in effect, act as agents of the originating carrier in the performance of such service from origin of the shipment to destination. The provisions of a bill of lading contract executed by an originating carrier are, therefore, binding on such originating carrier's connecting lines to the extent that such connecting line participates in joint rates and routes with such originating carrier.

In *National Furniture Conference* v. *Associated Truck Lines,* 332 I. C. C. 802, affirmed in *Associated Truck Line* v. *United States,* 304 F. Supp. 1094, 397 U.S. 42, the Interstate Commerce Commission found that the cancellation of through-route, joint-rate, and interchange arrangements on shipments of furniture while maintaining such arrangements on other commodities, was an unreasonable practice and unduly and unreasonably disadvantaged shipments of furniture and, hence, was unlawful.

When a damaged shipment is tendered by one carrier to another carrier in joint service, the receiving carrier (the one to whom the freight was tendered) may refuse to accept the shipment until it is prepared by the delivering carrier (the one offering the freight) in a manner to render further transportation thereof reasonably safe and practicable. In other words, a connecting carrier may properly refuse to accept in interchange a shipment not in proper condition for further transportation. If, however, such damaged shipment is repacked, recrated, or otherwise prepared in such manner as would render further transportation thereof reasonably safe and practicable, the connecting carrier may not lawfully refuse to accept even though damage in connection therewith may exist. The receiving carrier, of course, should insist upon an appropriate exception notation in the billing by the carrier offering such shipment in a damaged condition. Such procedure would afford ample protection to the carrier with respect to claims for damage.

A carrier has no justification for refusing to accept a shipment from a connecting carrier merely because there is a shortage of some of the goods. The receiving carrier should accept the remainder of the shipment and secure an appropriate notation covering the shortage and transport the goods to destination in accordance with applicable tariff and bill of lading conditions.

4

Specific Phases of Carrier Liability

Exceptions from Liability

The common carrier's liability is not limited to injuries arising from his own negligence, but is a special, stricter liability than that imposed on other bailees. While this liability is sometimes spoken of as that of an *insurer,* this term is unfortunate since it suggests a relationship which does not in fact exist between the common carrier and his shipper, and it also suggests an absolute liability. Even the statement in Hutchinson's *Law of Carriers* ([Chicago, Callaghan and Co., rev. ed., 1891], p. 199) that the common carrier by law "is regarded as a practical insurer of goods" may be misunderstood or misapplied by the careless reader. The distinction between a common carrier's liability and an insurer's liability was made in *Sarno* v. *Southern Poe, Co.,* 277 F. Supp. 628. The common carrier is charged with a strict liability: a liability under which he is made responsible for loss or damage from whatever cause, except those from which he is specifically expected by law or, where permissible by contract. The five common law exceptions to the common carrier's liability, which have been carried forward by the Interstate Commerce Act, are liability for those injuries caused by (1) an act of God, (2) an act of the public enemy, (3) an act of public authority, (4) an act of the shipper, and (5) the inherent nature of the goods. In order for the carrier to be excused from liability for loss or damage arising from one of these excepted causes, it must be the immediate and proximate cause of the injury (some cases hold that it must be the sole cause), one which could not have been anticipated and averted by the carrier, and one with which no action of the carrier intervenes or conjoins. We will consider these excepted causes of freight loss or damage in turn.

Act of God

A carrier is not liable for loss or injury to goods caused by an act of God. While the exception from liability is generally recognized, an exact definition is not generally applied or even recognized. Dobie (*Bailments and Carriers* [St. Paul: West Publishing Co., 1914], pp. 328-29) notes two distinct theories of carrier excuse from liability: the *passive theory* and the *active theory.* These theories accord with the general division between those events due to natural causes of whatever kind and those due to sudden violent events of nature.

The broad and narrow views of carrier liability are also described by Hutchinson, *op. cit. supra* at pages 201-204, wherein he discusses one of the most liberal decisions in this country on the subject. (*Colt* v. *McMechen* 6 Johns. 160) The carrier, a sailing vessel, had been sailing close to shore when the wind failed and the vessel went aground. The court set out the following rule:

> Upon a position so plain in my apprehension as the cessation of a wind which was competent, at the very moment when the vessel began to come about, for the avoidance of the shoal, was the act of God and did not arise from the fault or negligence of man, I am at a loss for further illustration.

The older theory which equates an act of God with an inevitable or unavoidable accident has now generally given way to the concept of an event due to natural forces rather than the consequence of any human agency. In the case of *Forward* v. *Pittard,* 1 T. R. 27, Lord Holt stated the definition as follows:

> Now what is the act of God? I consider it to mean something in opposition to the act of man; for everything is the act of God that happens by his permission; everything by his knowledge. But to prevent litigation, collusion, and the necessity of going into circumstances impossible to be unravelled, the law presumes against the carrier, unless he shows it was done by the king's enemies, or by such act as could not happen by the intervention of man, as storms, lightning, and tempests.

As for the reason for the rule, there is little discussion in the texts or in the cases. The reference in *Colt* v. *McMechen, supra,* to "the fault or negligence of man" gives little guidance because the liability of a common carrier is not predicated on negligence or fault, since he is held liable to the shipper or owner of the goods for all losses or injuries to freight in his possession, without regard to the question of negligence, except those losses or injuries resulting from the five narrowly defined causes. Holmes suggests a different reason (*Common Law* [Boston: Little, Brown & Co., 1881], p. 204):

> It is another form of the principle which has been laboriously reargued in our own day, that parties are excused from the performance of a contract which has become impossible before breach from the perishing of the thing, or from change of circumstances the continued existence of which was the foundation of the contract, provided there was no warranty and no fault on the part of the contractor. Whether the act of God has now acquired a special meaning with regard to common carriers may be left for others to consider.

But even this suggestion does not explain why a common carrier is excused from performance of a contract of carriage made impossible because the goods were destroyed in a fire caused by lightning, but not when the impossibility results from a fire started by human agency although without showing of carrier negligence.

The rule that an act of God is one which occurs without any intervention of man is now generally followed. In *Michaels* v. *New York Central R. Co.,* 30 N. Y. 564, the court said:

> It is agreed that the notion of exception is those losses and injuries occasioned exclusively by natural causes, such as could not be prevented by human care, skill and foresight. All the cases agree in requiring the entire exclusion of human agency from the cause of the injury or loss. If the loss or injury happen in any way through the agency of man, it cannot be considered the act of God; nor even the act or negligence of man contributes to bring or leave the goods of the carrier under the operation of natural causes that work their injury, is he excused. In short, to excuse the carrier, the "act of God," or *vis divina,* must be the sole and immediate cause of injury. If there be any cooperation of man, or any admixture of human means the injury is not, in a legal sense, the act of God.

An act of God, generally, is an event which could not happen by the intervention of man or be prevented by human prudence; it must be such that no skill or watchfulness could have foreseen the disaster. It includes extraordinary floods, storms, unusual lightning, sudden tempests, severe frosts, earthquakes, and the like. (*Gleeson* v. *Virginia Midland R. Co.,* 140 U.S. 435; *Little Rock Packing Co.* v. *Chicago B. & Q. R.,* 116 F. Supp. 213)

It is the common-law duty of a carrier to provide protection from ordinary weather conditions. A motor carrier operating open-top equipment with tarpaulins could not avoid liability for damage caused by rain leaking onto the cargo. But, for example, where lightning strikes a tree, causing a limb to fall and tear the tarpaulin, permitting the rain to reach the cargo, the carrier would presumably be able to defend against liability, absent any negligence after discovering the damage, on the ground that the injury resulted from an act of God. In *Southern R. Co.* v. *Smith,* 102 S. W. 232, an electrical storm was held to be an act of God. In *Vermont* v. *American Railway Express,* 222 S. W. 913, extraordinary hot weather at a time it could not reasonably have been anticipated was held to be an act of God. An unexpected drop in temperature which the carrier could not reasonably foresee has been held an act of God. (*Rezek* v. *Southern Pacific Co.* 181 N. Y. S. 117) However, a carrier is liable for freezing which occurs at a season of the year or in a climate where freezing weather is reasonably to be expected. (*Bernstein* v. *Illinois Central R. Co.,* 208 N. W. 679)

Although there are some differences of opinion regarding which events are and which are not acts of God, the authorities are in general agreement that for a carrier to avoid liability for loss or injury due to an act of God, it must be the proximate cause of the loss or injury. The carrier will not avoid liability if he has been negligent in exposing the goods to the danger or if he fails to take reasonable steps to reduce the extent of the injury once he discovers the danger. Thus, if the natural event can reasonably be anticipated, the carrier must take steps to protect the goods or remove them from the peril. (*The Majestic,* 166 U.S. 375) Even where the natural event was of such force or unexpectedness that is could not be anticipated the carrier must take reasonable care to minimize the injury. (*Morrison* v. *Davis,* 20 Penn. St. 171; *The Generous,* 2 Dodson 324) If the carrier, after becoming aware of an impending act of God, could, by the exercise of such care as a man of ordinary prudence would have exercised under like circumstances, have protected the goods or mitigated their injury, the carrier is liable, notwithstanding that the act of God was of an unprecedented nature and could not have been foreseen.

In *Chesapeake & O. Ry. Co.* v. *J. Wix & Sons,* 87 F. 2d 256, the court held that even though the storm was so unusual and unprecedented as to be considered an act of God, if negligence on part of the carrier concurred with such act of God and contributed to any degree to cause damage, the shipper could recover. In this case the carrier knew from weather forecasts that a storm of great intensity was due; yet, even after the storm commenced and it was apparent that it was such as was never previously experienced, the carrier delayed removing the cargo to a place of safety. The court in holding the carrier liable cited *Ferguson* v. *Southern Ry.,* 74 S. E. 129, wherein it is stated:

It requires no citation of authority to sustain the proposition that, after a carrier has discovered or by the exercise of reasonable prudence and diligence should have discovered, that goods in his possession are subject to the perils of an unprecedented floor, or other vis major, it is his duty to exercise reasonable care and diligence to save them from damage or loss.

See also *Johnson* v. *Chicago, M., St. P. & P. R.*, 400 F. 2d 968; *West Bros., Inc.,* v. *Resource Management Service, Inc.*, 214 So. 2d 431.

In *Lehigh Valley R. Co.* v. *Allied Machinery Co.*, 271 F. 900, the court stated that even in those cases involving an act of God, the carrier is obliged to show in addition that the loss was inevitable; that is, could not have been prevented by due care on its part.

In *Chicago & E. I. R. Co.* v. *Collins Produce,* 235 F. 857, the court stated, by way of dictum that "If the loss be occasioned by a commingling of the 'act of God' and the negligence of the carrier, the latter is not relieved from liability." Certain state court decisions are cited in support of this statement. This case was affirmed by the Supreme Court of the United States (39 S. Ct. 189), but the soundness of this dictum was not discussed.

The established rule in the federal courts is that where property is destroyed by an act of God which would not have been within the range of the destructive force except for the carrier's negligent delay, the act of God is the proximate cause of the injury and the carrier's negligent delay is too remote to make the carrier liable. In *Standard Brands, Inc.* v. *Boston & M. R. R.*, 29 F. Supp. 593, the court stated:

If the decision turned upon the failure of the defendant's (carrier's) employees to anticipate the extent to which the high waters of 1936 would exceed the highest recorded level, I would not be able to conclude . . . that such failure would deprive the defendant of its right to invoke the provisions of the contract excepting liability for damages arising from the acts of God. . . . This conclusion is further required because the failure cannot be deemed to be the direct and proximate cause of the damage.

See also *Little Rock Packing Co.,* v. *Chicago, B. & Q. R.*, 116 F. Supp. 213.

In *Whittier Mills Co.* v. *Southern Ry. Co.* 190 S. E. 433, the carrier of an interstate shipment was held free from liability for damage resulting from a sudden and unexpected rise of the tide. In this case, it appeared that the carrier had transported the goods to its destination terminal, unloaded it and placed it on a pier for delivery to a connecting water carrier, unloading it on the pier five minutes after the last boat calling on the pier that day to pick up freight had left. About nine or ten o'clock that night a storm came up which caused the tide to rise considerably but the carrier concluded that there was no danger and permitted its employees to disperse. During the night the tide receded by the next morning before a boat called at the pier for the shipment, the tide returned suddenly as a result of the storm and rapidly rose over the pier and engulfed the shipment. While warnings of the approach of the storm had been given by the weather bureau, there was nothing that would intimate to the public that the storm would be of unprecedented violence or more severe than the usual storms in that locality. The court held that the event was an act of God for which the carrier was in no way responsible, and that no negligence of the carrier, either by delay in the delivery of the shipment at the pier or in failure to move the shipment, or otherwise, proximately contributed to the damage. Similar holdings were made in *Kraft Hat Mfg. Corp.* v. *Universal Carloading and Distributing Co.*, 7 N. Y. S. (2nd) 679; *Farr Co.* v. *Union Pac. R. Co.*, 106 F. 2d 437; and *Standard Brands* v. *Boston & M. R. R.*, 29 F. Supp. 593.

In *Southern Ry. Co.* v. *International Vegetable Oil Co.*, 159 S. E. 773, the railroad accepted a carload of cotton seed for transportation from Blackville, South Carolina, to Augusta, Georgia. While the car was in the railroad's yards at Hamburg, South Carolina, near the Savannah River, a sudden flood arose which lasted two days and then began to recede. Three days later, however, and before the railroad had moved the car, another flood occurred which damaged the contents of the car. The plaintiff contended that the rail carrier's negligence in failing to move the shipment after the first flood constituted negligence. In deciding against this contention, the court stated:

> We have exhausted the brief of evidence in a vain effort to find any proven fact indicating any act of negligence, either of commission or omission, on the part of the railroad company, to which the damage to the car of cotton seed might be attributed, in the unusual, unexpected, and extraordinary circumstances of the case. . . . It is urged by counsel for the defendant in error that the railway company neither availed itself of information obtainable nor acted upon such information as it had, to the end that the car of cotton seed would be safely placed in anticipation of the sudden second flood. But we cannot see that the evidence anywhere warrants such an inference. Being of the opinion that, with reference to the question of negligence, the plaintiff below completely failed to sustain the burden of proof upon it by law, we hold that . . . the trial court erred. . . .

While it is the rule in some state courts that the duty is on the carrier to show that it was free from negligence in order to use an act of God as defense to liability, the rule in the federal courts is otherwise and the duty to show that the carrier was negligent where act of God is alleged as a defense is upon the claimant. *Firpine Products Co.* v. *Atchison, T. & S. F. Ry.*, 124 F. Supp. 906; but see *Johnson* v. *Chicago, M., St. P. & P. R.*, 400 F. 2d 968. State courts in deciding cases involving interstate shipment, of course, will follow the federal rule. This is discussed in *Louisville & N. R. Co.* v. *Finlay,* 170 So. 207, where the court said:

The federal courts hold that the burden is on plaintiff to allege and prove negligence when an act of God is the immediate cause, *Memphis & C. R. Co.* v. *Reeves,* 10 Wall, 176, 19 L. Ed., 909, though the Alabama cases hold that the burden to show due care is on defendant, as we will show, and this being an interstate shipment the rule of the federal courts prevail. *Barnet* v. *New York Cent. & H. R. R. Co.*, 222 N.Y. 195, 118 N. E. 625; *Hadba* v. *Baltimore & O. R. Co.*, 183 App. Div. 555, 170 N.Y. S. 769; *Continental Paper Bag Co.* v. *Maine Cent. Railroad Co.*, 115 Me. 449, 99 A. 259; *Nashville, C. & St. L. R. Co.* v. *Camper,* 201 Ala. 581, 78 So. 925; *Alabama Great Southern R. Co.* v. *Conner,* 227 Ala. 562, 151 So. 355. The rule in Alabama, as in other state courts, is that, so long as the duty of a common carrier continues, and it is an insurer, in order to be relieved from liability for loss or injury to goods so carried, by an act of God, it must trace the loss to such act without negligence by it. *Atlantic C. L. R. Co.* v. *Rice,* 169 Ala. 265, 52 So. 918, 29 L. R. A. (N. S.) 1214, Ann. Cas. 1912B, 389; *Alabama G. S. R. Co.* v. *Quarles & Couturie,* 145 Ala. 436, 40 So. 120, L. R. A. (N. S.) 867, 117 Am. St. Rep. 54, 8 Ann. Cas. 308; *Alabama, G. S. R. Co.* v. *Elliott & Son,* 150 Ala. 381, 43 So. 738, 9 L. R. A. (N. S.) 1264, 124 Am. St. Rep. 72. In the case of *Coosa River Steamboat Co.* v. *Barclay,* 30 Ala. 120, Judge Stone, writing for the court observed: "In my opinion, 'The act of God' and the operations of nature, unmixed with human agency or human negligence are synonymous." Also, "in thus laying down my views of the law it is not my purpose to shift the onus, or to relieve carriers from the strict diligence required of them in the older authors. To render the excuse valid, not only must the carrier trace the loss or injury immediately to the operations of nature, but must also convince the jury that such loss or injury resulted from inevitable necessity, 'which no human prudence could forsee or prevent.' " While there was in that case some difference between him and Rice, C. J., it is shown in the case of *Steele* v. *McTyer's Adm'r.*, cv *Ala.* 667, 676, 70 Am. Dec. 516, and in *Steel* v. *Townsend,* 37 Ala. 247, 256, 79 Am. Dec. 49, that there was no difference as to the burden of proof as declared by Judge Stone. It is said in the latter case: "The true view is, not that the carrier discharges his liability by showing an act of God, and is then responsible, as an ordinary agent for negligence; but that the intervention of negligence breaks the carrier's line of defense by showing that the injury or loss was not directly caused by the act of God, or, more correctly speaking, was not the act of God." And when a loss is sustained to goods in the possession of a carrier, though its common-law liability as an insurer does not apply, whether by contract or otherwise, and it is liable only for its negligence, the burden is on the carrier to show that it used due care and diligence. *Louisville & Nashville R. Co.* v. *Touart,* 97 Ala. 514, 11 So. 756; *Nashville R. Co.* v. *Oden,* 80 Ala. 38; *Louisville & Nashville R. Co.* v. *Gidley,* 119 Ala.

523, 24 So. 753. But in *Memphis & C. R. Co.* v. *Reeves, supra,* the United States Supreme Court, in respect to such a question observed: "A common carrier assumes all risks except those caused by the act of God and the public enemy. . . . Now, when it is shown that the damage resulted from this cause immediately, he is excused. . . . No question of his negligence arises unless it is made by the other party. It is not necessry for him to prove that the cause was such as releases him, and then to prove affirmatively that he did not contribute to it. . . . the proof of this must come from those who assert or rely on it." The later cases are cited and the rule is recognized in *Schnell* v. *The Vallescura,* 293 U.S. 296, 55 St. Ct. 194, 79 L. Ed. 373, lately decided. The rule declared by the federal courts must prevail when the shipment is interstate, as we have shown. But for the moment we are dealing with the question of pleading. But when, as here, the plea alleges that the act of God was the proximate cause of the loss, a general denial raises the issue of whether something else was the sole proximate cause. If the intervention of negligence breaks the line of defense so that the loss is not directly caused by the act of God, such is not a proximate cause, but the negligence is its sole proximate cause. The act of God is then only the condition on which defendant's negligence operates, and resembles the status of subsequent neglience. *Randle* v. *Birmingham Ry., L. & P. Co.,* 158 Ala. 532, 48 So. 114; *Seaboard A. L. R. Co.* v. *Laney,* 199 Ala. 654, 75 So. 15; *Godfrey* v. *Vinson,* 215 Ala. 166 (11), 110 So. 13; *Memphis & C. R. Co.* v. *Martin,* 131 Ala. 269 (4), 30 So. 827; *Southern R. Co.* v. *Cooper,* 172 Ala. 505, 55 So. 211. If the defendent had notice of impending danger from the act of God, or if it was foreseeable, in time to have avoided the loss by such means as were then available, and neglected to use them, such neglect was the sole proximate cause of the loss, and the act of God was a remote cause. So that the allegation in the plea that the act of God was the proximate cause presents the issue of negligence after notice of the danger or negligence in not appreciating the danger, regardless of where the burden of proof exists . . . There is "shown the intervention of such an extraordinary, violent and destructive agent, as by its very nature raises a presumption that no human means could resist its effect." *Steele* v. *Townsend, supra,* 37 Ala. 247, at page 256, 79 Am. Dec. 49. The flood was the highest ever known before to have occurred. There was no duty to guard against one so far in excess of all previous floods until it became apparent that it probably would become so dangerously excessive. The flood stage had never there exceeded 22.9 feet; but this one rose to 33.3 feet. A flood of the highest known, or in excess of it to a material extent, would not have destroyed or injured the goods in question. They arrived on March 13, 1929. Notice was promptly mailed, but not received until the flood came the next day. By night, March 14, the waters were up. The car in question was moved to a higher level. The forecast then made by the meteorologist was that the flood would reach a stage of 23 to 24 feet, and no forecast of a higher stage was at any time made. That would not be dangerous to this car of sugar. The rise was then very rapid and at night. Every one was apparently taken by surprise and was helpless. When it became evident that the car might be submerged, nothing could be done. In 1928, when the highest previous flood had occurred, the water on the tracks at the depot was eight to twelve inches deep. Such a flood would not have damaged this car of sugar. It was safe against any flood which was known ever to have occurred or which when then predicted by the meteorologist or reasonably then anticipated. As was said in *Smith* v. *Western Ry. of Alabama,* 91 Ala. 455, 8 So. 754, 11 R. A. 619, 24 Am. St. Rep. 929, so in this case: "No human power could have stayed the flood, or foresight or prudence anticipated such an overflow. . . . It is no proof of negligence that because after an injury has resulted it can then be seen how the injury might have been avoided. The question is, what notice or knowledge had the defendant, from which such an overflow could reasonably have been anticipated or foreseen?" As was held in that case, we think the undisputed evidence shows that defendant in this was entitled to the general charge, since it shows that it was not negligent either in not foreseeing the danger or in not avoiding if after it became apparent, and that the damage did occur as the proximate result of an act of God. Such was also the case of *Memphis & C. R. Co.* v. *Reeves, supra.*

The court in the foregoing case remanded it to the lower court for retrial and thereafter it was again appealed. *Louisville & N. R. Co.* v. *Finlay,* 185 So. 904) Upon retrial, plaintiff endeavored to show that the flood was not "unprecedented" and offered a witness, 89 years of age, who testified that in 1864 there had been a flood in the locality of equal or greater depth than the one of 1929. On this basis it was argued that the flood of 1929 was not an act of God. The court on the second appeal rejected this contention in the following language:

. . . we think too great a stress is laid upon the word unprecedented. The rule of exemption from liability, if the loss is the result of an "act of God," is founded upon reason and justice that one should not be held responsible for that which could not have been reasonably anticipated. Or, as stated in *Steele* v. *Townsend,* 37 Ala. 247, 79 Am. Dec. 49, and quoted in the opinion on former appeal, 170 So. 209, the "intervention of such an extraordinary, violent and destructive agent, as by its very nature raises a presumption that no human means could resist its effect." The expression "act of God" has been employed in various and broad senses by the various authorities, such as an "extraordinary convulsion of nature or a direct visitation of the elements, against which the aids of science and skill are of no avail," or an "accident produced by physical causes which are irresistible," and other expressions of like nature. 9Amer. Jur. 849. In *Barnet* v. *New York Cent. & H. R. R. Co.* 222 N.Y. 195, 118 N.E. 625, cited in our former opinion, the simple statement is made that "an extraordinary flood . . . is an act of God." (page 627) And the Virginia court in *Southern Railway Co.* v. *Cohen Weenen & Co.,* 156 Va. 313, 157 S. E. 563, states that (page 564) "an act of God, as the term is known to the law, is such an unusual and extraordinary manifestation of the forces of nature that it could not under normal conditions have been anticipated or expected." Like observation is found in our case of *Law* v. *Gulf State Steel Co.,* 229 Ala. 305, 156 So. 835. But the Virginia court also, in the same opinion, points out that it need not be unprecedented, observing in this respect that "a building destroyed by an earthquake would be a building destroyed by an act of God. Should it be rebuilt and again destroyed, the second shock would be as much an act of God as the first, but it would not have been unprecedented. If it could not have been anticipated, or expected, under normal conditions, that is sufficient." And the authorities appear generally to be in accord upon this question. 9 Amer. Jur. 852. The question of precedent, therefore, bears relation to the matter of reasonable anticipation, and opportunity to avert the consequences, and it is in that sense that the authorities have noted the "unprecedented" nature of the catastrophe.

Another interesting case which differentiates between the state and federal rule relative to burden of proof when an act of God and carrier negligence are involved is *Baltimore & O. R. Co.* v. *Johl & Bergman*, 177 So. 778, and the following quotation therefrom is offered because of its excellent review of the leading federal cases:

It is contended by the appellant that the direct proximate cause of the damage to the shipment in question was the act of God, in that the proximate cause of the loss or damage here was an unprecedented flood, and that the evidence in its behalf shows that it was guilty of no negligence concurring with, or contributing to, the act of God; and that in that state of the case the burden then was cast upon the appellee that, notwithstanding the flood, the loss could have been averted by the exercise of the carrier of reasonable care and skill in invoking the rule, as it contends, which is adopted by the federal courts, the Supreme Court of the United States, and many other state jurisdictions. . . . In *Memphis and C. Ry. Co.* v. *Recves*, 10 Wall 176, 19 L. Ed. 909, the Supreme Court laid down this rule: "When a common carrier shows that a loss was (caused) by some *vis major* as by flood, he is excused without proving affirmatively that he was guilty of no negligence. The proof of such negligence, if the negligence is asserted to exist rests on the other party. In case of a loss of which the proximate cause is the act of God or the public enemy, the common carrier is excused though his own negligence or laches may have contributed as a remote cause." This principle seems to have been first adopted in *York Mfg. Co.* v. *Illinois Central Railroad Company*, 3 Wall. 107, 18 L. Ed. 170, and seems to have consistently followed with variations as to the reason for the rule, which is a modification of the common-law liability of a common carrier. The common-law liability of a common carrier was that of an insurer, and the only exception thereto is the act of God or the public enemy; and the duty of the carrier was not only to show that the act of God was the proximate cause of the damage or loss, but the burden was further on it to prove the absence of negligence on its part, for the reason that the facts to be proven are within the knowledge of the carrier; and that is the rule in Mississippi as found in *Chicago, St. L. & N. O. R. Co.* v. *Moss & Co.*, 60 Miss. 1003, 45 Am. Rep. 428; *Newberger Cotton Co.* v. *Illinois Central R. Co.*, 75 Miss. 303, 308, 23 So. 186. The Carmack Amendment provides in part that the carrier shall be liable to the lawful holder of the property being transported for any "loss, damage or injury to such property, caused by it or by any common carrier, railroad or transportation company to which such property may be delivered." In *Adams Express Co.* v. *Croninger*, 226 U.S. 491, 33 S. Ct. 148, 57 L. Ed. 314, 44 L. R. A., (N. S.) 257, the Supreme Court of the United States said: "Right and remedies conferred by existing state laws, where a shipment accepted by a carrier for interstate transportation has been lost, injured, or damaged, were not continued in force by the provision in the Carmack Amendment of June 29, 1906, to the Act of February 4, 1887, § 20 (49 U.S.C.A. §20 (11)), that nothing therein contained shall deprive the holder of the receipt or bill of lading of any remedy or right of action which he has under existing law, but such proviso only preserves to such holder any right or remedy which he may have under existing Federal law at the time of his action." The court further said that "The intent of Congress to take possession of the subject of liability of a carrier under contracts for interstate shipment, and to supersede all state regulations with reference to that subject, so clearly appears from the Carmack Amendment of June 29, 1906 . . . as to invalidate, as applied to interstate shipments, the provisions of any state law nullifying contracts limiting the liability of a carrier for loss or damage to the agreed or declared value."

In the preceding cited case, the owner of the goods alleged that the carrier did not use due care in preserving the shipment after the water had receded. A witness testified that 75 percent of the damage could have been obviated if the wet white suede shoes of which the shipment consisted had been segregated from those which were dry. In disposing of this contention that the carrier failed to mitigate the damages, the court said:

> . . . they (the railroad) ought not to be held for the damage following therefrom, because of lack of facilities to meet such an exigency. The prime object of a railroad engaged in interstate commerce is to continue the operation of its trains in order that commerce may move to and from in this nation as far as possible. After the flood, the tracks and trains of the railroad had to be repaired and reconditioned to move on the stream of commerce. And the evidence is undisputed that no facilities at that time existed for unloading its vast amount of freight and reconditioning it while in transit. . . . If the position be taken that it was the duty of the railroad to cease operation and remove from the car these cartons of shoes, then by the same reasoning a court would be compelled to hold that it was the duty of the carrier to so treat all the shipments in the 23 cars flooded. . . .

The principle that the act of God must be the proximate cause of the damage is illustrated by the decision in *Atlantic Coast Line R. Co.* v. *Fugazzi,* 165 S. E. 840, wherein the court said:

> The defense was that the delay was caused by interrupted transportation due to washouts of the railroad bed caused by a flood, which, it was alleged, constituted an act of God, and that the defendant was not liable. The evidence authorized the inference that the delay in delivery of the goods, which constituted a shipment of fish was perishable, was not caused by the washout or an act of God, but was caused by a negligent delay in transportation prior to the washout. Civ. Code 1910 §2713; *Richmond, etc. R. R. Co.* v. *White & Co.,* 88 Ga. 805, 15 S. E. 802; *Lamb* v. *Mitchell,* 15 Ga. App. 759, 84 S. E.

213; *Southern Railway Co.* v. *Standard Grower's Exchange,* 34 Ga. App. 534, 130 S. E. 373; *Bugg* v. *Perry & Fair-Cloth,* 42 Ga. App. 523, 156 S. E. 708, 46 A. L. R. 308 note. In *Memphis & C. Railroad Company* v. *Reeves,* 10 Wall. 176, 19 L. Ed. 909, and *Southern Railway Co.* v. *International Vegetable Oil Co.,* 43 Ga. App. 489, 156, S. E. 773, the cause of the damage to the goods shipped was an act of God and was not any negligence of the carrier.

Another case illustrating the principle that the act of God must be the proximate cause of the damage in order to excuse the carrier is *Atchison T. & S. F. Ry. Co.* v. *Eddie,* 61 Pac 2d 681. At the time shipments in this case were accepted, heavy rains had been falling in the vicinity and the carrier signed a pencil provision on the bill of lading reading, "Subject to delay account high water." Meanwhile the water reached a flood stage and no train service was possible because of high water and washouts. The shipments as a consequence did not move from point of origin until some five days after being loaded. Upon arrival at destination, the consignee examined the cars and found that the roof and ceiling of a car containing bran had the appearance of water having leaked or splashed in and that the water in another car appeared to have been ten inches deep above the floor of the car and that the water had entered the car through the sides, and that water was still leaking in from the top. The rail carrier endeavored to attribute some of the dampness to sweating and that in general the damage was due to an act of God. In rejecting the carrier's contention, the court said:

> This argument (of the carrier) would be unassailable were it not for the above testimony, from which the jury might have drawn an inference of negligence in furnishing defective equipment. "An act of God, such as a severe blizzard and snowstorm, which will excuse a carrier for liability for loss, must not only be the proximate cause of the loss, but it must be the sole cause, and though the loss may have been caused by an act of God, yet if the negligence of the defendant commingles with such an act of God as an efficient contributing concurrent cause, and it appears from the evidence and the circumstances of the case that such injury would not have occurred except for such negligence, the company will be liable." *St. Louis & S. F. Railway Co.* v. *Dreyfus,* 42 Okla. 401, 141 P. 773, L. R. A. 1915D, 547.

The case of *Little Rock Packing Co.* v. *Chicago, B .& Q. R. Co.* 116 F. Supp. 213, also involving two other separate suits by other parties based on practically the same facts and consolidated for trial, presents some interesting comments relative to determination of "proximate cause" in actions against carriers where damage is alleged to have resulted from an act of God. In this case cattle buyers for the plaintiffs tendered shipments of cattle to the Chicago, Northwestern Railroad for transportation from Sioux City, Iowa, to destinations in Arkansas and Texas. The agent for the Chicago, Northwestern Railroad at Sioux City checked with its connecting carrier, the Missouri Pacific Railroad, to determine if it could accept these shipments at Kansas City in view of flood conditions and upon being informed that the shipments could not be handled by that carrier refused to accept the proffered shipments. Following the rejection of the shipments, the plaintiffs contacted the defendant Chicago, Burlington and Quincy Railroad and inquired if that carrier could accept the cattle, explaining that the shipment had been refused by Chicago Northwestern because of floods south of Kansas City. The Burlington checked and notified the shippers that the cattle would be accepted and go through on schedule. The various shipments were then accepted and all routed for interchange at Kansas City.

The shipments of cattle were approximately three hours late in leaving Sioux City and due to delays en route arrived in North Kansas City seven hours behind schedule, late in the evening of July 12, 1951. Four hours after arrival all of the cattle were taken to the Kansas City Stock Yards and unloaded for watering and feeding. Before the flood waters topped the levees and flooded the stockyards, civil authority had ordered that the area be vacated but before this order was given, the Kansas City Stock Yards Company on July 13 had driven all of the cattle in question to the second and third floor of its hog barn, which, though above the subsequent flood-water level, was open to the sun at the third floor. There, plaintiffs' cattle remained mingled with 5,000 head of cattle until shortly before noon on Monday, July 16. During the period of this confinement, with daily temperatures ranging as high as 96°, the cattle had only hay for feed and no water at all. When finally the cattle could be reached on the sixteenth, plaintiffs' cattle, and other cattle mingled with them, were in serious condition and some had died of heat exhaustion. The remainder were loaded on trucks and taken to feed lots where still more of the cattle died. The Burlington was unable to determine the ownership of the surviving cattle, most of which were in bad condition, and in order to avoid further loss, defendant consented to the sale of the surviving animals and allocation of the proceeds proportionately to plaintiffs as salvage, without prejudice to whatever further claims plaintiffs might later pursue.

The plaintiffs all brought suit to recover the value of the cattle less payments for salvage. The railroad then, as third-party plaintiff, joined the Kansas City Stock Yards as third-party defendant alleging that it had delivered all the cattle in question to the stock yard in good health, and that if the railroad is liable to the plaintiffs, then it should be indemnified by the third-party defendant on grounds that if any actionable negligence was committed it was that of the stock yard company while the cattle were in their possession. In deciding the case, the court first considered the question as to whether plaintiffs' losses were the result of concurring negligence on the part of the Burlington in failing to notify the shippers that there would be a delay in transportation of their cattle because its connecting carriers, as to those shipments, were known by it to be out of service as a consequence of the floods south of Kansas City, which fact was unknown by the shippers. Answering this question, the court said:

> We think answer thereto must be in the negative. Conceding delay in the transportation of the shipments from Sioux City, Iowa, to Kansas City, and liability on the part of the Burlington for any negligence of its connecting carriers resulting in unusual delay, yet the fact is that the claims here made are not for damages occasioned as a result of negligent delay in transit. (In light of the provisions of Section 205, Title 7 U. S. C. A., the third-party defendant Kansas City Stock Yards Company is here treated as a connecting carrier. Its liability for livestock to it as a "public utility" is tantamount to that of a common carrier. Cf. 59 Am. Jur., p. 660.) The cattle in question never arrived at the point of destination. The instant claims are for total loss of shipment destroyed as a result of alleged negligence while in transit. The measure of damages recoverable in the instant action from those recoverable under a claim for delay in transit point up the destination. Cf. 9 Am. Jur. 518, 778, etc.
>
> To sustain their instant claims, plaintiffs rely upon the rule stated in 13 C. J. S., Carriers, Sec. 199, p. 403, to the effect that "A carrier must advise the shipper of any circumstances likely to cause delay of which it knows or should know," irrespective of the nature of the cause, and, failing so to do, it will be held liable for damages for delay in delivering the shipment. In support thereof, plaintiffs among other authorities cite *Michigan Central R. Co.* v. *Mineral Springs Manufacturing Co.*, 16 Wall. 318, 83 U.S. 318, 21 L. Ed. 297; and *Atchison, T. & S. F. Ry. Co.* v. *Jarboe Livestock Commission Co.*, 10 Cir., 159 F. 2d 527, as typical applications of such rule, decisive of the present issue. Neither the rule nor the authorities cited are in point. Loss of goods in transit as result of accidental fire, as in the *Michigan Central* case, *supra*, is not a loss as a consequence of an act of God, (Cf. 1 C. J. S., Act of God, p. 1427; *Miller* v. *Steam Nav. Co.*, 10 N.Y. 431; *Merchants' Despatch Co.* v. *Smith*, 76 Ill. 542; *Chicago & N.W. R. Co.* v. *Sawyer*, 69 Ill. 285; *Pope* v. *Farmers' Union and Milling Co.*, 130 Cal. 139, 62 P. 384, 53 L. R. A. 673; *Dippold* v. *Cathlamet Timber Co.*, 111 Ore. 199, 225 P. 202) nor is knowledge of probable delay in transporting a shipment because of an existing Act of God, as in the *Jarboe* case, *suupra*, tantamount to a claim for loss in transit directly resulting from such an unforeseen, irresistible force. Regardless of the fact that claimants here may have asserted a claim against Burlington for failure to notify them of probable delay in shipment from facts known by Burlington at the time it received the shipments, yet the fact remains that, assuming such negligent act, it was not the proximate or direct cause of the claimants' loss. At the most,

it was antecedent and remote thereto. Failure to "deliver within reasonable time" is the *sine qua non* of liability under the rule relied on by claimants. Absent delivery, such rule is not applicable nor decisive of the issue of "causation" in this action.

The court then proceeded to determine whether the delay in transporting the cattle to Kansas City, the failure to make connection with trains which departed after arrival in Kansas City, and holding the cattle in that city for an allegedly unreasonable length of time were in the nature of "concurring cause" of plaintiffs' loss. In answering, the court said:

> Again, the answer must be in the negative. It is hornbook that an injury or damage cannot be attributed to a cause unless, without it, the injury or damage would not have occurred. In the law of negligence, the principles of proximate and remote cause, though variously defined at times, are readily perceived, notwithstanding their application is fraught with difficulty. To make a practical application of "causation" to the facts in the case at bar, it must be kept in mind that we are dealing with facts that reveal abnormal conditions of nature, which are conclusively established as producing the damage complained of, and as to which the charge is made that human agencies contributed to bring about the loss resulting therefrom. Without delving into the intricacies of "causation," we think what is said in *Restatement of the Law of Torts,* (§302, p. 818) regarding negligent acts which create a situation that involves an unreasonable risk, is apropos. In *Comment f* thereto, it is said:
>
> > The actor is not required to anticipate or provide against conditions of nature or the operation of natural forces which are of so unusual a character that the burden of providing for them would be out of all proportion to the chance of their existence or operation and the risk of harm to others involved in their possible existence or operation. It is therefore not necessary that a particular operation of the natural force be unprecedented. The likelihood of its recurrence may be so slight that in the aggregate the burden of constantly providing against it would be out of all proportion great as compared with the magnitude of the risks involved in the possibility of its recurrence.
>
> When the transportation involved began, floods in and about Kansas City, Missouri, were "really catastrophic." Evidence in the case at bar delineated the proportions thereof. We need not encumber the record with a detailed recital of such evidence. History already records it. Suffice to say that as to the Central Industrial District in Kansas City, Missouri, levees and flood walls had been erected so that there had been no penetration of that district by flood waters since 1908. . . .

The court then reviewed the various circumstances surrounding the flood and quoted from a Kansas City newspaper for the morning of July 13 a report that there was no danger to the central industrial district on the Missouri side from the flooding Kaw River. Such assurance circulated in this newspaper was indicated to be a report from the Chief of the Kansas City District of Army Engineers and was accepted by thousands who went into the district that morning to carry on their usual business. At that time, the court indicated, any reasonably prudent person would have assumed that the Kansas River, then being more than two and one-half feet from the top of the levees protecting the district, would not overflow. It was not until almost 10:00 A.M. that the Army Engineers issued an evacuation order applicable to the district. The court continued:

> In the above setting the shipments were transported and unloaded in the Kansas City Stock Yards. Whether they were delayed in transit, or retained in the Stock Yards an excessive length of time, and not delivered to connecting carriers, did not, and could not under the circumstances shown in evidence, have subjected them to apprehended probable danger, such as actually caused their damage or loss. Therefore, any delay in transportation of such cattle, failure to make connections, and causing their unloading at the Stock Yards, were antecedent acts committed by the Burlington, which in nowise contributed to or concurred to bring about the danger from which they were damaged. The proximate cause of their loss was the flood. The delay in arrival of the cattle at Kansas City and unloading in the Stock Yards were remote causes, so that the maxim, *causa proxima, non remota spectatur,* applies to such acts in premising liability, as was done in *Memphis & C. R. Co.* v. *Reeves,* 10 Wall. 176, 77 U.S. 176, 191, 19 L. Ed. 909; and *Empire State Cattle Co.* v. *Atchison,* T. & S. F. R. Co., 210 U.S. 1, 28 S. Ct. 607, 52 L. Ed. 931. The latter cited cases involved transportation of cattle into the Kansas City Stock Yard during the 1903 flood, under circumstances indistinguishable from those in the case at bar.
>
> Notwithstanding the delay in transportation to Kansas City, at the time the cattle actually arrived, there is no evidence before the Court which establishes a then impending danger if the cattle were unloaded in accordance with the 28-hour watering and feeding law (7. §U. S. C. A. 205). . . . *An efficient concurring cause with that of an act of God which will premise liability for loss must be such as was operative with the act of God at the time of the loss, and which acted contemporaneously therewith to produce the damage*; such as made manifest in *Pinkerton* v. *Mo. Pac. R. Co.*, 117 Mo. App. 288, 93 S.W. 849. As to factual situations, comparable to those in the case at bar, which reveal no concurring cause, see *Grier* v. *St. Louis Merchants' Bridge Terminal R. Co.*, 108 Mo. App. 565, 84 S.W. 158; *Moffatt Commission Co.* v. *Union Pac. R. Co.*, 113 Mo. App. 544, 88 S.W. 117. (Emphasis added.)

The court, in conclusion, found that the stock yard company had pursued all prudent acts for the protection of the cattle after danger became apparent and, in the light of its findings, held the carrier free from liability and dismissed the suit against the third-party stock yard defendant.

In *Firpine Products Company* v. *Atchison, Topeka & Santa Fe Railway Co.*, 124 F. Supp. 906, another case involving the 1951 Kansas City flood, the plaintiff alleged the defendant railroad was negligent in removing its property on July 11 and 12, 1951, from what proved to be places of safety at St. Joseph, Missouri, and bringing it into the Kansas City area while the flood was in progress but before it had reached unprecedented state. The court held, however, along the same lines as the *Little Rock* case, *supra,* that the railroad had a right to rely upon the fact that there had not been a flood in metropolitan Kansas City for more than forty years and none since the levees in that area had been built. The rail carrier had asked that the court take judicial notice of the catastrophic nature of the flood and in complying with this request, the court said:

> In *Gerber* v. *McCall*, 175 Kan. 433, 264 P. 2d 490, the Kansas Supreme Court took judicial notice that the 1951 flood in the Argentine district of Kansas City, Kansas, where the car involved in this suit was inundated, was an Act of God. The Court said, 264 P. 2d loc. cit. 493:
>
> > . . . In the first place this court takes judicial notice of the unprecedented magnitude of the flood in question and its devastating effects and results. History has already recorded them. Viewing the matter in the light of hindsight, it is undoubtedly a fact that everyone in the path of the flood, had he known of its proportions, would have taken steps and measures different from those which were taken. The trite but familiar expression—"Hindsight is always better than foresight," is all the more meaningful when that frailty of human nature is coupled with an Act of God such as occurred in the Kaw valley on July 13, 1951.
> >
> > Accordingly, this court takes judicial notice that the July 12, 13, 1951 flood in Kansas City, Missouri-Kansas was an unprecedented one, and in overflowing the dikes and area in that district, was an Act of God, unforeseen and unforeseeable.

Other cases involving the 1951 Kansas City flood and in which the court relieved the carriers of liability for loss and damage are *Ray-O-Vac* v. *Chicago & Northwestern Ry. Co.*, 121 F. Supp. 409; and *Missouri-Kansas-Texas R. Co.* v. *Roegelein Provision Co.*, 260 S. W. 2d 605.

Act of Public Enemy

The term *public enemy* as used in Section 1 (b) of the bill of lading includes the military forces of a nation at war with the domestic government, but bodies of men not organized and operating as a military force against the government do not come within the description of public enemy. A strike by shipper's employees and actions of labor organizations are not the acts of a public enemy such as would excuse failure for nondelivery. (*Montgomery Ward & Co.* v. *Northern Pac. Terminal Co.*, 128 F. Supp. 475) Neither are mobs or rioters considered to be the public enemy, nor has any authority been found for the consideration of such enemy to be other than the military forces of a nation at war with the domestic government. Insects, rodents, etc., while contributing nothing to the welfare of man are, nevertheless, not considered as within the term public enemy.

Act of Public Authority

Common carriers are subject to the control of public authority to the same extent as other persons, and must equally obey the orders of properly constituted government officials. If freight is lost or damaged as a result of obedience to such orders without any intervening fault of the carrier, the carrier will not be held responsible.

This, of course, is logical since it would be most unfair and inequitable to require the carrier to obey the law and surrender the shipment under threat of penalty for refusal, and then to penalize him in damages for his obedience. (See Dobie, *Bailments and Carriers* [St. Paul: West Publishing Co., 1914], p. 338.)

There are two different types of circumstances where the act of the public authority intervenes in and interrupts carriage. The first exists where the movement, or even the existence, of the goods violates the laws or regulation enacted under the police power, as in the cases of contaminated goods or contraband articles. In such a case the carrier is not liable if the goods are seized from him. (*Wells* v. *Maine S. S. Co.*, 4 Cliff. 228, Fed. Cas. No. 17, 401; *Bliven* v. *Hudson River R. Co.*, 35 Barb. 191, 36 N. Y. 403) Both Dobie, *op. cit. supra* at 338, and Hutchinson (*The Law of Carriers* [Chicago: Callaghan and Co., 2d ed., 1891], p. 233) note this exception applies to the losses caused by the act of the paramount public authority at the time being, even though it is a de facto government only. Thus the destruction of goods by the Confederate government in a state subject to its authority excused the carrier from his liability, citing *Nashville & C. Ry. Co.* v. *Estes*, 10 Lea (Tenn.) 749. The carrier must assure himself of the authority of the officer seizing the goods before yielding their possession. (*Bennett* v. *American Express Co.*, 22 Atl. 159)

The second situation in which the act of the public authority in the seizure of freight will not be charged to the carrier is when the goods are taken from the carrier's possession under legal process, as by a writ of attachment against the owner. This subject is discussed at length in

Hutchinson, *op. cit. supra* at pages 464-76. The process must be fair on its face. Dobie, *op. cit. supra,* page 339, n. 28. And the carrier must make reasonable efforts to give notice of the seizure or proceedings to the shipper or the owner so that necessary action can be taken to protect the shipper's or owner's interest. (*Thomas* v. *Northern Pac. Express Co.* 75 N. W. 1120; *Jewett* v. *Olsen,* 23 Pac. 262; *Bliven* v. *Hudson River Ry. Co.,* 36 N. Y. 403) The Supreme Court of the United States, in *Stiles* v. *Davis,* 1 Black, 101, the leading case on the point, said:

> It is true that these goods had been delivered to the defendant as carrier by the plaintiffs, to be conveyed for them to the place of destination, and were seized under an attachment against third persons; but this circumstance did not impair the legal effect of the seizure or custody of the goods under it, so as to justify the defendant in taking them out of the hands of the sheriff. The right of the sheriff to hold them was a question of law, to be determined by the proper legal proceedings, and not at the will of the defendant nor that of the plaintiffs.

In *Pingree* v. *Railroad Co.,* 66 Mich. 143, the court stated the reason for the rule as follows:

> Whatever may be a carrier's duty to resist a forcible seizure without process, he cannot be compelled to assume that regular process is illegal, and to accept all the consequences of resisting officers of the law. If he is excusable for yielding to a public enemy, he cannot be at fault for yielding to actual authority what he may yield to usurped authority.

Act of the Shipper

The fourth exception from the common carrier's strict liability is for loss or damage due to the act of default of the shipper. Shipper action or failure to act which may lead to loss or damage usually is in four areas: in the packing of the goods; in the loading or unloading of the goods, when that is done by the shipper or consignee; in the marking of the goods; and in the description of the goods in such a way as to lead to their loss or damage.

As a general rule, in order to absolve the carrier from liability for loss or damage arising from the act or default of the shipper, that act or default must not be readily apparent. The question most frequently arises with respect to the packing or loading undertaken by the shipper. The reason for the rule is that even though the improper packing or loading resulted from the shipper's act, the carrier is the ultimate judge of whether the packing or loading is properly done and, if the defective packing or loading is readily apparent when the goods are tendered to the carrier, they should not be accepted for transportation until the defect is corrected.

Neither can a common carrier knowingly accept freight improperly packed or loaded and avoid liability by a contract purporting to limit its liability, or by noting on its bill of lading such phrases as "Shipped at Owner's Risk" or "Carrier not responsible for damage from faulty packing." This is not to say that the carrier will be held liable for loss or damage occurring to "shipper load and count" shipments where the improper loading or checking is not apparent. The difference is between attempting to limit the carrier's liability for apparent defective packing or loading which should result in a rejection of the shipment by the carrier and evidencing the carrier's inability to inspect the loading and packing by the shipper. "Shipper load and count" shipments are discussed in detail below.

Now we will discuss in detail the various shipper acts or defaults which can relieve the carrier of liability for loss or injury.

Containers, Packing, and Packaging

Ordinarily a carrier is not liable for injuries due to improper packing of goods by the shipper where this defect is not readily apparent. This is one of the exceptions to the carrier's common-law liability. It should be kept in mind, however, that if the carrier is guilty of negligence without which the damage would not have occurred, it is liable even though the shipment was packed improperly. Further, since a carrier has the right, generally, to reject defectively packed goods tendered for shipment, if it accepts for transportation merchandise which it knows is defectively packed, or which by the exercise of reasonable care it could have observed was defectively packed, it assumes the care of the goods in the condition packed, and its common-carrier liability attaches even though the shipment was not packed in accordance with the requirements of the governing classification or tariff.

The major carrier classifications all clearly provide by rule that the carrier will refuse any article not in such condition or so prepared for shipment as to render it reasonably safe and practicable for transportation. Acceptance of the shipment therefore creates an inference that the carrier considered the packing proper. Of course he is not required to open each container and examine the inner packing. The shipper knows better than the carrier the manner in which the goods should be packed. If there is some defect in the packing which is not apparent to ordinary observation, the carrier should not be liable for damages resulting solely from the improper packing.

Some early decisions apparently held without qualification that the full duty of the carrier is simply to carry the goods in the condition offered, and that where goods are insufficiently packed, the carrier is not liable for injury due to the insufficient packing, whether or not it was apparent. (*Cohn v. Platt,* 95 N. Y. S. 535; *Nelson* v. *Stevenson,* 12 N. Y. S. 538; *Alabama & V. Ry. Co.* v. *American Cotton Oil Co.,* 249 Fed. 312) But the better rule is that the carrier, being entitled to reject defectively packed goods tendered for transportation, assumes the liability for damages resulting from defects in the packing of goods which it knows, or by the exercise of reasonable care could ascertain, are improperly packed. (*Northwestern Marble* v. *William,* 151 N. W. 419; *Mitchell* v. *Northern Pacific S. S. Co.,* 213 Pac. 293; *Southern R. Co.* v. *DeLatour, Inc.,* 135 So. 187)

In *Thomas* v. *Chicago, M. & St. P. Ry. Co.,* 217 N. W. 927, the court said that where goods are insufficiently packed and that insufficiency is discoverable by the carrier by ordinary observation and inspection "it is the duty of the carrier to refuse to receive the goods," and if it does accept them it cannot rely on the insufficient packing as a defense.

Obviously, much of the controversy in this area centers around whether the damage resulted from the improper packing, and whether the packing was, in fact, improper. In *Armour Research Foundation* v. *Chicago, R. I. & P. R. Co.,* 311 F. 2d 493, cert. den. 372 U.S. 966, suit was brought for damage to certain electronic equipment packed in a trailer and delivered to the carrier under padlock. The evidence showed the trailer was loaded five weeks before it was delivered to the carrier, and was transported over highways and a private railroad before delivery. The court found that the evidence warranted a finding that the plaintiff failed to prove delivery in good order, noting that possible defects may have resulted from the original loading which were not discoverable on ordinary observation. Since the trailer was padlocked and the bill of lading did not disclose the contents of the trailer, the court held that the carrier was relieved of the obligation to ascertain the contents or whether the contents were properly packed for shipment. These facts were also held to place on the plaintiff the burden of proving proper loading, a burden which was not met in view of the time lapse and handling between loading and delivery to the carrier.

Another problem area is where the carrier's negligence commingles with the shipper's negligence to produce the damage. As a general rule, the carrier cannot avoid liability on the ground of improper packing if its negligence contributes to the injury. (*Klauber* v. *American Express Co.,* 21 Wis. 21, 91 Am. Dec. 452) Generally, to excuse the carrier, negligence on the shipper's part must be the sole cause of the injury. (*McCarthy* v. *Louisville & N. R. Co.*, 14 So. 370; *Northwestern Marble and Tile Co.* v. *Williams,* 151 N. W. 419) In the latter case, the court explained why no effort is made in such cases to prorate the liability between the carrier and the shipper:

> The general rule is that, where the shipper packs articles for shipment, he cannot recover from the carrier for injuries due to improper packing. . . . It appears to us that the rules of contributory negligence have no application to such a case. Contributory negligence of plaintiff is a defense only in cases where the action is founded on negligence of defendant. Here the action is not founded on negligence of the carrier at all. The carrier's common law liability is founded, not on negligence, but "on broad principles of public policy and convenience, and was introduced to prevent the necessity of going into circumstances impossible to be unraveled." It would be a distinct extension of the doctrine of contributory negligence to apply it to a case of this kind, and an extension which we believe to be unwarranted.

In *Advance Air Conditioning* v. *Cain's Truck Lines,* 175 Pac. (2d) 338, the court pointed out that where loss of or injury to goods while in possession of a common carrier of freight is shown, a prima facie case is made against carrier, and, if carrier relies on exception to such rule of liability as a defense, burden is upon carrier to show that loss occurred from some cause exempting it from liability. The assertion by a common carrier of freight that damage to shipment was due solely to fault of shipper in that goods shipped were not properly crated and the improper crating was sole cause of damage, if sustained by evidence, constitutes a good defense to an action by shipper against carrier for damage if the evidence likewise indicates that the carrier did not know of the improper crating.

Carrier claim agents should remember that where defects in a shipment are readily apparent, it is the carrier's duty to refuse the shipment, and, if it elects to carry the shipment in its defective condition, it will not be permitted to urge the defect as a defense. On the other hand, the fact that the carrier accepted the shipment does not preclude it from showing that the loss occurred from a cause which existed but was not apparent when the shipment was accepted. (*S. Valentine & Co.* v. *Atchison, T. & S. F. Ry. Co.*, 220 Ill. App. 188)

In *Mitchell* v. *Northern Pac. S. S. Co.*, 213 P. 293, defendant, a common carrier by water, received from plaintiff a shipment of postal cards. They had been packed in new double cardboard boxes; some of these were placed in wooden cases and others were tied in a bundle. The evidence indicated that the carrier hoisted the containers aboard with a rope sling which broke and crushed the boxes on the outside which would not have occurred if it had used another type of sling. The carrier contended that the packing was insufficient and improper and that it was released from liability. The court held the carrier liable and stated:

> A carrier in this state cannot by any argument made in anticipation thereof exempt itself from liability for damage by the gross negligence, fraud, or willful wrong of itself or its servants. If goods are improperly packed, and this fact is not apparent or known to the carrier, it is not liable for loss or injury due to such improper packing if it is itself free from negligence. Conversely, if the carrier is guilty of negligence but for which the damage would not have occurred, the carrier is liable even though the improper packing is not apparent. . . . Here the appellant's negligence in loading the goods and the resulting damage was shown. . . . If the goods were obviously poorly packed when delivered to it, appellant might have refused to accept them, but having undertaken to carry them, it was not excused from liability for damage due to its negligence.

In *Devinne Hallenbeck Co., Inc.* v. *Autotyre Co.*, 154 A. 170, defendant was a manufacturer of bathroom fixtures. The plaintiff shipped 200 cardboard display screens to the defendant to be placed in windows for advertising purposes. These screens were received in good condition. The balance of the order was later shipped but arrived in damaged condition and defendant refused to pay for them on the grounds that they were carelessly and negligently packed and that this caused the damage. The carrier handling the goods gave the plaintiff a receipt indicating that the screens were received in apparent good condition and defendant contended that the carrier rather than the shipper was liable for the damage. The court in deciding this contention said:

> The acknowledgement of the receipt of the cases by the defendant's carrier in apparent good condition did not shift to the carrier the responsibility for the damage resulting from the improper packing, when the latter had no knowledge as to how the screens were packed, and there was nothing in the situation to indicate that it ought to have known. *10 Corpus Juris, p. 120.* The rule invoked by the plaintiff that, where goods are delivered to a carrier in good condition and arrive at their destination in damaged condition, the burden is upon the carrier to show that the damage did not arise from its negligence is not applicable to the facts of this case.

In *Michellod* v. *Oregon-Washington R. & Nav. Co.*, 168 P. 620, the court in discussing the carrier's liability when shipper improperly packs said:

> Such terms (apparent good order, contents and condition of contents of packages unknown) often have been held to be not conclusive upon any one who

transports property. They amount to a statement by the issuing carrier that it has received goods which the shipper describes in the language mentioned, but go no further, unless the character of the chattels thus delineated is openly visible. . . .

It is plain, therefore, that there was nothing in the terms of the bill of lading giving conclusive notice to the defendant of the inherent quality of the goods in question. . . . It is not even alleged that they were in good order . . . the shipper must show that the goods were in good order when delivered to the carrier because the latter ordinarily cannot open the packages and examine their contents. . . .

The words in the bill of lading refer only to the external appearance of the packages and bind the defendant to no greater extent in the absence of any further showing . . . it is the duty of the shipper to establish the condition of the goods at the time they were entrusted to the carrier. . . .

It was objected that the court was wrong in instructing the jury to the effect that the defendant could not be held liable for injury due to the improper packing of the bottles in the barrels. The defendant was not authorized to open the containers, but was bound to ship (carry) the goods in the form in which they were delivered to it, unless they were manifestly in bad order. Hence, if the loss was due to the manner in which the packages were constructed the defendant would not be liable provided it was not negligent in the matter of its actual transportation.

In *S. Valentine & Company* v. *Atchison, Topeka & Santa Fe Railway Co.*, 220 Ill. App. 188, the plaintiff shipped 150 barrels of china wood oil on the lines of defendant from San Francisco to Chicago. The oil had originated in China and on arrival at the port, some of the barrels were leaking. These were recoopered before being given to the defendant. The shipment arrived at destination with the majority of barrels in bad condition. Some had staves knocked in, some had no heads at all, and most had hoops off of them. The court held the carrier not liable, stating:

While the bill of lading acknowledges the receipt of the goods in apparent good condition, we think in this respect the bill of lading is only a receipt and can be contradicted by other evidence . . . it does not preclude the carrier from showing, in case of loss or damage, that the loss proceeded from some cause which existed, but was not apparent when he received the goods, and which if shown satisfactorily, will discharge the carrier from liability.

We think the proof offered for defendant at least made issue of fact for the jury as to whether the loss which occurred was or was not the result of the inherent nature or vice of the articles shipped; was or was not caused by defects in the barrels which were not apparent to the carrier. . . .

Loading, Unloading, and "Shipper's Load and Count" Shipments

In this section, the problems arising out of those instances where the shipper loads the goods or where the consignee unloads them will be discussed. Frequently the shipper will perform the loading of his carload or truckload shipments and consignee performs the unloading of them. Some of these large lot shipments will move as "Shipper's Load and Count" (SL&C) shipments and, in other instances, the shipper will perform the loading and counting but the bill of lading will not indicate that the shipper performed these functions. In other instances, due to the size or weight of an article, the shipper may be required to load the shipment and the consignee to unload it. These procedures occasionally lead to controversies between the carrier and claimant as to liability for loss or damage.

While generally it is the duty of the carrier to load and unload shipments properly and to assume liability for any loss or damage resulting from such loading or unloading, there are exceptions to this rule. (*St. Louis, etc. R. Co.* v. *Hudgins Produce Co.*, 177 S. W. 400; *Lewis* v. *New York, etc. R. Co.*, 104 N. E. 944; see 13 C.J.S. 123-24; 10 C.J. 103) If, for example, the shipper assumes the duty of loading or the consignee the duty of unloading, generally the carrier is relieved of responsibility for any loss or damage which is the proximate result of the loading or unloading. (*St. Louis-San Francisco Ry. Co.* v. *Glow Electric Co.*, 172 N. E. 425; *Association of Maryland Pilots* v. *Baltimore & O. R.*, 304 F. Supp. 548)

Generally, the shipper is liable for improper loading which is not apparent or which cannot be discovered by ordinary inspection. (*Armour Research Foundation* v. *Chicago, R. I. & P. R. Co.*, 311 F. 2d 493, cert. den. 372 U.S. 966; *Minneapolis, St. P. & S. S. M. R. Co.* v. *Metal-Matic, Inc.*, 323 F. 2d 903; *Trautmann Bros. Co.* v. *Missouri Pacific R. Co.*, 312 F. 2d 102)

If the improper loading is apparent on ordinary observation of the carrier's agents, the shipper's defective loading is not a defense. (*Thomson* v. *Chicago, M. & St. P. Ry. Co.*, 217 N. W. 927; *Robinson* v. *New York Central R. Co.*, 282 N. Y. S. 877; *Kennedy, Inc.* v. *O'Brien*, 175 A. 882; *Lewis Machine Co.* v. *Aztec Lines, Inc.*, 172 F. 2d 746; *Modern Tool Co.* v. *Pennsylvania R. Co.*, 100 F. Supp. 595) In *Central of Georgia Ry. Co.* v. *Griner and Rustin*, 127 S. E. 878, the court held that where the improper loading is apparent, the carrier must refuse to accept the goods for transportation until the defects are corrected.

In *Snowden* v. *Tremont & G. Ry. Co.*, 140 So. 122, the plaintiff shipped a carload of used opera chairs from Cincinnati, Ohio, to Winnfield, Louisiana, delivery being made by defendant rail carrier. The chairs were loaded on the car by a wrecking company from whom plaintiff had purchased them. The chairs were loaded without knocking them down, the car containing rows of chairs with lumber over the first layer and other chairs loaded on top, and so on until the car was filled. The defendant's witnesses testified that there was enough lumber in the car to build the defendant's depot at Winnfield. When the shipment arrived at destination, a large number of the chairs were broken and torn. Plaintiff brought suit for the value of the entire shipment alleging that the damage was due to rough handling of the car in transit. In denying recovery the court said:

> The law governing such cases as the one under consideration is stated in *section* 1348, *Vol.* 3, *Hutchinson on Carriers* (3d Ed.), as follows:
>
> "A connecting carrier who has completed the transaction and delivered the goods to the consignee in damaged condition or deficient in quantity will be held liable in an action for the damage or deficiency, without proof that it was occasioned by his fault, unless he can show that he received them in the condition he delivered them. The condition and quantity of the goods when they were delivered to the first of the connecting carriers being shown, the presumption will arise that they continued in that condition down to the time of their delivery to the carrier completing the transportation and making the delivery to the consignee, and that the injury or loss occurred while they were in his possession."
>
> Acts of this kind are *ex contractu,* and it is not necessary for the plaintiff to allege negligence of any kind. Primarily, all that is necessary to be alleged is (1) that the initial carrier received the shipment in good condition; (2) that the shipment was delivered in a damaged condition; (3) the amount of the loss sustained because of the damaged condition of the shipment.
>
> . . . there is no allegation in plaintiff's petition to the effect that the chairs . . . were in good condition when they were shipped. Unless, therefore, the pleadings have been enlarged by evidence on this point, the legal presumption that the chairs were delivered to the defendant in good condition necessarily cannot be relied upon. . . .
>
> We could rest the case upon the finding that the plaintiff has neither alleged nor proved the important condition precedent, viz: That the goods were delivered to the initial carrier in good condition. But there are other equally important features of the case which should be discussed.
>
> In addition to denying liability for any injury done to this shipment of chairs on account of not being guilty of any rough handling, carelessness, or negligence while they were in its possession, the defendant alleged that the chairs were loaded by the shipper, that the initial carrier did not inspect the shipment and did not guarantee the weight, number, or condition of the property, and that a statement to this effect was stamped on the original bill of lading. . . .

In discussing the improper loading by the shipper, the court commented:

It would seem that any one with ordinary judgment ought to have easily known that these chairs would not and could not stand the hardships of a trip as a part of a freight train. . . . This being true (improper loading and stowing of chairs), the shipper must bear the blame, especially in view of the fact that the initial carrier disclaimed responsibility by stamping it on the face of the bill of lading. . . .

In *Thomson* v. *Chicago, M. & St. P. Ry. Co.*, 217 N. W. 927, the court said:

. . . where a shipper tenders to a carrier goods for transportation, which are insufficiently crated, boxed, packed, or loaded, and such insufficiency is discoverable by the carrier upon ordinary observation and inspection, it is the duty of the carrier to refuse to receive the goods, and, that, if the carrier does accept the goods, it may not thereafter allege that any injury they sustained in the course of transportation was due to insufficient crating, packing, or loading. The rule is otherwise where the insufficiency is not disclosed by ordinary observation and inspection. . . .

In *Southern Ry. Co.* v. *Frank De Latour,* 135 So. 187, it appeared that the shipper loaded live turkeys in an ordinary poultry car causing a large number to die of asphyxiation. The shipment was accepted by the carrier under an "SL&C" notation. In holding the carrier not liable the court pointed out that the carrier may, in proper cases, refuse shipments where they are in an unfit condition for transportation, but continued the court:

It cannot be said, however, that the carrier must, at his peril, know that the goods are not in fact safely packed. The shipper usually knows better than the carrier the manner in which goods have been packed, and the manner in which they should be packed, and even though the carrier may have knowledge of some defect in the packing, still if it is not apparent to the ordinary observation of the carrier or his servants that the goods cannot be safely carried in the condition in which they are presented, the carrier should not be held to take the chance of injury from improper packing. *Northwestern Marble Co.* v. *Williams,* 128 Minn. 514, 151 N.W. 419, 420 L. R. A. 1915D, 1077.

While in these cases, the courts speak of *packing,* the principle applies with equal effect to *loading.*

In *David E. Kennedy, Inc.* v. *O'Brien,* 175 A. 882, the plaintiff purchased a planing machine from O'Brien Machinery Company. The machine was loaded on a truck of Royal Freight Lines and when it arrived at destination, one of the legs of the machine had pulled loose from the skids and the machine had fallen to one side and was broken. Plaintiff brought suit against O'Brien and Royal. The court denied recovery against the carrier and held O'Brien liable, stating that: "From the evidence, the judge sitting without a jury was justified in finding that the machine was not properly fastened to the skids and loaded onto the truck of the Royal Freight Lines, Inc. Therefore, the common carrier, the Royal Freight Lines, Inc., was not liable for any damage, but the shipper, the O'Brien Machinery Company, was the wrongdoer." In this case there was no reference to an "SL&C" notation on the bill of lading. In *Boh Bros. Const. Co.* v. *Perry Heavy Haulers,* 166 F. 2d 719, suit was brought against the carrier for damage to a ditching machine while being transported by the carrier. It was held that the fault of the shipper in loading the machine exonerated the carrier.

In *Ross* v. *Troy & Boston Ry. Co.,* 49 Vt. 364, 24 Am. Rep. 144, a piece of machinery was injured in transit due to the insecure fastening and insufficient packing. In holding the defendant carrier not liable, the court said: "It seems incongruous for the plaintiff to claim that the defendant should overjudge him in a matter in which he assumed to judge and to all that he required or supposed necessary to be done in the premises, and that the defendant should be responsible for the inadequacy of what the plaintiff adjudged and did." In the case of *Hines* v. *Buchanan,* 109 S. E. 219, the subject of the liability of a carrier for injury to a shipment, due to faulty packing or loading, was exhaustively reviewed. In reversing the judgment of the lower court and in holding the carrier not liable the court justified its finding by the fact that in its opinion the testimony showed clearly that *nothing happened en route to cause the injury to a properly packed car, and the injury was found to be due to the negligence of the shipper in the manner of loading and packing.* See also *Texas & Pacific Ry. Co.* v. *Klepper,* 24 S. W. 567; *Texas & Pac. Ry. Co.* v. *Edins,* 83 S. W. 253; *Peoples Saving Bank of Saginaw* v. *Pere Marquette Ry. Co.,* 209 N. W. 182; *St. Louis-San Francisco Ry. Co.* v. *Glow Electric Co.,* 172 N. E. 425. In *Annunziato* v. *New York N. H. & H. R. Co.,* 253 N. Y. S. 626, the court said:

> The duty of a common carrier of carload shipments in interstate commerce is simply that of transportation. The shipper is obliged to see that the shipment is properly loaded and braced so that it may be transported in a satisfactory manner. *Lewis* v. *New York, O. & W. R. Co.,* 104 N. E. 944. It follows, as the duty of the carrier is 'merely of transportation,' it is incumbent upon the plaintiff to show that the car was properly packed and braced so that the transportation could be made in a satisfactory manner, and the goods or merchandise was 'in good condition at the time of shipment.' *Orunsten* v. *New York Cent. R. Co.,* 179 App. Div. 465 at 467, 165 N. Y. S. 996, 998.

In *Robinson* v. *New York Cent. R. Co.,* 282 N. Y. S. 877, the court held that where a shipper undertakes to ship carload lots and to do his own loading, he should bear the loss sustained by improper loading, and mere knowledge on the part of the claim agent of the carrier of the negligent manner in which the shipment had been packed will not impose liability for this negligence on the carrier, where the shipper himself had expressly undertaken the loading and the injury sustained was not due to any negligence on the part of the carrier. Similarly, it was held in *Standard Hotel Supply Co., Inc.* v. *Pennsylvania R. Co.,* 65 F. Supp. 439, that there is no duty on the part of the carrier to supervise the shipper's own undertaking. The court discussed the problem in the following words:

> As indicated above the frozen meat was loaded by the shipper into a comparatively warm car. The loading was done by the shipper under a "shippers load and count" bill of lading which "placed upon the shipper the obligation of seeing that the car was properly loaded." *South Carolina Asparagus Association v. Southern R.* 4 Cir., 46 F. 2d 452, 454. The carrier is not liable for damages caused by improper loading under this type of bill of lading. See § 21 of *Federal Bill of Lading Act, Title 49 U.S.C.A. § 101.* The railroad is not required to have experts at loading points to advise shippers concerning the proper car temperature at which to load the many different kinds of perishable commodities. Each shipper is supposed to know the condition of his own commodity and the requisite amount and period of re-icing, if any, that the commodity requires. There is no duty imposed on the railroad to warn the shipper that he should wait a certain length of time after the car is iced, before loading his perishable goods into the refrigerator car. Indeed, it has been held that "mere knowledge on the part of the local agent of the carrier of the carrier of the negligent manner in which the shipment has been packed could not impose liability for this negligence on the carrier, where the shipper itself had expressly undertaken the packing and the injury sustained was not due to negligence on the part of the carrier." *South Carolina Asparagus Growers Association* v. *Southern R., supra.*

As will be noted from the preceding cases, where the shipper has the duty or undertakes the duty of loading the shipment and the carrier neither supervises or participates in such activity, the carrier is relieved of responsibility which is the proximate result of the shipper's negligence or lack of skill in loading and this rule applies irrespective of whether the shipment is moving under an "SL&C" notation, the principal effect of the notation being that the shipper should have been on actual notice of the carrier's responsibility. The use of the "SL&C" notation prevents the shipper from contending that the carrier participated in any manner in loading the shipment. As stated in *Blytheville Cotton Oil Co.* v. *Kurn,* 155 F. 2d 467:

The rule seems to be clear that when a fully loaded car is delivered to the railroad, the railroad company is responsible only for such defects as may be discoverable by such visual inspection as it is able to make, and it is not responsible for imperfect packing or other carelessness on the part of the shipper. *Alabama & V. Ry Co.* v. *American Cotton Oil Co.*, 5 Cir., 249 F. 308; *Alabama Great Southern R. Co.* v. *Morris & Co.*, 5 Cir., 249 F. 312; *Southern Cotton Oil Co.* v. *Atlantic Coast Line R. Co.*, D. C. E. D. Va., 17 F. 2d 411. The state cases are in accord. *Chesapeake & Ohio Ry. Co.* v. *Nat'l Fruit Products Co.*, 155 Va. 438, 155 S. E. 630, 72 A. L. R. 878; *Fordyce* v. *McFlynn*, 56 Ark. 424, 19 S.W. 961; *Central of Georgia R. Co.* v. *Chicago Varnish Co.*, 169 Ala. 287, 53 So. 832.

There has been considerable controversy over loading and unloading large or heavy shipments by motor carriers. For the most part, for-hire motor carriers of general commodities have built their operation around a one-man-per-truck pickup and delivery concept, based on pickup and delivery at the tailgate of the truck. Most of the general-commodity motor carrier tariffs provide that where an article in a single container weighs more than a given amount, usually 500 pounds, loading and unloading shall be performed by the shipper and consignee, respectively. This rule further provides that if requested carriers will undertake in behalf of the shipper or consignee to employ additional help, and no charge will be made for the labor performed by the truck driver but a specified charge per hour or fraction thereof will be made for each man furnished other than the driver. Where tariffs make provisions similar to this and the consignee elects to furnish labor to unload, the shipper or consignee should assume the liability for any damage occurring as result of the loading or unloading. On the other hand, if the shipper or consignee elects to have the carrier employ the additional help and agrees to pay for such service as provided in the tariff, the carrier should be liable for any damage as clearly such additional help would be working under the control and supervision of the carrier. In each instance, however, the problem should be determined by an examination of all the actual facts and circumstances to develop under whose control and supervision the loading and unloading were being performed and upon that party the responsibility should rest. Even if the carrier had the authority to insist upon the supervision and control of these services, if the customer undertook to assume those duties, the carrier's responsibility should cease. The cases cited all support that the one assuming the duty also assumes the responsibility.

In *Wajay Bakery, Inc.* v. *Carolina Freight Carriers Corp.*, 16 Fed. Carr. Cas. 81,754, the Florida District Court of Appeals dismissed the carrier as a party defendant, saying, "the duty to unload this heavy machine (1,800 pounds) was on the consignee and not on the carrier, and in aiding the employees of the consignee in the unloading the carrier's driver became the servant of (the consignee)."

A view somewhat contrary, however, was adopted by the court in *Hanaman* v. *Liberty Trucking Co.*, 11 N. W. 2d 130. In this case a 3,500 pound secondhand printing press was damaged by a fall from defendant's truck while being unloaded at plaintiff's warehouse. After judgment in the lower court for plaintiff, defendant appealed, claiming exemption from liability because (1) the truck driver exceeded his authority in proceeding to unload the truck because his superior had directed him not to unload it but return it to the defendant's terminal; (2) the plaintiff's own employees participated in unloading the press and caused the injury to it; and (3) item 990 of the tariff schedule filed with the I.C.C. applicable to the plaintiff read:

> Rates published in this tariff apply only on such articles as can ordinarily be handled by one man. If single pieces are such as to require more than one man for loading and unloading, then the . . . consignee shall furnish whatever additional number of men are needed to handle the article and shall assume full responsibility for the safe . . . unloading. Should the carrier be required to furnish such additional help, a charge of . . . ($1.10) per hour, or fraction thereof, per man shall apply.

The court dismissed defendant's first contention stating that facts showed that the driver had not exceeded his authority. On defendant's second contention, the court said:

> The reason given for this proposition is that one voluntarily participating in the conduct of another which would be violative of his rights if not assented to has no right of recovery for injury resulting to him from such conduct. . . . But the thing here assented to was the unloading, not negligence in unloading. . . . The (lower) court found that the driver of the truck was in charge of the unloading and the evidence supports this finding. . . . Thus the injury to the press was plainly due to (driver's) negligence.

This discussion relative to the driver's negligence strengthens the court's decision because it points out that actually the driver was supervising the consignee's employees during the unloading.

Relative to the tariff provisions, the court stated:

> The rule in the tariff schedule relating to unloading articles requiring more than the driver of the truck to unload them provides that the consignee shall furnish extra help, but this does not exonerate the defendant from the duty of unloading, especially as it is further provided that if the carrier is required to furnish the extra man or men required the consignee shall pay for the extra

men at a specified rate per hour. The latter provision declares the effect of the consignee's not furnishing help to the carrier and thus affects the tariff rate, but it does not shift to the consignee the duty of unloading. Those helping with the unloading were the agents of the defendant regardless of not being its regular employees . . .and the defendant was liable for injury caused by their negligence. . .

Here the court disregarded the determining factors of the exercise of authority, supervision, and control, all of which present questions of fact to be determined by examination of the evidence and the opinion deviates from the general rule. The court endeavored to strengthen its opinion by stating that if the plaintiff had not furnished its employees it would have been required to pay for extra help and that this made the employees assisting in the unloading "loaned" employees to the carrier but this overlooks the fact that the carrier had to accept the employees "loaned" and could not question their qualification or skill as unloaders. While the conclusion of the court affirming the carrier's liability may be sound in view of the fact that the evidence indicated that the driver was actually supervising the unloading, the statements relating to the tariff provisions and the theory of "loaned" employees are questionable.

In *Lewis Machine Company* v. *Aztec Lines, Inc.*, 172 F. 2d 746, the court held the carrier liable for toppling of a machine which had been loaded by the shipper and transported safely from Chicago to Cleveland where the injury occurred. The facts in this case were such that a conclusion that some negligence on the part of the carrier caused the injury was justified. In this case the carrier accepted a shipment of machinery at Chicago for transportation to Cleveland. The machine weighed about 6,000 pounds. It was mounted on skids and the carrier made no complaint about the skids or the way the machine was mounted thereon. The machine was loaded onto the carrier's trailer by the plaintiff's agents by use of a crane which lowered the machine on the open top trailer. The floor of the trailer was made of oak boards about two inches thick, and the sides of the trailer were of plywood inside and sheet iron outside and extended upward from the floor about six feet with stakes, to which the sides were fastened, about two feet apart. The rear of the trailer rested upon a single axle, and the front on the fifth wheel of the tractor which is just above the tractor rear wheels. The machine was in about the center of the trailer and equidistance between the sides thereof. The skids, which were parallel to the sides of the trailer, were nailed to the floor of the trailer with spike nails.

After the machine was loaded on the trailer, it was driven to Cleveland, and several times on the way it was inspected by the driver and nothing out of the ordinary was noticed or occurred. In Cleveland, another driver was assigned to the unit to make deliveries and while this driver was making a sweeping turn at a speed of five to seven miles an hour into an intersection, the machine toppled over, crashed through the side of the trailer, fell into the street and was destroyed. The driver had made other turns on that trip over the streets of Cleveland and nothing had happened. The carrier contended that the damage was due to the shipper's failure to load properly and relied on provisions in its tariff and classification which provide:

> Where an article or articles in a single container or shipping form tendered weighs 500 pounds or more, or if the greatest dimension exceeds 8 feet, or greatest and intermediate dimension each exceed 4 feet, loading or unloading shall be performed by the shipper or consignee, as the case may be.
>
> * * * *
>
> Skids must be constructed of material of sufficient strength and dimensions to afford safe handling and protection of the shipment, and so constructed as to enable skid and article thereto to be handled as a unit.

Aztec continued that it was the duty of the shipper in loading the machine to see that is was so fastened and secured that in the ordinary course of travel it would not tip over and fall from the truck. The court found that the plaintiff was not at fault in securing and fastening the machine to the truck, and if the loading by the plaintiff was defective, the defects were patent to the driver of the truck and to other employees of the carrier. Further, the court found that the damage resulted from the negligence of the carrier. In this case, it is clear that if the defective loading is such that the carrier reasonably should have been able to discover it, the carrier must take precautions to prevent damage. The inference in this case, however, is that the machine was properly loaded and the damage occasioned by the carrier's negligence.

It was held in *Loveless Manufacturing Co.* v. *Roadway Express, Inc.*, 104 F. Supp. 809, that a carrier that enters into an agreement of its own volition, without request by the consignee, to unload heavy equipment at the place of delivery, and thereby violates the terms of its tariff regulations prohibiting such service, will be liable for any damages resulting during such unloading. This is so even though the tariff places responsibility for unloading on the consignee, who is presumed to have constructive notice that the carrier cannot lawfully perform such service, the carrier being under a positive duty to inform the consignee of the tariff prohibition. In this case, Roadway transported a large shearing machine and parts weighing 17,500 pounds to the consignee's premises. This machine was to be unloaded on a concrete slab adjacent to the consignee's shop. Roadway driver asked Loveless how the machine was to be unloaded, and the driver was informed by Loveless that he had nothing to do with the unloading and that was Roadway's responsibility. Roadway's driver called his company, informed them of the situation and thirty minutes later another truck with a winch and flat bed trailer arrived at the Loveless premises. This equipment was owned by Edwards Transfer Company and Edwards' driver along with Roadway's attempted to unload the machine from the Roadway trailer onto the flat bed when the machine toppled over and was damaged. Loveless refused to accept delivery of the damaged machine and filed claim for its value which Roadway declined. Suit was instituted against Roadway and Edwards and its insurance company were brought in as third party defendants. In holding Roadway liable, the United States District Court said:

At the trial of the case, the evidence disclosed that Roadway upon its own volition, without any request of Loveless, and without informing Loveless of any tariff regulations, contacted Edwards for the purpose of acquiring equipment to unload the machine which was subsequently damaged. This arrangement with Edwards was made by authority of Roadway's manager. One of the main controverted facts was the status of Edwards, *i.e.*, whether it occupied the position of an independent contractor or whether the truck and driver of Edwards were hired by Roadway so as to make the driver of the Edwards truck a special servant of Roadway. From all of the testimony elicited at the trial, the court has concluded that the arrangement between Roadway and Edwards was that Edwards was hiring out the truck and driver on an hourly basis, and that Roadway had absolute control or the right to control the unloading operations as well as control over the Edwards truck and driver. It is true that the driver of the Edwards truck was in charge of the operation of the winch mounted on the Edwards equipment, but Roadway was the special master; and the driver of the Edwards truck was the special servant of Roadway due to the element of control being in the hands of Roadway. It should also be noted at this point that the truck rented to Roadway was not defective and was adequate for the work for which it was to be used.

From the complaint of Loveless, it is ascertained that recovery of damages is based upon a breach of the contract of carriage. To the complaint, Roadway answered alleging that the contract of carriage had been completed on its part, and that a tariff regulation made Roadway's employees the agents of Loveless in unloading. At the outset, it is to be noted that Roadway has consistently been inconsistent in its theory of the case. It was first alleged that Edwards was the agent of Loveless, and then in an amended third party complaint which superseded the original, it is alleged that Edwards was the agent of Roadway. Next, it is alleged that delivery of the machine was completed by Roadway and yet in the suggested findings of fact and conclusions of law filed by Roadway, it takes the position that Edwards was engaged to *complete* the delivery.

The common law rule is that a common carrier by land is to deliver to the door of the consignee. To the door, or the "place of delivery," means the unloading platform or the customary place used for delivery. Delivery is completed when there is nothing left to be done to finish the transportation. Here there was an element of transportation remaining, however short a distance it may have been. Ordinarily, the court would be disposed to view the case as being one of completed delivery or at least a valid tender of delivery. However, since the carrier itself takes the position that delivery was not completed, the court will not ignore such a position when there was in fact a small element of transportation still involved.

Assuming that there was a valid tender of delivery, the outcome as to liability of the parties would be the same. Upon the hypothesis that the transportation was at an end and a valid tender of delivery was made, the liability of Roadway would cease to be that of a common carrier or qualified insurer. At this point, the tariff regulation relied upon by Roadway would become important. This tariff is as follows:

> National Motor Freight Classification, Rule 21 Heavy or Bulky Articles, loading or unloading. Sec. 1. Where an article (or articles) in a single container or shipping form tendered, weigh 500 lbs. or more, or if the greatest dimension exceeds 8 feet or greatest and intermediate dimension each exceeds 4 feet, loading or unloading shall be performed by the shipper or consignee, as the case may be. If requested, carriers will undertake, in behalf of the shipper or consignee, as the case may be, to employ additional help. No charge will be made for labor performed by the truck driver, but a charge of one dollar and fifty cents ($1.50) per hour or fraction thereof, for each man furnished, other than the truck driver, shall apply from time vehicle arrives at the place of pick-up or delivery until shipment is loaded or unloaded, as the case may be.

Exception

There is numerous authority for the proposition that where motor carriers engaged in interstate commerce have on file tariffs stating their rates and regulations, that such tariffs are binding on all parties concerned and have the force and effect of law. *Jackson & Perkins Co.* v. *Mushroom Transportation Co.*, 351 Pa. 583, 41 A. 2d 635, certiorari denied 326 U.S. 733, 66 S. Ct. 42, 90 L. Ed. 427; Annotations to 49 U.S.C.A. §§ 319, 20 (11, 12). The tariffs bind the parties whether they have actual notice of them or not and are a part of the contract of carriage along with the bill of lading. The purpose of some of the tariffs is for regulation and uniformity to prevent unlawful discrimination by the rendition of various services to interstate shippers by common carriers which are not provided for in other tariffs. The tariff regulation above quoted is one of the regulatory tariffs, and Roadway had no choice, in order to abide by the law, but to heed the terms of such tariff which it had on file with the Interstate Commerce Commission.

Roadway relies upon the tariff to establish as a fact that its employees were the agents of Loveless. The case of *Columbus & Greenville Railway Co.* v. *Owens*, 153 Miss. 628, 121 So. 265, would seem to support this view, but the tariff there involved was materially different. In that case, mules were shipped to the consignee and the consignee was not there to receive them. The railroad employees unloaded and put the mules in a pen where they ate rust scales, resulting in death to a number of the animals. The court held that the railroad employees were agents of the owner on the strength of the Consolidated Freight Classification tariff to the effect that any assistance rendered by employees of a railroad or carrier in loading or unloading, shall be construed as purely voluntary and that any such employee shall be considered as the agent of the owner and not of the carrier.

In the case before this court, the evidence discloses that Roadway through its soliciting agent represented that it would unload the shipment on arrival. In addition to this, the evidence discloses that no request was ever made by Loveless to have the carrier employ additional help to unload, nor did Roadway ever call the attention of Loveless to the tariff involved. It cannot be denied that Loveless is charged with constructive notice of the tariff, but if ever the law put a duty upon a person to speak out, such law should be applicable to this case when Roadway was well aware of its own tariff regulations and did not call it to the attention of Loveless. Be that as it may, the fact remains that Roadway did undertake the unloading of the machine. It is immaterial that the tariff put the responsibility of unloading upon the consignee, or stating it negatively, that the carrier could not lawfully do the unloading. The mere fact that the tariff provides that the consignee shall do the unloading does not and cannot logically mean that the carrier could not violate the law or that its agents were the agents of Loveless. This is precisely and clearly stated in the case of *William Ramsey* v. *New York Central Railroad Company*, 269 N.Y. 219, 199 N. E. 65, 102 A. L. R. 511, 513, 514, where a similar tariff was involved. In the *Ramsey* case the court said:

> It is pointed out that the tariff provision made it illegal for the respondent railroad company to do the work of unloading the car, and that it must be presumed that it was not engaged in doing an illegal act. It is hard to see the distinction. So far as the legality of its act is concerned, what difference does it make whether we say it was unloading the car itself or that it loaned the crane and its operator to the construction company to do the work? In either case, it retained the absolute control of its machinery and its operator.
>
> The fact is undisputed that the respondent's crane was being operated by its servant over whom it retained complete control. *The rule of the Commission cannot change the facts. It would be strange indeed if the respondent, by violating the rule of the commission could by such violation or by loaning its servant to the construction company change its relation to the employee and make such employee the servant of the construction company without the consent of the servant or of the construction company either expressed or implied. . . .* (Emphasis added.)

In American Jurisprudence, Volume 9 Carriers, §467, it is stated that "A carrier which has assumed the duty of loading or the unloading the shipment is liable for such damages as result from its failure to do so properly." Roadway introduced testimony of its own employees who were engaged in the unloading operation that there was negligence on the part of some of the unloading crew. Over and above this, Roadway breached the terms of the contract as contained in the bill of lading. Section 4(a) of the bill of lading provides:

> SEC. 4(a). Property not removed by the party entitled to receive it within the free time allowed by tariffs, lawfully on file (such free time to be computed as therein provided), after notice of the arrival of the property at destination or at the port of export (if intended for export) has been duly sent or given, and after placement of property, for delivery at destination has been made, may be kept in vessel, car, depot, warehouse or place of delivery of the carrier, subject to the tariff charge for storage and to carrier's liability as warehouseman, only, or at the option of the carrier, may be removed to and stored in a public or licensed warehouse at the place of delivery or other available place, at the cost of the owner, and there held without liability on the part of the carrier, and subject to a lien for all freight and other lawful charges, including a reasonable charge for storage.

The identical section was involved in the case of *Textron, Inc.* v. *Lowell Trucking Corporation et al.,* 74 F. Supp. 322. In that case, the court held that even though the consignee refused to accept delivery after a valid tender that the carrier was liable for the loss of goods where the carrier did not comply with the terms of the contract of carriage. Here Roadway had no alternative after the attempted delivery, still assuming that a valid tender of delivery was made, but to comply with the provisions of the bill of lading herein set out. Instead, Roadway undertook to unload the machine in violation of the tariff.

It will be the judgment of the court that Loveless recover from Roadway the sum of $1660.00 plus the sale price of the damaged machine, $5,500.00, or a total of $7,160.00. The case is dismissed as to the third party defendant, Edwards, which effectively disposes of the third party complaint against the American Equitable Assurance Company of New York.

In *Roadway Express* v. *Gordon,* 277 P. 2d 146, the court held that the evidence supported a finding that the carrier had been free from negligence and that the damage occurred as result of negligence in cargo loading which had been participated in by shipper's employee, and supported a conclusion of law that the carrier was not responsible. However in *United States* v. *Savage Truck Line, Inc.,* 209 F. 2d 442 (cert. den. 347 U.S. 952), the court held that the primary duty as to the safe loading of property is on the carrier and if the improper loading was apparent as it was in this case, the carrier is liable notwithstanding the negligence of the shipper, since the carrier as a matter of right may refuse to accept the shipment which is improperly loaded. In *Emerson Electric Mfg. Co.* v. *Terminal R. Assn.* 262 S. W. 2d 323, the court held there was no duty on a terminal railroad to inspect cars and contents before accepting and transporting them to determine whether they were properly loaded so that, where defective loading was not apparent and carrier was free from negligence, carrier was not liable for injury due to improper loading of cars of steel.

While carrier liability with respect to "shipper's load and count" shipments has been referred to and discussed previously in this section in connection with the carrier's liability generally for damage where the shipper loads the goods, some additional discussion is offered in view of the fact that these shipments differ to some extent from others. Sections 20 and 21 of the Federal Bill of Lading Act govern carrier's liability for shipments received under "shipper's load and count." Contrary to popular conception on the part of some carriers, the endorsement of "shipper's load and count" on a bill of lading does not always relieve the carrier from liability for shortages or damages due to improper loading of such shipments. On the other hand, a proper understanding of Sections 20 and 21 and the observance of a few requirements will afford carriers a measure of relief which could not otherwise be secured.

Section 20 requires that carriers loading freight must count the packages of goods, if package freight, and ascertain the kind and quantity of bulk freight and, in such cases, are forbidden from endorsing on the bill of lading "shipper's weight, load, and count" or other words of like purport to indicate that the goods were loaded and described by the shipper. Section 21 provides, however, that when package freight or bulk freight is actually loaded by the shipper, the carrier may endorse on the bill of lading the words "shipper's weight, load, and count" or other words of like import, and if such statement be true, the carrier will not be liable for damage caused by the shipper's improper loading, or by nonreceipt or misdescription of the goods described in the bill of lading. Where a shipper of bulk freight has installed and maintains adequate weighing facilities, the carrier must, upon written request, and after reasonable opportunity to do so, utilize such facilities and ascertain the kind and quantity of such freight, and is forbidden in these circumstances from endorsing any words on the bill to indicate "shipper's weight."

In the event of shortage, the effect of Section 21 is to place upon the shipper loading the goods the burden of proving that the amount specified was loaded and that a lesser amount was delivered to consignee. If the shipper can establish these facts, then the carrier will be held liable for the shortage. Very often the shipper's employees are willing to testify that the amount shown on the bill of lading was actually loaded in full. In some instances, the shipper is able to present stock inventory records to indicate that this quantity must have been shipped. Under these circumstances the carrier, unless it can produce some evidence of its own, will be held liable for the shortage. This evidence cannot easily be found in most cases. Usually the truck has moved many miles to its destination, several drivers may have been in charge of the load, and it may have been left unattended at times. However, if the carrier takes the precaution of sealing the load in the shipper's or his representative's presence, endorses the seal number on the bill of lading, transcribes this seal record on all billings, and on delivery requires the consignee to note on delivery receipt the number of the seal removed from the vehicle, then the carrier will be able to establish a strong case that the shortage could not have occurred while the goods were in its possession and, under such circumstances, shipper's evidence that the full quantity was actually loaded would be entitled to little weight. It is not believed that carrier operating open-top equipment can realize much benefit from the provisions of Section 21 insofar as shortages are concerned.

In the event of damage due to improper loading, under the provisions of Section 21 a carrier is afforded some measure of relief where the shipper has loaded the vehicle. In *Robinson* v. *N. Y. C. R. Co.*, 282 N.Y.S. 877, aff'd 1 N. E. 2nd 985, the court stated:

> Placing on the bill of lading the words "Shipper's Load and Count" gives the shipper the privilege of loading as he pleases. Requiring the carrier to see that the shipper does his own business prudently, and making it responsible for his failure to do so, would not be just.

In another case, the shipper loaded bulk watermelons under bill of lading endorsed "SL&C," with knowledge that practically all such shipments will shift in transit; the court denied discovery for damage caused by bruising of some melons as result of normal shifting in the absence of any evidence of carrier's negligence. (*Leonard* v. *Pennsylvania R. Co.*, 15 F. Supp. 55) Carrier was also relieved of liability where shipper's employees loaded machine on truck for transportation to buyer and damage resulted from improper loading. (*Kennedy, Inc.* v. *O'Brien*, 175 A. 882) The shipper's improper loading, of course, is available to the carrier as a defense only when it is the direct cause of the damage to the goods. (*St. Louis-S. F. R. Co.* v. *Glow Electric Co.*, 172 N. E. 425)

The cases illustrating the effect of "SL&C" notations are numerous and the principles established so well recognized that very little purpose would be served by reviewing them here. It is believed, however, that review of some recent decisions illustrating the effect of the omission of the notation where, in fact, the shipper had actually performed the loading, will be of interest. In *Robinson Electrical Co.* v. *Capitol Trucking Corp.*, 79 A. 2d 123, the plaintiff had purchased some used machinery, including electric motors, from a concern in New York for which it paid

$915. Plaintiff claimed that in transporting the machinery from New York to Philadelphia the carrier failed to deliver two motors of the value of $600, some of the machinery was damaged to the extent of $125, and there was an overcharge of $62.16. The plaintiff asserted that the presumptive validity of the bill of lading reciting 23 motors, five exhaust fans, and one lathe was not overcome by the evidence in the record. The plaintiff's witnesses testified that only 21 motors were delivered, some of the machinery was damaged, and the shipment weighed 2,600 pounds. Defendant's evidence showed that the machinery was shipped as junk; the truck after loading was sealed until delivery was made to plaintiff in Philadelphia; nothing happened to the shipment in transit; five boxes of parts were included in the shipment but not listed on the bill of lading; the bill of lading was prepared by the consignor without definite knowledge as to the exact amount of goods shipped; and the weight of the shipment was 8,205 pounds. The plaintiff admitted receipt of one box not listed on the bill of lading. Upon delivery of the shipment, it was so intermingled with other machinery in the consignee's warehouse that it could not be identified. Inconsistencies appeared in the plaintiff's records including the fact that only 20 motors had been purchased from the consignor. The court held the carrier not liable and said:

> It was shown that the statements in the bill of lading did not conform with the goods received and delivered by defendant. There was also evidence of safe carriage and the improbability of loss and damage in transit. The bill of lading did not recite any boxes as a part of the shipment, and admittedly at least one box of parts was delivered to plaintiff, while defendent testified that five such boxes were in the shipment received and delivered. Consignor's employee who prepared the bill of lading did not know the exact number of motors shipped or the full extent of the shipment. *Defendant's truck driver receipted for the cargo without inspection or opportunity to check it.* At least it appears that the bill of lading was prepared and accepted under circumstances which disclosed a mistake as to description of the shipment. (Emphasis added.)

In *Modern Tool Corporation* v. *Pennsylvania Railroad Company,* 100 F. Supp. 595, the War Assets Administration, through the Frontier Contracting Co., Inc., consigned to Modern Tool Corporation two grinders together with one milling machine, comprising a carload shipment. The car was loaded by the shipper on its private siding and sealed. When the car arrived at is destination, it was discovered that the grinder at the brake end of the car had toppled over onto the grinder next to it located toward the center of the car, and damage to both was so great that they were sold as junk for $98. The plaintiff contended that as a matter of law it was immaterial whether or not the machines were properly loaded by the shipper. He contended that by accepting the shipment, the railroad accepted the responsibility for carrying the machines safely regardless of the question of the carrier's negligence. The carrier had failed to show on the bill of lading that the shipment was "shipper's load and count." In holding the carrier not liable the court said:

> Plaintiff cites *Commodity Credit Corp.* v. *Norton*, 167 F. (2d) 161 (C.A. 3, 1948) which holds that the carrier is responsible "without regard for the exercise of due care, unless, of course, the damage or loss flows from an excepted cause. . ." (at page 164). However, as that case clearly indicates, the carrier is not an insurer. At common law, the carrier had a duty to transport and deliver safely against all contingencies *except* an Act of God, the public enemy, or the act or default of the shipper. *Austin* v. *Seaboard Airline R. Co.*, 188 F. (2d) 239 (C. A. 5, 1951); *Farris Bros. & Co.* v. *P. R. R. Co.*, 98 Pa. Super. 123, 126 (1930); *St. Louis S. F. Ry. Co.* v. *Glow Electric Co*, 35 Ohio App. 291, 172 N. E. 425 (1929); *Ross* v. *Troy & Boston Ry. Co.*, 49 Vt. 364, 24 Am. Rep. 144 (1887); *Kassel Poultry Co.* v. *P. R. R. Co.*, 7 N. J. Misc. 301, 145 A. 316 (S. C. N. J. 1939). It should be noted that the very bill of lading for shipment here in question contained in Section 1(b) of its contract terms and conditions the exceptions noted above.
>
> The defendant contends that the machines were improperly loaded by the shipper, and that the damage was occasioned by this default. The carrier bears the burden of proving this contention. *Atlantic Refining Co.* v. *P. R. R. Co.*, 113 A. 570 (S. Ct. Pa. 1921); *Crump, et al.* v. *Thompson*, 171 F. (2d) 442, (C. A. 8, 1948).
>
> Where "shipper's load and count" appears on the bill of lading, and in fact, the goods were improperly loaded, the shipper is liable for the loss. *Robinson* v. *N.Y. Central R. Co.*, 282 N. Y. S. 877, 245 App. Div. 378, aff'd 1 N. E. 2d 985, 270 N.Y. 659 (1936).
>
> *The bill of lading here contained no such notation. There is nothing in the statute to indicate that the mere omission of the words "shipper's weight, load and count" in and of itself makes the carrier liable for damage to goods improperly loaded. The omission of the statutory words merely serves to shift upon the carrier the burden of proving that the goods were improperly loaded by the shipper, and that the damage ensued from that cause.* (Emphasis added.)
>
> * * * *
>
> The defendant thus (by its evidence of failure to observe carrier's rules and regulations for safe loading) established that the machines were improperly loaded in that all skids were fastened to the car floor, and the machine which toppled was not secured to its skid. The contention that the damage was caused by rough handling was refuted by introduction of evidence that during the course of shipment nothing occurred which would likely cause damage. *Snowden* v. *Tremont & G. Ry. Co.*, 140 So. 122; *Lever Bros. Co.* v. *Baltimore & Ohio R. Co.*, 164 F. 2d 738. The carrier cannot be held liable here for the act of the shipper in loading the car improperly. *Lever Bros. case, supra.* See also

Alabama & V. Ry. Co. v. *American Cotton Oil Co.*, 249 F. 308 (C. A. 5, 1918); *Austin* v. *Seaboard Airline R. C., supra*; *Shapiro* v. *P. R. R. Co.*, 83 F. 2d 581 (C. A. D. C. 1936); *Blytheville Cotton Oil Co.* v. *Kurn*, 155 F. 2d 467 (C. A. 6, 1946).

The contention was also made that the carrier is liable even if the goods were improperly loaded by the shipper for the carrier has a duty to inspect the car for proper loading, and failing this the carrier is liable. Although there is a school of thought which absolves the carrier from liability even if it is aware of the defect of loading upon accepting the goods (*Ross* v. *Troy & Boston R. Co., supra*) the majority and better view holds the carrier liable if the defect is patent. *Lewis Mach. Co.* v. *Aztec Lines, Inc.*, 172 F. 2d 746 (C. A. 7, 1949); *Perkel* v. *P. R. R. C.*, 148 Misc. 284, 265 N. Y. S. 597 (1933). As to defects not perfectly apparent the test is one of "ordinary observation," *Thompson* v. *Chicago M. & St. P. Ry. Co.*, 195 Wisc., 78, 217 N. W. 927, 929 (1928); 13 C. J. S. 124, section 67; 9 Am. Juris 866, 867. "Insofar as its condition could be ascertained by mere inspection." *Alabama & V. Ry. Co.* v. *American Cotton Oil Co., supra; Blytheville Cotton Oil Co.* v. *Kurn, supra.*

It develops then that the defect was not apparent to the railroad. As was stated in *Alabama & V. Ry. Co.* v. *American Cotton Oil Co., supra*, ". . . it can scarcely consist with public policy to encourage the furnishings by shippers of . . . defective loading, by excusing them from the results of their negligence" (at page 311).

Marking

Carrier classification rules require that the shipper plainly and durably mark, stencil, or tag each package or piece of each shipment. The rules further provide that marks on the freight must be compared with shipping order or bill of lading, and corrections, if necessary, made by the shipper before the receipt is signed.

In cases before the Interstate Commerce Commission involving additional freight charges resulting from the transportation of shipments to erroneous destinations due to the error of the shipper in marking the freight, it has been held that the marks on the package, and not on the bill of lading, control. In deciding *American Agricultural Chemical Co.* v. *Bangor & Aroostook Railroad Co.*, 28 I.C.C. 398, the Commission stated:

> The Commission has recently held informally that when a shipper prepares a bill of lading providing for the carriage of property to a particular destination and marks a different and erroneous address on the package, the carrier will not be held responsible for the freight charges incurred in transporting the property to the destination shown on the package, although the correct destination shown on the bill of lading.

In *Parlin & Orendorff Plow Co.* v. *United States Express Co.*, 26 I. C.C. 561, the shipper gave the carrier a shipment erroneously marked for "Ozark, Arkansas," and the carrier changed the receipt showing the correct destination of "Ozark, Missouri," to "Ozark, Arkansas," before signing it. In deciding the case, the Commission held that the carrier in issuing the receipt was not bound to call attention to the change in destination thereon, and should not be required to return the goods without charge.

It will be noted that the foregoing Commission cases in connection with mismarking involve rate matters. They are not controlling in connection with a loss and damage claim resulting from mismarking by the shipper. Since the bill of lading constitutes the contract between the parties, its provisions should govern in determining the carrier's duty in making delivery of the shipment. The receipt portion of the bill of lading recites that the property described is received "marked, consigned, and destined as shown below." Before signing the bill of lading, it is the carrier's duty to examine the shipment to assure that the marks on it correspond to those on the bill of lading. While the carrier's failure to take this precaution may not excuse the shipper from paying additional freight charges for transportation resulting from erroneous marking of the package as indicated under the aforementioned cited ICC decisions, it does not excuse the carrier from liability for failure to transport the shipment to the consignee and destination specified in the bill of lading contract.

It seems clear from the decisions in the following cases that since the bill of lading constitutes the contract between the parties, the provisions thereof should govern the carrier in making delivery of the shipment: *Union Pacific R. C. Co.* v. *Burke,* 225 U.S. 317; *N.Y.C.R. Co.* v. *Samuel Goldberg,* 250 U.S. 85; *New York Central R. Co.* v. *Lazarus,* 278 Fed. 900; *Guillaune* v. *General Trans-Atlantic Co.,* 3 N. E. 489; *Lewis Poultry Co.* v. *N.Y.C.,* 105 A. 109; *Ocean S.S. Co. of Savannah* v. *People Shoe Co.,* 81 So. 241; *L. G. Cohen & Co.* v. *Davis,* 142 N. E. 75; *H.&T.S.* v. *Southern Arch Cement Co.,* 245 S. W. 644; *Myers* v. *American Railway Express,* 137 N. E. 544; *Booth* v. *N.Y.C.,* 112 A. 894; *Old Dominion S.S. Co.* v. *Blakeman,* 105 S.E. 752.

While ordinarily the carrier is not liable for loss of the goods due to the negligent or wrongful act of the shipper in disregard of a known rule of the carrier which is reasonable and adopted for the mutual interest of carrier and shipper, or of a regulation of the Interstate Commerce Commission, the shipper's failure to mark a portion of the freight shipped as required by regulations does not relieve the carrier for loss where the carrier raised no objection and, in fact, failed to enforce the regulation. In *Grammes* v. *Central R. Co. of New Jersey,* 122 A. 532, the court said:

Where railroad by haste in moving freight prevented shipper from properly marking the freight, and where the railroad received such freight not properly marked, and issued a through bill of lading therefor, which did not show the markings on the freight, as required by the regulations of the company . . . it could not avoid liability . . . on the ground that the shipper did not mark the freight as required.

Had defendant observed its own regulations, and the loss been occasioned by plaintiff's failure to comply therewith, the point it now seeks to raise, viz., is a carrier responsible for a loss resulting from the shipper's failure to observe its rules: would have been up for consideration. Here, however, defendant by its haste prevented plaintiff from marking the freight as required, did not observe its own regulations—as the Act of 1910 relied on (by it) required it to do—in that it received freight which was not all properly marked, and issued a through bill of lading therefor which did not show the markings on the barrels, and yet seeks to escape the liability which the act of Congress imposes though the fault was all its own. This, of course, it cannot do. . . .

In *Arabian American Oil Company* v. *Kirby & Kirby, Inc.,* 90 A 2d 410, one of the carrier's grounds of defense was the shipper's failure to mark the goods as *fragile* and that this misled the carrier as to the risk assumed. The shipment consisted of earthenware sinks which were ultimately intended for export. They were packed by the manufacturer in wooden cases instead of crates, which are commonly used for domestic transportation. In refusing to free the carrier from liability, the Pennsylvania Superior Court said:

The only markings on the shipment were the words "This Side Up" on the top of each box. But the failure of the shipper to mark the packages as "fragile" does not relieve the carrier from liability under the circumstances. The principle of *Bell Tel. Co.* v. *Am. Rwy. Exp. Co.,* 92 Pa. Superior Ct. 180, on which appellant strongly relies, is not controlling here. In that case the shipment was a box of radio tubes of "delicate and fragile construction," which were destroyed in transit. Judgment was entered against the shipper "because of the failure of the plaintiff (as shipper) to mark on the package the fact that the contents were fragile, thus putting the defendant (carrier) on notice in order that care might be exercised in proportion to the greater risk involved in the shipment." The rule applied was the "established principle of law . . . that no responsibility rests on the (carrier) for the loss of property arising from a wrongful act of the shipper. . . . " But though charging the shipper with deceptive conduct, that case did not hold that failure to mark the package "fragile," in itself, was a fraud on the carrier. The carrier's bill of lading providing that packages containing fragile goods be "so marked and packed as to insure safe transportation . . . with ordinary care." The shipper in that case was charged with fraud, barring recovery, from the fact that the requirement of the bill of lading for such marking was reasonable and had not been met, with the result that the carrier was justified in exercising less care than the actual character of the goods required. In the instant case the carrier's contract with plaintiff did not demand such marking and the nature of the shipment did not require it. The bill of lading referring to the shipment as "earthenware" gave ample notice that the plumbing fixtures, accepted for carriage, were breakable. There was no attempt at concealment of the nature of the articles and the plaintiff here is not chargeable with imposition on the carrier in any respect.

The earthenware sinks were properly packed for shipment from Trenton to Philadelphia. It is therefore unimportant that they were consigned to defendant Gallagher for the purpose of testing the sufficiency of the packing to withstand rough handling by foreign stevedores and others in exporting them to Arabia, the ultimate destination of the shipment. In general a common carrier is regarded as an insurer against all losses. *Steamship Co.* v. *Smart,* 107 Pa. 492, 500. To avoid liability, since the contract here was one of common carriage, the burden was on the appellant to show that the loss was within an exception to the general rule. *Villari et al.* v. *James,* 155 Pa. Superior Ct. 155, 158, 38 A. 2d 379. Appellant's evidence failed to sustain the affirmative defense of fraud and concealment of the inherent fragile nature of the goods. The trial court upon sufficient evidence found that the sinks were properly packed and that the carrier had notice of the nature of the shipment. These findings, adverse to the appellant have the force and effect of a verdict of a jury and cannot be disturbed on appeal. *Villari et al.* v. *James, supra.* On the trial of the case this appellant's evidence did not account for the loss under circumstances absolving it from negligence. Appellant therefore has no just ground for complaint.

Misdescription by Shipper

No uniform rule can be given as to carrier liability in those instances where the shipper misdescribed the commodity shipped, as each case must be considered on its own merit. As a general proposition, the determining factor appears to be whether or not such misrepresentation by the shipper was intentional or fraudulent. The decisions of the courts are not in entire harmony as to the extent of the carrier's liability in all circumstances. It would appear, however, that as a general rule, where such misrepresentation by the shipper was neither intentional nor fraudulent and if the goods shipped were not of such nature that the classification or carrier's tariffs restricted the handling (such as jewelry or other valuable articles), or if the goods were not of a perishable nature, and such misrepresentation did not prevent the carrier from affording protective service, then the carrier is usually liable for the value of the goods shipped in case of loss or damage.

It has been held in a number of decisions that where the goods shipped were money, jewelry, or other valuables so concealed as to hide their value and mislead the carrier, the carrier would be discharged from any liability for any loss or damage. (*Lancaster* v. *Houghton,* 249 S. W. 113, error dismissed 266 U.S. 590) This rule is particularly applicable if loss results from the carrier's omission of precautions which ordinarily would have been taken had the carrier known the nature of the goods. (*Mobile, etc. R. Co.* v. *Phillips,* 60 So. 572)

Some cases hold that regardless of the fraud of the shipper, the carrier, although discharged of liability as an insurer, is nevertheless liable as an ordinary bailee of the property for hire and as such is charged with the duty of exercising *ordinary care* to keep and deliver the property. (*Head* v. *Pacific Express Co.,* 126 S.W. 682) It is the theory of these cases that a misrepresentation by the shipper as to the nature of the goods in order to obtain lower rates will not prevent a recovery from the carrier for loss thereof where the misrepresentation did not contribute to the loss by misleading the carrier as to the precautions required for safe transportation. Section 10(3) of part I and Section 222(c) of Part II of the Interstate Commerce Act, however, provide that any shipper knowingly securing any rebate, concession, or discrimination by means of a false statement shall be deemed guilty of a misdemeanor and upon conviction thereof be subject to fine. It is difficult to visualize a situation where a shipper would admit violation of the law in order to secure settlement of a claim.

Where the misrepresentation was not fraudulent, the shipper is entitled to recover the value of the goods. The carrier, of course, would be entitled to collect the difference in freight charges where the correct description would result in a higher rate. In *New York Central R. Co.* v. *Goldberg,* 250 U.S. 85, defendant railroad contended that there was no responsibility for loss of the furs that were shipped because they were goods not of the same, but of a different character from those described in the bill of lading, and were goods for the transportation of which a higher rate was established. The court answered this contention in the following language:

> Were there otherwise any difficulty in answering this contention, it would be wholly relieved by the fact that the precise contingency was anticipated in the preparation of the form of the bill of lading and provided by one of its conditions, which reads as follows:
>
>> The owner or consignee shall pay the freight and all other lawful charges accruing on such property, and if required, shall pay the same before delivery. If upon inspection it is ascertained that the articles shipped are not those described in this bill of lading, the freight charges must be paid upon the articles shipped.

Clearly, the effect of this is, that a misdescription of the character of the goods not attributable to fraud, merely imposed upon the shipper or consignee an obligation to pay freight charges according to the character of the goods actually shipped, and did not affect the liability of the carrier for a failure to deliver the goods.

The provision of the rail bill of lading cited in the foregoing opinion is similar to the last sentence in Section 7 of the terms and conditions of the motor carrier bill of lading.

Defect in the Property

The final exception from the common carrier's strict liability is for loss or damage due to defects in the goods. The older cases speak of losses caused by the inherent nature, vice, defect, or infirmity of the goods. (*Lester* v. *Railway Co.*, 1 K. B. 878; *Louisville & N. R. Co.* v. *Bigger,* 66 Miss. 319; *Illinois Central R. Co.* v. *Brelsford,* 13 Ill. App. 251; *Lawrence* v. *Denbreens,* 1 Black, 170) The usual situations involve damage from decay of perishable fruit and natural death or deterioration in livestock. It is sometimes suggested that this exception stems from the same principles as the act of God exception or even to be one aspect of it (Dobie, *Bailments and Carriers* [St. Paul: West Publishing Co., 1914], p. 340; Hutchinson, *Law of Carriers* [Chicago: Callahan and Co., 2d ed. 1891], p. 238), but it has historically been treated as a separate and distinct exception.

When goods are received by the carrier in good condition, delivered by it in damaged condition, and carrier alleges that the damage was due to some defect or inherent vice in the goods, the burden is on the carrier to show both that it was free from negligence and that the damage was due to one of the excepted causes.

Most of the controversy in this area is over the source of the damage. While in the case of spoilage of perishables that nature of the damage is clear, the cause of it is open to dispute. Spoilage is not a cause of damage but a symptom of it. The spoilage was caused by some other operative force, and the question is whether that force was some inherent defect of the property, some failure of the carrier to protect it properly, or some other source entirely. In some of the recent cases, the lower federal courts have indicated that where damage to perishable goods is in issue, the burden on the carrier is only to show its own compliance with the rules of the tariff and the shipper's instructions. This was the ruling of court in *Larry's Sandwiches, Inc.* v. *Pacific Electric Ry. Co.*, 318 F. 2d 690, relying on *United States* v. *Reading Co.*, 289 F. 2d 7; *Illinois Packing Co.* v. *Atchison, T. & S. F. Ry. Co.*, 236 F. 2d 908;

Delphi Frosted Foods Corp. v. *Illinois Cent. R. Co.*, 188 F. 2d 343. The court specifically held that at common law a carrier was not liable for damages occasioned by the inherent vice or nature of the goods *in the absence of negligence*, and that the Carmack Amendment codified this common-law rule. (See *Martin* v. *E. A. McCabe & Co.*, 113 So. 2d 879)

A similar ruling was made by the court in *Trautmann Bros. Co.* v. *Missouri Pac. R. Co.*, 312 F. 2d 102, a case involving damage to a shipment of melons. The shipper had precooled the melons and the evidence showed that the carrier re-iced at all regular icing stations. The precooling, however, had apparently melted much of the original ice. The defendant railroad did not know about the special precooling operation. In holding for the carrier, the court held:

> A common carrier is not absolutely liable for spoilage or physical deterioration during the course of shipment. So long as the carrier had discharged its duty of reasonable care, it is not liable for "damage to a shipment caused . . . by the operation of natural laws upon it . . ."; that is, the carrier is not liable for damages caused solely by the acts or direction of the shipper.

The court also held that tariff rules limiting carrier's liability for perishables to liability for "negligent failure reasonably to carry out instructions given by the shipper" did not violate Section 20(11) of the Interstate Commerce Act, because that section only bars a carrier from limiting "its liability for damage *caused by the carrier.*

At this point an action arose in the Texas courts involving damage to a carload of melons. The jury found that the melons were in good condition when shipped but arrived damaged, and also found that the railroads performed all required transportation services without negligence. The state court concluded, in view of the jury's findings, that although a common carrier is not responsible for spoilage or decay which is shown to be due entirely to the inherent nature of the goods, the railroad defendant had not established that the damage was caused *solely* by natural deterioration. The Supreme Court of the United States granted certiorari because of the conflict with the decision in *Larry's Sandwiches*, previously cited. In *Missouri Pacific R. Co.* v. *Elmore & Stahl*, 377 U.S. 134, the Supreme Court noted that there were, as far as this case was concerned, two undisputed effects of the Carmack Amendment making common carriers liable for the full actual loss, damage, or injury caused by them. First, "the statute codifies the common-law rule that a carrier, though not an absolute insurer, is liable for damage to goods transported by it unless it can show that the damage was caused by" one of the five excepted causes. The second effect of the Carmack Amendment noted by the court was that "the statute declares unlawful and void any rule, regulation, or other limitation of any character whatsoever" purporting to limit this liability.

Thus, the court said, in an action for damage, "the shipper establishes his prima facie case when he shows delivery in good condition, arrival in damaged condition, and the amount of damages. *Thereupon, the burden of proof is upon the carrier to show both that it was free from negligence and that the damage to the cargo was due to one of the excepted causes relieving the carrier of liability.*" The court said that the jury was apparently unable to determine the cause of the damage. The defendant argued that if the goods are perishable and the nature of the damage is spoilage, and further if the jury affirmatively finds the carrier free from negligence and that the carrier performed the transportation service required by the shipper, then the law presumes that the cause of the damage was the inherent nature of the property. The court said that the argument did not account for all bases of carrier liability, specifically referring to damage caused by third parties, for which the carrier is liable. The railroad argued for a perishable goods rule similar to the "livestock rule" which absolves a carrier from liability upon proof that the carrier exercised reasonable care and complied with the shipper's instructions, but the court said it was aware of no such "new rule of federal law."

It is important to understand what the court did *not* hold in *Elmore & Stahl,* as well as what it did hold. The court did not limit the exception to carrier liability for damage arising from the inherent nature or vice in the goods. What it held was that the general rule which place on the carrier the affirmative burden of bringing the cause of the damage within one of the specified exceptions to carrier liability applies to perishable commodities. It did not change the liability of the carrier.

In *Hamilton Mfg. Co.* v. *Chicago & N. W. Ry. Co.,* 277 F. 2d 652, the court said:

> Where rust damage to certain steel sheets occurred solely by operation of natural laws upon the steel, that is, the natural tendency of steel to rust from moisture caused by condensation due to temperature changes, carrier could not be held liable for such damage. Burden was on consignee . . . to establish that some negligence of carrier contributed to damage, and where no such proof was made, carrier could not be held liable.

The holding of the court that the natural tendency of steel to rust from condensation is an inherent defect or vice in the goods, and that damage from such cause should not be the liability of the carrier, is undoubtedly still the law. But the holding that the burden was on the consignee to prove negligence on the part of the carrier has undoubtedly been modified by *Elmore & Stahl.* Other cases placing the burden on the shipper to show negligence on the carrier's part also have undoubtedly been modified by *Elmore & Stahl;* e.g., *Standard Brands* v. *Boston & M. R. Co.*, 29 F. Supp. 593; *American Ry. Exp.* v. *Fegenbush*, 144 So. 320; *Gulf, C. & S. F. Ry. Co.* v. *Downs*, 70 S. W. 2d 318; *Seaboard Airline R. Co.* v. *Henry Chanin Corp.*, 66 S. E. 2d 113; W. E. *Roche Fruit Co.* v. *Northern Pacific Ry. Co.*, 52 P. 2d 325.

The procedure to be followed in cases of damage to perishables is for the shipper to show that the goods were delivered to the carrier in good order and that they arrived in bad order, *United States* v. *Mississippi Valley Barge Line Co.*, 285 F. 2d 381; *Inland Waterways Shippers Ass'n.* v. *Mississippi Valley Barge Line Co.*, 194 F. Supp. 818, 289 F. 2d 374, cert. den. 368 U.S. 876, or to show that the merchandise, when delivered to the carrier, was in better condition than when delivered by the carrier. (*Helm's Express, Inc.* v *United States*, 186 F. Supp. 521) When the shipper shows that, he establishes a prima facie case of liability on the carrier and the burden then shifts to the carrier to show both its freedom from negligence and that the damage resulted from an inherent defect or vice in the goods.

For cases dealing with sufficiency of evidence to establish delivery to the carrier in good order, see *Larry's Sandwiches, Inc.* v. *Pacific Electric Ry. Co.*, 318 F. 2d 690; *Harris Truck Lines, Inc.* v. *Cherry Meat Packers, Inc.*, 313 F. 2d 864, cert. den. 375 U.S. 821; *Armour Research Foundation* v. *Chicago, R. I. & P. R. Co.*, 311 F. 2d 493, cert. den. 372 U.S. 966; *Minneapolis, St. P. & S.S.M.R. Co.* v. *Metal-Matic, Inc.*, 323 F. 2d 903.

The principle that a carrier is not liable for loss caused by the inherent character of the goods shipped is illustrated very effectively in *Shapiro* v. *Pennsylvania R. Co.*, 83 F. 2d 581. In this case, the plaintiff brought suit against the railroad to recover damages for failure to safely refrigerate and transport a carload of peas and cauliflower from Auburn, Washington, to Washington, D. C. The shipment moved under standard refrigeration, with the addition by the shipper of almost five tons of ice on top of the crates and hampers. The carrier proved by its records that the car was properly iced at all the different icing stations en route and was always in good mechanical condition. Upon inspection after arrival at destination, the peas and cauliflower were found to be unmerchantable because of rot and deterioration. In holding that the damage sued for occurred as result of the inherent vice of the goods, and that the carrier was not liable therefor as insurer, the court said:

> The rule of liability applicable to freight shipments is well stated in *Northwestern M. & T. Co.* v. *Williams,* 128 Minn. 514, 151 N. W. 419, 420, L. R. A. 1915D, 1077, as follows: "A common carrier of goods in general insures the safe transportation of goods committed to him for that purpose, and he is responsible for all damage to the same while in transit, unless such damage is occasioned by certain exempted causes. These excepted causes are act of God, act of public enemy, the inherent quality of 'proper vice' of the articles themselves, or some act or omission of the shipper or owner." Or as recently stated by Mr. Justice Stone in *Schnell* v. *The Vallescura,* 293 U.S. 296, 304, 55 S. Ct. 194, 196, 79 L. Ed. 373: "He is a bailee intrusted with the shipper's goods, with respect to the care and safe delivery of which the law imposes upon him an extraordinary duty. Discharge of the duty is peculiarly within his control. All the facts and circumstances upon which he may rely to relieve him of that duty are peculiarly within his knowledge and usually unknown to the shipper. In consequence, the law casts upon him the burden of the loss which he cannot explain or, explaining, bring him within the exceptional case in which he is relieved from liability." Here the railroad has explained the damage and brought itself well within the excepted cases. . . . In the circumstances, it is manifest that the damage sued for occurred as the result of the inherent vice of the things shipped; and, in that view, it is equally manifest that the railroad is not an insurer and is not liable. A recent case illustrative of the principle we apply is *Cassone* v. *New York, etc., R. Co.,* 100 Conn. 262, 123 A. 280, 283. There the plaintiff sued for damages to grapes shipped from the West Coast to Connecticut. The bill of lading showed that the shipper ordered a dry car, but stipulated for ventilation. The court found that the defendant discharged its duty as to this service, and said: "The consignor took advantage of the choice, which was his, and contracted for transportation in a dry car without ice, relying upon ventilation to protect the fruit. A shipper cannot make that choice and then insist that the carrier must assume the peril of any loss that comes to the fruit in transit in the way contracted for, if it develops, on delivery of the grapes, that ventilation failed to keep the grapes from decay when refrigeration might have done so." To the same effect is *Chesapeake & O. R. Co.* v. *Thompson Co.,* 270 U.S. 416, 46 S. Ct. 318, 70 L. Ed. 654.

That a carrier is not an unqualified insurer of transportation of perishables is clearly illustrated in *Railway Express Agency* v. *H. Rouw Co.,* 128 S. W. 2d 989. In this case the record showed that the carrier iced the cars of strawberries at shipping point, that an adequate number of icing stations were provided en route, that cars were re-iced to capacity at each station, that diversion orders were promptly effected by the carrier, and that the inspector of the Railroad Perishable Inspection Agency who examined cars upon arrival at destination determined that deterioration of the berries was caused by their inherent nature and was of field origin. In holding in favor of the carrier, the court said:

It was said in the case of *Railway Express Agency, Inc.* v. *S. L. Robinson & Co.*, 43 S.W. 2d 543, that when the shipper proves delivery of the commodity in good condition, and failure to redeliver in good condition, that a prima facie case is made, and the burden shifts to the carrier to show that its negligence did not cause the damage which accrued to the commodity in its shipment. But it was held in that case that the carrier may show that it was not responsible for the damage, and in holding that the carrier had discharged this burden in that case it was there said: "The carrier did not content itself with introducing witnesses as to the general condition of the shipment of strawberries while in its hands, but introduced all persons employed by it who had part in the different transactions during transit. We do not mean that all the operatives of the train were introduced as witnesses, but we do mean that the carrier followed the shipment step by step from the place of shipment to the place of delivery. It was shown by competent evidence that a refrigerator car of the most approved type was furnished the shipper within which to carry the berries. The condition of car and its material, both as to equipment and construction, was detailed by the witnesses. It was shown that the carrier had a sufficient number of icing stations along the route for re-icing the car and that the car was properly inspected and well iced at all these stations. The evidence shows that the car of strawberries was in good condition at all these points. The car was diverted by the shipper from Kansas City, Mo. to Chicago, Ill. As soon as it arrived at its destination, the consignor was notified. An examination of the berries was made when they arrived at their destination, and they were found to be full ripe and watery. None of the crates were broken or damaged." In this case, as in the *Robinson case, supra,* none of the crates were broken or damaged, and it appears, from the facts herein recited, that appellant carrier has, in like manner, overcome the prima facie case, and the judgments (in favor of shipper) must, therefore, be reversed. . . .

The decision in *Joseph Miller Co.* v. *Gateway City Transfer,* 20 N. W. 2d 651, contains an excellent summary of the law on this subject:

The Royal Wine and Liquor Company in Chicago shipped two hundred cases of brandy to itself at LaCrosse, with directions to notify the J. Miller Company, 122 North 4th Street, LaCrosse, Wisconsin, on an order bill of lading on June 14, 1944, in sealed containers with bottles of brandy packed therein. The bill of lading acknowledged receipt of the shipment in apparent good order, except as noted (contents and condition of contents of packages unknown). The bill of lading provides that: "The surrender of this original bill of lading properly indorsed shall be required before the delivery of the property. Inspection of property covered by this bill of lading will not be permitted unless provided by law or unless permission is endorsed on this original bill of lading or given in writing by the shipper."

No right of inspection was endorsed on the original bill of lading or given in writing by the shipper. An inspection of the shipment was made after delivery of the goods to the plaintiff company at LaCrosse. The bill of lading contains the further provision: Sec. 1(b): "No carrier or party in possession of all or any of the property herein described shall be liable for any loss thereof or damage thereto or delay caused by the act of God, the public enemy, the authority of law, or the act or default of the shipper or owner, or for natural shrinkage."

The shipment left Chicago in one of the defendant's trucks at 10:20 p.m. on June 14th, and arrived at LaCrosse at about 10:30 on the morning of June 15th, and remained in the van in the parking lot of defendant until the afternoon of June 16th, when plaintiff took up the order bill of lading which was at the State Bank of LaCrosse, and delivered the order bill of lading to the defendant. Upon receipt of the order bill of lading defendant made delivery of the shipment to plaintiff within a few hours.

At the time of making delivery to the plaintiff leakage was found in some of the cases. Upon investigation it was found that on some of the bottles the wax had become softened, and the corks forced from the bottles. No bottles were broken. In forty-five bottles the liquor had leaked out, and in seventy-two bottles the corks were partially forced out but the contents were still in the bottles. On June 14th the temperature at Chicago was ninety degrees; on June 15th at LaCrosse it was eighty-eight degrees, and on June 16th it was eighty-five degrees.

There were twelve bottles in each case; twenty-four hundred bottles in all; thus, in 4.87% of the bottles the corks had been wholly or partially forced out. The bottles from which the corks had been wholly or partially forced out were scattered among many cases throughout the load. Besides the cork and wax method of bottling liquor, a screwcap method is sometimes used. The screwcap method allows for no expansion. Respondent contends that if that method had been used the bottles would have broken instead of pushing out the corks. The plaintiff grounds its action on two theories of liability on the part of the carrier. First, that under the decision in *Klauber* v. *American Express Co.*, 21 Wis. 21, 91 Am. Dec. 452, the carrier, having been apprised of the character of the shipment, is liable as an insurer where the goods were received in a good condition and were delivered in a damaged condition, where the carrier failed to prove that the loss was due to one of the exceptions which would relieve the carrier, namely, an act of God, the act of the public enemy, or the act of the owner. Secondly, that delay in delivery of the shipment to the plaintiff after it had arrived in LaCrosse constituted negligence as a matter of law on the part of the carrier.

The plaintiff's theory of liability on the ground of delay in making delivery after the arrival of the shipment at LaCrosse is without merit. This was a shipment made by the consignor to itself with instructions to notify the plaintiff company. It was an overnight shipment from Chicago to LaCrosse, arriving in LaCrosse at about 10:30 in the forenoon of June 15th. Draft with bill of lading was sent by the consignor to the State Bank of LaCrosse. The amount of the draft was approximately $9,384. Under the terms of the bill of lading the carrier was not permitted to make delivery until the plaintiff company had taken up the draft at the bank, procured the original order bill of lading, and delivered same to the carrier. Plaintiff did not do this until the afternoon of June 16th, and it appears that within two hours after the bill of lading had been procured from the bank and delivered to the carrier the shipment was delivered to the plaintiff. We think it must be held as a matter of law that the carrier was not negligent in the delay in making delivery of the shipment to the plaintiff after its arrival in LaCrosse.

* * * *

Aside from its theory of liability on the ground of negligent delay in making delivery to plaintiff after the shipment had arrived in LaCrosse, plaintiff contends that by leaving the brandy stand in the closed van exposed to the normal summer heat, the heat caused the contents of the bottles to expand and thus blow the corks.

There seems to be no escape from the conclusion that the blowing of the corks was due to the fermentation of the brandy in the bottles from which corks were blown, or to the expansion of the contents of the bottles due to the temperature during the time the brandy was in transit or while it remained in defendant's van awaiting delivery of the bill of lading to the carrier. In 13 *C. J. S., Carriers,* p. 155, § 79, it is said: "Applying the general principles here stated it has been held that the carrier is not liable for loss or injury due solely to such causes as fermentation, depreciation, drying, decay, heating merely as a result of transportation, spontaneous combustion, effervescence, putrefaction, or corrosion or rusting from the chemical union of parts of the goods shipped. Irrespective of the exemption from liability for injuries atttributable to the acts of God . . . , it may perhaps also be stated as a general proposition that the carrier is not liable for loss happening from the operation of natural causes without negligence or fault of the carrier. This rule has been frequently applied where the shipment was susceptible to injury by freezing and was so injured or destroyed, and it has been applied where the injury was due to warm weather, ..." As to the latter cause, citing *Nelson* v. *Woodruff,* 1 Black 156, 17 L. Ed. 97.

That case involved a shipment of molasses. The loss was due to the bursting of a hogshead by reasons of fermentation. In 1 *Black at page 161, 17 L. Ed., at page 99,* the court said: "The implied obligation of the carrier does not extend to such cases, any more than to does to a case when the liquid being carried, if it shall be conveyed with care, is entirely lost from its intrinsic acidity and fermentation, and bursting the vessel which contains it; as it was adjudged that the carrier was not liable when a pipe of wine during its fermentation burst and was lost, it being proved that at the time it was being carried carefully in a wagon commonly used for such a purpose." Citing *Farra* v. *Adams,* Bull, N. P. 69.

To same effect see 4 R. C. L. 728, sec. 200; 9 Am. Jur. 862, sec. 725. In the latter authority it stated: "Another established exception to the common law rule of liability as an insurer is where the loss or damage arises from the nature and inherent character of the property carried, ..."

In *Faucher* v. *Wilson,* 68 N. H. 338, 38 A. 1002, 39 L. R. A. 431, involving a loss while transporting a hogshead of molasses which burst while being unloaded, due to fermentation, it is said, 38 A. at page 1003: "If the defendent was a common carrier, he is not liable for the plaintiff's loss, since it happened from the operation of natural laws, which a common carrier does not insure against." See cases there cited.

The plaintiff's general manager testified that when heat is applied to brandy a steam or vapor pressure occurs, possibly caused by alcoholic fumes. The court's finding that "the owner (Royal Wine and Liquor Company) had no special knowledge of the character of the shipment of which they did not apprise the defendant carrier" is not sustained by the evidence. The only knowledge defendant had was that contained in the bill of lading. It disclosed that the shipment consisted of two hundred cases of brandy in glass. It recites that the two hundred cases were received in apparent good order. It further recites, "contents and condition of contents of packages unknown."

The brandy was in wooden boxes, not open to inspection at the time they were received by the carrier. The shipper is a wholesale liquor house; it is charged with the knowledge of the characteristics of the goods shipped and the effect of heat thereon. It also had knowledge of the temperature in Chicago on the date of shipment. The plaintiff's manager testified that they never notify carriers to protect brandy or whiskey from heat. If those engaged in the liquor business do not think brandy should be protected from heat, then the carrier ought not be required to afford such protection.

If fermentation of the brandy caused the corks to blow, the loss resulted from the operation of natural laws and the carrier would not be liable; and if it be true, as plaintiff's manager testified, that ordinarily there is no danger to brandy from heat, the fact that under certain circumstances heat may cause an expansion of the contents of a bottle of brandy to the extent that it blows the cork will not make the carrier liable for any resulting loss.

In *R. S. Austin, d b/a Evergreen Christmas Tree Co.* v. *Seaboard Air Line Railroad Co.*, 188 F. 2d 239, the court said:

The evidence reveals that on November 24, 1948, plaintiff delivered to the initial carrier at South Barre, Vermont, 606 bundles of spruce Christmas trees consigned to Miami Retail Grocers at Miami, Florida; that plaintiff loaded the shipment of trees in a heavy steel railroad box car provided by the initial carrier, and upon inspection found that the box car was in good and proper condition for the safe transportation of the shipment; that after the trees were loaded into the box car, the car was fumigated in accordance with the requirements of the United States Department of Agriculture, by turning into the car a liquid gas or chemical vapor designed to kill insects; that after fumigation of the car it was kept closed for several hours, and then opened and aired from four to eight hours, after which it was sealed tight to await shipment; that the car was delivered to Central Vermont Railway, Inc., and left South Barre, Vermont at 11 o'clock a.m. on November 26, 1948, and arrived in Miami, Florida, at 3:45 o'clock a.m. on Saturday, December 4, 1948; and that when the box car was opened at its destination, the inside of the car was wet, and heat and smoke in the car had caused all the Christmas trees to become burned and turn brown, so as to render the entire shipment a total loss. It was shown that plaintiff had been in the Christmas tree business at South Barre, Vermont for about twenty years; that he bought and cut its trees from sections in Vermont and Canada, and stacked them near the railroad siding at South Barre to await shipment from September to the last of November each year; that the trees comprising the shipment in question had been cut and left on the siding for sometime prior to the loading, and that heavy rains had made the trees wet and heavy to the extent that plaintiff had requested the carrier to make some allowance on the freight for this additional weight at the time of the shipment; that the temperature was approximately sixty degrees at the time and place of the shipment, but while the car was in transit and as it approached its destination the temperature increased to above eighty degrees. The evidence further discloses that the car containing the shipment was inspected by agents of the initial carrier, as well as by the plaintiff Austin; that further inspections were made along the route by each intervening carrier, and on each occasion the seal on the box car was unbroken and it was found to be in the same condition as when it was turned over to the initial carrier; and that the time required for delivery of the shipment was not unusual, but covered only a reasonable period.

The case was tried by the lower court without the intervention of a jury, and the court found from the evidence that the trees were loaded in a wet condition; that their damp condition when loaded, combined with the gradual increase in temperature while the shipment was en route, contributed to or caused the damaged condition of the trees; that the injury to the shipment was not caused by the defendent or connecting carrier, but that all reasonable care and diligence had been exercised by the initial and connecting carriers in the transportation of the shipment, and the damage or loss was therefore not chargeable to defendant. On appeal, the court said:

We are of opinion that district court properly held the defendant was not liable for the damage to this shipment. It is well settled that a carrier is not responsible for damage to a shipment caused solely by the operation of natural laws upon it, or by an act or default of the shipper which proximately causes the damage, *Shapiro* v. *Penn R. Co.*, 83 F. 2d 581; *Chesapeake & O. R. Co.* v. *A. F. Thompson Mfg. Co.*, 270 U.S. 416, 423; C. J. S., Carriers, Sec. 79a, ps. 152, 153; 9 Amer. Jur., Carriers, Sec. 728, p. 865.

Here, it was shown that the trees were loaded by plaintiff, and that an inspection was made by him before delivery of the shipment to the initial carrier. The box car furnished was in good condition, and was the type air-tight car ordered by plaintiff. Moreover, it is without dispute that the car was sealed, and that the shipment arrived at its destination with the seals unbroken. The evidence conclusively reveals that there was no unreasonable delay in the delivery of the shipment. Under such circumstances, the proof is more than adequate to overcome any inference of negligence on the part of the carrier, and the loss of the shipment must therefore be borne by the shipper. *Chesapeake & O. R. Co.* v. *A. F. Thompson Mfg. Co.*, 270 U.S. 416, 423; see also, *Atlantic Coast Line R. Co.* v. *Georgia Packing Co., et al.*, 165 F. 2d 169, 170.

We find no merit in the contention that because another car of Christmas trees left the point of shipment at the same time and in the same train as the shipment in question, and arrived in Miami undamaged, that defendant was therefore negligent in handling the damaged shipment in suit. It was not shown that the shipment in the other box car contained trees comprising the shipment in controversy. There is evidence that the damaged trees were cut a good length of time before they were shipped, and it is practically without dispute they were loaded in an almost air-tight box car by plaintiff in an excessively wet condition. It becomes patent that the heat and moisture in the car combined to scorch and damage the shipment en route without any fault on the part of the carrier. We therefore conclude there is no substantial evidence of negligence on the part of this defendant which proximately caused the loss of the shipment, and it is therefore not liable. *Chesapeake & O. R. Co.* v. *Thompson Co.,* 270 U.S. 416.

Tariff regulations purporting to provide that the publishing railroads shall be liable for in-transit loss or damage to shell eggs transported by them only to the extent that such loss or damage is in excess of specified percentages or *tolerances* were the subject of the decision of the Supreme Court in *Secretary of Agriculture* v. *United States,* 350 U.S. 162. The Commission in *Special Regulations, Eggs,* 284 I.C.C. 377, had concluded that since the tolerance represented preshipment and unavoidable damage not *caused by* the railroads, their deduction from damage claims could not limit the railroads' proper liability. However, the Supreme Court concluded that the facts as found by the Commission did not support this conclusion or establish that the tolerances permitted by the Commission's order would not operate to limit the carriers' liability in violation of Section 20(11) of the Interstate Commerce Act and set aside the Commission's order approving the tariff regulations. At 350 U.S. 170-173, the Supreme Court concluded its decision as follows:

A third major respect in which the Commission's report falls short of establishing that the tolerances will not limit liability results from its failure to consider the relationship between the physical damage represented by the tolerances and the legal loss for which damage claims are asserted. We have thus far assumed that "physical damage" could properly be equated with "loss" and have shown that, even on the assumption, the Commission has not shown the existence of a relationship between the damage represented by the tolerance and that included the damage claims which would justify the deduction authorized by the tariff provisions. In fact, however, it would appear that damage claims are based not on physical damage to individual eggs but rather on the loss of commercial acceptability of a case of eggs as a whole. As the Commission observed, the "commercial sound" case of eggs invariably contains some damage, and it is apparently only when the damage is so great as to make a case commercially unacceptable for its grade that it loses value. When a commercially unsound case is received, the consignee, rather than suffer the presumable greater loss that would result from selling it at a lower grade or as salvage, ordinarily "reconditions" the case by replacing the visibly damaged eggs and, if necessary, the packaging materials. From the character of this process as described by the Commission, it is apparent that the purpose is simply to make the case commercially sound and not to discover and remove all the damage present in the case. The damage claim, if liability is asserted against the carrier, then consists simply of the cost of reconditioning the case—that is, the labor and material costs plus the loss on the damaged eggs removed.

Viewed in the above terms, the probable effect of the tolerances on liability becomes even more apparent. Inasmuch as the highest grade specifications prescribed by the Department of Agriculture permit physical damage of 5%, a case of eggs received at destination with only the tolerance of 3% or 5% would presumably be considered "commercially sound" and be salable at the full price. Thus it would seem that presence of the tolerance damage by itself causes the consignee no loss and affords no basis for a damage claim, and that it is only when there is additional damage, making it necessary to recondition the case to make it commercially sound, that there is a loss for which a claim may be asserted. And if the *additional* damage is caused by the railroad, it necessarily follows that the cost of the reconditioning made necessary only because of that damage is a loss "caused by" the railroad within § 20(11). Any reduction of the damage claim in such circumstances would thus relieve the carrier of its proper liability.

The Commission's report thus leaves us not merely with uncertainty as to the impact of the tolerances, cf. *United States* v. *Chicago, M., St. P. & P. R. Co.*, 294 U.S. 499, 504-505, 510-511, but with the strong impression that they are likely to operate in a forbidden manner. The report contains no answers to the problems we have raised, if indeed the Commisison considered them at all. Since the report falls far short of establishing that the tolerances will not operate to limit carrier liability in violation of § 20(11), the order of the Commission approving the tolerances must be set aside, and the judgment below *Reversed.*

Condition of Shipment at Delivery to Carrier

In this section various aspects of carrier liability relating to the condition of the shipment when delivered to the carrier will be discussed. This generally involves questions of evidence—the manner of proof of the condition of the shipment. Problems arise primarily in two circumstances. First, carriers normally receive goods in packages and do not visually inspect the goods to verify their condition. The second type of problem arises because shipments are received in apparent good order by the carrier and delivered to the consignee in apparent good order, yet upon unpacking concealed loss or damage is discovered. These two situations are discussed in the following.

Apparent Good Order

The uniform standard rail and motor carrier bills of lading acknowledge receipt of "the property described . . . in apparent good order, except as noted (contents and condition of contents of packages unknown)." This means that as far as can be determined upon ordinary inspection, the shipment seems to be in good order. It is an admission that so far as external appearances are concerned the shipment is in good condition and this is sufficient to establish a prima facie case against the carrier that the goods were received in apparent good condition. If it later develops that the shipment was not in good order, the carrier may bring attention to this fact.

The Bill of Lading Act requires, in case of package goods, only that the carrier count the goods (49 U.S.C. sec. 101). Under these circumstances when a bill of lading acknowledges receipt of packaged goods and recites that the content and condition of contents are unknown, the bill is only prima facie evidence of receipt of the packages and does not establish the quantity or condition of the contents. (*Riff* v. *Yadkin R. R. Co.*, 127 S. E. 588) Such a recital relieves the carrier of liability for shortage of the contents of the package where the carrier can establish that the package was delivered in the same condition as received. (*Dworkutz* v. *N. Y. C.*, 129 N. E. 650) It renders the bill of lading insufficient prima facie evidence to show delivery of the purported contents of the package to the carrier. (*Shore* v. *N.Y.N.H. & H.R.R. Co.*, 121 A. 344) It is not an admission that the contents were in good condition. (*Louisville & N. R. Co.* v. *Hendricks*, 171 So. 273)

The effect of this recital that the goods were received in apparent good order, except as noted (contents and condition of contents unknown), is to place the burden of proof on the shipper to show delivery to the carrier of the contents of packages and their condition at time of delivery to the carrier. In other words, it becomes a question of fact as to whether the amount said to be in the package was actually in the package and in good order when received by the carrier for transportation.

In *Reider* v. *Thompson,* 197 F. 2d 158, a shipment of sheepskins and wool originated in Buenos Aires, Argentina, and was transported to New Orleans by steamship and there reshipped to Boston by rail. In commenting upon the certification as to "apparent good order" in the bill of lading issued by the rail carrier in New Orleans, the court said:

> The shipment in question followed an ocean shipment. Evidence was introduced to show that the exterior of the boxes were in good condition and there were no water stains apparent at the time of the issuance of the bill of lading and transshipment. The bill of lading recited receipt in "apparent good order," but that the "contents and condition of contents of packages (were) unknown." These provisions are considered to relate to the external condition of the packages and do not establish the condition of the contents. *The Neil Maersk,* 2

Cir., 91 F. 2d 932; *The Donde,* D. C., 287 F. 239. However, when packages are received by the carrier in acknowledged good *external* condition but are delivered by the carrier in a damaged or stained condition which could reasonably and logically be found to indicate that the discovered damage or deterioration of the contents resulted from the cause indicated by the condition of the external package, theretofore received in good condition, the trier of facts may infer from these circumstances that damage to the contents was occasioned by the negligence of the carrier in the respect indicated by the changed external condition of the package. "The outturn itself" may be considered as evidence. We, of course, do not anticipate the scope and effect of the evidence, or the weight and credit the trier of facts should accord it upon another trial when the testimony and all the circumstances of the case will be considered in the light of the applicable principle to which we have referred.

In *Flota Mercante del Estado* v. *Orient Ins. Co.,* 198 F. 2d 740, a shipment of aspirin was made by steamship company to Argentina and upon arrival some of the barrels containing the aspirin was found to be damaged. The goods had been receipted for by the steamship company as being received "in apparent good order and condition." The trial court found in favor of the claimant and upon appeal, among other things, the carrier contended that there had been no evidence presented that the aspirin was in actual good order and condition when received by it. In discussing this contention, the court said:

In support of its contention that appellee (claimant) must prove the actual good order of the aspirin at the time shipment was received by the carrier, as distinguished from its apparent good order and condition acknowledged by the bill of lading, appellant relies principally upon *The Chester Valley,* 5 Cir., 110 F. 2d 592, and *The Niel Maersk,* 2 Cir., 91 F. 2d 932. In *The Chester Valley, supra,* the goods were accepted by the carrier as being in apparent good order and condition and were delivered to the consignee in the same external condition in which they had been shipped. . . . In defense of the action to recover for damage to the goods, the carrier relied upon an exception in its bill of lading which absolved it from liability for loss or damage resulting from inherent vice, nature, defect of the goods, smell, taint, or evaporation from any other goods. It established by its evidence that the damage resulted from a cause in this execption. Under these facts, this Court held that in the absence of proof that the goods were in actual good order when received by the carrier, there could be no recovery.

In *The Niel Maersk, supra,* the carrier, in defense of an action to recover for loss or damage to a shipment of fish meal which was received by it in apparent good order, relied upon the failure of the libelants to prove the actual condition of the merchandise at the time of the shipment and also upon certain exceptions in the bills of lading which included inherent vice. The Court, observing that the tendency of fish meal to deteriorate depends on whether it contains an excess of moisture or oil held that in the absence of competent proof as to the moisture and oil content of the fish meal the libelants must fail in their efforts to recover damages against the carrier. Cf. *The Nichiyo Maru,* 4 Cir., 89 F. 2d 539.

In the present case there is no evidence as to inherent vice, or as to the nature of the particular shipment of aspirin, or of aspirin generally. The carrier made no attempt to prove that the goods were subject to spontaneous deterioration under any circumstances. Moreover, it was shown by the evidence that the loss of contents was due to breakage of the barrels and that the water damage was due to water which entered the broken barrels. It is clear that these barrels were not broken when accepted by the carrier for shipment. . . .

From the preceding case, it is clear that in those instances where a shipment is delivered at destination with the external appearance of the containers indicating damage to contents, the carrier is handicapped in its efforts to require the shipper to establish the actual good order of the contents at time of shipment. Where, however, there is no indication of damage to the containers, it appearing that the carrier delivered them in the same condition as received, it is incumbent upon the shipper to adduce by competent evidence the good condition of the contents when the shipment was delivered to the carrier in order to hold the carrier liable. While little fault can be found with this rule, it should be pointed out, however, that at least one court has adopted a contrary view. In *Morris Yuspeh* v. *Acme Fast Freight, Inc.,* 54 So. 2d 866, the plaintiff had purchased dry goods from a supplier in Chicago which were shipped to him via the services of the freight forwarder. It was alleged that when the goods were delivered they were in a damaged condition, the plaintiff allowing fifty percent depreciation on the merchandise which was water stained and bringing suit for the amount depreciated. A memorandum on the reverse of the defendant's freight bill, signed by defendant's agent, indicated that the goods had been recoopered by defendant and at that time they were soiled. Plaintiff alleged that the goods had been delivered to the freight forwarder in good condition in Chicago and had been damaged thereafter while in defendant's custody; this the defendant denied. Plaintiff was unable to produce the bill of lading issued by the defendant in Chicago and in lieu thereof had executed a bond of indemnity. Plaintiff did not secure depositions from the Chicago shipper as to the condition of the goods and containers at time delivered to the freight forwarder nor did plaintiff request the court to require the defendant to produce its shipping order copy of the bill of lading issued. In deciding the case the court said:

The failure of plaintiff to make proof that the carrier received the merchandise from the shipper in good condition is fatal to his case.

Under the Interstate Commerce Act. § 20, paragraph 11, as amended, 49 U.S.C.A. § 20(11) the delivering carrier under an interstate contract of affreightment or through bill of lading is liable for goods damaged in transit by it or any of the common carriers to which such property may be delivered or over whose line such property may pass. The liability of the carrier in such cases is for the full actual loss, damage or injury to the property at the place of destination at the time delivery of the goods should have been made.

In order for the consignee to make out a prima facie case against the carrier for damage to goods sustained in transit, it is necessary for him, under the principle so well established to allege and prove (1) receipt of the goods by the carrier in good order and condition, (2) that the shipment arrived at its destination in a damaged condition, and (3) the amount of the loss. *Bancroft* v. *Yazoo & M. V. R. Co.*, 194 La. 115, 193 So. 481; *L. Frank & Co.* v. *I. C. R. R. Co.*, 43 So. 2d 88; *Colotra* v. *Railway Express Agency,* 32 So. 2d 69; *Arwady* v. *T. & N. O. R. Co.*, 18 So. 2d 339. See also 9 Am. Jur., Carriers §§ 834-835.

Counsel for plaintiff argue that the presumption arises that the merchanise was in good condition when shipped, from the fact of the receipt of the goods by the carrier without objection or exception noted in its bill of lading or shipping receipt to the effect that the merchandise was otherwise than in good condition. We are cited to 13 C. J. S., Carriers, § 254(d), pp. 538-539, reading.

> No presumption exists that the goods were in good condition when delivered to the carrier. The presumption arises, however, from the fact of the receipt of the goods by the carrier without objection or exception noted in the bill of lading or shipping receipt, that as far as the condition was apparent on ordinary inspection the goods were in good condition.
>
> . . . If the damage to goods by water was apparent from exterior inspection on their arrival at destination, the carrier's failure to note the condition when receiving the goods, raises the presumption that the condition did not then exist. The burden is on the carrier to show that goods open to inspection were in bad condition when received by it. Where there is proof that the goods were damaged in transit, the burden is on the carrier to show that they were in bad condition at the time of shipment. . . ."

The argument proceeds on the premise that it was incumbent upon the carrier to issue a bill of lading, couched in terms fixed by the Interstate Commerce Commission, which contracts are made uniform throughout the United States in interstate shipments, and which uniform bill of lading is to be implied herein as the contract of shipment.

Counsel take the position that in the absence of the defendant's production of a copy of the bill of lading showing exceptions noted therein, the implication results that there were none, and that the merchandise was in good order and condition when accepted for transportation by the defendant.

We cannot agree with counsel that the burden rested upon defendant to produce its copy of the bill of lading. The law provides what must be proved by a consignee to make out a prima facie case against the carrier. Among other things, plaintiff carried the burden of showing to the court that when the merchandise was delivered to the Acme Fast Freight, Inc., in Chicago, the shipment was in an undamaged condition. The only evidence which plaintiff adduced regarding the condition of the merchandise is his statement that when the shipment reached him in New Orleans it was in a damaged condition as a result of having become wet.

It seems to us that if plaintiff's demands are valid, he could have made out his case, notwithstanding the loss or mislaying of the bill of lading, by introducing other available evidence going to show the sound condition of the merchandise when delivered to the carrier. For instance, he might have proved that fact, if true, by obtaining the evidence of the consignor. If it was plaintiff's choice to rely upon the bill of lading, means are provided by law whereby he might have secured the carrier's copy thereof; or he might have proved the recitals of the document by parol, after laying the proper foundation.

Plaintiff's testimony is silent so far as any mention of the bill of lading is concerned. He was content to submit his case on a showing that the shipment indicated that it had been damaged by water before delivery to him from defendant's truck. He now seeks to throw upon the defendant the burden of proving that the merchandise was not in such damaged condition when received for shipment, notwithstanding that the law clearly imposes that burden upon him. We have not been cited to any authority, and our own research reveals none, holding that it is the duty of the defendant carrier to establish that the shipment was not in good order when received, in the absence of any affirmative proof emanating from plaintiff that the merchandise was in good order and condition when accepted by the carrier for shipment.

Plaintiff also contends that whereas there is no objection or exception noted on the freight bill indicating that the property was in a damaged condition when received by the carrier, it should be assumed, in the absence of such notation on the freight bill, that the merchandise must necessarily have been in good condition. We do not think that because there was no notation on the bill for the carriage charges that such circumstance in any way militates against the defendant in this case, as we know of no provisions of law which make it mandatory for the carrier to note the condition of the shipment on the freight bill. We are unwilling to imply, solely because no such notation was made, that the merchandise, when received by the carrier, was in any condition other than that in which it was at the time of delivery in New Orleans.

While on first impression this decision may seem open to criticism for not taking into account the recoopering of the shipment and the poor condition of the shipment at the time of delivery as indicia of damage in transit, on close analysis there is little basis for quarreling with it. The dissenting judge would reach the result argued for by plaintiff through an assumption of a fact not in evidence and a questionable presumption based on that unproven fact. The dissent said:

I respectfully dissent. No bill of lading issued by the carrier appears in the record. Under the Carmack Amendment to the Interstate Commerce Act, 49 U.S.C.A. Sec. 20, it is provided that the carrier must issue a bill of lading in conformity with the provisions of the act, and as a result thereof, such contracts are uniform throughout the United States. A carrier has no authority to enter into any other contract. Contracts for interstate shipments must be evidenced by a bill of lading, which necessarily implies that such contracts must be in writing. Hence the provisions of such bill of lading cannot be varied by parol testimony.

Where a carrier accepts freight for interstate transportation but issues no bill of lading to the shipper, the uniform bill of lading prescribed by the Interstate Commerce Commission will be implied as the contract of shipment. *Western Maryland Railway Company* v. *Cross,* 96 W. Va. 666, 123 S. E. 572; *Standard Combed Thread Co.* v. *Pennsylvania Railroad Co.,* 88 N. J. Law 257, 95 Atlantic 1002; *Aman* v. *Dover and S. R. Co.,* 179 N. C. 310, 102 S. E. 392; and C. J. S. Verbo Carriers Section 123(b), test 58, page 237.

Therefore we must read into the instant case the uniform bill of lading as prescribed by the Interstate Commerce Commission; we then have before us a clean bill of lading with no exception noted thereon, which it prima facie proof that the shipment was delivered to the carrier in good condition. At this point of the instant case, the burden of proof shifted and it became incumbent upon the carrier, if it had actually issued a bill of lading with exceptions noted thereon to produce it as a matter of defense.

There is no proof by the carrier either as to the existence of a bill of lading or any exceptions noted thereon. If a bill of lading was issued by the carrier, with exceptions noted thereon, the defendants would certainly have produced their copy to establish this fact.

I am, therefore, of the opinion that plaintiff made out a prima facie case and has proven that the merchandise was delivered to the initial carrier in good condition and that the shipment arrived at its destination in a damaged condition.

It is clear from this quotation that the dissenting judge assumed that the carrier did not issue a bill of lading to the shipper: "Where a carrier . . . *issues no bill of lading* to the shipper. . . ." But this assumption is not supported by the record. Plaintiff did not allege that defendant had failed to issue a bill of lading. In fact, counsel's argument that defendant must produce its copy suggests that plaintiff knew or believed that a bill of lading was issued.

Following the dissenting judge's reasoning would throw the burden onto the carrier of establishing the condition of the shipment at the time it was received for shipment whenever the plaintiff, for whatever reason, failed to offer into evidence the bill of lading or other evidence of the condition of the goods at the time of shipment. In effect, the carrier would be presumed responsible for every *claimed* injury until he could prove to the contrary. But the burden is on the shipper, as the court recognized, to show that the goods were received by the carrier in good order and delivered by it in bad order, or at least to show that the goods were in better condition when received by the carrier than they were when delivered by it. Failing this, plaintiff has failed to make a prima facie case.

This is not to say that a claimant may never properly seek to have the carrier produce its copy of the bill of lading in the court. If plaintiff can explain the absence of his copy, the court will consider a request that the defendant produce its copy. But this was not done in the case at hand, and the unexplained failure of the claimant to produce the original bill of lading which should have been in his possession does not justify the presumption that no exception was taken on it and does not justify the shifting of the burden to the carrier to "disprove" its liability.

Concealed Loss and Damage

Concealed loss and damage claims are the source of frequent and acrimonious controversies between carriers and claimants. At least part of this comes about because of the prevalent notion that the carrier is absolutely liable for any loss or damage found after transportation—that he is an "insurer" of the good delivery of the goods. But there are exceptions to the carrier's absolute liability, as noted. One of those exceptions, for damage due to the act or default of the shipper, probably plays a much more significant role in concealed loss and damage than most people in transportation realize.

Concealed loss or concealed damage means that no one has noted any external evidence of the loss or damage which is discovered when the consignee (or, in some cases, the customer of the consignee) opens the package on or after ultimate delivery. Usually the circumstances surrounding a claim for concealed loss or damage are such that the claimant in the event of litigation would have serious difficulty in establishing a prima facie case of carrier liability.

The reasons for this are readily apparent. A carrier accepts packaged goods from a shipper for transportation and gives the shipper a receipt indicating that the property is received in "apparent good order (contents and condition of contents unknown)." The carrier takes the packages and hauls them to the designated consignee and receives a receipt for them indicating that the goods have been delivered in "good order," leading to the inference that the carrier delivered the goods in the same condition as received from the shipper. Later, the consignee opens the packages and in one or more of them discovers that some of the merchandise is missing or is in damaged condition. While the shipper and the consignee may firmly believe that the missing goods were lost or stolen while in the carrier's possession or that the damage was occasioned by the rough handling or carelessness of the carrier's employees, it is only natural for the carrier to entertain some doubts as to whether or not the loss or damage is its responsibility. After all, carriers do not have a monopoly on damaging freight or on employing "light-fingered" employees.

The nature of these claims and the absence of external evidence, particularly in the case of concealed damage, suggests that the packing may well be at fault. Concealed "loss" may frequently be no more than careless checking when preparing the shipment or careless checking on unpacking, with the goods being commingled with other stock before the "shortage" can be verified.

In no other phase of voluntary adjustment of freight loss and damage is the possibility for fraudulent claims more prevalent than in connection with concealed loss and damage claims. Yet traffic managers for some of this country's outstanding corporations have no hesitance in adopting an uncompromising attitude relative to securing payment of these claims, which in the vast majority of instances fall within what can be appropriately termed the "twilight zone" insofar as proved or prima facie carrier liability is concerned. Carriers endeavoring to point out that liability has not been clearly established and attempting to decline or settle on compromise basis, claims within this category are frequently told to "pay or else." Naturally the big shipper or consignee is enabled to play one carrier against another by threat of diversion of traffic, with the inevitable result that the small or occasional shipper or consignee is the victim of discrimination and the big shipper or consignee the recipient of an undue and illegal preference. The increase in number of concealed loss and damage claims filed in recent years together with the readiness with which they are paid has greatly contributed to a deterioration in shippers' efforts to properly package shipments and particularly, to their failure to provide proper and adequate interior packaging, and at the same time made a serious inroad upon the carriers' revenues. Suspicion of carriers sometimes is aroused after receiving an increase in rates to note that simultaneously claims of those having to pay the increased charges in the concealed category rise to a point to just about offset the additional revenue realized.

The statement that "a claim for concealed loss or damage is just as valid as any other claim" is frequently bandied around if this statement in itself automatically established the prima facie liability of the carrier.

The statement is in many instances paraphrased to "a concealed damage claim is just as *legitimate* as any other claim." A claim, however, is merely an assertion of liability against another; in and of itself no claim establishes carrier liability even on a prima facie basis. At most, a claim merely indicates that the claimant asserts that he is entitled to compensation for some injury for which claimant alleges another legally responsible. Subsequently investigation may and frequently does develop that for some of many reasons the carrier is not legally liable. All claims should be carefully investigated and particularly those involving concealed loss and damage; no claim should be paid until this investigation has been completed and the facts developed convincing to the carrier that its liability has been established as a result of some acts or omissions on its part while the goods were in its custody.

The difficulty in connection with claims for loss and damage of a concealed nature is in definitely locating responsibility with the carrier. Where the claim is for alleged concealed loss or damage, a prima facie case against the carrier frequently and in most instances does not exist. The facts will usually indicate that the carrier delivered the shipment in the same condition as received from the shipper, namely, in apparent good order. It therefore becomes the claimant's burden to establish in the case of alleged concealed loss that the missing merchandise was actually shipped and at time of delivery to consignee was actually missing from the shipment and, in the case of concealed damage, to establish that the goods were properly packaged in actual good condition within the container and at time of delivery to consignee were in damaged condition. Simply stated, claimant is required to establish that neither the shipper nor the consignee could have been responsible for the loss or damage and as a matter of logical deduction the loss or damage therefor must have occurred while the goods were in the carrier's possession. This is usually extremely difficult to establish.

A prima facie case of carrier liability usually is established where goods are received by carrier in apparent good order and at time of delivery observed and noted on the carrier's records as received damaged. In the case of concealed loss or damage, however, the carrier's receipt indicates that the goods were delivered in good order so the essentials of a prima facie case of carrier liability are lacking. The receipt, however, is only prima facie evidence that the contents of the container were in actual good condition. Like any other receipt, the actual facts may be established by clear and convincing evidence that the receipt does not properly reflect the actual conditions. The burden, however, of establishing this by clear and convincing evidence is upon the claimant. He must establish that all of the goods were in good condition and properly protected within the container when the carrier received them, and at time of delivery at destination all of the goods shipped were not within the container or that they were damaged when received.

Since the run-of-the-mill claim for concealed loss or damage is for a comparatively small sum, carriers have become lax in their investigation of them. Unquestionably unscrupulous claimants have been able to take advantage of carriers where such laxity exists. In many instances the person filing and signing claims of this nature will be compelled to rely upon the integrity of another regarding the validity of the claim. For example, numerous concerns have branch stores and warehouses located at many points and the traffic department at the concern's general office necessarily must depend upon the written record supplied by employees of the firm located many miles away and with whom there is no personal contact. While, as a general rule, in the conduct of business there is a natural desire to believe that most people are honest until circumstances clearly indicate otherwise, this principle must be governed by a rule of reason. Those who would never think of robbery by force sometimes in the conduct of business have no hesitation or qualms of conscience in parking illegally, speeding, and otherwise violating traffic laws. The consciences of individuals are not exactly alike.

For a receiving clerk of a branch store or warehouse and, in some instances, for his immediate supervisors, when shipments are received and receipted for in good order and subsequently damaged in opening the container or in handling after receipt or even after display upon the counter or shelves, there is a tremendous temptation to allege that the damage was the result of handling in transportation. This is not idle speculation; it is a known fact that this temptation frequently is encountered and a prevailing belief on the part of some that these claims are covered by the carrier's insurance quite often serves to encourage the filing of claims for what is loss or damage for which the consignee or his employees are fully aware no carrier liability exists. A carrier over a period of time usually is able to ferret out the dishonest claimant and careful investigation is devoted to his claims. Some receivers in fact would be shocked to learn the reputation they have established with the carrier industry. The reluctance on the part of the receiver's traffic department to publicize to receiving personnel the penalties for fraudulent filing of claims or to take other steps to discourage unjust shifting of responsibility to the carrier gives an inference of ratifying or condoning the practice.

In *Colotra* v. *Railway Express Agency,* 32 So. 2d 69, the plaintiff brought suit seeking recovery of $210.81 for damage to a large electric neon sign. Defendant had received the sign in Wisconsin packed in two boxes for delivery to plaintiff in Louisiana. Delivery was made upon examination it was found that eighteen pieces of neon tubing were broken. At the trial, the plaintiff failed to prove that the sign was in undamaged condition when delivered to the defendant in Wisconsin. The lower court in finding in favor of defendant stated:

> The provisions of the Interstate Commerce Act oblige a carrier to deliver merchandise entrusted it for carriage in the condition it was received. However, where a plaintiff seeks to recover under the provisions of said Act he must make some showing that the goods were in good condition at the time they were received by the carrier. . . . In a case of this character the plaintiff must at least make out a prima facie case of liability and where he fails to prove that the goods were in good condition when delivered to the carrier, he has failed to make out such a case.

In sustaining the lower court, the Louisiana Court of Appeals said:

> We fully agree with the trial judge's statement wherein he states that the Supreme Court, in the case of *Bancroft* v. *Yazoo & M. V. Railroad Co.*, 194 La. 115, 193 So. 481, held "that in order to recover it was necessary for the consignee to allege and prove that the carrier received the shipment in good condition, that the shipment arrived at its destination in a damaged condition, and the amount of the loss.

A review of court cases which indicate the type of proof necessary to establish carrier liability for concealed loss and damage clearly shows the difficulty which would be encountered by claimants if required to resort to litigation. This burden and the expense involved clearly point out that as a matter of convenience to both claimant and carrier it is desirable that these claims be adjusted on a voluntary basis with each party willing to "give and take." The uncompromising attitude on the part of some claimants to recognize the carrier's position from a legal viewpoint in regard to claims in the concealed category, however, often indicates a complete refusal to recognize the actual legal status of these claims. The refusal of some carriers likewise to investigate in detail these claims and the readiness with which they are frequently paid in full frequently as a result of actual or implied threat of "diversion of traffic" eventually, it is believed, must compel the enactment of legislation not only for the purpose of deterring the filing of fraudulent claims but also to prevent or at least reduce discrimination and undue preference. If such legislation is eventually enacted, the claimants and carriers have only themselves to blame. The decisions of the courts relating to these claims is definitely convincing that they cannot be readily regarded in the same light as other claims where prima facie carrier liability is more readily apparent.

In *Shore* v. *New York, N. H. & H. R. R. Co.*, 121 A. 344, Sweet, Orr & Co. delivered a box with contents described as shirts to rail carrier in Philadelphia consigned to plaintiff in Stamford. Delivery was made, consignee took possession, removed the box and delivered it back to defendant for return back to the shipper in Philadelphia. Neither plaintiff nor defendant had any actual knowledge of what was in the box as it remained securely closed. Defendant's receipt for the return movement read in part: "Received . . . property described below in apparent good order, except as noted (contents and condition of contents of packages unknown) 1 Box shirts." Defendant transported the box in the same condition as received from plaintiff to Elizabeth, N. J., where the box was given to a connecting rail carrier and later was lost. Plaintiff brought suit to recover for the value of the shirts. In denying recovery, the court said, in part:

> To support this action against the defendant, a common carrier of goods, the plaintiff must have established (1) the delivery of the goods to the carrier; (2) the undertaking on its part to transport them to the named consignee; and (3) the breach of its contract by the defendant through its failure to deliver the goods to the consignee . . . all that it (the evidence) shows is the delivery to the defendant of a box purporting to contain shirts. . . . The plaintiff relies upon the bill of lading as prima facie evidence of the receipt of the goods. Unexplained or uncontradicted, that proof would be sufficient to establish delivery if the bill of lading delivered by the defendant to the plaintiff recited an absolute delivery, without qualification as to quantity, condition, or contents of the box. . . . But this bill of lading does qualify the receipt of the box by its recital: "The property described below (1 box shirts) in apparent good order, except as noted (contents and condition of contents unknown)". . . . This constituted an express limitation upon the contract of carriage to the goods received. . . . It was still necessary . . . to show that he in fact delivered the goods to the defendant for which he sues. . . . It was therefore necessary for the plaintiff, since he had no means of proving the contents of this box at time of delivery to the defendant, to show its contents at the time of delivery to the railroad at Philadelphia. . . . Failing to prove the contents of the box when delivered to the defendant or to the railroad at Philadelphia, the plaintiff might have relied upon proof of the contents of the box when it left the possession of Sweet, Orr & Co., and supplemented this proof that the condition of the box remained the same when it was delivered to the railroad at Philadelphia, and of the fact that, thereafter its condition did not change. In either of these ways the plaintiff could have met its burden of proving the delivery of the goods to the defendant for which loss he sues.

In *Canfield* v. *Baltimore and Ohio R. Co.*, 75 N. Y. 144, the evidence indicated that the property was delivered to the defendant at Washington for transportation to consignee in New York. After delivery the goods were stored in plaintiff's basement and several days later upon opening the containers, loss of some of the contents was discovered and suit for loss instituted against the carrier. At the trial no evidence was given as to the care taken of the goods from the time of delivery to time the loss was discovered. In denying recovery, the court said:

> I cannot think however that there was any legal proof upon which a finding could be based that the goods were abstracted from the packages while in possession of the defendants or the Pennsylvania R. R. Co. and before they were delivered . . . in New York. This was necessary to be shown by the plaintiff as a condition of their recovery against the defendant. The burden was upon them to prove it and there was no presumption in their favor in regard to it. The affirmative resting upon them, it was not sufficient for them to show a state of facts as consistent with the loss having occurred after as before delivery of the property in New York, yet this is the most that can be made of the evidence.

Regarding plaintiff's failure to offer evidence as to the care taken of the goods, security of the storage place, and the time lapse from delivery to discovery of the loss, the court said:

> These proofs taking the view of them most favorable to the plaintiff, tended quite as strongly to show that the goods were abstracted while in the basement as while in the hands of defendant. The presumption, if any, was that they continued in the box, as they were delivered to the defendant, until after its delivery in New York, and the burden being upon the plaintiffs to prove affirmatively the loss while in the defendant's control, they failed to do so.

In *Breazeale* v. *American Railway Express Co., Inc.*, 137 So. 585, there was shipped to the plaintiff via the defendant carrier a lot of china and cut glass in two boxes, valued at $400. Shipment was delivered to the express company in apparent good order and delivered to the plaintiff in apparently the same condition. Some time after delivery, the packages were opened and breakage was discovered. Claim was filed for $250 and an effort was made to adjust the matter amicably. These efforts failed and suit was instituted. At the trial the claimant failed to prove just how the goods were packed for shipment. In holding the carrier not liable, the court said:

> Rule 18 of the Freight Classification Rules, provides as follows: "All shipments must be so prepared or packed as to insure safe transportation with ordinary care on the part of the Express Company." And further: "Glassware, other fragile articles, or article in glass or earthenware must be boxed, barreled, or crated and so packaged as to insure safe transportation with ordinary care; if

not so packed and plainly marked to indicate the nature of the contents, the company shall not be liable for damage to shipments, except when proved to be negligent." The only testimony as to how this glass was packed was by Mrs. Breazeale, who testified that, when the packages were opened, "they were packed in excelsior, and newspapers on the bottom and the top." There is no testimony as to the size of the packages, what they were composed of, how much excelsior was used, or the quantity of newspapers. It was not shown that the boxes were marked to indicate that the contents was glass, earthenware, or fragile articles. And there is complete lack of testimony as to defendant's negligence. The burden of the proof was upon the plaintiff to show that these articles were in fact, properly packed, and marked to indicate their contents. Failing in this, it was incumbent upon the plaintiff to prove defendant was negligent. In this, plaintiff also failed.

In *Elder & Johnston Co.* v. *Commercial Motor Freight, Inc. of Ind.*, 115 N. E. 2d 179, the court clearly refuted the contention of many receivers that damage discovered on opening of a container received from a carrier must be automatically presumed to have occurred during transportation. In this case, the court said:

The defendant, a trucking company, transported the mirrors from Louisville, Kentucky, to plaintiff's store in Dayton, Ohio, where the crates containing the mirrors were unloaded from the truck onto a loading platform on the first floor of plaintiff's store. The three crates, which in the aggregate weighed 1,215 pounds, were then put on skids, placed on the elevator and taken to the third floor of the store, where the crates were removed from the elevator and placed on the floor to be opened. A hammer was used to pry open the crates, which had been nailed. There were no marks on the outside of the crates showing damage or indicating mishandling. There is not a scintilla of evidence showing the care exercised by the plaintiff's employees in handling the crates from the time they were taken from the truck until they were opened on the third floor. *Before the presumption of negligence rule could have application it would have been necessary to rule out the possibility of damage to the crates after they were removed from the truck.* This was not done. Under the facts in this case a presumption of negligence on the part of the carrier did not arise, and, therefore, the plaintiff was unable to fix liability on the carrier in the absence of facts showing its negligence. (Emphasis added.)

The general rule is that where goods are received in good condition by a carrier for shipment and are delivered in a damaged condition at the destination a prima facie case of carrier liability is made out. (*Association of Maryland Pilots* v. *Baltimore O. R.*, 304 F. Supp. 458; *Condakes* v. *Southern Pacific Co.*, 303 F. Supp. 1158; *Thomas Electronics, Inc.* v. *H. W. Taynton Co.*, 277 F. Supp. 639; *Skaggs* v. *Midland Val. R.*, 233 F. Supp. 1004; *East Texas Motor Freight Lines* v. *Hutchinson & Son*, 241 S. W. 2d 759) Under the *Elder & Johnston* decision, this rule has no application where the goods, after being received, are transported by consignee's employees to another portion of his premises where damage is discovered and no evidence is presented as to care exercised by the employees handling and transported the goods after receipt. The decision in this case, as a practical matter must, however, be regarded and evaluated in the light of its own facts, as should all decisions. If the plaintiff in this case had gone to the trouble to present evidence as to the care exercised by its employees in removing the goods after unloading from the truck to the third floor of its store and the care exercised in opening the container, and such evidence was convincing that the discovered damage could not have occurred after receipt, undoubtedly the court would have decided in its favor on the grounds that plaintiff had established a prima facie case of carrier liability. The plaintiff ignored this basic and essential proof, however. It preferred instead, as many do, to rely on the erroneous assumption that once a container has been in the custody of a carrier damage discovered at any subsequent time must have been the result of carrier's negligence.

Today retail concerns have widely adopted the practice of advertising merchandise "in original factory container," evidently to assure the prospective purchaser that the item is not a floor sample or one which has been taken in trade or repossessed. Delivery of such merchandise still in the unopened original container is made by some form of transportation—the purchaser's own vehicle, the store's truck, or by common or contract carrier. After reaching the domicile of the purchaser and upon being opened, damage may be discovered and the item replaced, the store accepting the return of the damaged item. The transportation from the store may be only a few blocks or many miles; nevertheless, there is seldom reluctance in endeavoring to charge the carrier delivering the goods to the store for the damage. This problem of prior or subsequent transportation of goods in original unopened container is more fully covered in the following section but the preceding case is pertinent to indicate the weak legal status of trying to saddle the carrier with liability.

An indication as to the proof necessary to establish a prima facie case of carrier liability is found in *Railway Express Agency, Inc.* v. *Smith,* 212 F. 2d 47. In this case, the evidence indicated that two highly valued porcelian urns had been packed by a company which had more than forty years' experience in packing fragile articles for shipment. A witness from this company testified that he had personally supervised the packing of the urns which had been wrapped in cotton, packed in excelsior and placed in cardboard drums which were enclosed in slatted wooden crates. The witness stated positively that the urns were not broken when delivered to the express company. Upon arrival of the crates at destination, they were placed on the floor of the warehouse of the consignee in a place where they were out of the way of people moving about. They remained there two or three days before they were opened *in the presence of a representative of the express company.* The evidence clearly indicated that no one had touched the crates or moved them during the interim from delivery to opening. The warehouse worker who finally unpacked the goods had twenty years' experience in such work. The joint inspection report clearly indicated that the articles were packed in the manner alleged by the company packing the goods. On the basis of this evidence, the court held:

> In Tennessee which supplies the governing law of the instant case, it has been established for more than half a century that when property has been delivered in good condition to a carrier and has been damaged while in its possession (nothing else appearing), the necessary presumption is that the carrier has been negligent in handling the goods, leading to the inevitable conclusion that the burden is cast upon the carrier to remove this presumption.

In this case the plaintiff went to great particularity in establishing that the goods were properly packed and in good condition when delivered to the carrier at origin and in making out a prima facie case that the goods were not damaged during handling after receipt or while opening the containers; in fact, when the containers were opened, a representative of the carrier was present and witnessed the opening. Perhaps more evidence was adduced to establish prima facie carrier liability than would have been required, but claimant overlooked no possibility in this regard and put in all the facts available. On the other hand, in many instances claims are filed where the carrier has either not been notified of concealed damage, notified many days after delivery, not afforded an opportunity to make an inspection or, if afforded such opportunity, found upon arrival at consignee's premises that the container and packaging has either disappeared or been destroyed. Surprisingly, the claimant will often ignore these factors and vigorously insist upon claim payment. More surprising and perhaps disappointing, the carrier will frequently agree to pay!

As the preceding cases indicate, the claimant in concealed loss and damage has a definite burden to establish certain essential facts before there exists a prima facie case of carrier liability. It is seldom that these claims become involved in litigation for that very reason. Statistics indicate that carriers voluntarily pay millions of dollars for concealed loss and damage each year and that claims paid which fall in this category generally increase substantially each year. While the law as to proof of liability is equitable to the carrier, there is a growing reluctance to rely upon the law, many carrier representatives contending that courts of lower jurisdiction will not be receptive to the legal aspect favoring the carrier, others contending that expense of litigation makes it impractical to defend litigation, while others are simply indifferent to the strength of their position or yield to pressure and actual or implied threats of traffic diversion. The problem is not new; on the contrary, it has long been recognized. In fact, the carriers for many years have had in existence certain safeguards and requirements which, if observed, would greatly alleviate the problem. Although these requirements have existed for many years and are generally recognized as fair, reasonable, and necessary in order to prevent injustices such as rebates, discrimination, and undue preference, they are frequently subjected to severe criticism and attack by not only the inexperienced and novice but also by otherwise highly ethical and dedicated members of the traffic management profession. To assure its standing as a profession, the enactment by those interested in its advancement of a code of ethics to prevent the possibility of injustices in these matters eventually may be found necessary or, if this is not feasible, legislation may be required to achieve the ultimate objective.

Both motor and rail carriers have adopted to govern the members of their respective claim organizations a set of rules entitled "Regulations Governing the Inspection of Freight Before or After Delivery to Consignee and Adjustments of Claims for Loss or Damage Thereon." The motor and rail regulations in this regard are practically identical. The rules according to their preamble are prescribed "in order to avoid any discrimination" and "so that practices may be certain and uniform in the treatment of claims." These regulations among other things require that loss or damage discovered after delivery to consignee shall be reported by the consignee to carrier immediately upon discovery and, in any event, within fifteen days after receipt, and the contents and container held for inspection by carrier. Notice may be given carrier by telephone or in person but in either event shall be confirmed by mail. It is further provided that carrier shall make inspection within 48 hours and that this inspection shall include examination of the goods, checking of contents with invoice, weighing for comparison with shipping weight, and examination of the container. It is also provided that if investigation "develops that the loss (or damage) occurred with carriers, the fifteen-day clause shall not be invoked."

The fifteen-day period for reporting of concealed loss and damage was originally adopted by rail carriers in 1920 and at that time was "approved" by the National Industrial Traffic League, one of the nation's largest organizations of shipper-receiver traffic representatives. Carriers have never contended that the fifteen-day requirement has the sanction of the Interstate Commerce Commission or courts of law. The rules are simply what they purport to be, namely, reasonable and lawful carrier regulations which if observed will greatly expedite disposition of claims for concealed loss or damage on a voluntary basis. If the requirements are not observed and there is doubt on the carrier's part that the loss or damage occurred while the goods were in its possession, the carrier may refuse voluntary payment of the claim and leave the claimant to pursue his legal remedy.

It is often argued by claimants that the fifteen-day rule cannot be enforced at law against a claimant. This contention ignores the basic reason for this regulation of carriers. The rule in itself is a reasonable requirement and is not illegal as there is no statutory prohibition against carriers establishing reasonable requirements to prevent discrimination and to promote uniform treatment of claimants; on the contrary, reasonable regulations designed for these purposes when not specifically prohibited by statute would seem deserving of legal sanction. While no reported decision of any court involving the legal interpretation of the fifteen-day rule has been located, the absence of such decision after the fifty years' existence of the rule, and its wide observation are such as to indicate a widely prevalent custom concerning which a court might well take judicial notice.

As indicated by the decisions discussed in this section, the claimant in litigating a case involving concealed loss or damage would be required by the courts to produce sufficient evidence to establish that the loss or damage did not occur before shipper tendered the goods to the carrier or after the carrier delivered the goods to consignee and that the goods were properly packed. In the event of litigation, the carrier would usually be able to establish not only by documentary evidence that it delivered the goods in apparently the same condition as received but also by use of its own employees give corroboration to show that the exterior of the container at time of delivery showed no evidence of rough handling or pilferage while in transit, and that the shipment had received careful handling. The production of such evidence would provide strong support for establishing the defense of improper packaging by shipper or to indicate that the damage occurred after delivery to the consignee. The fifteen-day rule is simply meant to establish a line beyond which the carrier ordinarily will not go in the voluntary settlement of claims without some evidence from the consignee that the loss or damage could not have occurred while the goods were in its possession. In view of the quantity of proof which would be required of consignee if the case were litigated, the rule on its face is extremely liberal.

When the consignee fails to notify the carrier within fifteen days, the carrier should satisfy itself that the loss or damage occurred while the goods were in possession of its line or its connecting carrier before making voluntary payment. Sometimes there may exist quite reasonable grounds for suspicion that the loss or damage might have occurred after delivery through theft, pilferage or mishandling by consignee's own employees or others. Under these circumstances, it should be borne in mind that the goods were possibly in the possession of the carrier for only a few days. On the other hand, it will probably be true that the material was in the hands of the consignee and its employees for many times that period and quite often moved from place and not always kept under supervision. If the consignee can present a plausible case for carrier liability, regardless of the fact that no opportunity for inspection within a reasonable time was granted, then voluntary settlement will usually be made. If on the other hand claimant is unable to satisfy the carrier that the loss or damage is the carrier's responsibility, voluntary settlement will usually be refused.

The inspection rules recognize that basically it is not enough for a claimant to show merely that goods were damaged; in the case of concealed loss and damage, claimant must go just a little further and establish that the loss or damage occurred while the goods were in carrier's possession. The consignee observing the rules and making a reasonably prompt inspection of the goods after receipt from the carrier is given by these rules an opportunity of having an inspection promptly made by the carrier's representative while it is possible to develop more definite information as to the cause of the loss or damage. This inspection consists in recording in writing the available pertinent facts and the report is signed by both the consignee's and carrier's representatives. A copy of this report is left with the consignee and assists him in supporting his claim when filed.

Some claimants vigorously argue that the fifteen-day inspection rule violates Section 20(11) which prohibits carriers from establishing a period of less than nine months within which claims may be filed. However, these rules do not violate that statute as they do not attempt to outlaw the claim on the grounds of failure to file within a stipulated time. They simply establish a procedure for the inspection of freight on which loss or damage is discovered after delivery. Declination of claims because of failure to report concealed loss or damage within the fifteen-day period is not on grounds that claimant failed to file within the nine month period *but on the grounds that claimant failed to present sufficient evidence to locate responsibility for the loss or damage with the carrier.* A carrier always has the right to decline any seasonably filed claim which in its opinion is not its liability; in fact, it is the carrier's duty to pay only those claims which its investigation indicate are its liability.

It should also be remembered that these rules are not meant to provide an arbitrary basis for declining claims. If the concealed loss or damage is reported within the fifteen-day period, the rules provide that the carrier will make an inspection within 48 hours and in case no inspection is made by carrier, the consignee's inspection will be accepted by the carrier. Further, if the loss or damage is not reported within fifteen days, the carrier should for its own protection be agreeable to making a reasonably prompt inspection after report and request for inspection is received. An honest effort should be made by all parties concerned to determine responsibility for the loss or damage by investigating and recording all available factual information.

In some instances a consignee may not afford the carrier any opportunity to make an inspection of concealed damage. An interesting case involving this point is *Phoenix Insurance Company* v. *Cushman Motor Delivery Co.,* decided January 27, 1945, by the Municipal Court of Cincinnati, O., and reported in *4 Federal Carrier Cases* Paragraph 80, 214. In this case a printing company delivered 400 paper packages to the defendant for shipment to Joliet, Ill. The plaintiff issued its policy of insurance to the shipper to protect the shipper against loss and damage in transit. The shipper claimed that 30 of the cartons were damaged and on May 24, 1943, filed its claim with the carrier. On May 27, 1943, the carrier requested an opportunity to inspect the goods alleged to have been damaged. On June 1, 1943, defendant was informed by the shipper that it had destroyed the damaged goods and on March 22, 1944, the carrier declined the claim. The insurance company paid the shipper and brought suit against the carrier. In upholding the carrier's declination, the court said:

> The defendant, as a common carrier, is subject to the rules and regulations of the Interstate Commerce Commission. The purpose of requiring a claim to be filed as a condition precedent to payment by the carrier for loss claimed to have been sustained by the shipper, is to give the carrier an opportunity to make an investigation within a reasonable time, *while the matter is fresh and easily investigated,* in order to safeguard the carrier from false and fraudulent claims. *This is a rule of law* not only for the protection of common carrier, but also to protect honest shippers, who could otherwise be discrim-

inated against if carriers were permitted to pay claims without investigating and verifying them. If the carrier paid claims of shippers without first investigating them, he would lay himself open to the charge of secret rebating. (Emphasis supplied.)

There is no doubt in the mind of this court that some part of the shipment was damaged. . . . The consignee, claimed that thirty of the four hundred packages were damaged, but since these packages each contained a number of paper board boxes, it is possible that some of the boxes were still in good condition and useable. This fact could be ascertained only by an examination of the salvage. By destroying the salvage, the carrier was deprived of an opportunity to ascertain the exact amount of damage. It is an elementary principle of law that the amount of damage which a person sustained must be based on the evidence and should not be speculative.

The defendant made its request for an examination and investigation of the damaged goods three days after the claim was filed by the shipper with the defendant, which is certainly prompt and reasonable.

In view of the facts of this case the court is of the opinion that the defendant was justified in refusing to pay the claim for damages filed by the shipper and finds that plaintiff is not entitled to recover from the defendant and that defendant should be dismissed and recover his costs expended in this case.

Concealed Loss or Damage Where Prior Transportation Is Involved

Section 20(11) of the Interstate Commerce Act which sets forth the statutory liability of interstate common carriers subject to the jurisdiction of the Interstate Commerce Commission is specifically related to transportation rendered under a "through bill of lading." This is clearly expressed in the following words:

Any common . . . subject to the provisions of this chapter . . . shall issue a receipt or bill of lading . . . and shall be liable to the lawful holder thereof for any loss, damage, or injury . . . when transported on a through bill of lading. . . .

A through bill of lading is one issued by the origin carrier to a shipper to cover transportation from the origin point designated therein to the specific consignee and destination shown in the contract. This is the transportation contract under which the transportation services of the initial carrier and its connecting lines agree to perform the services specified. When delivery is made to the consignee designated in this bill of lading contract, the transportation services covered by the bill of lading contract have been performed. If there has been loss, damage, delay or other injury in connection with this transportation service, the lawful holder of the bill of lading covering this through transportation has the rights granted to him thereunder and by Section 20(11). In the vast majority of instances, the consignee receiving the goods is the purchaser of them for some specific purpose such as his own use or enjoyment of them for commercial purposes in connection with his business. In event the goods received are enclosed within a container, the container will usually be opened promptly after delivery and their condition readily determined. If upon examination after removal from the container loss or damage concealed at time of delivery is discovered, the consignee will usually contact the delivering carrier immediately for an inspection and as a matter of routine, usually file his claim promptly for the injury discovered.

This, however, in some instances is not done. Frequently the consignee may be a warehouse, a distributor, or a dealer and have no desire to open the container and examine the condition of the goods. In the case of a warehouse, the goods are moved from the receiving dock and stored for subsequent reshipment in the original unopened container, likewise, the broker or distributor will store the goods received as will the dealer. When the goods subsequently are sold, they will be delivered or shipped to the purchaser still in the original unopened container. This delivery or reshipment may be the same day on which they were received, a few days later, or in some instances many months later. If the goods are subsequently reshipped by common carrier, this transportation service is performed under a new bill of lading issued by the carrier accepting the shipment at the storage or warehousing point covering "through transportation" as specified therein.

Under these circumstances, there has not been any through bill of lading issued to cover through transportation from the initial origin point where the goods were packed in the container to the ultimate destination to which the goods were subsequently reshipped in their original unopened container. On the contrary, there have been two separate, distinct, and different through bills of lading issued and each covers the transportation service specified in a separate contract. If concealed loss or damage is discovered upon opening the containers at the ultimate destination, no one knows where such concealed loss or damage occurred. All that is known is that there has been loss or damage. Conceivably, the loss or damage could have occurred at the initial shipping point after the goods were enclosed in the container and before delivery to the common carrier by the shipper; likewise, it is entirely possible that the loss or damage might have occurred during the course of transportation to the warehousing or storage point while in the possession of the carrier or carriers performing the transportation under the initial bill of lading.

Further, the loss or damage could have occurred after the goods were received at the warehousing or storage point while being handled by the consignee receiving them and, of course, it is also possible that the damage could have occurred while the goods were in the possession of the common carrier or carriers performing the transportation service from that point to the ultimate consignee. It is even possible that the loss or damage could have occurred after delivery to the ultimate consignee. Admittedly, common carriers do not have a monopoly on careless, inefficient or "light-fingered" employees. Clearly, no one actually knows where the concealed loss or damage occurred and it is preposterous to contend that the damage must have occurred while in the hands of carriers when the manufacturer, the warehouse, distributor, dealer, or ultimate consignee have all handled the goods since enclosure within the container.

It is not always easy, however, for the consignee receiving such damaged merchandise to understand the position of the carrier delivering the goods to him. The consignee's immediate assumption is that the carrier delivering the goods to him should promptly pay him for the damage. Additionally the shipper, warehouse or distributor, although having no means whatever of knowing the condition of the goods at the time they were shipped, nevertheless strongly feels that the carrier performing the service from their facilities should absorb the claim of damage. Regardless of the handling which the goods may have received at the manufacturer's plant before being given to the initial carrier at the initial point of origin, the manufacturer likewise is apt to assume that the damage could not have occurred during its handling and therefore must be the full responsibility of some transportation agency. All three parties—the manufacturer, the warehouse or distributor, and the ultimate consignee—look to the carriers involved for full reimbursement for the damage without much consideration of the possibility that the damage might have occurred while the goods were in their possession.

The difficulty with claims involving prior transportation of goods in containers to a warehouse or distributor for subsequent reshipment arises from the fact that two separate and distinct bills of lading are involved. There is no "through" transportation under one bill of lading from the initial origin point (manufacturer) to the ultimate destination. The service from point of manufacture to the warehouse is performed under one bill of lading; the transportation service may be performed by a rail carrier, motor carrier, or freight forwarder. The subsequent transportation may be by an entirely different mode of transportation than the one used to bring the goods to the warehouse or distributor. The shipment into the warehouse may be a carload, truckload, or large lot. The subsequent reshipment from the warehouse may be LTL, LCL, CL, or TL lot. Since the entire transportation was not performed under a single through bill of lading, the delivering carrier cannot compel the carriers rendering the prior transportation to contribute to the payment of the damage after delivery. Section 20(11) of the Interstate Commerce Act imposing liability upon both the originating and delivering carrier applies only where a single through bill of lading is involved. From a legal viewpoint, if the ultimate consignee brought suit against the carrier or carriers performing delivery from the warehouse or distributor, it would be necessary for the claimant to establish that the shipment was in actual good condition at the time it was delivered to the carrier by the warehouse or distributor. This essential proof cannot be adduced, however, since the container was not opened and the goods examined to determine their condition before reshipment. Claimant as a matter of law, therefore, would be unable to recover anything from the carrier and many courts have so held. (See *Denton* v. *Ramsdell*, 31 So. 2d 873; *Colotra* v. *Railway Express*, 32 So. 2d 69; *House* v. *Wheelock*, 254 Ill. App. 149; *Gramling Electric Refrigeration* v. *Southern R. Co.*, 152 S. E. 670; *Goldberg* v. *N.Y.N.H. & H.R. Co.*, 153 A. 812; *Hines* v. *Warden*, 229 S. W. 957)

The bills of lading used by rail and motor carriers clearly recite that the property is received in apparent good order—"contents and condition of contents unknown." In *House* v. *Wheelock*, 254 Ill. App. 149, and *Gramling Electric Refrigeration* v. *Southern R. Co.*, 152 S. E. 670, it was held that the use of these qualifying words served to remove the ordinary presumption that the goods were in good order when received by the carrier. In *Goldberg* v. *New York, N. H. & H. R. Co.*, 153 A. 812, the court held that there is no presumption that goods were in good order when received by the carrier when such goods were not open to inspection. Further, in *Hines* v. *Warden*, 229 S. W. 957, the court held that where goods have been received by a warehouse and stored before their delivery to a carrier, the ordinary presumption of their good order at that time does not arise. In view of this, it would seem that the shipper at the warehouse would have the burden of establishing that the shipment was in actual good order at the time it made the reshipment. If the containers were not opened and examined at that time, it is obvious that the shipper could not sustain its burden of proof and accordingly the carrier would be justified in declining the claim.

A case directly in point with these prior shipment transactions is *M. H. Felder & Co.* v. *Atlantic Coast Line R. Co.*, 165 S. E. 730. In this case a shipment of potatoes moved by boat from Boston to Savannah. At Savannah the potatoes were reshipped by rail to South Carolina and plaintiff alleged that they were in bad order when unloaded. The claimant brought suit claiming that the shipment was a through movement and that the railroad was a connecting carrier and therefore liable regardless of where the damage occurred. The railroad contended that the reshipment was a new transportation contract and that therefore the presumption that damage was its responsibility did not arise. Claimant appealed from a directed verdict for rail carriers. On appeal recovery was denied on the grounds that plaintiff had failed to show that the potatoes were in good order when delivered to the defendant at Savannah. Citing *Copeland Co.* v. *Davis,* 119 S. E. 19, the court held "the burden is first upon the consignor or consignee to show the condition or quantity of the goods when first delivered to the first of the connecting carriers." (See also *Armour Research Foundation v. Chicago, R. I. & P. R. Co.,* 311 F. 2d 493, cert. den. 372 U.S. 966; *Inland Waterways Shippers Association* v. *Mississippi Valley Barge Line Co.,* 194 F. Supp. 818, 289 F. 2d 374, cert. den. 368 U.S. 876)

The problem is clearly illustrated in *Turner* v. *North American Van Lines,* 287 S. W. 2d 384. In this case the plaintiff, an officer in the United States Navy, was transferred to Japan and was confronted with the problem of moving and storing his household goods during this tour of duty. He employed the Alpha Van Line to move his goods from his home in Arlington, Virginia, for storage in their warehouse in Alexandria, Virginia, where they remained for over nine months and eventually were delivered to North American Van Lines for transportation to Tulot, Arkansas, where they were stored in a vacant house. Several months later, the plaintiff employed Needles Van Lines to move his goods to the warehouse of Fidelity Storage Company in St. Louis. About a month later, the plaintiff had the goods removed from this warehouse to a new home in Olivette, St. Louis County, Missouri. The plaintiff then for the first time since leaving Arlington made a detailed examination of his household goods and found that they had been damaged extensively. He brought suit against the North American Van Lines and the insurance company covering the goods while in transit and storage for $2,260.50 which he had expended for repairing his furniture. The lower court found in favor of the plaintiff but on appeal this decision was reversed, the court finding:

> There is no way to place the blame. The cause of the damage may have occurred when none was liable or it may have been caused when either was liable. It is a rule that when the evidence shows that the occurrence, which give rise to the injury complained of, may have resulted from two or more

causes, in order to hold a defendant liable the plaintiff must have substantial evidence tending to show that the cause for which the defendant would be liable was the actual cause of the occurrence. *Cole* v. *Uhlmann Grain Co.,* 340 Mo. 277, 100 S.W. 2d 311, loc. cit 317; *Waldron* v. *Skelly Oil Co.,* 363 Mo. 1146, 257 S.W. 2d 615; *Raftery* v. *Kansas City Gas Co.,* 237 Mo. App. 427, 169, S.W. 2d 105.

The evidence is therefore not sufficient to support a judgment against any of the named defendants. Although the plaintiffs urge us to indulge them with all reasonable favorable inferences that may be drawn from the evidence, which we do, we find none which will aid them. *There is no evidence from which it may be determined who was in the possession of the furniture when it was damaged.* Any conclusion as to when it happened would be conjecture and not an inference. This is not sufficient. *Waldron* v. *Skelly Oil Co., supra*; *Van Brock* v. *First Nat. Bank in St. Louis,* 349 Mo. 425, 161 S.W. 2d 258.

In the situation outlined in the foregoing case, there is natural sympathy for the plaintiff, a Naval officer, who handled a personal problem in what undoubtedly was about the only course of conduct readily available to him. On the other hand, one able to place himself in the position of the defending carrier can readily appreciate its position and reluctance to pay out its money for damages which could have been caused by others. Before compelling anyone to part with his money, it is fundamental that the court have before it clear evidence to justify the verdict. Mere conjecture is never sufficient and had the Naval officer been in a position of the defendant carrier, he, too, would have been reluctant to part with his money under the circumstances outlined. Yet apparently there was no hesitation on his part in undertaking the considerable expense of litigation which upon calm reflection he himself undoubtedly would have conceded was based upon flimsy evidence; and, surprisingly, the lower court was sufficiently swayed to find in his favor although there was no evidence before it to indicate which of many parties was responsible for the damages.

It will be observed from the cases reviewed that the courts clearly recognize that carriers do not have a monopoly on causing loss and damage. The claimant is rightfully compelled to establish a prima facie case before judgment will be rendered against the carrier defendant. It is incumbent upon the claimant to establish that the shipment was in actual good condition at time of reshipment; if he has not opened the container and examined the contents after receipt and before reshipment, he can adduce no evidence of such good condition and no presumption or inference that they were in good condition exists. When the goods moved under two or more separate and distinct bills of lading, Section 20(11) giving the claimant the right to proceed against an originating or delivering carrier and expect recovery regardless of carrier responsible for the loss or damage has no application.

Under these circumstances, carriers paying any portion of these claims are not only exceedingly liberal but serious question arises as to whether or not the filing of such claims by claimants and payment of them by common carriers does not warrant condemnation of both claimants and carriers, especially since the practice could readily be used in such manner as to give undue preference, rebates and to discriminate between claimants. In Great Britain, the transportation agencies only pay 50 percent of the damage proved under such circumstances. In this country, the common carriers generally follow a much more liberal policy although the justification for it is not readily apparent nor can it be justified from a legal basis.

Before the regulation of interstate motor common carriers was placed under the jurisdiction of the Interstate Commerce Commission, rail carriers through their national claim organization established the practice of having the delivering carrier handling the shipment from the warehouse of storage point pay the claimant 100 percent and then prorating the claim on a mileage basis between all carriers involved from initial origin point to the ultimate destination, providing the goods had not been warehoused in excess of 120 days before reshipment. While there was no legal basis for this practice, undoubtedly the rail carriers justified it on a moral basis choosing to assume that the concealed loss or damage probably occurred while in transit and ignoring the possibility that such loss or damage could have occurred during handling at the storage point.

This policy greatly encouraged manufacturers and others to ship large quantities of their products to distributors or warehouses at key points from which the goods were later distributed to purchasers or others in the surrounding areas with considerable saving in transportation expense and saving in time in delivering to the customer. This practice likewise eliminated the expense of opening the container at the storage point and examining the goods to determine if a loss or damage had occurred during the initial transportation under the first bill of lading or during handling after receipt and before reshipment. Unquestionably, the distribution system developed as result of this convenient system has considerable value from an economical viewpoint and it is today a recognized and common method of distribution.

With the advent of motor carrier transportation and its subsequent regulation by federal law, certain problems developed because quite frequently the rail carriers would handle the movement from manufacturing point in carload lots to the distribution point and motor carriers handle the small lot movements therefrom to the ultimate consignee. In some instances, the motor carrier would handle truckload movement into the storage point and the rail carriers the subsequent small lot reshipment therefrom. There was considerable reluctance on the part of both motor and rail carriers in prorating claims for concealed loss and damage under these circumstances and many controversies arose.

While many motor carriers during the early days of regulation followed the policy of paying 50 percent maximum on these claims, the pressure from the claimant consignee, the shipper at warehouse point and the manufacturer at initial origin point became so great that gradually both modes of transportation developed an unwritten agreement to prorate these claims. While as between the two modes of transportation there are no written rules providing for the proration of these claims between them, most motor and rail carriers are agreeable to prorating claims with other modes of transportation. Airline, steamship companies, and freight forwarders are usually reluctant to prorate with other modes of transportation. Both rail and motor carriers through their national claim organizations have established rules providing that as between their respective members such claims will be prorated; there are, however, no written rules governing the proration of these claims when the transportation into the storage point was by one mode of transportation and the transportation therefrom by another mode but, as mentioned, an unwritten "gentleman's agreement" usually is followed as between rail and motor carriers.

In order to secure 100 percent payment on these claims, it is essential that the identity of the shipment into the warehouse and transportation therefrom be maintained. In other words, reference to prior billing covering the prior transportation must be available and tied in with the subsequent transportation in order to establish to the carriers's satisfaction that the subsequent movement was at one time handled by the prior carriers. Rail carriers rendering the prior transportation until recently would not entertain these claims if the goods had been warehoused in excess of 120 days before reshipment; this proviso was abolished in the summer of 1952. Prior to that time, motor carriers did not have a similar 120 days' limitation in their rules but almost simultaneously with the rail elimination of their proviso, the motor carriers inserted the limitation. For competitive reasons, motor carriers subsequently eliminated the proviso from their rules. It is pointed out, however, that since two bills of lading are involved, it is essential that any claim for prorate from carriers rendering the prior transportation be filed with them within nine months after their delivery to the warehouse or distributor, since necessarily their obligations to claimant are governed by the date of delivery under their bill of lading.

Occasionally the carrier performing the prior transportation will insist that its liability for its proportion of the claim should be limited to the value of the goods at the time they were in its possession. Usually the value of the goods into the warehousing or storage point will be less than their value on the subsequent movement from that point. Inasmuch as there is no legal authority for adjusting these claims and their adjustment is purely on a voluntary basis as result of agreement or understanding between carriers, it is impossible to express any opinion as to whether this action limiting value is or is not proper.

It cannot be emphasized too strongly that the payment of any portion of these claims involving prior or subsequent transportation is entirely voluntary and not result of any carrier legal liability. The practice is so common, however, that many claimants overlook this feature and quite often are lulled into belief that they enjoy a legal right to such payments. This aspect is brought home to them in those instances where the identity of the shipments from initial origin point to final destination has not been maintained; when for some reason the prior or subsequent carrier may refuse to absorb its proportion; where the nine months limitation under the initial bill of lading for filing claim has expired; where the prior carrier insists upon limiting its proportion to the value of the goods while in its possession, or where the prior carrier may insist on prorating on a revenue or mileage basis and the subsequent carrier vice versa. As a matter of precaution, the carrier receiving the claim will for its own protection before payment in full determine the policy of the prior carriers and if, for any reason, prior carrier or carriers will not absorb in full their proportion, the carrier receiving the claim may limit its payment to claimant by deducting such deficiency.

The claimant deprived of 100 percent recovery under such circumstances is not inclined to any sympathy with the paying carrier's position or its liberality in voluntary paying any portion of his claim. This is particularly true of the small merchant and the occasional recipient of merchandise, but surprisingly the same is often true of even the largest shippers including the United States government, the largest of all. The tendency is for the claimant to regard erroneously the entire shipment from initial origin point to ultimate destination under two separate bills of lading as through transportation within the provisions of Section 20(11) and assert strongly that the carrier with whom claim is filed should pay the claim in full and proceed under Section 20(12) to secure reimbursement from the other carriers involved. Section 20(12), however, is applicable in only those instances where a carrier under the provisions of Section 20(11) has been compelled to pay a claim for which another was 100 percent responsible and this element, of course, is never present in any claim involving loss or damage of concealed nature irrespective of the prior transportation feature.

The inherent danger of developing procedures based on an alleged moral basis in complete disregard of legal liability results from the fact that in such voluntary matters uniformity is seldom possible and that once an inch is voluntarily given or relinquished, more concessions are sought, the voluntary aspect overlooked or conveniently ignored, and eventually chaos and confusion result. In the whole area of concealed loss and damage claims, the evils eventually will outweigh or negate the benefits sought by the carriers' liberal policy, and failing the establishment and observance of strict uniformity by the carriers the only apparent solution would seem to be through legislative enactment.

The liberal policy and the apparent lack of desire of carriers to protect their own interests encourage even greater demands and expectations on the part of claimants. For example, the development and expansion of private and contract carriage transportation has resulted in some claimants' insistence that the same theory by which carriers voluntarily pay or participate in prorating claims involving prior and subsequent transportation should be extended to these forms of transportation. While admittedly at some point there should be an end of a common carrier's liability for the condition of the contents of an unopened container, the growing contention on the part of claimants is to insist that such liability continue until the container is actually opened and the goods examined regardless of the time or handlings involved.

Connecting Carriers

While Section 20(11) of the Interstate Commerce Act specifically provides that both the originating and delivery carrier are liable for the full actual loss, damage, or injury occasioned to shipments transported, this provision by no means relieves intermediate carriers from liability for injury caused to the goods. Section 20(11) merely provides the claimant with a convenient means for satisfying its claim by filing it with either the originating or delivering carrier. This procedure against the originating or delivering carrier is not exclusive; the claimant is not compelled to seek satisfaction from them as the intermediate carrier responsible for the injury is liable to the claimant as the responsible party is always liable for his torts. The difficulty, from a claimant viewpoint, in proceeding against an intermediate carrier responsible for the injury is that it must show *affirmatively* that such carrier caused the loss whereas this burden is not required when the claimant proceeds against the originating or delivering carrier. In *Galveston, H. & S. A. Ry. Co.* v. *American Grocery Co.*, 36 S. W. 2nd 985, the court held that the claimant could bring action against all of the carriers involved in transporting an interstate shipment and the court could award judgment of the claimant against the carrier liable for the injury to the shipment.

Section 20(12) of the Interstate Commerce Act provides that when the originating or delivering carrier is required to pay a claim for which it was not responsible, it may recover the amount paid from the carrier which was responsible for the injury. The fact that another carrier was responsible for the injury does not, however, justify the originating or delivering carrier with whom the claim was filed in holding up settlement while awaiting payment from the connecting line responsible. In many cases, of course, delay is necessary under these circumstances to enable the carrier with whom claim is filed to complete its investigation to determine carrier liability as ordinarily complete information with respect to the injury will not always be in the possession of the carrier with whom the claim was filed.

The relief afforded the carrier paying a claim for which it was not responsible by Section 20(12) is available in only those instances where the carrier paying the claim is able to establish that its connection was responsible for the injury and, in the case of concealed loss and damage, this is exceedingly difficult to prove. (See *Interstate Southern Express* v. *T. S. C. Motor Freight Lines*, 200 F. 2d 797) Both rail and motor carriers have by freight claim rules provided that all carriers participating in the movement shall prorate loss and damage claims of a concealed nature, and thus a right to contribution is established. In the case of carriers which are not parties to such freight claim rules there will usually be no right of contribution. If the claim is paid without lawsuit, the paying carrier has no legal claim against connecting carriers unless it can prove that one was responsible. If the claim is paid after lawsuit, the paying carrier's right to contribution from connecting carriers would depend on the form of action. If the suit was in tort (which is usually an action based on negligence), a right of contribution seldom would exist; if the suit was on the bill of lading contract, the paying carrier would acquire a right of action against connecting carriers. Some relief might be afforded the defendant carrier by interpleading the other carriers involved as defendants if such right existed in the jurisdiction where suit was brought.

Very often the question arises as to the right of a carrier to compensation for transportation performed by it when the shipment is subsequently destroyed while in the possession of a connecting carrier. The factual situation with which this question deals is: A shipment originates on the line of Carrier A and is carried by it for its portion of the haul without damage and is then transferred to Carrier B. While in the possession of Carrier B the shipment is either lost or completely destroyed. Under these facts, it seems well settled that Carrier A cannot recover any compensation from the shipper for the portion of the transportation it performed. This conclusion is supported by *Sumner* v. *Walker*, 30 Fed. 261; *Scow No. 190 and 450 Bales of Cotton*, 88 Fed. 320, and *British and Foreign Marine Insurance Co.* v. *Southern Pacific Co.*, 72 Fed. 285.

The last named case, which was decided by the United States Circuit Court of Appeals for the Second Circuit and is therefore the most authoritative of those cited, dealt with several shipments of cotton originating in Texas and other southern points which were shipped by rail to New Orleans, by water to New York and while in New York awaiting export, were partially destroyed by fire. The owners agreed that the remaining undamaged bales should be sold for salvage in New York and this was done. The steamship company which had brought the cotton from New Orleans to New York attempted to recover the full freight charges due from the inland points of origin to New York. These shipments moved on through export bills of lading. In its decision, the court awarded freight charges on that portion of the shipment which was sold in New York, but denied freight charges on the portion which was destroyed on the theory that the contract of affreightment was not fulfilled as to those portions of the shipment which were destroyed, and was fulfilled as to those portions which were sold in New York by virtue of the owner's consent of sale which amounted to a modification of the original contract. In its decision the court stated:

> The shipper sought carriage for his goods, not to New Orleans, nor to New York, but to Europe; and when three carriers, having formed a combination for the entire carriage, take the goods under a contract by the terms of which the entire compensation for such carriage is made dependent upon delivery at final destination, there is no reason why a Court should alter those terms. Had the carriers chosen to apportion the freight in advance, and to require the shipper to pay separately for each successive stage of the voyage, it was competent for them to insert such provision in the contract. Not having done so, their contract must be interpreted as such contracts of affreightment always have been, and their right to demand freight must be held dependent upon delivery at destination.

The question as to whether or not Carrier A can recover compensation for the transportation it performed from Carrier B under the facts set forth above can be approached from three theoretical viewpoints, all of which lead to the conclusion that such compensation should be recovered. These are (1) if, as between two carriers, Carrier B is subject to the same high degree of liability to Carrier A as he would be to a shipper, then Carrier A could clearly recover unless Carrier B could prove that the loss or damage was occasioned by one of the recognized exceptions to a carrier's liability; (2) if, in their relation to each other, Carriers A and B do not stand in the special relationship which exists between carriers and shippers, but are merely two ordinary contracting parties, then Carrier A could assert that the relationship between it and B gave rise to an implied contract by B to carry the shipment to destination and recover for B's breach which caused A to lose its share of revenue; (3) Carrier A could disregard the contractual aspect of the case and sue in tort, alleging negligence on the part of Carrier B which resulted in a financial loss to A. While no authority has been discovered dealing with this matter and the foregoing is entirely theoretical, nevertheless it is believed to be sufficiently sound to warrant the conclusion that Carrier A would be entitled to recover from Carrier B.

The question sometimes arises as to the circumstances under which a local cartage company becomes primarily liable for loss and damage when performing service for a line-haul carrier. If no technical distinction is made between primary and secondary legal responsibility and the subject treated as one of ultimate responsibility it seems that the answer is as follows: A pickup and delivery carrier is liable under the Interstate Commerce Act as a carrier where the injury to the goods is sustained while the shipment is in possession of the pickup and delivery carrier, the line haul carrier paying the loss and asserting a right of subrogation against the pickup and delivery carrier responsible for the injury.

Under Section 20(11) the delivering and originating carriers are liable for any loss, and such carriers may recover from the company on whose line the loss, damage, or injury was sustained. In *Keystone Motor Freight Lines* v. *Brennon Signago Cigar Co.*, 115 F. 2d 736, the delivering local cartage company was held liable to the claimant for the loss of a shipment. In this case Hall, the over-the-road carrier, attempted to make delivery of cigars on Saturday but found the cigar company closed. By special contract Hill obtained the services of Keystone, who was to make delivery two days later. When Keystone opened for business on Monday, it was discovered that the cigars had been stolen, but not because it had been negligent. Both Hall and Keystone were common carriers operating under the Interstate Commerce Act; both were members of the same rate bureau and had on file tariffs providing for a division of interline revenues.

In this particular case Hall and Keystone made a special contract and the rate used was the same as the rate fixed for deliveries made under a regular contract which the parties used in the normal course of their business. Keystone was not a party to the bill of lading and the bill of lading subjected the carrier in possession of the property to liability as a common carrier for any loss to the property. Suit was brought by the consignee against Hall, who brought in Keystone as a third party defendant. Hall paid the consignee for the loss, claimed subrogation against Keystone and was allowed to recover. What the decision would have been if Keystone had been a contract carrier or if there had been no pickup or delivery tariff published is not certain. There is nothing in the opinion, however, to lead to a conclusion that the result would have been different.

In the case of *Olive Kent Park, Inc.* v. *Moshassuck Transportation Co.*, 71 N. Y. S. 2d 15, the facts were as follows: The Moshassuck Transportation Co., an over-the-road carrier, had an arrangement with Conboy Trucking Corp., a local truckman, to perform a portion of its pickup and delivery work. On August 13, 1946, Moshassuck turned over to Conboy, for delivery, 195 pieces of textiles valued at approximately $35,000. The goods were not delivered to the consignee because on the date mentioned Conboy's truck was hijacked and the goods stolen. There was no charge of negligence on the part of Conboy or his employees. Suit was brought against Moshassuck and this carrier brought in Conboy as a third party defendant.

In deciding the *Moshassuck* case, the court stated that the sole issue was whether or not Conboy was operating as a common carrier or, as it contended, a contract or private carrier. It was clear from the evidence that Conboy did not, at least in its dealings with Moshassuck, issue its own bills of lading or delivery receipts but used those of Moshassuck. The court concluded that the evidence when viewed in the light of the authorities justified the conclusion that Conboy was a common carrier and that as a common carrier a local cartageman is liable to the line-haul carrier for loss, damage and injury to goods transported for it.

Contamination

Carriers are liable for damage caused by leakage or contamination from other freight but, under classification or tariff rules, usually may refuse to accept shipments which are likely to injure other cargo or equipment, or may accept subject to delay for procuring suitable equipment. Once having accepted the goods, however, the carrier becomes liable for any damage by it to other shipments. Some commodities such as foodstuffs are highly susceptible to contamination by odor from other goods and, as a practical matter, the carrier must exercise precaution in loading goods susceptible to contamination by goods which are known to give off odors.

In connection with contamination of cargo, carriers are confronted with leakage from liquids in metal and other containers. As a result of a desire to secure every economy possible, some shippers of liquids will use and reuse metal drums until eventually the drums will simply wear out, with resulting leakage of contents which causes serious damage to other goods. Even though made of steel a used drum is just like any other container. It cannot last forever and eventually reaches the point where its continued use constitutes a hazard. Practically all large metal drums are constructed with their bottoms an inch or more above floor surface. While in use and particularly while in transportation, the heavy contents of the drums will cause the bottom to flex up and down. This flexing eventually results in a crack in the metal bottom and leakage of contents. Metallurgists describe this failure of the drum *fatigue injury;* the layman usually terms it as leakage resulting from *metal fatigue.* Simply expressed, this injury is identical with that which results when one takes a wire and bends it back and forth until it breaks. If as a result of drum failures the carrier had to reimburse the owner of the drum for only the loss of the liquid, the problem would be relatively simple. This, unfortunately, is usually only a small part of the damage; the damage to other cargo caused by leakage frequently will exceed many thousands of dollars.

To illustrate the problem, a shipper of liquids will repaint an old metal drum so that to all outward appearances it will look just as good as a new drum. At the time the carrier's agent accepts this drum for transportation, he has no way of knowing how long the drum has been in service or whether or not its seams are weak and some of the metal defective from rust. Later the carrier loads the drum together with other cargo for transportation to destination, and while in transit the liquid contents of the drum will be splashing around and the stress created may eventually cause the weakened seams, chimes, or rusty bottom or side to give way, with resulting leakage of the contents and damage to other cargo. The owner of the drum will file his claim with the carrier for the loss by leakage and the owners of other shipments will likewise file their claim for damage to their goods. The carrier will probably decline the claim filed by the owner of the drum on the grounds that the shipper failed to use a serviceable container and that this condition of the container constituted a latent defect which the carrier was unable to determine at the time the shipment was accepted. This defense, however, is not available against the owners of the other merchandise who are entitled to recover for their injury in full. On the other hand, it would appear that since the owner of the drum failed to exercise the proper degree of care in selection of the drum, the carrier would be entitled to look to him for reimbursement for the sums expended for the damage to other cargo by the drum's failure.

The liability of a shipper to the carrier for damage occasioned under these circumstances was the subject matter in *Eastern Motor Express, Inc. v. Maschmeijer, Jr., Inc.*, 247 F. 2d 826, reversing 141 F. Supp. 477, cert. den. 78 S. Ct. 535. In this case, the decision of the United States Court of Appeals for the Second Circuit was as follows:

On May 2, 1949, a trailer-truck belonging to Eastern Motor Express, Inc. (hereinafter called plaintiff), a common carrier, was being loaded at the plant of A. Maschmeijer, Jr., Inc., at Newark, New Jersey (hereinafter called defendant). The defendant's shipment consisted of 30 drums of methyl phenyl acetate (hereinafter abbreviated to m.p.a.). The driver's helper inspected the drums, found no leaks and gave the defendant a clean bill of lading.

The truck next stopped in Jersey City at the plaintiff's terminal where miscellaneous freight was put in the trailer. This freight was placed in the center while the drums were along the sides and front against the walls.

During the journey, the plaintiff's driver noticed moisture under the trailer and a strange odor. Upon inspection he found the floor damp, some of the miscellaneous freight soaked through, and notices a leak in one of the drums. The driver testified he had had no accident or collisions along the way. At its final destination, on May 5, the trailer was inspected by the head of the plaintiff's claims department. The odor was very strong and the trailer was not entered at that time, but it was observed that the underside of the trailer had lost all its paint. Later that day, the trailer was entered. Two drums were found to be leaking and nearby paint had blistered off the saddle tanks and some of the miscellaneous cargo was found to have been destroyed.

The drums had been consigned to Eli Lilly & Co., and some time after they were delivered the plaintiff paid Lilly for its loss from the leakage.

In this action the plaintiff is suing for damage to its truck-trailer, the amount paid to Lilly, and for damage caused to the miscellaneous freight belonging to other shippers.

After a trial without a jury, the District Court granted motions to dismiss the complaint. The plaintiff has appealed and the defendant has cross-appealed because of the Court's failure to make certain findings.

The plaintiff alleged claims based on negligence and on breach of warranty. The breach of warranty argument is two-fold. It asserts an implied warranty of fitness and in this connection cites Rule 5, subsection 8(a), of Tariff MF-ICC No. 17, National Motor Freight Classification No. 9. The pertinent part of this rule states: "Barrels . . . drums . . . must be made of wood . . . metal . . . or other materials of such strength as to afford safe handling, reasonable and proper protection of contents and to protect against damage to other goods." This rule, the so-called "Packing Rule," was part of the contract in legal effect —as are all properly authorized tariff rules and regulations published by carriers. *Davis* v. *Henderson,* 266 U.S. 92; *Louisville & Nashville R. Co.* v. *Chatters,* 279 U.S. 320, 331; *American Ry. Express Co.* v. *American Trust Co.,* 7 Cir., 47 F. 2d 16, Cert. den. 284 U.S. 629; *Standard Hotel Supply Co.* v. *Pennsylvania R. Co.,* 65 F. Supp. 439 (S.D.N.Y.).

The District Judge held that the above-quoted rule did "not require that a drum shall never leak . . ." but merely required that the drum afford reasonable protection. We disagree with that interpretation. Under the common law, a bailor impliedly warrants that the goods are fit for the use for which the bailment is made at least as against latent unfitness. *Hoisting Engine Sales Co., Inc.* v. *Hall,* 237 N.Y. 30, 142 N.E. 342. Thus a shipper in delivering packaged goods for shipment impliedly warrants that the containers, if not patently inadequate, are fit for the contemplated shipment. We think that the Packing Rule (Rule 5, subsection 8(a)), makes it plain that a shipper by motor carrier is within that rule. Indeed, the rule of the common law of bailment is peculiarly appropriate for application to the relationship between shippers and common carriers. For such carriers are under obligation to accept for shipment containers which are not patently unfit for such shipment. In this case, the undisputed facts imperatively required a finding that the defendant had breached an implied warranty existing under the common law as recognized by the Packing Rule. As a defense to the plaintiff's claim of breached warranty, the degree of care exercised by the defendant is irrelevant, for—with exceptions not pertinent here—the duty of the defendant, as bailor-warrantor is absolute. *Overbury* v. *Platten,* 2 Cir., 108 F. 2d 155; *Mulvaney* v. *King Paint Mfg. Co.,* 2 Cir., 256 Fed. 612.

Since we have sustained the plaintiff's claim of breach of implied warranty, there is no need for us to consider the plaintiff's second warranty claim based on an express certification in the bill of lading or to consider its claim of negligence on the part of the defendant.

Defendant has cross-appealed from the failure of the District Court to make certain findings. It is asserted that it was error not to find the plaintiff guilty of contributory negligence due to its failure to secure or brace the barrels or at least to place the other goods on skids or pallets so that they would be 4 to 6 inches above the floor level above the drums.

The District Judge found that the defendant had failed to prove that failure to brace the drums was negligence. This finding we think well-founded. However, no express finding was made as to the plaintiff's failure to use skids and pallets. The point is not material to the issue of liability under the plaintiff's claim of breach of implied warranty. If presented on remand on the issue of damages flowing from the defendant's breach the judge will doubtless give it due consideration and make any required findings. Skids and pallets apparently would not have avoided damage to other merchandise caused by the pervasive odor of m.p.a.

The defendant also asserts it was entitled to exclusive use of the trailer and thus it was not liable for damage to the other goods in the trailer. The District Judge made several findings on this issue and indicated that, if necessary he would decide adversely to the defendant. Such a finding is amply supported by the evidence.

The defendant also interposed deviation as defense, arguing that because the plaintiff's driver on the trip west did not follow the route described by the plaintiff, plaintiff was barred from recovering in this action. It cites the old cases dealing with a carrier's absolute liability once it leaves the route contracted for. But these cases are not applicable to the situation presented by the evidence below; none go further than to hold that a carrier who has deviated from the route contracted for may not in the event of a loss avail himself of a special limitation of liability to the shipper contained in the contract of carriage. Nothing in the deviation case suggests that a deviation by the carrier operates to relieve a shipper, who has breached his implied warranty of the adequacy of the containers from the consequences of his breach.

There is, however, no need to make a definitive ruling as to the effect of a deviation by the plaintiff on the defendant's liability because the record presented fails to show a deviation. In the operative bill of lading the space provided for statement of route was left blank and we find no evidence whatever to show that any particular route was agreed on by the parties or prescribed by the Interstate Commerce Commission. Cf. 49 U.S.C.A. 308 (a) and (b).

We hold also that the fact that the plaintiff compensated Lilly, the consignee, for its loss does not excuse the defendant for its breach even though the bill of lading expressly excepts from the carrier's liability loss due to the shipper's default as well as the Act of God. For the plaintiff made it plain in its accompanying letter that the payment was made for the preservation of customer relations and was not to be construed as an admission of liability on the part of the plaintiff. That letter also stipulated that acceptance of the plaintiff's check should constitute an assignment to the plaintiff of Lilly's claim against the defendant. Whether, by reason of this payment the plaintiff, as Lilly's assignee or otherwise, is entitled to recover from the defendant the amount of Lilly's loss, will be a question for the court below when it comes to determine the damages.

The defendant's cross-appeal is denied. The plaintiff's appeal is granted and the case is remanded for computation of damages flowing from the defendant's breach of warranty.

The United States District Court, Southern District, New York, which rendered the opinion in the *Maschmeiper case,* 141 F. Supp. 477, which was subsequently reversed as indicated, failed to give consideration to the classification requirement that containers offered for transportation must be of sufficient strength to afford safe handling, reasonable and proper protection of contents, and to *protect against damage to other goods.* While it went into considerable detail in reviewing the evidence offered by an expert metallurgist in connection with the allegation that the leakage resulted from fatigue which could not have been ascertained in advance by either the shipper or the carrier, as between the two innocent parties, it concluded that the carrier should be saddled with the loss. To a large extent the opinion was based on the following reasoning:

> Aside from the facts that one drum was two years old and the other six, there is no proof that defendant "knew" the drums had become weakened from reuse. Although it might be presumed that almost anything becomes weakened through reuse, there was no evidence to show at what point reuse of the drums constitutes dereliction.
>
> Further, since Dr. Brown stated that the cause of the fractures was metal fatigue and that the method he used was the only method for discovering the same, it would be ridicuolous to suppose that "reasonable care" obligated defendant to excise specimens from its drums in order to prevent occurrences similar to those in suit. Such an obligation carried to its logical extreme would require destruction of the drums to ascertain their life expectancy. (Loc. cit. 485.)

This theory the Court of Appeals dismissed emphatically in its holding that "the degree of care exercised by the defendant (drum owner) is irrelevant, for—with exceptions not pertinent here—the duty of the defendant, as bailor-warrantor is absolute." It should be kept in mind that the decision in the *Maschmeijer* case while clarifying the law as to liability in these matters does not purport to be new law but, on the contrary, merely affirms liability which has always existed under the common law. For example, it would appear that the entire controversy was anticipated and answered in Hutchison, *Carriers* (3rd edition, 1906) Vol. 1 at page 169:

> SEC. 163 (& 125) Recitals as to condition of goods, how far conclusive. It has likewise been determined that the usual recital in such instruments that the goods are in good order has reference only to the external appearance, either of the goods themselves or of the packages into which they are put. Hence, it is always competent for the carrier to show, notwithstanding such an admission, that the loss or damage was caused by the spoiling of the goods from natural decay before they could be delivered, *or that they had wasted from defects in the vessels in which they were contained,* or that it arose from the unskillful or improper manner in which they were packed, or that they had deteriorated or were damaged at the time they were delivered to him. He is not presumed to know the quality of the goods, nor can he refuse to carry them, whatever it may be, if they are fit to carry and are the kind he usually

carries, nor can he, ordinarily, know the condition of the contents of the packages or vessels brought to him for transportation. It cannot be supposed, therefore, that he intends by such a recital to admit more than that the goods are in an apparently fit condition for shipment. And such is the construction which these words have received. *If the damage has proceeded from any such "hidden cause, whether naturally inherent in the commodity itself or arising from the carelessness of the shipper, the loss must be borne by him."* The carrier is not then in fault, *nor is his acknowledgement that they have been received in good order or condition a warranty or insurance against such an event.* But if it can be shown that the loss might have been avoided by the use of the proper precautionary measures, and that the usual and customary methods for this purpose have been neglected, he will still be liable (Emphasis added.)

The classic case of *Lister* v. *Lancashire & Yorkshire Ry.*, 1 K. B. (1903) 878, 72 L.J.K.B. 385 also applies. In that case the shipper employed the defendant as a common carrier to transport an engine from his yard to a neighborhood station. The engine was on wheels and had shafts attached by which it could be drawn. En route, one of the shafts broke and the engine was upset and damaged. The shaft was rotten at the point where it broke, but this was not known either to the shipper or carrier, and could not have been discovered by any ordinary examination. In other words, it was a latent defect. The arguments accepted by the trial court and reversed on appeal are remarkably similar to the petitioner's contentions in the instant controversy. As stated in the reversing opinion:

The learned County Court judge was of opinion that common carriers were not only liable for negligence, but were insurers; that the fact that there was a concealed defect in the shaft prevented there having been any evidence of negligence on the defendant in drawing the engine the way they did, but that this did not of itself relieve them of liability. It was contended that when the injury results from an inherent defect in the article carried, the carrier is excused, but in the learned judge's opinion that was much too general a proposition and he could not see any principle upon which the defendants could claim to be excused the consequences of their act. He therefore gave judgment for the plaintiffs (shippers). (Parentheses added.)

In reversing on appeal the court said:

. . . the learned judge has limited the rule as to nonresponsibility of the carrier —the accident happening by the inherent vice or inherent defect when it is in the hands of the carrier—to an extent that he ought not have done. That being so, in my opinion, when you once get that the article is being carried in the ordinary way and every precaution has been taken consistently with that mode of carriage and the accident happens, as the learned judge has found, by the breaking down of the article itself, which causes the whole damage, then the carrier is not responsible. I think Mr. Lush (attorney for the plaintiff) who was very fair in the matter, must have contended, in order to succeed, that, even if the shaft had broken and no other damage had happened that the Railway Company would have been responsible for that shaft and would have had to put it back into its previous condition.

Williston on Contracts, revised edition, volume 4, sec. 1041, page 2907, states: "One who lets property for hire may reasonably be subjected to the same implied warranties as one who sells goods."

In the *Maschmeijer* case, it was argued by the shipper and supporting parties that the doctrine of implied warranty applied only to dangerous articles, citing *Brass* v. *Maitland,* 119 Eng. L. R. 940 (1856); *Bamfield* v. *Goole,* 2 K. B. 94 (1910); *Grt. No. Rwy.* v. *L. E. P. Trans. & Depos. Ltd.,* 2 K. B. 742 (1922). There appears to be no authority for limitation of the principle of these cases to dangerous articles only. In *Bradley* v. *Lake Shore & M. S. Ry. Co.,* 129 N. Y. S. 1045, specific reference is made to a failure of compliance with the provision of the classification filed with the Interstate Commerce Commission. On this basis, it was determined that the acids should have been differently packed before being shipped. It is only in obiter dictum that the residual reference is made to the common-law duty of the shipper concerning the dangerous commodity.

Similarly, in *Great Northern* v. *L. E. P. Trans. & Depos. Ltd.,* 2 K. B. 742 (1922), the commodity, perhydrol, was not packed in accordance with the classification. In finding a breach of implied warranty in reference to the tariff provision, it was stated: "The duty is at least as large as that which is imposed upon a person who tenders goods for carriage on a general ship which is the foundation of the warranty. . . ." It was also stated: "In my opinion, the foundation of those judgments is, that where a person requests another to perform a statutory duty, there is an implied promise to indemnify him if he suffers damage in the performance of it."

The nature of the product contained thus is not necessarily the legal test. The underlying rationale of the dangerous article cases is applicable to the *Maschmeijer* case in that the shipper failed to comply with the terms of the "Packing Rule" as required by the "law of the case." (*Bradley* v. *Lake Shore* & *M. S. Ry. Co.,* 129 N. Y. S. 1045)

In *W. A. Hover & Co.* v. *Denver & R. G. W. R. Co.,* 17 F. 2d 881, the shipper delivered a box containing two five gallon cans of carbon bisulphide, an inflammable liquid, to the carrier for transportation over its line. The box was properly labeled with a red label calling attention to its contents and containing the usual warning. The shipper certified on the bill of lading that the box was packed according to ICC regulations. This box was loaded into a car containing other cargo. The train was inspected periodically during its journey with nothing apparently being wrong. Later, the train went down a hill with a number of sharp curves at a speed of 12 to 18 miles per hour. The car swayed and rocked but no more than usual. At the next inspection point, it was discovered that liquid was dripping on a hot brake shoe at the rear of the car in which the carbon bisulphide was loaded, and was igniting. The conductor and brakeman were unable to extinguish the fire and the car was cut out of the train and burned completely.

The carrier paid claims of other shippers and brought suit against shipper of the carbon bisulphide, claiming negligence on the part of the shipper in using secondhand containers (gasoline cans) of 30 gauge metal for the shipment of the carbon bisulphide in violation of the ICC requirement of not less than 28 gauge metal containers. The carrier also claimed that it was deceived in accepting shipment by the shipper's certificate that it complied with these regulations. The shipper defendant denied that the fire was the result of any negligence on its part, or that it was negligent in any respect, and alleged that the carrier itself was negligent, and liable to it for $28, the value of the carbon bisulphide.

In deciding the *Hover case*, the federal court found that at the time the shipment moved, the Interstate Commerce Commission had not been authorized by Congress to regulate the packing requirements for inflammable liquids. The Act of March 4, 1909, pursuant to which the Commission had prescribed container specifications for carbon bisulphide, related only to prescribing regulations for the safe transportation of explosives. By Act of March 4, 1921, which was enacted subsequent to the date of this particular shipment, Congress amended the Act of March 4, 1909, and authorized the Commission to formulate regulations for the safe transportation not only of explosives but of other dangerous articles, including inflammable liquids. Because the ICC did not, at the time this shipment was moved, have the authority to prescribe container specifications for inflammables, the court said:

> We reach the conclusion that the regulation relied upon by the plaintiff as the basis for its claim of negligence on the part of the defendant, because unauthorized, imposed no duty upon shippers, and that its violation by a shipper could not, therefore, constitute negligence as a matter of law or evidence of negligence. It is therefore unnecessary to determine whether there was evidence to justify the conclusion that the regulation had been violated.
>
> But, even if the defendant was obligated to comply with this regulation and had failed to do so, there could still be no recovery by the plaintiff in this

case. . . . If there had been any evidence to show causal connection between the use of the second-hand gasoline cans of 30-gauge metal and the happening of the fire, the question of proximate cause would have been a question for a jury; but, under the evidence here, the whole matter was left in the realm of speculation and conjecture. The leaking of the cans may have been caused by many other things than the gauge of the metal. . . .

A study of the *Hover* case leads to the conclusion that the court as in the *Maschmeijer* case would have held the shippers liable for the fair market value of the goods destroyed if fault in packaging was shown by evidence to have caused the injury of the goods. In the *Hover* case, the carrier relied almost entirely upon the shipper's failure to observe ICC regulations as constituting negligence. In fact, the carrier almost was compelled to adopt this approach since the cans had been destroyed in the fire. In the usual used drum failure, however, the drum will be available to the carrier for use as evidence to establish the fact that the shipper used it in disregard of its obligation to employ a container which could withstand the normal hazards of transportation.

It is, of course, not easy for the average person to distinguish between a metal fatigue fracture and one resulting from mishandling. By the use of technical publications, however, the carrier's investigation can usually arrive at a fairly reasonable conclusion.

Conversion and Misdelivery

Conversion is an act of interference with the dominion or control over the property of another. Conversion may be committed by (1) acquiring possession of the goods with an intent to assert a right to them which is in fact adverse to that of the owner; (2) transferring the goods in a manner which deprives the owner of control; (3) unreasonably withholding possession from one who has the right to it; or (4) seriously damaging or misusing the chattel in defiance of the owner's right. Insofar as carrier liability is concerned, conversion is usually related to misdelivery. When a carrier has made misdelivery of a shipment, the resulting claim is technically not one for loss or damage because the goods have not actually been lost or damaged but merely delivered to someone not entitled to possession of them. Conversion of a shipment, however, constitutes an "injury" to the owner of the goods within the meaning of Section 20(11) of the Interstate Commerce Act for which the carrier is liable in the same manner as for "loss and damage" and for that reason comes within the purview of this text.

A carrier is liable to the owner of a shipment for delivery of the shipment to a person not entitled thereto, unless the misconduct or negligence of the owner induced the misdelivery. (*Marquette Cement Mfg. Co. v. Louisville & N. R.*, 281 F. Supp. 944, affirmed 406 F. 2d 731) Ordinarily a carrier is not liable for a misdelivery occasioned by the negligence of the shipper in addressing the goods as, for example, where shipper fails to indicate a street address and carrier delivers to the wrong party where there are two or more persons of the same name. If the loss resulted, however, from the negligence of the carrier, then the negligence of the shipper will not excuse the carrier.

The last duty required of the common carrier is that of delivery and every delivery must be made to the right person, at a reasonable time, at the proper place, and in a proper manner. But placement of frozen food in cold storage after failure of consignee to accept delivery of order-notify shipment is not conversion. (*Tri-State Produce Co.* v. *Chicago, B. & Q. R.*, 104 F. Supp. 452) If delivery to the consignee in person is required, it is the carrier's duty to seek him and make him a tender of the goods. Generally, no circumstances of fraud, imposition or mistake will excuse the carrier from responsibility for a delivery to the wrong person. If a person who applied for the goods is not known to the carrier, and there is any doubt as to his being the consignee, the carrier should require the most unquestionable proof of identity and as long as the carrier acts in good faith, the carrier will not be responsible for delay or conversion.

In *Price v. Oswego, etc., R. Co.*, 50 N. Y. 213, a swindler addressed a letter to the shipper in the name of a fictitious firm, requesting that goods be forwarded to the address of the firm. The shipper did not know the firm but assumed the order was honest and shipped the goods over defendant's line, consigned and directed as specified by the swindler. There was no firm as that in whose name the goods had been ordered and when the goods arrived at destination, a stranger to the carrier's agent called at their office, paid the freight charges, and accepted delivery of the goods. The carrier did not require any evidence as to the stranger's identity or his connection with the fictitious firm. The court held the carrier liable on the grounds that it was the carrier's duty to make inquiry as to the existence of such a firm as that to which the goods were shipped and, upon ascertaining that such a firm did not exist, it should have warehoused the goods for the shipper's account. The court indicated that since the goods were consigned to a firm, delivery should not have been made to an individual without inquiry.

In *Samuel* v. *Cheney,* 135 Mass. 278, a swindler, giving his address as "A. Swannick, P. O. Box 1595, Saratoga Springs, New York," sent a letter to plaintiff requesting a price list on cigars. Upon receiving the list, the swindler forwarded an order and the shipper filled it and shipped it by defendant, writing the swindler at the box number and informing him of the shipment. There was a reputable dealer in Saratoga Springs by the name of Arthur Swannick who did business as "A. Swannick" and who enjoyed favorable credit according to report secured by the shipper from a commercial agency. This dealer operated his business at the corner of Ash and Franklin streets; no other A. Swannick appeared in the Saratoga directory or was known to the commercial agency. About this time, however, a man appeared in the community, rented a store on Congress Street, hired post office box 1595, and used letterheads with his name printed as "A. Swannick, P.O. Box 1595" and it was this individual who corresponded with the shipper. Defendant carried the shipment safely to Saratoga Springs and since a previous shipment of cigars had been refused by the reputable dealer and the carrier had delivered them to the Swannick on Congress Street, the carrier likewise delivered this shipment which was addressed simply "A. Swannick, Saratoga Springs, N. Y." to the store on Congress Street where they were accepted. The court in holding the carrier not liable said:

> The plaintiff contends that he intended to send the goods to Arthur Swannick. It is equally true that he intended to send them to the person with whom he was in correspondence. We think the more correct statement is that he intended to send them to the man who ordered and agreed to pay for them, supposing erroneously that he was Arthur Swannick. It seems to us that the defendant, in answer to the plaintiff's claim, may well say, we have delivered the goods intrusted to us according to your directions, to the man to whom you sent them, and who, as we are induced to believe by your acts in dealing with him, was the man to whom you intended to send them; we are guilty of no fault or negligence.

The court in the preceding case referred to the case of *Price* v. *Oswego, etc., R. Co., supra,* but stated that the facts were distinguishable because in this case the carrier delivered the goods to the person intended by the shipper to be the consignee, while in the *Price* case the goods were consigned to a firm and delivered by the carrier to an unknown individual.

In *Fox River Butter Co.* v. *Lightning Motor Lines,* 210 N. Y. S. 172, a shipper received telephone orders from a swindler who identified himself as "William Evans, 4922 Fairmount Avenue, Philadelphia," which name the shipper found listed with satisfactory credit rating in mercantile reports, but without any address. The shipper made two shipments of butter to the swindler at the address given which was a store rented by the swindler. The court found that the carrier was not liable in making delivery to the address given since it was to the consignee as directed by the shipper. On the other hand, in *Turner Okl. Co.* v. *Yellow Cab & Baggage Co.*, 269 Pac. 1082, an unknown person called the shipper, a wholesaler, and ordered a shipment for the Palace Drug Co., Noble, Oklahoma, and advised that someone would call for the shipment. Subsequently, defendant received a telephone call and was requested to call at the shipper for the package and deliver it to an address in Oklahoma City. This the carrier did and received its charges after which the party receiving the goods absconded. The court held the carrier liable on the grounds that it was the duty of the carrier to deliver the shipment to the consignee or its authorized agent, and that delivery of the package consigned to the drug firm at Noble to an unknown person in Oklahoma City was contrary to its common carrier duty.

In *Chicago, M., St. P. & P. R. Co.* v. *Flanders*, 56 Fed. 2d 114, a swindler called on the shipper and represented himself as a reputable South Dakota farmer and the shipper sold him 35 head of cattle, giving him a bill of sale and shipping the cattle to him. The court held that the carrier was not liable for making delivery to the swindler since the shipper had clothed the swindler with apparent title whereby the carrier was induced to make delivery to him. In *Atlantic Coast Line R. Co.* v. *Seward*, 142 So. 881, the court held the carrier not liable where the shipment in question was delivered to the drayman whom the consignee had allowed for a long period of time to receive and sign for freight consigned to him at the depot, the consignee having clothed the drayman with an agency relationship.

Conversion embraces not only misdelivery but any act which constitutes a wrongful exercise of dominion over the property intrusted to it by some affirmative act contrary to the instructions, expressed or implied, and against the interest of the owner of the goods. Thus in *Pennsylvania R. Co.* v. *Gentile Bros Co.*, 191 N. E. 369, it was held that a carrier has no authority by virtue of the uniform bill of lading to sell a perishable shipment at destination without first attempting to communicate with the interested parties, and such a sale constitutes conversion. Likewise, in *St. Louis Southwestern Ry. Co.* v. *Kessinger*, 72 S. W. 2d 1105, the carrier was held liable for conversion where the consignee asked for his shipment several times and the carrier's agent denied he had the shipment on hand when, in fact, it had arrived and was in the station.

In *Panhandle & S. F. Ry. Co.* v. *Miller*, 64 S. W. 2d 1076, the shipper consigned a machine weighing 28 tons to its plant. The carrier unloaded the machine and placed most of it in the plant but left five parts lying on its right of way where they were subsequently found by the carrier, removed, and sold as junk. Although these five parts could be purchased separately from the supplier, the consignee brought suit for conversion of the entire machine. The court in holding that conversion would lie for only the five missing parts said:

> In cases like this, where separate parts of a machine engine, vehicle, or like property, must be assembled in order to make a completed whole that is capable of being used in accomplishing the purpose for which it was designed and manufactured, and there is a taking and conversion of one or more of the parts only, the value of the parts at the time and place of conversion, together with such consequential damages as followed the act, would be the limit of the amount recoverable.

In *Woodruff Oil & Fertilizer Co.* v. *Charleston & W. C. Ry. Co.*, 180 S. E. 793, the court held that it is not conversion for a carrier to permit a consignee to inspect a shipment, although as a result of such inspection the consignee refused to accept it. In this case, the claimant ordered a car of cottonseed meal shipped order notify, but due to an error on the part of the initial carrier it was billed on a straight bill of lading basis.

In *Wilson Freight Forwarding Co.* v. *C.C.C. Highway, Inc.* 57 N. E. 2d 796, a carrier was held liable for astray freight which was found in its possession and which belonged to another carrier. Both the plaintiff and defendant employed the same independent contractor in Hamilton, Ohio, to bring freight from the local customers to the dock belonging to the independent contractor, where each carrier took charge of that which was consigned to places on its route. The independent contractor collected cartons of blank bills of lading from the Hamilton Autographic Register Co. for shipment to McKay Company at York, Pennsylvania. In doing so, the contractor was acting for and on behalf of Wilson, the plaintiff. The cartons should have been taken by the plaintiff to York but someone actually took them to Cleveland where they were found on the defendant's dock. The plaintiff had issued bill of lading to the shipper and as the cartons were not delivered to the consignee, shipment was duplicated by the shipper and claim made against plaintiff. This was paid and the plaintiff took an assignment from shipper of the claim. Shortly thereafter, the defendant notified the plaintiff that the cartons had been found on its dock in Cleveland and tendered them to plaintiff who refused their return and demanded reimbursement of the amount paid the shipper. On refusal of reimbursement, plaintiff brought suit for conversion and the lower courts awarded judgment in its favor. The appellate court affirmed this judgment and said:

There is no direct evidence as to how or by whom these cartons were taken from Hamilton to Cleveland, and it is asserted that because of that fact there is an entire failure of proof. But there is proof that the defendant was in Hamilton at the time the cartons were there and that at a later date it was in Cleveland with these cartons in its possession. We believe that from these facts an inference of fact arises that it was defendant that took them from Hamilton to Cleveland. Certainly, if this were a criminal prosecution, such an inference would arise. . . . The distinction between a civil and a criminal action is entirely irrelevant to the inquiry of whether an inference arises from proven facts. The only difference we can see is that the consequence of drawing the inference are graver in one instance than in the other. . . . But it is said there is no evidence that the defendant knew the cartons were on its dock in Cleveland until it found them there just before it notified the shipper and that under such circumstances it cannot be charged with conversion. It is true the defendant stated in its letters that it just discovered the cartons on its dock and did not know how they had gotten there, but laying aside the rule against self serving declarations, its assertion of lack of knowledge did not conclusively prove the fact and the trial court's finding is in general terms for the plaintiff. . . . It is finally urged that the defendant cannot be held responsible for conversion of these cartons and contents because the action is based on negligence. If the premise were correct, the conclusion would follow, because conversion is based on affirmative acts and not on negligence or nonfeasance. . . . But the defendant was not merely negligent. Its action was more than nonfeasance. When it carried these cartons from Hamilton to Cleveland, it acted affirmatively and exercised an unjustified dominion over the shipper's property. That constituted a conversion and the fact that it was done through mistake does not destroy its affirmative character. It was done intentionally and the motive . . . is immaterial.

Delay

Section 2(a) of both the rail and motor carrier bills of lading terms and conditions provide that no carrier is bound to transport property other than with reasonable dispatch. What constitutes reasonable dispatch or a reasonable time is a question of fact. Generally it can be measured by comparing the time required for the shipment in question with the time usually required to transport comparable shipments between the same points via the same route. (See *Lapidus* v. *Chicago, B. & Q. R.*, 161 F. Supp. 664. Compare *Condakes* v. *Southern Pac. Co.*, 295 F. Supp. 121; *Pennsylvania R. Co.* v. *Newmeyer*, 100 A. 2d 456) Carriers are not liable for delay caused by an act of God or any of the excepted causes listed in the bill of lading, providing their own negligence did not contribute to the delay.

Where goods are offered to a carrier for transportation, the carrier has the duty of informing the shipper of any occurrence likely to delay the transportation of which it has knowledge and which is not within the knowledge of the shipper. Failure to observe this duty will impose liability upon the carrier for a delay in the transportation of the goods irrespective of the cause of the delay. (*Bussey* v. *Memphis, etc. R. Co.* 13 Fed. 330; *Missouri, etc. R. Co.* v. *Stark Grain Co.,* 131 S. W. 410; *West Bros., Inc.* v. *Resource Management Service, Inc.,* 214 So. 2d 431) The acceptance of shipments without notifying the shipper of facts known to the carrier which are likely to occasion delay implies that they will be delivered within a reasonable time except for delays resulting from occurrences not within the carrier's knowledge. When the carrier has given notice of likely delay with respect to shipments offered and the shipper then knowingly entrusts the goods to the carrier for transportation, the carrier will not be held responsible for delays which it cannot prevent even though the shipper did not expressly agree to exempt the carrier from liability.

In holding that the carrier was liable for failure to notify a shipper of manure that certain quarantine regulations existed which would prevent the shipment from being carried through to destination, the court in *Atlantic Coast Line R. Co.* v. *South Georgia Milling Co.,* 161 S. E. 282 said:

> It is the general rule as to domestic shipments that "where goods are tendered to a carrier for transportation, it is bound to advise the shipper as to any cause likely to delay transportation, which cause is within its knowledge, or within its fair and reasonable means of knowledge; and not within the knowledge of the shipper; and, if it fails in its duty in this respect, a delay in the transportation of the goods will not be excused, and that too irrespective of the nature of the cause. The acceptance of goods for shipment without notifying the shipper of the fact that they cannot be promptly delivered is tantamount to an assurance that they will be delivered within a reasonable time, except for the intervention of excusing causes or subsequent occurrences. This duty is in no way dependent on special agreement, but is a part of the duty imposed by law on carriers; and the reason why the law has imposed it on the carrier is to give the shipper an opportunity to exercise his own discretion as to the propriety of making the shipment—to choose between the different courses open to him." 10 C. J. 290, §412. . . .

In *Security Stove & Mfg. Co.* v. *American Ry. Express Co.,* 51 S. W. 2d 572, which involved a shipment of a furnace to Atlantic City, New Jersey, for exhibition purposes, the carrier defended the action against it for delay in delivering a portion of the shipment on the grounds that a carrier's promise to deliver a shipment at a specific time is nonenforceable and void under the Interstate Commerce Act. Concerning this contention the court said:

> It is well established that a shipper cannot recover on a special contract to move a shipment within a specified time, for such would work an unjust dis-

crimination among shippers. The only duty that the carrier is under is to carry the shipment safely and to deliver it at its destination within a reasonable time. *United States* v. *Am. Ry. Exp. Co.*, 265 U.S. 425, 44 S. Ct. 560, 68 L. Ed. 1087; *C. & A. R. R. Co.* v. *Kirby*, 225 U.S. 155, 164, 32 S. Ct. 648, 56 L. Ed. 1033, Ann. Cas. 1914A, 501; *A. T. & S. F. Ry.* v. *Robinson*, 233 U.S. 173, 34 S. Ct. 556, 58 L. Ed. 901; *Cicardi Bros. Fruit & Produce* v. *Pennsylvania Co.*, 201 Mo. App. 609, 213 S.W. 531. . . .

A similar holding that carriers are unable to make enforceable agreements to transport other than with reasonable dispatch is found in *Tribby* v. *Chicago & Northwestern Ry. Co.*, 252 N. W. 20. In this case the plaintiff brought suit for the carrier's failure to live up to its special contract to transport the shipment through on a nonstop train. In denying recovery, the court said:

Counsel for plaintiff urges that in every contract for shipment there is an implied condition binding the carrier to transport within a reasonable time, and cites *Elliott* v. *Chicago, M. & St. P. Ry. Co.*, 38 S. D. 371, 161 N.W. 347, in support of such contention. Such claim for damage is not presented by this record. The allegations of the complaint are for breach of a special contract, and are not based upon the carrier's liability for negligence in not transporting and delivering within a reasonable time. *Chicago & A. R. R. Co.* v. *Kirby*, 225 U.S. 115, 32 S. Ct. 648, 56 L. Ed. 1033, Ann Cas. 1914A, 501. A brief quotation from *Willer* v. *Chicago, M. & St. P. Ry. Co.*, 50 S. D. 319, 210 N.W. 81, will indicate the applicable principle: "Respondent contends that this complaint pleads a special agreement to transport and deliver plaintiff's cattle on a certain date, and that such agreement is illegal and void and against public policy. It is too well known to require argument that the contract which a railway company can make with a shipper is so controlled by statutes, orders of the Interstate Commerce and Railroad Commissions that very little latitude is left for special agreements between shippers and railroad companies. That such an agreement is void, unless open to all shippers alike, is well settled." The foregoing rule is not opposed in principle to *Elliott* v. *Chicago, M. & St. P. Ry. Co.*, *supra*, wherein this court sustained the right of recovery for failure to transport within a reasonable time.

In *Ozark Fruit Growers' Ass'n.* v. *St. Louis-San Francisco R. Co.*, 46 S. W. 2d 895, the court in discussing carrier's liability for failure to meet a market on a certain day, said:

It is also settled that a carrier cannot, ordinarily, be held liable for failure to deliver the goods at point of destination in time for a certain market. That all the carrier is required to do is to transport in the usual way, and that a carrier by reason of the federal statute cannot bind itself by contract or otherwise to transport upon any other than the regular scheduled time for the operation of its trains. Assume that to be true, and we think it is true, there is no claim that a contract of that kind was made in this case. If, however, there is a delay in the transportation caused by the negligence of the carrier, which delay deprived the shipper of the benefit of the market, on a certain day, and he is damaged thereby, the loss of that market may be considered in estimating his damages. *New York, Philadelphia & Norfolk R. R.* v. *Peninsula Produce Exchange of Md.*, 240 U.S. 34, 36 S. Ct. 230, 60 L. Ed. 511, L. R. A. 1917A, 183.

In *Florence B. Fallgren, Adm'x., Hartford Insurance Co. (plaintiff in interest)* v. *Railway Express Agency*, 100 A. 2d 835, the New Hampshire Supreme Court held that an oral agreement between a shipper and a carrier that a shipment would be delivered at a certain time is not enforceable against the carrier where the tariffs of the carrier, on file with the Interstate Commerce Commission, contain no provisions for any agreement with respect to time of delivery. In this case, the court said:

> If the uncontroverted evidence produced by the plaintiff that special representatives of the defendant represented to the plaintiff that chicks shipped on a Thursday afternoon would arrive the Saturday following between the hours of five and six o'clock in the morning could be taken as evidence of an oral agreement that they would so arrive (see *Blodgett* v. *Abbott*, 72 Wis. 516), the evidence would be inadmissible to vary the terms of the written contract issued on the day of shipment. *Long* v. *N.Y. C. R. R. Co.*, 50 N.Y. 76; *The Jean Jabot*, 14 F. S. 161. Moreover such a contract if proved would be unenforceable. The Official Express Classification containing the defendant's published tariffs was binding on the parties. The contract being for an interstate shipment, their rights and obligations are governed by the Acts of Congress, the uniform express receipt, and the tariffs duly filed with the Interstate Commerce Commission. *Nicholas Zeo, Inc.* v. *Railway Exp., Inc.* 317 Mass. 374, 378. The tariffs could not be avoided, enlarged, or varied by the shipper or carrier through express or implied contract. *Am. Ry. Exp. Co.* v. *Am. Trust Co.*, 47 F. 2d 16, 18, *cert. den.* 284 U.S. 629. See also *Davis v. Cornwell*, 264 U.S. 560, 562. In the absence of a published tariff providing therefor, any special agreement for delivery at particular time would be illegal because a preference and in violation of requirements of the Interstate Commerce Act. *Chicago & Alton Railway Co.* v. *Kirby*, 225 U.S. 155. See also, *Davis* v. *Cornwell*, 264 U.S. 560, *supra*; *Clegg* v. *St. Louis & S. F. R. Co.*, 203 Fed. 971; *L. & N. R. Co.* v. *Warren Co. Strawberry Grow. Assoc.*, 206 Ky. 482; *Roberts* v. *Railroad*, 135 Tenn. 48; *Johnson* v. *N.Y., N. H. & H. R. R.*, 111 Me. 263, 270.
> In the absence of an enforceable contract for delivery at a particular time, the defendant's undertaking was one to deliver within a reasonable time. *Chicago & Alton Railway Co.* v. *Kirby*, *supra*, 164, *Nicholas Zeo, Inc.* v. *Ry. Exp. Agency, Inc.*, *supra*, 381. . . .

Volume 13, *Corpus Juris Secundum*, Sec. 229, states a general rule that damages for delay in transportation must be such as might reasonably have been contemplated by the parties at the time the contract of carriage was made, and that "special" damages are recoverable only in cases where the shipper, at or before the time he tendered his goods for shipment, informed the carrier of the special circumstances which rendered prompt transportation and delivery necessary. The same consequences follow if the carrier had constructive notice of special loss likely to follow delay. The notice, to be effective, must be of such character and to such extent that it will be presumed to have contracted in reference thereto, that is, the shipper must communicate all facts which do not ordinarily attend the carriage for the peculiar character and value of the property. The notice ordinarily should disclose the purpose or use for which the shipment is intended, and the necessity of prompt shipment and delivery. The notice must be communicated effectively to the carrier.

The carrier is held to assume a liability only for damages which ordinarily attend failure to perform in the usual and ordinary course. He is not required to foresee unusual or "special" damages which result from the unknown special circumstances. The required notice also gives the carrier opportunity to protect himself by special precautions. Regarding effectiveness of notice, the court in *Pomona Products Co.* v. *Sou. Ry. Co.*, 294 F. 982 said:

> The purpose of notice from the carrier's standpoint it to enable it to decline the shipment, if by reason of unusual conditions it cannot transport promptly, or to enable it to take measures to insure necessary dispatch, if it does undertake the carriage. This can be met only by notice at or before receiving the shipment, and to an agent in position to act in the premises, or one whose duty it is to receive such knowledge and cause others to act thereon.

It therefore appears that the usual notation on a bill of lading regarding delivery at a certain time or date, if permissible, is not sufficient to make the carrier liable for "special" damages, both because it does not give notice to the carrier of the circumstances rendering the special dispatch necessary and because such notices are usually not brought to the attention of a party in a position to act. But the main argument against liability on such a special contract of carriage is that the contract is void unless open to all shippers alike. In view of the control by statute and orders of regulatory commissions, little area is left for special agreements between shippers and carriers. Any such contract made individually is generally held void and unenforceable. But compare *West Bros., Inc.* v. *Resource Management Services, Inc.*, 214 So. 2d 431.

In *Great A. & P. Tea Co.* v. *Chicago, Burlington & Quincy R. R.*, the carrier was held liable for a delay of five days in delivering a shipment of apples shipped from Selah, Washington to Chicago, Illinois. The evidence indicated that under the usual, scheduled and customary time for transportation and delivery of the apples between the points involved, they should have arrived five days earlier. This, the court held was "unreasonable delay in delivery."

In *Lamb* v. *Railway Express Agency, Inc.*, 320 P. 2d 644, a carrier was held liable for one day delay in delivering a carload shipment of cherries shipped from Reith, Oregon, to New York City. In this case the published schedules of the carrier for the "cherry special" provided for the car's arrival in New York City in time for the fourth subsequent morning auction. The train was delayed, however, with the result that the car did not arrive until one day later and had to be sold on the fifth morning auction for less than the cherries could have been sold for on the previous day. The court predicated the carrier's liability on "failure to transport with reasonable dispatch" and pointed out that while delivery was within the schedule for *regular* freight service, this shipment was not offered for regular service but for transportation on the *cherry special* which had a one day earlier arrival than the regular freight service. Because the carrier did not sustain its burden of proof that the delay arose from some cause other than its own negligence, damages were awarded on the basis of the one-day decline in market value.

A carrier is not excused from liability by a mere showing that its equipment broke down en route and had to be repaired. It must, in order to be excused from liability, show that the defects in the equipment were not known, and that by the exercise of ordinary care in the inspection of its equipment and prudent and proper management and operation, such defects, patent or latent, could not have been discovered and the delay incident thereto avoided. (*Seaboard Air Line R.* v. *Lake Region Packing Ass'n*, 211 So. 2d 125) In *Leo Lococo's Sons* v. *Louisville & N. R. Co.*, 82 S. W. 2d 332, the carrier required 57 hours to transport a car of bananas from Montgomery, Alabama, to Louisville, Kentucky, while the usual and customary time was 27 hours, the additional time being required to repair equipment. In deciding whether the carrier was excused, the court said:

> As to what is reasonable dispatch depends in a measure upon the character of the commodity as perishable goods and live stock demand greater expedition from nonperishable and inanimate freight. It is regarded sufficient evidence of reasonable promptness to show what is the customary and usual time between the points involved under ordinary conditions and the circumstances of the particular case, and, while the carrier's schedule is not conclusive, it is an important consideration. Only negligence will render the carrier liable for unusual delay and its consequences, unless there is a valid contract for delivery within a specified time. When a litigant presents this proof and shows that his shipment was materially delayed beyond the usual time, together with evidence of proximate loss, he makes out a prima facie case. It then devolves on

the carrier to explain and to show that the delay was not due to negligence on its part, but arose from some other cause. This burden is placed upon the carrier because the facts are peculiarly within its knowledge and are ordinarily unavailable to the shipper. Michie on Carriers, §908; 4 R. C. L. 737-740; 10 C. J. 283-287, 301; *Louisville & Cin. Packet Co.* v. *Bottorff*, 77 S.W. 920, 25 Ky. Law Rep. 1324; *Illinois Cent. R. Co.* v. *Holt*, 92 S.W. 540, 29 Ky. Law Rep. 135; *Adams Express Co.* v. *Burr Oak Jersey Farm*, 182 Ky. 116, 206 S.W. 173; *Louisville & N. R. Co.* v. *Crain*, 189 Ky. 431, 224 S.W. 1063; *Hines, Director General* v. *Harris*, 202 Ky. 75, 285 S.W. 930; *McCord* v. *Louisville & N. R. Co.*, 206 Ky. 501, 267 S.W. 766; *Maloney* v. *Cleveland, C. C. & St. L. Ry. Co.*, 207 Ky. 262, 268 S.W. 1103; *Chesapeake & O. R. Co.* v. *Coleman Fruit Co.*, 210 Ky. 794, 294 S.W. 463. The carrier is excused from the consequences of unusual or unreasonable delay in delivering the consignment in a safe and undamaged condition if it can justify the tardiness by showing that it was caused solely by the shipper or by an unavoidable accident or was due to such occurrences as could not have been anticipated in the exercise of reasonable prudence, diligence, or care. It is legal implication of contract that the shipper assumes those risks. *Louisville & N. R. Co.* v. *Crain, supra; McCord* v. *Louisville & N. R. Co., supra; Adams Express Co.* v. *Burr Oak Jersey Farm, supra;* 4 R. C. L. 741; Michie, § 908 et seq.; 10 C. J. 287, 290, 294.

Turning to the facts of the instant case, the court said:

The plaintiff having proved that it had taken 57 hours to transport his car of bananas from Montgomery to Louisville, and that 27 hours was the customary and usual time under ordinary conditions, he made out a prima facie case, requiring explanation or justification by the defendant. It undertook that burden and introduced the records pertaining to this shipment by the custodian, who was connected with the office of its superintendent of transportation in Louisville. Without objection, he testified that on the way the car left Decatur, Ala., at 11:30 A. M. December 21st, and, when the train was about 40 miles north, the front drawbar broke and the car was necessarily removed from the train. See Federal Safety Appliance Act, title 45, U. S. C. §1 et seq., (45 USCA §1 et seq.); *Louisville & N. R. Co.* v. *Cecil*, 145 Ky. 271, 140 S.W. 186; but in *United States* v. *Erie R. Co.*, 237 U.S. 402, 35 S. Ct. 621, 59 L. Ed. 1019, it was held that chains are permissible for drawing cars containing perishable freight where there is a defect in a coupling. Continuing, the record showed that the car was attached to the end of the next south-bound train and taken back to Decatur, the most convenient place, to be repaired, and reached there at 5:30 P.M., which was after the shops had closed for the day. The car was promptly repaired on special service order the next morning, and left for its destination on the next available train at 1:35 A.M. December 22nd. However, when the train got about Nashville, the mechanical stoker of the locomotive broke or failed to function on account of a piece of metal dropping into or in some way clogging its operation. It was necessary to procure another engine, and this was done in about 6 hours. Thus the delay of 30 hours is shown to have been caused by these two breakdowns in equipment. The issue therefore narrowed to whether this should be regarded as a matter of law as a sufficient legal excuse with consequent exoneration from liability for the shipper's loss, if any proximately resulted. It is argued by the appellant that the moving of the car south when it ought to have been going north and the use of defective equipment showed negligence; furthermore, that the repairs should have been more promptly made, particularly of the broken drawbar, for, if they had been, the car could have moved north on one of two trains which passed while it was in the shops. We think the evidence shows reasonable diligence in repairing the car, for a rail company is not required to have facilities for making such repairs all along its line or to keep its shop in operation during the night for the repair of a freight car.

But reasonable diligence in making repairs was not all that was required of the carrier:

But merely proving that the coupling pulled out and was diligently repaired, and that the engine broke down and was replaced within a reasonable time, is not sufficient to authorize the court to say as a matter of law there was no negligence but an unavoidable occurrence. It was the duty of the company to maintain it equipment in reasonably good working order. Results attributed to defective equipment do not excuse nonperformance of a carrier's duty to deliver a shipment at destination within the proper time. Michie, § 912; 10 C. J. 295. The company should have gone farther back and showed, if it could, that the defects were not known, and that, by the exercise of ordinary care in the inspection of its equipment and prudent and proper railroad management and operation, such defects, patent or latent, could not have been discovered, and the delay incident thereto thereby avoided.

The court then stated the full obligation of the carrier:

As stated in *Adams Express Co.* v. *Hundley,* 145 Ky. 7, 139 S.W. 1084, 1085: "The rule is that when the car breaks it makes out a prima facie case of negligence against the carrier, and there is nothing in the record to overcome the presumption arising from the breaking of the car without any adequate cause." It is true that the records showed that the car had been inspected at Decatur and the engine at the last terminal (not identified); and no defect was shown on the records; but the character of inspection was not disclosed. It may have been a good inspection or a poor inspection.. The fact of inspection of machinery does not negative negligence, for it may have been superficial, inefficient, or insufficient to detect defects. *Adams Express Co.* v. *Hundley, supra.* As stated in *Vencill* v. *Quincy, etc. R. Co.,* 132 Mo. App. 722, 112 S.W. 1030: "Where the injury to an engine which caused a delay in the transportation of plaintiff's cattle was due either to negligence of defendant's employees in making couplings or to a defective engine end sill, and there was no evidence that the engine had been properly inspected before it left defendant's division point, defendant was responsible for such delay, under the rule that only such causes as cannot be reasonably anticipated, controlled, or avoided by reaonable care will excuse a carrier's unusual delay." See, also *Cleveland, etc. Ry. Co.* v. *Heath,* 22 Ind. App. 47, 53 N. E. 198. We are of opinion, therefore, that whether the delay was unreasonable, whether it was due to defendant's negligence, and whether damage was proximately caused thereby, should have been submitted to the jury.

In *Carter* v. *Atlantic Coast Line R. Co.*, 192 S. E. 624, the question presented to the court was "Is the mere fact that a perishable commodity moving in interstate commerce does not reach destination for a particular market, the possibility of reaching which is indicated in the schedule, evidence of negligence sufficient to support a verdict when the contract under which the commodity is shipped contains a stipulation that 'no carrier is bound to transport said property by any particular train . . . or in time for any particular market or otherwise than with reasonable dispatch'?" The evidence in this case indicated that the shipment arrived in Boston on June 4 when according to the schedule it should have arrived on June 3. The court held that the matter was one which should have been submitted to the jury for decision, and stated:

> It is the contention of the appellant (railroad) that the shipment could not have been made earlier for the reason that the defendant would have had to have given the same priority in violation of the federal law. Of course, the defendant could not be expected to get the shipment off for the plaintiffs in a manner that would be in violation of the federal law, but whether the defendant transported the shipment in question as soon as reasonable, under the circumtances and conditions surrounding the case, or whether it neglected to do this was a question of fact for the jury.

But see *Great A. & P. Tea Co.* v. *Atchison, T. & S. F. Ry. Co.*, 333 F. 2d 705, cert. den. 379 U.S. 967.

In *Southeastern Express Co.* v. *Bowers, Inc.*, 109 S. W. 2d 851, the shipper gave the express company notice that unless the shipment of hats arrived at destination at a specified time, it would stand a chance of losing the sale, as the hats were sold subject to the condition that they be delivered in time for reshipment by the consignee by boat to a foreign country. The court in holding the carrier liable said:

> The action herein is not one for breach of an alleged contract to deliver the hats within a stipulated time, and the cases cited by counsel, holding that in the absence of a published tariff for such expedited shipments preferential agreements of this nature are invalid, are not in point. The ground of action laid in the warrant and that insisted upon by counsel for the plaintiff is that defendant, with notice of the conditions of the sale and with knowledge of special damages likely to accrue as a result of delay, negligently failed to load and ship the hats within a reasonable time. It is in evidence that, barring unusual delay in transit, if the goods had been loaded on the train leaving Knoxville at 9:10 P.M. they would have reached their destination on time, and it is

now admitted that they were not shipped on that train. The excuse offered that defendant was unable to do so because of an unusually large shipment of express loaded at Chattanooga is supported by evidence, and the question presented is whether defendant was absolved from liability by reason of this unusual press of business. . . . There is authority for the view that where the carrier cannot handle the shipment without unusual or unreasonable delay, because of an unexpected influx of freight to its line, it may refuse to accept shipments; but if the carrier knowing the situation accepts goods for transportation it is liable for such delay unless the shipper agrees to assume the risk of delay. *Marine Ins. Co.* v. *St. Louis, etc. R. Co.,* (C.C.) 41 F. 643; *Thomas* v. *Wabash, etc. R. Co.,* (C.C.) 63 F 200; *Ill. Cent. R. Co.* v. *McCelland,* 54 Ill. 58, 5 Am. Rep. 83; *Ill. Cent. R. Co.* v. *Cobb,* 64 Ill. 128; *Faulkner* v. *South Pac. R. Co.,* 51 Mo. 311; *Houston, etc. R. Co.* v. *Smith,* 63 Tex. 322; *Joynes* v. *Penn, R. Co.,* 235 Pa. 232, 83 A. 1016, Ann. Cas. 1913D, 964, and see notes p. 967. But it is also held that: Evidence merely at the time cars were ordered the carrier did not have sufficient cars to comply with the demand is insufficient to excuse the failure to furnish cars, since the carrier may have been negligent in providing for the ordinary conduct of its business, and the rule is that it is bound to provide cars sufficient to transport goods offered in the usual and ordinary course of business, although it is not bound to anticipate and prepare for an exceptional and extraordinary press of business. *So. R. Co.* v. *Atlanta Sand & Supp. Co.* (1910) 135 Ga. 35, 68 S. E. 807. "The isolated fact that carrier (defendant) did not have cars enough to meet the demand, or that it expected cars from other railroads, but failed to get them, will not, in themselves, excuse the carrier for failure to furnish cars, but these facts, in connection with other circumstances may be sufficient show that the carrier was not at fault." *Wadley So. R. Co.* v. *Kent & Downs,* (1916), 145 Ga. 689, 89 S. E. 765, 766. However, it is well settled by numerous cases that since the facts set up as an excuse for the delay are peculiarly within the knowledge of the carrier, the burden is on it to show every fact essential to the validity of the excuse offered. *Atchison, etc., R. Co.* v. *Word* (Tex. Civ. App.) 159 S.W. 375; *Ayres* v. *Chicago & N.W. R. Co.,* 71 Wis. 372, 37 N.W. 432, 5 Am. St. Rep. 226; *Hines* v. *Mason,* 144 Ark. 244, 221 S.W. 861. As we have seen, the inadequacy of shipping facilities is no excuse where an unusual press of business is relied upon, unless the carrier has provided reasonable facilities for all ordinary purposes [*East Tennessee & G. Railroad* v. *Nelson, supra,* (41 Tenn. 272)]; and, under the principles announced in the authorities cited above, we think it necessarily follows that where plaintiff has shown an unreasonable delay the burden of proof rests upon the carrier to show that its equipment is adequate for ordinary purposes and ordinary conditions, and that the delay occurred by reason of an unusual volume of business of which it had no notice at the time the shipment was accepted.

The claimant has the burden of proving that the carrier failed to deliver the goods within a reasonable time. Claimant must establish that a longer time was consumed than should have been necessary to complete the transportation. A prima facie case of negligent delay is established when evidence of unusual delay is adduced and the burden is then on the carrier to show an excuse for the delay which cannot be attributed to its own negligence or that of its employees. (*Texas, etc. R. Co.* v. *Martin,* 175 S. W. 707; *Atchison, etc. R. Co.* v. *Word,* 159 S. W. 375) Concerning the evidence necessary to establish delay, the court in *Chicago, R. I. & P. Ry. Co.* v. *White,* 41 P. 2d 847, said:

> The burden of proof is on the shipper to make out a prima facie case of negligence. This burden he meets when he makes a showing that the cattle did not reach the market within that period of time "ordinarily required by the carrier to transport such a shipment to its destination." *St. Louis & San Francisco Ry. Co.* v. *May, supra* (236 P. 888). The manner of proving whether or not the shipment moved within the time ordinarily required was laid down by this court in the case of *Chicago, Rock Island & Pacific Ry. Co.* v. *Haskell,* 117 Okl. 185, 245 P. 858, as follows: "In an action against a common carrier to recover damages for the negligent delay in the transportation of cattle from a point in this state to their destination in another state, witnesses, who, from past experience, are familiar with such transportation, may properly testify as to the usual and customary time required to make such shipment, and from this testimony and other competent testimony in the case it is the province of the jury to determine whether or not the time actually taken by the carrier for the transportation of the cattle alleged to have been negligently delayed was reasonable or unreasonable." In determining the factors to be considered as to whether or not a movement of cattle between two points is reasonable, in the case of *St. Louis and San Francisco Ry. Co.* v. *May, supra,* this court also said: "The number of cattle constituting the particular shipment, the general movement of cattle from the territory in which the shipment originates, the general movement of cattle over the carrier's line to market, the volume of traffic moving over the line, the available equipment for the movement of the freight, and the extent of railway equipment ordinarily required to transport the general traffic, are elements which enter into the question of determining the reasonable period of time which the railroad should require to move some particular shipment of cattle to market."

While the foregoing case refers to a shipment of cattle, the principles involved would be equally applicable to other goods, consideration, of course, necessarily being given to the nature of the commodity involved.

Upon arrival of the goods at destination, the carrier, upon demand, is required to make delivery to the consignee during regular business hours and the fact that the carriers may have an agreement or custom which would prevent such deliveries being made does not ordinarily excuse the carrier for any loss which the consignee may suffer because of delay in delivery. In *Union Pac. R. Co.* v. *Spano,* 59 P. 2d 75, a car of grapefruit arrived at Denver, Colorado about 10:40 A.M. on a given date and could have been delivered within 15 minutes to two hours as demanded by the consignee but because of an agreement among Denver carriers, delivery was refused until the next day. The court held the carrier liable for decline in market price.

Unusual weather conditions such as floods, snowstorms, bridge washouts, impassable highways, etc., ordinarily will constitute a sufficient excuse for delay. (*Missouri, etc. R. C.* v. *Truskett,* 104 Fed. 728, affirmed 22 S. Ct. 943) The authorities differ as to whether or not a strike of carrier employees is sufficient to excuse a carrier's delay. Some courts in decisions prior to the Wagner Act held that the carrier is liable for the negligent or wrongful acts of its employees, and therefore if its employees go out on strike the carrier is liable, as the delay results from the employees' wrongful act. Thus in deciding *Sinsabaugh* v. *Cleveland, etc. R. Co.,* 149 Ill. App. 430, the court held the carrier liable, stating: "A carrier cannot avoid its responsibility for damages resulting from unreasonable delay in transportation of goods received by it for shipment upon the grounds that its employees refused to perform their usual duties. In such case the delay is held to result from the fault of the employees of the common carrier, for which fault the common carrier is responsible." Today, however, the right of employees to strike is certainly not to be regarded as a "wrongful act" of employees of a carrier. The bills of lading of both rail and motor carriers provide that except in case of negligence the carrier shall not be liable for loss, damage, or delay occasioned from "riots or strikes." While the Supreme Court has never directly decided whether this exemption from liability due to strikes contravenes the provisions of Section 20(11), it seems to be held inferentially in federal courts that the strike clause is valid.

In *Pennsylvania Railroad Co.* v. *Olivit Brothers,* 37 S. Ct. 468, the Supreme Court considered the validity of a lower court's instruction to the jury in a case involving delay due to strike but did not pass upon the validity of the strike clause in the bill of lading. The fact, however, that seemingly none of the parties to the action or the court took issue with the provision seems to give justification for believing the provision valid. Accordingly, the best view seems to be that carriers are not liable for claims occasioned by delay due to strikes.

Unreasonable delay in transporting and delivering does not amount to a conversion by the carrier, making it liable for the value of the goods. The owner must accept the goods and is entitled to recover damages for the loss caused by the delay (*Railway Express Agency* v. *Huntress,* 51 Atl. 2d 379), unless the delay has been such as to make the goods entirely worthless. Ordinarily a consignee may not refuse to accept goods because of delay in delivery, and has the duty to receive the goods and file claim or bring suit for the damages caused by the delay. (*Chicago,*

R. I. & P. Ry. Co. v. *Albert Pfeifer & Bros.*, 119 S. W. 642; *Southern Ry. Co.* v. *Bunch*, 102 S. E. 462; *United Pants Mfg. Co.* v. *American Railway Express Co.*, 2 La. Appeal 7) A consignee of goods which are of little or trifling value and unsalable because of negligent delay on the part of the carrier may, however, refuse to accept them and recover damages therefor. (*American Railway Express Co.* v. *Pitts*, 91 So. 571)

Billing: Bills of Lading; Delivery

Frequently shipments are made under billing which calls for payment for the goods at or prior to the time of delivery. Claims may arise out of the carrier's action which results in the failure to collect such charges. Two types of such billing are considered in this section: shipments moving on order-notify bills of lading and COD shipments.

Other claim problems arise out of the delivery or tender of delivery of the goods. Various problems relating to delivery are also considered hereafter.

Order Notify Bills of Lading and COD Shipments

While the problems relating to order notify and COD shipments do not usually involve loss or damage, they are nevertheless frequently the basis for filing claims against carriers. These claims usually are the result of the carrier's failure to secure surrender of the original order notify bill of lading properly endorsed when making delivery of an order notify shipment or its failure in collecting the COD amount when making delivery of a COD shipment.

It is the carrier's duty to make delivery to the holder of an order bill of lading, properly endorsed, so long as the carrier has no notice of any defect in the title of the holder. (*Pere Marquett Ry. Co.* v. *J. F. French & Co.*, 254 U.S. 538) A carrier, however, is not justified in delivering the shipment if the order bill is not properly endorsed or if the carrier has knowledge that the person demanding delivery is not entitled to delivery. (*Davis* v. *Fruita Mercantile Co.*, 220 P. 983) As with all negotiable instruments, an endorsement by a holder with good title can be made in blank. In other words the notify party by paying the draft to the bank can secure possession of the bill which will bear the endorsement of the "order party" (shipper) and subsequently deliver the bill to another person who, in turn, could pass the bill on to still another person without making any endorsement on the bill. In this manner, the bill could pass among several persons with only the name of the order party (usually the shipper) appearing in the space provided for endorsements. Inasmuch as the bill would be properly endorsed since it bore the signature of the person to whose order the goods are deliverable under the bill, the carrier would not be required to have the person presenting the bill and demanding delivery to also endorse the instrument. In its decision in *John S. Hale & Co., Inc.* v. *Beley Cotton Co.,* 290 S. W. 994, the court said:

> The bills of lading in controversy had not been indorsed by Manget Bros., the persons to whom the carrier had undertaken to deliver the goods, when they came into the hands of the bank. They were not in shape that they might be negotiated by delivery (Section 30). They were not in negotiable form at all. The bank therefore did not acquire the title to the goods which the person who negotiated the bill might have conveyed under a negotiable bill of lading to a purchaser in good faith for value (Section 31), but acquired only that title to the goods taken by one to whom a bill of lading has been transferred (Section 31); that is, title "as against the transferor."

In *Adel Precision Prod. Corp.* v. *Grand Trunk West. R. Co.,* 51 N. W. 2d 922, cert. den. 344 U.S. 831, the court held that where a manufacturer of machinery, through error, sent an unendorsed original order bill of lading to buyer instead of to the seller of the machinery, and the buyer presented the bill of lading with an allegedly forged endorsement to the seller thereon to the carrier, the carrier's delivery of the machinery to the buyer was not authorized by the Bill of Lading Act. The court also held that whether the seller ratified misdelivery of the machinery to the buyer by offering to treat the delivery of the misdelivered goods as an open account was for the jury to determine.

In *Chicago & N. W. Ry. Co.* v. *Stephens Nat. Bank,* 75 F. 2d 398, the court held the carrier liable where its agent following a custom of eleven years standing had signed an order bill of lading for goods not actually received by the carrier, and which enabled the shipper to hypothecate such bills of lading with the bank. The court held that the fact that the bills of lading bore notation of shipper's load and count did not relieve the carrier. In *Boatmen's Nat. Bank* v. *St. Louis Southwestern Ry. Co.,* 75 F 2d 494, the shipper purchased ten carloads of clean rice of fine quality in Arkansas and the carrier issued its straight bills of lading stating that the shipment consisted of "clean rice" and that the shipments were "shipper's load and count." When the cars arrived at Stuttgart, Arkansas, the shipper unloaded the rice and reloaded the cars with rice screenings of a very low grade. Shortly thereafter the shipper presented to the carrier exchange or reconsignment order bills of lading, still describing the shipments as clean rice and as moving "shipper's load and count." The carrier's agent signed the reconsignment bills of lading and they were sold to a bank. The shipper subsequently became bankrupt and the bank lost a large sum because of its purchase of the bills. The bank brought suit against the rail carrier, claiming that the bills entitled it to receive, and required the carrier to deliver, not the screenings loaded at Stuttgart but the clean rice which had originally been loaded at point of origin. The court held the carrier liable on the ground that the carrier was not authorized to issue reconsignment bills of lading since the shipment had not been kept intact since the original loading at point of origin.

In *Evergreen Broom Mfg. Co.* v. *Atchison, T., & S. F. Ry. Co.*, the plaintiff brought suit against the rail carrier for damages resulting from an alleged misrepresentation contained in order bill of lading issued by the defendant. The bill of lading was issued to the order of the shipper and was endorsed and delivered to plaintiff upon payment of the sight draft attached. The bill covered a shipment of 73 bundles of broom corn and contained the statements that it was received in apparent good order, except as noted (contents and condition of contents of packages unknown) "shipper's load, count and weight." The plaintiff alleged that the carrier knew that the broom corn was wet at time it was accepted and knew that, being wet, it was subject to damage and deterioration in transit. Relying upon this statement, however, plaintiff had paid the sight draft and obtained delivery of the broom corn which was then wet, mouldy and discolored whereby it had suffered over $3,000 damages. Defendant carrier filed a motion to dismiss based on the provisions of 49 U.S.C. 101, which provides that the carrier may by inserting in the bill of lading the words "shipper's weight, load, and count" indicate that the goods were loaded by the shipper and description of them made by him; and if such statement be true, the carrier shall not be liable for damage caused by the improper loading or by the misdescription of the goods described on the bill of lading. The motion was denied. The court on the basis of the evidence presented decided that the carrier should be held liable because it was clearly evident to its agent accepting the shipment that the broom corn was not in apparent good order and this constituted a misrepresentation in reliance upon which the plaintiff suffered injury.

In *Griggs Trucking Company* v. *Stoker Service Co., Inc.*, 50 S. E. 2d 914, York-Shipley between January 7, 1947, and February 7, 1947, made twelve shipments of heating equipment from York, Pennsylvania, to Charlotte, North Carolina, on order-notify bills of lading. The consignee, Stoker Service Company, never paid the drafts on these shipments but the carrier made delivery of all of the shipments to it without securing surrender of the original bill of lading properly endorsed. The carrier also failed to collect the freight charges. On February 14, 1947, without the knowledge of the carrier, the shipper and consignee entered into a written contract whereby the consignee turned back eight of the shipments to the shipper, retaining four shipments for which consignee paid the shipper. This agreement also released the consignee from all liability with respect to the drafts and the shipper agreed to accept responsibility for all freight charges. The carrier brought action against the consignee for its freight charges and the consignee thereupon procured an order from the court making the shipper a party defendant. The shipper counterclaimed against the carrier for making delivery without securing surrender of the original bills of lading and the carrier sought to recover its freight charges from shipper because of its failure to sign the Section 7 nonrecourse clause on the face of the bills of lading. The lower court held the shipper liable for the freight charges on the twelve shipments and the carrier liable to the shipper for $805.47 which the shipper had expended in reclaiming the eight shipments from the consignee. On appeal the carrier contended that the shipper had ratified its delivery without securing surrender of the bills by its contract with the consignee and acceptance of return of the shipments. The appellate court affirmed the lower court's findings as to the respective liability of the carrier and shipper.

The court noted that the shipments moved under order bills of lading obligating the carrier to deliver the freight only on surrender of the original bill of lading properly endorsed. When delivery was made without the surrender of the original bill of lading, it was delivery to one not lawfully entitled to possession and the carrier became liable for any loss that the shipper sustained by such misdelivery. The court further noted that the shipper, York-Shipley, could have refrained from taking any steps to avoid or minimize the loss resulting from the wrongful delivery and sued the carrier for the full value of the goods at the time and place of conversion.

With regard to the question of ratification, the court noted that such ratification must be intended with full knowledge of all material facts, and that the burden of showing the ratification rests on the carrier. It concluded:

> Manifestly, the act of a shipper in ratifying the wrongful delivery of specified items of freight consigned under one or more bills of lading neither compels or justifies an inference that he thereby intended to ratify other wrongful deliveries of other property transported under other bills of lading. Moreover, we think the legal result would have been the same on the present record if all of the equipment had been shipped under one bill of lading for the reason

that the mere acceptance by the owners of payment for part of the goods delivered to the wrong person does not operate as a waiver of the wrongful delivery of the remainder. *Lester* v. *Delaware, L. & W. R. Co.*, 92 Hun. 342, 36 N.Y. S. 907; *Olvany* v. *Nyamco Associates*, 154 Misc. 807, 278 N.Y. S. 242.

The court distinguished this case from *Brown* v. *Vandalia R. Co.*, 163 Ill. App. 473, and *Blowers* v. *Canadian Pac. R. Co.*, 155 F. 935, involving acceptance by the shipper from the person to whom delivery was made of the entire purchase price or part payment with a promise to pay the balance.

Unauthorized delivery without surrender of the original order bill has not occurred where a carrier has unloaded part of a shipment but, upon consignee's indication of its intent to reject the shipment, has reloaded and taken it to a warehouse for storage. In *Strickland Transportation Co., Inc.* v. *American Distributing Co.*, 198 F. 2d 546, the court held such action may constitute an unauthorized inspection of the goods but does not permit the owner to reject the property and recover other than the actual damages. In this case the shipper consigned pinball machines to its order with instructions to notify Active Amusement Company, Anderson, North Carolina, on a regular order notify bill of lading. The connecting carrier ET & WNC Transportation Company notified the Active Amusement Company of the arrival and inquired if it had the original order bill in its possession. The notify party requested that the shipment be delivered the following morning at which time it would have order bill available for surrender. The next morning the shipment arrived by truck on the public street in front of the place of business of Active Amusement Company, and the driver informed those in charge that the shipment had arrived. The driver was told to go ahead and unload the machines. An employee of Active Amusement Company assisted the driver in unloading the machines. The driver did not ask for nor was a tender made of the original bill and, in fact, the original bill was never picked up from the bank nor was the sight draft paid.

After five of the fifteen packages or crates had been unloaded on the public street or sidewalk in front of the Active Amusement Company, its employees were able to see that there was damage to some of the machines and that all of them were dirty and scratched. The entire shipment was rejected and the machines which had been unloaded were reloaded and taken by the delivering carrier to its nearest terminal where they were placed in storage. Upon being informed of the circumstances the shipper refused to accept return of the machines and brought suit against the originating carrier for the balance of the purchase price of $3,000 because of delivery without surrender of the original order bill and because consignee was allowed to inspect the shipment contrary to the terms of the bill of lading. The trial court found that there had been "a casual and very unsatisfactory inspection of some of the fifteen crates." The testimony of the employees of the notify party indicated that there had been no inspection other than observing the general condition of the containers; no effort had been made to break the containers open or remove any of the wrapping. In deciding that the carrier was liable for only the actual damage to the machines and not for the amount of the draft, the court said:

> Assuming, however, an unauthorized inspection of the property, we are clear to the opinion that there was no such delivery or conversion as to make the carrier liable for the value of the goods. . . . The owner in the present case has no right to reject the property and recover its full value, but can hold the carrier responsible for any actual damage. *Robinson* v. *Georgia Savings and Trust Company,* 106 F. 2d. 944, 947, 948; 9 Am. Jur., Carriers, Sec. 560. The judgment is therefore reversed and the cause remanded for new trial.

In *O. A. Sutton Corp.* v. *McMaken Transfer Co.,* 233 P. 2d 717, the court found that the consignee deposited with the carrier a certified check for 125 percent of invoice price of merchandise shipped under an order bill of lading prohibiting inspection by consignee, in order to secure permission to inspect the shipment but with oral understanding with the carrier that the check would be returned if the shipment was rejected. The court held that the inspection as agreed upon was not wrongful or unauthorized and did not constitute a delivery of the goods to consignee. Therefore the consignee, having rejected the shipment, was entitled to recover from the carrier the proceeds of the check which the carrier had cashed. The court held that the provision in the tariff limiting inspection was for the carrier's protection and could be waived by the carrier. This case does not appear to be on strong grounds and it is doubtful if many courts would adopt this view.

Controversies will sometimes arise when a shipper attempts to convert an ordinary straight bill of lading into an order notify bill. This is a practice which the carrier should not permit but, admittedly, it is sometimes difficult to police since carrier employees may not always understand its importance. Generally the carrier's classification and tariffs will set forth an exact description of the order bill and requirements in connection with its use; additionally, sometimes the tariff will specifically provide that a straight bill of lading cannot be used for an order notify shipment. Shippers sometimes will ignore these provisions and tender a shipment on a straight bill showing the shipper's name as consignee with instructions to notify another party, and there is some authority that delivery to the notify party under such circumstances constitutes misdelivery and conversion for which the carrier is liable. In other instances, the shipper will simply use the straight bill and in the space provided for name of consignee insert the words "Order of (shipper) Notify: . . ." When this is done, there is a strong basis for arguing that the carrier would be liable for delivery to the notify party without an order in writing from the shipper (order party). Section 3 of the Federal Bill of Lading Act provides that a bill in which it is stated that the goods are consigned or destined to the order of any person named in such bill is an order bill. It provides further that any provision in the bill or in notice, contract, rule, regulation, or tariff that it is nonnegotiable will be null and void unless upon the face of the bill such provision is agreed to in writing by the shipper.

While practically all straight bills of lading are indicated as *nonnegotiable* as required by Section 6 (49 U.S. Code 86), in view of the provisions of Section 3, there seems to be conflict between these sections which undoubtedly will have to be resolved by litigation eventually. In this connection, the decision in *Kesselman* v. *Mid-States Freight Lines, Inc.*, 82 A. 2d 881, will be of interest. The plaintiff shipper using a straight bill of lading consigned two skids of aluminum sheets to itself with instructions to notify Americana Reclaiming Company, Apponaug, Rhode Island. The original bill of lading with sight draft attached for $1,576.94 drawn upon the notify party was sent by the shipper to a Providence bank for collection; the draft was not paid. When the goods arrived at the plant at Americana an official of the corporation requested the carrier to deliver the goods. Upon delivery, Americana signed a receipt therefor and paid the freight charges but did not surrender the original bill. The uncontradicted evidence was that on a nonnegotiable bill such as the one involved the custom is for the carrier to deliver the shipment without receiving anything from the consignee other than his signature on the delivery receipt. After delivery under these circumstances, the shipper received and accepted a payment ($200) from Americana to be applied to this purchase. Shortly afterwards Americana went into receivership and the shipper filed claim for the unpaid balance with the receiver, which claim was allowed in full by the receiver. When the receiver was unable to pay this claim, the shipper brought suit against the carrier for failure to deliver in accordance with the bill of lading. In deciding the case, the court said:

On the facts herein outlined the trial justice, after finding that plaintiff intended delivery of the goods to Americana and that he knew all the facts concerning such delivery, decided for the defendant. The plaintiff contends that this was error because under "Notify" in the bill of lading defendant had notice that the person so designated was not the consignee of the goods and that, since it had failed to obtain the duplicate bill of lading from the person to be notified, the delivery to Americana was a wrongful delivery in law which entitled him to recover damages from the carrier in the amount of his loss. . . . It is clear from the rescript of the trial justice that he rested his decision for the defendant on the ground that plaintiff by conduct had ratified the delivery to Americana. In our judgment he applied the correct rule of law to the undisputed facts of record. Broadly speaking, ratification means the adoption or confirmation by one person of an act performed on his behalf by another without authority. It is generally held that to constitute a valid ratification, which may appear in express language or be implied from conduct, the principal ordinarily must have full knowledge of all the material facts and circumstances relating to the unauthorized act at the time of confirmation, 2 *C. J. S. Agency*, §§34, 42. As this court said in *Brumbaugh System, Inc.* v. *Providence Live Poultry Co., R. I.* 39, at page 41, ". . . subsequent ratification of a contract may bind a principal as effectively as prior authorization."

In connection with COD shipments, the question frequently arises as to whether the carrier is permitted to allow the consignee to examine the goods before collecting the amount of the COD Corpus Juris Secundum (vol. 13, p. 385) indicates that ordinarily the carrier may allow the consignee to inspect COD shipments unless such inspection is forbidden by the consignor. Where the carrier's tariffs, however, indicate that inspection will not be permitted unless shipper gives the carrier written authority permitting it, the carrier must refuse to allow inspection by the consignee. (*Astugue* v. *American Ry. Express Co.*, 131 So. 62)

In *Bond Rubber Corp.* v. *Gates Bros.*, 70 A. 2d 115, the court held that where the carrier's tariff required the carrier to collect cash or certified checks for C.O.D. shipments, but the carrier accepted postdated checks and mailed them to the shipper with delivery receipts attached which clearly indicated the postdating and the shipper's bookkeeper entered "paid" against the consignee's account, the shipper had thereby ratified acceptance of the checks and could not hold the carrier liable because they were returned due to insufficient funds.

A carrier's contract to collect on delivery represents an undertaking entirely separate from its undertaking as a carrier. The carrier in such circumstances acts as bailee to transport the goods and as agent to collect the price and remit it to the party entitled thereto. Its liability to collect and remit constitutes a "trust relation." In view of this, it is not believed that Section 2(b) of the bill of lading requires that claims for "loss, damage, injury, or delay" be filed within nine months would apply where the carrier had made delivery and either failed to collect the charges or to remit them. Claims of this character would be governed by the applicable state statute of limitation.

In *Anthony* v. *American Express Co.*, 124 S. E. 754, the court held that a condition on an express receipt that claims must be made in writing within a specified time applied only to the express company's liability arising out of breach of duty as a common carrier, and not to claims for money collected on COD shipments and not remitted as required. No other cases dealing with this precise point have been located but it is known that many contend that Section 2(b) of the bill of lading is sufficiently broad to include all claims arising out of transportation of property including those relating to COD transactions. In *Nuside Metal Products, Inc.* v. *Eazor Express, Inc.*, the Pennsylvania Common Pleas Court, Mercer County, held that a requirement in a bill of lading that, as a condition precedent to recovery, claims must be filed in writing within nine months after delivery of the property was a requirement which did not apply to COD payments. The basis for this decision was the view that the responsibility of the carrier as collecting agent of the shipper for COD funds was independent of its responsibility under the common law as a carrier for the safe delivery of the goods shipped.

"Owner's Risk, Shipper's Risk," Etc., Notations

In an effort to limit their liability, some carriers will, when receiving shipments improperly packed or already damaged, insert qualifying notations on the bill of lading such as "Owner's Risk," "Shipper's Risk," etc. These notations on bills of lading covering interstate shipments are void and provide the carrier with no protection whatever. In deciding *Morris* v. *Clayman*, 46 M.C.C. 371, the Commission stated:

> Under the bill of lading the defendants were bound to deliver the shipment in the same condition it was when they received it from the complainant, and it was their privilege and duty to describe on the bill of lading the condition of the radio at the time they received it. We observe, however, that the phrase "at owner's risk," inserted by defendants in the bill of lading in an apparent attempt to limit their liability, was void for this purpose under the provision of section 20 (11) of the act, and that, except to the extent provided therein, this action by the defendant was unlawful.

Notice of Arrival; Notice of Refusal

Courts generally hold that the carrier's liability as such does not terminate and its liability as a warehouseman does not commence until the carrier has given notice to the consignee of the arrival of the goods and a reasonable time has been allowed after such notice for removal of the goods. Both the railroad and motor carrier bill of lading provide for such "notice of arrival" and state that property not removed within a specified time after such notice shall be given will be held subject to carrier's liability as a warehouseman only.

Since, as a general rule, motor carriers and express companies make physical tender of delivery to the consignee, it is seldom necessary for them to send consignee a notice of arrival. If, however, delivery is not accomplished, it is necessary to refer to the carrier's tariff to determine whether storage charges commence immediately or free time for removal is allowed. It has also been stated that where by usage, custom, or special contract it is customary for the carrier to tender delivery at consignee's place of business or residence and such attempt has been made, the consignee is still entitled to notice of arrival and a reasonable time thereafter in which to secure delivery of the goods before the carrier's liability as such terminates and its less stringent warehouseman responsibility attaches. (*American Ry. Express Co.* v. *Rhody,* 143 N. E. 640; *American Ry. Express Co.* v. *Stanley,* 92 So. 642; *So. Express Co.* v. *Holland,* 19 So. 66) The motor uniform bill of lading contains a provision not appearing in Section 4(a) of the rail bill of lading, namely, "property not received, at time tender of delivery of the property to the party entitled to receive it has been made" may be kept by the carrier under its warehouseman's liability, and this clause unless modified by the carrier's tariff would indicate that once the motor carrier offers delivery of the goods and the consignee refuses acceptance at that time, the carrier's liability as warehouseman attaches until a subsequent undertaking as carrier once more is assumed.

The notice of arrival when required must be given to the consignee or his agent in a manner which definitely and sufficiently informs him of the arrival of the goods. In *Holloman* v. *So. Ry.,* 90 S. E. 292, the carrier established by oral evidence that notice which has been given by mailing a postal card to the consignee, properly addressed, was sufficient and that in the absence of proof to the contrary, the court held, it would assume that the card was received. In *A. E. Wood & Co.* v. *M. C. R. Co.,* 151 N. W. 601, however, it was held that notice sent by the carrier to the consignee advising erroneously that a shipment of shoes was on hand was insufficient when, in fact, the shipment on hand consisted of velvet and the consignee was not expecting any shipment of shoes. In *Milne Lumber Co.* v. *M. C. R. Co.,* 57 S. W. 2d 732, it was held that where the consignee's address appears on the billing, or it is known, notification of arrival must be sent to that address but, as held in *Tex. & N. O. Ry. Co.* v. *Patterson & Roberts,* 192 S. W. 585, if the consignee's address is not known the carrier is not required to look for him at any place other than that of destination.

A consignee having acted on information received through telephone and telegraph operator in its office cannot, thereafter, object to the sufficiency of the notice of the arrival of the goods. *Ross* v. *Indiana Natural Gas & Oil Co.*, 130 N. E. 440. The notice of arrival must be given within the time specified, if any, by the carrier's tariffs or statute and, in any event, prompt notice must be given. In *Reeder* v. *Wells*, 113 P. 342, the court held that notice written before but not mailed until after the shipment was destroyed by fire was insufficient to free carrier from liability. Likewise, in *Hoyland Flour Mills* v. *M. P. R. Co.*, 5 S. W. 2d 125, "notice of arrival" sent prior to actual receipt of the goods by the carrier's destination terminal was insufficient to start the 48-hour free time inasmuch as such notice related to prospective arrival and statement therein that shipment was ready for delivery was false.

In *Brown* v. *Railway Express Agency*, 188 A. 716, the plaintiff delivered to the express company two trunks, a suitcase, and ten boxes of personal effects consigned to himself and addressed to Armitt Brown, Ellsworth, Maine. The goods were valued at $1,000. The goods arrived in Ellsworth on May 2, 1933, and a postal card notice, bearing postmark May 3, 1933, was mailed in a street letter box to the address on the trunks and boxes, stating that the goods were being held at consignee's risk. This card was returned to the express company by postal authorities marked "Addressee Unknown." Before return of the card, however, the goods had been destroyed by fire on May 27. The court in determining that at the time of the fire the carrier's responsibility was that of warehouseman, said:

> Attempt to give notice of readiness to deliver was fruitless. The consignee did not reside in Ellsworth; he had no agent there. No rule requires the carrier to do what by the exercise of due effort it cannot do. . . . Despite inability to give notice, common-carrier obligation did not terminate until reasonable opportunity had been afforded for the consignee to call, examine, and take his things from the premise of the carrier. . . . What is a reasonable time . . . depends upon a variety of considerations. The term is an elastic one of uncertain value in a definition. . . . Conclusion in the case in hand is that, when the goods were burned, defendant was no longer liable as carrier. Liability had been transmuted to that of warehouseman.

The authorities are in conflict on whether the carrier has the duty to give notice of the failure or refusal of the consignee to accept the goods. The general rule is that the carrier has a duty to give such a notice within a reasonable time. (*13 Corpus Juris Secundum* 178 b; *Atlantic Coast Line R. Co.* v. *Ousley Co.*, 150 S. E. 564; *Church* v. *Cleveland, C. C. & St. P. Ry. Co.*, 5 Ohio N. P., N. S., 585; *Chicago, R. I. & P. Ry. Co.*

v. *Waldo,* 216 P. 911; *Stoddard Lumber Co.* v. *Oregon-Washington R. & Nav. Co.,* 165 P. 363; *Texarkana & F. S. Ry. Co.* v. *Twin City Products Co.,* 208 S. W. 989; *Rountree* v. *Lydick-Barmann Co.,* 150 S. W. 2d 173; *Alton R. Co.* v. *Tucker,* 138 F. 2d 796) Some courts hold that the carrier's duty to notify the consignor of nondelivery is not absolute, however, but depends upon the circumstances involved. (*Porter v. Pennsylvania R. Co.,* 215 N. Y. S. 727; *Markowitz* v. *New York Central,* 172 N. Y. S. 233; *Epstein, Henning & Co.* v. *N. C. & St. L. Ry. Co.,* 4 Tenn. App. 412) Some cases hold that in the absence of a requirement in the bill of lading, the carrier is under no duty to give notice to the consignor. (*Trinidad Bean & Elevator Co.* v. *Pennsylvania R. Co.,* 72 F. 2d 371) Others hold the carrier responsible only when under the circumstances of the case reasonable care requires that such notice be given. (*Mull* v. *Pennsylvania R. Co.,* 38 Pa. Super. 416)

In view of the provisions in carrier tariffs relating to storage and demurrage which in practically all instances require that the carrier notify shipper of consignee's refusal to accept delivery, it would seem that the prevailing rule is rather clear. It is not believed, however, that it can be unqualifiedly stated that in all instances it is the carrier's duty to notify the consignor of consignee's failure to accept the goods. Such obligation is subject to the qualification that the carrier's obligation is to exercise reasonable diligence to give such notice within a reasonable time. What constitutes reasonable diligence and a reasonable time will depend upon the facts and circumstances of each given case. A study of the old cases and the recent decisions involving the obligation to give the consignor notice clearly indicates a continuous trend in avoiding an inflexible, unqualified rule.

In *Trinidad Bean & Elevator Co.* v. *Pennsylvania R. Co.,* 8 F. Supp. 888, affirmed 72 F. 2d 371, plaintiff shipped two cars of beans from Idaho to Philadelphia on an order notify bill of lading consigned to itself with instructions to notify Elkan B. Marks. When the cars arrived, Marks was promptly notified but refused to take delivery of the goods. The shipper after inquiry was finally informed about three weeks after arrival that the cars were on hand at a warehouse which was holding them as agent for the carrier awaiting surrender of the original bill of lading. The plaintiff sold the beans and brought suit for its loss based on decline in market value. The lower court submitted to the jury the question whether notice had been given within a reasonable time and the jury found that it had not. On appeal the court said:

> The question involved in this motion is whether the defendant railroad company was under a duty to give the plaintiff any notice at all of the failure of

the notified party to accept the goods. It is conceded that no term of the bill of lading imposes such a duty. . . . Following the Pennsylvania rule and what appears to be the rule of the federal courts, I hold that in the absence of a provision in the bill of lading, there is no duty upon a carrier to notify the shipper of non-delivery of goods.

The Massachusetts Supreme Judicial Court adopted a view contrary to that of the federal courts in the *Trinidad* case, *supra,* in *Lapp Insulator Co., Inc.* v. *Boston and Maine Railroad,* 112 N. E. 2d 359. This case also involved shipments moving on order-notify bills of lading. The notify party was unable to accept delivery upon arrival at destination of two order-notify shipments because of being unable to pay the sight drafts, and requested the carrier to store the goods at its expense. The shipments had arrived on August 16 and 17 and the carrier was still holding the goods on November 3 when the goods were destroyed by a fire of unknown origin. The carrier then notified the shipper of the nondelivery of the goods, their storage, and their destruction by fire. The court stated that the shipper (order party) had "no prior notice of any kind."

We are disposed to reject the view that there is no duty on the part of the terminal carrier to notify the consignor in a situation like the present. Where the "notify party" does not accept the shipment it is not unreasonable, we think, to require the terminal carrier to inform the shipper of that fact so that he may take the necessary steps for the repossession, storage, or disposition of his property. Whether the duty to notify is absolute as in *Stoddard Lumber Co.* v. *Oregon-Washington Railroad & Navigation Co.* 84 Ore. 399, 405, or depends on the attendant circumstances as in *Porter* v. *Pennsylvania Railroad,* 217 App. Div. (N.Y.) 49, 53-54, need not be decided. It cannot be said as matter of law that the circumstances here were such that the defendant was under no duty to notify the plaintiff. The granting of the plaintiff's third, fourth and tenth requests indicates that the general finding for the plaintiff can be supported on either view. It is agreed that no notice of the nonacceptance of the goods was ever given by the defendant to the plaintiff. Hence a finding was warranted that there was a breach of contract on the part of the defendant.

In *Missouri, K. & T. R. Co. of Texas* v. *Sealy Oil Mill & Mfg. Co.,* 123 S. W. 2d 948, the court held that actual knowledge on the part of the shipper from the consignee as to refusal is sufficient notice even though the railroad fails to notify the shipper promptly. In this case, the plaintiff on April 24, 1935, shipped a carload of cotton seed hulls over defendant's lines and those of connecting carriers. When the shipment arrived at the billed destination, it was reconsigned to Plainview, Texas. On May 3, plaintiff received a wire from the consignee stating "Hulls received have strong musty odor will try to handle at a discount." On receipt of that wire the plaintiff had the defendant's agent at point of origin wire the agent at Plainview for time of arrival and delivery of the car. The destination agent wired in effect that the shipment arrived and was delivered on April 30. On May 7, the consignee again wired the shipper asking for disposition of the car and on May 8, consignee notified the carrier that delivery was refused. On May 9 or 10, the carrier notified the consignor that the car had been rejected by consignee. The plaintiff abandoned the car to the railroad and brought suit for damages. The court held in favor of the carrier and said:

> Obviously, then even if it was a duty, the plaintiff has not only failed to prove a violation of that duty, but the facts affirmatively show that it was not violated. . . . The damage to the plaintiff was caused by the rejection, not by anything which the defendant in this case did, and the plaintiff does not for one minute contend that the defendant had anything to do with the rejection. This is a plain case of a shipper trying to hold the railroad responsible for damages caused by its consignee, when the cause-of-action obviously was against the consignee and not against the carrier.

The requirements of giving notice to the consignor prior to sale of goods by carrier is set forth in Sections 4(b) and 4(c) of the uniform bill of lading and discussed herein under Sale of Goods.

Delivery to Consignee and Delivery Receipts

The duty of the consignee to accept delivery of shipments consigned to him is not ordinarily excused by the fact that the goods are damaged, unless such damage rendered the property practically valueless, having due regard to the expense of acceptance and use and to the purpose for which the goods were intended. (*Crinella* v. *Northwestern Pac. R. Co.*, 259 Pac. 774; *Pacific Heater Co.* v. *Southern Pac. Co.*, 188 Pac. 600; *Houston E. & W. T. Ry. Co.* v. *Brackin*, 191 S. W. 804) In case of partial loss or injury which does not render the property worthless, the consignee should accept delivery and file claim for its loss, or if the property is injured to such extent as to be worthless, consignee should refuse delivery and hold the carrier liable for full value of the shipment. The unlawful refusal by the consignee to accept damaged goods, however, is of no consequence where it appears that no different result would have resulted had the consignee accepted the merchandise in injured conditioned and filed claim for damages suffered (*Gulf, etc. R. Co.* v. *Pitts*, 83 S. W. 727)

The carrier's duty is not merely to convey goods safely but also to deliver them to the party designated by the terms of the shipment, or to his order, at the place of destination. This duty to deliver to the proper party is absolute. If the carrier delivers goods to a person not entitled to receive them it is liable to the person who is entitled to receive them irrespective of its good faith in making delivery. No question of care arises, for in such case the carrier acts at its peril and is responsible regardless of negligence. (*New York & O. R. S. Co.* v. *McGowin Lumber & Export Co.*, 284 Fed. 513)

The primary purpose of a receipt is to afford a written record of facts existing at the time the receipt is executed. If, at a time subsequent to its execution, the receipt is found to be erroneous, it will be amended to reflect the conditions which actually existed. Generally, courts hold that correction in a receipt will be made only upon showing by the clearest and most convincing evidence that it does not properly reflect the actual facts existing at the time of its execution. A carrier's signed delivery receipt reciting that the property was received in apparent good order is only prima facie evidence of that fact, and it is competent to show as between the parties thereto that a different quantity was actually received or that the goods were not in fact received in good order. The law on this subject is the same as the law governing that portion of the bill of lading which serves as a receipt.

The law does not require that a person or corporation sign a receipt in any particular way. The important thing is that the party making the signature, regardless of the means by which it is affixed, adopts such signature as his own act. For this reason pencil signatures, pen signatures, "X" marks and rubber stamp signatures either by facsimile or printed type will be given full effect. The practice, however, of using a rubber stamp without written signature of an individual is one which has very little to commend it.

Frequently, some consignees will accept delivery of shipment from a carrier but indicate on the carrier's delivery receipt that the shipment is received "subject to further check," "subject to recount," "subject to our count, weight, and inspection," or other qualification to the notation "received in apparent good order" which generally appears on the delivery receipt. Carrier should insist that delivery receipts state exactly the number of pieces delivered. Vague, general exceptions as to either count or condition serve no useful purpose and are often the source of controversies. As a strict matter of law, the placing of such notations on delivery receipts should not prejudice carriers. A receipt is prima facie evidence only of the matters it contains, and upon a clear and convincing showing that the facts stated are not correct, the effect of the receipt will be modified to reflect the true conditions. It is upon this theory, for example, that carriers honor claims for concealed loss and damage although a clear receipt was obtained at time of delivery.

Despite the generally applicable rules of law, many carriers seem to labor under the same impression as some consignees that the giving of a qualified receipt in some way strengthens a consignee's position in case of later dispute. It is probably true that some courts might give undue weight to a qualified receipt and for this reason plus the fact that the use of such receipts encourages gross carelessness on the part of consignee and driver, the acceptance of qualified receipts should be forcefully avoided.

The carrier has a right to demand a receipt for the goods as a condition of delivery and may insist on a receipt for the entire shipment. (*Skinner* v. *Chicago, etc. R. Co.*, 12 Iowa 191; *Morris, etc. R. Co.* v. *Ayers*, 29 N. J. Law 393) Section 8 of the Bill of Lading Act, U. S. Code, title 49, section 88, provides that a carrier, upon demand, must deliver goods to the party lawfully entitled thereto, if such demand is accompanied by, among other things, "a readiness and willingness to sign when the goods are delivered, an acknowledgement that they have been delivered, if such signature is requested by the carrier." It would appear that there could be little doubt that a so-called receipt bearing the notation "received subject to later count and inspection" or other vague general notation would in fact not constitute a bona fide receipt which a carrier would have to accept when making tender of delivery.

The primary purpose of a delivery receipt, from the viewpoint of both carrier and honest consignee, is to preserve a precise record of facts which existed at time delivery was made so far as these facts can be reasonably ascertained. From the carrier's viewpoint, the time of delivery affords the last chance to verify the number of pieces actually delivered. Certainly, as a matter of logic, the carrier is entitled to a written record of delivery of the property entrusted to its care. From the consignee's viewpoint, the signing of an exact statement at time of delivery will be very helpful. In the event a claim is found necessary, a positive statement by not only a responsible employee of receiver but also by the delivering carrier's driver will help to properly support a claim for shortage. A consignee's memorandum or carrier's delivery receipt which states exact facts as to number of pieces delivered, or apparent condition of property when delivered, will serve to assist claimant and carrier in determining validity of claim. On the other hand, a receipt which is subject to some general qualifications will only open the way to almost interminable argument between carrier and claimant.

The use of qualified delivery receipts is usually for the sole attempted purpose of "covering-up" inefficiency at the receiving point. Their use is a constant encouragement for carelessness on the part of the consignee's employees. Instances have been cited where material has been taken directly from the receiving docks to production departments without proper records, and claim later asserted against the delivering carrier solely as a result of carelessness on part of consignee's employees developed as a result of using qualified receipts.

When a claim is filed against a carrier for shortage of an entire package or other item listed on delivery receipt and the delivery receipt carries no notation of shortage other than a vague notation such as shipment "received subject to recount," the carrier should promptly decline the claim. In the final analysis in such cases, it is the carrier's driver's word against the consignee's employee's word and the carrier should certainly stand by its own records and employee. There are few things more absurd than a delivery receipt for one or two pieces of merchandise boldly signed by the consignee as "received subject to recount."

Where carrier through error or otherwise has misdelivered a shipment, it has the right to recovery of the goods or their value from the person to whom they were delivered on refunding the freight charges, if paid. (*Hartford Metal Product Corp.* v. *Tidewater Express Lines,* 36 A. 2d. 677)

A carrier is not liable when, in good faith, it delivers the merchandise to the person to whom they were actually sent although such person may be perpetrating a fraud upon the consignor. If, however, the successful perpetration of the fraud was due to the negligence of the carrier, then it will be liable. A carrier delivering an order-notifying shipment to a person on surrender of an unendorsed bill of lading which has been improperly obtained is liable for misdelivery. (*Florence, etc. R. Co.* v. *Jensen,* 108 Pac. 974)

Section 10 of the Bills of Lading Act provides that where a carrier delivers goods to one who is not lawfully entitled to their possession, the carrier shall be liable to the party having title or right of possession in the goods if the consignee to whom delivered is other than the party named in a straight bill of lading or other than the lawful holder of a properly endorsed order bill of lading. This provision does not excuse a shipper, whose goods were misdelivered, from a compliance with a stipulation in the bill of lading relieving the carrier from liability if claim were not made within a stipulated time after a reasonable time for delivery had elapsed. (*Davis* v. *Roper Lumber Co.,* 269 U.S. 158)

In *Williams-Richardson Co.* v. *New Orleans & N. E. R. Co.,* 115 So. 358, plaintiff delivered to defendant at New Orleans a case of cotton goods consigned to W. H. Magee & Company at Prentiss, Mississippi, whereas plaintiff's intentions were to ship the goods to Purvis, Mississippi. When the shipment reached Prentiss, the agent of the connecting carrier, never having heard of W. H. Magee & Company, assumed that a clerical error had been made and delivered the goods to J. T. Magee & Company, which he knew frequently received consignments of goods from the plaintiff. Subsequently, the mistake was discovered and plaintiff sued to recover the value of the goods. The court held that the carrier was bound to deliver the shipment to the consignee named in the bill of lading and was not excused for failure to make such delivery because the shipper had negligently consigned the shipment to W. H. Magee & Company at Prentiss, Mississippi, instead of at Purvis as intended.

Section 4(f) of the contract terms and conditions of the bill of lading provides in part: "Property destined to . . . landing or other place . . . shall be entirely at the risk of owner after unloaded . . . and, *except in case of carrier's negligence,* . . . shall be at owner's risk until the cars are attached to and after they are detached from locomotive or train . . . or if property is transported in motor vehicle trailers or semi-trailers . . . *after they are detached from power units.*" *Arkansas Railroad* v. *Winters,* 265 S. W. 967, held that the liability of a common carrier ceases when delivery of car is made at destination according to directions of consignee. *Davis* v. *Gossett & Sons,* 118 S. E. 773, held a carrier not liable for damage which occurred after delivery of car to side track of consignee. *Ward v. Pere Marquette Ry. Co.,* 204 N. W. 120, held that where a carrier pursuant to custom placed a car of lumber on a private siding thus relinquishing all dominion over the shipment and placing it in consignee's possession and control, carrier's common-law liability ceased. In *Republic Carloading & Dist. Co.* v. *Missouri Pac. R. Co.,* 302 F. 2d 381, the court held that common carrier liability ceases upon delivery of the shipment to the consignee, and that delivery of a carload shipment is normally effected when the car is placed on a team track or is spotted. In *Carter* v. *St. Louis-S. F. Ry. Co.,* 18 S. W. 2d 376, the court held that the carrier delivering a shipment to another at the oral direction of the consignee named in the bill of lading could not be held liable for wrongful delivery.

Delivery to Connecting Carrier

Generally, the requirements in connection with delivery to a connecting carrier are the same as delivery to a consignee. In some instances, however, there may be some differences occasioned by arrangement between carriers. In this connection, *Pratt* v. *Railway Co.,* 95 U.S. 43, is considered as the leading authority. In this case the Grand Trunk Railway was sued for the loss of goods carried over its roads from Montreal to Detroit. The goods reached Detroit on October 17, 1865, and on the night of the eighteenth were destroyed by fire. The Grand Trunk claimed to have delivered the goods to the Michigan Central Railway, a connecting carrier, and thus to have discharged itself from liability before the fire.

The Grand Trunk had no freight depot at Detroit except a single section or apartment in the Michigan Central's freight depot, which was a large building under one roof divided into sections without any partition wall between them. In the center of the building was a railway track for cars to be loaded with freight. The only use the Grand Trunk had of its section was for the deposit of all property which came over its railroad or was delivered for shipment over it. This section, in common with the rest of the building, was under the control and supervision of the Michigan Central. The Grand Trunk employed in its section two men who checked freight that came into it. All freight that came into the section was handled exclusively by the Michigan Central's employees, for which the Grand Trunk paid Michigan Central a flat rate per hundred weight. Goods that came into the section from the Grand Trunk's road, destined over the Michigan Central's road were, at the time of unloading from Grand Trunk's cars, deposited by the Michigan Central's employees into a certain place in the section from which they were loaded into Michigan Central cars by its employees when the road was ready to receive them; after they were so placed, Grand Trunk's employees did not further handle the goods.

Whenever the agent of Michigan Central would see any goods deposited in the section set apart for the use of the Grand Trunk, destined over the Michigan Central's line, he would call upon the agent of the Grand Trunk in the depot and from a waybill exhibited to him by that agent would take a list of the goods and then also, for the first time, learn their ultimate place of destination and the freight charges due on them. From this information, a waybill would be made out by the Michigan Central for the transportation of the goods over its line. The Supreme Court in its opinion said:

> We are all of the opinion that these acts constitute a complete delivery of the goods to the Michigan Central Company, by which the liability of the Grand Trunk Company was terminated.
>
> 1. They were placed within the control of the agents of the Michigan Company.
> 2. They were deposited by the one party and received by the other for transportation, the deposit being an accessory merely to such transportation.
> 3. No further orders or directions from the Grand Trunk Company were expected by the receiving party. Except for the occurrence of the fire, the

goods would have been loaded into cars of the Michigan Central Company, and forwarded, without further action of the Grand Trunk Company.

4. Under the arrangement between the parties, the presence of the goods in the precise locality agreed upon, and the marks upon them, "P & F., St. Louis," were sufficient notice that they were there for transportation over the Michigan road toward the city of St. Louis; and such was the understanding of both parties.

The facts in the case of *Great Coastal Express, Inc.*, v. *Fidelity & Guaranty Fire Corp.*, 43 A. 2d 96, involving two motor carriers, are somewhat similar to those involved in the foregoing cited case. In the *Great Coastal* case, the question was whether at the time of a fire which detroyed certain goods, the goods had been delivered to a connecting line. Great Coastal operated between Richmond, Virginia, and Baltimore, Maryland, with Washington, D. C., as an intermediate stop. Lambert's position in this terminal was separated by partition walls from space used by two other carriers. A corner of Lambert's space, about 12 feet square, had been partitioned off as an office.

In the course of its business, Great Coastal customarily accepted shipments to points served by Lambert and delivered such shipments to Lambert to be delivered by it to the consignee, especially consignees in Baltimore and Washington. Lambert would also pick up freight from shippers and at its terminal deliver to Great Coastal. Local shippers in Baltimore also would deliver freight to Lambert to be carried elsewhere by Great Coastal; Lambert had no part in hauling or delivering such freight.

For these purposes, Great Coastal "leased dock space" in Lambert's terminal and paid Lambert $25 per month as "compensation for dock space and one helper to load shipments from Lambert's dock or to unload shipments left with Lambert's." Lambert received specified pickup and delivery charges for shipments to Baltimore or Washington. Coastal's leased space was not designated by markings, barriers or anything of that kind. Space near the front of the terminal and also near the inner door of the office was generally used for Coastal. All freight left at the warehouse by Coastal was to be delivered by Lambert. Freight delivered by local shippers at the terminal, to be carried elsewhere by Coastal, would bear Coastal's name and be placed in Coastal's space until the Coastal's truck picked it up. Except while one of Coastal's trucks was delivering or receiving shipments, Coastal had no employees at Lambert's terminal.

When freight was brought by Coastal to the terminal for delivery by Lambert to the consignees during office hours. Coastal's drivers would have waybills in Coastal's name and a manifest listing the shipments they had for Lambert's which would refer to the freight bill number and would include the number of pieces and weight of the shipment. After the shipments were checked, Lambert would receipt the manifest, the freight would be deposited in the terminal, and Lambert would make delivery.

If one of Coastal's trucks arrived after office hours, the watchman would open the doors for Coastal's driver and allow him to unload his freight. The driver would unload the freight in the terminal and leave his manifest and other papers at the office so they could be checked the following morning. When Lambert's manager came in, he checked the freight against the manifest and either mailed the receipted manifest to Coastal at Richmond or sent it down on Coastal's next truck.

During January 1942, five shipments consigned to Baltimore, Washington, and other points served by Lambert were transported by Coastal from Richmond to Baltimore and as they arrived during the night were placed by Coastal's drivers "inside the door" of Lambert's terminal for delivery to the consignees, and the freight bills and manifest covering the shipments were left in Lambert's office as customary. While the shipments were in the terminal, they were destroyed by fire which occurred during the same night they were left at the terminal. The value of the goods destroyed was in excess of $2,000; Coastal's insurers paid the several shippers for their loss and then brought suit against the insurer of Lambert contending that at the time of the fire the merchandise had been delivered and was in the possession of Lambert.

In deciding this case the Maryland Court of Appeals, citing *Pratt* v. *Railway Co.*, 95 U.S. 43, as authority, held that where by agreement or tacit understanding, evidenced by practice and usage, a carrier regularly received for transportation property deposited at a particular place by a preceding carrier, deposit of property at that place, without notice by the one carrier to the other, constituted a constructive delivery of the property, although the succeeding carrier had not yet taken actual custody of it. The court stated:

> Checking the freight against the manifest, receipting the manifest and handing it to one of Coastal's drivers, or mailing it, were not part of the delivery or acceptance, but merely verification by Lambert's of the correctness of the previous delivery and acceptance.

Compare *Republic Carloading & Dist. Co.* v. *Missouri Pac. R. Co.*, 302 F. 2d 381.

Labor Disturbances

The liability of a carrier for loss, damage, delay or injury to shipments caused as a direct result of employees' strike is not entirely clear.

H. C. Lust in *The Law of Loss and Damage Claims,* 3rd edition (1931), on page 300 states: "The author is of the opinion that since the Cummins Amendment expressly prohibits every limitation of liability, the strike provision (in the bill of lading) is void."

However, the same authority on page 310 states: "The author believes . . . the strike provision in the bill of lading is probably valid, but it is not a universal bulwark to the carrier. For instance, if there is a strike in the carrier's freight yard at Chicago, that does not necessarily excuse the delay to a shipment at Kansas City. Under the bill of lading provision, the strike must cause damage or delay to the shipment involved."

The foregoing quotations by the same authority are in conflict. It is believed, however, that the last quotation reflects the proper view. The first quotation, it will be noted, is predicated on the assumption that *"the Cummins Amendment expressly prohibits every limitation of liability."* This assumption is erroneous. Section 20(11) expressly provides that a common carrier shall be liable to the lawful holder of a bill of lading for the full actual injury to property *"caused by it* or by any common carrier . . . to which such property may be delivered or over whose lines such property may pass." Under the provision, the question arises as to whether an employee strike occasioning injury to shipments can fall within the term *"caused by it,"* which of course would include carrier's negligence, its acts of omission as well as commission. Certainly it would appear unreasonable to hold that the carrier actually *caused* a strike of its employees since strikes are usually a result of supposedly voluntary action of employees.

The liability of an interstate common carrier for damages due to a labor disturbance was considered by the 9th Circuit Court of Appeals in *Pensick & Gordon, Inc.* v. *California Motor Express,* 323 F. 2d 769, cert. den. 375 U.S. 984, but the final statement on the problem is yet to be made. The *Pensick & Gordon* case was before the court of appeals twice and the Supreme Court of the United States once, the highest court denying certiorari the second time. On the first appeal to the court of appeals, 302 F. 2d 391, the court held the district court was without jurisdiction to determine whether or not motor carriers failed to provide service as required by the Interstate Commerce Act, because the Act vested such jurisdiction exclusively in the Interstate Commerce Commission. On certiorari, the Supreme Court remanded the proceeding to the court of appeals for further consideration. (371 U.S. 184)

On remand, the court of appeals held that a common-law cause of action for failure to serve did survive the enactment of the Motor Carrier Act (part II of the Interstate Commerce Act). However, the court held that the effect of that statute or any other federal statute upon the surviving common-law cause of action would have to be determined in further proceedings in the district court. The court expressly affirmed its prior holding that the Interstate Commerce Act did not create a statutory cause of action cognizable in the federal courts in the first instance.

The starting point for further proceedings in the district court sounding in common law will rest, said the court of appeals, "upon the long recognized doctrine that a cause of action does exist against a common carrier for unjustified failure or refusal to transport freight." The decision cites a number of cases so holding. However, the court of appeals went on to say that, "In further proceedings, the District Court can determine to what extent, if any, the common-law right has been affected or qualified or supplemented by the Motor Carrier Act, . . . or the Labor Management Relations Act, . . . – either, neither, or both." Specifically, the court said the evidence "may well disclose a situation where the common-law rights of the parties must be balanced in the light of pertinent federal statutes. Indeed, a balance may have to be striken in measuring the conflicting impacts of apparently conflicting federal statutes upon those common-law rights."

No report has been found of further action on remand of this case to the district court.

The subject of carrier liability for injury to property occasioned by labor disturbance has been discussed on several occasions in the "Questions and Answers" column of *Traffic World*, a weekly transportation publication, and this authority contends that the strike provision of the bill of lading relates only to the liability of carriers while the shipment is stopped and held in transit upon the request of the shipper. In support of this condition, *Traffic World* cites the Commission's decision in *Bills of Lading*, 51 I.C.C. 671, wherein on page 705 the following appears:

> From our study of the question we think that even in the absence of express stipulation the carrier's liability, under the circumstances contemplated, would be that of warehouseman, only, while the property is stopped and held in transit upon request of the shipper, owner, or party entitled to make such request.
>
> Although the matter is not brought in issue, we are not satisfied with the carrier's claim of exemption, which is included in this clause, from loss, damage, or delay on account of strikes or riots. We are of the opinion and find that this provision should be amended so as to provide that carriers shall not be liable for "delay caused by riots or strikes"; as thus modified we think that the condition proposed by the carriers would be in accord with the law and just and reasonable.

It seems to be the contention of *Traffic World* that all of the exceptions in this provision of the bill of lading related to carrier liability while the property is stopped and held in transit on the request of the owner. This view is difficult to accept. The clause in the bill of lading, Section 1 (b), reads:

> Except in case of negligence of *the carrier* or party in possession (and the burden to prove freedom from such negligence shall be on the carrier or party in possession), the carrier or party in possession *shall not be liable for loss, damage or delay* occurring while the property is stopped and held in transit upon the request of the shipper, owner, or party entitled to make such request, or *resulting* from a defect or vice in the property, or from county damage to cotton or *from riots or strikes.*

The italicized portion of thc foregoing quotation reads "the carrier shall not be liable for loss, damage, or delay . . . resulting from riots or strikes." If the "or" preceding the word "resulting" in the above provision had been omitted, the *Traffic World* contention would appear to be on stronger grounds. The fact that the word "or" is included, however, seems to remove the wording following entirely from any relation to the clause relating to stoppage in transit.

Further, it will be noted from the quotation from the Commission's decision that its objection to this provision runs to that portion which attempts to exempt carriers from liability for loss and damage due to riots or strikes. The Commission indicated that this clause should be modified to provide for exemption for liability for "delay caused by riots or strikes." The usual injury occasioned to shipments by strikes or riots is delay of the shipment. The carrier is usually able to take the necessary precautions to protect shipments from loss or damage when a strike or riot is in progress; the exemption from liability for delays would thus afford carriers a large measure of relief. Regardless of this, however, the present bill of lading terms appear to exempt carriers from liability for loss, damage, or delay resulting from riots or strikes except in those instances where the carrier is negligent, the burden in all instances being upon the carrier to prove freedom from negligence. Further, this exemption does not appear to contravene any of the provisions contained in Section 20(11).

The liability of a carrier for destruction of cargo as result of a strike and riot arising out of a controversy between the shipper and its employees is discussed in *Bowman Dairy Co.* v. *Megan,* 15 N. E. 2d 878. In this case a milk strike had been called by farmers. News concerning the strike was mentioned in newspapers, including a report that the farmers had threatened violence to anyone transporting milk. The court held that such reports were not sufficient to establish negligence on the part of the carrier in failing to take extra precautions to guard against the violence of the strikers who attacked the train and dumped the shipper's milk. The bill of lading under which the transportation service was performed contained the usual clause protecting the carrier "for loss, damage or delay . . . resulting from . . . riots or strikes." The court, in holding the carrier not negligent, said:

> Where liability was fixed upon the carrier, however, the courts have invariably found evidence that there was ample time between threats of violence and the knowledge thereof, on the part of the carrier to protect the shipment, and in such cases the courts have said that common prudence would have suggested the propriety of keeping a lookout where a mob bent on destruction, was operating in close proximity. The evidence in the case at bar presents no situation of this kind, and the undisputed facts disclose that nothing occurred, up to the time that these milk cars were delivered to the carrier, which would reasonably have led one to suppose that the train transporting them would be attacked and the contents of the cars destroyed.

Although a strike may excuse a carrier for a delay in transportation, and does constitute such excuse when the bill of lading so provides, nevertheless it is the duty of the carrier to inform the shipper of any cause likely to delay transportation which is within its knowledge or within its fair and reasonable means of knowledge; and if it fails in this duty, a delay in transportation of the goods will not be excused. In *Southern Pacific Company* v. *M. Rothstein & Sons,* 304 S. W. 2d 383, a strike had been in existence a long time before the shipment was tendered to the initial carrier and an embargo had been issued, by virtue of which railroads were authorized to disregard routing shown on waybills and reroute traffic so as to expedite movement. The embargo notice further provided that the carrier "shall notify each shipper at the time each car is rerouted or diverted and shall furnish to such shipper the new routing. . . ." The trial court found that the carrier did not give notice to the shipper at time of acceptance of the shipments that they would be rerouted. In holding the carrier liable for delay, the court said:

> The evidence in this case, from defendant's own witness, shows that the strike relied upon was in progress in the areas mentioned long prior to the time the shipments were tendered to defendant, and that at the time they were tendered, railroads in the areas affected had issued embargoes as a result thereof. The burden was on the defendant to show, not only the existence of the strike but also that it gave notice to the shipper at the time of shipment, and not having done so it cannot rely on the strike as an excuse for the delay.

A related problem is the obligation of a carrier to pick up and deliver shipments at the striking establishment of a shipper or consignee. The tariffs of both rail and motor carrier have contained "impractical operation" rules, a typical version of which reads as follows: "Nothing in this tariff shall require the carrier to pick up or deliver freight when prevented from doing so because of the existence of riots or strikes, either at consignor's or consignee's place of business or elsewhere." In *Pickup and Delivery Restriction, California Rail,* 303 I.C.C. 579, the Commission held such rules to be unjust and unreasonable, saying:

> Additionally, the carriers have always been privileged to make reasonable rules to regulate the manner of their operation, a matter quite distinct from failure to render impartial service. At no time has the sanctity of the general rule which assures nondiscriminatory treatment of shippers been violated unless it could be demonstrated that the intervening forces were outside the legal control of the carrier and were susceptible of proof by objective facts. The intangible barriers of peaceful picket lines coupled with union contractual provisions acquiesced in by the carriers constitute something less than the physical obstructions historically acceptable at common law. Indeed to accept such an excuse would be diametrically contrary to the accepted legal doctrine that parties may not by entering into a contract alter the rights of third parties.

Embargoes

Every common carrier is under a duty to receive for transportation and to transport any property tendered to it for transportation, provided the property is such as it holds itself out as willing to carry, or as it usually carries; this duty, however, is not absolute and is subject to reasonable limitations and conditions. Whenever necessary to the proper conduct of its business, a common carrier may lay an embargo on transportation for a definite or indefinite period. An embargo has been defined as a notice issued by a carrier refusing to receive or carry certain kinds of freight on its line or between points. Conditions which may justify the imposition of an embargo are numerous and varied. Among them are floods and other acts of God, congestion, shortage of equipment, strikes, and requirements of law or government order. An embargo must not be unjustly discriminatory or unduly prejudicial.

When goods are tendered for transportation a carrier is obligated to inform the shipper of any cause, within its knowledge but not within the knowledge of the shipper, which is likely to delay delivery, and if the carrier fails in this duty the delay will not be excused. Since embargoes are not published in the same manner as tariffs, and shippers are not chargeable with constructive knowledge of the terms of embargoes, it is the duty of the carrier to give actual notice to each shipper. Usually the shippers obtain notice of embargoes only when they tender freight or make inquiry of carriers.

Embargoes usually are directed against the further acceptance of freight and do not affect shipments already accepted for transportation. The carrier's duty with respect to freight already accepted is fixed and cannot be altered by a subsequent embargo. If the conditions causing the issuance of embargo operate also to delay the shipment already accepted and that delay is excusable under the bill of lading the carrier, of course, is excused.

Fire

Carriers are liable for loss or damage occasioned by fire to shipments in transit. This liability begins with the carrier's acceptance of the goods into its custody and continues until it has either delivered the goods as a carrier or, for some reason not within its control, has been unable to accomplish delivery and holds the goods as a warehouseman. If the fire results from an act of God or other cause excepted from common liability, the carrier, of course, is not liable. Cases discussing carrier's liability for loss by fire are *New Jersey Steam Nav. Co.* v. *Merchants' Bank*, 6 How. 344, 12 L. Ed. 465; *Hale* v. *N. J. Steam Nav. Co.*, 15 Conn. 539, 39 Am. D. 286; *Porter* v. *Chicago, etc., R. Co.*, 20 Ill. 407; 71 Am. D. 286; *Farley v. Lavary*, 54 S. W. 840; *McFadden* v. *Mo. Pac. R. Co.*, 4 S. W. 689; *Miller* v. *Steam Nav. Co.*, 10 N. Y. 431; *Berry* v. *Southern R. Co.*, 30 S. E. 14; *Gulf, etc. R. Co.* v. *Roberts*, 85 S. W. 479; *Oregon Short Line R. Co.* v. *Blyth*, 119 P. 875; *A. Arnold & Son Trf. & Stge. Co.* v. *Weisiger*, 6 S. W. 2d 1084; *Wagner* v. *T. S. C. Motor Freight Lines*, 181 So. 625.

In *Anderson, Clayton & Co.* v. *Yazoo & M. V. R. C.*, 141 So. 453, shipment of cotton was delivered to the carrier and the car containing it closed and sealed. Before the cotton moved, it was destroyed by fire although the evidence indicated that there was no fire in or about the station during the loading of the shipment. It was developed, however, that on several occasions during the ginning season of the year in which the cotton was burned, cotton was baled with fire concealed inside the bale. One of the bales intended to go with this shipment was detected and thrown aside because it contained fire inside and was burning. The claimant won a verdict for the loss of the cotton in the lower court and the carrier appealed. In affirming the carrier's liability, the appellate court said:

While the evidence points rather strongly to the hypothesis that the cotton was destroyed by reason of the fact that the shippers delivered a bale with fire concealed in it, of which neither they nor defendant had knowledge, nevertheless this does not appear with legal certainty. The evidence which is circumstantial, does not exclude every other reasonable hypothesis as to the cause of the loss except the hypothesis that it was occasioned in the manner advanced, namely, by the delivery of what is known as a fire bale, or that it was occasioned by any other act of the shippers.

Freight Charges

The law of "self-help" while being one which is quite often used is nevertheless one which has no basis in statutory law insofar as loss and damage claims are concerned. For the average occasional claimant, however, this is not easily understood. The ordinary person who orders merchandise shipped to him and receives it in damaged condition cannot be condemned for concluding that the carrier has a great audacity in asking him to pay the freight charges for such transportation when it is quite obvious that it is going to require a sum, which sometimes is greatly in excess of the amount demanded, to repair or replace the merchandise received. It is understandable that the consignee would prefer to retain the amount demanded for freight charges and apply it to the repair of his goods and demand any additional sum required from the carrier. Certainly he feels he is entitled to deduct the reasonable estimate of cost of repair from the carrier's bill.

Until regulation of carriers by the government, it was a common practice for the consignee to follow this procedure and even today some consignees will refuse to pay freight charges on a shipment where loss and damage are involved. The collection of freight charges, however, and the adjustment of loss and damage claims are entirely separate transactions. The carrier is required to collect the tariff rate for his services; the adjustment of claims for failure to perform the transportation services is another matter which has no relation to the collection of charges. If, after the charges have been paid, it is determined that some of them, a portion of them, or all of them were not properly earned, they will be refunded. But controversy over loss and damage should not be permitted to interfere with the carrier's duty to collect its charges. The justification for this rule is that unless it were applied, the carrier would be able to discriminate and give preference to some of its customers by using alleged controversy over claims as a means of extending credit for its services.

Before federal regulation of interstate motor carriers, it was not unusual for claimant to deduct the amount of his freight claim from the carrier's freight charges. Under federal regulation, however, this method of "settlement" is no longer permissible as is also true with rail carriers.

Administrative Rule No. 65, issued under date of August 3, 1937, by the former Bureau of Motor Carriers reads as follows:

> Question: May a comomn carrier by motor vehicle lawfully postpone the collection of its lawfully established charges for the transportation of property in interstate or foreign commerce because the consignor or consignee has filed with such carrier a claim for damage to the property so transported or for damages to other shipments, or because the consignor or consignee has a claim against the carrier for services or supplies furnished the carrier?
>
> Answer: No. The carrier must collect its lawfully established charges or must use every reasonable legal means to enforce such collection.
>
> A claim for damages filed by consignor or consignee or a claim for services or supplies furnished the carrier are matters entirely distinct from the collection of established charges for transportation and do not in any way relieve the carrier from the duty to collect such charges.

The foregoing is not a formal ruling of the Commission. It does represent the best thought of the bureau and very probably would be supported by the Commission should the question ever arise in a formal way.

In the event of legal action by a carrier against the consignee for collection of freight charges, the courts will allow the consignee to set off the amount of loss and damage claims. In the case of *Chicago and N. W. Ry. Co.* v. *Lindell,* 50 S. Ct. 200, Lindell delivered to the railroad a shipment of grapes for transportation to Chicago which was delivered to consignee without collection of freight and other charges amounting to $683.79. Because of unreasonable delay and failure to use reasonable care to keep the car properly iced, the grapes were damaged. The carrier sued to recover the freight charges and claimant by answer set up the loss. While claiming to have suffered damages of $1,011.70, claimant asked no affirmative relief but only that the loss be held to be a setoff against the carrier's claim. The Supreme Court of the United States allowed the setoff, stating:

> The practice of determining claims of shippers for loss or damage in suits brought by carriers to collect transportation charges is not repugnant to the rule prohibiting the payment of such charges otherwise than in money. The adjudication in one suit of the respective claims of plaintiff and defendant is the practical equivalent of charging a judgment obtained in one action against that secured in another. Neither is to be distinguished from payment in money.
>
> It is well understood that the payment by carriers to shippers under the guise of settling claims for loss and damage may in effect constitute discrimination that the act was intended to prevent. But it is not suggested how opportunity for collusion in respect of such matters would be lessened by abolishing counter-claims in cases such as this. Collusion and fraud may be practiced in the de-

fense and settlement of separate actions brought on such claims, as well as when the same matters are put forward as offsets or counterclaims.

The foregoing decision indicates that although in a court action a claimant may set off the amount of a claim against freight charges, carriers by law are prohibited from permitting claimant to do so otherwise than in a legal action. The credit regulations of the Interstate Commerce Commission require that freight charges be paid within a stipulated time and, obviously, if the consignee complies with the law and pays the freight charges within the lawful period, the charges will be paid before any lawsuit could be instituted.

In *Wells Fargo & Co., Express, S. A.* v. *Tribolet,* 50 P. 2d 878, the claimant shipped tomatoes from Mexico to the Wells Fargo Express Company at Nogales, Arizona. The express company was acting as agent for a tomato growers' association at Sonora where the shipment originated. Claimant, however, demanded possession of the cars upon arrival at Nogales but failed to tender the freight charges for same. In holding that it was claimant's duty to tender freight charges at time possession was demanded, the court said:

> We think as a general proposition of law the owner of goods, whether he or some one else be designated as consignee, may stop the goods enroute and demand their possession before they reach their destination, and that the carrier, especially if it have knowledge of such ownership, is legally bound to surrender the possession to the owner. 10 C. J. 261 §276. However, before the SP Company of Mexico was under any duty to deliver goods to plaintiff, she must have either paid or tendered payment of the freight charges and other expenses, incurred by the defendant under the laws of Mexico and the United States. This is expressly provided for in the bill of lading. . . .

While the claimant is under a duty to pay the freight charges at the time the carrier surrenders its lien at time of delivery, if delivery is accomplished without collection of the charges and the carrier later brings suit for their collection, the consignee is not prevented from setting up its claim for loss and damage as a counterclaim. (*Great Atlantic & Pacific Tea Co.* v. *Lexington-Hazard Express Co.,* 54 S. W. 2d 631; *New York Cent. R. Co.* v. *De May,* 277 N. Y. S. 17) In the latter case, the court discussed the problem in the following manner:

> The action was one brought to recover freight charges due on an interstate shipment. The counterclaim is one for damage alleged to have been caused by the improper handling of the shipment by the plaintiff. The argument of the plaintiff is that permitting the counterclaim to stand would be against public policy. . . . But an examination of the books shows that the cases in

New York, both in state and federal courts, are opposed to the contention herein of the plaintiff, and that such a counterclaim may be interposed as against a claim for freight charges.

In the event the carrier refuses to deliver because of consignee's refusal to pay freight charges in excess of the amount lawfully due according to carrier's tariff and unwillingness to accept the lawful charges, such refusal has been held to constitute conversion even though only a small excess over the legal rate is demanded and the carrier's agent acts in good faith in demanding the excess. (*Pecos & N. T. Ry. Co.* v. *Porter,* 183 S. W. 98; *Brooklyn Eastern Dist. Terminal* v. *Unex Credit Corp.,* 123 N. Y. S. 2d 88) In *Colley* v. *Chicago & N. W. Ry. Co.,* 187 N. W. 98, 107 Neb. 864, it was held that the carrier's refusal to deliver because of consignee's unwillingness to pay illegal storage charges which had been assessed constituted conversion, even though the consignee made no express or formal demand for the goods.

Government Claims

The United States government is this nation's most important shipper of freight. More government freight is transported than that of any other shipper. The obligation of the carriers for the safe delivery of government freight and their liability for in-transit loss or damage are not materially different than they are in the case of commercial movements, and generally the discussions of specific phases of common carrier liability throughout this book apply as well to government shipments as to commercial shipments. The greatest difference is in the manner of processing claims for loss or damage. Because of its unique bargaining position, the government frequently does not feel obliged to assume the burden of proving the validity of its claim; rather it imposes upon the carrier the burden of proving that the government's claim should not be honored. The following is a brief outline of the loss or damage procedure followed by most government agencies.

The difference in the claims procedure for government shipments and commercial shipments begins with the issuance of the bill of lading. Most shipments of government freight are made upon the government bill of lading prepared by the issuing officer for the agency ordering the transportation and usually assuming the liability for the transportation charges.

The government bills of lading, as they are generally referred to, are pre-numbered, and the accountable agency is expected to exercise careful control over their issuance. The government bills of lading are made up in sets of seven parts each, and in completing the face of the form the issuing officer simultaneously prepares (1) the original bill of lading, which contains the terms and conditions of the contract of transportation, the description of the articles comprising the shipment, and evidence of delivery, and which subsequently will be used as supporting evidence for the voucher covering the transportation charges involved; (2) the shipping order, which is to be retained by the carrier's agent at the shipping point; (3) the freight waybill-original, which is to accompany the shipment or to be otherwise conveyed to the destination point in accordance with the instructions of the carrier; (4) the freight waybill-carrier's copy, which is to be disposed of in accordance with the instructions of the carrier; and (5) three memorandum copies of the bill of lading, which are to be retained by the shipper for administrative purposes.

The liability of the carrier commences with its acceptance of the tendered shipment and its execution of the bill of lading. Upon tender of the government property to the carrier for transportation, the agent of the initial carrier inserts the name of his company in the space provided therefor on the face of the original government bill of lading, his signature and the date. The shipping order, the freight waybill-original, the freight waybill-carrier's copy then are surrendered to the carrier's agent. The original government bill of lading, receipted by the carrier's agent, promptly is forwarded by the shipper—the issuing officer or the agency's transportation officer—to the consignee in order that it will be in his possession upon arrival of the shipment at destination, at which time it will be receipted and surrendered by him to the destination carrier for billing. However, in those instances in which it is apparent to the shipper that the mailing of the original government bill of lading to the consignee will result in arrival of the shipment prior to the arrival of the original government bill of lading, for example, in the case of single-line truck movements or shipments by air express, the original government bill of lading may, by agreement with the carrier receiving such shipment, be surrendered to the carrier or its agent to accompany the shipment or otherwise be transmitted to destination.

In signing the government bill of lading the agent for the initial carrier acknowledges that there has been "Received by the transportation company named above, subject to the conditions named on the reverse hereof, the property hereinafter described, in apparent good order and condition (contents and value unknown) to be forwarded to destination by the said company and connecting lines, there to be delivered in like good order and condition to said consignee." Several conditions on the reverse side of the government bill of lading are relevant in the processing of loss or damage claims. One condition provides, "Unless otherwise specifically provided or otherwise stated hereon, this bill of lading is subject to the same rules and conditions as govern commercial shipments made on the usual forms provided therefor by the carrier." This condition is modified, however, by another providing, "In case of loss, damage, or shrinkage in transit, the rules and conditions governing commercial shipments shall not apply as to period within which claim therefor shall be made or suit instituted." Another condition reads, "This shipment is made at the restricted or limited valuation specified in the tariff or classification at or under which the lowest rate is available, unless otherwise indicated on the face hereof." A fourth condition provides, "Receipt of the shipment is made subject to the 'Report of Loss, Damage, or Shrinkage' noted hereon."

Upon delivery of the shipment of government freight at destination, the destination transportation officer completes the "Consignee's Certificate of Delivery" and surrenders the original government bill of lading to the delivering carrier for the collection of the freight charges. The consignee or his agent inserts the name of the transportation company effectuating delivery and the actual point of delivery, the gross weight of the shipment, the date of delivery and his signature in the appropriate places therefor. In completing the certificate the consignee certifies that he received "the property described in this bill of lading in apparent good order and condition, except as noted on reverse hereof." This certification permits the destination carrier to collect the freight charges on the shipment and serves as the carrier's receipt for the delivery of the shipment in apparent good order, subject, of course, to the subsequent detection of concealed loss or damage. However, if the loss or damage is apparent at the time of delivery, the consignee completes the "Report of Loss, Damage or Shrinkage" on the reverse side of the government bill of lading.

The report frequently cannot be reliably completed by the consignee at the time he accepts the shipment and executes the "Consignee's Certificate of Delivery" in advance of surrendering the original government bill of lading to the delivering carrier for the collection of the freight charges. However, the report simply serves as the notice to the carrier of the loss or damage. It is not a claim upon the carrier to settle for the loss or damage in the amount of stated invoice value or cost of repairs. Such amount ordinarily is an estimated figure, and settlement for the loss or damage usually is delayed until the consignee submits a claim or notifies the carrier of the imminence of deductions from charges otherwise due the carrier.

Collection of the freight charges is made upon Public Voucher for Transportation Charges. The voucher includes a recapitulation of the government bill of lading numbers and the freight charges due on each. The carrier attaches the original government bills of lading in support of the amount claimed on the voucher and submits the voucher together with the accomplished government bills of lading to the government agency shown on the government bills of lading as the agency to be billed for the freight charges.

In the course of pre-auditing the vouchers and attached accomplished government bills of lading, the reverse sides of all government bills of lading are inspected for notations of loss or damage. The detection of the notation of loss or damage on the reverse side of the government bill of lading is the initial step in the freight claim procedure. Occasionally the notations of loss or damage are found to have been completed in sufficient detail to permit action to be taken against the carrier solely on the basis of the information furnished. Most frequently the notations are deemed to be inadequate, however, and further investigation as to the nature of the loss or damage, its extent and cause must be undertaken. As previously indicated, the reason that the notations usually are incomplete is that the information called for is not available at the time of accomplishment of the government bill of lading.

Informal correspondence generally is initiated to compile all pertinent data relating to the noted loss or damage. Specifically, the answers to three questions are sought: (1) Did the loss or damage occur while the government property was in the possession of the carrier? (2) Is the carrier responsible for the loss or damage? (3) What was the extent of the monetary value of the loss or damage? If the information received reveals that the loss or damage occurred while the government property was in the possession of the carrier and that the carrier should be held liable and the value of the items lost or the cost of having the damaged items repaired has been ascertained, claim is filed with the carrier.

The carrier is allowed 90 days within which to remit payment in settlement of the loss or damage claim or to question the validity of the claim. The carrier is afforded ample opportunity to challenge the determination of liability in the amount claimed; the carrier can assert whatever defenses may be appropriate—that the loss or damage did not occur in transit, that the loss or damage resulted from an excepted cause, that the amount claimed exceeds the fair market value of the items lost or the reasonable cost of repairing the items damaged and so on. The carrier can request a conference and may submit documentary proof in support of its allegations. Only if the carrier fails to respond to the claim filed within the 90-day period will deductions be ordered from payments otherwise due the carrier. If the amount claimed has not been substantially or completely collected within an additional 180 days, the claim is forwarded to the General Accounting Office for collection.

When the shipment is lost or destroyed altogether, the destination carrier ordinarily is unable to collect the accomplished original government bill of lading from the consignee, and there is no notation of loss or damage on the reverse side of a government bill of lading presented for payment of the freight charges to initiate the freight claim procedure. In that event a thorough investigation of the loss or damage is made by an appointed surveying officer or board. If the report of survey is approved and carrier liability is established, a claim is filed with the originating carrier. The consignee is requested to forward the original government bill of lading for attachment to the loss or damage claim file. In the event the shipment believed to have been lost subsequently is delivered free astray, the original government bill of lading will be surrendered to the delivering carrier, properly accomplished by the consignee, so that the carrier will be able to collect the freight chages due on the shipment.

Claims for loss or damage to army property are submitted in duplicate. The claim form is supported by a copy of the memorandum form of bill of lading. An itemized statement of the prices of the items lost or destroyed is entered on the reverse side of the claim form, and the carrier is requested to remit the amount claimed within 90 days or within that period to furnish documentary evidence proving nonliability. If the carrier does not remit within the 90-day period or offer proof of nonliability, collection is made by deductions from sums otherwise due the carrier.

The armed forces are a large shipper of household goods. While the household effects of armed forces personnel are the property of the individuals and not the government, shipments nevertheless are made upon government bills of lading. The transportation of such household effects is arranged and the government bill of lading issued by the transportation officer of the facility from which the serviceman is being detached. However, the procedure followed in the event of loss or damage to household effects is not as outlined. Initially at least, claims for loss or damage to household goods shipped upon government bills of lading are for adjustment between the owner of the property and the carrier involved.

Even though loss or damage to household goods may have occurred in transit and be apparent at the time of delivery, the serviceman or his agent is expected to sign the Consignee's Certificate of Delivery on the original government bill of lading and surrender the government bill of lading to the delivering carrier for the collection of transportation and accessorial service charges due on the shipment. It is the serviceman's responsibility to submit a claim for the loss or damage and to attempt to collect the amount claimed. Under certain circumstances, the transportation officer of the facility to which the serviceman has been assigned, his commanding officer or even the Department, such as the Household Goods Division, Bureau of Supplies and Accounts, Navy Department, may intercede with the carrier on the serviceman's behalf. However, none of this in any way alters the liability of the carrier; the per pound per article limitation afforded by the released rates upon which the shipments were made restrict the carriers' liability.

Under recent legislation, the Military Claims Act, a serviceman can be reimbursed by the armed services for any loss or damage to his personal effects for which he has not recovered from the carrier up to $6,000. This measure does not absolve the serviceman from his obligation of proceeding against the carrier; it simply affords him greater protection. Where the Department, such as the Bureau of Naval Personnel, Navy Department, reimburses the serviceman for the loss or damage, it is considered to have been subrogated to his rights and can proceed against the carrier just as he could. This procedure has resulted in a certain amount of confusion in instances where trip-transit insurance has been purchased by the serviceman. Where the serviceman has purchased trip-transit insurance and has made partial recovery of the amount claimed for the loss or damage to his household goods from the insurance company and then has been reimbursed for the balance by the Department; the Department cannot recover from the carrier even up to per pound per article limitation; the insurance company, the first assignee of the serviceman's rights, will already have proceeded against the carrier for the full extent of its liability. The carrier need pay the amount per pound per article for which it is liable under the released rates, approved in Interstate Commerce Commission released rates order but once.

As previously indicated, where the government agency making claim upon a carrier for loss or damage is unable to effect collection within a reasonable period, frequently 180 days after a claim not honored by the carrier has been put in line for collection by deduction from sums otherwise due the carrier, the agency forwards its loss or damage claim file to the General Accounting Office for collection. The Transportation Division of General Accounting Office serves as the central point for the collection of amounts due from carriers for loss or damage to government property transported.

If it be determined by the Transportation Division as to a particular carrier's bill that the carrier claimed and was paid a sum in excess of that deemed properly due for the services rendered, there is prepared a notice of overpayment, setting forth in detail the basis of the difference established as to each bill of lading found to have been overpaid and citing applicable tariff references and other data, including the occurrence of loss or damage, relied upon to support the statement of differences. These forms request prompt refund of the amount found overpaid. If the amount found overpaid is not promptly refunded or properly protested by the carrier within sixty days after date of dispatch of the notice of overpayment, the Transportation Division requests the various agencies of the government to make deduction therefor from some unpaid bill of the carrier. If collection cannot be thus effected, there is issued to the carrier a letter requesting refund of all amount due in connection with shipments for all government agencies and, as a final resort, such matters are forwarded to the Department of Justice for collection by suit or otherwise.

It is in connection with the consideration by carriers of notices of overpayment that the area of great difficulty has presented itself. It should be emphasized that the Transportation Division, like any properly operated commercial organization, cannot await indefinitely the decision of a carrier to refund or properly to protest the basis of determination of the overpayment. Carriers can provide material assistance to the government and to themselves if they promptly refund or properly protest the basis of the overpayment cited. It is not sufficient that a carrier merely protest in so many words; each such protest should set forth fully and completely the basis on which the carrier disagrees with the determination reached and the tariffs or other information relied upon to refute the government's position. Each such protest is separately considered and the carrier is advised whether the particular notice of overpayment has been cancelled, revised, or sustained. If the information furnished by the carrier requires a revision in the amount determined originally as overpaid, a new notice of overpayment is issued and the prior one cancelled.

Too much emphasis cannot be placed upon the difficulties which are avoided by prompt servicing of notice of overpayment received by carriers. Failure to refund promptly or protest each such form promptly will involve a deduction from an unpaid bill which would not otherwise be involved in the transaction. This may involve a crossover as to the carriers' accounts with different federal agencies and with bills presented long after payment of the bill on which the overpayment occurred. If a carrier agrees in part with the statement of overpayment on the notice of overpayment, the amount conceded to have been overpaid should be promptly refunded and the balance protested with an appropriate explanation.

It should be understood clearly that the refund of an amount determined as overpaid by the Transportation Division of the General Accounting Office does not stop a carrier from subsequently filing its claim (supplemental bill) for settlement in the General Accounting Office for all or a part of the amount refunded, if later consideration of the matter or the discovery of new and material evidence indicates the presence of error. When carriers have not complied with requests for refunds to the various government agencies or have not refunded in response to notice of overpayment there are marshalled all amounts due from that carrier and the matter is forwarded to the Department of Justice for collection by suit or otherwise of the total amount then due the United States. In such instances there is for consideration the inclusion of interest from date of original payment as to any amount due the United States.

Many carriers are not aware of the limited authority vested in the Transportation Division in disposing of claims involving loss or damage findings by the various government agencies. In those cases in which the various agencies determine that a loss or damage has occurred in connection with a shipment on a government bill of lading, the reverse of that document is annotated at the time of delivery and prior to accomplishment of the consignee's certificate. The amount for which the carrier is administratively determined to be liable may be withheld from payment by a disbursing officer in paying the particular bill of lading or may be collected by deduction subsequently from other unpaid bills forwarded to a disbursing officer if the carrier does not voluntarily remit.

The withholding by the carrier of a bill of lading involving loss and damage will not, however, prevent the determination and collection of the value of the property lost or damaged. The Transportation Division is not usually advised of the basis upon which the notations on bills of lading are predicated. Loss and damage situations involve questions of fact and the information relative thereto is within the knowledge of only the carrier and the agency for which the service was performed. If the carrier objects to the amount deducted or stated for deduction, or as to whether a loss or damage actually occurred, or if it is believed that the shipment was actually delivered or delivered in an undamaged condition, or was subsequently located after being reported lost, it is necessary that correspondence be conducted with the agency involved. Communications addressed to the Transportation Division must be referred by it to the pertinent agency for administrative consideration and usually involves subsequent correspondence between the agency and the carrier. Time can be saved if the matter is presented directly to the installation or agency which determined that a loss or damage occurred.

If the Transportation Division, as a result of a report received from a government agency, has collected by refund or deduction a sum to cover loss or damage as to which the carrier has a real basis for denying liability, the carrier's protest to such collection action should be supported by whatever evidence may be available and the letter protesting the action should set forth in the greatest detail every fact relied upon for denying liability. Decisions reached in these matters are based necessarily upon the written record and evidence available. A deficient record presented by a carrier serves only to delay a final determination or results in a conclusion against the carrier. It is incumbent in these cases that carriers submit factual and written evidence which will adequately support their position.

Insurance

Section 2(c) of both the rail and motor carrier bill of lading provides that any carrier liable on account of loss of or damage to any property transported shall have the full benefit of any insurance that may have been effected upon or on account of the property, so far as this shall not avoid the policies or contracts of insurance, provided that the carrier reimburse the claimant for the premium paid thereon. Very little benefit accrues to the carriers as a result of this clause since the usual inland marine certificate of insurance contains a clause similar to the following:

> Warranted by the Assured free from any liability for merchandise in the possession of any carrier or other bailee, who may be liable for any loss or damage thereto, and for merchandise shipped under a bill of lading containing a stipulation that the carrier may have the benefit of any insurance thereon.

Clauses such as the foregoing make Section 2(c) inoperative; otherwise the insurance policy would be void. In *Arabian American Oil Co.* v. *Kirby & Kirby, Inc.*, 90 A. 2d 410, the plaintiff shipper secured from its insurer the value of the damaged goods under a "borrowed and loan" agreement. Under this agreement, the amount paid to the shipper plaintiff was repayable to the insurance company to the extent of its subsequent recovery from the carrier. Arrangements of this nature based upon a loan receipt have been a common practice for many years. The carrier argued that the provision of the bill of lading giving the carrier the benefit of insurance effected by the shipper absolved it from liability. Rejecting this contention, the court said:

> Historically the reason for such agreements, based on a loan receipt, was to enable the shipper to preserve its right of action against a carrier, notwithstanding a provision of the bill of lading that the carrier should have the benefit of any insurance effected by the shipper. The device was necessary for the protection of the insurer since if the shipper were paid outright the insurer's subrogation rights would be extinguished. Ever since the exhaustive opinion in *Luckenbach* v. *McCahan Sugar Co.*, 248 U.S. 139, 39 S. Ct. 53, the legality of such agreements cannot be questioned and they must be given effect regardless of the stipulation of any bill of lading that the carrier shall have the benefit of insurance effected by the shipper.

Where the motor carrier's cargo policy insures the legal liability of carrier to any shipper for loss or damage to property, and the shipper's optional policy insures shipper's cotton against loss and damage by fire in any place, the policies do not insure either the same interest or against the same casualty. The carrier's cargo insurance company has no right of contribution from shipper's insurer, where cotton owned by shipper is damaged by fire while being transported on the carrier's truck. (*Lucas* v. *Garrett,* 41 S. E. 2d 212)

In *China Fire Insurance Company* v. *Davis, Director General of Railroads,* 50 F. 2d 389, cert. den. 284 U. S. 58, the 2nd Circuit Court of Appeals held invalid a clause in carrier's bill of lading giving it the benefit of any insurance on shipments secured by the shipper on the grounds that this would give the carrier greater compensation than collected from others for similar services. A similar holding was made in *National Garment Co.* v. *New York, Chicago & St. L. R. R.* Co., 173 F. 2d 32.

Practically all rail carriers are self-insurers. Very few motor carriers, however, have received Interstate Commerce Commission authority to self-insure. In the absence of authority to self-insure, interstate motor common carriers are required by the Commission to file evidence of effective cargo insurance.

While generally a motor carrier's cargo insurance covers only loss and damage resulting from catastrophes such as fire, collision, upset, etc., the endorsement makes the insurance company liable within the limits set forth for loss or damage to cargo for which the carrier is legally liable regardless of cause. It is provided, however, that as between the motor carrier and the insurance company, the policy to which the endorsement is attached will prevail, and in the event the insurance company is required to pay any claim as a result of the endorsement for which it would not otherwise be liable, it will have the right to secure reimbursement from the carrier.

It is a common practice for claimants having difficulty securing payment of a claim from a motor carrier to write the Interstate Commerce Commission to secure information as to the identity of the carrier's cargo insurer, the policy number, etc., and use this information for filing the claim with the carrier's cargo insurance company. When such claims are received by the cargo insurance company, the claimant is usually advised that the insurance company can pay the claim only after the carrier's legal liability has been established and the impression is given that it will be necessary for the claimant to secure legal judgment against the carrier through court action. It is not believed that this position is sound; if the claim filed by claimant is properly supported by all necessary documents and the facts are such as to clearly indicate the carrier's liability, claimant should not be required to reduce its claim to judgment. On the other hand, if liability is not clearly established an insurance company cannot be criticized for refusing to pay, since payment would be at its peril as reimbursement can be secured from only the carrier for those claims for which it is legally liable.

The protection afforded to the public by the BMC-32 endorsement in the event the motor carrier becomes insolvent is extensive. Claims for which otherwise no recovery could be secured become the liability of the cargo insurer within the limits specified in the endorsement quoted in the foregoing.

The decision in *Lewis Machine Company* v. *St. Paul Fire and Marine Ins. Co.*, 172 F. 2d 746, indicates that courts will probably be stringent in holding insurance companies to observing the Interstate Commerce Commission rules and regulations regarding cancellation of policies on interstate common carriers. In this case, the plaintiff sued and secured judgment against the Aztec Lines and Anchor Insurance Company and St. Paul Fire and Marine Insurance Company, cargo insurance carriers insuring Aztec's cargoes, for the loss of a valuable piece of machinery. The St. Paul Company appealed from so much of the judgment as found it liable to the shipper for $1,000 with interest on the grounds that Aztec had given it notice of cancellation of its policy, effective May 1, 1947, and secured from Anchor a policy effective the same date covering the same risk. The cancellation of the St. Paul policy was pursuant to the terms thereof and Anchor's policy had been filed with the Interstate Commerce Commission. No notice of the cancellation had been given to the Commission although its regulations require that a policy may not be cancelled until 30 days' notice has been given.

The court pointed out that insurance policies are filed with the Interstate Commerce Commission in order to protect the public, the shipper and consignee, and that no cancellation could become effective as to the public until the insurance company had complied with the Commission regulations. "If this were not true," said the court, "the shipper could never ascertain from the public records whether he was covered but would have to examine the records of the carrier and the insurer and determine at his peril whether the insurance company of record was on the risk." *York-Buffalo Motor Express* v. *National F. & M. Ins. Co.* 63 N. E. 2d 61; *Amalgamated Casualty Ins. Co.* v. *Winslow,* 135 F. 2d 663; and *Maryland Casualty Co.* v. *H. A. Moss & Son,* 267 N. W. 810, were cited by this court in support of its holding.

In *Ward Trucking Corp.* v. *Philadelphia National Insurance Company of Philadelphia,* 67 A. 2d 480, the plaintiff had delivered seventeen shipments to City Line Express, a connecting carrier. While the property was in this connecting line's terminal, it was destroyed by fire. Plaintiff thereafter secured a judgment in the sum of $2,999.69 against its connecting carrier and since it was unable to obtain satisfaction of this judgment instituted suit against the connecting line's fire insurance company under the endorsement to the policy. The lower court allowed judgment against the insurance company but restricted it to $2,000 and both parties appealed. The higher court in refusing to allow greater recovery said:

> The lower court in construing the above quoted-language (the BMC-32 endorsement) rejected the plaintiff's contention that it insured each individual shipper to the extent of $2,000; instead, it concluded that the maximum liability imposed by the endorsement, independent of any other policy undertaking, was $2,000 for the aggregate losses resulting from the fire at the assured's premises. Our study of the endorsement, supported by the pertinent history of its preparation by the Interstate Commerce Commission, has led us to the same conclusion. After the passage of the Motor Carrier Act of 1935, the Commission, upon investigation, determined that a reasonable minimum amount of insurance to cover loss or damage to property of shippers or consignees would be:

> For the loss or damage to property carried on any one motor vehicle, $1,000; for loss of or damage to or aggregate of losses or damages of or to property at any one time and place, $2,000.

The insurance company argued that Ward should not recover the full $2,000 because shipments belonging to many other shippers other than the seventeen shipments of Ward were destroyed in the fire. The insurance company contended that it should be permitted to interplead the sum of $2,000 and join the other shippers and consignees as party to the action in order that the $2,000 could be prorated among the claimants. The court pointed out that over four years had elapsed since the fire, no proceedings had been instituted on behalf of these other shippers and consignees and it was entirely possible that none of them would ever commence such actions. The court said: "It seems to us that in view of the omission from the endorsement of any express provision for prorating, the plaintiff's diligence, in contrast to the inaction of the other shippers and consignees, entitles it in this proceeding to a full recovery against the defendant." The court also allowed the plaintiff carrier to recover interest from that date of its judgment against its connecting carrier.

The liability of an insurance company for loss by fire occurring while the insured line-haul carrier's shipments were on the docks of the freight depot operated by another is discussed in *American Alliance Ins. Co.* v. *Brady Transfer & Stge. Co.*, 101 F. 2d 144. In this case the cargo of Brady was located at a freight depot referred to as the Motor Freight Terminal and operated by one Hermann, when destroyed by fire. The evidence indicated that the Motor Freight Terminal was used by Brady as an agency in picking up and delivering shipments in Des Moines. When the Terminal picked up goods for Brady or when the latter delivered freight to it for delivery, the freight was placed in a space on the dock which was referred to as "Brady Dock" and all the freight there was in the custody and control of one Cavanaugh, an employee of Brady. These goods were transported by Brady under its own bills of lading and tariffs. The insurance policy issued by the plaintiff insurance company to defendant Brady by its terms applied to shipment "while in the custody and control of the assured, while in or on docks . . . depots . . . during due course of transfer to other insured trucks for distribution, from time of leaving warehouse, store, residence or factory of shipper or place of pickup until safely delivered to warehouse, residence, or factory of consignee or place of delivery, . . . but this policy shall cover only while goods are actually in transit, and in no event shall this policy cover any goods after same have ceased to be at the risk of the assured."

The insurance company based its defense on the grounds that the insurance of the Motor Freight Terminal rendered its own policy inoperative except as to the excess, if any; further, that at the time of the fire, the goods were not in Brady's custody or control and hence they were not covered by its policy. The court held that as to those shipments which plaintiff had clearly established as being under the custody of Cavanaugh, the insurance company was liable to the extent that the carrier had established the value of such shipments.

The right of a cargo insurance company to recover from a party whose negligence resulted in destruction of its assured's cargo is discussed to some extent in *Automobile Insurance Co.* v. *Pennsylvania R. Co.,* 14 N. E. 2d 613. In this case the insurance company had issued a policy to Roadway Express protecting its property and property of its shippers from damage. While transporting cargo owned by Goodyear Tire & Rubber Company, its truck was struck by a train of the Pennsylvania Railroad Co. The insurance company paid Roadway and Goodyear for their losses and secured subrogation against the rail carrier. The lower court which tried the case denied the insurance company's action as assignee of Roadway against the railroad on the grounds that Roadway's driver had been contributorily negligent, but it did permit the insurance company to recover as assignee of Goodyear on the grounds that the contributory negligence of Roadway's driver could not be imputed to the owner of the cargo. This holding as to Goodyear, however, was reversed on appeal, the court stating: "The rights of the insurer, however, under subrogation can be no greater than those of the insured (the carrier), from whom they are derived, and if the insured could not recover from the third person the insurer is likewise barred from recovering for the same reason . . . there cannot be contribution among joint tort-feasors, and . . . there cannot be contribution between indemnitors of joint tort-feasors after one of them has paid in full the claim of a third person who was injured by them." In support of its holding, the court cited *City of New York Ins. Co.* v. *Chicago, B. & Q. Ry.,* 140 N. W. 373; *Royal Indemnity Co.* v. *Becker,* 173 N. E. 194; and *United States Casualty Co.* v. *Indemnity Insurance Co. of N. W.,* 195 N. E. 850.

In *Automobile Ins. Co.* v. *Eastern Machinery Co.,* 25 N. E. 2d 954, the plaintiff insurance company issued its policy covering a shipment of freight while in transit and insuring the defendant against loss or damage, from specified causes, while it was in transit from Evansville to Cincinnati, Ohio. While in transit, the shipment was damaged from a cause other than one covered by the policy but under circumstances which led both the insured and the insurer to believe that the carrier was liable to respond in damages and the insured to believe that the insurer was liable under the policy. On inspection of the policy, however, it was found that the damage resulted from a cause not covered therein.

Nevertheless, the insurance company issued a draft to the insured worded as follows: "Pay to the order of the Eastern Machinery Company the sum of $990 as a loan pending recovery from carrier for loss or damage by damage to machinery in transit," etc. Endorsed on this draft was the following: "Received of the Fire and Marine Underwriters Agency of the Automobile Insurance Company of Hartford, Connecticut, the amount entered on the face of this draft as a loan in connection with claim for: Shipment November 14, 1934, to Eastern Machinery Company of Cincinnati, Ohio, via L. & N. Road. Said amount shall be returned to the Fire & Marine Underwriters Agency of the Automobile Insurance Company when and to the same extent recovered from any other person or persons. In consideration of said loan, it is agreed that we will institute and prosecute any and all suits and proceedings in our name for that purpose as we may be requested by . . . (insurance company) . . . at their expense."

The defendant endorsed this draft and secured the money. While it did file a claim with the carrier for $990, the carrier offered only $37 in full settlement of the claim and rejected the balance. The defendant failed to file suit against the carrier although requested by the insurance company to do so and after lapse of almost two years the latter instituted suit to recover on the draft. The court held that the terms of the draft and endorsement thereon made it unnecessary to determine if the insurance company were liable under the policy, but in holding the insured liable to the insurance company for its failure to bring suit against the carrier said:

> It (the insured) received the draft on the assumption that it had a claim in that amount and agreed to institute and prosecute an action for that amount. If there was some defense or defect in its claim that would have prevented a recovery of the full amount, or if the carrier was insolvent, and for that reason satisfaction of the claim could have been obtained, and for that reason defendant would be excused from paying all or any part of the amount received from the plaintiff such fact or facts should have been pleaded as an affirmative defense and proven by it at the trial. In the absence of any such allegation and proof, the plaintiff, prima facie, would have recovered the full amount through the action, which the defendant promised but neglected and refused to prosecute.

The meaning of the word *overturning* as used in a cargo insurance policy is discussed in *Moore* v. *Western Assurance Co. of Toronto,* 195 S. E. 558. In this case the motor carrier cargo insurance policy included, among other perils, coverage for damage resulting from "overturning of the motor truck and/or trailer." Due to traffic congestion, the carrier's vehicle was forced off the concrete surface into a soft shoulder which caused the cargo to shift its weight and break the truck's side boards and fall on the ground, with resulting damage. The court held that a "slight overturning is as much an overturning as a complete overturning" and permitted the carrier to recover from the insurer for the damage. "In the construction of insurance contracts," the court said, "it is vitally essential that the courts do not ignore the fact the primary object of all insurance is to insure, and that, in case of doubt, uncertainty, manifest ambiguity, of susceptibility of two equally reasonable interpretation, since the language used is the selection and arrangement of the insurer, such contracts must be liberally construed in favor of the insured."

In *Barish-Sanders Motor Co.* v. *Fireman's Fund Ins. Co.,* 278 N. W. 374, the court held that under a transportation floater policy insuring against loss or damage to goods while loaded for shipment or in transit on the described vehicles, by collision of the truck with any other automobile, vehicle or object, the insurance company was not liable for damage to automobiles which were being transported when they collided with and struck an overpass, where no part of the truck itself came in contact with the overpass. In this case, the court pointed out that the policy did not cover damage resulting from the cargo itself colliding with an object and the rule to construe ambiguous and inconsistent terms of insurance contracts against the insurer did not extend to imposing risks on the insurance company which were not assumed. In *Garford Trucking* v. *Alliance Ins. Co., of Philadelphia,* 195 F. 2d 381, the court held the insurance company liable where the policy insured against damage to cargo from collision of vehicle, overturning "or other accident to the conveyance." In this case a turbine being carried on one of the carrier's vehicles hit an overhead bridge and the court placed considerable stress on "other accident to the conveyance" since it was indicated that there was no "collision of vehicle" or "overturning."

The violation by a motor carrier of a requirement in its insurance policy that the alarm equipment on the truck be set in the "on" position on long distance hauls did not impair the right of the shipper to enforce for its own benefit the obligation of the insurer to the extent of $1,000 under the endorsement. (*Bolta Rubber Co.* v. *Lowell Trucking Corp.,* 23 N. E. 2d 873) In this case, however, it was also held that the motor carrier because of its failure to observe the requirement lost its right under the policy terms against its insurers.

In *Carolina Transp. & D. Co.* v. *American Alliance Ins. Co.*, 200 S. E. 411, it was held that in an action by the owner of the cargo for loss thereof against the carrier of which the insurance company had notice and an opportunity to defend, a judgment secured by the owner of the goods against the carrier is conclusive as to the insurer.

In *Phoenix Insurance Co.* v. *Cushman Motor Delivery Co.*, Municipal Court of Cincinnati, Hamilton County, Ohio, January 27, 1945, the court held that a carrier must be afforded an opportunity to investigate a claim and establish liability and extent thereof, if any. While the *Phoenix* case is from a lower court, it is believed that it would be followed by all courts in instances where a carrier is not given a chance to inspect concealed damage and the claimant by other evidence is unable to prove loss.

Jurisdiction

Except insofar as the provisions of the Interstate Commerce Act relating to rebates, concessions, and discrimination are involved, the Interstate Commerce Commission has no jurisdiction over loss or damage claims. In deciding *Morris* v. *Clayman*, 46 M.C.C. 371, the Commission stated:

> It is well settled that the Commission does not have jurisdiction over so-called loss and damage claims. Whether or not the bill of lading, as drawn by the defendants, properly described the condition of the radio when received from the complainant, and the extent of the defendant's liability, if any, under the bill of lading, are matters to be determined by a court of competent jurisdiction, as provided in section 20(11) of the act.

A discussion of jurisdiction of federal district courts and of removal from the state court to federal district court of matters involving interstate freight loss and damage claims is contained in *Strickland Transportation Co., Inc.* v. *American Distributing Co.*, 198 F. 2d 546.

Ownership of Goods

The determination of the passage of title to goods is by no means a simple matter. Bugan, in his treatment of the subject (Bugan, *When Does Title Pass*, [Dubuque: Wm. C. Brown Company, 1951]) devotes twenty-four chapters and 500 pages in covering the problem from all angles. It obviously is impossible to more than very briefly discuss the problem in this book and the general rules presented here are subject to numerous exceptions. There has been a tendency on the part of carriers and industrial traffic managers to treat this subject lightly and to endeavor to apply the test "who pays the freight charges?" in order to determine ownership of goods at time loss or damage occurred. Actually this test in itself is meaningless, as this is only one of the factors to be considered and by no means is the single factor controlling.

In present day commercial practices sales are made "FOB point of origin," "FOB Origin, freight charges deducted by consignee," "FOB origin, freight charges prepaid," "FOB origin, Order Notify or COD," "FOB destination," and on other arrangements such as those giving the consignee the right to return, etc. These arrangements frequently are complex and the fact that it is often necessary for the parties involved to resort to litigation to determine ownership of the goods at a particular time fully indicates this complexity.

As between buyer and seller of merchandise shipped, the question of determining when title passes from one to the other usually depends upon the intentions of the parties. In the absence of an agreement to the contrary, ordinarily a delivery by the consignor to the carrier conveys title to the merchandise to the consignee. This, however, would not be true in those instances where the shipper retains the right of stoppage in transit. (*Savannah Chemical Co.* v. *Grace,* 293 Fed. 145, cert. den. 264 U.S. 590; *Garfield, etc. Coal Co.* v. *Penna. Coal, etc. Co.*, 84 N. E. 1020) Upon delivery to the carrier designated by the buyer, or in absence of such designation to one usually employed in the transportation of goods from the place of the seller to that of the buyer, the carrier becomes the agent or bailee of the buyer so that the seller is not liable for injury to the goods in transit, or for delay in delivery by the carrier, without fault on the shipper's part, and the fact that no bill of lading is sent to the buyer is immaterial.

Where the provisions of a sale provide that the sale is FOB point of origin, title as a general rule will pass to the consignee when delivery is made to the carrier. If the provisions of the contract are, however, that the sale is FOB destination, title does not as a rule pass until the goods arrive at destination. (*Capehart* v. *Furman Farm Impl. Co.*, 16 So. 627; *Macgruder* v. *Gage,* 3 Am. Rep. 177; *Detroit So. Ry. Co.* v. *Malcomson,* 107 N. W. 915; *McNeal* v. *Baum,* 23 A. 687; *Weiser* v. *Granger Mercantile Co.,* 237 S. W. 328)

The prepayment of freight by the shipper is evidence to show that seller assumed the duty of delivering the goods at point of destination but not necessarily conclusive proof of this issue. (*Neimeyer Lumber Co.*

v. *Burlington & M.R.R. Co.*, 74 N. W. 670; *McLaughlin* v. *Marston*, 47 N. W. 1058; *Heert* v. *Ridenour-Raymond Grocer Co.* 108 Pac. 968)

The owner of goods lost or damaged during interstate shipment by a common carrier is a proper party to recover under the Interstate Commerce Act despite the fact that such party is neither named in the bill of lading or receipt nor is the holder thereof. In *Delaware, Lackawanna and Western Railroad Co.* v. *United States of America*, 123 F. Supp. 579, machinery was shipped under a bill of lading naming the Union Switch and Signal Company as consignor and the Ithaca Gun Plant as consignee. In allowing the United States to recover for the damage on this shipment, the United District Court for the Southern District of New York said:

> Section 20(11) Title 49 U. S. C. A. defines the liability of the delivering carrier, stating that any common carrier, railroad or transportation company delivering property received by it and transported shall be liable to the lawful owner of the receipt or bill of lading or to any party entitled to recovery thereon, whether such receipts or bill of lading has been issued or not.
> The stipulated facts do not state whether the United States is the present holder of the bill of lading. The fact that it has been conceded that the United States is the owner of the machinery gives it the right to bring the suit to recover damages without proof of actual possession of the bill of lading.

Cf. Chicago, Milwaukee & St. P. and Pac. Ry. Co. v. *Acme Fast Freight, Inc.*, 336 U.S. 465, 487, 488, footnote 27; *Atchison, Topeka & Santa Fe Ry. Co.* v. *United States*, 94 F. Supp. 677, 679; Restatement of Agency, Secs. 302 and 310.

The true owner of goods transported by a carrier has the right to have his consignment while in transit withheld or diverted at any intermediate point through which it passes, but unless diversion order emanates from one who has authority to divert, carrier alters destination at its peril. Consignee is presumptively the owner of goods in transit, and unless carrier is advised that shipper has retained title, carrier is justified in complying with consignee's request to deliver goods at some other destination than that designated by the consignor and incurs no liability to consignor by so doing. (*Missouri Pac. R. Co.* v. *Clay*, 182 S. W. 2d 467) That there has been a delivery of goods by a shipper to a common carrier for transportation to a consignee named in a bill of lading does not compel conclusion that title to goods thereby passed to named consignee, and such naming of a person as consignee is some evidence that title is in him but it is not conclusive, and burden of proving title to goods is one person claiming them. (*American Garment Co.* v. *Taylor*, 33 N. E. 2d 296)

The relationship between buyer and seller with regard to passage of title may well be affected by the Uniform Commercial Code which has been adopted with varying modifications in several states. When questions arise regarding ownership of goods and the right to file claim, advice of counsel should be secured.

Protective Service

Claims for damages by freezing of merchandise or spoilage due to excessive heat are often presented to carriers and controversies over the disposition of these claims are frequently litigated in our courts. Decisions of the courts, unfortunately, have not been uniform and the overzealousness of some of the courts in endeavoring to find some ground upon which carrier liability may be attached has made it impossible to establish fully acceptable general rules for guidance which in themselves would not be in almost direct conflict with some court decision. And yet, fundamentally, the courts rendering the conflicting opinions will pay "lip service" to certain recognized general principles but in reaching their conclusions find reasons for departing from the general rule.

In the early days of the law, damage due to weather conditions was considered as constituting "an act of God." This doctrine, however, was quickly discarded and the courts now hold generally that freezing is not an act of God when it occurs at seasons of the year and in latitudes where freezing is to be normally expected; the same principle is followed in those cases where the damage is due to warm weather. The problem today is in determining whether the carrier was under obligation to provide other than normal service to the goods and, if under a duty to provide protective service, whether it fulfilled its obligation to do so without negligence; or, if the carrier owed no duty to provide protective service, whether the carrier was negligent in some other respect. It is particularly in connection with this phase that the court decisions are at wide variance and often appear to be weak on grounds. In view of the definition of negligence, it is difficult to square decisions which imply that the carrier was under no duty to provide protective service yet seemingly for no other reason than the failure to supply such service, hold that it was at the same time negligent in not providing it.

The liability of rail carriers for damage resulting from weather conditions is more easily determined than the liability of motor carriers. This results from the fact that rail carriers publish protective service tariffs which clearly outline the type of protective service available, the conditions under which it will be rendered, and the charges which will be made therefor. The practices of motor carriers differ; some publish protective service tariffs similar to rail carriers; others do not publish such tariffs but advertise and provide such services; and still others do not hold out to supply or render such services under any conditions.

When the motor carriers were subjected to regulation by the Interstate Commerce Commission and required to file tariffs covering their services and charges with that body, there was considerable disagreement among them as to whether the industry should follow the policy of rail carriers and publish and file protective tariffs. Many in the industry owned, operated, or leased equipment with mechanical refrigeration or heater units; others had insulated equipment suitable for transportation of perishables with dry ice or portable heater units. These carriers had employed this equipment as a sales' inducement to shippers of goods requiring protection and in many cases the argument had been that the service would be provided without additional charge. It is understandable that under such circumstances there would be a reluctance for competitive reasons to instituting overnight a charge for this service which had been looked upon more as a sales expense than a service or operating expense.

Inasmuch as the problem seemed one upon which the industry could not agree, it was decided that action on a national basis by publication of a national protective service tariff should be avoided and the matter should be left for the determination of each individual carrier either by publishing agent handling the matter in agency tariffs. Accordingly, Section 2, Rule 23, of National Motor Freight Classification has always provided that ratings published therein on freight requiring protection from heat or cold do not obligate a carrier to provide refrigeration or heater service or trucks especially equipped for such protection except as otherwise provided in the carrier's tariffs. Since a carrier's duty with respect to goods transported is governed by not only the bill of lading but also the carrier's tariffs, it is essential that the shipper of perishables carefully review these tariffs to determine if a carrier provides protective service and, if so, the manner in which such service may be obtained and the charges therefor if any.

Though it would appear that the liability of a common carrier for damage resulting from failure to provide protective service should present a question of law which by this date should be firmly established by the decisions of the courts, an examination of the reported decisions shows a wide variance of opinion. To a large extent this variance probably results from the courts evaluating the problems involved from the viewpoint of the claimant plaintiff, with corresponding failure to take into consideration the practical aspects of transportation confronting the carrier. Many shippers of perishables undoubtedly are fully informed as to the provisions of the tariffs of the carriers; in any event, they have constructive notice of their contents which admittedly are binding upon them. Practically all shippers of perishables are fully aware that generally carriers seldom offer other than ordinary service for less-than-carload or less-than-truckload shipments; provisions of such service either by a heating or refrigerating unit on a single carload or truckload for the protection of one or two small shipments would in many instances cause considerable damage to other commodities which require neither service. Some shipments in a carload or truckload may require heater service, others refrigeration service, and some will be endangered by the provision of either. As a practical matter, it would be impossible for the carrier to provide all of the services which the inherent nature of the commodities on a mixed carload or truckload might require.

Further, it must be recognized that carriers daily accept hundreds, often thousands, of shipments for transportation. These are in most instances tendered to and accepted by pickup drivers and other carrier representatives who are ordinarily not in immediate touch with the carrier's traffic department or its management. In the ordinary course of business, these employees may occasionally be tendered shipments of commodities which the shipper is fully aware require some form of protective service to assure delivery in good condition at destination; the carrier employee unfortunately may not be aware of such requirement or if so may assume that the shipper knows what he is doing. In other instances, the bill of lading will contain instructions such as "Protect from Cold," "Protect from Heat," "Perishable," etc. Quite often there will be no instructions on the bill of lading as to these requirements but the containers of the shipment will be marked indicating that such service is required. Obviously when a carrier employee accepts a shipment with the bill of lading or packages or both indicating "Protect from Freezing" on a cold day in December, frequently miles away from his terminal, the merchandise in the shipment may be completely frozen before he can return to the terminal and call the attention of his supervisor to such instructions.

More than anyone else, the shipper knows the inherent nature of the products which he ships; more than anyone else he knows the risk which he assumes under these circumstances; and more than anyone else he should be concerned about their protection. As the early cases point out, a shipper shipping commodities at a season of the year when their inherent nature is such that they are liable to damage by freezing or destruction by heat assumes the risk of those natural occurrences. Motivated by a selfish desire to ship during all seasons of the year, however, these shippers often knowingly ship when fully aware of the risk assumed and when damage occurs seek to impose liability upon the carrier for the loss and, unfortunately from the carrier viewpoint, usually receive sympathetic consideration from courts that apparently are more concerned with the *moral* than *legal* aspects of the litigation.

There can be very little sympathy for the carrier that sends its salesmen out with instructions to solicit the transportation of commodities which it knows require some type of protective service it is unable to provide in all or any instance. For example, during the cold months practically all carriers can safely transport most commodities which require protection from heat; during warm months, most can safely transport commodities which require protection from cold. This not only the carrier but also its patron knows. Further complicating the matter are those instances where a carrier does have some equipment to provide the protective service requested but due to shortage of such equipment occasionally or frequently takes the risk of using ordinary equipment for transportation of shipments known to require protective service. When these matters become the subject of litigation, there is an understandable, though questionable, tendency on the part of courts to resolve the matter on what may be believed to be the requirement of "justice" or "equity" rather than on strict legal principles.

If the carrier by its conduct has misled the shipper, or if the carrier has been negligent in providing service which is offered by is tariffs or which it has promised to render, then clearly the carrier's misconduct should not relieve it from responsibility. On the other hand, in those instances where the shipper is fully aware of the inherent nature of its commodity, the known requirements of protective service and the possible inability of the carrier to provide it, there would seem to be a duty upon the shipper to conduct some reasonable investigation to determine its availability either by reference to publish tariffs or by discussion of the problem with the management of the carrier. In most of these matters there will be equities, responsibilities, and duties on both sides and those which fall upon the shipper should be no less exacting than those which fall upon the carrier.

Strictly as a matter of law, it seems well established that a carrier is under no duty to provide other than those services set forth in its tariffs. Section 217 of the Interstate Commerce Act, 49 U.S.C. 317, specifically provides:

> Every common carrier by motor vehicle shall file with the Commission, and print, and keep open to public inspection, tariffs showing all the rates, fares, and charges for transportation, and all services in connection therewith. . . .

A similar requirement applicable to rail carriers is contained in Section 6(1) of the Act, 49 U.S.C. 6(1). The Supreme Court of the United States in *Chesapeake & Ohio Railway Co.* v. *Martin,* 238 U.S. 209, stated:

> . . . the parties to a contract of interstate shipment . . . made pursuant to the Interstate Commerce Act, could not waive its terms, nor could the carrier by its conduct give the shipper the right to ignore those terms which were applicable to that conduct, and hold the carrier to a different responsibility from that fixed by the agreement made under the published tariffs and regulations. A different view would antagonize the clear policy of the Act and open the door to the very abuses at which the Act was aimed. . . .

It would seem this decision by the nation's highest court should establish the "law of the land," namely, that a carrier is not liable for failure to provide protective service unless such service is required or available under some specific provision of the carrier's tariff. As the court specifically states to hold otherwise would antagonize the clear policy of the Act and open the door to the very abuses at which the Act was aimed. In deciding *Jackson & Perkins* v. *Mushroom Transp., Co., Inc.,* 41 A. 2d 635, cert. den., 326 U.S. 733, the court seemed to have faced the problem presented specifically from its legal aspects, giving full weight to the holding of the highest court that the carrier had no other duty than to provide the services set forth in its tariff. The carrier was held not liable for freezing of rose bushes shipped in cartons labelled "This Box Contains Live Plants—Highly Perishable—Must Be Kept from Extreme Heat or Cold." The court said: "Defendants omitted nothing, provided by the tariffs, that would prevent subjecting the plants 'to extreme heat or cold' while in transit or at rest. . . ." As to the cause of the damage, the court said: "The evidence supports the conclusion that the damage resulted from the shipment of property liable to freeze during the low temperature stated above, in unheated transportation facilities, and that defendants performed the contract of carriage without negligence."

The decision in *American Writing Ink Co., Inc.* v. *New York, N. H. & H. R. Co.,* 80 F. Supp. 694, is in accord with the *Mushroom Transp.* case. The plaintiff in the *American Writing Ink* case in January 1948, shipped 55,000 bottles of ink via the defendant consigned to U.S. Naval Supply Depot, Oakland, California. The rail carriers took 25 days to complete this delivery although normally the schedule was only 12 days. On the bill of lading, plaintiff had inserted the following instructions:

"War Material—Urgent, Rush—Do Not Delay" and "Keep on Most Southerly Route to Avoid Freezing." The plaintiff did not specify a particular type car or that the car be heated so defendant provided an ordinary box car. When the ink reached destination, it was found to have been damaged as result of freezing. The shipper brought suit for the damage suffered and alleged that the railroad was negligent in not supplying a heated car and also because of delay. The court denied these contentions and stated:

> A reasonable person would have anticipated that this shipment of ink was not going to go through on pre-war schedule. Similarly, a reasonable man would have anticipated the likelihood of some freezing taking place in a product such as ink shipped in the coldest month of the year. Since the railroad provided a heater service at a higher tariff, it stood ready and willing to accept a contract for such service, which would of course have made it an insurer for all intents and purposes. This plaintiff, either by reason of ignorance or neglect, did not choose to avail itself of this service. It took a chance that the weather would be so mild that no damage would result to its product. I cannot find that the delay or routing contributed in any way to the freezing of the ink; in fact, the ink may have been frozen, for all that the evidence shows, before it left Boston.

A carrier's duty with respect to goods transported is governed not only by the bill of lading but also the carrier's tariffs, schedules, and the other governing rules and regulations of the Interstate Commerce Commission. In *Mobile & O. R. Co.* v. *Jensen,* 139 So. 840, the claimant had shipped bees by railroad freight from Louisiana to Mississippi. Some days before the bees were shipped the claimant informed the destination agent of the carrier of the necessity for immediate unloading upon the arrival of the bees and requested the agent to notify him of the arrival immediately. The bees arrived on March 21, 1929, at about 5:30 A.M. and the agent deposited in the mail at 11:00 A.M. a notice to the consignee concerning the arrival. The claimant who had been expecting the arrival of the bees on this date contacted the agent in the afternoon at about 4:30 P.M. and learned of their arrival, and on the following morning began to unload them and found that a large number of colonies had been injured as a result of lack of ventilation after arrival. In defense of claimant's suit for damage to the bees, the carrier introduced in evidence copy of its tariff which provided that notice of arrival would be sent or given to the consignee within 24 hours after arrival and urged that this regulation is controlling and any agreement made between carrier and shipper or consignee not authorized by this regulation is void. In upholding the carrier's contention, the court said:

The tariffs, rules, and regulations adopted by the Interstate Commerce Commission are controlling in all interstate shipments. Their purpose was to bring about uniformity and equality in rates, as well as in the rules, regulations and practices of the carriers. The cardinal purpose was to prevent discrimination and favoritism among shippers. The tariffs and rules and regulations of the Interstate Commerce Commission have the effect of law and cannot be added to, altered, amended, or changed by an oral agreement. The contract between the shipper and the carrier is made up, not of the bill of lading alone, but of the bill of lading, plus the tariffs, schedules, and the other governing rules and regulations of the Interstate Commerce Commission.

In *Denver-Chicago Trucking Co., Inc.* v. *Oyama,* 188 Pac. 2d 442, the shipper forwarded a shipment of ginger root from Tampa, Florida to Denver, Colorado, via lines of Acme Freight Lines and defendant. Upon delivery the shipment was found to be in a frozen condition and worthless. Plaintiff alleged that the shipment was in good condition when originally tendered and this the defendant admitted but went on in its answer to plaintiff's complaint to allege that the damage "was not caused by any fault or negligence on its part but that it resulted from freezing weather 'without any concurring fault of defendant'; that said property was shipped under a uniform bill of lading which provided that it was 'Received, subject to classifications and tariffs in effect on the date of the issue of this bill of lading'; that the published classification and tariffs in effect did not provide for heater service; . . . that by reason of the inherent nature of the shipment it was frozen by the lowering of the temperature while the property was in transit." The lower court found for the claimant but on appeal this decision was reversed, the court stating:

The law in this jurisdiction is that, where there is no defect in the service rendered by the carrier and the damage to the goods is due to their inherent nature and qualities, the carrier is not liable. We so held in *Fort* v. *Denver & R. G. R. Co.,* 69 Colo. 441, 447, 195 P. 109, 111. . . . In affirming the judgment we said: "It is the rule of the common law that a carrier is not liable for losses or injuries resulting from the inherent nature of the goods, which could not have prevented by the exercise of ordinary care upon its part, or for loss or injury to goods caused by an inherent defect in the goods themselves, the existence of which was unknown both to the shipper and the carrier."

Carriers were not insurers of perishables at common law; their duty was only to exercise ordinary care. In *Singer* v. *American Express Co.,* 219 S. W. 662, the court said:

A carrier is not an insurer of perishable fruit, if the damage is caused by it perishing; but he is an insurer in all other respects, just as if it were not perishable, as, for instance, it be injured in a wreck, or fire, or any other cause not the act of God or the public enemy. Therefore, it is not correct to say, broadly, that a carrier is not an insurer of perishable fruit, and it follows that he should exculpate himself by showing that the loss charged resulted from perishing, and the burden is on him to do that, unless the case made by the plaintiff shows it. In this case plaintiff himself has shown that the berries were damaged by reason of their perishable nature, and therefore defendant is not liable in the character he was sued, viz. an insurer.

Unless the carrier has by some negligence on its part actually contributed to the ordinary result of the laws of nature and if it has not unreasonably delayed the shipment, it would seem that damage by freezing or spoilage occurring to the goods in transportation would be recognized as the result of the inherent character of the goods for which the carrier is not liable, unless by its tariff it has offered to provide protective service and the shipper has complied with the tariff in order to secure such service. It is elementary that under the law the shipper has constructive notice of the contents of these tariffs and neither the shipper nor the carrier can waive compliance herewith. With these established principles in mind, it is enlightening to review some of the recent decisions.

In *Watson Bros. Transp. Co., Inc.* v. *Feinberg Kosher Sausage Co.,* 193 F. 2d 283, Watson's freight solicitor called on Feinberg and solicited its refrigerated freight business to California, advising that his company had recently instituted a refrigerated service to California. Feinberg relied upon this information and secured an outlet for its meat products in California and advised Watson that it would be up to them to see that the products were transported properly. Two shipments were given to Watson in April and handled through to destination without refrigeration and without spoilage. Other shipments were given to Watson consigned to intermediate points between Minnesota and California and were handled safely without refrigeration.

On May 2 and May 6, 1949, Feinberg gave Watson two shipments in good order consigned to Los Angeles. When these shipments arrived at Watson Brothers' dock there, although not refriegrated previously, they were packed in dry ice and delivered to the consignee in that refrigerated condition. The packages were not opened at time of delivery and were immediately placed in a cooler by the consignee, apparently in good condition. When opened and inspected, the shipments were found to be spoiled. Feinberg did not note on the bills of lading that refrigeration was required but appears to have relied on its understanding with Watson Brothers' solicitor that refrigeration would be provided. The products were packaged in new fiberboard boxes prominently marked, "Perishable. Keep Cool and Dry."

The tariff under which Watson operated contained the following clause: "Except as otherwise provided in individual items, rates named in tariffs made subject to this tariff include the cost of protecting shipments from damage by heat or cold, providing that the shipper states specifically on the bill of lading that such protection is required." Other tariff items provided: "The obligation to accept articles for shipment shall be subject to capacity and appropriate type of vehicles and to requirements of ordinances or laws limiting or regulating the transportation of the property or use of the vehicles" and "Rates or ratings provided on freight requiring protection from heat or cold do not obligate the carrier to provide refrigeration, heater service or vehicles specifically equipped for such protection, except as otherwise provided in carrier's tariffs." Watson Brothers defended upon the grounds that (1) it did not have the duty to refrigerate these shipments in the absence of a specific request on the bill of lading; (2) it used the degree of due care required by its contract or at common law in the transportation of these shipments; and (3) the plaintiff had failed to sustain its burden of proof by substantial evidence that the products were spoiled at time of delivery to consignee. The case was tried before the lower court without a jury and the court found in favor of the shipper. In appeal to the 8th Circut United States Court of Appeals, the decision was affirmed.

The court agreed that the tariff clause did not state that protection would be given to shipments only if the shipper requested protection, a conclusion based in part on the defendant's own action with respect to the tariff clause. The court also noted that the tariff clause concerns the amount of the rate to be charged and not what must be done by the shipper to obtain protection. The second ground for holding against the carrier is the conflict of the carrier's interpretation with the Carmack Amendment:

Section 20, Subdivision (11) of the Interstate Commerce Act, 49 U. S. C. A. §20, Subd. (11), prohibits the exemption of carrier from liability for any loss or injury to shipments caused by the carrier, notwithstanding any limitation thereof in any receipt or bill of lading or in any contract, rule, regulation, or in any tariff filed with the I.C.C. And the Act of Congress specifically provides that any such limitation is unlawful and void. To hold that a carrier may charge the rate to be applied for refrigerated transportation service under a contract requiring reasonable care for the protection of perishable goods and then relieve itself of that responsibility by a provision inserted in the tariff that it would not be responsible for exercising reasonable care unless the shipper specifically requested it on the bill of lading would effectively relieve the carrier of the responsibility imposed upon it by the Interstate Commerce Act and nullify the pertinent provisions thereof. Hence, if the clause of the tariff in question means what appellant contends it means, the proviso is void. *Adams Express Co.* v. *Darden,* 265 U.S. 265, 44 S. Ct. 502, 68 L. Ed. 1010; *Union Pac. R. Co.* v. *Burke,* 255 U.S. 317, 41 S. Ct. 283, 285, 65 L. Ed. 656. See also in principle *Chicago M. & St. P. Ry. Co.* v. *McCaull-Dinsmore Co.,* 253 U.S. 97, 40 S. Ct. 504, 64 L. Ed. 801.

It must be admitted by all that the court in the Feinberg case was presented with a perplexing problem. The carrier had solicited the business on the basis that it would provide protective service and by its course of conduct caused the shipper to rely upon it to provide such service. The rates in its tariff were the same when the service was supplied as when it was not supplied. It is not believed, however, that the court's reasoning that the shipper was not required under the tariff on the bill of lading that the service was required is sound; nor is it believed that this requirement as a matter of law is void. Words must be accepted in their ordinary meaning. Further, while Section 20(11) of the Interstate Commerce Act does prohibit carriers from limiting their liability except under certain specified condition, this law definitely states that carriers are only liable for loss, damage, or injury to property "caused by it," and damage caused by weather condition is not caused by a carrier but another and more powerful force.

It is believed that the court in the Feinberg case erred in its reasoning in its effort to find the carrier liable. The case would be on sounder legal grounds if the court had simply admitted that it was imposing liability upon the carrier because by its course of conduct it had waived compliance with its tariff requirement on notice of need for protective service, and it would be an injustice to permit the carrier to use its own misconduct as a defense. This would accord with *Hopper Paper Co.* v. *Baltimore & Ohio R.R. Co.,* 178 F. 2d 179, where the court held in effect that compliance with the carrier's regulations would not have accomplished anything in view of the carrier's awareness of all existing facts.

In *Watson Bros. Transp. Co.* v. *Domenico,* 194 P. 2d 323, the court simplified its problem by refusing to discuss whether or not the carrier was required to give refrigerated service and held the carrier liable on the broad grounds of negligence. As is true in most cases involving perishables where a carrier is found liable because of negligence, the court did not discuss just what the carrier should have done to avoid liability for negligence other than provide refrigeration. There is an implication, however, that the carrier probably should have made periodical stops enroute and opened the trailer doors to ventilate the shipment or should have kept the rear doors opened during the entire transportation. In this case a shipment of eggplant was received by Watson in good condition on September 4 which it delivered to the consignee in bad condition two days later. According to the findings of the lower court, the loss was caused by overheating. Watson defended on the grounds that the loss was occasioned by the inherent nature of the goods and that no duty rested on it in law or contract to furnish refrigeration to prevent spoilage. In sustaining the judgment in favor of the claimant on appeal the court said:

> The . . . circumstances are sufficient to establish a prima facie case in favor of plaintiff and create a rebuttable presumption of negligence of defendant, casting upon the latter the duty of absolving itself from liability by showing that the damage was due to no fault or negligence on its part. . . . Defendant introduced no evidence to overcome the above presumption of negligence, and failed to show any effort to keep down excessive heat or prevent the loss. . . . The perishable nature of the shipment does not relieve the carrier from the primary duty he owes the shipper to protect the goods. On the contrary there was imposed upon the defendant the obligation to exercise a higher degree of care. . . .

The court based its decision on the principle that the carrier's exemption from liability resulting from the inherent nature of the goods is predicted upon a showing of absence of negligence on the carrier's part and that by showing delivery to the carrier in good condition and arrival at destination in bad condition, the claimant establishes a prima facie case and shifts the burden to the carrier. While some of the early cases held that the carrier need only show the damage resulted from the inherent nature of the goods under circumstances not shown to be negligent to shift the burden to the claimant to prove the carrier's negligence, *Standard Brands* v. *Boston & Maine R. Co.*, 29 F. Supp. 593; *American Railway Express Co.* v. *Fegenbush*, 144 So. 320, recent decisions follow the *Domenico* case rule. (See *Missouri Pacific R. Co.* v. *Elmore and Stahl*, 84 S. Ct. 1142; cf. *Larry's Sandwiches, Inc.* v. *Pacific Electric Ry. Co.*, 318 F. 2d 690. Other recent cases dealing with carrier's liability for damages to perishables are *United States* v. *Reading Co.*, 289 F. 2d 7; *Trautmann Bros. Co.* v. *Missouri Pacific R. Co.*, 312 F. 2d 102)

In *R. C. A. Truck Lines, Inc.* v. *Georgia Rug Mill, Inc.*, 77 S. E. 2d 442, the court noted that a common carrier is not bound to accept for transportation a commodity it knows cannot be transported without damage, and when the evidence shows that the carrier had notice of the perishable nature of the shipment "and yet recklessly accepted the same for carriage," and if the evidence further shows that the damage resulted from a failure to furnish protective service, then a finding for the plaintiff is authorized. In *Johnson Motor Transport* v. *United States,* 149 F. Supp. 175, the court also referred to the carriers' right to refuse to accept shipments outside their tariff holding out and said: "In view of the carrier's privilege of refusal, it would seem unfair to permit them, after having accepted the shipments and agreed to transport the meat in refrigerated trucks, to avoid liability for breach of contract on the ground that the defendant should not have placed any reliance on their promise because their commitment to transport the meat in refrigerated trucks was beyond the scope of their tariff provisions." The court went on to hold that the carrier should be found liable for negligence for failure to exercise reasonable care in protecting the freight.

In *Van Lierop* v. *Chesapeake and Ohio Railway Co.,* 57 N. W. 2d 431, the carrier's tariffs specifically provided for the protective service which was available and the shipper requested such service in the manner outlined in the published tariffs. Request was also made for "Standard Ventilation" although this service was not mentioned in the tariff and, according to the carrier furnishing ventilation in connection with carrier protective service, was prohibited. In holding the carrier liable for damage to shipments of gladiolus bulbs which was apparently due to failure to ventilate, the court said:

> In *Southern Pacific Company* v. *Fred Itule,* 74 P. (2d) 38, 115 A L R 1268, it was held to be the carrier's duty to handle a shipment in a reasonably prudent manner as to all matters not covered by instructions. In our opinion, the duty to transport the bulbs without negligence was upon the carrier. Under the weather conditions existing at the time of the shipments, ventilation or artificial heat was necessary in order that the bulbs could have a degree of temperature that would not cause freezing or overheating.

In *Newmark* v. *Pacific Freight Lines,* 155 P. 2d 68, the court in finding against the carrier does present a plausible basis for concluding that the carrier was actually negligent. While this case involves an intrastate shipment, it nevertheless will illustrate the type of negligence which could be found in the case of interstate shipments. Briefly, the shipper employed the carrier to transport about three and a half tons of chilled fresh sausage from Los Angeles to Camp Roberts, California. Due to a heavy rainfall, the highway to the camp was closed so the carrier did not forward the sausage immediately but held it at the Los Angeles terminal for about 48 hours. The sausages when loaded were sufficiently chilled to prevent spoilage for about 30 hours. The carrier did not notify the shipper of the two days' delay but did place about 50 pounds of dry ice on the sausages before proceeding to the camp. When shipment was finally delivered, it had been loaded on the truck for about seventy hours and was unfit for human consumption. The court in holding the carrier liable said:

> Even if the rains caused the roads to be in such condition that defendant was justified in delaying the shipment, the question remained as to whether defendant used reasonable care to protect the sausage after it knew there would be a delay. . . . If defendant had notified the shipper that there was a delay, even as late as 4 P.M., Saturday when it iced the sausage, such notice being given about 24 hours after the sausage was taken from the refrigerator would have afforded the shipper sufficient time to properly protect the sausage. The defendant failed in its duty to notify the shipper of the delay. By reason of such failure the shipper was deprived of an opportunity to protect the sausage.

In *Ozark Fruit Growers' Assn.* v. *St. Louis-S. F. R. Co.*, 46 S. W. 2d 895, the court held that a carrier is not an insurer of perishable fruit if damage results from their perishable nature but if there is negligent delay in transportation and the delay keeps the fruit off the market until by its nature it decays, the carrier is liable therefor. It is presumed that damage to a shipment received by a carrier in good condition and delivered in bad condition was caused by the carrier's negligence and this is rebuttable only by a preponderance of evidence. In *American Ry. Express Co.* v. *Fegenbush,* 144 So. 320, it was established that a shipment of beans was received by the carrier in good order, transported on schedule, and delivered in bad condition and this was held to create a presumption of the carrier's negligence and to place upon the carrier the burden of establishing that the damage resulted from an inherent vice in the goods to which its own negligence did not contribute. (*Missouri Pac. R. Co.* v. *S. L. Robinson & Co.*, 61 S. W. 2d 700; also 62 S. W. 2d 965 and 66 S. W. 2d 1055; *Railway Express Agency* v. *McCarrick*, 69 S. W. 2d 803)

In *Bonfligio* v. *New York, N. H. & H. R. Co.*, 198 N. E. 236, a carrier was held liable for cinder damage to shipment of watermelons in a ventilator car, the court pointing out that a carrier whose business is transportation is held to have knowledge of any perils which goods shipped in the facilities it provides would ordinarily encounter. A shipper may relieve the carrier from its duty if it assumes the risk of damage resulting from a known condition or unsuitability of a car or has voluntarily selected or accepted a car for transportation of his goods with the knowledge of its defects or unsuitability, relying on his own judgment and not on the judgment or duty of the carrier. If a shipper selects or accepts a car without knowledge of a defect therein or of its unsuitability relying not on his own judgment but on that of the carrier, however, the latter is not relieved from liability. (*Ogdenburg & L. C. Railroad Co.* v. *Pratt*, 22 Wall. 123, 22 L. Ed. 827; *Harris* v. *Northern Ind. R. Co.*, 20 N. Y. 232; *F. D. Forrester & Co.* v. *Southern R. Co.*, 61 S. E. 524; *Frohlich* v. *Pennsylvania Co.*, 101 N. W. 223; *Louisville & N. R. Co.* v. *Dies*, 18 S. W. 266; *Alabama G. S. R. Co.* v. *Morris & Co.*, 249 F. 312; and *Louisville & N. R. Co.* v. *Carr*, 81 So. 779)

In *Railway Express Agency* v. *Rouw Co.*, 42 S. W. 2d 761, the court held that even in those instances where the carrier provided refrigerated service, its duty was limited to exercising ordinary care in properly icing and re-icing the cars. The court held the instruction of the lower court "that it is the duty of the carrier to furnish proper shipping facilities for the kind and character of commodity which it undertakes to carry, and in this case it was the duty of the defendant (carrier) to furnish a refrigerator car sufficiently iced to preserve the strawberries loaded therein and keep said car sufficiently iced for such purpose until the same was delivered at destination" was in error. The court, in discussing this instruction, said:

> The suit was based on negligence of the carrier, and it was its duty to exercise ordinary care to properly ice and re-ice the car, thereby keeping the proper temperature. Instead of telling the jury that it was its duty to do the things mentioned, the court should have told the jury that it was appellant's duty to exercise ordinary care. The suit being based on negligence, the burden was upon appellee (shipper) to show by the evidence that the appellant was guilty of negligence, causing the damage.

Where an express company had indicated to the shipper that refrigeration would be provided if weather conditions warranted and the shipper relied thereon, the carrier was held liable for failure to protect the goods even though the shipment was less-carload and the express company's tariffs provided for refrigeration only in connection with carload shipments. (*Gehrke* v. *American Ry. Express Co.*, 240 N. W. 321) The court said:

> In the instant case the poultry was perishable and was received by the defendant in good condition, and the burden was on it to show that the damage did not result from any cause for which it was legally responsible. *Beard* v. *Illinois C. R. Co.*, 79 Iowa 518, 44 N.W. 800, 7 L. R. A. 280. . . . The defendant offered no proof to overcome the burden, and the judgment must be and is affirmed.

In the foregoing case, the express company's agent by promising refrigerated service induced the shipper to tender its goods. While the shipper may have had constructive notice of the carrier's rules, regulations, and tariffs, its agent in response to the customer's inquiry actually misrepresented these regulations, and in reliance thereon the shipper was induced to ship its goods. This case can be distinguished from others in that here the shipper made inquiry of the carrier as to the available service and was not properly advised.

The court in *Akerly* v. *Railway Express Agency,* 77 A. 2d 856, in holding the express company liable for freezing of shipments of "hatching eggs" gave considerable weight to the nature of the business provided by that agency, pointing out its continual solicitation of commodities requiring protective service and its holding out to the public its services in providing heating cars and furnishing safe transportation service, regardless of the season. Further, the court found that the carrier's failure to provide a specific charge for protective service in its tariff did not excuse its failure to provide service since the service was made available to all without special charge. This court was "of the opinion that the service of heating was implicit in the defendant's general tariff without specific mention, and the defendant was under the duty to render the service. . . ."

In *Close* v. *Missouri Pac. R. Co.,* 191 So. 596, the court refused to accept the argument of the claimant that the carrier must not only prove that it exercised due care and prudence as regards a shipment of perishable products where loss or damage occurs enroute, but also must prove the precise cause of the loss and that it did not result from a fortuitous or uncontrollable event. Where the shipper or claimant alleges that the carrier's negligence was responsible for the damage, such negligence must be established by competent evidence. (*American Railway Express Co.* v. *Cole,* 42 S. W. 2d 772)

Routing

The problems relative to carrier's observance of routing instructions arise more often in connection with overcharge claims than loss and damage claims. While the routing observed by the carrier in transporting goods from origin to destination may quite often affect the rate assessed, it seldom has any relation to the carrier's liability for loss or damage. The problem does occur occasionally, however, where the claim is for delay or where an act of God is involved.

The Interstate Commerce Act gives the shipper the right to control the routing of shipments via rail carriers and a carrier is liable for any injury occasioned to the owner of the goods by any deviation from the shipper's routing instructions. Although the Interstate Commerce Act does not give shippers the right to route freight which is moving via motor carrier, the Commission nevertheless has held on several occasions that charges were unreasonable where a carrier failed to route freight via the cheapest reasonable route available. For example, with respect to a carrier participating in a through rate, the Commission has held that charges based on a combination of local rates via some other route were unreasonable.

The Commission cannot award reparations against a motor carrier, but its finding of unreasonableness of routing may be utilized in a court action for damages. In *Hewitt-Robins, Inc.* v. *Eastern Freight-Ways, Inc.*, 371 U.S. 184, the question was raised whether a common-law remedy for misrouting survived the Interstate Commerce Act. The United States District Court and the Court of Appeals held that the Act neither provided any reparations remedy nor preserved one at common law. (187 F. Supp. 722, 293 F. 2d 205) The Supreme Court of the United States reversed, holding that the survival of a damage claim for misrouting appears entirely consistent with the Act. In its decision, the Supreme Court noted with approval the practice of referring the question of the unreasonableness of the routing to the Commission and the question of damages to the courts. Subsequently, Congress enacted Public Law 89-170, amending Section 204a of the Interstate Commerce Act to permit actions for reparations against motor carriers for unjust, unreasonable, or discriminatory transportation charges. The effect of this statute on the common-law remedy for damages for misrouting has not yet been presented to the courts.

The former Bureau of Motor Carriers of the Interstate Commerce Commission issued two informal rulings regarding routing by motor carriers. Both were issued before the *Hewitt-Robins* decision. The first question concerned the right of a motor carrier to discontinue a through-route arrangement with another motor carrier. The Bureau said, in part, that a motor carrier of property may always cancel through-route arrangements and joint rates without Commission permission, but only upon 30 days' notice. In answer to the second question, the Bureau stated that the Commission has no power to require motor carriers of property to observe shipper's routing. The Act does, however, furnish such authority as to rail carriers in Section 15(8).

Because of the misunderstanding occasioned by the decision in *T.I.M.E., Inc.* v. *United States*, 359 U.S. 464, and to direct attention to the *Hewitt-Robins* decision, the Commission issued an "interpretative opinion" in August 1963, advising motor carriers to adjust claims caused by misrouting. The Commission said: "If a carrier misroutes a shipment and thus causes extra expense to the shipper over and above the legal charges applicable over the route that should have been used, and responsibility for its error is admitted by the carrier," he should make the necessary refund. The Commission emphasized two prerequisites to such refunds: an admission by the carrier of responsibility for the misrouting error and the willingness of that carrier to bear the entire expense of the refund without recourse upon any other carrier.

In *Planters Nut & Chocolate Co.,* 31 M.C.C. 719, the Commission held that a carrier was under an obligation to accept interchange traffic from a connecting carrier with which it had joint routes and rates.

Sale of Goods

As security for his compensation for transportation and for any advances which the carrier has been required to make upon a shipment, the carrier has what is called a lien upon the goods. A lien is a claim, a hold, or a charge upon goods for the satisfaction of a debt. At common law the carrier's lien, like the lien of other bailees, gave only the right of possession or detention until those charges legally due have been paid, and the right or power to sell the goods did not exist. (*State* v. *Aetna Casualty & Surety Co.,* 145 A. 172)

Under the terms of the standard uniform bill of lading of motor and rail carriers, Section 4 sets forth the procedure to be followed by carriers in selling refused and unclaimed shipments. The receipt portion on the face of the bill of lading specifically recites that the property received for transportation is received subject to the terms and conditions set forth on the reverse of the bill of lading of which Section 4 is a part. It would seem, therefore, that at the time the shipper and carrier enter into the bill of lading contract, the shipper specifically authorizes the carrier to sell the goods in the manner outlined in Section 4 and that all of the requirements of a binding contract sufficient to bind the shipper to such authorization have been complied with.

Despite this contractual agreement and authorization for sale in the manner outlined in Section 4, Lust in his *Law of Loss and Damage Claims* expresses some doubt as to the validity of sales under Section 4 and states that "there is good ground for argument that Congress has not so occupied the field of interstate commerce with respect to the liability of carriers concerning interstate shipments as to sanction such provision which is at variance with the statutes of any states" (Lust, *The Law of Loss and Damage Claims,* 3rd ed., p. 206). This authority adds that "the interstate transportation having ended when the property has arrived at destination, it would seem that the statutes of the states where the property is at the time it is unclaimed should govern as to the sale." It is submitted, however, that at the time the contract for interstate transportation was entered into the shipper by his signature to the bill of lading waived the carrier's compliance with the requirements of the statutes of the state to which the property was consigned. Further, the provisions of Section 4 require that the carrier notify the consignor concerning any proposed sale of the property, and it would appear that after receiving such notice the shipper would be estopped from claiming any injury resulting from the sale of the property after compliance with the procedure which he had previously authorized.

Section 4(c) of the bill of lading provides that where perishable property which has been transported to destination is refused by the consignee or party entitled to receive it, the carrier may, in its discretion, to prevent deterioration or further deterioration, sell the goods to best advantage at private or public sale. If time serves for notification to the consignor or owner, however, the carrier is required to give notice and request disposition before the property is sold.

In connection with nonperishable goods, the carrier is required by Section 4(b), in event consignee or the party entitled to receive the goods does not do so within 15 days after notice of arrival has been given, to notify the consignor that the property has been refused or remains unclaimed, and that it will be subject to sale under the terms of the bill of lading if disposition is not arranged for. Prior to selling nonperishables, however, the carrier must publish a notice containing a description of the property, the name of the party to whom consigned, or, if shipped order-notify, the name of the party to be notified and the time and place of sale, once a week for two successive weeks in a newspaper of general circulation at the place of sale or nearest place where such paper is published. Before publishing such advertisement, Section 4(b) provides that 30 days must have elapsed from the date that the consignor was notified concerning the refusal by consignee or his failure to claim the property.

Section 4(e) of the contract terms and conditions of the bill of lading further provides that the proceeds of any sale shall be applied by the carrier to the payment of freight, storage, and other lawful charges, including the expense of advertising and selling. Should there be any balance after these expenses, it is to be paid to the owner of the property sold. In instances where ownership of the property might be open to question, and particularly where a substantial amount is involved, it might be necessary to have a court determine the identity of the true owner of the goods. Carriers should secure advice of counsel in connection with the sale of merchandise in order that provisions of local statutes will be observed.

Some carriers are under the mistaken belief that they can retain a shipment for nine months and then sell it without complying with the provisions of Section 4. The basis for this belief is the fact that the claim of the owner of the goods is barred if filed after expiration of nine months from date of delivery or, in case of nondelivery, within nine months after a reasonable time for delivery has elapsed. While it is true that a claim for loss and damage would be barred after the expiration of the nine-month period as provided, it is fundamental in law that "no one can transfer to another a better title than he has himself" and the carrier's sale of the goods belonging to others without compliance with the bill of lading terms would constitute conversion for which the carrier would be liable.

A thief does not secure title to property regardless of the length of his possession and there is no basis for applying a different rule to a carrier—admittedly only a bailee of the property in his possession—which sells the goods of another without strictly complying with the provisions of Section 4 by giving the owner notice and an opportunity to specify the disposition desired. This same principle would apply to over-astray freight in the carrier's possession which bears marks indicating shipper or consignee, thus placing the carrier on notice as to the possible interest of others in the goods and requiring the carrier to make a reasonable investigation of the extent of such interest and possible ownership before disposition of the goods in a manner prejudicial to such possible interest. In *Southern Express Co.* v. *Smith,* 122 N. E. 427, it was held that the requirements for notice of claim for loss , damage or detention did not apply to an action based on conversion of the property. Similar holdings were made in *Southern Ry. Co.* v. *Harris,* 80 So. 101; *Chicago, etc. R. Co.* v. *Fifth Nat. Bank,* 59 N. E. 43; *Bardwell* v. *American Express Co.,* 28 N. W. 925; and *Ridgway Grain Co.* v. *Pennsylvania Railroad Co.,* 77 A. 1007.

An unauthorized sale of goods by a carrier is generally held to constitute a conversion. (*F. W. Brockman Commission Co.* v. *Missouri Pac. R. Co.,* 188 S. W. 920; *Standard Lumber Co.* v. *Pennsylvania Railroad Co.,* 139 A. 881; *Dobbins* v. *Delaware, L. & W. R. Co.,* 163 N. Y. S. 849) Further, where notice must be given the shipper as in the case of nonperishable property, a sale without such notice will constitute a conversion rendering a carrier liable for the value of the goods. (*Boshell* v. *Rec. of*

St. L. & S. F. R. Co., 76 So. 282; *Indiana Harbor Belt R. Co.* v. *Alpirn*, 296 N. W. 158; *Pa. R. Co.* v. *Gentile Bros. Co.*, 191 N. E. 369)

Where a carrier waives prepayment of freight charges and the consignee refuses to accept the goods and pay freight charges and the carrier, in strict conformance with the law, sells the goods to enforce its lien and there still remains a balance due, the consignor is liable to the carrier for such balance which the carrier is bound to collect. (*Jelk* v. *Phila., etc. R. Co.*, 80 S. E. 216; *Bewley-Darst Coal Co.* v. *W. & A. R. Co.*, 87 S. E. 702; *B. & O.* v. *Luella Coal & Coke Co.*, 81 S. E. 1044)

It is the carrier's duty to sell the goods for the best market price obtainable at the time and place of sale but the sale need not be made at point of destination but may be made at some point where the carrier may be able to sell at less cost and for a better price. (*Slayden-Kirksey Woolen Mill* v. *Houston, etc. R. Co.*, 132 S. W. 77) In *Horton* v. *Tonopah, etc. Co.*, 325 F. 406, the carrier sold certain carload lots of lumber, title to which was in the plaintiff as consignor, but which consignee had refused to accept, for freight and demurrage charges. These were sold together with shipments belonging to others to a purchaser who was acting secretly as agent for the carrier which was the real purchaser. The court held that the sale consituted a conversion of the lumber belonging to plaintiff.

An academic question often presented in connection with "overstray" is, "What is the legal status of a piece of over freight?" The reason this question is asked is that some carriers erroneously regard all over freight as their own property and eventually dispose of it by sale or in some other manner. Search of the authorities does not indicate that the exact question as to legal status of over freight has ever been before the courts. However, see *Wilson Freight Forwarding Co.* v. *C.C.C. Highway, Inc.*, 57 N. E. 2d 786, where the court held a carrier liable for conversion of over freight belonging to another carrier which was not promptly reported.

It is entirely possible that the carrier's relationship to the over freight could be considered as that of a gratuitous bailee, and undoubtedly where property of another comes into possession of the ordinary individual without some definite understanding, that relationship is created. A common carrier, however, occupies a position entirely different from that of the ordinary individual. Common carriers are engaged in the business of receiving, transporting, and delivering freight and have certain definite obligations in connection with property of other persons in their possession. Further, it is elementary that a common carrier always has a lien on the goods for its charges and it can be assumed that it will be compensated for its services before being required to make delivery of the property. One of the foremost obligations of a common carrier is its duty to issue a bill of lading for property received by it for transportation. Section 20(11) provides, in part, as follows:

> . . . any common carrier . . . receiving property for transportation . . . shall issue a receipt or bill of lading therefor . . . and shall be liable . . . for any loss, damage or injury caused by it . . . and any such common carrier . . . so receiving property . . . shall be liable . . . whether such receipt or bill of lading has been issued or not. . . .

Under the foregoing quoted statutory provision it would appear that with respect to over freight found in a carrier's possession which the carrier is unable to "tie in" with one of its bills of lading, an obligation is created toward the unknown owner of the property which is greater than the nominal obligation of a gratuitous bailee. The fact that the property is in the carrier's possession indicates that it was received from some source and, in all probability, was received under a bill of lading. Likewise, the inference follows that the property was received for transportation, since that is the nature of the carrier's business. The fact that no bill of lading was issued at the time the property was received from the unknown source does not necessarily, in itself, free the carrier from liability, since the quoted portion of the statute imposes liability irrespective of whether or not a bill of lading has been issued. Under these circumstances the carrier's duty toward over freight would not appear to differ in any respect from its duty toward other freight.

Salvage

As a general rule, the fact that goods are injured while in transit through causes for which the carrier is responsible does not of itself justify the consignee in refusing to receive them, but he must accept them and hold the carrier responsible for the injury. If the goods are so injured, however, as to be practically worthless and to cost as much to repair them as to replace them, the consignee is justified in refusing to receive the shipment and holding the carrier liable for the full actual loss. (*Thomas, etc. Co.* v. *Railway Co.,* 62 Wis. 642) The consignee may not refuse to accept the goods unless the condition of the goods is such that they have no value or very little value for the purpose for which they were intended. Where a shortage exists, consignee is not justified in refusing to receive the balance, but is bound to accept them and hold the carrier for the missing portion. (*Gulf, etc. Ry. Co.* v. *Booton,* 15 S. W. 502)

Since it is the duty of the consignee to accept the injured goods, it follows that it is likewise the duty of the consignee to make every effort to mitigate the damages by disposing of the injured goods to the best advantage, the carrier being liable for the difference between the value of the injured goods and their value in the condition in which they were originally delivered to it for transportation. Considerable confusion has been occasioned by the insistence on the part of some carriers that it is the carrier's privilege to determine whether or not injured goods will be delivered to the consignee. No legal authority for this contention can be found. Not only is it the carrier's basic duty to deliver property entrusted to it for transportation to the party entitled to receive it, but it is elementary that the only right a carrier has in the goods its transports is a lien for its freight and other lawful charges and, upon payment of these charges, the owner of the goods is entitled to their possession. Quite often it occurs that acceptance of damaged goods by the consignee will increase the carrier's damages as the goods, if refused, could be sold by the carrier for more than it would cost to replace them. Nevertheless, it is the consignee's right to demand delivery of the goods and hold the carrier liable for the cost of repairs and other actual loss suffered. This right, however, is subject to a rule of reason; obviously, the consignee cannot arbitrarily repair goods which are practically worthless in the condition received and hold the carrier liable for the cost of repairs. It is the consignee's duty to make every effort to mitigate the damages and, in any event, carrier's liability is limited to the destination value of the goods.

In *Phoenix Insurance Company* v. *Cushman Motor Delivery Co.,* 4 Fed. Car. Cas. par. 80, 214, it was held that where a consignee destroyed the salvage, thus depriving the carrier of an opportunity to ascertain the amount of damages, the carrier was justified in declining payment of claim.

Stoppage in Transitu

The right of stoppage *in transitu* arises after a vendor has delivered the possession of the goods to a carrier but before delivery discovers that the consignee who has purchased the goods on credit has become insolvent. The reason for this right is to prevent the property of one person from being applied to the debts of another. Where the shipper exercises this right, the carrier is excused from making delivery.

In exercising this right, all that is required of the shipper is that by some act of his own, or his agent, he countermands the delivery by giving a simple notice to the carrier stating his claim and forbidding delivery to the consignee or requiring that the goods shall be held by the carrier subject to his further instructions. It is always proper for the carrier to inquire into the authority of the person demanding the withholding of the goods from the consignee and, if it be ascertained that the person giving the instructions is without authority, it is the carrier's duty to make delivery. To make the notice of stoppage *in transitu* effective, it must be given to the person who has the immediate custody of the goods, or if given to the principal, whose servant has the custody, it must be given at such a time as to enable the principal, by the exercise of reasonable diligence, to communicate it to his employee having custody of the goods in time to prevent the delivery.

The right of stoppage *in transitu* usually does not exist where the goods shipped are covered by an order bill of lading. Further, an actual or constructive delivery of the goods to the consignee defeats the shipper's right to stoppage. The consignee's insolvency is essential to the existence of the right of stoppage *in transitu.* If the consignee in fact is not insolvent, the carrier if he knows this fact will not be justified in refusing to make delivery irrespective of shipper's instructions to the contrary. If the carrier is unable to determine whether or not the right exists to stop the goods, the carrier may, instead of refusing to obey the shipper's instructions, require that he be allowed sufficient time to investigate the condition of the buyer. If, after investigation, he shall be unable to determine whether or not the right exists, he may for his own security resort to legal proceedings to have the question determined, as in the case of adverse claimants.

In *Weyerhaeuser Timber Co.* v. *First National Bank,* 38 P. 2d 48, the court, in commenting upon the right of stoppage *in transitu,* said:

> As a general rule, both at common law and under statutory provisions in some jurisdictions, where the right has not been waived, an unpaid seller, who has parted with the possession of goods to a carrier for transportation to the buyer, may, if the buyer is or becomes insolvent, stop the goods in transit; that is, he may resume possession of the goods so long as they are in the course of transit, and may retain them until payment or tender of the price, 55 C. J. 907, § 889. The right may be exercised by any person who, as between himself and the buyer, may be considered as an unpaid seller. 55 C. J. 910, § 892. There is no particular method required for exercising this right. *Frame* v. *Oregon Liquor Co.,* 48 Or. 272, 85 P. 1009, 86 P. 791. The right of stoppage in transitu extends, not only to the property itself, but also extends to the proceeds of the property. 55 C. J. 910, § 891. The right may be asserted, not only against an

insolvent buyer, but also against ordinary purchasers or transferees of the buyer to whom a bill of lading has not been properly transferred, and against an assignee for the benefit of creditors, or a receiver appointed for the estate of the buyer. 55 C. J. § 893. The right of stoppage in transitu is not terminated until there has been final delivery of the goods to the vendee or his agent at the place named by the vendee to the vendor as the place of final delivery or ultimate destination of the goods. Delivery at an intermediate point or delivery to a person acting as a carrier or forwarding agent will not terminate the right. *Aguirre* v. *Parmelee,* 22 Conn. 473; *Markwald* v. *His Creditors* 7 Cal. 213; *Blackman* v. *Pierce,* 23 Cal. 508.

In *Hines* v. *Chaddick,* 63 S. W. 2d 263, the court held that a carrier's agent is not justified in refusing to allow to a shipper the right of stoppage *in transitu* merely because when such instructions were given the bill of lading was not presented as proof of ownership. Chaddick shipped 50 bales of cotton from Texas to Lumberton, North Carolina, with a stop in Greenville, Texas, for compression, the shipment moving on an order-notify bill of lading. While the cotton was in possession of the railroad at Greenville, the shipper notified the railroad's agent at McKinney, the point of origin, that the notify party in Lumberton had refused to pay for the cotton. The shipper advised this agent that it was still the owner of the cotton and the holder of the original order-notify bill of lading and requested the agent to have the cotton stopped in Greenville and turned over the bill of lading to the McKinney agent. The shipper also telephoned the railroad's agent in Greenville and explained all of these circumstances and requested that the shipment be held there. These instructions were disregarded and the cotton loaded through to Lumberton where it arrived and was sold by the shipper for 19 cents a pound, which was much less than shipper could have realized if its instructions had been observed. The court in holding the carrier liable for the loss said:

> We believe the facts of this case warrant the holding that a duty rested upon the agent at the point of shipment, as well as the agent at the intermediate point where the cotton was to be compressed, to exercise the care of a reasonable prudent person to aid the shipper in his right of stoppage and the failure to do so, under the circumstances stated, is imputable to the carrier for whom he was employed in that character of business.

In *Louisville & N. R.* v. *Campbell Lumber Co.,* 166 S. E. 252, the shipper had sold goods to the consignee for cash. The goods were shipped on a straight bill of lading but consignee failed to pay the draft which was drawn on him with the straight bill of lading attached. The shipper instructed the carrier not to deliver the goods but the carrier failed to observe the instructions. The shipper brought suit against the carrier for the contract price and the carrier defended on the ground that the shipper was indebted to the consignee and it was for this reason the consignee refused to pay the draft. The court held, however, that the indebtedness of the consignor did not afford the carrier any defense, since under the law the shipper had the right to stop the delivery of the goods.

Carrier's Liability as Warehouseman

A carrier's custody and possession of goods in the capacity of warehouseman is an undertaking separate and distinct from that of transportation. As warehouseman a carrier is bound to take ordinary care of the goods and if he suffers them to be damaged or lost, for want of such ordinary care or by his failure to keep them in a safe and suitable place or to store them properly, he will be liable. (*Tarbell* v. *Shipping Co.*, 17 N. E. 721) The standard of care of a warehouseman is such as an ordinarily prudent person would take of his own property under the same or in a similar situation. (*Brown* v. *Railway Express Agency,* 188 A. 716)

Under Section 4(a) of the rail bill of lading, property not removed by the party entitled to receive it within the free time allowed by tariffs shall be held by the carrier subject to its responsibility as warehouseman, the free time to commence after notice of arrival has been given to consignee. The motor carrier bill of lading differs slightly in this regard from the rail bill of lading. Section 4(a) on the motor carrier bill of lading provides, in part, as follows:

> . . . Property not received, at time tender of delivery of the property to the party entitled to receive it has been made, may be kept in . . . warehouse or place of business of the carrier, subject to the tariff charges for storage and to the carrier's responsibility as a warehouseman, only. . . .

There is no reference to "tender of delivery" in the rail bill of lading. Under the rail provision, it would appear that if delivery is tendered and the shipment refused by the party entitled to receive it, the rail carrier's liability as warehouseman would not commence until the free time allowed for removal by consignee has expired. The motor carrier bill of lading provides, on the other hand, that liability as warehouseman will commence upon refusal of consignee to accept delivery. In view of the fact that tariffs contain provisions relating to storage, notification of shipper in event of refusal, etc., these provisions should be consulted to determine when the carrier's liability as warehouseman actually commences, since these regulations are incorporated into the bill of lading contract.

The effect of placement of the car on a team track is discussed in *Republic Carloading & Dist. Co.* v. *Missouri Pacific R. Co.*, 302 F. 2d 381.

An interesting discussion of the degree of care required of the carrier as a warehouseman is contained in *Marsh* v. *Pennsylvania R. Co.*, 167 S. E. 274. The action arose out of theft of potatoes from a railcar on a siding. Accepting that the carrier held the freight as a warehouseman, the court said: "It is well settled that in the absence of a special contract, an ordinary warehouseman is not an insurer against theft, and cannot be held liable for loss of the property by this means without negligence on his part," citing *Firestone Tire and Rubber Co.* v. *Pacific Transfer Co.*, 120 Wash. 665, 208 P. 55. The court held, however, that the mere showing of theft does not establish the carrier's negligence. The plaintiff argued that the fact the railroad left the siding unguarded, coupled with its failure to explain the loss, made it guilty of negligence as a matter of law. The court rejected this position, saying, "It implies that a railroad company is under a duty to guard all loaded cars which may be stored on its side tracks. The situation did not present a case which demanded extraordinary and unusual precaution." In addition, the court noted, the danger of theft was just as obvious to the plaintiff as to the railroad "and if he was aware of any such danger he should have warned the railroad company."

In *Simon* v. *Universal Carloading and Dist. Co.*, 1 N. Y. S. 2d 249, the carrier was found not liable for the destruction of a COD shipment it had on hand which it was unable to deliver to the consignee. The evidence showed that the shipment arrived at destination on February 1 and was placed on defendant's warehouse platform, and a notice of arrival was sent to the consignee by mail. On February 17 the carrier received an inquiry from the shipper about the disposition of the shipment. The next day the carrier contacted the consignee, who informed the carrier the shipment could be accepted Saturday, February 20. This information was transmitted to the shipper by air mail the same day, February 18.

Delivery was attempted February 20 but consignee did not accept it. On Monday, February 22, Washington's birthday, the carrier's warehouse was burned by a fire of undetermined origin and plaintiff's shipment was totally destroyed. The court held: "The goods while in possession of the defendant, while its status was that of a carrier, suffered no damage or injury; when the loss by fire occurred, the defendant's status was that of a warehouseman only, and, as such, it is not liable, in the absence of affirmative proof that the fire was due to the negligence of the defendant, of which there was none." The court cited *Southern Railroad Co.* v. *Prescott,* 240 U.S. 632; *Weed* v. *Barney,* 45 N. Y. 344; *Hasse* v. *American Express Co.*, 94 Mich. 133, 53 N. W. 918.

The plaintiff also contended that the carrier was under a duty to notify it that the goods had not been taken up, but the court rejected this claim, saying:

> In absence of any agreement, there was no duty or obligation upon the defendant's part to do so. *Weed* v. *Barney, supra.* Upon notice to defendant by the consignee that they were not then ready to take up and pay for the goods when offered, it became the further duty of the defendant, common carrier, to store the goods and hold them a reasonable time to enable the consignee to pay, but the liability of the carrier, however, in such event, is that of a warehouseman only.

The carrier as warehouseman does not have the high degree of care with respect to the property as required in its capacity as carrier. As warehouseman, the carrier is not an insurer, and is liable only for failure to use ordinary care. This duty of ordinary care has been defined as "such care as men of reasonable prudence ordinarily exercise for the safety of their own goods under such circumstances." (*American Ry. Express Co.* v. *Rhody,* 143 N. E. 640; *Chalmers* v. *New York Central,* 161 N. Y. S. 577) With respect to its duty as a carrier of goods, the carrier has the responsibility of proving freedom from liability on its part in actions brought against it.

As warehouseman, however, the burden of proving the carrier's negligence is upon the party instituting the action. Since it is the duty of a warehouseman to deliver upon proper demand, his failure to do so, without excuse, will usually be regarded as establishing a prima facie case of negligence. If, however, it appears that the loss is due to some catastrophe that fact in itself, in the absence of circumstances permitting the inference of lack of reasonable precautions, does not suffice to show neglect, and the claimant has the burden of establishing negligence by affirmative evidence. (*Wood* v. *L. & A. R. Co.*, 104 So. 306; *Southern R. Co.* v. *Prescott,* 240 U.S. 632; *Allen* v. *Southern R. Co.*, 126 S. E. 722)

If the shipment moves under tariff provisions calling for protective service, the degree of "ordinary" care which would be expected to be exercised would be considerably greater for a perishable product than it would be where the commodity was not perishable or did not require protective service. A shipment of eggs, for example, would call for a higher degree of care on the part of a carrier than a shipment of iron castings. As a warehouseman, a carrier is bound to take ordinary care of the goods and if he suffers them to be damaged or lost for want of such ordinary care, or by his failure to keep them in a safe and suitable place or to store them properly, he will be liable. (*Tarbell* v. *Shipping Co.*, 17 N. E. 721)

5

Measure of Damages

Section 20, paragraph 11, of part I of the Interstate Commerce Act (which is applicable to rail and motor carriers and freight forwarders) provides, in part, as follows:

> That any common carrier . . . (operating in interstate commerce) . . . shall issue a receipt or bill of lading . . . and shall be liable to the lawful holder thereof for any loss, damage, or injury to such property caused by it or any common carrier . . . to which such property may be delivered . . . and no contract, receipt, rule, regulation, or other limitation of any character whatsoever shall exempt such common carrier . . . from the liability hereby imposed; and any such common carrier *shall be liable* to the lawful holder of said receipt or bill of lading or to any party entitled to recover thereon . . . for the *full actual loss, damage or injury to such property* caused by it or any such common carrier. . . . (Emphasis added.)

Under the provision of the law as quoted, the question as to measure of damages is usually one of fact—*what was the actual loss to claimant?* The law does not contemplate, generally, the making of a profit out of a carrier's misfortune in losing or damaging freight; rather the law is concerned with restoration of the claimant to the same position he would have occupied had there been no loss or damage. The court in *Atlantic Coast Line Ry. Co.* v. *Roe,* 118 So. 155, accurately stated this principle in the following language:

> The basic thought underlying the federal statutes which define the liability and prescribe the measure of damages in cases of this kind is that the owner shall be made whole by receiving the proper money equivalent for what he has actually lost, or, in other words, to restore him to the position he would have occupied, had the carrier performed its contract.

As in any factual question, opinion of the adversaries will often be at wide variance. For the claimant who is inconvenienced by loss, damage, or delay of his shipment, there may be an understandable desire to seek the highest amount which he thinks he can persuade the carrier to pay. This is not unusual especially since many patrons of carriers labor under the misapprehension that eventually the carrier's insurance company will reimburse the carrier so in the long run not even the carrier suffers. The growing cost of public liability and property damage insurance on passenger vehicles reflects a fundamental misunderstanding on the part of the general public as to who pays for the judgments rendered. The profit incentive has become so ingrained in many of us that the question (which sometimes is fundamentally only a moral one, namely, whether it has been *earned*) seldom receives much if any attention. Specifically, the law set forth by Section 20(11) is that the claimant is entitled to only his full *actual loss*—no more no less.

After the enactment of Section 20(11) it was inevitable that some claimant would seek to secure a court determination as to the exact recovery allowable. The first case which was considered by the Supreme Court of the United States was in *Chicago, M. & St. P. Ry. Co.* v. *McCaull-Dinsmore Co.*, 253 U.S. 97, commonly referred to as the *McCaull-Dinsmore* case. This case, however, must be evaluated entirely upon the facts involved. Commonly, this case is cited for the principle that the claimant is entitled to recover for the destination value of the shipment in the quantity shipped. Actually, the case only held that a stipulation in the carrier's tariff that the claimant was limited to recover only the value at the time and place of shipment (point of origin) was invalid in view of the provisions of Section 20(11), which specifically allowed claimant recovery for his "full actual loss, damage, or injury." In studying this case it is important to remember that the claimant was the shipper as well as consignee and that the commodity shipped (grain) was not sold but was being forwarded to destination for sale on the established open market existing at time of arrival. In deciding this case, the Supreme Court stated:

> The grain was shipped under the uniform bill of lading, part of the tariffs filed with the Interstate Commerce Commission, by which it was provided that "*the amount of any loss or damage for which any carrier is liable shall be computed on the basis of the value of the property at the place and time of shipment under this bill of lading, including freight charges if paid.*" (Emphasis added.)

From the foregoing it will be observed that the shipment involved in the *McCaull-Dinsmore* case moved under a bill of lading incorporating into the transportation contract the terms of the carrier's tariffs which contained a provision limiting recovery for loss or damage to the value of the property at the time and place of shipment (point or origin). The question involved in the case therefore was whether or not this limitation was valid and, if not, upon what basis recovery would be allowed. The decision in the case does *not* involve determination of whether the proper measure of damages in such *cases is always the market value* at destination. Continuing, the Supreme Court stated:

> The petitioner (carrier) has paid $1,200.48, being the amount of the loss so computed (on value at point of origin), but the value of the grain at the place of destination at the time when it should have been delivered with interest, less freight charges, was $1,422.11. The plaintiff claimed the difference between the two sums on the ground that the Cummins Amendment to the Interstate Commerce Act made the above stipulation (tariff provision) void. The district Court gave judgment for the plaintiff, 252 Fed. 664, and the judgment was affirmed by the Circuit Court of Appeals, 260 Fed. 835. The Cummins Amendment, Act of March 4, 1915, c. 176, 38 Stat. 1196 (Comp. St. §86040a), provides that the carriers affected by the Act shall issue a bill of lading and shall be liable to the lawful holder of it "for any loss, damage or injury to such property . . . and no contract, receipt, rule, regulation, or other limitation of any character whatsoever, shall exempt such common carrier . . . from the liability herein imposed," and further that the carrier "shall be liable . . . for the full actual loss, damage, or injury . . . notwithstanding any limitation of the amount of recovery or representation or agreement as to value in any such receipt or bill of lading, or in any contract, rule, regulation, or in any tariff filed with the Interstate Commerce Commission; and any such limitation, without respect to the manner or form in which it is sought to be made is hereby declared to be unlawful and void." Before the passage of this amendment the Interstate Commerce Commission had upheld the clause in the bill of lading as in no way limiting the carrier's liability to less than the value of the goods, but merely offering the most convenient way of finding the value. *Shaffer* v. *Chicago, Rock Island & Pacific Ry. Co.*, 21 I.C.C. 8, 12. In a subsequent report upon the amendment it considered that clause was still valid and not forbidden by the law. 33 I.C.C. 682, 693. The argument for the petitioner suggests that courts are bound by the Commission's determination that the rule is a reasonable one. But the question is of the meaning of a statute and upon that, of course, the courts must decide for themselves. We appreciate the convenience of the stipulation in the bill of lading and the arguments urged in its favor. We understand that *it does not necessarily prevent a recovery of the full actual loss,* and that if the price of wheat had gone down the carrier might have had to pay more under this contract than by the common law rule. But *the question is how the contract operates upon this case.* In this case it does prevent a recovery of the full actual loss, if it is enforced. The rule of the common law is not an arbitrary fiat but an embodiment of the plain fact that the actual loss caused by breach of a contract is the loss of what the contractee would have had if the contract had been performed, less the proper deductions, which have been made and are not in question here. It seems to us, therefore, that the

decision below was right, and as, in our opinion, the conclusion is required by the statute, neither the convenience of the clause nor any argument based upon the history of the statute or upon the policy of the later Act of August 9, 1916, c. 301, 39 Stat. 441 (Comp. St. §§8592, 8604a), can prevail against what we understand to be the meaning of the words. Those words seem not only to indicate a broad general purpose but to apply specifically to this very case. (Emphasis added.)

As a result of the foregoing decision, many claimants are quite insistent that the correct measure of damage is the *market value at destination;* however, the *McCaull-Dinsmore* case cannot be cited as authority for that proposition as that case is authority for only the following principles:

1. *As to law:* Any attempt by carrier to limit its liability to less than the full actual loss suffered by the claimant is void unless accomplished in the manner provided in Section 20 (11).
2. *As to facts:* Where shipper shipped grain to a specific destination for sale on the open market at the prevailing price, it is entitled to the market value of the grain at destination at time when it should have been delivered in event of loss by carrier, notwithstanding any stipulation between the shipper and carrier to the contrary.

Since the facts in the *McCaull-Dinsmore* case were such that the claimant would have received the market value at destination had the carrier not lost the property, the claimant was allowed to recover the market value. While in the *McCaull-Dinsmore* case the claimant was entitled to the market value at destination, it does not necessarily follow that in other cases where the facts differ the claimant is entitled to the market value at destination. Even in the *McCaull-Dinsmore* case, which is erroneously cited as holding measure of damage to be market value at destination, the Supreme Court clearly indicated that it would be possible for the value at point of origin in some instances to represent the proper measure of damages, since the court said that the stipulation of the parties that the value at point of origin should be the measure "does not necessarily prevent a recovery of the full actual loss," but if applied in this particular case, "it does prevent a recovery of the full actual loss."

It is admitted that shippers often are entitled to the market value at destination because in many instances, as in the *McCaull-Dinsmore* case, the market value at destination will represent the claimant's full actual loss; but each case must be determined on its own merits to answer the controlling question, "*What was the actual loss to this claimant?*" In answering this question, in some instances it will be found that the claimant is entitled to less than the destination market value. All of the circumstances surrounding the purchase, sale, and transportation of the goods must be considered such as whether it was necessary to replace the goods at destination in order to fill contract of sale, whether the seller has lost a sale because of nondelivery of the goods or damage to them or whether the claimant has earned a retail profit by a contract of sale.

Section 20(11) makes a carrier liable to the *lawful holder* of the bill of lading. In some instances, it is entirely possible that there may be a material difference in the amount of the damages suffered, depending upon who is the lawful holder of the bill of lading (owner of the property). For example, "X Sales Company may sell $1,000 worth of goods to "Y Consuming Company" and purchase the goods from "Z Manufacturing Company" with instructions to ship to "Y Consuming Company" and on this deal the mark-up by "X Sales Company" may result in its securing a $500 profit. If during transportation, the goods are destroyed, the "X Sales Company" will through the carrier's negligence have suffered a $500 loss of profit which it is entitled to recover from the carrier plus the $500 purchase price.

In this situation, there is no dispute that the profit has been *earned* and would have been realized except for the carrier's negligence. In other instances, the claimant may be, as in the *McCaull-Dinsmore* case, both the shipper and consignee; for example, where a manufacturer ships to its own warehouse for storage pending sale and distribution as sales are made on the best price obtainable which may fluctuate according to demand and competition from day to day or week to week. Obviously, the situation is very different where goods are shipped under these circumstances, and the facts of the particular situation are exceedingly important and must be weighed carefully where no sale has actually been made to clearly establish a loss of *earned* profit.

Generally, the rule is that the maximum recovery to which the claimant is entitled is the *market value in the quantity shipped;* however, in order to secure this *maximum* the evidence must clearly indicate that it has been *earned.* In case of *special damages,* if the carrier was made aware of their possibility the claimant may recover even more than ordinary market value. On the other hand, where no sale has been made to justify recovery of market value, as is generally most frequent, the claimant will be limited to recovery only of the landed cost of the merchandise at destination except in those cases where the goods are within that class which enjoy an acknowledged and established open market value at destination. Quite often *Illinois Central R. Co.* v. *Crail,* 281 U.S.

57, is cited as authority for the principle that the claimant is entitled to recover the wholesale value at destination. This case, however, like the *McCaull-Dinsmore* case and all other cases involving the question, must be evaluated upon its own facts.

As pointed out previously, the value at destination does not always represent the correct measure of damages but in those instances where it does (and there are many), the question as to whether retail or wholesale value is to be used depends upon the answer to the controlling question in all such cases: "*What was the actual loss of this claimant?*" If the actual loss to claimant was the wholesale value, then that is the proper measure; on the other hand, if the retail value represents the loss suffered, then that is the proper measure.

In the *Crail* case, claimant, a coal dealer, purchased while in transit a carload of coal. On delivery at destination, there was a shortage of 5,500 pounds. At the time of arrival the coal dealer had not sold any of the coal. It was intended to be, and was, added to his stock of coal for resale, but the shortage did not interfere with the maintenance of his usual stock. He lost no sales by reason of it, and purchased no coal to replace the shortage, except in carload lots. Both before and after the shortage, the coal dealer purchased coal similar to that lost in carload lots at $5.50 per ton plus freight. The retail value for this coal was $13.00 per ton, which included $3.30 freight. The coal dealer endeavored to hold the carrier liable for the retail value. In rendering its decision, the Supreme Court stated:

> By the Cummins Amendment the holder of a bill of lading issued for an interstate rail shipment is entitled to recover for failure to make delivery of any part of the shipment without legal excuse, "the full actual loss, damage, or injury to such property" at point of destination. *C. M. & St. P. R. R. Co.* v. *McCaull-Dinsmore Co.*, 253 U.S. 97, 40 S. Ct. 504.

The foregoing quotation, it will be noted, while indicating that the law entitles claimant to recover the full, actual loss at point of destination, does not state that this recovery is the destination *market value.* Continuing, the court said:

> It is not denied that a recovery measured by the wholesale market price of the coal would fully compensate the respondent, or that the retail price, taken as the measure of recovery allowed below, includes cost of delivery to retail consumers which respondent did not incur, and a retail profit which he had not *earned* by any contract of resale. But respondent contends, as was held below, that the established measure of damage for nondelivery of a shipment of merchandise is the sum required to replace the exact amount of the shortage at the

stipulated time and place of delivery, which, in this case, would be its retail value, and that convenience and the necessity for a uniform rule require its application here.

This contention ignores the basic principle underlying commonlaw remedies that they shall afford only compensation for the injury suffered, *Milwaukee, etc. R. R. Co.* v. *Arms et al.*, 91 U.S. 489, 23 L. Ed. 374; *Chicago, etc. Ry. Co.* v. *McCaull-Dinsmore Co.*, supra; *Robinson* v. *Harmon*, 1 Ech. 850, 855, Sedgwick, *Damages* (9th Ed.), 25 Sutherland, *Damages* (4th Ed.), § 12; Williston on *Contracts*, § 1338; and leaves out of account the language of the amendment, which likewise gives only a right of recovery for "actual loss." The rule urged by respondents was applied below in literal accordance with its conventional statement. As so stated, when applied to cases as they usually arise, it is a convenient and accurate method of arriving at an amount of recovery which is compensatory. As so stated, it would have been applicable here if there had been a failure to deliver the entire carload of coal, since the wholesale price, at which a full carload could have been purchased at point of destination, would have afforded full compensation . . . or, in some instances, if respondent had been under any constraint to purchase less than a carload lot to repair his loss or carry on his business, for in that event the measure of his loss would have been the retail market cost of the necessary replacement, *Haskell* v. *Hunter*, 23 Mich. 305, 309. But in the actual circumstances the cost of replacing the exact shortage at retail price was not the measure of the loss, since it was capable of replacement, and was, in fact, replaced in the course of respondent's business from purchases made in carload lots at wholesale market price without added expense.

There is no greater inconvenience in the application of the one standard of value than the other and we perceive no advantage to be gained from an adherence to a rigid uniformity which would justify sacrificing the reason of the rule, to its letter. The *test of market value is at best but a convenient means of getting at the loss suffered. It may be discarded and other more accurate means resorted to if, for special reasons, it is not exact or otherwise not applicable.* See *Wilmoth* v. *Hamilton* (C.C.A.), 127 F. 48, 51; *Theiss* v. *Weiss*, 166 Pa. 9, 19, 31 A. 63, 45 Am. St. Rep. 638; *Pittsburgh Sheet Mfg. Co.* v. *West Penn Sheet Steel Co.*, 201 Pa. 150, 50 A. 935; Williston on Contracts, § § 1384, 1385. In the absence of special circumstances, the damage for shortage in delivery by the seller of fungible goods sold by quantity is measured by the bulk price, rather than the price for smaller quantities, both at common law and under Section 44 of the Uniform Sales Act. Likewise, we think that the wholesale market price is to be preferred as a test over the retail when, in circumstances like the present, it is clearly the more accurate measure. *Brown Coal Co.* v. *Illinois Central R. R. Co.*, 196 Iowa 562, 192 N.W. 920. See *State* v. *Smith*, 31 Mo. 566; *Wendnagel* v. *Houston, supra* (155 Ill. App. 666, 667); *Wood Co.* v. *Chicago, Milwaukee & St. Paul Ry. Co.*, 320 Ill. 341, 151 N.W. 229. Compare *Heidritter Lumber Co.* v. *Central R. R. of N. J.*, 100 N. J. Law 402, 122 A. 691, 125 A. 926; *Leominster Fuel Co.* v. *New York, N. H. & H. Ry. Co.* 258 Mass. 149, 154 N. E. 831, 50 A. L. R. 1464, cited as supporting the conclusion of the court below. In these cases it does not clearly appear whether the consignee suffered special damage by reason of the shortage, measured by the retail price, or whether he did or could replace it at the wholesale price in the ordinary course of business.

The court below thought that the fact that the award to respondent of the expense and profit, included in the retail price to consumers, did not militate against the rule it applied, for the reason that the wholesale price, as is often the case where market price is the measure of the loss, likewise included a profit over mine cost plus freight. But respondent had done every act and incurred every expense prerequisite to procurring delivery at destination. Any profit included in its market value at the stipulated time and place of arrival was, therefore, appropriately included in the measure of his loss. In this respect it is distinguishable from the expense and *prospective* profit not actually incurred or earned by respondent, represented by the retail price. See *Central of Georgia R. R. Co.* v. *American Coal Co.*, supra (28 Ga. App. 95, 110 S. E. 320); *Yazoo & M. V. R. Co.* v. *Delta Grocer Co.*, supra (134 Miss. 846, 98 So. 777). Compare *Cincinnati, N. O. & T. P. Ry. Co.* v. *Hansford,* 125 Ky. 37, 100 S. W. 251; *Smith* v. *N. Y. O. & Western Ry. Co.*, supra (119 Misc. Rep. 506, 196 N. Y. S. 521); *Quanah, A. & P. Co.* v. *Novit,* supra (199 S. W. 496). Reversed. (Emphasis added.)

In the foregoing quotation it will be observed that the court points out that a projected or anticipated loss is not the measure of damage required by Section 20(11). The court states that the "basic principle underlying common-law remedies" is "that they shall afford only compensation for the injury suffered. . . ." Any other argument, the court says, "leaves out of account the language of the amendment (Sec. 20, paragraph 11), which likewise gives only a right of recovery for 'actual loss.'" Any attempt to recover more than the actual loss by any lawful holder of the bill of lading must be limited by the court's decision in the *Crail* case. But the "actual loss" must depend upon the facts in each case.

In recent years there has been a growing tendency upon the part of some claimants to inform carriers of their *inability* to supply a copy of invoice covering shipment involved in a claim. In lieu of the invoice, these claimants make a certification upon their claims reading similar to the following: "This is to certify that the amounts set forth above do not exceed destination market value in the quantity shipped." A certification of this nature occasions considerable suspicion from a carrier's viewpoint. Investigation of claims with this certification frequently reveals that the price set forth is usually equal or in excess of the prevailing retail price at destination of competitive products and the particular product involved. If the product had not been lost or damaged, it would have been delivered to the consignee, stored in its warehouse, eventually placed in stock, and possibly months later sold on a highly competitive market at perhaps a loss and involving considerable expense for storage, handling, advertising, and selling.

Frequently, the product involved may be so unique that it enjoys very little public acceptance and while the mark-up may be high the expense of selling it may be a substantial portion of its eventual selling price. A casual glance at any newspaper reveals highly competitive prices on the same merchandise depending upon the nature of the seller's business; frequently, after the end of a season, surplus unsold merchandise will be dumped on the market at less than cost and many of the consuming public make a practice of buying only off-season goods. Until merchandise is actually sold to the ultimate consumer, no one knows the profit, if any, which may be earned in excess of its actual cost of production and landing at that point where the ultimate purchaser takes custody.

In the *McCaull-Dinsmore* case and the *Crail* case, the commodities involved were goods (grain and coal) which not only were fungible but those upon which it was easy to determine the prevailing open market price on the day upon which they should have arrived. Grain, coal, livestock, meats, fruit, and vegetables, while highly competitive, are subject to ready grading, and prevailing market prices both wholesale and retail are easily ascertainble by consulting reliable daily market quotations. It is possible at this date to determine the wholesale auction price in New York City, Philadelphia, or any other large metropolitan center on a specific date twenty or more years ago for these products. Actually those purchasing these products are not concerned with the producer's cost of placing the goods on the local market nor with the identity of the actual owner or producer of the goods, since the price is governed primarily by supply and demand. Assuming, as is generally true, equal quality, the price on a particular day will be subject to very little fluctuation but on a day-to-day basis as supply increases or decreases the fluctuation will differ considerably.

Generally, these commodities are seldom stored or warehoused at destination; usually they are sold directly to the purchaser from the rail car or motor vehicle in which they arrived and the purchaser takes immediate possession. Frequently they are sold while in transit and diverted for delivery to the purchaser. These products differ greatly from those ordered to replenish stock of a wholesaler, retailer, or distributor of goods which must be warehoused, displayed, advertised, and often sold many months after arrival at destination, these costs frequently representing a considerable portion of the selling price if eventually sold. Unfortunately, erroneous interpretation of the *McCaull-Dinsmore* and *Crail* cases over the years have led to the assumption by many that in all cases the claimant was entitled to the wholesale destination market price on all commodities. To illustrate the extreme that this misinterpretation finally reached, one need only consult *Texas and New Orleans Railroad Co.* v. *The H. Rouw Co.*, 271 S. W. 2d 666, decided by the Texas Court of Civil Appeals, which is discussed hereafter in *Missouri Pacific R. Co.* v. *The H. Rouw Co.*, 258 F. 2d 445.

The former case concerns an attack upon the market rule of damages applicable in the case of damages to an interstate shipment of perishables. As the court pointed out, it involved the same set of facts as it had previously decided in *Thompson* v. *H. Rouw Co.*, 237 S. W. 2d 662, holding that commissions should not be deducted from the damages computed on the basis of the wholesale market value. The argument of the carrier was that if it paid the wholesale market value at destination this amount would include commissions and other items which had not been incurred, and the shipper would receive more for the merchandise which arrived in a damaged condition than it would receive for merchandise delivered without damage. The court awarded these *unearned* profits, thus permitting the claimant to recover more than it would have realized had the goods been delivered in good condition and sold, in which case the claimant would have received only the sales price less commission for selling. Although, as indicated, the reasoning of this court was subsequently repudiated in a similar case by the United States Court of Appeals, Fifth Circuit (*Mo. Pac. R. Co.* v. *The H. Rouw Co.*, 258 F. 2d 445), the pertinent portions of its decisions as a matter of information are given as follows:

An important and controlling fact is that there was a wholesale market for each shipment at destination in both the *Thompson* case and in this case. Precedents which determine damages by methods other than a resort to a market value because none existed are inapplicable to the decision in this case. At the outset, also, it should be observed that there is nothing new, unusual nor exceptional about the market value rule of damages. There is no room for any misgivings about the *Thompson* case disturbing settled law, but should we depart from the rule there announced, we would disturb the law of long standing. In *McCaull-Dinsmore Co.* v. *Chicago, M. & St. P. Ry. Co.*, 252 F. 664, affirmed in 260 F. 835, the question was whether a bill of lading which fixed value at the point of origin was a limitation of liability. Mr. Justice Stone, speaking for the Circuit Court of Appeals, struck down the carrier's contention that the disputed clause in the bill of lading was inserted for the mere purpose of seeking certainty and stated: "There was no uncertainty as to the time or place of estimating value under the rule of common law—it was the destination." The court stated also, "The fair market value of the shipment at destination at the time when it should have been delivered, with interest, and less freight charges, was $142.11." That was the rule of common law, and that was the amount awarded by the court. Mr. Justice Holmes, speaking for the Supreme Court, affirmed the two lower courts and in so doing followed the common law rule of damages, measured by the wholesale market value. *Chicago Milwaukee & St. Paul Railway Company* v. *McCaull-Dinsmore Co.* (1920), 40 S. Ct. 504, 253 U.S. 97, 64 L. Ed. 601. Scores of cases in an unbroken line confirm the rule, *S. S. Ansaldo San Giogia* v. *Rheinstrom,* 55 S. Ct. 483, 294 U.S. 494, 79 L. Ed. 1016; *Pennsylvania R. Co.* v. *Wm. H. Muller & Co.,* 15 Fed. 2d 535, cert. denied, 47 S. Ct. 449, 273 U.S. 748, 71 L. Ed. 872; *American Ry. Express Co.* v.*Ewing Thomas, etc.,* 292 F. 335; *Bussey* v. *Memphis & Littlerock R. Co.,* 13 F. 330; *Railway Exp. Agency* v. *Smith,* 116 F. Supp. 609; *Rio Grande & E. P. R. Co.* v. *Austin Co.,* Com. App., 25 S.W. 2d 306; *Texas Mexican Ry. Co.* v. *Slaughter,* 241 S.W. 2d 749; *Thompson* v. *Tebbe & Sons,* 241 S.W. 2d 627; *Thompson* v. *Tankersley,* 238 S.W. 263; *Thompson* v. *Associated Growers of Brownsville,* 162 S.W. 2d 754; *American Ry. Express Co.* v. *McDaniel,* 20 S.W. 1104; *Coulter* v. *Gulf C. & S. F. Ry. Co.,* 286 S.W. 559; *Gulf C. & S. Ry. Co.* v. *Stewart,* 141 S.W. 1020; 8 Tex. Jur., Carriers, §227; 9 Am. Jur., Carriers, §781; 13 C. J. S., Carriers, §264 (notes 24 and 25).

From what has been said, it does not follow that the absence of a market value at destination prevents a shipper's recovery. When no market exists at destination, resort is made to other means to prove damages, as exceptions to the rule. The general rule is not abandoned, however, when all facts exist by which it can be applied. Appellant's authorities are exceptions to the general rule . . . . We find no instances applying exceptions when a wholesale market actually exists. In the *Thompson* case we sought to point out that there was a wholesale market.

Appellant urges that the phrase, "full actual loss, damage or injury to such property," used in Title 49 U. S. C. A. 20(11), was a statutory departure from the common law rule of damage, and that since its enactment, some measure other than the market value measure was adopted. We find no cases so stating, but the many cases cited above hold to the contrary. Some cases have expressly so stated. *Chicago Milwaukee & St. Paul Railway Company* v. *McCaull-Dinsmore Co., supra; Meltzer* v. *Baltimore & O. C. T. R. Co.,* 38 Fed. Supp. 391; *Piazza* v. *Louisiana & Arkansas Ry. Co.,* 46 So. 2d 670; *Gore Products* v. *Texas & N. O. R. Co.,* 34 So. 2d 418; *Thompson* v. *A. J. Tebbe & Sons Co.,* 241 S. W. 2d 627, 629; *Thompson* v. *Rouw, supra*; *Matthews-Carr* v. *Brown Express,* 217 S.W. 2d 75, 77; 13 C. J. S. Carriers, §264 (note 25, citing many cases). Appellant's attack upon the *Thompson* case ignores the general rule, and would read into the words, "full actual loss, damage or injury," a meaning different from the settled market value rule. Appellant would convert it into a "cost to the shipper" rule.

One exception to the general rule is that a shipper may recover in some instances on a basis other than market value when there is no market. *United States* v. *Palmer & Parker Co.,* 61 F. 2d 455. Appellant has briefed this exception to the general rule. We shall examine those cases. In *Baltimore & O. C. T. R. Co.* v. *Becker Mach. Co.,* 272 F. 933, the court properly refused to fix the market price at the price to individual purchasers of specifically manufactured machines when the manufacturer controlled the price. That, of course, was not a valid market price. In *Wierton Steel Co.* v. *Isbrandtsen-Moller Co.,*

126 F. 2d 593, certain parcels of tin plate were damaged. The tin was intended to be made into oil cans, and the tin was used for that purpose apparently at no loss in price. If the case is applicable at all, there was no proof with reference to the wholesale market value of tin at Hong Kong, the destination. In *Waterman S. C. Corp.* v. *United States S. R. & M. Co.*, 165 F. 687, thirteen sheets of steel were lost overboard into the sea. The sole evidence of value was the replacement value at Seattle, which was the destination, and the Court stated: "No other evidence in the record exists as to the value of the steel plates at Seattle. . . . In absence of any contrary evidence, 'the value at Seattle' *may be taken as the market value.*" In *Continental Distributing Co.* v. *Reading Co.*, 168 F. 2d 967, there was no proof of market value at destination of wine, the commodity which had been lost. Only one witness testified with reference to values and he undertook to prove value of the wine at Chicago by the cost method, which is the cost method appellant here sponsors. The witness fixed the value of wine by testifying to cost in New York rather than at destination. He then added to that costs necessary to get it to Chicago, and also tax and duty. The method and the evidence were properly rejected. *Meletio Sea Food Co.* v. *Gordons Transports*, 191 S.W. 2d 983, states the general rule as we have stated it. The case concerned a special food preparation, and the case makes no mention of its having a market price. The facts show that the only proof of a market was the one customer to whom the food preparation was shipped, and that of the sale was not lost. *Matthews-Carr* v. *Brown Exp.*, 217 S.W. 2d 75, was decided against the shipper because he made no proof of damage to the commodity in question. Significantly, however, the court stated: "There was no testimony as to the cash market value of the Mexican chewing gum at the various points of destination where the consignees were located, either in the condition in which it should have been delivered or in its damaged condition." The Court stated that fact two other times in the course of the same opinion. *Reider* v. *Thompson*, 197 F. 2d 158, was a case where there was proof of the market value of the commodity at destination. The Court reversed the trial court for dismissing the shipper's suit upon such prima facie proof. We find that on remand, the court correctly applied the market value measure of damages. *Reider* v. *Thompson*, 116 Fed. Supp. 279; *United States* v. *Northern Pac. Ry. Co.*, 116 F. Supp. 277, concerned damages to a shipment of potatoes and it is the only case called to our attention which in our opinion varies the settled rule. It awarded the contract price rather than the market value, but it should be observed even there that the potatoes belonged to the United States under the Price Support Program and were not a part of free commercial market at all. Hence, appellant's authorities are those wherein there was no valid market value, and, of course, resort was then made to other rules.

This case and the *Thompson* case are readily understandable if we keep in mind the general wholesale market value rule of damages, and then further keep in mind the fact that certain exceptions to that rule become operative, when, for some reason, it is impossible to prove a wholesale market value. *American Ry. Express Co.* v. *Parisian Hat Co.*, 240 S.W. 947. The precedents relied upon by the appellant are not holdings inconsistent with the general rule, but are well recognized exceptions to the general rule, which are not applicable here, where there was a readily ascertained market and it was proved. 15 Am. Jur., Carriers, §125; 13 C. J. S., Carriers, §264 (c, d).

Appellant insistently urges that the *Thompson* case varies the rule of damages announced by the United States Supreme Court in *Illinois Cent. R. Co.* v. *Crail,* 50 S. Ct. 180, 281 U.S. 57, 74 L. Ed. 699, 67 A. L. R. 1423. The two cases are in complete harmony. The trial court in the *Crail* case stated the general rule as we have stated it and then refused to allow the consignee of a coal shipment, damages computed at retail prices for a small quantity of coal that was was lost in shipment. The court held that damages measured by retail prices would be improper and that the correct measure was the wholesale market value on the basis of the entire carload of coal. The Supreme Court affirmed this view, expressly stating that the circuit court erred in awarding damages based on the "retail value of the coal," and that the trial court correctly awarded "judgment for the wholesale value of the coal not delivered." That is exactly what we held in the *Thompson* case, and the case is not authority that something less than the wholesale value should be awarded, as appellant urges upon the Court here by insisting that commissions should be subtracted from the wholesale market value. The *Crail* case rejects a retail price and accepts a wholesale value as the basis for measuring damages. The case by no construction can mean that the wholesale value should also be rejected. The Court stated in part:

> In the absence of special circumstances, the damages for shortage in delivery by the seller of fungible goods sold by quantity is measured by the bulk price rather than the price for smaller quantities, both at common law (see *Morgan* v. *Gath,* 3 Hurlst. & C. 748, 159 Eng. Reprint, 726; *Avery* v. *Willson,* 81 N.Y. 341, 37 Am. Rep. 503) and under §44 of the Uniform Sales Act. Likewise, we think that the wholesale market price is to be preferred as a test over the retail when, in circumstances like the present, it is clearly the more accurate measure. *Brown Coal Co.* v. *Illinois C. R. Co.,* 196 Iowa 562, 192 N. E. 920. See *State use of Hayden* v. *Smith,* 31 Mo. 566; *Wendnagel* v. *Houston, supra* (155. Ill. App. 666, 667); *Wood & Co.* v. *Chicago, M. & St. P. R. Co.,* 320 Ill. 341, 151 N. E. 229. Compare *Heidritter Lumber Co.* v. *Central R. Co.,* 100 N. J. L. 402, 122 Atl. 691, 125 Atl. 926; *Leominster Fuel Co.* v. *New York, N. H. & H. R. Co.,* 258 Mass. 149, 50 A. L. R. 1464, 154 N. E. 831, cited as supporting the conclusion of the court below. In these cases it does not clearly appear whether the consignee suffered special damage by reason of the shortage, measured by the retail price, or whether he did or could replace it at the wholesale price in the ordinary course of business.

There are other reasons that the market value must be followed rather than the adoption of a new rule based on actual costs to a shipper or consignee. *Kyle* v. *Laurens R. R. Company,* 10 Rich Law 383, with reference to the claim that commissions should be deducted, used the following language which accords with the *Thompson* case:

> The answer to the second question (whether or not the Defendant railroad company was entitled to deduct the commission), cannot, I think, be well doubted after it is properly considered. If, as in the case of *Bridges* v. *Austin,* 4 Mass. 115, he undertook to transport and sell and for so doing he was to have 5% commission, it may well be in the case of a loss he would have the right to deduct commission, for that was

> part of his compensation for his services touching the article lost. But in these cases the carrier had nothing to do but deliver in Charleston. If a factor might have sold, it was a matter in which the Laurens R. R. had no interest whatsoever. To illustrate still further, suppose the cotton had reached Charleston depot and carrier had refused to deliver and trover had been brought what would have been the plaintiff's damage? The value of the article, deducting the freight, and adding interest on the net value. In such a case, commission could not have been talked about. How, in any case, can any deduction be made for that which was to be subsequent to carrier's discharge of liability, by delivering the parcel? The authorities are, I think, clear against such allowance. Sedwick on Damages, C. 13, P. 369, tells us the rule whereby the damages are fixed as a rule of law. At pages 370, 371, he tells us that the rule as to carriers is the value of the article lost or not delivered at the place of destination, deducting his freight. The same is substantially the ruling is *Gillingham* v. *Dempsey*, 12 Serg. N. R. 183.

If, as the carrier urges, "full actual loss, damage or injury to such property," means that the actual cost to a shipper or consignee should be the rule when the wholesale market value of produce is strong and high, it very well could be that the shipper, when the wholesale market is weak and low, may join the carrier in its contentions and urge that it should be permitted to total its "full actual costs" as a measure without regard to the market price. The rule, so applied equally, would then make the carrier an insurer that the shipper would never lose its costs on any shipments, whatever the market may be. Such has never been the rule in either instance.

The trial court, acting under the impression that the *Thompson* case announced strange law, made strong findings with the suggestion to counsel that this Court may avail itself of the opportunity to overrule our former opinion. The findings are an overstatement of the case, as reflected by some of the account sales, which on their face show that commissions were owing and that some had actually been paid; but appellee, winning its case anyway, made no objections, and we take the findings without limitation. They include the findings that the shipper would collect and keep the full amount of the judgment, that no commissions were to be paid to the commission agent, that the market value rule gives to the shipper a full market value recovery without having to pay commissions which he would have paid if the produce had arrived in good condition and been sold. The trial court concludes as a matter of law that the shipper recovered more than would have made him whole.

We are at a loss to know how the court could make a judgment that would bind a commission agent as against the shipper when the agent is not a party to the suit. Whether the agent will sue and recover against the shipper was not before the court, and the court could write no judgment in this case denying him his rights should he seek to assert them. Those findings and conclusions, so far as the rights of the commission agent are concerned, are suppositions.

But it makes no difference to the correct rule. Title 49 U. S. C. A. 20 (11) states who may sue and what he may recover. It states that the carrier "shall be liable to the lawful holder of said receipt or bill of lading or to any party entitled to recover thereon." In *Thompson* v. *Rouw* we stated, as forcefully as we could, that either the shipper or the consignee could sue and recover for all. But we shall say it again. "The matter of accounting between a shipper and consignee is of no concern to the carrier." *Thompson* v. *Rouw,* 237 S. W. 2d 662, 666. The consignee, or the commission agent has an interest in the shipment, and in our former opinion we stated the reasons and cited many authorities so holding. We did not discuss the authorities, thinking that they could be studied without lengthening the opinion. We shall, however, quote from one of them by way of summing up what the cases hold. 13 C. J. S. Carriers, §249(k), in part states:

> One who has a special property in the goods shipped or a beneficial interest in the performance of the contract, such as a broker, factor, or bailee, may sue the carrier to recover for loss of, or injury to the goods, although the general owner may also sue.
>
> One who has a special property or interest in the goods shipped, or a beneficial interest in the performance of the contract, is entitled to maintain an action for their loss or injury.
>
> A bailee has such special property in goods as entitles him to maintain an action for loss of or injury thereto.
>
> If the consignee has a special property in the goods as factor or broker, he has such an interest in the shipment as will entitle him to maintain an action for loss of or injury thereto. It is not necessary to his capacity as a plaintiff that he is entitled to all the damage, although he may recover the full damage done; the judgment would bar another action by the real owner, and the owner's share would be held by the consignee to be accounted for by him.
>
> General or Special Owner. The right of one having a special or beneficial interest in the goods shipped to maintain the action as stated above, does not preclude an action by the general owner. Either one may sue, and whichever first obtains damages it is a full satisfaction.

Hence, under the statute, the shipper may sue and make "full" recovery for every one having an interest in the shipment, and the trial court, in concluding that the shipper received more than would make him whole, failed to take into account that the statute intends for the plaintiff against a carrier to recover for himself as well as for others. A conclusion that others will be unable to recover, by suit or otherwise, from the shipper is in violation of the Federal statute, and the trial court ruled correctly when it disregarded its own conclusion. The judgment is affirmed.

The extreme to which the Texas Court of Civil Appeals had extended the argument of destination wholesale value could only result in further litigation and especially so since these particular cases involved perishables moving from the Southwest to markets everywhere and involving millions of dollars. On 27 August 1958, the United States Courts of Appeals, Fifth Circuit, 258 F. 2d 445, with one dissent, held that in computing damages to be allowed for interstate shipments of perishables damaged by the negligence of common carriers by rail, it was error to fail to deduct, from gross amount of difference in market values, sales commissions, and other charges figured on amount of differences in market values between delivery in good order and delivery in bad order. In this case, the court said:

This appeal presents the question of the correct measure of damages which should be allowed the owner (or the party entitled to recover) of an interstate shipment of perishables damaged by the negligence of a common carrier by rail. Based upon two Texas cases the court below held that "the measure of damages . . . (was) the difference between the wholesale market price of the commodities had they arrived in the condition they should have been had they been properly and promptly transported and the same market value in the condition in which they were delivered."

The rule stated by the court below is undoubtedly the rule of general application, and both sides admit that this is true. But appellant claims that, under the facts of this case, the court should have deducted from the gross amount of this difference in market value, the necessary expenses shown by the evidence to have been included in the award made by the court attributable to such difference. Appellee contends, on the other hand, that the court correctly allowed it the gross difference between the actual market value of the shipments as received and the market value which would have been realized if they had not been damaged in transit. We agree with the position of appellant.

The shipment involved here being interstate, the liability of the carrier and the measure of damages are determined by the Interstate Commerce Act and the decisions of the Courts of the United States construing it. *Georgia, Florida, & Alabama Ry. Co.* v. *Blish Milling Co.*, 1916, 241 U.S. 190, 36 S. Ct. 541, 60 L. Ed. 948; *St. Louis, I. Mt. & So. Ry. Co.* v. *Starbird, etc.*, 1916, 243 U.S. 592, 37 S. Ct. 462, 61 L. Ed. 917; and *Southern Pacific Co.* v. *Stewart*, 1917, 245 U.S. 359, 38 S. Ct. 130, 62 L. Ed. 345. There can be no doubt that the damages allowed by the court below faithfully reflect the rule as worked out in the two Texas cases, which discuss ably and at great length various decisions of the United States Courts of Appeal and of the Supreme Court. The two Texas Courts concluded that the rule followed by the court below was one of universal and invariable application even though they conceded that it was merely a rule of convenience.

We are unable to agree with the conclusions reached in these two cases upon which the court below relied. Here, as there, the problem is simplified by the fact that the property constituting the damaged shipments had, in every instance, a market value at destination. The two Texas decisions took freight charges into consideration in arriving at the difference in market values, but declined, as did the court below, to take into account other items of necessary expense which, in our opinion, ought to be deducted in arriving at the true actual loss and damage. The rule of convenience quoted from the opinion of the court below would result, if applied thus categorically to the shipments here involved, in recovery by the appellee of more than its actual loss. Such a recovery would violate principles of law as universal in their application as that which the court below used as the basic and inflexible rule governing recovery in this case. These principles are well set forth in 15 American Jurisprudence, Damages, § 13, p. 402:

> The fundamental principle of the law of damages being compensated for the injury sustained, the plaintiff in a civil action for damages cannot . . . hold a defendant liable in damages for more than the actual loss which was inflicted by his wrong. . . . The law will not put him in a better position than he would be in had the wrong not been done or the contract not been broken.

The evidence before the court below fairly established that shippers, including appellee, universally paid brokers a commission to dispose of such shipments at destination. That commission represented a charge each shipper was bound to pay upon the full amount received, so that a carload of tomatoes would yield to the owner the amount for which it was sold, less the commission incurred in making the sale. By allowing appellee the gross amount of the difference between the market value of the shipments in damaged conditions and the value which would have been applied if the shipments had not been damaged, the court did not deduct from this difference the amount of commissions which would have been incurred in selling them.

The action of the court below in awarding appellee damages in the full gross amount of the differences between the two market values necessarily resulted, therefore, in the enrichment of appellee to the extent of the nondeducted commission, and permitted it a rec very of more damages than actually suffered. This is, in our opinion, in derogation of the general rule above quoted from American Jurisprudence.

The rule adopted by the court below can be applied as herein set forth so as to make the shipper whole and not require the carrier to pay more than indemnity. What the Supreme Court said in *Chicago, Milwaukee & St. Paul R. Co.* v. *McCaull-Dinsmore Co.*, 1920, 253 U.S. 97, 100, 40 S. Ct. 504, 64 L. Ed. 801, indicates that the rule should be applied in such a way as to achieve fairness and justice:

> But the question is how the contract operates upon this case. . . . The rule of the common law is not an arbitrary fiat but an embodiment of the plain fact that the actual loss caused by breach of a contract is the loss of what the contractee would have had if the contract had been performed, less the proper deductions, which have been made and are not in question here.

The Supreme Court, in *Illinois Central R. Co.* v. *Crail*, 1930, 281 U.S. 57, 50 S. Ct. 180, 74 L. Ed. 699, demonstrated clearly that the market value rule should be applied in such a way as to dove-tail with the rule permitting recovery of compensatory damages only. A carload of coal shipped to Crail was 5,500 pounds short, and both the District Court and the Circuit Court of Appeals awarded him recovery of $9.70 per ton, which was the amount he would have to pay to replace the coal at retail. The coal actually received was placed in Crail's large stock of coal held for resale, and he did not actually go into the market to purchase coal to replace that which had been lost in transit.

The Supreme Court refused to approve the hard and fast application of the "market value" rule because it would permit Crail to recover more than his actual loss. Its language (281 U.S. at pages 63-64, 50 S. Ct. at page 181) points the way to the correct decision here:

> It is not denied that a recovery measured by the wholesale market price of the coal would fully compensate the respondent, or that the retail price, taken as the measure of recovery allowed below, includes costs of delivery to retail consumers which respondent did not incur, and a retail profit which he had not earned by any contract of resale. But respondent contends, as was held below, that the established measure of damage for nondelivery of a shipment of merchandise is the sum required to replace the exact amount of the shortage. . . .
>
> This contention ignores the basic underlying common-law remedies that they shall afford only compensation for the injury suffered, (citing authorities) and leaves out of account the language of the amendment, which likewise gives only a right of recovery for "actual loss." The rule urged by respondent was applied below in literal accordance with its conventional statement. As so stated, when applied to cases as they usually arise, it is a convenient and accurate method of arriving at an amount of recovery which is compensatory. . . .
>
> There is no greater inconvenience in the application of the one standard of value than the other, and we perceive no advantage to be gained from an adherence to a rigid uniformity, which would justify sacrificing the reason of the rule, to its letter. The test of market value is at best but a convenient means of getting at the loss suffered. It may be discarded and other more accurate means resorted to, if, for special reasons, it is not exact or otherwise not applicable. . . .

We think that the rigid application of the market value rule here resulted in awarding appellee more than its actual loss; and there is ground to believe that the court below had the same feeling.

We are not, however, undertaking to weigh or appraise the evidence as to damages. We hold simply that the judgment appealed from clearly includes the award of some damages to which appellee was not entitled, growing out of the holding of the court below that no deduction should be made of sales commissions and other charges figured on the amount of the difference in market values between delivery in good order and delivery in bad order. Appellee's recovery should be based upon this difference in market values, but not exceed indemnity.

The dissenting opinion failed to discuss the merits of the majority opinion and simply alleged that the majority had rejected "weightier matters of law" and for that reason aligns with the Texas courts which the majority opinion had reversed. It is disappointing that the dissent did not go into greater detail by setting forth the law believed to entitle claimants to recover more from the carrier than they would have received had the carrier actually performed their contractual duty under the bill of lading by delivering the goods without damage. The effect of the majority in its final analysis can be regarded simply as closing a *loophole* by which claimants in the Southwest had been receiving a *windfall* out of the carrier's misfortune in handling shipments of perishables. As a practical matter, no actual injury resulted to the claimants by restricting them to their "full actual loss, damage, or injury" as provided by the governing law (Sec. 20, paragraph 11, part I of Interstate Commerce Act).

As indicated in the introduction to this chapter, the problem of measure of claimant's recovery is primarily a factual question—*what was claimant's actual loss*? To answer this question on a particular set of facts requires that the claimant have the ability to fully understand and appreciate the carrier's position and the carrier to fully understand and appreciate the claimant's position. It is exceedingly difficult, however, for any individual to consider and respect the viewpoint of an antagonist completely. For the claimant there is an understandable desire to secure maximum recovery from the carrier, even though in many instances the allowance of such recovery would be to give to the claimant more than he had actually *earned* upon the delivery of the undamaged goods. Similarly, from the carrier's viewpoint, its desire to restrict the claimant to the lowest possible amount of recovery can be readily understood.

Considering all authority including that of the United States Supreme Court, it is believed that the Court in deciding *Atlantic Coast Line Ry. Co.* v. *Roe,* 118 So. 155, best stated in the fewest words the proper interpretation of Section 20(11) of part I of the Interstate Commerce Act in pointing out that: "The basic thought underlying the federal statutes which define the liability and prescribe the measure of damages in cases of this kind is that the owner shall be made whole by receiving the proper money equivalent for what he has actually lost, or, in other words, to restore him to the position he would have occupied, had the carrier performed its contract." As the court in *Missouri Pacific R. Co.* v. *H. Rouw Co.,* 258 F. 2d 445, stated the objective should be "to make the . . . (claimant) . . . whole and not require the carrier to pay more than indemnity." Any profit realized out of the carrier's misfortune in losing or damaging the goods must from the state of facts involved be clearly established as *earned,* and this actually was the principal holding of the *Crail* case. And, as the United States Supreme Court said in the *McCaull-Dinsmore* case "the actual loss caused by breach of contract is the loss of what the contractee would have had if the contract had been performed, *less the proper deductions. . . .*"

In the voluntary settlement of claims, there is a growing tendency to use the invoice price as the basis for measuring the damages. From the carrier's viewpoint, this practice has much to commend it, but it should always be remembered that insofar as the law is concerned the carrier is liable for the "full actual loss, damage, or injury." As indicated the application of this measure presents a question of fact and each case must be determined on its own merits. Generally the claimant's full actual loss will be the invoice value plus freight charges, if paid. The vast majority of claims are adjusted upon this basis and except in unusual cases as, for example, where some special sale is lost or seasonable goods are delayed or lost, this will be the claimant's full actual loss.

In *Atlantic Coast Line Ry. Co.* v. *Roe,* 118 So. 155, plaintiff shipped three cars of grapefruit destined for ultimate delivery to a purchaser in Chicago. The shipment was made on an *order-notify* bill of lading and the shipper drew drafts on the purchaser for $1,593. The delivering carrier delivered the shipments without securing the original bills of lading and the draft was never paid. Action was brought by shipper against the carrier and claimant was awarded judgment in amount of $5,360.85 by the lower court, representing, apparently, the market value at destination with interest to date of judgment. In deciding this case, the court held:

What the plaintiff has actually lost, therefore, by reason of the carrier's default is, not the market value of the goods, but the amount he would have received from the purchaser if the carrier had performed his contract. Of the latter amount, and nothing else, has the plaintiff been deprived by the transportation company, and under the particular circumstances of this case he is made whole by receiving that amount, with interest. The contract of transportation is, of course, not affected by the terms of the contract for the sale of the goods between the plaintiff and his purchaser, but under the rule of "full actual loss" fixed by the statutes, the value of the goods to the plaintiff at destination, as fixed by his existing contract of sale with the purchaser, upon the payment of which the carrier could have properly delivered the goods under the delivery directions existing at the time of the wrongful conversion, determines the plaintiff's actual loss under the circumstances of this case, and is, therefore, of controlling force in determining the amount recoverable from the carrier. The plaintiff was not compelled by the default of the carrier to secure equivalent goods in the open market in order to complete his contract with the purchaser. If he had been, the amount of recovery might be otherwise. The purchaser has received the goods, but, due to defendant's wrong, the shipper has not received the stipulated price which he would have received had the carrier performed its duty. Under those circumstances, he is entitled to recover that purchase price, but no more. If the circumstances were such that plaintiff's "actual loss" was the market value of the goods at destination, and not merely a loss of the agreed and stipulated purchase price of the goods, the former value would constitute the proper amount of recovery. The rule as to the measure of damages for wrongful delivery of interstate shipment is very plainly stated in *Chicago, M. & St. P. Ry. Co.* v. *McCaull-Dinsmore Co.*, as also in *G. F. & A. Ry.* v. *Blish Milling Co., supra,* and in *Leominster Fuel Co.* v. *N. Y. N. H. Hartford R. R. Co.*, 258 Mass. 149, 154 N. E. 831, 50 A. L. R. 1464. Under the facts in those cases, the plaintiff's "actual loss" was properly measurable by the market value of the goods at destination. But the facts in those cases bearing upon the question of the amount of recovery—that is, the amount which will compensate the plaintiff for his actual loss—distinguish those cases from the case at bar. Those cases were suits by consignees from whom goods had been wrongfully withheld at destination, their only recourse being to secure like goods in the open market at destination to replace those wrongfully delivered or lost. Therefore, the "actual loss" of the consignee plaintiffs in those cases was the market value of the goods. Had the carrier in this case performed its contract, and carried out existing delivery directions, for the breach of which duty the plaintiff recovers his "actual loss" in this form of action, plaintiff would have received the contract sales price from the purchaser, not the market value of the goods at destination. Had the plaintiff received the amount of the drafts at the time of the wrongul delivery, he would have suffered no loss under the circumstances. Having lost the amount of the drafts by a wrongful delivery, that amount is plaintiff's actual loss under the circumstances. . . .

There are two cases by state courts which have caused considerable confusion in determining measure of damages, and an understanding of their background is desirable to remove this confusion. Both of these cases will be reviewed here. The first case, entitled *H. V. Kell Co.* v. *Southern Railway Co.* was decided by the Supreme Court of Georgia in Peach Superior Court, Macon Circuit and, since not rendered by the state's highest court, is unreported and for that reason alone entitled to little weight as an authority, involved the loss of a shipment of 30,000 cigarettes shipped by the R. J. Reynolds Tobacco Co., Winston-Salem, North Carolina to a wholesale grocer at Fort Valley, Georgia. The cigarettes were sold at a trade discount of 12 percent, making the purchase total $168.96, which the wholesaler paid and then sued the carrier for, claiming that the price at which it would have sold them was $192, which would include its profit. The court in deciding the case said, in part:

The defendant admits the loss of the cigarettes and the only issue in the case is the real actual loss sustained by the plaintiff growing out of failures to deliver any part of the shipment of cigarettes. All other questions either of law or of fact are virtually settled by the construction of the Interstate Commerce Act, as finally amended by the Cummins Amendment, in the case of *Chicago, St. Paul and Milwaukee Ry.* v. *McCaull-Dinsmore*, 253 U.S., page 97. This case is recognized as settling the legal principle that the loss in interstate shipment of goods must be accounted for by payment of the real value of the property at the place at which it was contracted to be delivered at the time it should have been delivered.

In the foregoing quotation it will be noted that the court misinterprets the Supreme Court's holding in the *McCaull-Dinsmore* case, since that case held only that any attempt by a carrier to limit its liability to less than the full actual loss suffered by claimant is void and, while claimant was permitted to recover market value at destination under the facts of that case, it provided no authority for application of that recovery in all other situations. After stating the above erroneous premises, the court continues:

The facts agreed upon (by the parties to the suit) are as follows:

1. That the plaintiff is a jobber or wholesale dealer in cigarettes, and inferentially that the cigarettes in question were bought in Winston-Salem, N. C., to be resold to retailers in and around Fort Valley, Ga.
2. That shipments of cigarettes, in quantities of 30,000 were being sold to jobbers in Fort Valley at the time (February 5, 1925) for $192, with a discount privilege if paid in a limited time.
3. That on the same date, Fort Valley jobbers bought cigarettes on these terms and at this price, and were selling them to their retail customers for $6.40 per thousand with no discount privilege.

The point is made that it does not appear that the market in Fort Valley in which jobbers bought for the purpose of reselling fixes the price by which the plaintiff's loss is measurable, the further contention being that discount privilege of 12 percent reduces the real value of the property to $168.96 and that $192 is not the cash value because Camel cigarettes in quantities of 30,000 could be bought in Fort Valley at a discount of 12 per cent from that price.

The defendant alleges in the written argument, and I think it appears that there were on February 5, 1925, three markets in Fort Valley for the purchases of cigarettes, to wit: the market in which the jobbers bought; the market in which the jobbers sold; and the market in which the retailers sold.

According to a well-known principle, referred to in the brief of defendant's counsel, in a market where only smaller quantities of goods or merchandise are sold the price is naturally higher than where the quantities are larger. So the wholesale price is, under normal conditions, always less than the retail price of the same or similar goods.

The stipulation of fact in the record, to the effect that Camel cigarettes were being sold by the wholesalers to jobbers in the vicinity of Fort Valley to dealers or retailers at $6.40 per thousand, with no discount, fixes, in my opinion, the market value in that kind of a market. As much so as if the shipment should have been sold before it was due to arrive at Fort Valley.

While it is true that the question is not what was the personal or peculiar value to the plaintiff the cigarettes possessed, yet this does not prevent the ascertaining of the loss by the value of the undelivered cigarettes in the market where the defendant must have known the same were to be sold, or possibly had already been sold.

It is true that speculative profits are not recoverable, but only the actual loss that can be certainly ascertained, but the cigarettes were worth what the plaintiff could sell them for in the only market in which he sold, to wit, the market to retailers in and adjacent to Fort Valley. According to the agreement of fact in the case his loss is fairly ascertainable, and cannot be defeated by a speculation that possibly the delivery of the cigarettes, according to the contract of shipment, might have demoralized the market and reduced the price therein.

Wherefore, the finding and judgment of the court is that the plaintiff do recover of the defendant the sum of $192 principal sum, and interest thereon at 7 per cent from February 5, 1925.

The foregoing case, decided prior to the Supreme Court's decision in the *Crail* case which did much to clarify the decision in the *McCaull-Dinsmore* case, for some reason has been widely distributed to claimants although it is unreported in any of the law reports. While of historical interest, the case is not authoritative and without question the reasoning of the court is clearly unsound when considered in the light of the *Crail* case. The other case referred to which is frequently cited by claimants and which is not authoritative is *Nashville, C. & St. L. Ry.* v. *W. L. Halsey, Grocery,* 121 So. 16, decided by the Alabama court in 1929, and prior to the Supreme Court's decision in the *Crail* case. The decision in this case resulted from the state court's reliance upon the decisions of the federal circuit court of appeals and the federal district court in the *Crail* case which were subsequently reversed by the Supreme Court in its decision. The following extract from the Alabama court's decision is presented as of historical interest since frequently it is erroneously cited as an authority by claimants:

Two cases of cigarettes were shipped to the plaintiff at Huntsville, Ala., from Durham, N. C., and defendant, as one of the connecting carriers, admits liability for nondelivery thereof, but insists the damages should be limited to the purchase price at Durham. The price to plaintiff at Durham was $64 per case, with a trade discount of 10 per cent, making the true invoice price $57.60. The trial court awarded the damages at $64 per case upon the undisputed evidence that this sum represents the market value of the cigarettes at Huntsville, the point of destination, as it appears from the proof this was the sum for which the cigarettes would sell at Huntsville and the price plaintiff would have to pay if purchased at that point. The shipment was interstate and the case is here controlled by the federal statute and decisions. Pursuant to what is known as the "Cummins Amendment," the federal statute now provides that the liability of the carrier to the holder of the bill of lading should be the "full actual loss" sustained . . . notwithstanding stipulations to the contrary in the bill of lading. This statute received consideration, and was given application, in the case of *Chicago, Milwaukee & St. Paul Ry. Co.* v. *McCaull-Dinsmore Co.*, 253 U.S. 97, 40 S. Ct. 504, 64 L. Ed. 801, the holding of the court being succinctly stated in the headnote as follows:

> Under the Cummins Amendment of March 4, 1915, which provides that the carrier shall be liable for the full actual loss, damage or injury, notwithstanding any limitation of liability, limitation of amount of recovery, or representation or agreement as to value in the receipt, bill of lading, etc., and which declares any such limitation unlawful and void, a shipper, in case of loss, is entitled to damages on the basis of value at the place of destination at the time when the property should have been delivered if that is greater than the value at place and time of shipment, notwithstanding the Uniform Bill of Lading provided for computing damages on the latter basis.

It will be noted that the state court places great reliance on the headnote to the *McCaull-Dinsmore* case which is not sustained by the decision itself. Headnotes are never authoritative unless supported by the decision to which they form a part and in all instances a headnote should be carefully considered in conjunction with the decision itself. Continuing, the court stated:

In the course of the discussion in the (McCaull-Dinsmore) opinion, the (Supreme) court said: "The rule of the common law is not an arbitrary fiat but an embodiment of the plain fact that the actual loss caused by breach of a contract is the loss of what the contractee would have had if the contract had been performed, less the proper deductions, which have been made and are not in question here." In the more recent case of *Hicks* v. *Guinness*, 269 U. S. 71, 46 S. Ct. 46, 70 L. Ed. 168, treating a different state of facts, but giving application to the same principle, the court cited the above noted authority with the following expression: "The loss for which the plaintiff is entitled to be indemnified is 'the loss of what the contractor would have had if the contract had been performed.'" Among the more recent federal cases citing and giving application to the decision of *Chicago, Milwaukee & St. Paul Ry.* v. *McCaull-Dinsmore Co. supra*, is that of *Crail* v. *Ill. Cent. R. Co.* (C. C. A.), 13 F. (2d) 459. See also *Crail* v. *Ill. Cent. R. Co.* (D. C.), 21 F. (2d) 836. *These decisions are in point and here controlling.* (Emphasis added.)

At this point in the foregoing quotation the state court clearly indicates its reliance on the decisions of the federal circuit court of appeals and lower federal district court which were subsequently reversed by the Supreme Court. Continuing, after stating the above premises, the court said:

> This court applied the same measurement of damages in *So. Ry. Co.* v. *Northwestern Fruit Exch.*, 210 Ala. 519, 98 So. 382, allowing to the plaintiff the market value of the merchandise at the point of destination, though this was in excess of the value at the place of shipment with freight added. Holding to like result in the case of *Yazoo & M. V. R. Co.* v. *Delta Gro. Co.*, 134 Miss. 846, 98 So. 777. Defendant directs attention to *H. T. Cottam & Co.* v. *Ill. Cent. R. Co.*, 3 La. App. 240. That case seems to have been differentiated in *Crail* v. *Ill. Cent. R. Co.* (D. C.), 21 F. (2d) 836, upon the theory that "contemplated profits" occupied an important place in the decision; but in the light of federal authorities noted above, as well as from this State, more minute consideration of the Cottam case is deemed unnecessary. Defendant cites, among other authorities, *L. & N. R. Co.* v. *Sullivan Timber Co.*, 138 Ala. 379, 35 So. 327, as to the duty of one injured, either in tort or by breach of contract, to exercise reasonable diligence to minimize the injury, and insists that plaintiff should be held to the price of $57.60 at the place of shipment, as he could have ordered another shipment at that same figure as shown by the proof.
>
> But we do not think the foregoing principle is properly to be extended to such situation as here present, for, as held by the court in the *Ill. Cent. case, supra,* answering a like argument, no duty rested upon the plaintiff to order another shipment to replace the lost goods.

While the Alabama court correctly states the view of the lower federal courts in the *Crail* case, the Supreme Court in reversing those decisions limited recovery to the wholesale value at point of destination since there was no evidence to indicate that the consignee lost any sale by the carrier's failure to deliver.

Another case illustrating the principle that the shipper is not permitted to realize more than he would have secured had the carrier faithfully performed his duties is *Southern Pac. Co. of Mexico* v. *Gonzalez,* 61 P. 2d 377. In this case the shipper claimant had contracted to sell the carload of tomatoes to the consignee for $2.75 per case, but on arrival and due to damage, they were only worth $1.25 per case. The shipper brought suit based on the destination market value of tomatoes in good condition which was $3.25 or $3.50 per case and the lower court allowed judgment on this basis. On appeal, the court reversed this decision holding that if the goods had been delivered for sale on the open market, the plaintiff's contentions would be correct; but since they were sold before arrival for only $2.75 per lug, that is all he would have received if they had arrived in good condition, and therefore he was not entitled to recover more.

The consignee or claimant has the burden of establishing his damages. In *Railway Express Agency* v. *McCarrick,* 69 S. W. 2d 803, involving injury to a shipment of perishables, the court held that it was necessary for the claimant to establish (1) the market value of the shipment on the day it arrived in the condition in which it arrived and (2) its value had it arrived in good condition. The court said:

It was incumbent upon appellee to prove the market value of these radishes on January 20, 1930, the day they were received by the consignee. There is no proof as to this fact. The witness Herman L. Goldstein did testify that the radishes were sold for the best price obtainable, but he does not say on which date, nor that the best obtainable price was the reasonable market price. *Houston & T. C. Ry. Co. v. Lewis,* (Tex. Civ. App.) 185 S.W. 593; *Gulf, C. & S. F. Ry. Co.* v. *Peacock,* 60 Tex. Civ. App. 250, 128 S.W. 463; *M., K. & T. Ry. Co.* v.*McLean,* 55 Tex. Civ. App. 130, 118 S.W. 161. In the absence of proof of the reasonable market value of the radishes on the day they arrived at the destination and in the damaged condition in which they did arrive, there is no way to properly determine the amount of appellee's damages.

Another case holding that plaintiff must establish the value of the goods is *Max Biederman, Inc.* v. *Henderson,* 176 S. E. 433. In this case the carrier had contracted to transport two Dodge automobiles from Detroit to Huntington, West Virginia. While enroute, he was forced off the road and the cars were damaged. In a suit brought against him, he contended that the measure of damages was the value of the shipment immediately before the accident and the value of the cars in their damaged condition immediately after the accident. The trial court permitted plaintiff to recover upon the basis of the list price of the cars. It appeared, however, that the model of such cars was going to change in about 30 days and further that plaintiff made only one attempt to sell the cars. On appeal, the appellate court overruled the trial court and allowed recovery based on market value rather than list price, stating:

The next contention of the defendant is that the case was tried on the wrong theory as to the measure of damages. Plaintiff was permitted to recover additional transportation charges caused by the accident, and in getting the cars repaired at Columbus, Ohio, the cost of the repairs, and on one of the cars, the difference between what was actually received by the plaintiff when the repaired automobile was sold and the retail list price which, presumably, the plaintiff would have received for the same automobile had it not been wrecked. Defendant (plaintiff in error) argues, we think correctly, that the market value of the cars immediately before the wreck and immediately after is the true basis for figuring the damages. As a usual thing, the measure of damages, where personal property is damaged, is the fair market value of that property before the damage, from which is subtracted the fair market value of the same property immediately after the damage. *Broadie* v. *Randall,* 114 Kan. 92, 216 P. 1103, 32 A. L. R. 708, and note; *Gass* v. *Agate Ice Cream, Inc.,* 264 N.Y. 141, 190 N.E. 323; *Lake Erie & W. R. Co.* v. *Molloy,* 78 Ind. App. 72, 134 N. E. 913; *Blanke* v. *United Rys. Co. of St. Louis,* (Mo. App.) 213 S.W. 174; *Huddy, Cyc. of Automobile Law,* vol. 17-18, pp. 520, 546. If, for some peculiar reason, there is no market value for the article injured and this fact is proven, then some other test of damages may be adopted. *Jacksonville, T. & K. W. R. Co.* v. *P. L. T. & Mfg. Co.* (pt. 34, syl.), 27 Fla. 1, 157, 9 So. 661, 17 L. R. A. 33, 57, 65. The courts vary widely in their statement of this rule, but it is our belief that a close scrutiny of the decided cases will result in the conclusion that the apparently variant principles laid down by the courts are in fact merely different evidentiary methods of getting at the determining factors of market value immediately after the injury subtracted from the market value immediately before the injury, the remainder being the actual damage. Different elements, according to the circumstances of each particular case, of course, must be considered as repairs, cost of transportation, etc. *Rhodes* v. *Firestone Tire & Rubber Co.,* 51 Cal. App. 569, 197 P. 392. In this case, the witnesses for the plaintiff did not qualify themselves as familiar with the market value of the damaged automobiles. Instead, the retail list price was substituted for market value before the injury, and the price for which they were sold by the plaintiff was substituted for market value after the injury. These prices may or may not have represented the actual fair market value of the automobiles. The model of this make of cars was about to change, and would change according to the testimony within thirty days. Possibly the retail list price for them could not have been procured under these circumstances. It is not shown that any more than the one effort was made to sell the cars after the injury to them. It is possible that on the resale the plaintiff did not procure the fair market value. What actually was done in the one transaction concerning the injured automobiles is, of course, probative for the purpose of showing that plaintiff actually got the fair market value for the automobiles after the injury, but it is not the test of fair market value. This must be shown by witnesses who are qualified on the question, as, for example, by virtue of their experience in the line of business in which the damaged articles moved. The damages must be shown by evidence along this broad line, and then it must appear that the specific transaction was based on the fair market value thus shown. Segregated transactions are not the proper test. Since the automobiles were obviously intended for the retail trade, we believe that the retail market would control. A different rule might apply where the contract of carriage is entered into with knowledge on the part of the carrier of a specific resale of the property to be carried so that the contract of carriage might be said to contemplate that very transaction. But that is not this case.

In *Bachos* v. *Chicago, R. I. & P. Ry. Co.,* 61 S. W. 2d 416, it was held that plaintiff's description of used motors as *junk* motors did not preclude his recovery of their actual value. In this case, a party bid at government auction for used motors and secured them at his own price of $69. He directed that they be shipped to him, and the carrier's agent in his absence described them as *junk* motors. Upon arrival at destination they were seriously damaged and had to be sold as junk realizing only $16. The court in dealing with the question said:

There is no question but that, in an interstate shipment like this where the shipper describes a shipment as belonging to a certain classification and obtains a rate corresponding to the same, he is not entitled to recover damages according to a higher value or better classification in case there is a loss in transit. *Hart v. Pennsylvania R. Co.*, 112 U.S. 331, 340, 5 S Ct. 151, 28, L. Ed. 717; *Russell & Co.* v. *Quincy, Omaha, etc., R. Co.*, 177 Mo. App. 186, 164 S.W. 164. The trouble with defendant's contention is that, so far as the evidence discloses, there was no obtention of the lesser rate by classifying the shipment as "junk." It is true the agent in describing it in the bill of lading described one of the motors as crated "junk motor" and the others as "2 junk motors," but no valuation was stated, nor was any rate of transportation fixed according to that valuation or corresponding to that classification. Furthermore, it is not disputed that the plaintiff delivered the motors at the station to be shipped, but had no dealings with the agent, nor was the bill of lading made out and given to the plaintiff then, for the latter in order to catch his train left and the bill was afterwards made out and sent to him. Plaintiff does not claim they were *new* motors, but that he bought them and had them shipped as *used* motors, so that the description inserted in the bill was noting more than the agent's *conclusion* as to what they were. Under the plaintiff's description of their condition at the time they were delivered to the railroad, they were far from being "junk," but according to both sides, they were unquestionably junk when the railroad had them for delivery in Kansas City. It is true, the Lawton agent (of the railroad) in his deposition testified, when asked if he had "any independent recollection as to this particular shipment," said "*I have in this way*: They were billed as junk motors and so receipted for at the request of the shipper." He was then asked this further question: "Had they been usable or serviceable motors they would have been shipped as serviceable motors and *would* take the class rate higher than that which was used?" But, for all that the evidence shows, the agent merely shipped them on his *ex parte* conclusion as to what they were. The jury heard the plaintiff's evidence as to the condition the motors were in, not junk but used motors, when delivered for shipment, and heard their condition afterwards when on their way and when finally delivered at destination. Shoemake, the shipping agent, did not testify to their condition when shipped but merely that they "*were billed as junk*." No special rate is shown to have been given plaintiff. He paid the usual regular rate on said bill totaling $36.06.

Under the evidence showing the condition of the motors at the point of shipment and the difference in their condition and value at destination, the jury, under instructions of where there is no complaint, found for the plaintiff. The fact that an auction, where plaintiff was the only bidder, he got them at his own price, is not conclusive as to their valuelessness.

Considerable confusion has arisen as result of a growing tendency on the part of some claim agents and attorneys to argue that claimant is never entitled to include any profit in his claim. This belief is probably founded on the repeated statement that the law does not contemplate, generally, the making of a profit out of a carrier's misfortune in losing or damaging freight. This statement, however, does not mean that if the claimant has *earned* a profit which he would have obtained if the carrier had performed its duties properly, he must be deprived of it because of the carrier's negligence in performing its duties. Certainly the law does not contemplate that the claimant should suffer financially as result of carrier's misfortune in losing or damaging the freight. The law contemplates the restoration of the claimant to the same position he would have occupied had there been no loss or damage and if this involves allowing the claimant to recover profit which he has earned, the law has no objection to its recovery since it is only by this allowance that the claimant will realize his "full actual loss." As has been pointed out in the review of the decision in the *Crail* case the claimant therein while being denied recovery of the retail price of the coal which was lost on the grounds that he had done nothing to *earn* the retail profit, nevertheless was permitted to recover the wholesale price which allowed him a profit above mine cost plus freight. The claimant in the *Crail* case, the court pointed out, had done all that was necessary to *earn* the wholesale price.

To a large extent the confusion relative to recovery of profit resulted from two decisions by the St. Louis (Missouri) Court of Appeals. These decisions are unique in that the doctrine announced is completely contrary to the overwhelming weight of authority of other state and federal courts. The first of these cases was decided in 1924 and entitled *Bernet, Craft, & Kauffman Milling Co.* v. *New York, C. & St. L. R. Co.*, 260 S. W. 508. In this case the plaintiff shipped a carload of flour from Mr. Carmel, Illinois, to New York City over the lines of the defendant and others. While in transit 287 sacks of the flour were lost and other flour damaged. The car had been shipped on an order-notify bill of lading, the notify party being Bliss-Dallet & Co. and the draft was paid by this concern on the basis of $8.50 a barrel. The shipper replaced the flour lost and brought suit against the defendant on basis of the market value in New York City at the time the flour should have been delivered. The railroad contended that the correct measure of damage was the price that the consignee had agreed to pay for the flour ($8.50 a barrel). The court held:

> As plaintiff replaced the flour lost, its full actual loss, damage, or injury was the cost of manufacturing the flour replacing that lost, *not less than the controlling contract price.* (Emphasis added.)

There is nothing seriously wrong with the holding in this decision except that entirely too often the words shown in italics are overlooked and this decision cited as holding that the claimant was allowed to recover only his manufacturing cost which decidedly is not correct. The court did state that the shipper should be permitted to recover his cost of manufacturing the flour used to replace that lost and damaged, but it specified that if this cost of manufacturing the replacement flour was less than the contract price ($8.50 a barrel) then claimant was entitled to recover the contract price. On the other hand, if the cost of manufacturing the replacement flour exceeded $8.50 a barrel, under this decision the claimant is allowed to recover his exact cost of manufacture.

In 1946, the St. Louis Court of Appeals rendered its decision in *Meletio Sea Food Company, Inc.* v. *Gordon's Transports, Inc.*, 191 S. W. 2d 983. This case originated in the justice's court in Missouri and was appealed to the St. Louis Circuit Court, and finally to the St. Louis Court of Appeals. The opinion was written by a commissioner and was concurred in by the judges of the Court of Appeals.

The plaintiff in this case had consigned a shipment of foodstuff to a customer in New Orleans. The invoice price to plaintiff's customer was $13.20 per hundred pounds. The cost of the goods to the plaintiff before taxes was $10.349 per hundred pounds. The shipment was damaged in transit and refused by the consignee and returned to shipper. The shipper made a replacement shipment to the consignee on the same basis as the refused shipment and at the same original cost to itself. Plaintiff likewise expended $13.34 in examining the returned goods in order to determine the question of the extent of damage to the shipment.

Claim was filed with the carrier for the invoice price of the refused shipment which the carrier declined on the basis that the damages should have been calculated at plaintiff's cost price, especially in view of the fact that plaintiff, having replaced the damaged shipment, lost no profit on the transaction. The legal question thus presented was whether the plaintiff, as consignor of a shipment which was damaged in transit, was entitled to recover from the carrier the full price contracted to be paid by the consignee where the shipment, after loss or damage, had been replaced by the consignor at the same agreed price to the consignee, or whether plaintiff should be limited in its recovery to the actual cost price to itself. The court held:

> The important factor in the case is the fact that plaintiff, upon the happening of the loss, replaced the damaged merchandise at the identical invoice price to its customer in New Orleans, and at the identical cost price to itself. Con-

sequently, having sustained no ultimate loss on the transaction with its customer, its actual loss was obviously the cost of replacing the damaged merchandise, plus the incidental expense incurred in examining the shipment in order to ascertain the extent of the loss. In delivering the substituted shipment to its customer, in New Orleans at the original invoice price, it still gained its contemplated profit on the transaction, whereas to require defendant to pay the claim upon the basis of the invoice price to the customer would result in giving plaintiff a double profit on the single transaction, that is, a profit on the damaged shipment as well as a profit on the substituted shipment. As between plaintiff and its customer, the matter stands precisely as though there had been no damage to the original shipment; and to hold defendant to the invoice price, and thereby require it to pay a profit which plaintiff had not lost, would be to accord plaintiff more than full compensation for the injury actually sustained.

If the foregoing decision is accepted in its literal sense, a manufacturer could be forced to operate its plants for months without any profit whatever in order to replace at cost goods lost or damaged by a carrier, and conceivably the manufacturer could be forced into bankruptcy while operating its facilities for the benefit of carriers. The law certainly never contemplated a result of this nature and the aforementioned decision is contrary to the general law on this subject. In 1948, this decision was relied upon as an authority in *Gore Products, Inc.* v. *Texas & N. O. R. Co.*, 34 So. 2d 418, and the court's comment upon it is certainly worthy of note. This decision by the Court of Appeals of Louisiana contains such an excellent review of the law on the subject that is reproduced in full.

This suit involves the question of what is the proper measure of damages to be assessed against a common carrier for the lost part of the goods which constituted an interstate shipment. The facts of the case are succinctly set out in the brief of defendant as follows:

Plaintiff contracted with defendant for the interstate transportation of four containers of medicine to a customer in Mexico City who was to pay fourteen hundred and forty dollars for the lot, or three hundred sixty dollars per container, freight included. In removing these containers from the plaintiff's place of business, defendant's employees broke one, thereby causing the loss of its entire contents; defendant thereupon requested and received from plaintiff an identical container of medicine to replace the broken one, and the shipment was carried to destination under the original contract of carriage, delivered to the consignee and payment of the full purchase price made to plaintiff.

Plaintiff promptly made claim upon defendant for its loss by submitting an invoice for three hundred sixty dollars, the amount for which it had billed (and which it had received from) the consignee of the shipment. Defendant admitted its liability to the extend of plaintiff's actual loss and declined payment at the figure named by plaintiff on the ground that this was not plaintiff's cost and therefore did not represent the true measure of its actual loss. Plaintiff made no claim or showing of special damages, but insisted that this was the identical price made to its local customers as well as to the consignee of the broken container (which is admitted by defendant)and although admitting that this amount included its profit, refused to divulge the cost to it of the medicine. Being thus effectually prevented from making tender of the amount it believed to be due, defendant could only decline payment of the claim in full and this suit followed.

Plaintiff brought judgment for $360 (the price for which it had sold the destroyed goods), and recovered that amount, subject however, to a credit of $3.52 for freight charges. Defendant has appealed.

It is agreed by both parties that the measure of plaintiff's recovery is to be governed by the Cummins Amendment to the Interstate Commerce Act, which provides that in case of loss, damage, or injury to property which is the subject of carriage, the carrier "shall be liable . . . for the full actual loss, damage or injury to such property." Act of March 4, 1915, c176, 38 Stat. 1197, 49 U. S. C. A. (par) 20 (11).

It is defendant's contention that, under the circumstances of this case, the "full actual loss" specified by the statute means the cost of the article to the claimant, and there should be no consideration given to the price for which the articles might have been sold.

In this argument, counsel for the defendant first points to the case of *Illinois Cent. R. Co.* v. *Crail,* 1930, 281 U. S. 57, 50 S. Ct. 180, 181, 75 L. Ed. 699, 67 A. L. R. 1423. There plaintiff purchased in transit a carload of coal in which a 5,500 pound deficiency was found to exist upon delivery; the deficiency was replaced with coal purchased for the same price in wholesale lots. Plaintiff contended that the measure of damage should be the retail value of the undelivered coal, which included the cost of delivery to his customers. He had not contracted to resell any of the coal when the car arrived. The court held that under the circumstances peculiar to the case, the more accurate measure of damage of the shortage would be the wholesale price, since it was capable of replacement and was in fact replaced, in the course of the consignee's business from purchases made in carload lots at wholesale market prices without added expenses. The court said:

> There is no greater inconvenience in the application of the one standard of value than the other, and we perceive no advantage to be gained from an adherence to a rigid uniformity, which would justify sacrificing the reason of the rule, to its letter. The test of market value is at best but a convenient means of getting at the loss suffered. It may be discarded and other more accurate means resorted to, if for special reasons, it is not exact or otherwise not applicable. See *Wilmoth* v. *Hamilton,* 3 Cir., 127 F. 48, 51; *Theiss* v. *Weiss* 166 Pa. 9, 19, 31 A. 63, 45 Am. St. Rep. 638; *Pittsburgh Sheet Mfg. Co.* v. *West Penn Sheet Co.,* 201 Pa. 150, 50 A. 935; Williston on *Contracts,* (par) 1384, 1385. In the absence of special circumstances, the damage for shortage in delivery by the seller of fungible goods sold by quantity is measured by the bulk price rather than the price for smaller quantities, both at common law, see *Morgan* v. *Gath,* 3 Hurl. & C. 748; *Avery* v. *Wilson,* 81 N.Y. 341,

> 37 Am. Rep. 503, and under section 44 of the Uniform Sales Act. Likewise, we think that the wholesale market price is to be preferred as test over the retail when, in circumstances like the present, it is clearly the more accurate measure. . . .

Counsel also directs our attention to the case of *H. T. Cottam & Co.* v. *Illinois Cent. R. Co.*, 3 La. App. 240, decided by this court. The plaintiff in that case sued the carrier for recovery of the loss sustained as a result of defendant's failure to safely carry certain goods. Judgment was rendered for plaintiff in the lower court for the cost price of the damaged or lost merchandise, and the plaintiff sought before us an amendment of the judgment, so as to increase the amount allowed to the price at which it could have sold the goods at their reasonable wholesale cash value at the destination. We denied plaintiff recovery for its anticipated profits, *because there was no proof that the goods in question had been sold* by plaintiff before or while in transit, or that they formed any part of any contract which plaintiff was bound to fulfill upon the date of delivery at the destination. We said:

> . . . The evidence establishes that there was no wholesale buyer of such goods in New Orleans, except the plaintiff, who bought not at New Orleans, but at the point of shipment involved in this case. However, there are innumerable buyers of such goods in New Orleans, buying exclusively of plaintiff, and if plaintiff's contention should here prevail, the effect would be to enlist defendant as an additional customer in plaintiff's New Orleans trade. We cannot give such effect to the contract. *There is no proof that the goods in question had been sold* by plaintiff before or while in transit, or that they formed parts of any contracts which plaintiff was bound to fulfill upon due date of delivery at New Orleans. There is nothing to show that the plaintiff had contracted for the resale of these goods upon expectation of their timely delivery by the defendant.

Defendant's counsel also cites the case of *Silverman* v. *St. Louis I. M. & S. R. Co.*, 51 La. Ann. 1785, 26 So. 447, 450, which he contends is authority for the proposition that a carrier is not expected, in the case of loss or damage, to purchase the lot at the shipper's price with anticipated profits added. The Silverman case has no application here. The shipment consisted of clothing, etc., made up largely of shopworn and secondhand goods, and plaintiff sued not only for the cost price, but also for ten percent advance on values at time of shipment, rent, clerk's hire, and twenty-five per cent loss of profit on goods *which he would have sold,* and also for personal expenses and loss of time. The freight car in which the goods were loaded was broken into by an unauthorized person, and eight of the thirty-six boxes in shipment were opened and some depredations committed upon the goods. In denying plaintiff's claim, the court used the following expressions:

> These being the facts disclosed by the evidence, we find no principle of law upon which to predicate a judgment for the plaintiff. It may be conceded that the defendant was at fault for leaving plaintiff's property in an insecurely fastened and isolated car, with no one to watch it. Nevertheless, the plaintiff cannot recover, without proving what, if any, injury this negligence of the defendant has caused him.

> The preponderance of evidence leads to the conclusion that plaintiff's goods were *neither lost or damaged.* As far as we can see, there was no sufficient reason to have prevented his taking possession of them on the morning of October 5th, and if, in doing so he had been subjected to trouble and expense, in collecting and repacking them, the defendant would have been liable therefor. He, however, refused at that time, and and has since refused, to receive the goods, or any part of them, or to have anything to do with them; and the defendant was obliged to accept the alternative of taking such steps as seemed prudent for the preservation of the goods thus left on its hands and for its own protection against the claim with which it was threatened, and it accordingly collected the goods and repacked them. *We do not understand that, in case of loss or damage of part of a lot of assorted goods the carrier is bound to purchase the whole consignment,* at the shipper's price with expected profit added.

In *Anderson, Clayton & Co.* v. *Yazoo & M. V. R. Co.,* 174 La. 762, 141 So. 453, 455, the value of a shipment of cotton which had been destroyed was involved, and our Supreme Court stated the rule for assessing damages as follows:

> The general rule is that, when goods delivered to a carrier for shipment are lost in transit, the carrier will be liable for the market value of the goods at the place of destination at the time when delivery of the goods should have been made, less the freight charges to the point of destination if they have not been paid.

The *Anderson, Clayton & Co.* case was cited with approval in *Brancroft* v. *Yazoo & M. V. R. Co.,* 194 La. 115, 193 So. 481, 482 as follows:

> . . . The liability of the carrier in such cases is full actual loss of property at the place of destination at the time delivery of goods should have been made. *Anderson, Clayton & Co.* v. *Yazoo & M. V. R. Co.,* 174 La. 762, 141 So. 453; for the consignee to allege and prove (1) that the initial carrier received the shipment in good condition, (2) that the shipment arrived at its destination in a damaged condition, and (3) the amount of the loss.

Plaintiff contends that it is immaterial whether it had sold the medicine which defendant destroyed at a profit or a loss. Counsel argues that the price at which plaintiff had contracted to sell the goods, before turning them over to the defendant for shipment, was both the market price in New Orleans and in Mexico, the destination, and should constitute the true measure of damages, as that is the price plaintiff would have received for the goods had they been safely delivered by the defendant.

The syllabus in the case of *Wilson* v. *Hines,* 58 Utah 38, 196 P. 1007, reads:

> Where plaintiff shipper had sold to the consignee the peaches shipped at the place of shipment, he was entitled to recover as damages for delay injuring the peaches, the difference between the price for which he had sold the peaches, which was their market value at the place of shipment, with freight loading, and war tax added, and their market

value in their damaged condition at destination when he was notified of their nonacceptance by the consignee.

The United States Supreme Court, in *Chicago, M. & St. P. R. Co.* v. *McCaull-Dinsmore Co.*, 253 U.S. 97, 40 S. Ct. 504, 64 L. Ed. 801, in adjudicating an action for the loss of a shipment of grain, said:

> . . . The rule of the common law is not an arbitrary fiat but an embodiment of the plain fact that the actual loss caused by breach of a contract is the loss of what the contractee would have had if the contract had been performed, less the proper deductions, which have been made and are not in question here. . . .

The Supreme Court of Alabama, in the case of *Nashville, C. & St. L. Ry.* v. *W. L. Halsey Grocery Co.*, 219 Ala. 16, 17, 121 So. 16, permitted a consignee to recover the value of goods estimated at their price for which it had purchased them at the place of shipment. The court said:

> . . . no duty rested upon the plaintiff to order another shipment to replace the lost goods.

In *Amer. Jur. Carriers*, Sec. 783, a summary of the law is given as follows:

> The contract price, rather than the market value of goods may constitute the proper basis for estimating the damages for their loss or injury where they are shipped under, or pursuant to, a contract of sale.
>
> . . . Where the contract price is the only evidence of the market value it should be taken as the measure of damages.

The language used in 13 *C. J. S.*, Carrier, (par) 264b (1), is:

> The rule as to the measure of damages for loss of property shipped applies both in actions of tort and in actions based on breach of contract; and its operation is not affected by the fact that the shipper was permitted to substitute other animals in place of those lost, or that the livestock was to be kept for use and was not intended for sale." Citing, among other cases, *El Paso, etc. R. Co.* v. *Lumbley,* 56 Tex. App. 418, 120 S.W. 1050 and *H. W. Little & Co.* v. *Atlantic Coast Line R. Co.*, 168 N. C. 658, 85 S. E. 18.

And in (par) 264e we find:

"Where property is shipped for sale at a specified price or is sold in transit, the damages recoverable are based on the contract price or on the market value at destination, according to the circumstances of the case." Citing cases *Bernet, Craft & Kaufman Milling Co.* v. *New York C. & St. L. R. Co.*, Mo. App. 260 S.W. 508, which held that where more goods were manufactured to replace those lost the recovery would be cost of manufacture, *but not in any event less than the contract price.*

In addition to relying upon the *Crail, Cottam and Silverman* cases, defendant relies more strongly upon the case of *Meletio Sea Food Co.*, v. *Gordons Transport,* Mo. App. 191 S.W. 2d 983, and contends that the issues in the latter case are identical to those now before us. The plaintiff in that case, which was a manufacturer like the present plaintiff, replaced from its stock goods damaged by the defendant carrier. A recovery for the amount of the price at which plaintiff had contracted to sell the goods was denied, and the measure of damages was fixed at the cost to plaintiff of manufacturing the goods which replaced those that had been lost. The *Meletio* case, however, originated in a justice's court in Missouri and was appealed to the St. Louis Circuit Court, and finally reached the St. Louis Court of Appeals. The opinions were written by a commissioner and was concurred in by the judges of the Court of Appeals. *The doctrine established in the Meletio case is contrary to that announced by our own Supreme Court and other courts deciding the cases cited by plaintiff, and our opinion is that the Meletio case should not be used as a criterion here.* Under the circumstances present in the instant case, there is a distinguishment between it and the *Crail* and *Cottam* cases. In neither of those cases had the shipper contracted to sell the goods which constituted the shipment, and the courts denied recovery for expected or anticipated profits. In addition, in the *Crail* case the goods were fungible, and plaintiff replaced them by purchasing other wholesale lots; furthermore, the retail price on which plaintiff's claim was premised included the cost of delivery to his customers.

In the case now before us, the plaintiff, which is the manufacturer, had *already sold the goods to its customer* in Mexico by contract, and in line with the authorities cited by plaintiff we feel that in this case *the measure of plaintiff's loss is the price which it would have received from its customer in Mexico,* which price was also the market price prevailing at New Orleans the place or origin of the shipment. There are no special circumstances in the present case to warrant a holding that the sale price, which is also the market price at destination, should be discarded and the cost of manufacture adopted as the standard of defendant's liability.

It is true that plaintiff delivered to the carrier a carboy of medicine to substitute for the one which was destroyed, but we do not think that the defendant's liability should be fixed at the amount required to reimburse plaintiff merely for the cost of manufacturing one carboy of medicine. What would be the situation if the second carboy had been lost, or even a third or fourth? Could plaintiff be required to continue to manufacture goods for the defendant at cost? Furthermore, if plaintiff's business was an extensive one it might be quite difficult to compute with exactness the cost of one carboy of medicine.

For the reasons assigned, the judgment appealed from is affirmed. (Emphasis added.)

No greater mistake can be made by claimants and carriers than to endeavor to apply a uniform rule to determine measure of damages unless that measure is: "*What was the full actual loss, damage or injury to the claimant?*" This rule is the only criterion authorized by the Cummins Amendment and in every case it presents essentially a question in fact, requiring each claim to be reviewed in the light of all the circumstances involved. It is not easy, however, for a carrier's claim agent to place himself in the position of his claimant in order to properly evaluate the claimant's actual loss. The same is true of the claimant who often is unable to properly evaluate the carrier's obligation to simply restore him to the same position which he would have occupied if the carrier had faithfully performed his duty by delivering the goods and all of them in proper condition.

In applying this rule, the position of the claimant to be considered is *the position he would have occupied at the time the goods should have been delivered complete and in good order*—not the claimant's position at the time the shipment was originated at point of origin. If it is apparent that the claimant would have received a profit without any additional undertaking if the goods had been delivered complete and in good order, then the claimant has *earned* a profit which he is entitled to recover. It should be remembered that a manufacturer by the very process of manufacturing usually produces a product which is valued in excess of its cost of manufacture. Our entire distribution system embraces the selfish motive of profit and usually the movement of commercial goods is for the very purpose of realizing a profit.

With respect to grain, produce, livestock, coal, etc., most large cities have established markets and published quotations are usually available to supply a reliable basis of their market value on a certain date. In many instances at the time the carrier receives such goods, the shipper does not know the exact destination at which he intends ultimately to sell the goods. The carrier knows that the goods may be reconsigned while in transit to a more favorable market than the one originally selected. Unless the goods have been sold by contract or while en route, the shipper does not know the exact value of his goods until the goods finally reach the market selected. If the shipper sells the goods, he knows exactly what he will receive at the time of delivery and if the goods are lost or damaged, he is entitled to his contract price in event the purchaser consignee refuses to accept delivery.

On the other hand, the purchaser consignee of such goods in the event they are delivered in good order may be in possession of goods with a ready market value in excess of the price he paid to the shipper; it is also possible that they will be worth less than what he has paid or agreed to pay for them. If there has been a decline in the market under what he agreed to pay, the purchaser consignee will be on the lookout for reasons to refuse to accept delivery and abandon the goods to the carrier and if this occurs, the shipper is entitled to the contract price which he would have received if the refusal has been on a proper basis. Again, if there has been a favorable market and the goods have increased in value since their purchase, the consignee will usually be readily agreeable to accepting the goods and disposing of them to best advantage and holding the carrier liable for loss suffered by failure of the carrier to deliver the shipment complete and in good order. It is in transactions of this nature that market value plays such an important part.

If a shipper or jobber ships goods to a customer at a stipulated price and loss or damage occurs while in the carrier's possession, the shipper or jobber will usually be fully compensated by payment on the basis of the price he would have received from the customer if the carrier had fulfilled its transportation contract. Likewise, the purchaser will usually be fully compensated by the contract price, as the goods can usually be replaced for the same amount. On the other hand, the goods may have been purchased to fulfill a contract of sale, and the carrier's failure to perform its duties properly may cause the consignee to lose the sale and, in this event, the contract or invoice price received by the shipper would not fully compensate the consignee.

Carrier claim agents in their day-to-day handling of loss and damage claims are engaged in what is technically known as the "voluntary settlement of claims." In other words, the claim agent is adjusting and paying claims voluntarily without compulsion from any court. There are many factors which enter into the merits of a particular claim other than the amount which the claimant is entitled to recover in event of carrier liability. While the claimant usually adopts the attitude that his claim is "legitimate," the amount claimed correct, and the carrier legally liable, there may be some doubt and, in some instances, considerable doubt on the carrier's part as to its actual legal responsibility and, if admittedly liable, as to whether the amount claimed is correct. Under such circumstances the measure of damage or the basis of settlement may be the lowest amount which the claimant will accept—*the best bargain that the claim agent can secure.*

There is nothing inherently morally or legally wrong with the adjustment of claims on this basis. Often a compromise adjustment of opposing contentions is the most economical means for concluding disputes involving only a nominal sum and in most instances neither party to such controversies is 100 percent correct. There usually is some merit on both sides and a proper determination of respective liability wholly dependent upon a question of fact which is not often easily resolved. In the final analysis, the patrons of carriers pay the bill for loss and damage and it is to the customer's interest as well as the carrier's that loss and damage costs be kept as low as possible.

The remainder of this chapter deals with specific problems in determining claimant's "full and actual loss" and his recovery in those instances where the carrier has been authorized to limit its liability by extending a lower rate in return for lower liability.

Actual Value Rates

Actual value rates must be carefully distinguished from released rates or ratings. In the case of the former, different rates are imposed according to the variation in the value of the articles shipped. The purpose is to give proper weight to value as an element of rate-making. The approval of the Interstate Commerce Commission is not required for publication of actual value rates. Carriers are liable under Section 20(11) for the full actual value of goods moving under actual value rates in case of loss or damage, but any intentional understatement of value by the shipper constitutes false representation for the purpose of securing transportation at less than the applicable rate and is subject to the penalties provided in Section 222 (c) (49 U.S.C. 322).

Beyond question, the shipper is in a better position to know the value of goods shipped than the carrier. It is true, however, that some shippers are under the impression that actual value rates are published to provide them with an election of declaring a value lower than the actual value of the goods in order to secure a more favorable rate. While this election does exist in connection with released rates authorized by the Commission, it does not exist in connection with actual value rates. Actual value rates are rates based precisely on actual value and shippers should exercise care to be certain that the actual value of the goods is specified on the bill of lading in the exact terminology of the carrier's tariff.

Since shippers are in the best position to know the value of their goods, it is quite obvious that a carrier will look with askance upon a claim filed for more than what the shipper has previously specified as the actual value. The readiness of the shipper to admit an error in understating the value at the time the shipment was made and willingness to have the carrier issue a corrected billing based on a higher rate will seldom remove the carrier's doubt of the shipper's good faith. Manufacturers of glassware and other commodities customarily moving under actual value rates are generally fully aware of the importance of specifying the actual value on the bill of lading. Where claims are filed by such shippers for an amount greater than the previously declared actual value, the carrier is certainly justified in believing that a misrepresentation has knowingly been made which should be reported to the proper authorities. Before paying such claims, carriers should make careful investigation in an effort to determine whether or not the claimed value is correct. Where there is doubt as to the validity of the claim, carrier is justified in refusing voluntary payment.

The Interstate Commerce Commission considered the distinction between "actual value rates" and "released rates" and gave a sound rule for distinguishing them in *Crown Overall Mfg. Co.* v. *Director General,* 100 I.C.C. 471, in which it said, in part:

> The distinction should be clear between an "agreed valuation," which, to use the language of the Supreme Court in *Hart* v. *Pennsylvania Railroad Co.*, is "the one on which the minds of the parties met, however it came to be fixed, and the rate of freight was based on that valuation, and was fixed on condition, that such was the valuation, and that the liability should go to that extent and no further"; and a value given not as a measure of the extent to which the liability of the carrier shall go, but as a description for determination of what the particular commodity is that is being shipped.
>
> The estoppel in the former case is based upon the fact that the shipment was received for transportation with the understanding that the carriers' liability should extend only to the amount indicated. In the latter there is no such understanding or representation, but the representation as to value is made solely as establishing the identity of the commodity. Furthermore, under section 20 as amended any attempted limitation of the shipper's right of recovery for the full actual loss, damage, or injury to property received for transportation is "declared to be unlawful and void" except when the limitation is published under an order from us; and it follows that any attempt on the part of a carrier to set up a defense or limited liability as to goods shipped under actual-value rates not published under order from us would fail.
>
> And there can no longer be any rates, even upon a declaration of value which is less than the actual value and at the reduced rate, [which] does not operate as a limitation upon the shipper's right to recover for the full actual loss, damage or injury, as this question was squarely decided by the Supreme Court in *Adams Express Co.* v. *Darden,* 265 U.S. 265. For the reasons set forth herein, released rates and actual-value rates may, in our opinion, be fairly and effectively differentiated.

Allowances, Discounts, Free Goods

While usually only very small amounts are involved, there are nevertheless frequent arguments between carriers and claimants as to whether or not the carrier is entitled to take advantage of any cash discount which the claimant may have secured by making prompt payment to the vendor. The practices of carriers vary in this regard. For many years, the

"Question and Answer" column appearing in *Traffic World* has answered this problem by holding that if the consignee actually realized a saving by making prompt payment then the carrier is entitled to this advantage. For example, the following is quoted from page six of the March 26, 1949, issue of *Traffic World.*

> The invoice price with deduction of the cash discount is, in our opinion, what the shipper is entitled to, if the condition under which it is made, namely, payment within the stipulated time has been fulfilled by the purchaser. This, for the reason that the invoice price based upon a cash payment, or a payment within thirty days or less, is a price separate and distinct from one which contemplates the extension of credit for a longer period of time, and should be recognized in settling claims for loss or damage.

When the shipper vendor is the claimant, the *Traffic World* answer seems reasonable because if the carrier had faithfully performed its duty, it is clear that from a financial viewpoint the shipper would have benefited only to the extent of payment received from the purchaser, i.e., the invoice price less discount. The answer, however, is not quite so apparent when the consignee purchaser is the claimant. From a bookkeeping and auditing view, the purchase account is usually charged in full with the total invoice price less trade discounts, but any reduction secured by reason of prompt payment (cash discount) is not reflected in the purchase account but under an account usually headed "Discounts," "Other Income," etc. If furniture valued at $100 is purchased, the purchaser usually debits the "furniture and equipment account" with $100 and credits the "discount account" with two dollars, this account being used to reflect *earnings* from prompt payments. Similar procedure is usually followed in connection with merchandise purchased for resale, the cost of an item ordinarily being determined from the invoice price less trade discounts but without deduction of any saving realized from a cash discount.

In other words purchasers usually regard any savings realized by prompt payment as something *earned* apart from the value of the goods. There is considerable merit in this contention that technically carriers are not entitled to the advantage of the nominal saving secured by the consignee in making prompt payment. It is pointed out, however, that many carriers in making voluntary payment of loss and damage claims will insist that if the purchaser has actually made prompt payment and secured the cash discount then the amount of the claim should be reduced to that extent. Certainly, where the discount allowed for prompt payment exceeds the nominal percentage usually allowed in commercial practices there is often reason to believe that the discount is more in the nature of a trade discount than an allowance for prompt payment; where the discount exceeds two percent, the carrier is strengthened in its position that it should be allowed this advantage.

Motor carriers in meetings with shipper representatives have vigorously argued that they are entitled to the cash discount where the claimant has secured it by prompt payment, and generally the shipper representatives have raised no serious objections and have in fact, to some extent, agreed to accept that basis for voluntary settlement. It has been the author's position that the carrier should seek to secure the advantage; but if it is observed that the claimant intends to argue over the matter, the best solution is to eliminate the cash discount, providing of course the discount is not so large as to cause suspicion that it is actually a disguised trade discount. The carrier is, of course, entitled to trade discounts and other allowances which definitely are an integral part of the actual cost to the claimant.

Container Damage and Loss

To the ordinary purchaser the crate, carton, box, or barrel which the shipper vendor uses to protect the merchandise shipped during transportation has little, if any, value. In fact delivering carrier employees frequently have difficulty in convincing the consignee that it is not the carrier's duty to unpack the goods and cart the container and packaging away. To the shipper in many instances the container used represents an expense of operation which he is constantly trying to curtail by reducing its cost to a minimum so that it will serve only to meet the established requirements of carriers, and incidentally protect the goods during transit to the purchaser. If the carrier loses the merchandise or damages it to such extent it is worthless, the consignee will seldom if ever accept delivery of the container itself without the goods so it is understandable that from a carrier viewpoint the simple function of the usual container is solely to protect the goods during transportation in its services. There are, however, certain types of containers which are used and reused many times; for example, exhibit containers, rental machinery containers, steel drums, carboys, etc. These containers, the carrier knows, are to be reused and in event of their loss or damage the carrier unquestionably is liable for their depreciated value at the time of loss or for the reasonable cost of their repair in event of damage.

An entirely different problem, however, results where there is damage to an ordinary container which may nevertheless be of some value to the consignee. For example, it is often the intent of the consignee to reship the goods received in their original container to another purchaser and if the container is damaged, he must repair or replace it before he can offer it for transportation. In connection with this problem, the practices of carriers differ; some will compensate the claimant for repairing or replacing the containers while others refuse to pay voluntarily for such cost. There is merit on both sides but, as a matter of law, it is believed that most courts would allow claimants to recover for the actual loss suffered by reason of damage to the container. It must be recognized, however, that a container depreciates in value during transportation and if it is damaged and repaired, its value will probably be enhanced and the carrier should not be expected to pay for providing the consignee with a better container than he would have had if the carrier had delivered it without any injury.

Further, it is pointed out the mere fact that a container arrives in damaged condition does not in itself establish that the carrier was responsible for such damage. The container may have been inadequate at time of shipment; it may have disintegrated from some inherent defect during transportation; it may have been loaded improperly by the shipper. All of these factors must be considered by the carrier. Likewise, claimant's alleged cost of repairs may be inflated; more repairs than reasonably necessary may have been made; the fact that the claimant is taking the trouble to claim damage to the container in itself is some indication that the claimant's attitude may be to extract the very last penny of compensation from the carrier and the purpose for this may not be from a commendable motive but from a desire to reduce its transportation costs by a fraudulent claim. For these and other reasons, carriers are extremely reluctant to make voluntary payment of claims for damage to ordinary containers with the objective of discouraging a practice which conceivably could soon get out of control. Further, many consignees regard claims of this nature as trivial and vexations to the carrier and refuse to file them and this attitude is to be commended.

Section 3 of the bill of lading terms and conditions provides that the owner of the goods shall bear the cost of baling or cooperage except where such service is required on account of the carrier's negligence. Under this provision it is entirely possible for the carrier to recooper merchandise before delivery and include a recooperage charge in the freight bill, refusing delivery until such charges are paid, alleging that the recoopering was required because the container was inadequate and did not withstand normal handling. This practice would be annoying to the consignee and result in needless controversy. In view of the reasonableness of the position of both carriers and claimant, the author's position has been to discourage the filing of claims including amounts of damage to ordinary containers unless the carriers have been placed on notice or reasonably should have known that they will be held responsible for such damage. This notice affords the carrier the opportunity of making close scrutiny of each container at the time it is received from the shipper and of making the repairs necessary at its own expense before delivery if such repairs are required. In other words, it is probably best in the long run for all concerned to regard damage to ordinary containers as in the nature of special damage rather than incidental damage which it more probably is.

Delay

For unreasonable delay in the transportation of goods the shipper is ordinarily entitled to recover the difference in the market value of the goods at the time and place when delivery should have been made and their market value when delivery was actually made.

Delay in the delivery of the goods, even though it is such as to render the carrier liable, does not constitute conversion, and the person entitled to the goods cannot on that account refuse to receive them and sue for the full value. (*Buston* v. *Pa. Ry. Co.*, 116 Fed. 235; *St. Louis R. Co.* v. *Dreyfus,* 132 Pac. 491; *Hackett* v. *B. C. & M. C. R. Co.*, 35 N. H. 390; *Fishman* v. *Pratt,* 90 N. Y. S. 354; *C. & O.* v. *Saulsburg,* 103 S. W. 254; *Spalding* v. *Chicago R. Co.*, 73 S. W. 274)

The carrier's liability is to compensate for the damages growing out of the delay and not for loss; and the remedy of the party entitled to the goods is to sue for the damages he has sustained by reason of the delay. *Moody* v. *Southern Ry. Co.*, 60 S. E. 711; *Southern Express Co.* v. *Hanaw*, 67 S. E. 944. This, as a rule, is the difference between their market value at the time they should have been delivered and when they were delivered, less freight, if unpaid. *E. T. V. & G. Ry. Co.* v. *Johnson & Shahan,* 11 S. E. 809; *Gooden* v. *Southern Ry. Co.*, 54 S. E. 720.

While the *market value* rule is generally the basis of the measure for delay, it is not the only basis. This was discussed by the court in *Great Atlantic & Pacific Tea Co.* v. *Atchison, T. & S. F. Ry. Co.*, 333 F. 2d 705, cert. den. 379 U.S. 967. This most recent decision on carrier liability for delay also points up the necessity of the claimant proving the injury claimed. The action was for damages for "unreasonable and unexcused delay" to a shipment of plums. The evidence showed that the plums were shipped from California on June 2 and under the carriers' usual schedule would have been delivered in New York before 9:00 A.M., Sunday, June 10, for sale on Monday, June 11. Delivery was actually made at 5:30 A.M. on June 12. The plums were sold at retail in plaintiff's stores. Had they been sold wholesale on June 12, the day of delivery, the average price would have been 74 cents a crate less than if they had been sold wholesale on June 11, the first market day after the due date. That was the basis of the claimed loss.

The evidence showed that plaintiff neither bought nor sold plums in the wholesale market on any day during the critical period. The plums in question were bought for sale at retail and were so sold. Plaintiff sent daily price lists to its store managers. The store managers had authority to lower the prices shown on the lists but not to raise them. The price lists did not reflect any change in the price of plums between June 10 and June 15. These price lists and advertisements were the only records plaintiff had of retail price. The court found that plaintiff had no record of (1) whether all the plums were sold, (2) the date or time of sale, (3) the stores where sales were made, (4) whether the delayed plums were commingled with other plums, or (5) any facts about the sale, including the price. The evidence showed that there was no physical damage or deterioration in the plums because of the delay.

The court first discussed the market value rule:

> The general common law rule of damages in cases of unreasonable delay and damage to goods in shipment is the market value of the goods at the date and in the condition they were contracted to arrive at their destination and the date on and the condition in which they actually arrived.

This rule was followed in *New York, L. E. & W. R. Co.* v. *Estell*, 147 U.S. 591; *Mitsubishi Shoji Kaisha* v. *Davis*, 291 F. 882, cert. den. 263 U.S. 706; *Sangamon and Morgan R. Co.* v. *Henry*, 14 Ill. 156.

The court emphasized that the measure of damages in delay is the actual damages and said, "the market value rule has been adopted as a method to ascertain actual damages. Its adoption is due to its simplicity in application, the probability that it comes close to actual damages in most cases and the policy that 'as against the wrong-doer, the law is willing to disregard the possibility that an award of market value at the time of the wrong may be too much.'" The court cited for this reasoning: McCormick, *Damages*, sec. 48, at 184 (1939). "The wrong-doer shall bear the risk of the uncertanty which his own wrong has created," citing *Bigelow* v. *RKO Radio Pictures*, 327 U.S. 251. The court noted that the market value rule is but a method of computing damages and will not be used when another rule will better compute actual damages. It said, "It has been held that the burden of proving that the market rule will not result in a just measure of actual damage is on the carrier," citing *Reider* v. *Thompson,* 197 F. 2d 158. The court then quoted from *United States* v. *Palmer & Parker Co.,* 61 F. 2d 455, 459, a suit for damages due to delay, as follows:

> We think the court below erred in applying the market value of logs to this case. There is only one rule, of universal application, and that is to give compensation for the loss suffered. Frequently, this ideal is found impossible of complete attainment; perhaps generally the market value rule is found to be the nearest approach to reaching the actual loss. But the market value rule is inapplicable when, on the facts, it is not the nearest practicable approach to an ascertainment of the actual loss. Each case must be governed by its own facts.

The court then noted that the Carmack Amendment does not change this common-law rule, citing *Wood & Co.* v. *Chicago, M. & St. P. Ry. Co.,* 151 N. E. 229, and *Fort Worth and Denver Ry. Co.* v. *United States,* 242 F. 2d 702. The court cited *Illinois Central R. Co.* v. *Crail,* 21 U.S. 57, "The test of market value is at best but a convenient means of getting at the loss suffered. It may be discarded and other more accurate means resorted to, if, for special reasons, it is not exact or other wise accurate."

In the absence of a showing of, for example, decline in retail price, physical damage or deterioration, or sale at a reduced price on a "quick-sale" counter due to delay and anticipated spoilage, the court said, "We fail to see how A&P has established actual damage." The court noted, "Unexcused and unreasonable delay establishes a wrong, but in the absence of proof of actual damage such wrong is not compensable under the Carmack Amendment or the common law." For cases distinguishing between proof of wrong and proof of damages, see *Crail* case, *supra; Missouri Pacific R. Co.* v. *Rouw Co.,* 258 F. 2d 445; *Weirton Steel Co.* v. *Isbrandtsan-Moller Co.,* 126 F. 2d 593; *United States* v. *Palmer & Parker Co.,* 61 F. 2d 455, and cases cited therein.

Because of plaintiff's failure to prove damages, the court found for the carrier.

Where goods are of a special design and of no value to other than the party to whom consigned and this value is destroyed by the unreasonable delay in transportation by the carrier, the carrier is liable for the full value of the goods. (*Uhrich Mill Work Co.* v. *Missouri Pac. Ry. Co.,* 212 Pac. 654)

Special damages for delay in the delivery of goods are recoverable only in case the shipper, at or before the time he tendered the goods to the carrier, informed the carrier of the special circumstances which rendered the prompt transportation and delivery of the goods necessary. (*Simons-Mayrant Co.* v. *Atlantic Coast Line R. Co.*, 207 F. 387; *Clyde Coal Co.* v. *Pittsburgh, etc. R. Co.*, 226 Pa. 391, 75 A. 596) To render effective the notice of special circumstances, it must be given at or before the time of the making of the contract of shipment. A notice which is given after the shipment has started on its way and before it has arrived at destination or after the damage has already occurred or after a reasonable time for delivery has elapsed is insufficient. (*Chicago, etc. T. Co.* v. *Planters Gin, etc. Co.*, 113 S. W. 352; *Illinois Central R. Co.* v. *Nelson*, 97 S. W. 757)

In *Security Stove & Mfg. Co.* v. *American Railway Express Co.*, 51 S. W. 2d 572, the court held that the shipper could recover as damages its expenses incurred in renting space at exhibit which it was unable to fully utilize as result of the carrier's unreasonable delay in delivering all of the exhibit goods. In this case the plaintiff rented exhibit space in Atlantic City, New Jersey, and inquired from the defendant as to time required to handle a shipment from Missouri to Atlantic City and gave the shipment to the defendant for transportation to that destination two days in advance of the date specified in order to be certain that the shipment would arrive in time. The shipment consisted of a special combination oil and gas burner to be exhibited at a convention of the American Gas Association. The burner was not to be exhibited for purpose of immediate sale but for show and advertising purposes.

When the president of plaintiff's company arrived in Atlantic City, he found the exhibit set up but missing one important part which was later found in the defendant's overroom in St. Louis. This part was forwarded to Atlantic City but arrived too late for the convention. The exhibit of the plaintiff was not successful because the important part did not arrive. The plaintiff asked damages including express charges on the exhibit, freight charges for return of the exhibit to Missouri, railroad and pullman fares to and from Atlantic City, hotel room for two (a workman went with president), time of the president, wages of the other employee, and the cost of renting the booth, making a total claim of $801.51. The lower court allowed recovery of this amount and the carrier appealed. In affirming the carrier's liability for this amount and rejecting its contention that the carrier could be held liable only for loss of profits, the court said:

> In support of its contention that plaintiff can sue only for loss of profit, if anything, in a case of this kind, defendant, among other cases cites that of *Adams Exp. Co.* v. *Egbert*, 36 Pa. 360, 78 Am Dec. 382. That case involved the shipment of a box containing architectural drawings or plans for a building to a building committee of the Touro Almhouse, in New Orleans. This committee

had offered a premium of $500.00 to the successful competitor. These plans arrived after the various plans had been passed upon and the award made to another person. It was sought in that case to recover the value of the plans. The evidence, however, showed that the plans would not have won the prize had they arrived on time. The court held that the plans, under the circumstances, had no appreciable value and recovery could not be had for them and there was no basis for recovery for loss of the opportunity to compete for the prize. The opinion states that in denying recovery for the plans it is contrary to the English rule in such cases. Other cases cited by defendant involve loss of profits or the loss of opportunity to compete in such events as horse racing and the like. In one case, *Delta & Chair Co.* v. *R. R.*, 105 Miss. 861, 63 So. 272, it was held that the plaintiff could recover for loss of profits that might have been made in the sale of its commodity, as a result of exhibiting a sample at an exhibition, where the shipment was delayed too late for the exhibit. Some of the cases cited by defendant hold that such profits in those classes of cases are not recoverable and others to the contrary. Defendant contends that plaintiff is endeavoring to achieve a return of the status quo in a suit based on a breach of contract. Instead of seeking to recover what he would have had, had the contract not been broken, plaintiff is trying to recover what he would have had, had there never been any contract of shipment; that the expenses sued for would have been incurred in any event.

The Court then stated the general rule:

It is no doubt, the general rule that where there is a breach of contract the party suffering the loss can recover only that which he would have had, had the contract not been broken, and this is all the cases decided upon which defendant relies, including *C., M. & St. P. Ry.* v. *McCaull-Dinsmore Co.*, 253 U.S. 97, 100, 40 S. Ct. 504, 64 L. Ed. 801. But this is merely a general statement of the rule and is not inconsistent with the holdings that, in some instances, *the injured party may recover expenses incurred in relying upon the contract although such expenses would have been incurred had the contract not been breached.* See *Morrow* v. *Railroad,* 140 Mo. App. 200, 212, 213, 123 S. W. 1034; *Bryant* v. *Barton,* 32 Neb. 613, 616, 49 N.W. 331; *Woodbury* v. *Jones,* 44 N. H. 206; *Driggs* v. *Dwight,* 17 Wend. (N.Y.) 71, 31 Am. Dec. 283. In *Sperry et al.* v. *O'Neill-Adams Co.* (C. C. A.), 185 F. 231, the court held that the advantages resulting from the use of trading stamps as a means of increasing trade are so contingent that they cannot form a basis on which to rest a recovery for a breach of contract to supply them. In lieu of compensation based hereon the court directed a recovery in the sum expended in preparation for carrying on a business in connection with the use of the stamps. The court said, loc. cit. 239, "Plaintiff in its complaint had made a claim for lost profits, but, finding it impossible to marshal any evidence which would support a finding of exact figures, abandoned that claim. Any attempt to reach a precise sum would be mere blind guesswork. Nevertheless a contract, which both sides conceded would prove a valuable one, had been broken and the party who broke it was responsible for resultant damage. In order to carry out this contract, the plaintiff made expenditures which otherwise it would not have made. . . . The trial judge held, and we think rightly, that plaintiff was entitled at least to recover those expenses to which it had been put in order to secure the benefits of a contract of which defendant's conduct deprived it."

The court reviewed other cases involving the measure of damages:

Gilbert v. *Kennedy*, 22 Mich. 117, involved the question of the measure of plaintiff's damage, caused by the conduct of defendant in wrongfully feeding his cattle with plaintiff's in the latter's pasture, resulting in plantiff's cattle suffering by the overfeeding of the pasture. The court said loc. cit. 135, 136: "There being practically no market value for pasturage when there was none in the market, that element of certainty is wanting, even to those cattle which were removed from the Pitcher farm to the home farm of the plaintiff for pasturage; and, as it could not apply to the others at all, and there being no other element of certainty by which the damage can be *accurately* measured, resort must be had to such principle or basis of calculation applicable to the circumstances of the case (if any be discoverable) as will be most likely to *approximate* certainty, and which may serve as a guide in making the most probable estimate of which the nature of the case will admit; and, though it may be less certain as a scale of measurement, yet if the principle be just in itself, and more likely to approximate the *actual damages*, it is better than any rule, however certain, which must certainly produce injustice, by excluding a large portion of the damages actually sustained." In *Hobbs* v. *Davis*, 30 Ga. 423, a negro slave was hired to make a crop, but she was taken away by the owner in the middle of the year, the result of which the crop was entirely lost. The court said, loc. cit. 425: "As it was, the true criterion of damages was, perhaps the hire of the negro, the rent of the land and all expenses incurred, and actual loss sustained by the misconduct of the defendant, rather than the conjecture of the witness, as to what the crop would have been worth." Compensation is a fundamental principle of damages whether the action is in contract or in tort. *Wicker* v. *Hoppock*, 6 Wall. 94, 99, 18 L. Ed. 752. "*One who fails to perform his contract is justly bound to make good all damages that accrue naturally from the breach; and the other party is entitled to be put in as good a position pecuniarily as he would have been by performance of the contract.*" *Miller* v. *Robertson,* 266 U.S. 243, 257, 258, 45 S. Ct. 73, 78, 69 L. Ed. 265.

The court then turned to the facts in the instant case:

The case at bar was to recover damages for loss of profits by reason of the failure of the defendant to transport the shipment within a reasonable time, so that it would arrive in Atlantic City for the exhibit. There were no profits contemplated. The furnace was to be shown and shipped back to Kansas City. There was no money loss, except expenses, that was of such a nature as any court would allow as being sufficiently definite or lacking in pure speculation. Therefore, unless plaintiff is permitted to recover the expenses that it went to, which were a total loss to it by reason of its inability to exhibit the furnace and equipment, it will be deprived of any substantial compensation for its loss. The law does not contemplate any such injustice. It ought to allow plaintiff, as damages, the loss in the way of expenses that it sustained, and which it would not have been put to if it had not been for its reliance upon the defendant to perform its contract. There is no contention that the exhibit would have been entirely valueless and whatever it might have accomplished defendant knew of the circumstances and ought to respond for whatever damages plaintiff suffered. In cases of this kind the method of estimating the damages should be adopted which is the most definite and certain and which best achieves the fundamental purpose of compensation. 17 C. J. p. 846; *Miller* v. *Robertson*, 266 U.S. 243, 257, 45 S. Ct. 73, 78, 69 L. Ed. 265. Had the exhibit been shipped in order to realize a profit on sales and such profits could have been realized, or to be entered in competition for a prize, and plaintiff failed to show loss of profits with sufficient definiteness, or that he would have won the prize, defendant's cases might be in point. But as before stated, no such situation exists here. While, it is true that plaintiff already had incurred some of these expenses, in that it had rented space at the exhibit before entering into the contract with the defendant for the shipment of the exhibit and this part of plaintiff's damages, in a sense, arose out of circumstances which transpired before the contract was even entered into, yet, plaintiff arranged for the exhibit knowing that it would call upon defendant to perform its common law duty to accept and transport the shipment with reasonable dispatch. The whole damage, therefore, was suffered in contemplation of defendant performing its contract, which it failed to do, and would not have been sustained except for the reliance by plaintiff upon defendant to perform it. It can, therefore, be fairly said that the damages or loss suffered by plaintiff grew out of the breach of the contract, for had the shipment arrived on time, plaintiff would have had the benefit of the contract, which was contemplated by all parties, defendant being advised of the shipment. The judgment is affirmed. (Emphasis added.)

In *Lamb* v. *Railway Express Agency, Inc.*, 320 P. 2d 644, 51 Wash. 2d 616, a carload of cherries arrived at destination one day late. Because there was evidence of unusual delay, the court held that the burden of proof was on the carrier to prove that the delay arose from some cause other than the carrier's negligence. Because the carrier did not sustain this burden, damages were awarded on the basis of the one-day decline in market value; interest, however, was denied. In deciding this case, the court said:

The trial court found that respondents delivered the carload of cherries, consisting of 1,568 lugs, to appellant at Milton, Oregon, at seven o'clock A.M., June 27, 1948. At about 9:10 A.M. of that day, the car was forwarded to Reith, Oregon, on Union Pacific train No. 361. At Reith, it was included in a train referred to as the cherry special, which originated at Reith and departed therefrom at about one o'clock P.M., June 27, 1938. The car in question was originally destined for Chicago, Illinois, but was later timely diverted in transit to New York City. The published schedules of the appellant for the cherry special provided for its arrival in New York City in time for the fourth subsequent morning auction. The train was delayed, with the result that the respondents' carload of cherries arrived one day late and had to be sold on the fifth morning auction for less than they would have brought the day before.

Appellant contends that the burden is on respondents to show that appellant was negligent, in addition to showing unreasonable delay in delivery.

We think the better-reasoned rule is as stated in 13 C. J. S. 421 § 216:

> It is clearly the majority rule, as stated in Corpus Juris, which has often been quoted and cited as authority therefor, that when evidence of unusual delay is adduced, a prima facie case of negligence is made out, and the burden then devolves on the carrier to explain or excuse the delay and to show that it arose from some cause other than the carrier's negligence, or that of its agents or servants. . . .

The appellant contends it does not guarantee its schedules. The recovery in this case is not sought under a guarantee of delivery for a particular market or transportation on a particular train, but it is predicated on a failure to transport with reasonable dispatch. *New York, Philadelphia & Norfolk R. Co.*, v. *Peninsula Produce Exchange,* 240 U.S. 34, 60 L. Ed. 511, 36 S. Ct. 230. . . .

Appellant assigns error to the finding that respondents were damaged by the market decline from July 1, 1948, to July 2, 1948. Victor Joseph qualified as an expert and testified that he had represented Washington and Oregon cherry shippers during June and July, 1948; that his company sold the cherries in question, and he had been present at the auctions and observed the condition of the cherries on both days; and that the New York Daily Fruit Reporter is generally accepted by the trade, the carriers, and the appellant as being correct, and, based upon that and upon his observation and experience, he was of the opinion that the cherries in question suffered a net decline in market value from July 1, 1948, to July 2, 1948, of $2,973.64. He further testified that the July 1, 1948, market was a special market, because the cherries sold on that auction would be on the retail market on the three-day week end immediately following, but cherries sold on July 2, 1948, would have to be held over until July 6, 1948 for the retail market, at which time they would compete with fresher cherries.

The court's finding is supported by the record.

In *Great A. & P. Tea Co.* v. *Chicago, B. & Q. R. R.*, the carrier contended that the claimant's recovery should be measured by the decline, if any, of the retail selling price, since the nature of claimant's business was retail rather than wholesale. This contention, however, the court rejected. Two issues were presented in this case. First, was a delay of five days by defendant railroad in delivering applies shipped from Selah, Washington, to Chicago, Illinois, an unreasonable delay? Second, assuming carrier liability for unreasonable delay, was claimant entitled to recover the decline in the value of the apples on the basis of a decline in the wholesale market price? In deciding these issues, the court said:

We believe the law to be well settled that a common carrier must deliver goods without unreasonable delay unless excused by uncontrollable circumstances. In *Behn* v. *Southern Pacific Co.*, 2 Ill. App. 2d 62, heard by this court, an unexplained delay of four days in the shipment of carrots was held to be an unreasonable delay in delivery.

Since the usual, scheduled and customary time for delivery of the apples in question to A & P in Chicago would have been on January 25th, 1956, and since they were not delivered until January 30th, a delay of five days, we hold such delay to be unreasonable and that the circumstances in law did not excuse the delay.

We come now to the most difficult question raised in this controversy, namely, the rule of law to be applied in measuring damages.

This court feels that the greater weight of authority supports the wholesale market theory as a rule to measure damages.

In *Wabash Railroad Co.* v. *Campbell,* 219 Ill. 312, at page 320:

> The rule, adopted by the court in regard to the measure of damages, is the same which was announced by this court in the recent case of *Cleveland, Cincinnati, Chicago and St. Louis Railway Co.* v. *Patton,* 203 Ill. 376.
>
> In the latter case it was held that the measure of damages, in an action for injuries to horses in shipment, is the difference between what the horses were worth when received for shipment, and what they were worth when they reached their destination; and it was also there held that, where plaintiff, in an action for injuries to horses in shipment, was obliged to keep the horses for a month after their arrival at their destination on account of their damaged condition, evidence as to what they sold for after he prepared them for market was immaterial, and its admission was properly refused.
>
> Appellant here complains that it was not allowed to ask questions of the witnesses of appellees for the purpose of showing what the cattle were subsequently sold for, but under the ruling in the *Patton* case, *supra,* such testimony was properly excluded.

Both the *Campell* and the *Patton* cases referred to, hold that the measure of damages is predicated upon the depreciation of market value and is not concerned with what the shipper subsequently does with the goods shipped.

In further support of this theory we cite the *Behn* case previously referred to. In the *Behn* case, the Court said at page 64:

> Under these circumstances, the measures of damage for unreasonable delay in delivery by common carrier, as established in many cases, is the difference between the market value of the consignment at the time and in the condition it should have arrived and its fair cash market value and condition at the time it actually did arrive at its destination.

And, then a number of cases are cited. . . .

> *Idaho Sheep Co.* v. *Oregon Short Line R. Co.,* 188 Ill. App. 591, 599; *Hutchinson Grocery Co.* v. *Louisville & N. R. Co.,* 230 Ill. App. 291, 295; and *Stern, McGiveny & Co.* v. *Keeshin Motor Express Co., Inc.,* 310 Ill. App. 337, 341.

The *Behn* case is of recent date, having been decided in 1954.

The court disagrees with defendant's interpretation of *Illinois Central R. R.* v. *Cobb, Blaisdell & Co.*, 72 Ill. 148, as being inconsistent with this view of the market value rule. Here's what the court said about the market value rule in this case at page 150:

> It is clear that if appellant failed to transport the grain to its point of destination within a reasonable time, and the price of the grain declined in the market at Cairo, the point to which it was consigned, then appellees would be entitled to recover the difference between the market price at Cairo when it should have arrived and the time it actually arrived";

And, the court continuing on page 151:

> If appellees sold oats in Cairo at that time for seventy-five cents per bushel, that was a fact proper for the consideration of the jury, tending to establish the market price of the grain at that date, and we are unable to conjecture upon what principle appellant was denied the right to establish the market value of oats at that time.

In other words, in permitting this kind of testimony the cases disclose that the only time the courts are concerned with what the shipper does with the goods subsequent to the delivery date, namely, the amount received from a resale, is for the purpose of establishing a market value on the date of the delayed delivery where there is no established market or where a market value cannot be determined.

This is precisely what happened in the *Cobb, Blaisdell* case just cited and is consistent with the doctrine enunciated in *Reider v. Thompson,* 17 F. 2d 158. Indeed, this doctrine has been recognized in Illinois for over a century. See *Sangamon and Morgan Railroad* vs. *Henry,* 14 Ill. 156, 158.

Now, in the *Behn* case this court was confronted with this kind of a situation: Ordinarily, the market value of carrots was governed in the particular area by what is known as the Cincinnati reports. However, there were no Cincinnati market quotations for California carrots at this particular time and so the court permitted evidence of the original sales price of the commodity and the price at which the shipper was obliged to sell as furnishing some basis for determining the market value.

The court has given considerable weight to the *Ward* case which supports the market value rule. In *Ward* v. *New York Central Ry.*, 47 N.Y. 29 at page 32, the court said:

> Where a carrier from mere negligence, from plain violation of duty, omits to transport merchandise beyond a reasonable time and its market value falls in the meantime, the true rule of damages in my judgment both upon principle and authority, is the difference in its value at the time and place it ought to have been delivered and the time of its actual delivery. The rule is simple, and though it may sometimes operate harshly, easily applied.

Defendant railroad argues that to apply the wholesale market rule to plaintiff would do violence to our elementary concept of the law of damages, that the payment of $147.00 damage to plaintiff would put plaintiff in a better position by that amount than if the delay had not occurred.

Now, this argument has some appeal but no real merit in law. Could not this same kind of argument be made against one engaged in the wholesale business?

Since the courts are not concerned with what the shipper does after receiving merchandise from the carrier other than to establish market values where there are none, what practical difference is there, in the light of the authorities cited and all of which we have examined, whether the shipper is engaged in the wholesale or retail business?

It seems to this court that many of the arguments advanced by the defendant go to the very nature of the market value rule generally and could be applied from the viewpoint of the defendant to a shipper whether he be engaged in the wholesale or retail business.

Here the rights of the parties become fixed on the date of actual delivery of the apples by the Burlington to A & P, and it is not relevant what disposition of the apples A & P intended to make or did in fact make.

This court finds that, since there was an unreasonable delay in the delivery of the apples in question, the rule of damages to be applied, in the light of the many cases examined by this court, is that plaintiff was not required to offer evidence of resale at wholesale or retail. Therefore, the measure of damages to the plaintiff is the decline in the wholesale market price between the date on which the apples should have been delivered and the date of actual delivery.

Aside from the foregoing, this court finds considerable merit to the arguments advanced by plaintiff that to require a retail shipper to prove damages by retail prices would be a most cumbersome and difficult rule to apply and particularly would enable each shipper to set his own special measure of damages. In short, it would be impractical to trace merchandise to resale at retail.

In *H. C. Parker, Inc.* v. *Herrin Transp. Co.*, 183 So. 606, a shipper who had given carrier notice was awarded profit which it would have made if the carrier had delivered a shipment of sample furniture in time for consideration in awarding a contract. The court said:

The damage consists of the profits plaintiff would have made on the contract (which should have been awarded to it by the Police Jury of St. Martin) if its bid had been received and considered by that body. It is not disputed that the Police Jury of Martin Parish had given written notice that it would receive bids, for the purpose of purchasing furniture and office equipment to be installed in the new Courthouse. . . . The record also discloses that the plaintiff company prepared a bid in accordance with these specifications; that the bid was the lowest one submitted and that the only reason why it was not considered was because the samples of its furniture, which were to be displayed . . . did not arrive in St. Martinville on the date the defendant had agreed to make delivery. . . . In addition to this, plaintiff's evidence justified the conclusion that, if the bid it submitted had been considered and accepted, it would have made a profit of 11% of the contract price. Counsel for defendant nevertheless argues that the damages which plaintiff seeks to recover are conjectural and that there is no assurance that plaintiff would have been awarded the contract, even though it was the lowest bidder, since the Policy Jury, in its proposal, reserved to itself the right to reject any and all bids submitted. To maintain this contention would be to recognize the wrong and refuse a remedy. And in denying relief, we would be compelled to assume that the Policy Jury would have arbitrarily and capriciously refused to award the contract to the lowest bidder. Such a result would be manifestly unjust and indefensible. Counsel also insists that the profit plaintiff expected to make in performing the contract is too speculative and remote to be a fit subject for consideration in the assessment of damages. He points out that a rise in price, an increase of overhead or other expenses could have easily reduced plaintiff's anticipated profits on the contract. If counsel is correct in this contention, then there could be no case in which apprehended gains could be the subject of a recovery in damages for breach of contract.

Where because of unreasonable delay the goods become worthless or, in other words, where the delay has caused the equivalent of a total loss to the owner, an exception exists to the usual rule that the consignee must accept delivery and hold the carrier liable for the difference in the value of the goods at the time they arrived and when they should have arrived. In *Baumann* v. *New York, etc., R. Co.*, 35 Misc. 223, 71 N. Y. S. 632, a carrier receiving summer goods on July 10 and not delivering them until August 8 was held liable for their full value after the consignee had refused to accept them. In *Lambert-Murray Co.* v. *Southern Express Co.*, 59 S. E. 991, the carrier was held liable for the market value of a box containing souvenirs which it failed to deliver within a reasonable time and which on their arrival were valueless even though the carrier had no notice of the importance of promptly completing delivery.

In *Steinberg* v. *Erie R. R.*, 172 N. Y. S. 92, the court held, however, that mere delay in itself in accomplishing delivery does not establish that the goods even though seasonal in nature are worthless, and while late arrival might cause an unusual loss, it does not create an exception to the usual rule that the goods should be received and the carrier held liable for the difference in market value between the time of arrival and the time when they should have arrived. A consignee of goods which are of little or trifling value and unsalable, however, may refuse to accept them when tendered after a negligent delay in transportation, and may recover his damages therefor. (*American Ry. Express Co.* v. *Pitts*, 91 So. 571)

Duty of Consignee to Accept Freight

The duty of the consignee of goods transported by a carrier to accept delivery thereof is not ordinarily excused by the fact that the goods are damaged, unless such damage rendered the property practically valueless, having regard to the expense of acceptance and use and to the purpose for which it was intended. (*Crinella* v. *Northwestern Pac. R. Co.*, 259 Pac. 774; *Pacific Heater Co.* v. *Southern Pac. Co.*, 188 Pac. 600; *Sipple* v. *Seaboard Airline,* 114 S. E. 39; *C.C.C. & St. L. R. Co.* v. *Bement-Rea Co.*, 154 N. E. 32; *Quanah, A. & P. R. Co.* v. *Novit,* 199 S. W. 496) The consignee's remedy in case of partial loss or damage not rendering the property worthless is to accept the goods and sue for damages or, in the case the damage renders the goods valueless, to reject the shipment and sue for its full value. A consignee of goods which are of little or trifling value and unsalable, however, may refuse to accept them when tendered after a negligent delay in transportation thereof, and may recover full damages. (*American Ry. Express Co.* v. *Pitts,* 91 So. 571)

The unlawful refusal of the consignee to accept damaged goods, and his action in bringing suit for their value, is of no consequence where it does not appear that any different result would have been reached had the consignee received the goods in their injured condition and then sued for damages.

It is the duty of the owner of goods to make reasonable effort to minimize the damages, and the carrier cannot be held liable for damages which such efforts would have prevented. It is the duty of the property owner where the goods have been damaged to use all reasonable means to render the effect of the injury as light as possible, but failure to prevent additional damage does not preclude recovery for that part of the damage not due to such failure but solely to the carrier's negligence.

In *Norfolk & Western Ry. Co.* v. *Keystone Packing Co.*, 195 N. E. 403, the carrier was held free from liability for goods it delivered in good condition which were salvaged with a portion of the goods that were damaged. If a shipment composed of several cartons arrives at destination with one or two cartons short or damaged, the consignee has the legal duty of accepting the shipment and holding the carrier liable only for the missing goods or the loss caused to the damaged goods delivered. Likewise, if a carton containing, for example, 24 bottles arrives with four bottles broken and the remaining 20 in good condition, the consignee has the legal duty of accepting the goods and looking to the carrier for compensation for only the four damaged bottles.

If the consignee fails to observe its legal obligation and the goods are abandoned to the carrier, such abandonment is at consignee's peril because the carrier will be liable only to the same extent as if consignee had accepted the goods and observed its legal duty. The usual practice when goods are abandoned to the carrier under these circumstances is for the carrier to salvage the goods for the best price obtainable, turn over the proceeds received for the undamaged goods and pay claimant for its full actual loss suffered on the goods actually lost or damaged at time of delivery. Since the carrier usually is unable to salvage merchandise even when undamaged for as much as can be realized by the consignee, it is to the consignee's advantage to observe its legal obligation, accept the goods, and salvage them for the best interest of all concerned.

The carrier has the duty of showing the manner by which the claimant could have mitigated the damages. In *Perkel* v. *Pennsylvania R. Co.*, 265 N. Y. S. 597, the carrier was held responsible for damage to a carload of watermelons. The railroad argued that the claimant, instead of unloading the cars and segregating the damaged melons and then selling the undamaged melons for the best price obtainable, simply sold the cars in the condition in which they arrived. This appeared to be in line with the custom followed at the market. The court rejected the carrier's contention and said:

> The burden of showing how the plaintiff could mitigate the damages falls upon the defendant (carrier), and no evidence was offered that such action by the plaintiff would mitigate the damages. Opposed to this lack of evidence is the affirmative showing by the plaintiff that a car contains 800 to 1,200 melons, and that to adopt the procedure suggested by the defendant would entail an expense of 2 cents per melon for unloading and another 2 cents per melon for reloading, would result in a delay of at least one day in the sale, and in addition would depreciate the value of the car, since it would not be a fully loaded car. From this proof it appears that, instead of mitigating the damages, the procedure suggested would enhance them.

A similar holding was made in *Schwalb* v. *Erie R. Co.*, 293 N. Y. S. 842, in which the court said:

> The damaged portions were disposed of in accordance with the usage and custom of the trade and the burden of going forward with proof to show that a disposition of the damaged portions of the shipments in a manner other than was adopted by the plaintiff would have mitigated the plaintiff's damages rested upon the defendant. Defendant failed to produce any evidence of any method of salvage by which plaintiff's loss could have been lessened.

In *Wagner* v. *T. S. C. Motor Freight Lines,* 181 So. 625, it was held that the claimant cannot hold the carrier liable for the total value of the goods where the damages can be mitigated by repairs at reasonable cost. In this case the plaintiff shipped a machine to a prospective customer for demonstration purposes and when the prospective customer found that the machine did not meet his requirements, plaintiff ordered that the machine be returned by defendant carrier. While in the act of loading the machine on the truck, defendant's employee permitted it to fall to the ground and, as a result, it was damaged. The machine was later returned by the defendant to its warehouse in New Orleans in order that the extent of the damage might be determined. It was inspected by both the plaintiff and the carrier. Plaintiff contended that the machine was a total loss since it was damaged beyond repair. The carrier, on the other hand, took the position that the device could be placed in perfect working order at a cost of $205. Plaintiff refused to agree to having the machine repaired and brought suit for its value. The court in holding the carrier liable only for cost of repairs said:

> In an attempt to prove that the machine was damaged so badly that it constituted a total loss, plaintiff produced two witnesses, viz., a Mr. Jensen, Sales Manager of the Triumph Manufacturing Company (plaintiff's vendor) and a Mr. Lane, a mechanic doing business in New Orleans. Jensen stated that he inspected the machine after it had been stored in defendant's warehouse and that it was worthless because it had been damaged beyond repair. On cross-examination, however, he admitted that he was not a mechanic and, while he is somewhat familiar with the mechanism of the device (being in the business of selling these machines), he is unable to state what was wrong with it or why it could not be restored to its former condition. We cannot accept his statement as expert testimony as it is patent that the conclusions he seeks to establish are mere guesses and are not founded upon a requisite knowledge of mechanics. The evidence of Lane does not sustain plaintiff's contentions that the machine was damaged beyond repair. On the contrary, on cross-examination, he stated as follows: "Q. The machine could be fixed so that it could operate satisfactorily, couldn't it? A. It could be fixed, I would prefer to use the word 'rebuilt'." He further said that he was not in position to state what it would cost to repair the device and did not know whether the estimate of $205.00 by defendant's witness, E. E. Longley, was reasonable or not. On the other hand, defendant produced Mr. Longley, who is engaged in the welding business in New Orleans and who inspected the machine at the time it was stored in the warehouse. He stated that he has had considerable experience in repairing machines similar to the one in controversy; that his examination of it revealed that the damage consisted of a break at its base; that its frame was chipped, the hopper cracked, the extended shafts and burr wheels bent and that the guards of the protecting gears were broken. He further declared that the machine could be satisfactorily repaired for $205.00 and he

made a written offer to the defendant to perform the work for that price. In view of the foregoing testimony, we have no hesitancy in finding that the plaintiff has failed to prove that the damage to the machine constituted total loss. It was his duty to minimize his damage and he had no right to assume that the apparatus could not be repaired. Moreover, he was not justified in relying upon the conclusion of Mr. Jensen, who was devoid of mechanical knowledge. The testimony of his other expert, Mr. Lane, did not sustain his claim. We see no reason to doubt the statement of Mr. Longley and, as it is the only evidence in the record tending to establish the extent of the damage to the machine, we accept the figure given by him as the amount which plaintiff is entitled to recover. . . .

In *Biltmore Manufacturing Co., Inc.* v. *Overnite Transportation Co.*, 157 F. Supp. 891, the court held that a consignee upon examining a portion of shipment offered for delivery and finding it in a highly damaged condition is justified in refusing acceptance of the entire shipment, even though subsequent events develop that some of the shipment was actually undamaged. In this case, the plaintiff, a clothing manufacturer, shipped nine cartons of merchandise to Sears, Roebuck and Co., in Chicago. This shipment was refused because of late delivery and subsequently, the manufacturer authorized it returned. When the shipment was offered to Overnite in Richmond by a freight forwarder, all of the containers were in such bad shape that Overnite refused to accept them but eventually was prevailed upon to take them under a blanket exception indicating damage to all containers and with the understanding that if refused at destination, the freight forwarder would accept their return.

Upon arrival of the shipment and at the time of its attempted delivery, it was determined that all of the cartons had been damaged and were watersoaked; four of them at least had been broken open, and all had been roughly handled and were soaking wet. Four of the cartons were actually removed from Overnite's delivery truck and placed on the claimant's platform. The remaining five cartons were on the truck, evidently were not broken open, were not examined other than from the outside, but were found to be wet and otherwise damaged. Plaintiff refused to accept any of the shipment and it was thereupon returned by Overnite and delivered to the freight forwarder's warehouse in Richmond. Subsequently, it was determined by the freight forwarder that while the containers had been damaged to some extent, the goods contained therein for the most part were in good condition and constituted first class merchandise. The forwarder thereupon notified the manufacturer, requested disposition, and commenced to assess storage on the goods. In holding that the consignee was justified under the circumstances in refusing to accept delivery of the apparently seriously damaged goods, the court said:

> Since this is a diversity case the rule in estimating such damage as plaintiff may have suffered is that rule as set out in the decisions of the North Carolina courts, however it would appear that the doctrine adopted here is the universally accepted one, and that. . . .
>
>> As a general rule, the doctrine that where goods are injured the owner may abandon them as for a total loss, and sue for their value, does not apply to contracts of affreightment. The fact, therefore that the goods were injured upon the journey through causes for which the carrier is responsible, does not of itself justify the consignee in refusing to receive them, but he must accept them and hold the carrier responsible for the injury. 3 Hutchison on Carriers, sec. 1365.

In *Wilkins* v. *Atlantic Coast Line R. Co.*, 160 N. C. 54, 58, 75 S. E. 1090, 1092, which was a case of total loss:

> In contracts of affreightment, the consignee under an ordinary bill of lading may not as a general rule reject the goods because the same have been wrongfully damaged in the course of shipment. Under usual conditions, he must receive the goods and hold the company for the injury done, and he is required further to do what good business prudence would dictate in the endeavor to minimize the loss. The principle, however, does not obtain when the 'entire value of the goods has been destroyed and the injury amounts practically to a total loss.' In such cases the consignee is justified in refusing the goods, and may sue for the entire amount.

In *Whittington* v. *Southern Railroad Co.*, 172 N. C. 501, 90 S. E. 505, 506, the Supreme Court through Mr. Justice Allen goes fully into the applicable law and reaffirms among other things the doctrine theretofore held by the court, and notes, however,

> That when the loss is partial the doctrine is that the owner cannot reject the goods and recover the value, and not that he cannot recover the damages actually sustained, and this distinction is found in all the authorities.

The court in its decision likewise approved the charge given by the trial judge that the measure of damage was "the difference between the value, reasonable market value of the shipment at the time it reached (its destination), in the condition it then was and what would have been a reasonably fair value of that same shipment at (its destination) at the same time but for the damage suffered by it or sustained to it, owing to the negligence of the defendant," and the court then goes on to say "this rule is not only supported by authority, but seems to be reasonable and just, and it imposes no additional burden on the carrier."

It would certainly seem that from the description of the nine cartons when each was being unloaded on the plaintiff's platform and their appearance, that plaintiff was warranted in assuming that the damage found in the four cartons which were fully examined would likewise prevail in the other five cartons not then removed from Overnite's truck, and that plaintiff would be justified in refusing the shipment as worthless, and if perchance, as appears in this case, it would subsequently develop that this assumption was not wholly borne out, that plaintiff, even though it had refused said shipment would yet be entitled to recover its damage suffered and sustained under the rule as set out in the above cited case.

The preceding case must be evaluated upon its particular facts. Normally, water damage to new clothing greatly reduces its value. Four of the containers examined by the consignee in the case were "sopping wet" and the remaining containers appeared to be similarly damaged. While after "drying out," it appeared that the clothing was "first class;" this observation on the part of the freight forwarder was self-serving and open to question, it being seriously doubted if a purchaser with knowledge of all the facts would be willing to buy such goods when other goods were available, an understandable reluctance. The consignee manufacturer naturally would have great reluctance in accepting return of its goods which had been water damaged and assuming the expense and trouble of minute inspection to determine that there had been no deterioration in quality.

Extraordinary Value

In *Hart* v. *Railroad Co.,* 112 U.S. 331, the court said:

As a general rule and in the absence of fraud or imposition, a common carrier is answerable for the loss of a package of goods, though he is ignorant of its contents, and though its contents are ever so valuable, if he does not make a special acceptance. This is reasonable, because he can always guard himself by a special acceptance, or by insisting on being informed of the nature and value of the articles before receiving them. If the shipper is guilty of fraud or imposition, by misrepresenting the nature or value of the articles, he destroys his claim to indemnity, because he has attempted to deprive the carrier of the right to be compensated in proportion to the value of the articles and the consequent risk assumed, and what he has done has tended to lessen the vigilance the carrier would otherwise have bestowed.

Section 5 of the uniform standard bill of lading of both motor and rail carriers provides that "No carrier hereunder will carry or be liable in any way for any documents, specie, or for any article of extraordinary value *not specifically rated in the published classification or tariffs* unless a special agreement to do so and a stipulated value of the articles are endorsed hereon." Carriers' classifications and tariffs also usually provide that "unless otherwise provided" certain named items "or other articles of extraordinary value" will not be accepted for transportation.

It will be observed that the provisions of the bill of lading provide that articles of extraordinary value will not be accepted "unless specifically rated in the carrier's classification." A review of carriers' classification, however, clearly indicates that the compilers have endeavored to list and classify every conceivable commodity. Many of these commodities are so specifically described that there is no room for doubt as to the identity of the commodity intended to be covered. For example and purely for illustration, one might find under furniture: furniture, wood; furniture, iron; furniture, steel; furniture, paper; and finally after all conceivable types of furniture have been listed, the words—*furniture, noi.* (or *noibn.*). These *noi.* or *noibn.* ratings are *catch-all* ratings. In other words they serve to provide a classification on commodities which are "not otherwise indexed (listed or described) by name." This is necessary because carriers are required by law to publish and file their rates in advance and they must have some means of providing ratings for commodities for which they have not established a more specific rating. It would appear, therefore, that Section 5 of the bill of lading does not afford the carrier much protection as to transportation of articles of extraordinary value because the carriers by their classifications and tariffs have provided specific ratings on most high valued commodities.

An interesting decision in *Hecker Products Corp.* v. *Transamerican Freight Lines, Inc.*, 296 N. W. 297, indicates that the court had some understanding of the carrier's problem, which justified some relief. In this case, the shipper described its shipment as consisting of various soap and washing compounds and several filing cabinets, desks, and cases of records. While the shipment was en route, the truck collided with a train and claim in the amount of $1,155.82 was later made covering damage to the desks and file cabinets as well as loss of various credit reports. The carrier declined to pay for the commercial credit reports, contending that they were excluded by the bill of lading and tariffs on file with the Interstate Commerce Commission. The court in its decision after citing Section 217 of the Motor Carrier Act, Rule 3 of the National Motor Freight Classification, and Section 5 of the bill of lading, rejected the plaintiff's contention that Section 20(11) of the Interstate Commerce Act made these provisions void as an attempt to unlawfully limit liability.

The court said with respect to this contention: "There is no limitation of liability on the part of the defendant. Its agreement was that it would not be liable in any way for articles of extraordinary value not specifically rated unless a special agreement was entered into and stipulated articles were indorsed thereon. No value whatsoever was placed on the shipment nor was any special agreement entered into by the parties." Further, the court held that, "The exclusion of a commodity from all classes is a classification of it in as real a sense and with as definite effect as to include it in any one of the usual classes," citing *Director General* v. *Viscose Co.*, 254 U.S. 498. The theory of the court was that the provision in regard to nonliability for documents and articles of extraordinary value were not of limitation as prohibited by Section 20(11), but of *exclusion*, and in view of this the plaintiff could not recover.

From a carrier viewpoint, however, the *Hecker* case is limited in the protection it affords. The *Hecker* case involved a claim for damage to a commodity which the carrier's tariff clearly indicated would not be accepted; further, the documents were not described on the bill of lading and there was an element of misdescription or concealment of value. The problem which the carrier confronts is in those instances where the highly valued goods are described in the classification or tariff. For example, the carrier may receive a shipment of machinery parts and have no knowledge of their value until they are lost or damaged, when it is discovered that what the carrier believed was worth only a few dollars actually was worth thousands of dollars. From the shipper's viewpoint, the shipment may not be regarded as being of extraordinary value because precision machinery parts always have a high value and it considers the value of it shipments the normal value of such parts. It is not believed that where the carrier has provided ratings and rates for the transportation of named commodities it can be relieved of liability for their actual value simply because such value is high. On the other hand, if the carrier has excluded the commodity from transportation by provisions in its tariffs and the shipper who has either actual or constructive knowledge of such provision nevertheless tenders shipments of such commodities and fails to describe them properly, the carrier would not be liable for their full value in event of loss or damage.

Fraudulent Claims

Claimants in certifying to carriers the amount of damages claimed must know the amount claimed is correct. A person making a false loss and damage claim on behalf of his employer, and who certifies to an account sales, is guilty when he knows, or should have known, that he was falsely certifying to a document which is to be used in support of a claim against a carrier. In *United States* v. *Wishnatzki,* 7 F. Supp. 313, 77 F. 2d 357, defendants were indicted for filing false loss and damage claims against interstate rail carriers for more than their actual damages in order to secure rebates on legally established rates for the transportation of vegetables in carloads. In this case it was established that for years it had been the custom in determining amount of damages to carloads of tomatoes to take the weighted average of the sales prices of the sound lugs in a car and apply this average to the damaged lugs. The court held that when claims were presented on this basis on the actual facts and real prices at which the undamaged lugs were sold, no criminal offense would be committed, but where it appeared that the defendant certified that certain sound lugs had been sold for $3.00 per lug and the rest had been sold for $2.75 per lug, when actually there had not been any sales of any lugs out of that particular car for $3.00, the defendant would be guilty of the criminal offense of filing false and fraudulent claims and subject to fine and imprisonment or both, as provided in the law.

A common expression of claimants is "we file only legitimate claims" or "our claim is legitimate." The use of expressions of this nature indicates a misunderstanding of the nature of a claim. The fact that a claim is legitimate does not in itself establish carrier liability; on the contrary, it only indicates that the claim is filed in good faith—that the claimant honestly believes that he is entitled to compensation. The fact that the carrier may decline the claim is not be construed as indicating that it believes the claim to be *fraudulent* or *not legitimate* but only that, in the carrier's opinion, its liability for the claim has not been established; in other words, the opinion of the carrier is that the claim is not in order and that under the law it is not liable for the loss claimed. The declination is not by any means a reflection upon the party filing the claim but only an indication that there is a disagreement as to liability or as to the amount of it.

Until a court has definitely adjudicated a controversy through litigation of the parties involved, no one can say that a particular claim is one which should or should not be paid. As long as the claimant filing it honestly believes that the carrier or carriers involved are liable, the claim is "legitimate." On the other hand, the fact that the carrier may decline the claim by no means indicates that the good faith of the claimant is questioned; on the contrary, the ordinary declination simply means that the carrier does not agree with the claimant as to its contention as to the liability of the carrier. In the voluntary settlement of claims, the carrier has every right to determine the merits of the claim as filed, and its declination under ordinary circumstances is to be respected as representing its best judgment concerning its liability based upon the claim as filed and its own investigation.

Thousands of claims are filed every day and a small portion of them are declined; this is to be expected. In most instances the claimant readily accepts the carrier's grounds for declination. In other instances, the claimant may still feel that his claim should have been paid. It is not unusual for parties to honestly and sincerely disagree over a commercial transaction. The only methods for adjusting such controversies are by a compromise or by litigation in the courts which are established for that purpose. It is seldom in any controversy that either antagonist is one-hundred percent correct—it is natural that disagreements will arise—and it is extremely poor taste for any claimant to self-servingly declare that his claim is "legitimate." It adds nothing to the merits of the claim to deny that it is fraudulent and should be remembered that disagreement as to merits does not imply a belief on the part of the carrier that the claim was not filed in good faith.

Freight Charges

Where the value at destination is a factor in measuring the damages, unpaid freight charges should be deducted from that value under the theory that the value of the goods was enhanced from origin to point of destination to the extent of such charges. If the charges have been prepaid, they likewise are not recoverable from the carrier. However, where the invoice is used as the measure of damages, plaintiff is entitled to recover in addition thereto the freight charges if paid and *not* included in the invoice. Generally, if the shipment moved prepaid the freight charges will be included in the invoice price to consignee. If the shipment moves collect and part of the shipment is lost or damaged, consignee paying freight charges on the entire shipment is entitled to recover the proportionate freight charges on the lost or totally destroyed portion. In *Uhrich Mill Work Co.* v. *Missouri Pac. R. Co.*, 212 Pac. 654, the court said:

> One item of damages, the freight charges, was erroneously allowed. The railway company cannot be required to respond in damages for the full value of the door and give up its freight charges also. *Kennedy* v. *Railway Co.*, 104 Kan. 708, 181 Pac. 117, 5 A. L. R. 149; 100 C. J. 314; 4 R. C. L. 931, 932. That

would make the plaintiff $14.03 better off because of the delay in transportation than it would have been if the door had been transported with promptness and dispatch.

Household Goods

Where household goods or personal effects are lost or damaged, the measure of damages is the actual loss or fair value which the goods have to their owner. In case of damage to such property, the claimant is entitled to recover for their depreciated value or reasonable cost of repairs. Household goods and personal effects usually move subjects to rates based on agreed or declared value. In some instances, however, these goods may move on an unreleased basis. The following two cases are illustrative of the problem presented in determining value where the goods have not been released.

The case of *Shikany* v. *Salt Creek Transp. Co.*, 45 P. 2d 645, contains an excellent review of the law relating to the proper measure of recovery for loss or damage to household goods or other articles having no ready market because of having been used. In this case, claimant delivered to the carrier a shipment of household goods that included an oriental rug valued at $2,500 which was lost and suit was brought for this amount. The jury returned a verdict for $725. The evidence indicated that plaintiff's deceased husband had bought the rug in Europe 38 years before and that the purchase price paid by him was not known. The carrier contended there was no evidence as to the value of the rug and that the mere statement of the owner that the rug was worth such an amount was insufficient. The appellate court upheld the verdict of the jury and discussed the issues involved in the following manner:

> The great weight of authority is to the effect that secondhand household goods in use do not have a market value in the ordinary sense, and that the measure of damages in case of loss or conversion is not the price which could be realized by a sale of the goods in the market, but the actual money loss resulting to the plaintiff, that is to say, the actual value of the property, or, as it is sometimes said, its value to the owner; excluding, however, any mere fanciful or sentimental value which might be placed thereon. 8 R. C. L. 488; 26 R. C. L. 1149; 10 C. J. 398; 65 C. J. 153, 154; cases cited in exhaustive notes to 63 A. L. R. 240; L. R. A. 1917D, 495; 3 Ann. Cas. 889; 62 Am. St. Rep. 772; Ann. Cas. 1917B, 585; *St. Louis, etc., R. C. Co.* v. *Dunham*, 36 Okl. 724; 129 P. 862; *Barber* v. *Motor Inv. Co.*, 136 Or. 361, 298 P. 216. And see *Lake Shore, etc., Co.* v. *Warren*, 3 Wyo. 134, 6 P. 724.

The court reviewed the testimony presented to the trial court relative to the value of the rug. This testimony, briefly, went as follows:

Q. What in your opinion, Mrs. Shikany, was the value of the rug at the time shipped?
This was objected to on grounds that no proper foundation was laid; the objection was overruled.
Q. Tell the jury, in your opinion, what is the value of this rug?
A. Well, value about $2,500 to me.
Q. I do not want to know what its value is to you. What, in your opinion, is the market value of the rug? What could you sell it for?
A. Well, in my opinion, it is worth over two thousand dollars to me.
Q. I do not want to know what it is worth to you. What can you sell it for?
A. I can't sell less than two –
Q. (interrupting) It isn't what the rug is worth to you, it is, what can you sell it for?
A. Well, I will sell it for twenty-five hundred dollars.
Q. I want you to tell the jury what, in your opinion, was the value of the rug —not to you or anyone else, but what could you sell it for?
A. For twenty-five hundred dollars.

On cross examination, the witness testified that she had never been offered $2,500 for the rug—she "had never put it on sale." Later she testified that the rug in her opinion was worth $2,500. Another witness who claimed to be an expert on oriental rugs testified concerning the manner in which oriental rugs were produced and that "the older they get the better they are" but that he could not tell the value of the rug which was lost without seeing it. The carrier presented no evidence as to the value of the rug. Commenting on the testimony as to value, the court said:

The fact that the witness, in answer to several questions, stated the value *to her*, surely does not necessarily show that her subsequent answers refer to the same thing. Nor are we as confident as counsel seems to be that the testimony of plaintiff as to the value *to her*, while not, perhaps, to be commended, is of no force whatsoever, when taken in connection with all of her testimony. The very authorities cited by him (e.g., Elliott on Railroads [3d Ed.] § 2748) hold that, in the absence of market value, the fair value *to the owner* should be allowed in cases like that at bar. That, it is true, does not include purely fanciful or sentimental value, but it does include any actual value to the owner. If, for instance, a piece of household goods which has been used is substantially as good as new for all practical purposes, it would hardly be just that the owner should have compensation merely upon the basis of a secondhand piece of goods. And if, in addition, actual use has in fact increased the value thereof, no reason exists why that should not be considered. Of course, if it appeared that the plaintiff, when she testified as to the value *to her*, meant, not the actual value to her, in the sense above stated, but merely sentimental value, or value which had no relation to actual value, the situation would be quite different. It was said in *Gleason* v. *R. Co.*, 49 Utah 405, 164 P. 484, 486, that "neither this or any other court, so far as we know, has ever gone to the length of permitting a plaintiff to prove the value of property by merely showing what he assumed it to be worth or what it was worth to him." And see 22 C. J. 582. But it is clear from the examination of the case that the court referred to value other than actual value.

In the instant case the court found:

Plaintiff's testimony in the respect mentioned does not show what plaintiff included in her estimate, and counsel for the defendant did not take the trouble to find out. The jury may have understood the testimony in a sense different from that in which it is understood by counsel for defendant. Counsel argues that the jury necessarily merely speculated on the value, as shown by the fact that they fixed the value at $725, whereas the plaintiff's testimony fixed it at $2,500, and that for that reason the judgment should be set aside. A like contention was made in the case of *Dyer* v. *Barnes* (1929), 128 Me. 131, 145 A. 741, 742. In that case the plaintiff sued for the value of his services in digging a well, and fixed such value at $825. That was the only testimony on that point. The jury returned a verdict for $666.60. The defendant appealed. It was argued that the judgment should have been for the whole amount or none. The Supreme Court, in brushing the argument aside, stated: "Where there exists a fixed standard or scale by which damages may be calculated, a jury will not be permitted to depart from it. . . . But no such standard is applicable to the case at bar. Damages were not liquidated, nor were they capable of being reduced to certainty by arithmetical calculation, so the criterion was how much the plaintiff deserved for drilling the well. He was allowed to express his opinion from personal knowledge of a transaction in the ordinary affairs of life. *Snow* v. *Boston & Maine Railroad, supra.* See, also, 64 C. J. 1083.

* * * *

We do not say that the rule should be applied in all cases and as to all classes of personal property. It must be applied reasonably. Owners ordinarily have a fair understanding of the value of the property in their possession and use. That is the basis of the rule. By reason thereof they are prima facie qualified as witnesses; they are presumed to know the value, unless the contrary appears. Note, L. R. A. 1917D, 506-507; *Meyer* v. *Express Co.*, 240 Mass. 94, 132 N.E. 672; *Taylor* v. *R. Co.* (Mo. App.), 256 S.W. 499; *Parmelee* v. *Raymond*, 43 Ill. App. 609; *Wrenn* v. *Storage & Furniture Co.*, 236 Ill. App. 601; *Union Pac. D. & G. Co.* v. *Williams*, 3 Colo. App. 526, 529; 34 P. 731; *Tubbs* v. *Garrison*, 68 Iowa 44, 48, 25 N.W. 921. The rule mentioned by Wigmore, *supra*, has often been applied to household goods and personal belongings. 22 C. J. 582.

The court cited cases based on the testimony of a single witness:

Nor are the cases lacking in which the testimony of a single witness, not specially conversant with values, has been held sufficient to carry the case to the jury on that point. The case of *State* v. *Finch*, 70 Iowa 316, 30 N.W. 578, 69 Am. Rep. 443, was a criminal case, involving larceny, in which we would expect the rules of law to be somewhat stricter than in a civil case. Insofar as it has any bearing herein is shown by the following excerpt from the opinion of the court: "It was insisted below that there was no legal proof as to the value of the overcoat. The only witness who testified to the value of the overcoat was one Arnold. He showed that he had never seen a seal-skin overcoat bought or sold, and did not show he had any knowledge of the value of such an article, except such as any man of ordinary intelligence might be presumed to have. We do not think, however, that we should be justified in wholly discarding his testimony. He might not be a very accurate judge of the value of such an article, but we think that, having seen and examined the coat, he might form some opinion about it. He doubtless could judge with considerable accuracy of the value of such overcoats as are in common use, and he could judge, we think, though perhaps not as accurately, how this compared in value with the best of such coats. We think that his testimony was not inadmissible, and if not, the verdict was not without support." In the case of *Hood Van & Storage Co.,* 178 Cal. 150, 172 P. 594, 595, the facts and the conclusion of the court appear in the opinion of the court as follows: "The only evidence offered touching the question of the value of the goods destroyed was that of plaintiff herself. Appellant insists not only that she failed to qualify as a witness competent to testify upon the subject, but that her testimony was so uncertain and contradictory that it was not entitled to any weight whatsoever in considering the question. The value of her evidence and weight thereof was a question for the determination of the trial judge. Her testimony, however uncertain and contradictory was nevertheless the only evidence offered bearing upon the subject, and since it satisfied the trial judge that the value of the goods alleged in the complaint to be worth upwards of $3,000 was in fact $1,500, it is not the province of this court, upon a review thereof to determine otherwise." The case of *La Compagnie, etc.,* v. *Persaglio,* (C. C. A.) 165 F. 638, 639, involved the loss of personal belongings shipped in a trunk. It seemed that the defendant, against whom judgment was rendered, complained both of the competency of the witness as well as the sufficiency of the evidence to support the amount of the judgment. The plaintiff was the only witness. He was permitted to testify that the value of the goods was $400, although he had no personal knowledge. The court said: "The witness had said that his wife had bought the clothes; that he could not tell the prices she paid, but gave her the money for them. This does not prove that he was unable, independently as a father of a family, to give a fair estimate of the value of the wearing apparel, and therefore the trial judge was justified in refusing to strike out his testimony for the reasons assigned. The value of the clothing of a family of steerage passengers does not admit of very accurate proof, and as the jury and the trial judge were both satisfied, and we think the verdict reasonable, we are not astute to amplify the defendant's expectation."

On the scope of the rule the court said:

Ordinarily, it is true, the rule of Wigmore, supra, has been applied to household goods and personal belongings in common use and generally purchased by everyone. See, e.g., *Berry* v. *Ingalls,* 199 Mass. 77, 85 N.E. 191; *Erickson* v. *Drazkowski,* 94 Mich. 551, 54 N.W. 283; *Tubbs* v. *Garrison,* 68 Iowa 44, 48, 25 N.W. 921. But in *Colby* v. *W.W. Kimball Co.,* 99 Iowa 321, 68 N.W.

786, it, and the rule of presumption above stated, was applied in a case involving the conversion of a piano. In *Fredericks* v. *Sault,* 19 Ind. App. 604, 49 N. E. 909, a witness was held to be qualified to testify as to the value of a piano, when it appeared that she was a pianist, that she had experience in the use of pianos, and that she was asked to select the instrument when it was purchased, and that she did select it. In the case of *F. W. Bromberg & Co.* v. *Norton,* 208 Ala. 117, 93 So. 837, involving the conversion of a valuable diamond, there was considerable testimony showing that the witness was qualified. So, while the case is not strongly in point, the rule of Wigmore, nevertheless, was approved. In the case of *Graham* v. *Cohen,* 111 Cal. App. 131, 295 P. 46, a case of conversion of a valuable diamond, the plaintiff, apparently without qualifying himself specially, was permitted to testify to the value of the property in suit. There was no other evidence in the case on that question, and the court said "there is no doubt under the authorities that the owner of an article, whether he is generally familiar with such value or not, is entitled to testify as to its worth, and that a finding of value based upon such evidence may not be disturbed on appeal."

Dealing with the evidence before the jury the court said:

In the case at bar the property involved is an oriental rug, presumably of the value of $725. Defendant did not see fit to crossexamine plaintiff as to her knowledge of value. The rug had been in the possession and use and ownership of the plaintiff for a period of 38 years, and it would seem that it would not be out of place to apply the rules above mentioned to her. Hence we cannot say that her testimony as to value was worthless. Furthermore, we think that counsel is wrong in wholly ignoring the testimony of the witness Peterson, from which it appears that oriental rugs are more valuable than domestic rugs, that the former are of better make and workmanship, and that they increase in value with age. Sight must not be lost of the fact that this and all other testimony in the case was to be construed by the jury in the light of their own knowledge and experience. True, the ordinary rule is that a verdict must be based upon the testimony in the case, and the modification of that rule, that the jury can apply their own knowledge to the facts in a case, is limited in extent. But that it can be applied as to matters upon which men in general have a common fund of knowledge and experience is just as settled as the main rule. 16 R. C. L. 303, 304. Wigmore on *Ev.* (2d Ed) § 2570; 64 C. J. 1021-1024; Sedgwick on *Damages* (9th Ed.) § 171a. In fact, in some cases damages may be fixed by a jury upon the mere disclosure of the facts without testimony as to the estimate of the damages. Sedgwick, supra, § 171a. Thus in *Denver Consol. Tramway Co.* v. *Riley,* 14 Colo. App. 132, 59 P. 476, 479, involving the value of the services and companionship of a wife who was injured, the court said that "the husband is entitled to compensation in money for their loss, and the amount of that compensation is to be determined by the jury, not from evidence of value, but from their own observation, experience, and knowledge, conscientiously applied to the facts and circumstances of the case." Again, it has been held that life expectancy may be determined by the jury, without the aid of mortality tables, but from their common knowledge, if they have seen the person whose expectancy of life is in question. *Kawamura*

v. *Honek,* 127 Cal. App. 509, 16 P. (2d) 150; and see additional cases where the value of property was in question. Thus in *Hartman* v. *Pittsburgh Incline Co.*, 159 Pa. 442, 28 A. 145, 146, involving the question of damages for injury to a house, the facts were given, but no estimate of the cost of repair. The court said that "the ordinary intelligence and experience of jurors is sufficient to enable them to say, with reasonable accuracy, how much it would cost to repair damages such as were described by the witnesses in this cae."

Other cases involving measure of damages were cited:

In *Bradford* v. *Steamship Co.*, 147 Mass. 55, 16 N.W. 719, 722, the goods of the plaintiff were valued at about $3,500. They were damaged by salt water and soda ash, against which the defendant had insured the plaintiff. The only evidence offered as to the estimate of the damage was the report of an appraiser, since deceased, who had fixed the damage at about $1,500. This report was held inadmissible, both in the trial and the appellate court. Notwithstanding that the lower court ruled that the jury could find damages against the insurance company in the sum of $500. Said the (Mass.) Supreme Court through Justice Holmes: "We cannot say that a jury would not be warranted in finding, as a matter of common experience, that damages of such a nature, to such goods, could not be less than $500, or somewhat under a third of the value of these goods which were all soaked with the alkali." The case of *Salter* v. *Furniture Co.*, 144 Miss. 194 109 So. 704, 705, involved the value of household goods. The court, after remarking that such value is a matter of opinion, stated: "In addition to the evidence of the witnesses, the jury had the right to apply their own knowledge along with the evidence in the case, and deduce from the whole their judgment as to the value of the property." In *Westerfield & Meeks* v. *Catlett*, 153 Miss. 228, 120 So. 458, 459, the court, after approving what was said in the *Salter* case, further stated that, "in questions of value where there is no market value, but depending upon the character and use of property, and its condition, etc., the law has, of necessity, relaxed the rule of strict, definite, specific proof, and has authorized the jury to take all the available facts pertinent to the question, apply their common sense and experience to such facts, and therefrom deduce the value of the property or the extent of the damages or injury." The case of *Murdock* v. *Sumner*, 22 Pick. (Mass.) 156, was a case of trover for goods. The court held that, if a juror knew of any fact, he should testify to that in open court, and that such fact should not otherwise be considered. But they also said: "The facts were stated by the witness, and also his opinion. But the jurors had full opportunity to exercise their own judgment on the facts, and form their own opinion of the value. . . . The jury may properly exercise their own judgment and apply their own knowledge and experience in regard to the general subject of inquiry. In the present case, the jury were not bound by the opinion of the witness; they might have taken the facts testified by him, as to the cost, quality and condition of the goods, and come to a different opinion as to their value." See, also, *Green* v. *City of Chicago*, 97 Ill. 370, 372; Sedgwick, supra, § 171, and cases cited. But see contra, to some extent, *Chicago, etc., R. Co.* v. *Parsons,* 51 Kan. 408, 32 P. 1083.

Concluding, the court said:

> We need not go as far as some of the cases from which we have quoted, and need not assume that jurymen have general knowledge or experience as to the value of oriental rugs. It would, however, seem that we are justified, from what has been said, and from the authorities from which we have quoted, to come to the following conclusion: The use of common, domestic rugs is so universal that all the members of a jury may well be presumed to have some general knowledge of the value thereof. They had the right to take such general knowledge, and their experience, into consideration in determining the case. They knew, accordingly, without evidence on the subject, at least the fact that such ordinary, domestic rug is of some substantial value. They knew from the testimony, and probably from their general experience, that oriental rugs are of greater value than domestic rugs. The rug in question was in good condition, and special care had been taken thereof. Then there was the age of the rug, which, according to the witness Peterson, made the rug still more valuable. These combined factors were sufficient to show that the rug in controversy had a value of a substantial amount. Further, the jury had the testimony of the plaintiff that the rug was worth $2,500. They discounted that testimony to a considerable extent, which they had a right to do, and they believed that the value was $725. The writer would be more satisfied with the verdict if the amount had been fixed lower, but his judgment, too, would be a mere estimate, based partially on the want of recognition of appreciation of antiques or near antiques. Counsel for defendant states in this brief that, had there been any evidence of value, he would have produced testimony that a new Surac oriental rug could be bought in Denver for $295 to $395. Counsel misjudged the effect of the testimony, and it might have been better if he had produced the testimony mentioned, although, of course, the evidence of the age of the rug in question would still have to be considered. All in all, the value fixed by the jury, and approved by the trial judge, does not seem to be so unconscionably high as to warrant us to interfere. Moreover, counsel for defendant has not contended that the amount fixed by the jury is excessive, if there is evidence legally warranting the jury to give judgment for any amount. We think there was such evidence, and it is accordingly doubtful that, in view of counsel's position, we could give consideration to the amount of the verdict.

In *St. Louis Southwestern Ry. Co.* v. *Kessinger*, 72 S. W. 2d 1105, claimant had shipped certain household goods and wearing apparel from Corsicana, Texas, to Longview, Texas, and although claimant asked for them several times, the railroad agent at destination denied having received them. After suit was brought the railroad located the goods and offered to deliver them. The court held the railroad liable for conversion of the goods and allowed claimants to recover the actual or intrinsic value of the goods since their market value would not fully compensate them. The court said:

The plaintiffs alleged that the defendant converted said freight to its own use and failed and refused to safely and promptly transport and deliver same as per the contract, and that by reason thereof plaintiffs were entitled to recover the value of said property. The case was tried before the court without a jury, and resulted in judgment for the plaintiffs for the sum of $201. . . .

It is appellant's contention that the freight in question was promptly transported by it from Corsicana to Tyler; and from thence to Longview by its connecting carrier, the Southwestern Transportation Company; that upon arrival of the freight at Longview the consignee, after proper notice, failed to call for same, and as a result said freight was stored as required by law. It now offers to deliver the freight upon payment of the storage charges, and here contends that under such circumstances it cannot be held for conversion of the property. On the other hand, Mrs. Kessinger and various other witnesses testified that they made repeated demands at the office of said connecting carrier at Longview for delivery of said freight, and that the agent in charge denied having received same. Two of said witnesses testified that said agent finally admitted having received the freight, but claimed to have delivered the same to a Negro for storage, and that said Negro was then using a part of the household goods; that said agent promised to have said property ready for delivery the following day, but when called upon for that purpose the next day he denied having received the freight. Like demands for delivery of said freight were made upon appellant at its office at Tyler, but with no avail. Mrs. Kessinger and others representing her claim to have sought delivery of said freight over a period of several months.

The court then affirmed the trial findings:

The trial court found that Mrs. Kessinger made repeated demands upon the appellant and its connecting carriers and associates for delivery of said freight, but that they each refused and still refuse to deliver the same. The evidence is sufficient to sustain these findings of the trial court, and the same are therefore binding on this court. Under the findings of the trial court the defendant was liable for conversion for the value of the goods in question. 8 Tex. Jur. 293; *Panhandle & S. F. Ry. Co.* v. *Talmadge* (Tex. Civ. App.), 206 S.W. 862. The trial court found that some of the articles of wearing apparel and household goods sued for were secondhand and slightly used, and that their market value, if any they had, would not adequately compensate appellees for the loss sustained by them. Consequently the court allowed a recovery for the actual or intrinsic value of such articles. The trial court did not err in this respect. 13 Tex. Jur. 156; *Dallas Hotel Co.* v. *Blanchette,* (Tex. Civ. App.), 246 S.W. 1065, par. 5.

Large movements of household goods are usually handled by specialized motor carriers under a bill of lading which differs slightly from the standard uniform bill of lading used by rail and motor carriers hauling general commodities. The tariffs and bills of lading of household goods carriers usually require that the shipper release the goods to "not exceeding . . . cents per pound, per article" while general commodity rail and motor carriers usually provide for release to "not exceeding . . . per pound."

In *Glickfield* v. *Howard Van Lines, Inc.*, 213 F. 2d 723, the court refused to accept the claimant's contention that the carrier should be held liable for full value of the goods because of the carrier's failure to use the exact bill of lading prescribed in its tariffs, inasmuch as the claimant had accepted the lower rate and the different bill of lading used did not in any manner mislead him. The household goods carrier's tariff by rule therein provided that "Unless otherwise provided, when property is transported subject to the provisions of tariff, the acceptance and use of the *Uniform Household Goods Bill of Lading as described herein is required.* The rates shown herein are reduced rates *conditioned* upon the use of the Uniform Household Goods Bill of Lading." The bill of lading used by the carrier differed from the form prescribed in the tariff which has a provision for the declaration of excess valuations for named articles for which an additional charge, not exceeding two percent of excess value, must be made. The form actually used by the carrier, however, provided only that *all* the articles were released to 30 cents per pound per article and "if more than 30 cents per pound per article, strike out 30 cents and insert figure."

Glickfield argued that the bill of lading used contained no provision enabling a shipper to protect certain specified articles by making a declaration of excess valuation as to them. The evidence showed that the bill of lading was not issued for Glickfield's goods until they were picked up by the carrier and, at that time, Glickfield had left New York and the person who tendered the goods to the carrier had no authority to list any particular item for excess valuation even if the proper bill of lading had been presented. Further, it was established that the carrier's agent had when discussing arrangements with Glickfield explained the liability feature but Glickfield had informed him that he was going to get his own insurance from his broker. At that time Glickfield signed an "order for service" in which it was clearly stated in bold type that the goods were released to not exceeding 30 cents per pound per article. In view of these facts, the court in overruling the claimant's contentions said:

> Clearly, therefore, neither the shipper nor the carrier with his insurer were prejudiced by the deviation in the form of the Bill of Lading used. In fact, insofar as the instant shipment was concerned, the issued Bill of Lading spoke the truth and covered every relevant requirement of the Interstate Commerce Act and Commisison's regulations.

While it is true that the provisions of the tariff, as published, are binding upon both the shipper and the carrier as a matter of law, . . . those provisions are not to be read or applied in a manner which would lead to an unjust or absurd conclusion. Where the shipper has not been misled by the deviation, or there is no allegation or proof of an intention or conspiracy to avoid the applicable law it seems to us that the denial of the reduced rate to the shipper or the requirement that the full value should be paid for the damage would be the acme of adherence to form and contrary to the plainest principles of fair dealing. . . .

Section 20 (11) of the Interstate Commerce Acts . . . permits a carrier to limit its liability where it does so in conformity with a Commission authorization for rates dependent upon "the value declared in writing as the released valuation of the property." The Commission, as we have heretofore adverted, has set forth a formula upon which a carrier may base a released value rate. One of the requirements of the Commission's order is that the carrier permit a shipper to protect specified articles in a shipment by declaring an excess value, provided an additional amount not exceeding 2% of the total excess value is charged.

The shipper was charged a rate which had been duly filed and approved by the Commission, and which was based upon a written declaration of released valuation as to the property. Since Glickfield, the eventual shipper, asked for and was quoted the lowest rate and, as we have already related, expressed himself as unconcerned with further details for the reason that he was himself insuring against possible shipment losses, the absence of a provision in the bill of lading for a declaration of excess value on specific items was of no primary importance. The shipper got what he bargained for, and the carrier got what he was entitled to under the statute. . . .

We turn next to Howard's cross-appeal relating to the district court's application of the thirty cents per pound formula in assessing damages. Howard contends that such an award is not supported by the evidence, since the shipper, Glickfield, failed to prove a prima facie case in damages in that he failed to establish that the property was delivered to the carrier in good condition, and he failed to show the nature and extent of the claimed damage and the amount of loss, if any, sustained. The record does not support either of these claims. The main point argued by Howard is that Glickfield estimated the damages by considering their worth in New York and their worth in Los Angeles and in some way by using the difference as an element in assessing damages. It is true that the record shows some confusion caused by a commendable and successful effort to shorten the testimony by stipulation. A memorandum prepared by Glickfield and used by him in his testimony was admitted in evidence under the stipulation that Glickfield would testify in accord with it. The memordanum set out values "in New York" and values in Los Angeles. The witness clearly testified however that the "in New York" phrase as used, meant, not New York values at all, but meant values of the goods shipped in their condition when the carrier picked them up in New York. He explained that all his testimony as to values related to the difference in value in Los Angeles between their condition as the carrier took possession of them and their condition as the carrier delivered them in Los Angeles.

Incidental, Speculative, Rentals, Etc.

A carrier is liable for incidental damage naturally and proximately arising from the loss of, or injury to, property in its possession for transportation, including expenses reasonably and necessarily incurred. Thus in one case involving damage to machinery in transit, the owner's loss of the use of the machinery during the time necessary to repair it was held to be an element of damage and the owner was permitted to recover the rental which would have been earned during the period the machine was undergoing repairs. *Western Machinery Exchange* v. *Northern Pac. Ry. Co.*, 254 P. 248. Remote or speculative damages are not recoverable from the carrier. In *Crichfield* v. *Julia*, 147 F. 65, cert. den. 206 U.S. 593, the Court defined speculative damages as follows:

> The term "speculative damages" is usually applied in cases of breach of contract where money is sought for loss of uncertain or remote profits not within the understanding of the parties, or where there is uncertainty as to whether the party has been, in fact, damaged or whether the damages result from the act of the other party, or where they are wholly uncertain in measure or extent. *Anvil Mining Co.* v. *Humble*, 153 U.S. 540; 8 *American and English Encyclopedia of Law* (2 Ed.) 609. The rule against the recovery of uncertain damages has been generally directed against uncertainty as to cause rather than uncertainty as to measure or extent; that is, if it is uncertain whether the defendant's act caused any damage, or rather, the damage proved flowed from the defendant's act, there may be no recovery of such uncertain damages; whereas uncertainty which affects merely the measure or extent of the injury suffered does not bar recovery.

Special damages, however, are not recoverable in an action against a carrier for loss of, or injury to, property shipped, unless the carrier had notice or knowledge of the peculiar circumstances from which such damages would flow. Where the carrier does have notice or knowledge of the circumstances, special damages may be recovered. Ordinarily, in an action for loss of or damage to goods shipped, only such damages are recoverable from the carrier as were originally contemplated, or which might reasonably have been contemplated, by the parties.

Corpus Juris Secundum, Volume 13, page 618, paragraph 226, cites *Western Manufacturing Co.* v. *The Guiding Star*, 37 F. 641, and *Martin* v. *Delaware, etc., R. Co.*, 141 N. Y. S. 942, for the principle that a carrier is not liable for expense incurred in determining whether there has been injury to a shipment. Further, in *Emery & Co.* v. *Chicago, B. & Q. R. Co.*, 170 N. W. 540, the court held that a shipper could not recover expenses incurred in sending a representative to inspect the goods at point of destination.

Under the head of incidental damages it has been held that any reasonable expense in searching for or attempting to locate or regain possession of goods lost or delayed may be recovered. Thus it has been held that the amount spent in telegraphing and telephoning to trace a shipment is a natural result of the wrongful delay and may be recovered. (*Murrell* v. *Pac. Express,* 14 S. W. 1098; *Haberzettle* v. *Trinity R. Co.,* 103 S. W. 219) There must, however, be a necessity for incurring such expense. (*St. L., etc., R. Co.* v. *Mudford,* 3 S. W. 814; *Lichterman* v. *Barrett,* 157 N. Y. S. 882) Recovery of the amount spent for telegrams, telephone calls, etc., depends upon whether the expenses incurred resulted *in a benefit to the carrier* by lessening the amount of its liability. If the only result of the expenditure was a benefit to the owner of the goods, the expenses are not recoverable.

Volume 13 of *Corpus Juris Secundum,* page 617, defines *incidental damages* as those "naturally and proximately arising from the loss of, or injury to, property in its (carrier's) possession for transportation, including expenses reasonably and necessarily incurred by the plaintiff." Strictly construed, incidental damages must be the result of the loss or injury of the goods. A recent case which illustrates incidental damages is *Illinois Central R. R.* v. *Zucchero,* 221 F. 2d 934, in which damage to a carload of bananas necessitated an additional expense to the claimant for segregating and cutting out the damaged bananas. The incidental expense was made necessary by the damage to the shipment while in the carrier's possession.

Interest; Attorney Fees; Punitive Damages

In the voluntary settlement of claims, interest ordinarily is not allowed by carriers. In the case of suit, courts usually allow interest on the amount recoverable from date of the loss, though in some instances the award of interest is a matter of discretion with the jury. (*Atlantic Coast Line Ry. Co.* v. *Roe,* 118 So. 155; *Ford* v. *Wabash Ry. Co.,* 300 S. W. 769; *Copeland Co.* v. *Davis,* 119 S. E. 19; *Lehigh Valley R. Co.* v. *State of Russia,* 21 F. 2d 396, cert. den. 275 U.S. 571; *International & G. N. Ry. Co.* v. *Reed,* 203 S. W. 410; *Gulf, C. & S. F. Ry.* v. *Morrow,* 66 S. W. 2d 481)

Attorney's fees in the case of suit for loss or damage to an interstate shipment are not allowable. While some state statutes provide for allowance of attorney fees, such statutes can apply only to intrastate shipments. Section 20(11) of the Interstate Commerce Act provides that carriers are liable to the owner of property for the full actual loss, damage, or injury to such property and it would thus seem that attorney fees would not fall within the meaning of damage "to such property."

Some state statutes provide a penalty in a sum stated if a carrier does not pay the claimant for loss or damage within a stipulated period. These statutes do not apply to interstate shipments. Further, a carrier's liability for "loss, damage or injury" to property transported precludes the recovery of punitive damages on interstate shipments. In *Huddy* v. *Railway Express Agency,* 188 S. E. 247, the trial court awarded the plaintiff $2.40 actual damages and $1,000 punitive damages for delay in making delivery of a suitcase containing wearing apparel. In reversing the award of punitive damages, the court said:

> The shipment being admittedly interstate, the measure of damages is governed by the federal law and even though the state of South Carolina permits the recovery of punitive damages against a corporation for breach of public duty, . . . the character of the damages in this case is not to be measured by that law, but by the federal statute and the common law is interpreted by the federal courts in the case of an interstate shipment. *Charleston & W.C. Ry.* v. *Varnville Furn. Co.,* 237 U.S. 597, 35 S. Ct. 715, 59 L. Ed. 1137.

Other cases holding that punitive or exemplary damages cannot be recovered are *Lake Shore, etc., R. Co.* v. *Prentice,* 147 U. S. 101; *Turman* v. *Seaboard Airline Ry.,* 89 S. E. 655; *LeLoach* v. *Southern Ry. Co.,* 90 S. E. 701; *Harman* v. *Southern Ry. Co.,* 90 S. E. 1023.

"Mail Order Company" Claims

Considerable confusion exists on the part of numerous carriers in handling loss and damage claims filed by so-called "mail order" houses which have retail stores located in large cities. This confusion has resulted because the shipments of these companies are sometimes direct to their retail store for over-the-counter sale; on other occasions the shipment will be forwarded to the consumer as a result of mail order purchase; and, in some instances, the shipment will be destined to a "catalog order office" to await delivery to ultimate consignee. In each of these situations, the measure of damages varies to some extent and each will be discussed to indicate the basis upon which carriers are generally settling such claims.

On shipments moving *from the general warehouse* of a mail order company *to one of its branch stores or branch warehouses,* the correct measure of damages would be the mail order company's cost (including warehousing and handling expense at the central warehouse) and freight charges, when freight charges to destination have been paid. Under no condition should damages on these shipments be calculated on the retail basis unless it definitely can be shown that a specific sale has been lost.

On shipments from the mail order company *direct to its customer,* the claim will usually be made upon the customer's price, as shown on the customer's invoice from the mail order company. In the event the shipment was lost, the shipper is entitled to receive what he would have received had the carrier completed delivery—the invoice price. The fact that the shipment may be duplicated and the shipper actually realize two profits is not material, since there is no duty on the consignee to order a replacement nor upon the shipper to send a replacement. If the shipment is damaged, the carrier is liable for the depreciated value or reasonable costs of repairs. The carrier should be afforded a reasonable opportunity of negotiating with the customer in regards to having repairs made or having the consignee accept an allowance for the damage, and the shipper should refrain from shipping a replacement until the carrier has had this opportunity.

The third situation in connection with mail order company claims arises out of shipment made from mail order companies to what are termed "catalog order offices." These offices are usually located in communities where the mail order company does not have a retail store, although some are operated in conjunction with retail stores. The agent of the catalog order office will not carry any stock on hand and customers merely come into the order office, look over the catalog, and decide what merchandise they wish to purchase. At the end of a specified period, the agent at the order office consolidates all orders he has received and forwards them to the mail order company. In time a consolidated shipment, filling all orders received from the particular order office will be forwarded in bulk and move under one bill of lading, showing the mail order company as shipper and the order office as consignee. These shipments are not made direct to the customer and the customer has a right to inspect the goods upon arrival at the order office. Pending acceptance at the order office by the customer, therefore, they remain the property of the mail order company. The correct measure of damages in such instances is the mail order company's cost (including warehouse and handling expense) plus freight, if paid.

It is obvious that a carrier is at a great disadvantage in verifying the mail order company's cost in connection with claims in which the measure of damages is the company's cost plus warehousing and handling expense. Likewise, it is no easy matter for these large shippers to determine or approximate these amounts accurately. In the voluntary settlement of claims there is a growing tendency on the part of shipper and carriers to compromise these claims on the basis of 85 percent of invoice (catalog) price. From a practical and legal viewpoint, there is considerable merit to the argument that the claimant is entitled to full retail price since this merchandise is shipped to fill a contract of sale, but if the shipment is replaced this argument is weakened considerably.

While this discussion relates primarily to mail order company claims, it should not be thought that carriers handle claims for such shippers on basis different from the claims of other shippers. Claims of other shippers similar to the factual situation involved in connection with mail order company claims as discussed are handled in the same manner.

When No Market at Destination

In *Green* v. *Railroad Co.*, 128 Mass. 221, in connection with determining the measure of damages where goods were not intended for sale or have no market value, the court said:

> The general rule of damages . . . for not delivering the goods undoubtedly is the fair market value of the goods. But this rule does not apply when the articles sued for are not marketable property. To instruct a jury that the measure of damages for the conversion or loss of a family portrait is its market value would be merely delusive. It cannot with any propriety be said to have any market value. The just rule of damages is the actual value to him who owns it, taking into account its cost, the practicability and expense of replacing it, and such other considerations as in the particular case affect its value to the owner.

In *International, etc., Ry. Co.* v. *Nicholson,* 61 Tex. 550, the lost articles were secondhand clothing, books, and furniture, which the court held could not have had differing values to plaintiff at different places. Neither could plaintiff have duplicated the goods in the open market. The court held that in these circumstances the value of the goods to their owner was the proper measure of damages: "Not any fanciful price that he might for special reasons place upon them, nor, on the other hand, the amount for which he could sell them to others, but the actual loss in money he would sustain by being deprived of articles so specially adapted to the use of himself and his family."

Where articles which cannot in any fair sense be said to be marketable and have a market value, or at least to have a market value which is fairly indicative of their real value to their owner and of his real loss by being deprived of them, the proper measure of damage for their loss or conversion is their value to the owner based on his actual loss considering all the circumstances and conditions, but not including any sentimental or fanciful value which he may for any reason have placed upon them. (*Twersky* v. *Pennsylvania R. Co.*, 273 N. Y. S. 238)

Reconditioning, Assorting, Etc.

Where the consignee in an effort to mitigate the damages incurs expenses for reconditioning or assorting goods, such being required because of carrier's failure to perform its duties properly, the carrier will be liable for the reasonable cost of such services. In *Collins* v. *Texas & P. Ry. Co.*, 123 So. 504, the claimant was allowed to recover expenses of reconditioning the goods where such service was necessitated by the carrier's negligence. Such allowance, however, is authorized only when the expenditures are made in a just expectation of reducing carrier's liability by the amount expended. *Kennedy* v. *Atchison, T. & S. F. Ry. Co.*, 181 P. 117. From the court cases, it is clear that in order to recover the expense of reconditioning and assorting goods the claimant must establish that the expenditures incurred were in the interests of the carrier and as a result the carrier's liability was reduced.

Where separate shipments of pig iron becomes mixed while in transit, the carrier becomes liable for the reasonable cost of assorting the goods upon delivery. In *Inland Waterways Corp.* v. *Sloss Sheffield S. & I. Co.*, 136 So. 849, the plaintiff shipped through the Southern Railway a shipment or shipments of eight cars of pig iron. Four cars contained the pig iron marked with "red" dots and the other four held pig iron marked with "white" dots for the purpose of classification. The carrier issued two separate and distinct bills of lading, one for the four cars with the "red" dotted pig iron and one for the four cars with the "white" dotted pig iron. During transportation the pig iron in the eight cars was mixed and the court held the carrier liable for the reasonable cost of assorting the shipment of destination.

Reconsigned Shipments

The measure of damages in connection with reconsigned shipments is the same as in those instances where there has been no reconsignment, the correct measure usually being the difference in the value of the shipment in the condition it arrived and the value it would have had if it had arrived without injury.

Released Rates

An exception to the general rule that the carrier shall be held liable for the "full actual loss, damage, or injury" is provided by Section 20(11) of the Interstate Commerce Act, which permits the establishment of rates based upon the declared or released value of the property transported, which declared or released value thus becomes the measure of the carrier's maximum liability. The pertinent provision reads as follows:

> The provisions hereof respecting liability for full actual loss, damage, or injury . . . shall not apply . . . to property . . . received for transportation concerning which the carrier shall have been or shall hereafter be expressly authorized or required by order of the Interstate Commerce Commission to establish and maintain rates dependent upon the value declared in writing by the shipper or agreed upon in writing as the released value of the property, in which case such declaration or agreement shall have no other effect than to limit liability and recovery to an amount not exceeding the value so declared or released, and shall not, so far as relates to value, be held a violation of section 10 of this part to regulate commerce, as amended; and any tariff schedule which may be filed with the Commission pursuant to such order shall contain specific reference thereto and may establish rates varying with the value so declared and agreed upon; and the Commission is hereby empowered to make such order in cases where rates dependent upon and varying with declared or agreed values would, in its opinion, be just and reasonable. . . .

The foregoing procedure furnishes the only way in which a carrier validly may restrict its liability to less than the "full actual loss, damage or injury." Historically, the development of released rates as presently authorized goes back to the enactment of the Carmack Amendment to Section 20 of the Interstate Commerce Act, which prohibited limitations of liability.

The purpose of Congress in passing the Carmack Amendment was two-fold—to completely regulate all commerce, and to hold the initial carrier liable for loss, damage, or injury caused by it or a connecting carrier. (*Atlantic Coast Line* v. *Riverside Mills,* 219 U.S. 186; *Adams Express* v. *Croninger,* 226 U.S. 491)

Although Congress under the Carmack Amendment provided that a carrier was liable for "any loss, damage, or injury," the Supreme Court in deciding the *Croninger* case held that a carrier by a fair, open, just, and reasonable agreement could limit the amount recoverable in case of loss or damage to an agreed value made for the purpose of obtaining the lower of two or more rates or charges proportioned to the amount of risk. The *Croninger* case was soon followed by a series of similar decisions. (*Boston & Maine R. R. Co.* v. *Hooker,* 233 U.S. 97; *Atchison, T. & S. F. Ry. Co.* v. *Robinson,* 233 U.S. 173; *Kansas City So. Ry. Co.* v. *Carl,* 227 U.S. 639) In all of these cases the Supreme Court held that tariffs filed with the Interstate Commerce Commission were conclusively presumed to be a part of the transportation contract, and therefore binding upon both the carrier and shipper.

The situation created by the *Croninger* and similar cases resulted in the enactment of the first Cummins Amendment to Section 20 on 4 March 1915, which contained the following provision:

> Provided, however, that if the goods are hidden from view by wrapping, boxing, or other means, and the carrier is not notified as to the character of the goods, the carrier may require the shipper to specifically state in writing the value of the goods, and the carrier shall not be liable beyond the amount so specifically stated, in which case the Interstate Commerce Commission may establish and maintain rates for transportation, dependent upon the value of the property shipped as specifically stated in writing by the shipper.

The effect of the first Cummins Amendment was to overcome the Supreme Court's decisions in the *Croninger* and similar cases and, generally, to restore the principle of full liability for property transported except where the goods were hidden from view, etc., in which case the carrier could require the shipper to specifically state their value in writing, and the carrier's liability would not be for more than the amount so stated. The first Cummins Amendment was found to be impractical and as a result the present second Cummins Amendment was enacted and became effective 6 August 1916. This amendment eliminated the proviso relating to goods hidden from view, etc., and substituted the present wording.

The only purpose in publishing rates dependent upon the declared or released value of the property transported is to limit the carrier's liability in case of loss or damage. Under the present statutory requirements, the released rate not only must be *expressly* authorized by the Interstate Commerce Commission but the carrier's tariff filed with the Commission pursuant to a released rate order must contain specific reference thereto. The mere publication of released rates under authorization of the Commission is not sufficient to effectively limit the carrier's liability, however, as the second Cummins Amendment further provides that such rates can be established only in connection with "value *declared in writing* by the shipper or *agreed upon in writing* as the released value of the property."

The ground upon which a declared or agreed value is upheld is that of estoppel. (*American Ry. Exp. Co.* v. *Lindenberg,* 260 U.S. 584;

Union Pac. R. Co. v. *Burke,* 255 U.S. 317) It would not be just to have a shipper understate the value of his property for the purpose of reducing the rate and then recover a larger value in case of loss. (*Hart* v. *Pennsylvania R. Co.,* 112 U.S. 331) On the other hand, if the specified amount does not purport to be an agreed valuation but has been fixed arbitrarily by the carrier without reference to the real value, or if the specified amount, while purporting to be an agreed valuation, is in fact purely fictitious and represents an attempt to limit the carrier's liability to an arbitrary amount, the carrier cannot be heard to complain if the stipulation is held to be no bar to the recovery of the full and actual value of the loss or damage. (*In re Released Rates,* 13 M.C.C. 550)

The most frequent use of released rates is in the transportation of household goods. Movers generally limit their liability by the establishment of rates based upon a declared or released value of 30 cents per pound per article, and their tariffs publishing such rates aptly serve to illustrate the ways in which shippers affirmatively declare the value or simply agree upon a released valuation and how the carrier's corresponding charges are assessed.

The suggested form of "Combined Uniform Household Goods Bill of Lading and Freight Bill" contained in such tariffs provides spaces for the shipper's declaration of value, his signature, and the itemized listing of articles having a value in excess of the declared value of the balance of the shipment. The table of transportation rates that makes up the bulk of such tariffs is limited in its application to shipments released to a value declared not to exceed 30 cents per pound per article. When household goods are shipped pursuant to tariffs published under released rates orders, it is customary for the carrier to point out to the shipper the advisability of purchasing insurance to provide greater protection than is afforded under the carrier's released rates. The fact that the shipper has purchased trip transit insurance does not relieve the carrier of its liabiltiy for loss or damage to the household goods shipped. On the contrary, the trip transit insurance policy ordinarily contains a subrogation clause permitting the insurance company to proceed against the carrier in the shipper's stead and, where the shipment has been made at the base rate, the insurance company will seek to recover from the carrier such amounts as it has paid in settlement of the shipper's claim, subject, of course, to the limitation upon the carrier's liability.

Some of the court cases dealing with the carrier's liability for loss or damage to shipments made upon released rates shed further light upon the measure of the carrier's liability.

In *Caten* v. *Salt Lake City Movers & Storage Co., Inc.,* 149 F. 2nd 428, the plaintiffs arranged with the defendant carrier to ship their household goods and personal effects from Gouverneur, N. Y., to Pawtucket, R. I. While the goods were en route defendant's van caught fire and the shipment was totally destroyed. The defendant had undertaken to transport plaintiffs' property following the receipt of a letter from Robert Caten containing a list of the goods and a request for the approximate cost of the service. The defendant replied by letter, giving an estimate of the weight and of the cost figured upon that basis. Later the goods were loaded by defendant and taken to be weighed.

After the weight was ascertained, defendant telephoned Caten and informed him of the weight (4,650 pounds) and asked what valuation was to be placed on the shipment, saying, "You are allowed 30 cents a pound under the Government bill of lading." Caten replied that he carried insurance on it to the amount of $3,000 and was informed by the carrier that $2,000 in insurance in addition to the 30 cents per pound liability would cost $5.00, making the entire charge for freight and insurance $153.25. Caten instructed the carrier to procure the insurance and at once sent the defendant a check for $153.25, which was duly received. There was no declaration of value by the shippers other than as embraced in the related transactions, and no bill of lading or receipt was issued and delivered to the shippers, although a bill of lading was made out in which the rate was based on a valuation of 30 cents per pound. That bill was carried by a van when it started for Pawtucket and it was destroyed in the fire without ever having been seen by the shippers. In deciding that the carrier was liable for the full actual loss, the court stated:

The statute makes it abundantly clear that the carrier's common law liability for full actual damages whether or not caused by its negligence is imposed when it accepts goods for carriage, unless a certain specified agreement limiting that liability has been made as the result of an equally certain specified action by the shipper in respect to a voluntary valuation of his goods. Even then the carrier is not permitted to contract against liability for its own negligence. Only by giving the shipper an opportunity to choose between higher and lower rates based upon valuation can the carrier place the shipper who has selected a lower rate in the prescribed manner in the position where he is estopped to assert loss or damage to an amount in excess of the declared valuation upon which the rate was fixed. (*Boston & Maine R. R.* v. *Piper,* 246 U.S. 439; *Hart* v. *Penn. R. R.* 112 U.S. 331; *Union Pacific R. R.* v. *Burke,* 255 U.S. 317) Here nothing was done by the shippers which amounted to written action by them as to valuation and any agreement limiting the defendant's liability to less than the actual value was void. Therefore it was correct for the District Court to instruct the jury that the defendant was liable for the full value of the plaintiff's goods.

Thus, in the *Caten* decision the court indicated that even where released rates are authorized by the Commission and the carrier's tariff makes proper reference thereto, the statute further requires some affirmative, direct and positive act which the court terms *written action.* This written action constitutes a condition precedent to a carrier's right to make an effective limitation of liability.

Written action does not necessarily mean that the shipper's signature must be affixed to the declaration or writing although, as indicated in the *Caten* case, the signature "does furnish good evidence that he did declare or agree in writing." It is enough, according to the U.S. Supreme Court's decision in *American Railway Express Co.* v. *Lindenburg,* 260 U.S. 584, if the shipper accepted the bill of lading containing a limited valuation clause and the benefits accruing from the lower rates. In *Loeb* v. *Friedman's Express, Inc.,* 65 N. Y. 2d 450, cert. den. 331 U.S. 851, a bill of lading was issued by the carrier and received and signed for by the shipper. The released valuation clause was not filled in and the freight charges were not prepaid. The evidence further indicated that a bill for freight charges was not rendered to plaintiff until after the carrier became aware that the entire shipment had been lost. In deciding this case, the court stated:

> Here the charges constituting the freight rate were not entered in writing on the bill of lading, nor were those charges prepaid by the shipper. It could not be said, therefore, that having accepted the benefit of the lower rate dependent upon a specified valuation, the shipper is estopped from asserting a higher value; nor could it be said in this case even on the basis of a presumption of knowledge on the part of the shipper of the rate-valuation relationship, that there was anything in writing on the bill of lading to constitute an agreement as to valuation.

In *Rabb* v. *Railway Express Agency, Inc.,* 95 N. E. 2d 784, it was held that the agreement of released value must be delivered to the shipper at the time the goods are accepted for transportation or as soon thereafter as practicable and, where the receipt is not given until after the loss has occurred, the carrier is not exempted from full liability. In this case, Ida Rabb had purchased a mink coat in 1943 in New York City at the wholesale price of $1,800. The coat was thereafter insured by her with an insurance company for the amount of the purchase price. In 1946, Mrs. Rabb delivered the coat to her husband, Ben P. Rabb, for shipment to New York City for cleaning and storage. The coat was enclosed in a box addressed to the consignee, and Mr. Rabb, an attorney, took the package to his office and instructed his secretary to call the express company to pick up the shipment. Bernard Oros, a uniformed driver for the carrier, came to Rabb's office. It was undisputed that Rabb and his secretary asked Oros for a receipt before delivering the package to him and that the driver was unable to give a receipt as his blank forms had been left in the truck. Both Rabb and his secretary testified that they gave him the package after taking his badge number and upon his promise to make out a receipt upon returning to his truck and to return it to Rabb's office. Also, it was testified that Oros was instructed to insure the coat for $3,800. Oros, however, testified that he was told that the package contained a cloth coat valued at $100. He further testified that Rabb was in a hurry and instead of waiting for the driver to go to the truck and return with the receipt apparently was satisfied with the notation made from his badge number.

Upon reaching the truck, Oros made out a uniform receipt in quadruplicate. The first carbon of the receipt was placed upon the package and the second and third copies were turned in at the express office; the original, which should have been delivered to Rabb, the driver destroyed. About two weeks later, upon learning that the coat had not been delivered, Rabb wrote to the defendant notifying them of that fact and requesting that a search be made for it. Three days later, an employee of the defendant called on Rabb for the purpose of collecting the freight charges of 67 cents. This employee had with her the payment receipt which was the second carbon copy of the uniform receipt. This receipt indicated that the declared value of the package was $100. At that time Rabb denied that he had given this amount of valuation but paid and accepted the receipt anyhow because he had not other evidence of shipping the coat. Suit was instituted against the carrier by Mrs. Rabb and the insurance company. In holding the express company liable for full value the court said:

> We find no dissent from the general rule that a uniform receipt or bill of lading limiting the liability of a carrier for damages must be delivered to the shipper at the time the goods are accepted for transportation or promptly mailed to the shipper in due course of business unless there is an agreement that such instrument shall be delivered at a later time. *Harris* v. *Great Northern R. R.*, 96 Pac. 334; *Clubb* v. *Hetzel*, 198 Pac. (2d) 142, 165 Kan. 594; *Behrends* v. *Chicago Rock Island Pac. Ry.*, 198 Ill. App. 236.

In *Chicago, R. I. & P. Ry. Co.* v. *Geissler*, 61 P. 2d 14, the court held that a shipper of household goods having elected to ship under a certain rate, the rate automatically fixed the value of the shipment, and shipper could not thereafter recover a greater value for the damage to or loss of his property. The railway company's agent had solicited the carriage of the household goods from San Francisco to Oklahoma City and told the plaintiff that the rates of competing lines were uniform and specified by the Interstate Commerce Commission. The plaintiff prepaid the freight charges and directed that the goods be shipped.

The agent made out a bill of lading releasing the goods to $10.00 per hundredweight. The plaintiff did not sign this bill of lading or see it until some time after the goods arrived at destination. Plaintiff was not asked to declare the value, did not know of this limitation until the claim arose, was not informed that the carrier's tariff established five classes of values and that his goods were to be released to the lowest value provided. Plaintiff contended that the bill of lading did not constitute the shipping contract because of his lack of assent thereto and the illegality of such contract as a limitation upon defendant's common law liability. In refusing to accept this contention, the court said:

> In the case before us, the uniform straight bill of lading under which these goods were shipped constitutes the contract of the parties by virtue of the force of law; the rate for carriage agreed upon between the parties carried with it all of the legal effects prescribed by the laws of the United States and the rules and regulations of the Interstate Commerce Commission thereunder; and the plaintiff's ignorance thereof or inattention thereto make no difference. The plaintiff's recovery, if any, is limited by the terms of the shipping contract. The judgment of the trial court is reversed, and the cause is remanded.

In *Glickfield* v. *Howard Van Lines, Inc.*, 213 F. 2d 723, the shipper who requested and paid the base rate was limited in seeking to recover for loss or damage to the releasd value of 30 cents per pound per article, as set forth in the applicable tariff, even though the form of the bill of lading differed from that set forth in the tariff.

In *Stricker* v. *Chicago & Northwestern Railway System,* 40 N. W. 2d 30, the plaintiff's son-in-law in Iowa arranged with the carrier's agent to have fourteen boxes and crates of household goods picked up and shipped to California. The agent was instructed to present the bill for the freight charges to the local bank and that arrangements had been made with the bank to pay the charges. The agent had a local drayman pick up the goods. When the drayman turned over the goods, the agent billed the shipment out but failed to indicate in the printed release rate clause the amount, if any, to which the goods were released.

Under the section of the bill of lading entitled "Description of Articles," the agent indicated that the shipment consisted of personal effects and household goods and inserted the words "Rel @ 20.00 cwt." Neither the plaintiff or anyone in her behalf ever signed the bill of lading or any other instrument connected with the shipment. When the goods arrived at destination, the carrier collected additional charges from the consignee and advised that the shipment was two boxes short. Plaintiff brought suit for $850, the value of the goods lost. The carrier argued that its liability was limited to $121.57 upon the theory its liability was limited to $20.00 per hundred pounds weight of the lost boxes. In denying that the words "Rel @ 20.00 cwt." constituted an effective limitation of value, the court said:

> Plaintiff contends this language is insufficient to comply with the statute. It is not a common expression. Nor is its meaning generally understood. Defendant deemed it necessary to explain such meaning to the court by the testimony of Shearman "the letters . . . meant released at $20.00 per hundred weight." However, no explanation was made to the housewife consignee or her son-in-law who was listed as shippers, neither of whom was shown to have had any special knowledge of shipping. They should not be bound by cryptic symbols whose meaning is unintelligible to the average shipper. . . .
>
> We hold the expression "Rel. @ 20.00 cwt." under the heading, "Description of Articles," etc., was insufficient to constitute a declaration of value or an agreement fixing the released value of the property, within the requirements of the statute.

In the preceding case, the carrier also argued that the plaintiff was presumed to know the tariffs and limitations of values based thereon, and it contended that, having accepted the benefits of the lower rate dependent upon the specified valuation, plaintiff was estopped to assert a higher value. The court denied this contention and pointed out that the goods were billed out by the carrier without any disclosure, suggestions or instructions by plaintiff or her son-in-law concerning valuation and rates, and there had been no course of conduct to justify the carrier in assuming that transportation at the lower rates with reduced liability was desired. The court found that the present case was subject to the same rule as applied in the *Caten* case, as well as *Smith* v. *Pippin,* 188 Va. 869, 51 S. E. 2d 159, and *Clubb* v. *Hetzel,* 165 Kan. 594, 198 P. 2d 142.

In *White* v. *Southern Railway Co.,* 38 S. E. 2d 111, the court noted that even though ordinary shippers are unfamiliar with the provisions of carriers' tariffs, nevertheless by law they are charged with constructive knowledge of the applicable tariffs and "conclusively presumed" to know their provisions. The plaintiff and his wife had moved from West Virginia to South Carolina and instructed a storage company to forward four trucks of household goods and personal effects to him when notified and also arranged to have his father-in-law ship his household furniture. The freight charges in both instances were prepaid and the carrier presented evidence that at the time of prepayment the bills of lading indicated that the goods were released to ten cents per pound and that this had been written on the bills by the carrier's rate clerk. The plaintiff failed to produce the original bills of lading, and since under the law it was the carrier's duty to issue bills of lading, the court would not presume that the carrier had not observed its legal duty and concluded that plaintiff's agents must have received bills of lading from the carrier when the shipment was made. The court limited plaintiff's recovery in this case to the released value, even though it was not evident that plaintiff or his agents had been informed that by paying a higher rate greater liability would be imposed.

In *Miller & Miller Motor Freight Lines* v. *Gilliland,* 232 S. W. 2d 886, Gilliland negotiated with Hearne Motor Freight to ship household goods from New Mexico to Texas. Hearne delivered the goods to Miller & Miller at Lubbock to transport to destination. There was no bill of lading issued to Gilliland, but *after the goods were shipped,* Hearne issued and delivered a bill of lading to Gilliland's mother in Hobbs, New Mexico, and she later mailed it to Gilliland. When the shipment was delivered at Wichita Falls, a box of tools worth $322.50 was missing. Gilliland brought suit for this amount, and the carrier defended on the grounds that recovery should be limited to $13.00, based on release at 10 cents per pound as shown by the bill of lading issued after the shipment moved. The court relied upon the *Caten* case and allowed the claimant to recover full value since the requisite "written action" on the part of the shipper had not been established.

In *Emily Shops, Inc.* v. *Inter-State Truck Line, Inc.,* 139 N. Y. S. 2d 561, affirmed 161 N. Y. S. 2d 46, cert. den. 355 U.S. 815, the court held that where the carrier agreed with the shipper on a flat charge in excess of the tariff charge, such disregard of its proper rates by the carrier precluded it from profiting from limited liability set out in the bill of lading. In this case the plaintiff delivered merchandise to the carrier in New York for transportation to Pennsylvania. The bill of lading contained a release of value under the terms of which the "carrier will not assume any liability in excess of 50 cents per pound, or 50 dollars minimum." At time of shipment, the plaintiff and the carrier agreed upon "the flat sum of $115.00" as freight charges. Under the applicable tariffs filed with the ICC, the freight charge for the shipment should have been $35.59 if, as was the case, it was released, or if shipped unreleased, the charges should have been $69.18. The goods were lost in transit. Plaintiff claimed that it was entitled to recover from the carrier the full value of the goods ($6,155.93) while the carrier argued that it was only liable for 50 cents a pound which amounts to $75.00 and for excess freight charges it collected. The court in awarding full recovery said:

> The flat sum deal made by this defendant was not a choice of rates either at common law or under the Interstate Commerce Act. Where the statute and the rates are completely disregarded and there is actually no choice of rates, the liability limitations of the statute do not apply.

While it is clear that carriers can effectively limit the amount of recovery by complying with the released rate proviso of Section 20, it is equally clear that having done so it is not always easy to determine in case of loss or damage the amount to which claimant is entitled. If the limitation of liability is lawfully affected, the maximum recovery is the total released or declared value in the event all of the goods are lost or destroyed. Where there is only partial loss or damage, however, there are several schools of thought as to the proper procedure in measuring the amount of recovery.

The great difficulty in connection with measure of recovery under released rates arises in those instances where it is necessary to give some consideration to the actual value of the goods in determining the measure of recovery. The only purpose of released rates is to effectively limit the carrier's liability to less than the full value of the goods, and there is no serious difficulty in ascertaining the measure of recovery until an effort is made to give some weight to actual value of the goods.

The law is well settled that in cases where a contract of carriage fixes the value of a shipment as so much per pound, per hundredweight, per ton, or by some other unit of weight or measure and the rate is calculated upon such agreed value, the recovery in case of partial loss is limited to the agreed value, per unit, of that part of the shipment which was lost, for the claimant is estopped from asserting any unit to have a greater value than the per unit value declared. *Kansas City So. R. Co.* v. *Carl,* 227 U.S. 639; *Western Transit Co.* v. *A. C. Leslie & Co.,* 242 U.S. 448; *United Lead Co.* v. *Lehigh Valley R. Co.,* 141 N. Y. S. 310, affirmed 109 N. E. 1094; *Boyle* v. *Bush Terminal Co.,* 210 N. Y. 389, 104 N. E. 933.

A review of rail and motor carrier authorized released rates indicates, generally, that the shipments are released on the basis of so much per 100 pounds or per pound. The rail and motor carrier uniform straight bills of lading in the released rate clause on their face provide that the agreed or declared value is stated to be not exceeding" . . . per . . ." The wording of this clause and the manner in which common carrier released rates generally are established are sufficient, it is believed, to provide clearly that in event of partial loss or damage, the claimant's recovery is limited to a ratio basis. In the case of *Western Transit Co.* v. *Leslie, supra,* the Supreme Court said:

> The contention was also made that the judgment below was correct, even if the bill of lading be held to govern the warehousing at Buffalo; because the agreed valuation clause properly construed fixes an amount far greater than the actual value for which judgment was rendered. The "released" or agreed valuation is "$100 per net ton." There were 25 tons in this shipment. It is insisted that, as the 25 tons constituted a single lot, $2,500 is recoverable for loss of or damage to the whole or any part of the lot. This construction does violence to the language used and is unreasonable. The valuation clause fixes not an arbitrary limit to recovery but a ratio.

Where a shipper declares the value of his shipment, it is still incumbent upon the claimant to prove the true value. In *Rothstein* v. *Railway Express Agency,* 170 A. 406, the claimant brought suit against the carrier for $100 each on five shipments of merchandise on which the value of each shipment had been declared as $100. In holding that the claimant was still required to establish the value of the goods, the court said:

> While a carrier such as defendant may limit its liability to an amount declared in writing by the shipper or agreed upon in writing, the plain language of the statute provides that such declared value "shall have no other effect than to limit liability and recovery to an amount not exceeding the value so declared or released." Such being the case, the carrier was not bound by the value declared by the shipper and to recover it was incumbent on the shipper to prove the true value, the same not having been admitted by the pleadings.

Even though a state law may permit the recovery of punitive damages against a carrier, the measure of damages on interstate shipments is governed by federal law and the common law as interpreted by the federal courts. In *Pastime Amusement Co.* v. *Southeastern Express Co.,* 186 S. E. 283, the state (South Carolina) court upheld a verdict for $1,500 damages as a result of the failure of the express company to deliver a movie film in time to be shown, as advertised, on Labor Day, September 1, 1930, and the following two days even though the express bill of lading limited the carrier's liability to $50.00. This holding upon appeal was reversed by the United States Supreme Court. The facts in this case indicated that the film entitled *Anybody's War,* weighing less than 100 pounds, was shipped from Jacksonville, Florida, on August 29 in sufficient time to arrive in Charleston, South Carolina, before Labor Day. The express receipt covering the shipment provided that under the rate charged, "The shipper agrees that the (express) company shall not be liable in any event for more than fifty dollars for any shipment of 100 pounds or less. . . ."

Although the shipment was properly marked, the express company sent it to Charlotte, North Carolina, and this error prevented the film's arriving in Charleston until too late on September 3 to be of any value to the plaintiff. Suit was instituted for $3,000 actual and punitive damages and a verdict was returned for $1,500. The South Carolina appellate court affirmed this verdict on the ground that a carrier could not contract against its liability for negligence, that the action arose in tort for damages rather than for breach of contract, that the defendant had knowledge that if delivery was not made promptly special damages would result, and that failure to deliver promptly was not only a breach of the carrier's duty but a violation of public duty. In reversing this decision in *Southeastern Express Co.* v. *Pastime Amusement Co.*, 57 S. Ct. 73, the United States Supreme Court said:

> The broad purpose of the federal act is to compel the establishment of reasonable rates and to provide for their uniform application. Special contracts are not permitted to give any advantage to a particular shipper. *Chicago & Alton R. Co.* v. *Kirby*, 225 U.S. 155, 166, 32 S. Ct. 648, 56 L. Ed. 1033. Ann. Cas. 1014A, 501. *The liability in this instance is thus governed by the provisions of the applicable tariff and no recovery could be had in excess of the amount permitted by its terms. New York, Philadelphia & Norfolk R. Co.* v. *Peninsula Produce Exchange*, supra, 240 U.S. 34, at pages 41, 42, 36 S. Ct. 230, 60 L. Ed. 511, L. R. A. 1917A, 197; *Southern Railway Co.* v. *Prescott*, 240 U.S. 632, 638, 36 S. Ct. 469, 60 L. Ed. 836; *American Railway Express Co.* v. *Daniel*, 269 U.S. 40, 42, 46 S. Ct. 15, 70 L. Ed. 154. (Emphasis added.)

Where the carrier has converted goods to its own use, it cannot invoke the released value for its protection but, on the contrary, will be liable for the full value of the goods converted. In *Van Dyke* v. *The Pennsylvania Railroad Co.*, 8 Federal Carrier Cases, paragraph 80, 742 the plaintiff shipped from Washington, D. C., a trunk weighing 550 pounds, containing personal effects and released to value of 10 cents per pound. When the truck arrived in Dover, plaintiff presented her bill of lading to the freight agent of the carrier and requested delivery of the shipment. Although the bill of lading indicated that charges had been prepaid in Washington, the agent refused to make delivery because his records indicated that the shipment was to move on a collect basis. Twelve days elapsed before the agent verified that the charges had actually been prepaid and that plaintiff was entitled to have her trunk without paying additional charges.

The trunk, however, had disappeared and plaintiff brought suit to recover $665, the full value of its contents, on the grounds that the railroad by its refusal to make delivery at the time demanded had converted the trunk to its own use. The court denied this contention pointing out that while the carrier can never invoke protection of the released value where there has been a *true* conversion of the goods by the carrier itself for its own gain, in this case it had not been established that the carrier had converted the trunk to its own use and gain, and said: "The wrongful conduct as alleged on the part of the defendant's agent in this case falls within the same classification as indicated in cases involving failure to deliver, including misdelivery and nondelivery, negligence, embezzlement by agent, and such other courses of conduct which under the Carmack Amendment do not render inapplicable the stipulation relating to the restriction of liability." In *Normann* v. *Burnham's Van Service*, 73 So. 2d 640, recovery for the loss of 48 pounds of garments and liqueurs shipped by a Naval Reserve office, and assumed to have been fraudulently taken by the carrier's employees, was limited to $14.40 in the absence of proof of the actual conversion of the goods by the carrier for its own use.

Cost of Repairs

The carrier is liable for the reasonable cost of repairing damaged merchandise. This not only includes cost of labor and material but may also include a reasonable amount for *overhead*. It is pointed out, however, that the carrier's liability for damage to goods transported is the difference between the value of the property at the time and place of delivery in uninjured condition and its value in the depreciated condition in which it was delivered, less freight charges to point of destination if not already paid. In addition to the damages directly resulting from damage to the goods, the carrier is also liable for any other incidental expense reasonably and necessarily incurred in reconditioning or putting the goods in salable condition. (*Olcovich* v. *Grand Trunk Ry. Co.*, 176 P. 459; *Galveston, H. & S. A. Ry. Co.* v. *Standard Rice Co.*, 34 S. W. 2d 619; *Western Machinery Exchange* v. *No. Pac. Ry. Co.*, 254 P. 248) The effect of repairs, however, must be to enhance the value of the goods at least to the extent of the cost of the repairs. If the repairs serve only to increase rather than mitigate the damages, they are improper and cannot be recovered.

Replacement Costs

Generally, the carrier's maximum liability in case of loss or damage is the destination value of the goods shipped. As to many commodities, however, the goods shipped have no readily ascertainable market value. In many instances, the goods ordered by the consignee may be a commodity entirely new to the community and perhaps one in which no one else would have any interest. In most of these instances, the invoice value of the goods will provide a ready method for measuring the claimant's full actual loss, damage, or injury but this is based on the assumption that the consignee can reorder the goods on the same basis as the lost, destroyed, or damaged, or damaged shipment. In some instances, however, the consignee may under certain circumstances be compelled to replace the goods by a purchase on the local market or he may have to reorder from the same source or another source but at a price in excess of the invoice on the shipment injured. In this event, the carrier usually is held liable for the increased replacement cost. The carrier is, of course, entitled to the salvage where the goods have been replaced.

The United States Supreme Court said in *Illinois Central R. Co.* v. *Crail,* 50 Sup. Ct. 180:

> But respondent contends, as was held below, that the established measure of damages for nondelivery of a shipment of merchandise is the sum required to replace the exact amount of the shortage at the stipulated time and place of delivery, which in this case, would be at its retail value, and that convenience and the necessity for uniform rules require its application here. This contention ignores the basic principle underlying common law remedies—*that they shall afford only compensation for the injury suffered. . . .*

As the court said in *Gore Products, Inc.* v. *Texas & N. O. R. Co.,* 34 So. 2nd 418:

> It is true that the plaintiff delivered to the carrier an (article) to substitute for the one which was destroyed, but we do not think that the defendant's liability should be fixed at the amount required to reimburse plaintiff merely for the cost of manufacturing one (article). What would be the situation if the second (article) had been lost, or even a third or fourth? Could plaintiff be required to manufacture goods for the defendant at cost?

In *Bachos* v. *Chicago, R. I. & P. R. Co.,* 61 S. W. 2nd 416, the claimant bought some used motors at a government auction at his own price of $69. He directed that they be shipped to him and the carrier, in his absence, shipped them under a bill of lading describing them as *junk motors.* Upon arrival at destination the motors were found to have been damaged in transit and they had to be sold as junk. The carrier contended that since the motors were described as junk and sold by the claimant as such, claimant got their full value. The court, however, denied this contention and allowed claimant to recover for the value of *used motors.*

Retail Price

If profit has been *earned* by the claimant but is lost because of carrier failure to perform its duties properly by delivering all of the goods in good order, the claimant is entitled to recover such profits as an element of his full actual loss, damage, or injury. For example, a store may accept an order from a customer for a $100 bed, while in transit the bed may be damaged and as a result the customer may refuse to accept it and demand either refund of his money or a replacement. If the shipper refuses to refund the money or to replace the shipment, it is obvious that the consignee purchaser is entitled to recover his purchase price from the carrier because without question that represents his full loss. Likewise, if the consignee simply refuses to accept delivery because of the damage, refuses to accept a replacement, and demands refund of his purchase price if paid, it is obvious that the shipper has lost a sale because of carrier's negligence and is entitled to receive the invoice (retail) price because that represents his full actual loss. Further, if consignee refuses the shipment but agrees to accept a replacement, the shipper (or consignee) is entitled to recover the price paid or agreed to be paid because there was no duty upon the consignee to accept a replacement nor was there a duty upon the shipper to replace it and in reality two separate sales have taken place.

There is a prevailing objection on part of carriers to the words *retail price* because the words are often considered in connection with a wholesale shipment to a store of goods to be advertised and sold to the retail trade and under such circumstances, of course, the store cannot recover retail price from the carrier since such recovery would include profit which has not been earned. A different situation exists in those instances where a retailer has sold merchandise to the retail trade and earned his profit and thereby justified recovery of what he would have obtained if the carrier had properly performed its duties. Again, it is possible that a store may have sold merchandise to a customer which in order to secure the purchase price requires that it have the goods shipped to it by its supplier. If the sale has been completed and the only remaining task is to deliver the goods and carrier's failure to do this properly results in loss of sale, the store is entitled to recover the contract price which it has earned but lost due to the carrier's negligence.

In other instances as result of carrier's failure to perform its duties properly, the consignee may be compelled to replace goods injured or lost by purchasing locally or from a source at a higher price, and under such circumstances the claimant is entitled to recover the replacement or retail cost if the circumstances warranted this procedure. Where a lost or damaged shipment is capable of replacement, the consignee is entitled to recover the actual cost of replacing the lost or damaged goods and this, of course, would not include the profit which consignee anticipated making by selling the goods. In other words, if the article lost or damaged is to be placed in stock and it is not necessary to purchase at destination an article to replace that injured or destroyed, recovery of the difference between invoice price and the retail price cannot be had.

This question was fully explored in *Gore Products, Inc.* v. *T. & N. O. R. Co.*, 34 So. 2d 418, where the court distinguished between claims including *prospective* profits and those where the goods actually were sold and moved under a contract of sale. Of the latter type, the court said:

> In the case now before us, the plaintiff, which is the manufacturer, had already sold the goods to its customer in Mexico by contract, and in line with the authority cited by plaintiff we feel that in this case the measure of plaintiff's loss is the price which it would have received from its customer in Mexico, which price was also the market prevailing at New Orleans the place of origin of the shipment. . . .
> It is true that plaintiff delivered to the carrier a carboy of medicine to substitute for the one which was destroyed but we do not think that the defendant's liability should be fixed at the amount required to reimburse plaintiff merely for the cost of manufacturing one carboy of medicine.

One of the questions most frequently asked concerns situations in which it is proper to include an amount labelled *profit* in claims filed for freight loss, damage, or delay. When a carrier damages goods which are later sold at a markdown from the usual retail price, what is the measure of damages? What is the proper measure of recovery when claims are filed on goods moving from distributors to retail dealers? May a consignee recover the profit on a sale which was made before the goods were lost or damaged? May a claimant recover the profit on a sale made before shipment if goods are returned for reason other than carrier fault? May a consignee recover the full cost of repairs to damaged goods even though he is able to make an advantageous trade with the repaired goods so that the net effect is to leave him in a better position than before the injury?

There is no formula covering every situation. Section 20(11) of the Interstate Commerce Act provides that carriers shall be liable for the claimant's "full actual loss, damage, or injury." While this is a uniform rule for determining the measure of damages, the Act does not spell out the method of ascertaining the full actual loss, damage or injury. The problem has been litigated frequently and carriers may look to court decisions which state the rule in similar instances. Unfortunately not every conceivable set of facts has been before the court, and even when a case or cases are found which seem in point, it is difficult to find a court decision on an identical fact situation.

What was the actual loss to the claimant? The law, generally, seeks to restore an injured party to the position he would have occupied except for the injury. The court in *Atlantic Coast Line Ry. Co.* v. *Roe,* 118 So. 155, stated: "The basic thought underlying the federal statutes which define the liability and prescribe the measure of damages in cases of this kind is that the owner shall be made whole by receiving the proper money equivalent for what he has actually lost or, in other words, to restore him to the position he would have occupied, had the carrier performed the contract." The law does not generally contemplate that a profit shall be made out of the misfortune of one liable for an injury. The law will not, however, prevent collection of a profit already earned solely because recovery is made from one injuring the goods and thereby preventing the contract from being executed in the usual manner. As a general rule, a claimant is entitled to his profit if he has done every act necessary to complete his contract and the only act remaining undone is delivery. In many instances, the question of profit may be resolved by determining whether the goods had been sold before the injury and were moving under a contract of sale at the time of injury. In such a situation, no further act is required of the shipper and he has *earned* his contract price, which includes profit.

When damaged goods are sold for a markdown from the normal retail price, the amount of markdown is a convenience measure of the damage experience and frequently is the only measure. When the sale was completed before injury and the injury is the cause of the parties being unable to complete the contract, the measure of recovery is, as stated, the contract price. But if the contract could not be executed, even had there been no injury, no profit has been *earned* and none should be recovered. This generally occurs when goods, though sold, are undeliverable for other than carrier fault and are lost or damaged while awaiting instructions from the shipper or on the return movement. The fact that the claimant is able to make an advantageous trade of the repaired goods does not entitle carrier to avoid part or all of the cost of making repairs. The *profit* results from claimant's trade, which is a separate transaction from the damage and repair for which the carrier is liable.

Goods Returned to Shipper

The determination of claimant's recovery for loss or damage to goods which are being *returned* depends upon the factual situation involved in each particular case in an effort to develop the answer to the controlling principle—"What was the claimant's full actual loss?" Some merchandise is shipped to consignee on a consignment or inspection basis and is later returned to the original supplier. Clearly, in these instances, a sale has not been accomplished and the original shipper has failed to *earn* a full profit. Nevertheless the terms of the sale may be such that until the returned goods actually are received by the original supplier the party returning them is charged with their invoice price. If, as a result of the carrier's negligence, the party returning them is compelled to pay the invoice price then obviously the extent of the claimant's full actual loss is the invoice price, as it is evident that if the carrier had completed its contract the party returning the goods would have received credit equivalent to that price. While the determination of the amount of recovery under such circumstances presents a close question, it is believed that failure to allow the claimant recovery of the invoice price would fall short of allowing him his full actual loss. If the carrier had faithfully performed its duties, claimant would have received the invoice price and no sound reason for denying him this recovery is readily apparent.

In other instances, the claimant will return defective merchandise to his supplier for full credit or for an adjustment. Until the supplier has received this merchandise and examined it, no credit or adjustment is allowed by the supplier. As a general rule, defective merchandise has no market value other than as junk or scrap, such values being nominal, and yet to the party returning such goods in expectation of receiving credit or adjustment, the value of the goods is much higher. As a matter of law, where goods have no market value their value is determined by their worth to the owner. While no court cases directly involving the point have been located, it is believed that under such circumstances the owner would be entitled to recover the credit he would have received but for the carrier's negligence unless the goods have been described in such manner as to indicate to the carrier that they had a lesser value.

Goods Salvaged by Consignee

As has been pointed out, the consignee has the legal obligation to accept delivery of goods which have not been damaged to such extent as to be worthless for the purpose for which intended and to take all necessary and reasonable steps to mitigate the damages. The extent of a carrier's liability for damage is generally the difference between the value of the goods in the condition delivered and their value in the condition in which they should have arrived. The consignee in disposing of damaged goods must make every reasonable effort to realize the best price obtainable. Damaged merchandise should not be sacrificed against the carrier's interests. In *D'Olier* v. *New York Cent. R. Co.*, 98 N. Y. S. 649, the plaintiff brought suit for damage to certain cases of cotton yarn. The shipment consisted of 14 cases of yarn on cones. Upon arrival at destination, five of the cases were broken and the yarn in them damaged. There was no damage to the other nine cases. The plaintiff, however, sold the entire shipment as damaged goods. The court in its decision, however, held that the carrier was liable for only the five cases which arrived in damaged condition:

> In awarding damages as if the whole shipment had been damaged, the (lower) court followed the speculative and fanciful testimony of plaintiff's witnesses, to the effect that the fact that a few cases out of a shipment had been injured would so affect the reputation of the whole shipment in the eyes of the trade, that a fair price could not be obtained even for the uninjured merchandise; a proposition which appears to be quite unreasonable. . . . If the plaintiff's assignors suffered the loss for which they sue, it is because they took no pains to reduce their damages, or to obtain a fair price for so much of their equipment as was uninjured.

In *Cleveland, C. C. & St. L. Ry. Co.* v. *Stormont*, 187 N. E. 838, the carrier's contention that claimant was entitled to recover only the difference in value of a shipment of eggs in good condition and their value after reconditioning was overruled, the court holding that plaintiff was entitled to recover the difference in value of the eggs had they arrived in good condition and their value in the damaged condition in which they arrived. The evidence in this case indicated that if the eggs had arrived in good condition they would have been reasonably worth $2,760. Due to carelessness of the carrier, however, upon arrival a large number of eggs were found to be broken and cracked and the remainder stained and discolored to such extent that their market value was depreciated to $2,160. Claimant contended that he was entitled to the $600 difference but the defendant carrier pointed out that the consignee did not sell the eggs in the condition in which they arrived but reconditioned them and sold them for a price in excess of $2,160 and that to permit him to recover $600 would allow him to make a profit on this suit. In this case, the claimant was able to present evidence to indicate the value of the goods in damaged condition. This, however, is not always possible. Usually the consignee will repair or recondition the goods and hold the carrier liable for the difference in value of the goods in their reconditioned or repaired condition and their value in the condition in which they should have arrived plus cost of repairs or reconditioning.

In *Railway Express Agency* v. *McCarrick*, 69 S. W. 2d 803, it was held that the fact that a witness states that a car of radishes which arrived in a damaged condition was sold for the best price obtainable, but does not state the date nor that such price was the reasonable market price, does not sufficiently establish the market value of the shipment at the time it arrived.

In *Cedar Rapids Hide and Fur Co.* v. *Railway Express Agency, Inc.*, 46 N. W. 2d 545, the court held that a verbal agreement made between a carrier and consignee prior to acceptance of a damaged shipment which fixed an agreed amount of damages to be paid by the carrier upon tender of claim by consignee did not contravene the Interstate Commerce Act. In this case, the shipper delivered a shipment of green muskrat pelts to defendant and when they arrived at destination some of them had become spoiled and damaged due to delay enroute. When the consignee was about to refuse the shipment because of the damage, the carrier requested him to accept the shipment at once in order to salvage as much as possible and thus decrease the damages. A joint inspection report was prepared stating the cause of the damage as delay and fixing the salvage value of each skin at fifty cents and the loss on each skin at $1.05 and the shipment was then accepted. The carrier denied, however, that any promise was made that the claim would be paid but the trial court found otherwise. The carrier's motion for a new trial was denied and the case was appealed on the grounds that any agreement as alleged would have been a special contract and void because of being in violation of the Interstate Commerce Act. This the appellate court rejected, saying:

> The promise of the defendant to pay these damages was in no way in contravention of any provision of the Interstate Commerce Act or of its amendments. The plaintiff's claim for damages was a legitimate one. . . . It was in con-

sideration of the initial damages, and the plaintiff's acceptance of the shipment and salvaging service, that defendant agreed to pay the claim. One of the objects of the Interstate Commerce Act and the various amendments thereto, was to prevent unjust discrimination against some shipper and preferments to others. It does not prohibit legitimate settlements of damages caused by carriers, or arrangements made with a shipper to salvage property so damaged.

Goods Transported to Shippers' Warehouses

In some instances, a shipper will consign its merchandise to a warehouse or branch store where the goods are to be held for its account pending sale or distribution. This merchandise may or may not be covered by an invoice. On occasions the invoice may indicate that the consignee warehouse or branch store is charged with the price for which the goods are to be sold, and in these instances the invoice is used more for accounting purposes than for reflecting the value of the goods. Some concerns such as chain clothing stores, oil well suppliers, distributors, etc., have established their bookkeeping procedures under a system which does not reflect that their outlets earn any profits whatever; in other words, the goods consigned to such branches are charged to the outlet on the basis of the price which will be obtained when the goods are sold to purchasers. It is obvious, however, that until such goods have been sold such profit as reflected in the charge to the branch has not been *earned* and the expense incident to earning such profit has not been incurred. In settling claims for loss and damage on movements under these circumstances, profit which *has not been earned* should therefore be excluded.

Where a manufacturer has produced a product or a business concern obtained a product, an investment motivated by anticipated profits has been made and definite steps toward earning that profit undertaken. It is therefore no easy matter to determine at a stated time exactly how much profit has been made above manufacturing costs or investment in purchase. Where it is possible to determine the wholesale selling price of the merchandise or similar merchandise, a good indication of value is secured. Where the goods are sold on a commission basis at an established or ascertainable retail price, the reduction of the retail selling price by the amount of such commission will usually properly reflect the value. In *Baltimore & O. C. T. R. Co.* v. *Becker Milling Mach. Co.*, 272 F. 933, the plaintiff manufactured a special type of milling machine which it sold through agents. Due to tremendous demand plaintiff was unable through its own facilities to manufacture sufficient machines to supply the market and engaged the Miehle Company to fabricate 200 of these machines for it for $1,850 each. While some of these machines were in transit to Boston, they were damaged and the question as to amount plaintiff should be permitted to recover was presented to the court. The court held that the plaintiff was entitled to more than the manufacturing cost but less than the price for which the agents sold the machines. The court said:

> Manifestly the cost of replacement was more than $1,850 for we know from common knowledge that the expense of maintaining engineering and experimental departments in factories, as well as expense for superintendance and all other proper items of overhead, must be apportioned to products and charged as parts of the manufacturing cost. Defendant engaged to deliver the machines at Boston, and therefore must compensate plaintiff for the loss caused by failure to deliver. . . .

In ascertaining damages there is no objection to profits as such where profit has been *earned,* and it is only when an attempt to ascertain profits leads to conjecture and speculation that profits are rejected. The court in the foregoing case, in any event, said: "Plaintiff in no event would be entitled to more than compensation for its actual loss; and the burden was on the plaintiff to show what that loss was with that degree of certainty of which the case is capable." In view of this, it would seem that under this case the plaintiff's recovery would depend upon its proof of actual loss and that the value of the machines would approach the selling price to the public less the agent's commission.

While in general the courts have in the past based their decisions upon the rule that the destination value is the measure of carrier's liability, the tendency in the more recent decisions is to restrict the owner, whether consignor or consignee, to his actual loss as determined from the evidence put before the court, depending upon the terms of the contract of sale, the business methods of the plaintiff, and the circumstances under which the shipment was made. See, in this connection, *Bernet, Craft & Kaufman Milling Co.* v. *N. Y. C. & St. L.,* 260 S. W. 508.

Carriers are liable to the claimant for the "full actual loss, damage, or injury" suffered by the owner of the goods shipped. This presents a question of fact, i.e., what was the claimant's actual loss? In answering this question, the facts of each case must receive consideration. Manufacturers have invested enormous sums in equipment and other facilities with the expectation of deriving some profit from these expenditures. If the manufacturer should be restricted to his actual manufacturing costs, it would be possible for him to spend thousands of dollars manufacturing an article, thousands to sell it for a profit and then lose the entire investment as a result of carrier's negligence in failing to perform the service it had agreed to perform under its bill of lading contract.

In the carrier industry, for-hire carriers make their services available to the public with the expectation of deriving profit from service rendered. No patron expects the carrier to give such service purely on a cost basis and, likewise, carriers cannot expect manufacturers to operate their equipment solely for the benefit of a carrier which has through negligence lost or destroyed the shipper's merchandise. If the carrier loses the merchandise or damages it completely, the owner has the right to expect the carrier to compensate it fully and restore it to the same position it would have enjoyed had there been no loss or damage.

By the very process of manufacture, the manufacturer usually creates a product which has value in excess of the cost of raw material, labor, and overhead. Most manufactured products have a market value (retail selling price) and while additional effort after manufacture is necessary to *earn* this profit, certainly it would seem unjust to restrict claimant to its cost of manufacture when the product has an established retail price which the claimant is well on the way to earning.

It would appear that the correct measure of damages for loss of goods moving from point of manufacture to the manufacturer's warehouse is the wholesale selling price less wholesaler's commission. In the *Becker Milling Machine* case, *supra,* a similar problem was involved and the court restricted the owner of the goods to his actual loss, i.e., its wholesale price less commission, stating that this would be the measure of damages whether the goods were sold through "manufacturer's agents" or branch houses of the manufacturer. The court excluded the selling costs (commission) on the ground that they had not been borne by the manufacturer and could not therefore be charged against the carrier. If the shipper is merely a distributor and secures merchandise from a supplier and adds nothing to its value, such distributor could probably be limited to its cost of securing replacement, etc., where a sale had not been completed.

Special Damages

Special damages are not ordinarily recoverable from the carrier unless the carrier actually knew, or reasonably could be expected to know, that such special damages would naturally follow upon failure to safely and promptly transport the property. Black's Law Dictionary defines special damages as:

> . . . those which are the actual, but not the necessary, result of the injury complained of, and which in fact follow it as a natural and proximate consequence in a particular case, that is, by reason of special circumstances or conditions. Hence, general damages are such as might accrue to any person similarly injured, while special damages are such as did in fact accrue to the particular individual by reason of the particular circumstances of the case.

Unless the carrier is informed by the shipper at the time of shipment of the urgency and the circumstances requiring unusual dispatch or handling, or reasonably might be expected to have known them, it cannot be held liable for special damages. The reason for this rule is well founded on the principle that if one of the parties to a contract is to be made liable for extraordinray damages, it is right that before the contract is made he should have notice of the exceptional circumstances that may warrant them, in order that he may decline, if he wishes, to make a contract which will increase his risk. As a common carrier, if he receives an article for transportation after having received notice of the special circumstances, he is conclusively presumed to have contracted with reference to the enlarged liability and afforded the opportunity of using special diligence and employing extra precaution to guard against the increased risk. (*American Express Co.* v. *Jennings,* 86 Miss. 329, 38 So. 374)

A carrier is not liable for loss of profit as result of delay in transportation where it had no notice that the goods were intended for immediate resale and special damages would result if delayed. In *Missouri Pacific R. R.* v. *S. L. Robinson Co.,* 65 S. W. 2d 902, appellees ordered from the shipper four or five cars of strawberry crates to be shipped as ordered from time to time during the strawberry season. When the first car was ordered it came from origin to destination in three days. Knowing from this the approximate time required for transportation, appellees when they began to run low on crates ordered additional crates about four days in advance of the time they anticipated running out of stock on hand. When they ordered the second car shipped, they notified the carrier's agent at destination to start tracing the car so that it would not be delayed. Appellees sold the last of the crates in the first car the night before the second car should have arrived. If the second car had arrived in the same time as the first, appellee would have had the crates on hand to supply demand without interruption. The second car, however, was two days late and appellees were unable to supply demand and suffered a net loss of $260.94 in profits. When the car did arrive, appellees sold the crates at a net profit of $260.94. The appellees argue that since they were out of the crate selling business for two days during the season they are entitled to recover the profit which they would have made if the car had been delivered promptly.

In rejecting this contention, the court said:

> In this case there is no evidence tending to show, either that appellees had already made contracts to sell the crates, or that they gave any notice to the carrier, at the time of the shipment of the fact that the crates were desired for immediate sale or that there would be any special damages because of delay. There is no claim that any notice of special damages were given. Such notice must be given in order to recover special damages, or the evidence must show that the carrier had knowledge of the special circumstances, and this notice or knowledge must be at or before the shipment is made.

See also *Chicago, R. I. & P. Ry.* v. *Newhouse Mill & Lumber Co.*, 90 Ark. 452, 119 S. W. 646. In *Southwestern Bell Tel. Co.* v. *Carter,* 181 Ark. 209, 25 S. W. 2d 448, the court gave the rule for assessing special damages: if the party in default had notice that more than ordinary damages would result from the failure to perform, or if such knowledge "be brought home to the party sought to be charged under such circumstances that he must know that the party he contracts with reasonably believes that he accepts the contract with the special condition attached to it."

In contrast, in *Chicago, R. I. & P. Ry.* v. *Miles,* 92 Ark. 573, 123 S. W. 775, the court held that, "Having notice of the special damages that would result to appellee if he failed to get his cattle to that auction sale, and having contracted with appellee after such notice to deliver them for that sale, appellant cannot be heard to say that the damages that appellee sustained by reason of the loss of that particular sale were not in contemplation of the parties to the contract." See also *Chicago, R. I. & P. Ry.* v. *Thomas,* 118 Ark. 406, 176 S. W. 681. As to one manner of acquiring notice, see *St. Louis-S. F. R. Co.* v. *State,* 179 Ark. 1128, 20 S. W. 2d 878.

Where the carrier is given notice that unless the shipment arrives promptly loss of a sale is likely, the carrier is liable for special damages in the event it fails to transport the goods with reasonable dispatch. In *Southeastern Express Co.* v. *Bowers, Inc.,* 109 S. W. 2d 851, the shipper had in stock a large number of size 6-7/8 hats which appear to be in demand only in foreign countries, and had entered into an agreement to sell 50 dozen of these hats for six dollars per dozen upon the condition that they be shipped to arrive in New York City on May 2 so that they could be reshipped to South America by boat on that date. The evidence indicated that when the express company's truckman arrived at plaintiff's premises to pick up the hats he was notified that unless the shipment arrived at destination May 2, plaintiff would probably lose the order. There was also evidence indicating that some one at the express office was informed similarly over the telephone. Due to the defendant's negligence, the hats did not arrive in time and were refused. Plaintiff brought suit for $300, the contract price. The court held that plaintiff was entitled to recover on this basis but that the carrier was entitled to some credit since the hats were not entirely worthless. The court said:

> If the carrier accepts the goods for transportation with full notice that the goods are sold subject to being seasonably delivered, the consignor is entitled to recover the difference between the contract price and the value of the goods when actually delivered, if by reason of unreasonable delay in transportation he loses the sale.

The law of damages does not supersede the contractual principle that one may refuse to enter a contract which will impose an extraordinary liability upon him. In *Kansas City, M. & O. R. Co.* v. *Bell,* 197 S. W. 322, and *Conn.* v. *Texas & N. O. Ry.*, 14 S. W. 2d 1004, the courts held that each successive carrier is bound by the knowledge of the originating carrier as to likelihood of special damages. This, however, would relate to the connecting lines' liability to the claimant and if the originating carrier failed to pass on to its connecting lines the knowledge as to urgency, etc., as between carriers the originating carrier would be liable to reimburse its connecting carriers for any special damages they were required to pay.

Taxes, Recapture when Included in Claims

A great deal of uncertainty exists with respect to whether or not taxes can be properly included as an item in the measure of damages on loss and damage claims filed with carriers. These questions usually arise in connection with shipments of distilled spirits and shipments of tires and other commodities upon which an excise tax has been paid.

In connection with shipments of distilled spirits, uncertainty exists because of a provision in the Internal Revenue Code which was changed in 1942. Prior to 1942 the Code provided, in substance, that where distilled spirits upon which the internal revenue tax had not been paid were lost by theft, accidental fire, or other casualty while in the possession of a common carrier subject to the Transportation Act of 1920, no tax should be assessed or collected upon the distilled spirits so lost. It will be observed that two conditions were present in this part of the Code: (1) The tax had *not* been paid, and (2) common carriers were limited to those subject to the Transportation Act of 1920, the railroads. This section of the Code was amended in 1942, and the protection offered to the railroads under the old section was expanded to cover all types of common carriers and made more specific.

Section 2901 of the Code, as amended in 1942, now provides that the Commissioner of Internal Revenue may, under regulations, abate any internal revenue taxes accruing on distilled spirits if he finds that: (1) The distilled spirits were not stolen or intentionally destroyed, but were lost otherwise than by leakage and evaporation while being transferred between buildings constituting the same internal revenue bonded warehouse, or while being transferred by common carrier from the premises of a registered distillery to an internal revenue bonded warehouse of such registered distillery's premises, or while being transferred by a common carrier between internal revenue bonded warehouses; (2) the distilled spirits were withdrawn for use in the fortification of sweet wines and were not stolen or intentionally destroyed but were lost, otherwise than by leakage or evaporation prior to such use while being transferred to, or while stored in, the fortifying room of the bonded winery premises; (3) the distilled spirits were lost by theft from the premises of a registered distillery, or while being transferred between buildings constituting the same internal revenue bonded warehouse, or while being transferred by common carrier to an internal revenue bonded warehouse of such registered distillery premises, or while being transferred by a common carrier between the internal revenue bonded warehouse, and that such loss did not occur as a result of connivance, collusion, fraud, or negligence on the part of the distiller, owner, consignee, consignor, bailee or carrier, or the employee of any of them; and (4) the distilled spirits were withdrawn for use in the fortification of sweet wines and were lost by theft prior to such use while being transferred to, or while stored in, the fortifying room on the bonded winery premises, and that such loss did not occur as a result of connivance, collusion, fraud, or negligence on the part of the distiller, owner, consignor, bailee, or carrier, or the employes of any of them.

When in any of the foregoing instances the tax is paid *subsequent* to the loss or destruction, as the case may be, the Commissioner is authorized to refund such tax. This indicates that in all of the situations the tax is not paid at the time the loss occurs, and the Code provision is limited to very few situations where carriers are suffering losses.

There is levied on all distilled spirits a tax by the federal government, the provisions of which are found in Section 2800 (a)(1) and Section 2800 (c) of the Internal Revenue Code. The tax, which amounts to a specified sum per gallon, is paid by the distiller or importer when withdrawn from bond or imported and attaches to distilled spirits, alcohol, or alcoholic spirits as soon as this substance is in existence as such. Once the tax has been paid and the liquor has been removed from the bonded warehouse, none of these exemptions found in the Code, Section 2901, apply. Most of the difficulties encountered by motor carriers are under circumstances where the liquor has left the bonded warehouse and is being transported to either wholesalers or retail merchants. There are no provisions in the Code for any refund of taxes after the tax has been paid and the liquor has left the bonded warehouse. Consequently, where claim is made for loss of liquor being transported after payment of the tax, the amount of the tax must be considered as part of the value of the liquor and computed in the claim for any loss or damage.

An entirely different situation from the federal excise tax on distilled spirits is found in connection with the excise taxes on such commodities as tires. In these situations, the tax involved is a tax on the sale by a manufacturer, producer, or importer. To determine whether or not the tax is applicable, it therefore must be further determined whether or not a sale has actually been consummated. Ordinarily where goods are sold F.O.B. destination, they would remain the property of the shipper until they had reached destination in good order. Upon reaching destination, ownership would be transferred to the purchaser and only then would the sale be consummated and the tax attached. Where goods are shipped F.O.B. point of origin, the usual case, a different situation would ordinarily prevail. Immediately upon delivery of the goods to the carrier the sale would be completed and the merchandise would become the property of the purchaser. The sale having been completed, the tax would be attached and could not be recovered, even though the shipment might be destroyed while in possession of the carrier and before delivery to the purchaser.

The Internal Revenue Service has ruled informally that in all cases where the manufacturer replaces stolen or destroyed merchandise subject to excise tax on no-charge basis, the excise tax should not be included in the claim paid by the carrier for such stolen or destroyed shipment. The service holds that only one sale has been completed even though the manufacturer has made a replacement shipment, and consequently only one tax is due. In connection with this ruling, tire manufacturers have represented that:

1. It is not standard practice in the tire industry to physically replace tires lost in transit on a no-charge basis.

2. It is standard practice in the tire industry, to sell to dealers on the basis of F.O.B. point of shipment, which means that title passes and the sale is complete when the goods are delivered to the carrier. It is common practice in the tire industry for the manufacturers to undertake to collect claims for goods lost in transit as a service to the dealer. In so acting, the manufacturer is an agent of the dealer, because title has already passed to the dealer at point of shipment.

The service, on the basis of the foregoing representations, has ruled that:

1. If the tires are not physically replaced on a no-charge basis, the carrier is liable for the tax if the sale has been completed.
2. If the tires are sold to dealers on the basis of F.O.B. factory, freight allowed, title has passed and a complete sale has been made, subjecting the tires to the applicable excise tax.

Carriers should not hesitate to determine whether or not the manufacturer is actually the agent of the consignee in filing a claim by demanding that the manufacturer present evidence of an assignment of consignee's interests. The determining factor as to whether or not the tax is properly included in any claim depends upon whether there has been a completed sale and, in the case of a replacement, whether there has been one or two sales. Where the merchandise has been lost or completely destroyed and shipper makes replacement on a no-charge basis, there is only one sale and consequently only one tax.

6

Freight Forwarder Claims

Definition of Forwarders

Section 402 of the Interstate Commerce Act, 49 U.S.C. §1002, defines the term *freight forwarder* to include any person who (otherwise than as a carrier subject to parts I, II, or III) holds itself out to the general public as a common carrier to transport or provide transportation of property, for compensation, in interstate commerce, and who, in the ordinary and usual course of its undertaking (A) assembles and consolidates or provides for assembling and consolidating shipments of such property, and performs or provides for the performance of break-bulk and distributing operations with respect to such consolidated shipments; (B) assumes responsibility for the transportation of such property from point of receipt to point of destination, and (C) utilizes, for the whole or any part of the transportation of such shipments, the services of a carrier or carriers subject to part I, II, or III of the Act. The operations of freight forwarders are described in *Chicago, Milwaukee, St. Paul & Pacific R. Co.* v. *Acme Fast Freight, Inc.*, 336 U.S. 465.

Statutory Liability of Forwarders

Statutory liability of freight forwarders (as in the case of rail and motor carriers) is found in the Interstate Commerce Act.

Section 413, 49 U.S.C. §1013, provides:

The provisions of section 20(11) and (12) of part I of this Act, together with such other provisions of such part (including penalties) as may be necessary for the enforcement of such provisions, shall apply with respect to freight forwarders, in the case of service subject to this part, with like force and effect as in the case of those persons to which such provisions are specifically applicable, and the freight forwarder shall be deemed both the receiving and delivering transportation company for the purpose of such section 20(11) and (12). When the services of a common carrier by motor vehicle subject to part II of this Act are utilized by a freight forwarder for the receiving of property from a consignor in service subject to this part, such carrier may, with the consent of the freight forwarder, execute the bill of lading or shipping receipt for the freight forwarder. When the services of a common carrier by motor vehicle subject to part II of this Act are utilized by a freight forwarder for the delivery of property to the consignee named in the freight forwarder's bill of lading, shipping receipt, or freight bill, the property may, with the consent of the freight forwarder, be delivered on the freight bill, and receipted for on the delivery receipt, of the freight forwarder.

Widely different results flow from transportation by rail carriers for freight forwarders when compared with effect of movement of forwarder shipments by motor carriers. Where freight forwarder shipments are transported by rail carriers (at least in the case of the great majority of tonnage) an individual bill of lading contract is made between the forwarder and rail carrier covering the rail movement, and the rail lines apply a rate published to apply upon the rail transportation. In such instances, the rail carriers are not concerned with the actual origin of the shipments nor their ultimate destinations, as there is no arrangement for a through movement, rate, etc. Since a bill of lading contract covers such rail movement, the freight forwarder stands in relationship of a shipper and consignee to the rail carrier and is bound by all of the contract terms and conditions of the bill of lading, including the time limitation of nine months for filing claims. See *Republic Carloading and Dist. Co.* v. *Missouri Pacific R. Co.*, 302 F. 2d 381.

Claim Relations with Other Carriers

In utilizing the services of motor carriers, two methods are available to freight forwarders. One method can be described as *assembly and distribution service,* the other as *linehaul service.* In utilizing motor carriers for assembly and distribution, the motor carrier employed does not issue its bills of lading when receiving the goods from shippers nor does it utilize its own bills or delivery receipts in making delivery to the consignees. In performing these services, the motor carrier serves the freight forwarder as its agent and the pickup and delivery is made in the name of and on documents of the freight forwarder. In other instances, the forwarder may use the motor carrier's service in the same manner as any other shipper and, in this event, its relation to the carrier is exactly the same as any other shipper.

Freight forwarders are subject to the provisions of Section 20(11) and (12) of the Interstate Commerce Act in the same manner as motor and rail carriers, but with the additional provision that for the purposes of these sections the forwarder shall be considered both the receiving and delivering transportation company. In view of this, a motor carrier would not be statutorily liable to a claimant where the claim arose out of a shipment moving under a forwarder through rate; any liability of the motor carrier to claimant would therefore have to be based on common law. In the absence of statutory liability and proof of common-law liability, an originating or delivering motor carrier is justified in refusing to accept a claim filed by a shipper or consignee on a forwarder shipment where the carrier's records failed to indicate that the injury to the shipment occurred while the shipment was in its possession. As a practical matter, however, when motor carriers receive such claims they usually investigate them and handle them direct with the forwarding company in order to facilitate disposition. It is clear, however, that under Section 413 (see p. 380), unless the originating or delivering motor carrier was responsible for the injury to the shipment, the motor carrier cannot be held liable for the full actual loss, damage, or injury under the provisions of Section 20(11).

In its decision in *Bill of Lading of Freight Forwarders,* 259 I.C.C. 227, the Commission stated:

> Under section 413 the forwarder, as above indicated, is made the "receiving and delivering transportation company" for the purpose of section 20(11) and (12). It is not a connecting carrier within the meaning of the act. From the standpoint of the shipper, the forwarder is the "transportation company" upon whom responsibility is placed by section 20(11) for the issuance of a receipt or bill of lading and for any loss, damage, or injury to the property caused by it or any common carrier, railroad or other transportation company to which such property may be delivered or over whose lines such property may pass.

In deciding *Rhea Manufacturing Company* v. *Acme Fast Freight, Inc.,* 47 M.C.C. 280, the Commission said:

> As stated, . . . from the standpoint of the shipper the forwarder is a "transportation company" under section 413 of the act, but it is not a connecting carrier within the meaning of the act. In relation to the common carrier, however, the forwarder has the characteristics of a shipper. In view of this twofold relationship, when these shipments were consigned to Milwaukee care of Acme at Baltimore they were actually consigned to Acme as intermediary agency between the consignee and common carrier and not as a connecting carrier.

> Thus, under general rules of law, the delivery of the goods by the consignor to the common carrier Red Line and the issuance by latter of the bill of lading showing Acme as the consignee insofar as the carrier was concerned, placed the shipment subject to the control of Acme upon execution of the bill of lading at Danville. . . .

In *Chicago, Milwaukee, St. Paul & Pacific R. Co.* v. *Acme Fast Freight, Inc.*, 336 U.S. 465, the Supreme Court of the United States held that Section 413 of the Interstate Commerce Act while making forwarders liable to the claimant as receiving and delivering carriers under the provisions of Section 20(11), nevertheless did not place forwarders in the category of connecting lines under the provisions of Section 20(12), and that as to line-haul carriers subject to parts I, II, and III, of the Interstate Commerce Act, forwarders stood in the same relationship as other shippers and thus were compelled to observe the nine months' limitation for filing claims. In rendering its decision, the court said:

> The Act thus leaves the freight forwarder in substantially the same position it had previously held with respect to its liability to shippers and its rights against underlying carriers. The hearings, committee reports and debates are bare of any suggestion that forwarders needed relief from the requirement that they file their claims against carriers like other shippers. They have done so for over a century. They have continued to do so since enactment of the Freight Forwarder Act. See, *e.g.*, *Merchant Shippers Assn.* v. *Kellogg Express & Draying Co.*, 28 Cal. 2d 594, 170 P. 2d 923 (1946); *J. R. Kelly Freight Forwarder Application*, 260 I.C.C. 315, 318 (1944); *Hugh F. Gannon, Inc., Freight Forwarder Application*, 260 I.C.C. 219, 220 (1944). We would require a much clearer showing than has been made to find that Congress intended, without increasing the liabilities of forwarders regulated by the Act, to give them a right-over against railroads, ship lines, and linehaul motor carriers as initial carriers under § 20(12).

While the *Acme Fast Freight* case established the right of the freight forwarder to proceed against the underlying carrier, a Texas decision of a few years ago indicated that recovery against the underlying carrier may be had by the shipper as well as by the freight forwarder. In *Thompson* v. *American Abrasive Metals Company*, 253 S. W. 2d 83, a less-than-carload shipper who held a bill of lading from a freight forwarder was permitted to recover directly from the rail carrier performing the underlying transportation.

7

Filing of Claim

Notice of Claim

The requirement that a carrier allow no less than a specified period of time for the filing of claims for the loss of or damage to goods transported was added to the Carmack Amendment by the first Cummins Amendment enacted in 1915. The amendment contemplated that the claimants give notice of claims in advance of actually submitting their claims, the added language providing, in part, as follows:

> That is shall be unlawful for any such common carrier to provide by rule, contract, regulation, or otherwise a shorter period *for giving notice of claims than ninety days* and *for the filing of claims* for a shorter period than four months, and for the institution of suits than two years. . . . (Emphasis added.)

The second Cummins Amendment, enacted in 1916, continued this same provision, authorizing carriers to make provisions with respect to time limitation for giving *notice* of claim as well as for *filing* of claim. The provisions with respect to time limitation for giving *notice* of claims, however, were eliminated by an amendment to Section 20(11) enacted in 1930. The law now provides:

> That it shall be unlawful for any such receiving or delivering common carrier to provide by rule, contract, regulation, or otherwise a shorter period for the *filing of claims* than nine months, and for the institution of suits than two years, such period for institution of suits to be computed from the day when notice in writing is given by the carrier to the claimant that the carrier has disallowed the claim or any part or parts thereof specified in the notice. (Emphasis added.)

Since 1930 reference to the term *notice of claim* is entirely misleading, and its use in claim handling and court decisions should be avoided inasmuch as the present provisions of the law and the bill of lading now only relate to *filing* of the claim. Either a claim is *filed* with the carrier or a claim is not filed; whether or not the carrier was given *notice* of the claim is no longer material.

Time Limit for Filing Claims

The bills of lading normally issued by rail and motor carriers specify that written claim be made upon the carrier within nine months after the delivery of property damaged or delayed in transit or after a reasonable time for delivery of property lost altogether has elapsed. Condition 2(b) of the straight bill of lading provides:

> As a condition precedent to recovery, claims must be filed in writing with the receiving or delivering carrier, or carrier issuing this bill of lading, or carrier on whose line the loss, damage, injury or delay occurred, [or carrier in possession of the property when the loss, damage, injury or delay occurred], within nine months after delivery of the property (or, in case of export traffic, within nine months after delivery at port of export) or, in case of failure to make delivery, then within nine months after a reasonable time for delivery has elapsed; and suits shall be instituted against any carrier only within two years and one day from the day when notice in writing is given by the carrier to the claimant that the carrier has disallowed the claim or any part or parts thereof specified in the notice. Where claims are not filed or suits are not instituted thereon in accordance with the foregoing provisions, no carrier hereuder shall be liable, and such claims will not be paid. (Portion shown in brackets appears only in motor carrier bill of lading.)

The provisions of Section 20 of the Interstate Commerce Act and Section 2(b) of the bill of lading do not constitute a *statute of limitation.* Section 20 merely provides that it shall be *unlawful* for carriers to provide a shorter period than nine months for filing claims and a shorter period than two years for bring suits on claims. Under these provisions, it would be lawful for carriers to provide in their bills of lading that claims must be filed within one year after delivery; the law authorizes the carrier to establish any period just so long as the period is not less than nine months. Under these provisions, carriers have established a period of nine months within which claims must be field in writing and a period of two years and one day after declination in writing in which suits must be instituted. These requirements are not *statutory;* they are *contractual* in nature and therefore it is improper to refer to them as statutes of limitation.

The leading case in point is the decision of the Supreme Court of the United States in *Louisiana & W. R. Co.* v. *Gardiner,* 273 U.S. 280, wherein the court said:

> The bills of lading issued by petitioner undertook to restrict the institution of suits for loss to two years and one day after delivery of the property. This restriction does not accord with the Transportation Act which declared unlawful any limitation shorter than two years from the time notice is given of the disallowance of the claim, and is therefore ineffective. See *Chicago & N.W. R. Co.* v. *Bewsher* (C. C. A. 8th) 6 F. 2d 947. But neither the above quoted provision from the Cummins Amendment nor the one from the Transportation Act was intended to operate as a statute of limitation. They restricted the freedom of carriers to fix the period within which suit could be brought—prohibited contracts for any shorter period than the one specified.

See, also, *Neuss Hesslein & Company, Inc.* v. *Louisville & N. R. Co.,* 50 So. 2d 855; *Watson-Higgins Milling Co.* v. *Pere Marquette Ry. Co.,* 43 N. W. 2d 43; *Boderman Clothing Co.* v. *Railway Express Agency,* 95 N. Y. S. 2d 802.

Accordingly, the usual rule that the United States government shall not be bound by a statute of limitations not expressly made applicable to it has no pertinence when it maintains an action for loss or damage, and the government has been held to be bound by the time limitation in the contract of shipment into which it has entered with a carrier. (*East Texas Motor Freight Lines* v. *United States,* 239 F. 2d 417; *United States* v. *Chicago, R. I. & P. R. Co.,* 200 F. 2d 263; *Delaware, L. & W. R. Co.* v. *United States,* 123 F. Supp. 579) Nevertheless, filing claim within the specified time is a condition precedent to recovery by a claimant. (*Northern Pacific Ry. Co.* v. *Associated General Contractors,* 152 F. Supp. 126; *Railway Express Agency* v. *General Shoe Corporation,* 276 S. W. 2d 725)

Determining when the nine-month period allowed for filing claim should start running is frequently a matter of dispute between the claimant and the carrier. In *National Distillers Product Corp.* v. *Companhia Nacional de Navegacao,* 99 F. Supp. 458, the railroad issued one bill of lading for twelve cars which departed from Philadelphia on different dates between April and June 1944. The plaintiff contended that it was under no duty to present the claim until nine months after the last car was delivered and further that it was for the convenience of the railroad that the shipments had been split into twelve cars on different dates, as it would have preferred to have them all transported at one time. The court, in holding for the railroad, said:

> We are not here concerned with a situation where a consignee might be unaware of a shortage until a final shipment is received. The trouble here was in a leakage of a certain amount of pipes in a carload lot and therefore the type of loss that was at the time of delivery immediately brought to the attention of the consignee, and which in my judgment, the consignee is required to promptly call to the attention of the carrier.

In *Erie R. Co.* v. *Callahan Co.*, 184 N. E. 264, there was a shortage on a carload of sugar as well as decline in market value due to delay. The shipment moved via the Erie Railroad Company and the Wabash Railroad. The claimant filed with the Wabash for the shortage and accepted that carrier's payment for the shortage. Thereafter, claimant filed a claim with the Erie for the loss due to market decline caused by delay. In holding that claimant could maintain its action for market decline, the court said:

> It is contended by appellant that since both carriers acted under the same contract, appellee's action in filing a claim with the Wabash Railroad for the shortage of sugar, and accepting payment therefor, barred this action against the appellant under the rule that where one has cause of action against another he must assert all of his damage in a single action and not split his cause of action. . . . The reason for the rule against splitting of actions fails in this case. There is nothing in the findings to indicate that the payment was intended by the parties as full satisfaction of all claims existing between them, and, therefore, the payment would not bar this action under the accord and satisfaction rule.

In the event of nondelivery, Section 2(b) of the bill of lading requires that claim must be filed within nine months after a reasonable time for delivery has elapsed. The question of what constitutes a reasonable time for delivery is one of fact rather than law and as a result there is little uniformity in the holdings of the courts. In its decision in *Chesapeake & Ohio R. R. Co.* v. *Martin,* 283 U.S. 209, the Supreme Court stated:

> What constitutes a reasonable time depends upon the circumstances of the particular case. As applied to a case like this, it means such time as is necessary conveniently to transport and make delivery of the shipment in the ordinary course of business, in the light of the circumstances and conditions surrounding the transaction. *Hazzard Co.* v. *Railroad Co.*, 121 Me. 199, 202-203. Compare *First Nat. Bank* v. *Pipe & Contractors' Supply Co.*, 273 Fed. 105, 107-108.

In *Herrin Transportation Company* v. *Southeastern Electric Co.*, 310 S. W. 2d 343, a crate of electric switches, shipped with two boxes of iron and steel hardware, was never delivered. As the two boxes of hardware were delivered on 7 June 1954, the carrier contended that the claim for the loss of the crate of electrical switches, submitted 22 November 1954, nine months and eighteen days after the date of the bill of lading, was not timely filed. The court held otherwise, saying:

> We have found no case in point on the question before us. After a careful consideration of the provisions of Section 2(b) of the bill of lading, we have concluded that inasmuch as the crate of electric switches was separate and apart from the two fiber boxes of iron and steel hardware, it cannot be said that it was such an integral part of the whole shipment that the delivery of the two fiber boxes of iron and steel hardware could in any wise warrant the conclusion that the whole shipment covered by the bill of lading was being delivered. Neither is there any ground upon which it can be reasoned that there was a delivery of the property contained in the crate of electric switches at the time the two fiber boxes of iron and steel hardware were delivered. As a separate entity, the crate of electric switches simply remained undelivered.

The court had less trouble in finding for the carrier in *Henderson* v. *National Carloading Corp.*, 92 S. E. 2d 593, wherein it said:

> . . . the time for filing a claim had expired, whether nine months began to run on the day the balance of the shipment was delivered to the plaintiff, or on the day the tender of the box *short* on the original delivery was made. In no event could the date on which plaintiff was advised that the property had been sold be used to start the running of the nine-month period provided for in Section 2(b) of the contract of lading.

The time ordinarily required for transportation between the points involved is not the only factor to be considered. Evidence relating to war conditions and the influenza epidemic should have been taken into consideration, the court held in *Moore* v. *American Ry. Exp. Co.*, 107 S. E. 6. Likewise, strikes, floods, weather conditions, embargoes, and other factors which may occasion delay should be considered as affecting the time of expected arrival. In *Cohen v. Southern Ry. Co.*, 193 N. E. 480, there was a controversy involving delay of one day in filing of the claim. At the trial it was stipulated that the normal transit time between the two points was five days and that the shipment actually arrived on 3 July 1929. The consignee mailed his formal claim on 3 January 1930, and this was received by the carrier on January 6. The carrier argued that the filing time expired on January 5 which was six months plus two days after arrival date, the two days being allotted for that amount of free time allowed after arrival. The court, in discussing this problem, said:

> The Fourth of July, a national holiday, intervened on the day following the delivery of the goods to Melrose Park, and it is a circumstance to be considered that no draft could have been taken up at any bank on that day nor any mail delivered had notice been mailed instantly upon arrival of the goods. . . . In order to bar the plaintiff's claim under the six months rule it would be necessary to assume that he either had, or should have had, the knowledge on July 5, that the goods were at the depot and that he was not entitled to as much as twenty-four hours in which to take up the draft and accept the delivery. Upon consideraion of all of the circumstances in this particular case we cannot so hold, nor that the trial court erred in finding that the claim was filed within six months after a reasonable time for delivery.

The nine-month limitation applies whether the action for the loss of a shipment is based on the common law right to sue for conversion or whether it is based on the contract. This was the holding of the Tennessee Supreme Court in *Railway Express Agency* v. *General Shoe Corporation,* 276 S. W. 2d 725, wherein the court said:

> The provision in the express receipt as to making claim within a specified time does not deprive the holder of that receipt of any remedy to enforce a right of action given by the common law for conversion. It only requires as a condition precedent to such enforcement by appropriate remedy that the holder of the receipt shall make claim within the required time. Although there are decisions to the contrary, we think that any other construction would render inconsistent these two provisions [of section 20(11)] in the Federal Statute separated by only one fairly short sentence.

The limitation does not apply, however, to claims for money collected under C.O.D. agreements. (*Nuside Metal Products, Inc.* v. *Eazor Express, Inc.,* 12 Fed. Car. Cas., paragraph 81, 176)

There is sufficient compliance with the requirement for filing claim in writing within the stipulated time if claimant mails its claim to the carrier in time to reach it within the time limit in the ordinary course of the mails. In *Wichita Valley Ry. Co.* v. *Davis,* 275 S. W. 169, it was held that testimony of plaintiff's attorney that letter to carrier's agent, notifying him of claim for damage, was forwarded through due course by mail, raised a presumption that letter was received by such agent and agent's denial of its receipt merely raised issue of fact, which was for decision of jury, or court in cases tried without jury. Similar holdings were made in *Johnson* v. *New York, etc., R. Co.,* 88 A. 988; *Vencil* v. *Quincy, etc., R. Co.,* 112 S. W. 1030. Notice by mail, however, will not be sufficient unless mailed in time to be received within the time fixed by the contract. (*St. Louis, etc., R. Co.* v. *Furlow,* 117 S. W. 517) The limitation of nine months refers to calendar months and not to 270 days. In other words, if the shipment were delivered on February 10, the time limit for filing claim with the carrier would expire on midnight of November 10 of the same year.

The bill of lading provision for a time limit for filing claims is mandatory and may not be waived by the carrier. (*B. A. Waterman Co.* v. *Pennsylvania R. Co.,* 295 F. 2d 627; compare *Reading Co.* v. *Commodity Credit Corp.,* 289 F. 2d 744)

What Constitutes a Claim

Whether or not a particular document constitutes a claim in a given situation is a question which depends upon the facts. The decisions of the courts as to what constitutes a claim are not in harmony; some courts are exceedingly liberal and will go to great lengths to construe a given document as constituting a claim in writing; other courts are more exacting in their requirements and their decisions indicate a full appreciation that the carrier is entitled to an opportunity to make a reasonably prompt investigation of the facts and circumstances involved and that there must be some reasonable time limitation on a carrier's responsibility. As a practical matter and for simple, good business reasons, carriers cannot be as liberal as some courts in construing documents as constituting claims in the voluntary settlement of claims.

Even in those instances where the carrier has good reason to believe that if the claimant resorted to litigation, the attitude of the court would be liberal and the document or documents involved would be construed by the court to fulfill the requirements of the claim in writing; the carrier, nevertheless, is usually justified in refusing to so construe the document or documents as fulfilling these requirements and in declining voluntary payment. Under the law the carrier is prohibited from waiving the requirements relating to the filing of claims, and its own interest requires that it insist that claimant comply fully with these requirements in order that all claims can be investigated promptly and that its liability be kept within reasonable limits. If carriers adopted a liberal attitude in this regard, the provisions with respect to claim filing would soon become meaningless, discrimination and preferences would result, estimate of outstanding liability on claims would be impossible, opportunity for prompt investigation would be lost, and dilatory claim filing greatly encouraged. Further, motor carriers under the BMC-32 endorsement to their cargo insurance policies would undoubtedly be compelled to pay much higher premiums. While, as indicated, court decisions at the present time are not in harmony as to what constitutes a claim, the trend today is becoming more exacting and ultimately the courts will probably all become more technical in requiring a substantial compliance with Section 2(b) of the bill of lading.

The word *claim* is usually defined as meaning to demand or assert as true. Insofar as relations between carriers and their customers are concerned, the word can be considered as meaning *a demand* and in filing a claim, the person filing it is demanding compensation for loss, damage, or injury caused by the carrier to the property of the claimant. While the courts have not specifically discussed the matter and probably it would not be favorable if they did, a document in order to fulfill the legal requirements of a claim should be one on which the carrier could, if it so desired, authorize payment. If a document or several documents are filed with a carrier but the substance of the document or documents is such that the carrier, even though admitting its liability, still does not have in its possession sufficient information on which to authorize payment of the claim, it would certainly seem that the claimant has not fully complied with the requirements of filing a claim in writing with the carrier. If before the carrier can pay the claim something still must be done by the claimant, then the carrier does not have a claim before it for consideration.

Courts in their decisions generally emphasize that in filing a claim no particular form is necessary, that neither formality nor technical exactness is necessary, and that a substantial compliance with the stipulation that a claim in writing be filed is all that is required. One of the leading cases which discusses this matter and is frequently cited is *Bond Stores* v. *Overland Package Freight Service,* 13 N. Y. S. 2d 928. While this is a decision of a state court, it was decided upon the basis of the federal law applicable to interstate shipments. The evidence indicated that on 27 May 1936, the consignor delivered to the carrier in New Brunswick, New Jersey, a carton of men's clothing, the carton being numbered 604 and consigned to Chicago, Illinois. The carton was never received by the plaintiff's store in Chicago and the evidence indicated that it was stolen from the carrier's truck in Chicago. On June 15, plaintiff wrote to the defendant at its New York address advising that the shipment made on May 26, covered by invoice number 604, to the Bond Stores in Chicago had been received with a shortage and that "We are this day filing claim for same and would thank you to please acknowledge receipt of this letter." On June 18, defendant's claim agent wrote to plaintiff acknowledging receipt of the letter and stating that "We will be pleased to entertain your claim upon receipt of proper supporting documents."

The plaintiff alleges that thereafter on December 17, a further letter was written to the carrier and mailed but the carrier denies receiving this letter. Thereafter, on 25 February 1937, plaintiff wrote another letter to the carrier referring to prior communications and the fact that the shipment was made from New Brunswick on May 26, and the further fact that it was not received by the plaintiff at the designated Chicago address. Defendant acknowledged receipt of this letter on March 4. Plaintiff on April 2 referred the matter to a claim adjuster and a letter was sent by the adjuster to defendant's claim agent enclosing various documents to support "the above captioned claim." On May 24 defendant responded to that letter declining to consider the claim because it had not been received within the nine-month period set forth in the bill of lading. The court in holding that there had been a substantial compliance with the requirements for filing a claim in writing stated:

> It would appear that in order to constitute a claim the transfer agency should be advised by the consignor or the consignee that, first, a loss has occurred, second, the nature of the loss, third, the nature of the shipment involved, fourth, the approximate date of the shipment and its point of origin and destination, and finally, that the parties to the shipment expect restitution or reimbursement. Concededly there is no requirement that any precise language be followed or that any detailed specifications be filed.

In response to the contention that supporting documents should have been filed within the claim period, the court said:

> There is, of course, no requirement under the law that any supporting documents be filed within the nine months' time limit established by the "Uniform Bill of Lading" in order to perfect a claim. . . . While nowhere in the correspondence does the plaintiff set forth the kind of merchandise contained in the carton, the quantity thereof, or the value which they attribute to the contents of this carton, there seems to be no requirements in law that they do so within the nine months, limitation in order to establish a claim.

Georgia, Florida & Alabama Ry. v. *Blish Milling Co.*, 241 U.S. 190, cited as controlling by the court in the *Bond Stores* case, without doubt is the leading case on the question of the formality and exactitude with which a claim must be filed. Generally speaking, the Supreme Court there liberally construed the filing requirements, and the decisions that have followed it since then have relied upon that opinion in support of their acceptance of communications between the shipper and carrier as possessing the essential elements of a valid claim.

In the *Blish Milling Co.* case, the shipper consigned a carload of flour under a uniform bill of lading from Seymour, Indiana, to Bainbridge, Georgia. Upon arrival it was placed on the consignee's side track without requiring payment of the draft and surrender of the bill of lading. In the course of unloading, the consignee found that some of the flour was wet and he thereupon reloaded the car and returned it to the carrier which sold the contents. The carrier did not notify the shipper of the situation and his representative appeared on the scene. The shipper then wired the carrier that "*We will make claim* against railroad for entire contents of car at *invoice price.* Must refuse shipment as we cannot handle." (Emphasis added.) In construing whether this and preceding telegrams were sufficient to comply with the requirement that a claim be filed in writing, the court in affirming that they did, said:

> In the preceding telegrams which passed between the parties, and are detailed by the state court in stating the facts, *the shipment had been adequately identified, so that this final telegram, taken with the others, established beyond question the particular shipment to which the claim referred, and was in substance the making of a claim within the meaning of the stipulation, the object of which was to secure reasonable notice.*
> We think that it sufficiently apprised the carrier of the character of the claim, for while it stated that the claim was for the entire contents of the car "at invoice price," this did not constitute such a variance from the claim for the value of the flour as to be misleading and it is plain that no prejudice resulted. Granting that the stipulation is applicable and valid it does not require documents in a particular form. It is *addressed to a practical exigency and it is to be construed in a practical way.* The stipulation required that the claim should be made in writing, but a telegram which, in itelf, or taken with other telegrams, contained an adequate statement, must be deemed to satisfy this requirement. . . . (Emphasis added.)

In *Dillon* v. *Goldstein Refrigerator Line,* 268 P. 2d 699, the Colorado Supreme Court viewed an exchange of correspondence between the shipper and carrier, started within nine months of a reasonable time for delivery of a lost shipment, as constituting a claim. The court said:

> Following the reasoning of Mr. Justice Hughes in the case of *Georgia, Florida & Alabama Ry Co.* v. *Blish Milling Co.,* 241 U.S. 190, we determine that the real effect and object of the letters . . . apprised the carriers involved of the character of the claim well within the nine-months' period, and in view of the fact that the stipulation contained in the bill of lading does not require the documents to be in any particular form, it is sufficient if the carrier is advised within the required period in a manner sufficiently clear, that the shipment for which the loss is alleged can be identified.

In *Johnson* v. *Missouri Pacific Ry. Co.*, 187 S. W. 282, it was held that bad order notations on the freight bill do not take the place of filing a written claim. See *Lucas Mach. Div.* v. *New York Central R.*, 236 F. Supp. 281.

The authorities are not altogether in agreement as to whether the writing must include a demand for payment in order to constitute a claim. A strict view was taken by the Supreme Court of Michigan in *Dawlen Corporation* v. *New York Central R. Co.*, 43 N. W. 2d 887, wherein the court said:

> Substantial compliance with the claim requirement is necessary, and a letter may suffice. *Snyder* v. *King*, 199 Mich, 345, 165 N.W. 840, 1 A. L. R. 893. Yet a claim within the the provision of the bill of lading is more than a notice of loss; it must include a demand for payment of damages. *Douglas Shoe Co.* v. *Pere Marquette Railway Co.*, 241 Mich. 297, 217 N.W. 12. The letter of December 13, 1946, was only a request to trace the shipment and was not sufficient to constitute a claim.

A similar conclusion was reached in *Louda* v. *Prague Assurance-National Corporation*, 106 N. E. 2d 757, as follows:

> We are of the opinion that the letter of October 17, 1946, did not constitute a claim in writing for damage to plaintiff's goods. Although the letter is entitled "Re: Claim of Frantisek Louda," there is no indication therein that a claim is being made against the defendant. The letter relates a request . . . to obtain the inspection papers from the railroad handling the shipment and requests the certificate at an early date.

To the contrary, the United States District Court for the Southern District of New York in *Delaware, L. & W. R. Co.* v. *United States*, 123 F. Supp. 579, stated,

> The written notice which is to be considered in a "practical way" is sufficient if a carrier can not draw any inference from it other than a claim for damages was contemplated, even if the writing does not contain a formal demand for damages. See *Benson* v. *Davis*, 194 N.W. 771; *Fiske Rubber Co.* v. *N.Y., N. H. & H. R. R.*, 132 N. E. 714, 715; *Payne* v. *Smith*, 238 S.W. 243.

In *Thompson* v. *Levy Bros. Drygoods Co.*, 180 S. W. 2d 212, it was held that a letter from consignor giving date of shipment, name and address of consignee, nature or value of shipment, and stating that consignee had advised that the shipment had not been received, and asking the carrier to prove delivery was sufficient compliance with the bill of lading terms. This case differs from the *Bond* case in that while not making an unqualified demand for payment, at least it did indicate the value of the goods and supply the carrier with sufficient information to investigate the alleged loss and pay the claimant if the record indicated loss of the shipment. In *Minot Beverage Co.* v. *Minneapolis & St. Louis Ry. Co.*, 65 F. Supp. 293 a letter identifying the shipment, indicating contents, weight, points of shipment and destination, declaring that the goods were damaged, and reciting that in a short time "claim will be filed" for loss, was in itself a "claim" within the provisions of the bill of lading notwithstanding use of future tense, since facts in their entirety controlled.

In *Southern Ry. Co.* v. *Black*, 196 S. E. 291, the court held that the filing of a written notice of claim with the defendant carrier the day after arrival of apples designating the car number, the day of its arrival, stating that the shipment arrived in damaged condition caused by the negligence and improper service of the defendant connecting carrier, describing in detail the nature of the damage, giving the names of the employees of the defendant who inspected the car, constituted sufficient compliance with the bill of lading requirements even though it failed to set out any specific sum claimed as damages. While no particular form of written claim is required, said the court, it is essential in order to constitute substantial compliance with the bill of lading requirements that the writing possess the characteristics of a demand for compensation or amount to a notice of intention to claim compensation for loss suffered.

The statement of an approximate amount sought to be recovered was held to satisfy the claim requirements in *Reider* v. *Thompson*, 116 F. Supp. 279, the court saying:

> A reasonable compliance . . . is all that is necessary, and a statement as to the amount of loss is not required. A claim specifying a lesser sum than the damage actually sustained is no bar to recovery of the correct amount. . . . This principle is applicable, *a fortiori*, when the amount of a claim is stated explicitly to be shown only for immediate compromise, with express reservation of the right to base recovery on arrived sound value if the compromise is not affected.

A "Statement of Protest" which included the notation "This is consignee's claim for $150.00 more or less" and a "Placement Notice" purporting to be a "claim for $100.00 subject to correction for such loss, damage and/or delay" were relied upon as claims in *Thompson* v. *James G. McCarrick Co., Inc.*, 205 Fed. 2d 897.

Many claimants today still file documents with carriers which are entitled "Tracer and Notice of Claim," "Notice of Claim," etc., and a reading of these documents reveals that they relate to an alleged shortage, seek only proof of delivery, and seldom make any demand upon the carrier for payment of any specified sum. Within recent years, some claimants have included a statement which in substance usually states that if proof of delivery cannot be supplied then the document is to be considered as a claim for "$100 more or less." It is not believed that Section 20 of the act or Section 2(b) of the bill of lading contemplates facetious technical compliance of this nature and perhaps one should not condemn the carrier, upon receiving a document containing a clause of this nature, for replying in this manner:

> We have before us your printed form dated .... entitled "Tracer and Claim" and have noted that you wish us to consider it as your claim for "$100 more or less." We regret that you have not supplied us with sufficient information to consider this as your claim. If this document actually constitutes a claim, we certainly do not know how much you wish us to pay but since it implies that you might be satisfied with less than $100, we are enclosing an unused one cent U.S. postage stamp and until more specific information is supplied, you may consider your alleged claim for any greater amount as declined. The enclosed payment does not constitute an admission of liability.

While handling in this manner certainly has very little to recommend it any more than the use of the printed form to which it replied, carriers generally are replying to this form and similar ones for "$100 more or less" by simply acknowledging receipt of the document and advising that "your alleged claim for $100, more or less, is respectfully declined and we are enclosing standard claim forms for your use in resubmitting this matter to us for further consideration if desired." By dedeclining the alleged claim the two-year provision for bringing suit commences, and in many instances if the claimant does not submit additional information within the nine-month period, the carrier will decline voluntary payment when the information is submitted on the grounds that the document filed within the nine-month period entitled "Tracer and Claim" or similarly did not fulfill the requirements of a claim.

Under the *Minot* and *Thompson* cases, *supra,* it might be argued that the ordinary tracer forms used by shippers would constitute a claim especially since many of these forms indicate that claim will be filed. It is pointed out, however, that in the *Minot* and *Thompson* cases the shipments involved were *damaged,* whereas usually the tracers used by shippers as a matter of routine to expedite delayed shipments relate to *shortages.* The receipt of a communication from a consignee indicating that a shipment was received in damaged condition and setting forth the other information contained in the communication involved in the *Minot* and *Thompson* cases certainly acquaints the carrier with the actual fact that consignee expects some reimbursement. On the other hand, the usual shipper or consignee tracer only informs the carrier that a shipment is being delayed in transit or has gone astray. Frequently, the shipment is located and delivered to consignee in the ordinary routine of the carrier's business. On occasions delivery is made to consignee by some other carrier. The carrier on receiving the tracer does not actually know whether or not it has lost or misdelivered the merchandise and the function of the tracer is merely to set in motion the carrier's facilities for searching for and expediting the shipment. For these reasons, it is not believed that the *Minot* and *Thompson* cases provide any support for the contention that an ordinary tracer constitutes a claim where the tracer relates to shortages.

Actual Notice

Considerable doubt has arisen within the past decade as to whether a claimant needs to submit a written claim within the nine-month period when the carrier has had actual notice of the loss or damage. The confusion stems from a decision of the United States Court of Appeals for the Seventh Circuit in *Hopper Paper Co.* v. *Baltimore & O. R. R. Co.*, 178 Fed. 2d 179, cert. den. 339 U.S. 943. In that case, the plaintiff on 10 August 1945, consigned 18 skids of paper to the Government Printing Office, Washington, D. C., over the lines of the defendant rail carrier under the standard commercial bill of lading. While in transit on August 16 the paper, except for some salvage, was destroyed in a wreck between two of defendant's trains. The salvage was sold by the carrier without the plaintiff's knowledge for $100 and no accounting was ever made for this sum. On August 18, the carrier advised the consignor and the Government Printing Office by telegrams that the shipment had been destroyed. On 30 July 1946, almost 11 months after the date of the shipment, the defendant received a letter from the consignor and attached thereto was a written claim for $4,224.96 for the loss of the 18 skids of paper. The railroad declined this claim on the grounds that it was not filed within nine months as provided by Section 2(d) of the contract terms and conditions of the bill of lading. The shipper brought suit, the case was tried without a jury, and a judgment was entered in favor of the plaintiff shipper which the defendant carrier appealed. In affirming the judgment of the lower court, the court stated:

> In the instant case it is undisputed that defendant and its agents were fully aware and cognizant of the existence of all the facts concerning the wreck and destruction of the carload of paper. In such a situation a formal notice by plaintiff to the defendant could not have accomplished anything more. Hence,

we conclude that the carrier may not use the provision of the bill of lading to shield itself from the liability imposed upon it by the statute and the common law for its negligent destruction of the shipper's property. To hold otherwise would not be construing the bill of lading "in a practical way."

The holding of the *Hopper* case has been questioned in several cases. Of it the United States Court of Appeals for the First Circuit in *Insurance Co. of North America* v. *Newtowne Mfg. Co.*, 187 Fed. 2d 675 said:

Hopper Paper Co. v. *Baltimore & Ohio R. R. Co.*, 178 F. 2d 179, seems perhaps out of line with the other cases; but there at least the carrier knew that the loss had occurred during the transportation on its line and had so advised the shipper by telegram. In the present case the carrier's stated position was that it had no record of having accepted any such shipment, that it had no knowledge of the loss, and no responsibility for it if it occurred. Even though Newtowne might previously have made an oral claim upon the carrier it does not follow that the carrier would necessarily be aware of the shipper's determination to press the claim to litigation after being informed of the carrier's disclaimer of responsibility as the result of investigation. It would not have been unduly burdensome upon Newtowne, and there was ample time remainaing after such disclaimer, to make a written demand upon Holland as a condition precedent to bringing suit.

The United States Court of Appeals for the Fifth Circuit found the *Hopper* case not controlling in *East Texas Motor Freight Lines* v. *United States*, 239 F. 2d 417. There the lower court had held that written notice of the claim did not have to be given the carrier "if and when the carrier knew that the damage had actually occurred in the shipment which it had carried." The appellate court reversed, saying:

We think this holding was, under the facts of this case, contrary to the law as established in an unbroken line of decisions of the Supreme Court holding that this requirement of notice is valid and must be observed by shippers and carriers alike. . . .

Appellee stakes its chief reliance on *Hopper Paper Co.* v. *Baltimore & Ohio R. R. Co.*, 7 Cir., 1949, 178 Fed. 2d 179, certiorari denied 339 U.S. 943, 70 S. Ct. 797, 94 L. Ed. 1359, and *Loveless* v. *Universal Carloading Co.*, 10 Cir., 1955, 255 F. 2d 637. Hopper involved the complete loss in a train wreck of a carload of paper. The salvage was disposed of by the railroad for a nominal amount without consultation with or accounting to the owner. The carrier promptly advised consignor and consignee in writing of the destruction of the shipment. The Court felt that these facts charged the carrier "with actual knowledge of all the conditions as to the damage that a written notice could give." See also, *Atlantic Coast Line R. R.* v. *Pioneer Products, Inc.*, 256 F. 2d 431.

We do not have that situation here.

In *Delphi Frosted Foods Corporation* v. *Illinois Central Company,* 188 F. 2d 343, cert. den. 342 U.S. 833, shipments of fruit in carload lots were involved. When the cars arrived at destination, they were found to be damaged. The appellant shipper neither gave nor attempted to give notice to the originating or delivering carrier as to the damage. Certain of appellant's customers who had contracted to purchase portions of the shipment gave notice to the delivering carrier with reference to the damaged condition of the goods. The customers brought suit against the shipper for refund of amounts paid for the fruit and the court held that title had not passed to them and that they were entitled to recover their purchase money. Appellant brought suit against the carrier for loss of these sales and contended that the requirement of the bill of lading for filing claim in writing had been substantially complied with. The court denied this contention in the following manner:

> The District Court correctly concluded that the notice contemplated by the bill of lading is to be given by the claimant and not by others. Notice to the delivering carrier was sufficient; but the assertion of damages by persons who had contracted for some portion of the goods, title to which had not passed, persons who were not agents of the appellant, did not constitute such a claim as was required. A bill of lading is valid and has the sanctity of a contract. *Chesapeake & Ohio Ry. Co.* v. *Martin,* 283 U.S. 209. To hold that the filing of the claim is dispensed with under the circumstances of this record would be to "alter the terms of a contract, made in pursuance of the Interstate Commerce Act and having, in effect, the quality of a statute of limitation, and thus to open the door for evasion of the spirit and purpose of the act to prevent preferences and discrimination in respect of rates and service." *Chesapeake & Ohio Ry. Co.* v. *Martin,* supra, 222. While the purpose of the notice is to give the carrier an opportunity to investigate the claim, *Georgia, Fla. & Ala. Ry. Co.* v. *Blish Milling Co.,* 241 U.S. 190, the identity of the claimant is a material feature of any such investigation. As stated in *Appalachian Electric Power Co.* v. *Virginia Ry. Co.,* 126 W. Va. 626, the bill of lading clearly contemplates that the person damaged shall file the claim. . . .

In *Northern Pacific Railway Company* v. *Mackie & Lewis,* 195 F. 2d 641, after the carrier had delivered the shipment involved to the consignee, an employee of the carrier inspected the shipment and made a written report, a copy of which was given to the consignee. The report noted damage, extent unknown, and that the consignee would call for a final inspection. The report stated that it was not an acknowledgement of liability and contained a provision indicating that claims must be filed in accordance with bill of lading requirements. A final inspection was never requested or made, the shipments being refused and eventually sold by the shipper who suffered a net loss of over a thousand dollars.

In oral conversation one of the partners discussed the claim with the chief clerk in the railroad's freight claim department and advised him of his intention of filing claim and further that none had been filed because of necessary delay to determine the extent of loss. More than nine months after delivery a written claim was filed and this was declined. The court in upholding the carrier's declination said: "A study of the federal decisions, including those of the Supreme Court makes it clear that some sort of written notice of claim is mandatory. It is not enough that the carrier had actual knowledge that damage occurred, or that an oral claim for damage was made."

The weight of authority clearly is to the effect that actual notice by the carrier of the loss or damage to goods entrusted to its care does not relieve the claimant of the obligation of filing written claim within the nine-month period. (*Penn State Laundry Co.* v. *Pennsylvania Railroad Co.*, 134 F. Supp. 955; *Rhode Island Tool Co.* v. *New York, N. H. & H. R. Co.*, 114 A. 2d 404; *White Cross Hospital* v. *Chesapeake & Ohio Ry. Co.*, 125 N. E. 2d 363; *Union Pacific R. R. Co.* v. *Denver-Chicago Trucking Co., Inc.* 253 P. 2d 437; *Louda* v. *Prague Assurance-National Corporation*, 106 N. E. 2d 757; *Public Service Electric & Gas Co.* v. *Reading Co.*, 85 A. 2d 548; *Berg* v. *Schreiber*, 92 N. E. 2d 88, cert. den. 340 U.S. 851; *Wood & Selick, Inc.* v. *Wabash Railroad Co.*, 104 N. Y. S. 2d 488; *Everest* v. *Railway Express Agency*, 230 P. 2d 900)

The only case to follow the *Hopper* case has been *Loveless* v. *Universal Carloading & Distributing Co., Inc.*, 225 F. 2d 637. There the court said:

> Lovelace leans heavily upon the holding and philosophy of the *Hopper* case, as indeed he may, for we think his facts outweight the considerations which prompted the court's decision in the *Hopper* case. In both cases the carrier acknowledged the damages and the cause thereof. In the *Hopper* case, however, the extent of the damages was immediately known and nothing prevented the immedaite filing of a formal claim for the complete loss. In our case the extent of the damages was not at once ascertainable, the parties agreeing that when they were the shipper would file a claim "at some future date." Universal so notified the originating and intermediate carriers. After the damages were ascertained, a formal written claim for the amount thereof was filed, and the carrier does not now contend that it was in any manner prejudiced by the failure to receive the formal claim within the nine-month period.

While clearly contrary to the weight of authority, the *Hopper* case and the buttressing *Loveless* case, representing, as they do, the views of at least two circuit courts that a claimant's failure to file written claim upon the carrier within the nine-month period necessarily is no bar to recovery for loss and damage, should put carriers on notice that some courts will not tolerate their taking refuge in mere technicalities when they have had actual notice of the loss sustained by the claimant.

Who Must File

In *Texas & N. O. R. Co.* v. *Rosenblum,* 195 S. W. 2d 433, the court held that notice of exceptions prepared by inspection service and offered to delivering carrier on date of delivery and report to carrier made by railroad perishable inspection agency constituted neither a demand for compensation for loss resulting from improper carriage nor notice of intention to claim compensation for such loss within the provisions of the bill of lading requirements that a written claim be filed within nine months after delivery. In *Lewis* v. *Roth,* 69 N. E. 2d 510, it was held that the shipper by giving oral notice to carrier's claim adjuster of damage to goods while in transit was not relieved from filing his written claim within nine months after date of delivery as required by the bill of lading. Likewise, in *Louisville & N. R. Co.* v. *Patton,* 156 S. W. 2d 474, it was held that where consignee advised a weighing bureau, which was an alleged agent of the carrier, of shortage of wheat and requested it to give the consignee "weight on said shipment" and in a letter from the bureau to the railroad the weight on the shipment was supplied, the claimant was not relieved from filing its written claim even though the shortage had been discussed orally with the railroad representatives.

A similar conclusion was reached with respect to a "Statement of Protest" filed with the Railroad Perishable Inspection Agency in *James G. McCarrick Co.* v. *Thompson,* 227 S. W. (2d) 832. This decision was distinguished by the court in *Thompson* v. *James G. McCarrick Co., Inc.,* 205 F. 2d 897, as follows:

> We do not consider the case of *James G. McCarrick* v. *Thompson,* 227 S.W. (2d) 832, here controlling as to the validity of these instruments as claims. Appellee contends that in the case the Texas Court of Civil Appeals "did not decide that the statement of protest was insufficient as a claim." While the opinion does contain some language intimating that instruments similar to those were not sufficient as claims, the holding is based almost entirely on the lack of evidence to establish the agency of the R. P. I. A. to receive them for the carrier. Apparently only one witness testified in that case with reference to the authority of the R. P. I. A. to receive claims, and his testimony was without dispute that such authority did not exist. However, in the case before us the testimony introduced by appellee, including that of the representative of the inspection agency, and the Articles of Incorporation of the R. P. I. A. all tend to establish the agency of the R. P. I. A. to receive such claims for the delivering carrier. Without detailing the evidence at length, we think the authority of the R. P. I. A. in this regard is clearly established.

Claim filed upon the carrier's assistant general livestock agent was deemed to be adequate in *Nichols* v. *Atchison, T. & S. F. Ry. Co.*, 229 P. 2d 52.

On the other hand, it is of little consequence to the carrier by whom the notice in writing is made, as long as it is advised and put on notice of the loss. (*Dillon* v. *Goldstein Refrigerator Line*, 268 P. 2d 699) Thus the claim can be filed by someone other than the owner. (*Franck* v. *Railway Express Agency*, 112 N. E. 2d 381; but see *Delphi Frosted Food Corp.* v. *Illinois Cent. R. Co.*, 188 F. 2d 343)

In *Silver Motor Freight Lines* v. *Automatic Web Guide Co.*, 249 P. 2d 994, the court discussed the obligation of the carrier to notify the shipper when it is unable to effectuate delivery of a shipment. The court said:

> There is no provision either in the act of Congress or the bill of lading requiring the defendants to give notice to plaintiff in the event they are unable to make delivery of the shipment. Even if such duty rested upon it at common law, as stated in some of the cases cited by plaintiff, the carrier, under the decision in *Chesapeake and Ohio R. Co.* v. *Martin*, could not waive compliance with the provision or by its conduct in failing to give notice the shipper the right to ignore the terms of the provision in the bill of lading. . . .
>
> We are unwilling to hold that under the circumstances in this case as disclosed by the evidence above referred to, plaintiff was absolved of the duty to file its claim within the required time. By the terms of the statute and the provisions in the bill of lading, it was required to exercise some diligence to ascertain whether or not the machine had been delivered, so that if it had not been delivered it could file its claim within the required time. That the plaintiff exercised no diligence whatever to ascertain whether or not the machine had been delivered is clearly disclosed by the testimony of its president.

As has been indicated in the preceding text and review of court decisions, carriers are not at liberty to waive compliance with the bill of lading requirements regarding the filing of claims. In Section 241(a) of Volume 13, *Corpus Juris Secundum*, the following statement is made:

> It has frequently been held or recognized, so far as interstate shipments are concerned, a stipulation in the shipping contract for making a written claim, a stipulation in the shipping contract for notice of claim, or for notice of loss or injury, cannot be waived, and that such a waiver would contitutes an invalid dicrimination. . . . Since the decision in *Georgia F. & A. R. Co.* v. *Blish Milling Co.*, 36 S. Ct. 541, 241 U.S. 190, 60 L. Ed. 948, some state courts have regarded the rule as settled that there cannot be a waiver of stipulations of the type here under consideration in the case of interstate shipments. . . .

It is the general rule that it is not only proper for carriers to decline claims not filed within the nine-month period but that it is their duty to do so, since it is the overwhelming weight of authority that a carrier cannot waive the provisions in the bill of lading. While some authorities disagree with this they are very much in the minority, as the Supreme Court of the United States and many of our lower federal and state courts have held that the provisions of the bill of lading have the effect of law from which neither carrier nor their customers may deviate. A few of the many cases in point are *Chicago & A. R. Co.* v. *Kirby,* 225 U.S. 155; *Kansas City So. Ry.* v. *Carl,* 227 U.S. 639; *Phillips* v. *Grand Trunk Ry.,* 236 U.S. 662; *Southern Ry.* v. *Prescott,* 240 U.S. 632.

The basis for the decisions cited is twofold. In the first place, the bill of lading is a published tariff provision from which it is unlawful to depart. In the second place, departure in one instance, but not in another, would constitute discrimination which is prohibited by the law. In *Chesapeake & O. Ry. Co.* v. *Martin,* 283 U.S. 209, where the shipment was misdelivered due to misunderstanding or negligence on the part of the carrier, claimant contended that the carrier should not be permitted to invoke the provision of the bill of lading requiring claims to be filed in writing within a specified time; since carrier's own negligence prevented or hampered claimant's compliance, the court held nevertheless that the carrier could invoke the provision.

Time Limit for Suits

There is nothing in the law which prevents a claimant from entering suit against a carrier within the nine-month period for filing claims. The bill of lading provision limiting the maximum time for entering suit applies in only those instances where the carrier has disallowed the claim or a portion thereof in writing. No provision of the law or the bill of lading establishes any minimum time limit before which suit cannot be instituted after written claim has been filed. In fact, there is nothing to prevent an aggrieved claimant from resorting to legal action against the carrier at any time within the nine-month period for filing claims even though a written claim may not have been presented to the carrier.

An offer by the claim department of a carrier of a certain amount in settlement of a claim for damages to an interstate shipment is a notice of the disallowance of the claim and suit must be instituted by the claimant within two years and one day thereafter. In *Tribby* v. *Chicago & N. W. Ry. Co.,* 264 N. W. 185, the plaintiff filed his claim with the carrier on 15 October 1929. The claim was rejected and suit was commenced thereon on 19 August 1930. From a judgment for plaintiff, defendant appealed and the appellate court reversed the lower court and sent the case back for retrial. Subsequently, the case was dismissed without prejudice on 30 June 1934, and on 5 July 1934, another action was instituted.

As a defense, defendant pleaded the bill of lading provision that suits must be instituted within two years and one day after carrier has disallowed the claim or a portion thereof. The carrier contends that notice of disallowance was given to the plaintiff in a letter dated 20 May 1930, which read: "However, to give you the benefit of any doubt on the claim, I will be willing to send you a check for $300. Please advise me if you wish to accept this amount in full settlement of the two claims." The plaintiff declined this offer and correspondence between the parties continued until litigation finally resulted. The plaintiff contended that there was nothing contained in the correspondence between the parties that constituted a disallowance of the claim. The court in holding for the carrier said:

> We do not agreee with this contention (of plaintiff). True, defendant does not state in so many words, nor in the language contained in the bill of lading, that plaintiff's claim was disallowed either in whole or part, but we think it is sufficient to convey the understanding that such was defendant's meaning and that it was so understood by the plaintiff is clear from the fact that he immediately commenced his action. . . .

It does not matter whether or not the disallowance was proper; the mere fact that there has been a disallowance starts the running of the two-year period. (*H. Rouw Co.* v. *Texas & N. O. R. Co.*, 260 S. W. 2d 130) Negotiations for the settlement of the claim carried on between the carrier and the shipper after the carrier has disallowed the shipper's claim do not operate to extend the period within which the shipper may bring suit upon its claim. (*Burns* v. *Chicago, M., St. P. & P. R. Co.*, 192 F. 2d 472) The suit against the carrier is deemed to have been timely begun when the complaint is drawn and dated within two years after notice by the carrier that the claim has been disallowed even though actual service of the complaint may have been delayed until after the period has run. (*Lapp Insulator Co., Inc.* v. *Boston and Maine Railroad*, 112 N. E. 2d 359) Where the complaint embraces more than one shipment, the carrier can insist that the separate causes of action be set forth in separate counts as "the cause of damage might well be different as to each shipment, and the defenses available to defendant may likewise vary in regard to each shipment." (*Marianao Sugar Trading Corporation* v. *Pennsylvania Railroad Co.*, 11 F. R. D. 288)

Once the claim is seasonably filed in writing with the carrier, the claimant is not precluded from amending the claim to a greater amount than originally sought. This privilege, however, is lost after claimant accepts payment from the carrier unless it can be shown that such payment was not intended in full satisfaction of the claim. In the event of litigation, the claimant is not restricted in his suit to the amount set forth in his written claim filed with the carrier. (*Texas, etc., R. Co.* v. *McMillen,* 183 S. W. 773; *Pecos, etc. R. Co.* v. *Holmes,* 177 S. W. 505; *Parham* v. *Chicago, M. & St. P. Ry. Co.,* 189 P. 227; *Caston* v. *Schaff,* 185 P. 33)

Time Limit Between Carriers

When a shipment handled jointly via several carriers on a through bill of lading becomes the subject of a claim, the nine months limitation on claim filing time applies only as to the original claimant. This limitation will not apply as between the several carriers participating in the joint through movement. Under Section 20(11) of the Interstate Commerce Act, courts have held that notice to one of the several carriers is notice to all. (*Denver-Chicago Trucking Co.* v. *Republic Drug Co.,* 306 P. 2d 1076; *Overton* v. *C. R. I. & P. Ry.,* 160 S. W. 111; *Gulf, etc., R. Co.* v. *Bogy,* 178 S. W. 577; *Olsen* v. *R. Co.,* 250 F. 372)

If a movement of goods is handled under more than one bill of lading, each one controls the filing of claims thereunder. For example, if a shipment moves via motor carrier from the west coast to New York and the motor carrier upon reaching Chicago, the end of its line, is unable to find a connecting motor carrier to handle it to destination and turns the shipment over a rail carrier accepting its bill of lading, filing of claim with the motor carrier within the nine-month period does not constitute seasonable filing with the rail carrier, and unless a claim is filed with it within the nine-month period the rail carrier is released from liability.

Section 20(12) of the act gives a carrier which is required to pay a claim on a joint movement the right of recovery against the carrier actually responsible for the loss or damage for which payment is made. While that section contains no express limitation of time within which action asserting interline liability must be begun, at least one court has held that the two-year limitation of Section 20(11) is applicable. The court in *Flanzbaum* v. *Klein,* 10 Fed. Car. Cas. 80,924, said:

> As the original complaint was filed (by the shipper) on December 23, 1948, and the defendant (originating carrier) served his answer on February 27, 1950, three years had expired since the service of the answer when on February 23, 1953, the defendant sought to bring in the third party defendant (delivering carrier). The action is barred by Section 20(11), Title 49 U.S.C. A., and by the terms of the bill of lading.

8

Carrier Claim Regulations

Inasmuch as a considerable amount of goods received for transportation by carriers moves over the lines of two or more carriers, claims filed for loss, damage, or delay frequently will involve the interests of several carriers. As pointed out in the preceding chapters, Section 20(11) of the Interstate Commerce Act provides that the originating or delivering carrier is liable to the owner of the goods for the full actual loss, damage, or injury irrespective of whether or not the loss, damage, or injury occurred while the goods were in that carrier's possession. Section 20(12) provides that any carrier required to pay a claim under Section 20(11), for which another carrier was responsible, may recover the sum expended from the carrier responsible for the injury. It is not always possible, however, to determine the carrier responsible for the injury as, for example, in the case of concealed loss or damage. For this reason, both rail and motor carriers have established national claim organizations composed of member carriers of their respective industries. In this connection the Supreme Court of the United States in *Chicago, M., St. P. & P. R.* v. *Acme Fast Freight,* 336 U.S. 465, said:

> Elaborate freight-claim rules have been established (by rail carriers) covering the investigation, settlement, and defense of claims and the allocation of liability between carriers when, as is frequently the case, responsible for loss or damage cannot be precisely ascertained. Arbitration boards settled disputes arising between carriers under the rules. As a practical matter, the right-over given by § 20 (12) is very little used by carriers, and indeed it is of no value when responsibility cannot definitely be placed upon any one carrier.

The Freight Claim Division of the Association of American Railroads was founded in the early 1890s and practically every major railroad is a member. The National Freight Claim Council of the American Trucking Associations, Inc., was founded in 1938 and has over 1,000 member motor carriers. The purposes of both groups are substantially the same; namely, (1) the prompt and equitable apportionment among carriers of amounts paid in settlement of freight claims, (2) the prompt and lawful settlement of freight claims with claimants, and (3) the study of causes of loss and damage in connection with freight traffic and the suggestion of measures for prevention thereof. Both groups have developed comprehensive regulations for the apportioning of claim liability as between their members; however, such rules have no application to the settlement of claims with claimants. Copies of the rules of both organizations are available to those interested.

Both of these groups have adopted principles and practices for the investigation and disposition of freight claims, as well as regulations governing the inspection of freight before and after delivery to the consignee. The investigation principles and practices of both groups set out their purposes as (1) uniformity in claim settlement and treatment of claimants, (2) the preservation of harmonious relations in freight claim matters between carriers and with patrons, and (3) prompt and efficient service in the investigation and disposition of freight claims. The principles and practices of each group are binding on its members and since most of the major carriers of each mode are active supporting members of their respective claim organizations, this means that the vast majority of freight loss and damage claims are handled in accordance with these principles and practices. The inspection regulations of these groups are likewise applicable to the majority of freight claims. In both instances, investigation principles and inspection rules, the regulations are designed to achieve the prompt, efficient and equitable settlement of freight claims, and major shippers and receivers of freight in the United States, recognizing their purpose and their soundness, attempt to observe them. The recognition by all claimants that the carrier regulations are not designed to thwart the payment of claims, but to assist in the necessary investigation, will result in prompt and equitable claim handling and disposition.

While the Interstate Commerce Commission has issued no formal rulings in connection with investigation of claims by motor carriers, the following rulings in connection with investigation by rail carriers probably reflect its view as to motor carriers as well:

> It is not a proper practice for railroad companies to adjust claims immediately upon presentation and without investigation. The fact that shippers may give

a bond to secure repayment in case, upon subsequent examination, their Claims prove to have been improperly adjusted does not justify the practice. Carriers that have adopted that practice will be expected promptly to discontinue it. (Conference Ruling No. 236)

* * * *

A carrier cannot shield itself from responsibility in paying a claim by accepting the authority of a connecting line to pay it, but must ascertain the lawfulness of the claim and allow it or not upon the basis of its own investigation. This is not to be understood, however, as requiring each carrier interested in the claim to make an independent investigation. The principle of direct investigation embodied in the rules of the freight claim association, whereby the carrier against which a claim is presented undertakes to make the investigation for itself and for the other carriers concerned in the joint movement out of which the claim arises, is approved by the Commission as a means of expediting the adjustment of claims. In all cases, however, the investigation so made must be thorough and must disclose a lawful basis for payment before the claim is adjusted. (Conference Ruling No. 462)

In Ex Parte Docket No. 263, by order dated 24 February 1972 (as amended 5 October 1972), the Interstate Commerce Commission promulgated principles and practices for the investigation and voluntary disposition of loss and damage claims and processing salvage, as follows (49 C. F. R., Part 1005):

Part 1005—Principles and Practices for the Investigation and Voluntary Disposition of Loss and Damage Claims and Processing Salvage.

SEC. 1005.1. Applicability of regulations.
The regulations set forth in this part shall govern the processing of claims for loss, damage, injury, or delay to property transported or accepted for transportation, in interstate or foreign commerce, by each railroad, express company, motor carrier, water carrier, and freight forwarder (hereinafter called carrier), subject to the Interstate Commerce Act; *Provided, however,* That with respect to the acknowledgment and disposition of cargo claims filed against motor common carriers of household goods, carrier action shall be in accordance with the provisions of section 1056.17(a) and (b) of these regulations.

SEC. 1005.2. Filing of claims.
(a) *Claims in writing required.* A claim for loss or damage to baggage or for loss, damage, injury, or delay to cargo shall not be voluntarily paid by a carrier unless filed in writing, as provided in subparagraph (b) below, with the receiving or delivering carrier, or carrier issuing the bill of lading, receipt, ticket, or baggage check, or carrier on whose line the alleged loss, damage, injury, or delay occurred, within the specified time limits applicable thereto and as otherwise may be required by law, the terms of the bill of lading or other contract of carriage, and all tariff provisions applicable thereto.

(b) *Minimum filing requirements.* A communication in writing from a claimant filed with a proper carrier within the time limits specified in the bill of lading or contract of carriage or transportation, and (i) containing facts sufficient to identify the baggage or shipment (or shipments) of property involved, (ii) asserting liability for alleged loss, damage, injury, or delay, and (iii) making claim for the payment of a specified or determinable amount of money, shall be considered as sufficient compliance with the provisions for filing claims embraced in the bill of lading or other contract of carriage.

(c) *Documents not constituting claims.* Bad order reports, appraisal reports of damage, notations of shortage or damage, or both, on freight bills, delivery receipts, or other documents, or inspection reports issued by carriers or their inspection agencies, whether the extent of loss or damage is indicated in dollars and cents or otherwise, shall, standing alone, not be considered by carriers as sufficient to comply with the minimum claim filing requirements specified in subparagraph (b) above.

(d) *Claims filed for uncertain amounts.* Whenever a claim is presented against a proper carrier for an uncertain amount, such as "$100 more or less," the carrier against whom such claim is filed shall determine the condition of the baggage or shipment involved at the time of delivery by it, if it was delivered, and shall ascertain as nearly as possible the extent, if any, of the loss or damage for which it may be responsible. It shall not, however, voluntarily pay a claim under such circumstances unless and until a formal claim in writing for a specified or determinable amount of money shall have been filed in accordance with the provisions of subparagraph (b) above.

(e) *Other claims.* If investigation of a claim develops that one or more other carriers has been presented with a similar claim on the same shipment, the carrier investigating such claim shall communicate with each such other carrier and, prior to any agreement entered into between or among them as to the proper disposition of such claim or claims, shall notify all claimants of the receipt of conflicting or overlapping claims and shall require further substantiation, on the part of each claimant of his title to the property involved or his right with respect to such claim.

SEC. 1005.3. Acknowledgment of claims.

(a) Each carrier shall, upon receipt in writing of a proper claim in the manner and form described in these regulations, acknowledge the receipt of such claim in writing to the claimant within 30 days after the date of its receipt by the carrier unless the carrier shall have paid or declined such claim in writing within 30 days of the receipt thereof. The carrier shall indicate in its acknowledgment to the claimant what, if any, additional documentary evidence or other pertinent information may be required by it further to process the claim as its preliminary examination of the claim, as filed, may have revealed.

(b) The carrier shall at the time each claim is received create a separate file and assign thereto a successive claim file number and note that number on all documents filed in support of the claim and all records and correspondence with respect to the claim, including the written acknowledgment of receipt. At the time such claim is received the carrier shall cause the date of receipt to be recorded on the face of the claim document, and the date of receipt shall also appear in the carrier's written acknowledgment of receipt to the claimant. The carrier shall also cause the claim file number to be noted on the shipping order, if in its possession, and the delivery receipt, if any, covering such shipment, unless the carrier has established an orderly and consistent internal procedure for assuring (1) that all information contained in shipping orders, delivery receipts, tally sheets, and all other pertinent records made with respect to the transportation of the shipment on which claim is made, is available for examination upon receipt of a claim; (2) that all such records and documents (or true and complete reproductions thereof) are in fact examined in the course of the investigation of the claim (and an appropriate record is made that such examination has in fact taken place); and (3) that such procedures prevent the duplicate or otherwise unlawful payment of claims.

SEC. 1005.4. Investigation of claims.
(a) *Prompt investigation required.* Each claim filed against a carrier in the manner prescribed herein shall be promptly and thoroughly investigated if investigation has not already been made prior to receipt of the claim.

(b) *Supporting documents.* When a necessary part of an investigation, each claim shall be supported by the original bill of lading, evidence of the freight charges, if any, and either the original invoice, a photographic copy of the original invoice or an exact copy thereof, or an extract made therefrom, certified by the claimant to be true and correct with respect to the property and value involved in the claim; or certification of prices or values, with trade or other discounts, allowance, or deductions of any nature whatsoever and the terms thereof, or depreciation reflected thereon; *Provided, however,* That where the property involved in a claim has not been invoiced to the consignee shown on the bill of lading or where an invoice does not show price or value, or where the property involved has not been sold, or where the property has been transferred at bookkeeping values only, the carrier shall, before voluntarily paying a claim thereon, require the claimant to establish the destination value in the quantity shipped, transported, or involved and to certify the correctness thereof in writing.

(c) *Verification of loss.* When an asserted claim for loss of an entire package or an entire shipment cannot be otherwise authenticated upon investigation, the carrier shall obtain from the consignee of the shipment involved a certified statement in writing that the property for which the claim is filed has not been received from any other source.

SEC. 1005.5 Disposition of claims.
Each carrier subject to the Interstate Commerce Act which receives a written claim for loss or damage to baggage or for loss, damage, injury, or delay to property transported shall pay, decline, or make a firm compromise settlement offer in writing to the claimant within 120 days after receipt of the claim by the carrier; *Provided, however,* That, if the claim cannot be processed and disposed of within 120 days after the receipt thereof, the carrier shall at that time and at the expiration of each succeeding 60-day period while the claim remains pending, advise the claimant in writing of the status of the claim and the reason for the delay in making final disposition thereof and it shall retain a copy of such advice to the claimant in its claim file thereon.

SEC. 1005.6. Processing of salvage.
Whenever baggage or material, goods, or other property transported by a carrier subject to the provisions herein contained is damaged or alleged to be

damaged and is, as a consequence thereof, not delivered or is rejected or refused upon tender thereof to the owner, consignee, or person entitled to receive such property, the carrier, after giving due notice, whenever practicable to do so, to the owner and other parties that may have an interest therein, and unless advised to the contrary after giving such notice, shall undertake to sell or dispose of such property directly or by the employment of a competent salvage agent. The carrier shall only dispose of the property in a manner that will fairly and equally protect the best interests of all persons having an interest therein. The carrier shall make an itemized record sufficient to identify the property involved so as to be able to correlate it to the shipment or transportation involved, and claim, if any, filed thereon. The carrier also shall assign to each lot of such property a successive lot number and note that lot number on its record of shipment and claim, if any claim is filed thereon.

Whenever disposition of salvage material or goods shall be made directly to an agent or employee of a carrier or through a salvage agent or company in which the carrier or one or more of its directors, officers, or managers has any interest, financial or otherwise, that carrier's salvage records shall fully reflect the particulars of each such transaction or relationship, or both, as the case may be.

Upon receipt of a claim on a shipment on which salvage has been processed in the manner hereinbefore prescribed, the carrier shall record in its claim file thereon the lot number assigned, the amount of money recovered, if any, from the disposition of such property, and the date of transmittal of such money to the person or persons lawfully entitled to receive the same.

Postscript

A book replete with the misadventures of freight should end on a brighter note. Reading only of the lost, damaged, or delayed shipments can distort one's viewpoint and raise a question whether any freight goes through intact. Every day thousands, possibly millions, of shipments are delivered by carriers of all modes without loss or damage. Only a very small percentage of shipments are not delivered intact. The rail and motor carriers of this country and the other modes of transportation as well, have established enviable records in the careful, efficient handling of freight. In no small measure, the achievement of this outstanding record is the result of the work done in the AAR Freight Claim Division and the ATA National Freight Claim Council. The major, continuing efforts of both groups are directed toward improved freight handling and claim prevention. While the constant, continuing efforts of these groups, in cooperation with shippers and receivers around the country, may not eliminate freight claims, they are forcing the number of lost and damaged shipments down to the irreducible minimum.

Table of Cases

Index